PRE-COLUMBIAN CITIES

PRE-COLUMBIAN CITIES

Jorge E. Hardoy

Walker and Company · New York

First published in the United States of America in 1973 by the Walker Publishing Company, Inc.

Published simultaneously in Canada by Fitzhenry & Whiteside, Limited, Toronto.

ISBN: 0-8027-0380-1

Library of Congress Catalog Card Number: 77-186182

Printed in the United States of America.

Cover photograph: The main plaza of Tenochtitlán *INAM, México (autorizada)*.

CONTENTS

INTRODUCTION

I BEGAN TO EVOLVE the idea of writing a book about the cities of Latin America early in 1955. In March of that year, I spent several days in Lima where I had my first opportunity to look closely at a Colonial city and to visit the ruins of pre-Columbian centers near the Peruvian capital. From that moment until the publication of the first Spanish edition of this book, almost nine years passed, part of which time I spent traveling through Latin America and reading and classifying a large body of material.

During 1960 and the better part of 1961, I was associate researcher in the Joint Center for Urban Studies of Harvard University and Massachusetts Institute of Technology, which enabled me to work in the libraries and consult the map collections of Harvard, Brown, and Yale Universities, the American Geographical Society, the New York Public Library, and the Library of Congress in Washington. Most of the material initially gathered for this book on *Pre-Columbian Cities* has been derived from these sources. I also had access to the collections in a number of public and private libraries in various cities of Mexico, Peru, Brazil, and Argentina, as well as Caracas and Guatemala City, which allowed me to broaden considerably the general scope of this work.

Four institutions collaborated in various ways to make this study possible, and I am profoundly grateful to them. I should like to thank the National Council of Scientific and Technical Research of Argentina and the Guggenheim Foundation for their support which enabled me to travel through Latin America and work during 1960 and 1961 in the centers mentioned; the School of Mathematical Sciences of the National University of the Littoral, for their permission to leave my teaching and research duties in the Institute of Regional and Urban Planning and in the School of Architecture of that institution; finally Martin Meyerson and Lloyd Rodwin, directors of the Joint Center for Urban Studies, for having welcomed me in that excellent interdisciplinary research center, and for having placed its facilities at my disposal.

Many people have helped me in different ways. Among them, my special thanks goes to Olga Linares of the Peabody Museum of Harvard University, who read the entire manuscript at the beginning of 1963 and whose knowledge of pre-Columbian cultures prevented me from committing too many errors; to Dr. Gordon Willey of Harvard University who helped me work out a basic bibliography for the subject covered in this book that was little discussed back in 1960; to Dr. Alberto Rex González of the University of La Plata, for reading part of the manuscript and giving me his comments; to Dr. K. Chang, then of Harvard and currently professor at Yale University, for his commentaries on three essays I presented in his seminar on "Prehistoric Settlement Patterns," upon which I based Chapter II, parts of Chapter VIII and the Preface of this work, and to Dr. Ignacio Bernal, of the National Institute of Anthropology and History of Mexico City, for his valuable suggestions concerning the bibliography.

I have utilized information and suggestions given to me personally or by letter from Emilio Harth Terré, Luis Miro Queseda and Luis Dorich of Peru and Carlos Ponce Sanginés of Bolivia. As happens with everyone who has been connected with Harvard's Department of City and Regional Planning, the expert advice of Miss Katherine McNamara proved invaluable in preparing the bibliography.

Almost eight years have passed between the Spanish and the English editions of this book. During these years, I have concentrated my studies on Latin America's urban history and on analyzing the urbanization process in the Colonial period, but I never lost sight of my interest in pre-Columbian urbanization.

The second half of the decade following 1960 was a favorable period for studies of pre-Columbian cultures, as evidenced by the number of works undertaken and published. This wide-ranged activity, leading to the analysis of some of the principal pre-Columbian cities, is reflected in the bibliography of this edition, adding some hundred and twenty titles to those already included in the Spanish version. The work of Michael Coe,

William Coe, Willey, Murra, Donald Thompson, Schaedel, Millon, Sanders, Parsons, Rowe, Menzel, Lanning and Flannery of the United States; Bonavía, Engel and Lumbreras of Peru; Ponce Sanginés of Bolivia: González and Cigliano of Argentina; Zuidema of Holland, and researchers of Mexico's National Institute of Anthropology and History, among others, has been of enormous importance during these last eight years.

The opportunity to publish this book in English has enabled me to bring the Spanish edition up to date. During the years intervening between these two editions, I have traveled frequently through Latin America and have kept in close contact with most of the researchers mentioned. I thank them all for explaining their work to me. My greatest debt of gratitude is to Dr. Duccio Bonavía of the National Museum of Anthropology and Archeology of Lima, who made valuable corrections and suggestions for those chapters dealing with South America's pre-Columbian cultures.

Buenos Aires, *October, 1971.*

PREFACE

THIS VOLUME IS THE FIRST in an extensive study on the evolution of cities in Latin America. It deals only with those cities where America's Indian civilizations lived until the arrival of the Spanish in the first decades of the sixteenth century. A second book on Colonial cities is in preparation, and the study will conclude with a third volume discussing urban evolution from Independence to the present time.

Research for this work was done in libraries and archives in the United States and Latin America, and at the sites and ruins of the majority of these cities and ceremonial centers. In a work of this kind, there is no substitute for personal impressions. The grandeur of Teotihuacán cannot be appreciated without walking down the Avenue of the Dead from one end to another. To realize the importance of irrigation in the formation and development of Indian civilizations on the Peruvian coast, you must visit the desolate beaches of the Pacific, wander among Chan Chan's walls and the ruins of Pachacamac or fly over the Paracas Peninsula and the Nazca or Moche Valleys. It is difficult to comprehend 1,500 years of urban life without studying the marvelous creations of Indian gold and silversmiths, weavers, sculptors, and potters. Detailed study of the ground plans and excavations of Maya civic-ceremonial centers indicates the stupendous visual sweep which Indian architects achieved by their use of plazas, stairways, open courts, and terraces, but nothing can take the place of a walk through Tikal, Palenque or Uxmal for bringing home the scale in which all these elements were utilized. Maya architects, like those of Xochicalco and Monte Albán, were masters in the use of topography to create changing vistas and subtle impressions experienced only by an attentive visit to the partially reconstructed ruins.

The descriptions, maps, and excellent photographs of Machu Picchu that I have seen give only a faint glimpse of one of the most impressive urban settlements in existence. At the sites themselves, we can appreciate the superhuman effort which, voluntarily or by coercion, was required of these peoples, and so understand the organization of these societies, their technical limitations, and the demands of their religion.

Research in libraries and archives is fundamental. By organizing information taken from the chronicles of conquistadors and travelers who came into contact with the Indian civilizations and classifying the fragmentary information yielded by archeological and anthropological studies of the last fifty or sixty years, I assembled the bibliography necessary to learn about the societies that built Latin America's pre-Columbian cities to determine the periods of occupancy of those cities and perhaps find interrelationships between them.

All the cities and ceremonial centers mentioned in this book are now abandoned. Many of them had already been deserted when the sixteenth century Spaniards wrote the first sketchy descriptions of them. Nevertheless, there are still undiscovered centers of Indian life prior to the Conquest. From time to time, newspapers or magazines report new ruins found in the forests of the Petén or Quintana Roo. There are also villages, even cities, still buried beneath the sandy deserts along the Peruvian coast. The list of known archeological sites in Mexico and Peru is so extensive that only a few have been studied in detail.

The Spaniards founded many of their first settlements on the ruins of the Indian cities and in the densely populated territories they had conquered (Hardoy, 1965). The locations of Mexico City and Cuzco, the two principal cities during the first years of the Spanish Colonial Period, were determined by their previous existence as capitals of the two most advanced civilizations of Mexico and South America at the time of the Conquest. Similar circumstances decided the founding of Cholula, Mérida, Oaxaca, Trujillo, Lima, Bogotá, and other Colonial cities. As a result, many of the most extensive Hispano-American cities were built over layouts often incompatible with the colonial plan. Within a few years, Christian churches replaced native temples, the palaces of Aztec and Inca princes gave way to those of the conquistadors, and ancient cities yielded their stones to construct the new cathedrals, mansions for governors and bishops, municipal buildings, and urban land improvements. Only a few decades saw a culture, foreign to that continent, spring up upon the disintegrating remains of a thousand-year-old heritage. Reasons of state, strategy, and economy demanded it. Neither Conquest nor Colonial rule respected the Indian cities, nor did the Latin American governments of the first century of Independence do anything to protect the monuments of ancient civilizations. Today we can find nothing of Tenochtitlán, Texcoco or Azcapotzalco. We can admire Inca Cuzco only in the stone walls bordering some streets. Even its great ceremonial plaza is destroyed. The impressive bulk of Cholula's pyramid is all that remains to mark the city of temples that aroused the wrath of Cortés. Cempoala, Machu Picchu, Chan Chan, Mitla, and Tulum—living cities up to the time of the Conquest—have been deserted for centuries.

Industrialization in certain Latin American countries has produced a concentration of economic, administrative and cultural activities in their capitals. As a result, the population and size of these cities has multiplied ten and twenty times in less than two generations. Present-day capitals in the majority of Latin American countries are those of the Viceroyalty and seats of Colonial justice which were often built directly over the cities of existing Indian states. Continuous occupation of the same site throughout several centuries has wiped out all vestiges of the indigenous cultures. Mexico City extends over Tenochtitlán, the ancient Aztec capital, as well as over the ruins of its allies, Texcoco and Tlatelolco; over Azcapotzalco and Tenayuca, and over the remains, buried or barely intimated, of former occupations representing more than two thousand years of urban life. Within Lima's metropolitan area, we can still glimpse parts of the eroded temples of a prehistoric people.

Indian urban life, like the civilizations which produced it, has almost totally disappeared. In some villages of Guatemala and southern Mexico, in Ollantaytambo and the agricultural communities in the highlands of Peru and Bolivia, we can still observe a modified version of the way of life developed by the most densely populated, if not precisely urban, Indian societies. But gone forever are Tenochtitlán and Cuzco, Chan Chan and Texcoco, Dzibilchaltún and Cempoala, Cholula and Tlaxcala, Cajamarca and Jauja, once centers of the culture and dominion of the Aztecs, the Inca and the peoples they ruled.

While Moctezuma II, from the height of the Templo Mayor in Tenochtitlán, proudly showed his city to Cortés, the Inca lords were gathered thousands of miles away in Cuzco where their Empire's political structure was reflected in the urban arrangement of that highland capital. Each in its own way, Tenochtitlán and Cuzco, symbolized the culmination of the two most advanced civilizations which the Spaniards encountered.

Urban evolution of Latin American cities was interrupted in the first half of the sixteenth century, and from then on the principal cities began losing their inhabitants or were abandoned outright. Only at the end of the nineteenth century did Mexico City regain the population the Spanish conquistadors had reported in 1520, when, known as Tenochtitlán, it had been the capital of the Aztec Empire. Cuzco soon ceded its position of eminence to Lima, to become the tranquil provincial town visited by today's tourists.

From the moment of the meeting of the two cultures, the Indian cities began to be transformed by the Spanish Christian influence. What visitor to Mexico City without knowing her history could imagine that under the transept of a Christian cathedral lie the remains of the *tzompantli,* the sinister skull rack of the Aztec religion? How many people passing through the suburbs of Guatemala City suspect that those curious, elongated grass-covered mounds once were part of Kaminaljuyú, one of the oldest urban centers of America? And who would guess that Cholula's churches and chapels cover the ruins of one of the religious centers most venerated by pre-Columbian Mexicans?

A CITY FOR ITS TIME AND PLACE

In a study about cities, the word "city" appears constantly in the text. But what was a city in pre-Columbian America and how should it be defined?[1] What physical, social, and economic characteristics distinguish a city from a village or a ceremonial center? What institutions can be found in a city that are different from those in a village?

In a well-known article, Childe points out the ten prerequisites he considers essential for a society to reach a "civilized" stage (Childe, 1950).[2] As he himself admits, not all societies in Indian America fulfilled these requirements. In some cases we have no concrete proof, but we assume that these requirements were met. Most of Childe's ten prerequisites emphasize cultural aspects of a technical nature, which indicate the emergence of an increasingly complex society characterized by class divisions, progressive specialization of its members, and the support of a centralized government, creating a distinct way of life which we qualify as urban.

Although this study is basically about cities, I will analyze them from a point of view different from Childe's. My concern is with the plan and physical features composing these cities, their streets and plazas, their architecture and facilities. I am also interested in the reasons why the Indians built them and lived in them only to ultimately abandon them. Analysis of the physical environment in which these cities developed is important because of its influence on the structure of the urban societies and the circumstances which led to the choice of a particular site. I wanted to know how these cities were inhabited, to find an explanation for their urban form and use of their land and, whenever possible, to compare the characteristics of Indian societies themselves to the cities they created.

Once I had determined the objective of this study, I had to define a city and establish the necessary criteria to distinguish it from other forms of territorial settlement, as a guide to the analysis of those urban examples selected. Today many traditional differences between rural and urban areas such as literacy, sanitation, income level, etc., have disappeared or are minimized, but this has not been the case in underdeveloped countries. I feel that some of the accepted criteria currently applicable were also valid in pre-Columbian America, such as nonagricultural life, class differences and even that type of housing we call a multiple dwelling, an essentially urban grouping.

The term "city" is always used loosely. We all have a general idea of what we mean when we use it, but there is still no clear standard for its definition. Having based a good part of this book on data from archeologists, my confusion as to the correct use of the term grows upon learning that they too, in spite of the excellent systematization of their research, use the terms "city" and "urbanization" as loosely as other specialists. To standardize the presentation of the urban examples in this book, I have used contemporary criteria employed less by archeology than by urbanists, sociologists, economists, geographers, historians, architects, and other scholars who seek to define the city of today. With these criteria, I have tried to establish which urban concentrations can be considered cities in Latin America before the arrival of the Spaniards.

In general, we acknowledge a city to be a collection of separated yet relatively concentrated dwellings (Weber, 1958).[3] Let us look at some definitions. For a sociologist such as Wirth, a city is a permanent establishment, relatively large and thickly populated by socially heterogeneous individuals. Wirth prefaces these criteria by stating that to classify a community as urban on the sole basis of its size is totally arbitrary (Wirth, 1938). Another sociologist, Sjoberg, sees a city as contrasted to a village, having greater size, density and heterogeneity and including a wide variety of nonagricultural specialists among whom the most significant are the *literati* (Sjoberg, 1960).[4]

In a comparative analysis of the characteristics and elements defining urbanism according to eighteen sociologists, eleven chose heterogeneity of the urban society, seven cited the impersonal relations that a city produces, six mentioned anonymity, five, division of labor, three emphasized a nonagricultural life and two, commercialization (Dewey, 1959). I consider the last three elements to be fundamental in differentiating rural from urban, and as pertinent today in Latin America as during pre-Columbian times.

For one urbanist, the city is a permanent establishment, relatively large and densely occupied by people engaged in different economic activities (Bartholomew, 1955). Weber defines the city as "a market," explaining that we speak of a "city" only in such cases where local inhabitants satisfy a substantial economic part of their daily needs in the local market and where there is an essential balance in commodities which the local population and that of the immediate hinterland produce for sale in the market (Weber, 1958). Sombart states that in an economic sense, a city is a large concentration of persons who depend for subsistence on the production of the farmers.

The position of Linton, an anthropologist, is somewhat similar to that of Sombart and Weber. He defines the difference between a city and a village by describing the city as a community of people whose survival depends on the exchange of products and services for food and raw materials (Linton, 1957). Two other students of the contemporary city, Queen and Carpenter, speak of it as a collection of persons and buildings, extensive for its time and place, and characterized by a variety of different activities (Queen and Carpenter, 1953).

There are other views worth mentioning. Two historians defined the relationship on the basis of the greater size and larger number of inhabitants of the city as compared with the village (Mundy and Reisenberg, 1958). An architect, Le Corbusier, defined a city as an object to be used, a center of intense life and work (Le Corbusier, 1924). G. von Below list-ed a city's characteristics as market, fortification, jurisdiction, political independence, and certain privileges. We also have a large number of authors who describe cities as "fortified villages."

During the twentieth century, the Census Bureaus of various countries have tried a more realistic and technical approach, but their main concern is with those characteristics which separate urban from rural, rather than any new definition of a city.

Each country defines an urban area differently.[5] In the United States of America, Mexico, Argentina, Belgium, Switzerland, Holland, Spain, Japan, India, Canada, and other countries, an area is considered urban or an inhabited center if it has a certain number of inhabitants. The range, however, is broad and fluctuates from slightly more than one thousand in Canada to twenty thousand or more in Holland. In Egypt, they call the principal cities of provinces or districts urban areas; in Peru, populated centers of any size qualify, whereas in Israel, any community falls into the urban category if it has less than one third of its population economically involved in agricultural work (Woytinsky, 1953).

In recent years, the United States Bureau of the Census has introduced new classifications to define urban areas: that is, an area occupied by a minimum density of not less than 500 houses or about 2,000 persons per square mile (781.2 persons per square kilometer), and having a cohesive street network (United States: Bureau of the Census, 1959). The Bureau also specifies that areas dedicated to commercial, industrial, transportation, and other uses within the area defined as urban, must bear a functional relationship to the central city.

It is easy to understand that concepts of a city and an urban area are largely conditioned by each person's education and where he lives. I have mentioned the different approaches of specialists interested in the problem, but I think we still lack the opinion of the average man who constitutes the bulk of a city's population, today as in the past. A *gaucho* from the Argentine *pampas* would certainly have a different idea of city than a *porteño* living in Buenos Aires. I am sure that an artisan working at Teotihuacán would conceive of his city quite differently from his counterpart working near Tikal in the Petén forest during the seventh century A.D.

The concept of a city changes with time and place, conditioned by the environment, socioeconomic structure, and technological level of the observer's own society. Some of the criteria I have adopted are common to several of the selected definitions. Basic factors of size, density and permanence appear frequently in these and other definitions not included in this book. An important criterion for this work emphasizes the difference between an urban plan and a rural one based on a relatively tightly knit street system. We must also take into consideration structural and spatial adaptability and the location of dwellings and palaces in the overall plan as evidence of more or less prolonged residence.

In my opinion, most of these criteria could be established through superficial archeological studies, guided by a thorough analysis of aerial photographs of suitable scale where the terrain makes this feasible. I would supplement this data with a previous reconstruction of the possible urban evolution of the site based on tests of soil resistance and on the detailed study of all excavations, archeological reports and other sources of information.[6]

Frankfort points out that technical and economic reasons usually dictate a sample excavation of a city, a technique which provides a most incomplete picture of its urban aspects (Frankfort, 1950). As a result, we can never really know the layout of its streets nor the spatial relationship between the various parts of the city and other urban features. Nevertheless, there are interesting studies on the application of aerial photography to the surveying of urban archeological sites and as an aid in determining the specific uses of the terrain (Castagnoli, 1956).

The four criteria discussed up to now are based on the physical aspects of a city: size, density, layout, and permanence. They are best analyzed in relation to known written chronicles and histories, and compared with the probable climate, topography, water supply, and other particulars of the environment that prevailed when the locality and the site were occupied.

There are basic laws of urban development common to all cultures, which may be different and unrelated yet are going through similar stages in their social and economic evolution. Political and administrative structures also condition the location and the range of territorial influence of population centers.

Societies tend to locate their centers of living so as to encompass increasingly broader areas as their technological level evolves and their social structure grows more complex. These aspects of the relationship between the city and its zone of influence deserve a detailed study, but I have only touched briefly upon them in this work so as not to stray from my subject.

A city also has elements which we will call cultural. Certain institutions and a particular kind of political organization may be common to a village as well as to a city, but are differentiated by the variety and intensity of use of these institutions, by the different size of their areas of influence, and whether they are predominantly administrative, commercial, religious, or educational. A city has urban features, such as well-delineated plazas, houses with interior courtyards, and general sanitation services. It also has urban characteristics such as houses aligned along streets, superior architectural quality, and other attributes rarely found in rural hamlets or villages.

Social characteristics of cities vary according to their economic bases (Wirth, 1938), but even today, according to Patrick Geddes, the late British philosopher and regional planner, we classify cities in terms of their social and economic functions as centers that serve production and distribution or provide specific facilities. This probably was not the case in pre-Columbian America where urban functions were not so clearly defined.

In other words, the city is a center of government and the military; a market place for the products manufactured by its inhabitants whose subsistence depends on agricultural activity in which they do not participate; a place where the population lives and works (Dickinson, 1947) and which serves as a center for technological progress and services, exchange and innovation for its surrounding rural area; a social phenomenon (Korn, 1954) inhabited by a heterogeneous society which has developed a different psychological attitude (Redfield and Singer, 1954); a core from which future cities radiate with growing social interaction; a focus for the development of a distinct way of life.

Before going further, we should establish the difference between the concept of sedentary existence and that of urbanization and the city. Among the prerequisites suggested by Childe, at least one criterion did not pertain in Indian America (Childe, 1950). But the lack of a form of writing did not prevent some Indian cultures from reaching the Urbanist stage if we think of this as represented by human concentrations of a scale and density unknown before in those regions. Given the required environmental and technical conditions, we can be almost certain that a sedentary culture will advance to the Urbanist stage without its inhabitants necessarily gathering in actual cities. The few facts I have show that during the beginning of the Florescent or Early Intermediate Period on Peru's north coast, specifically the Early and possibly the Middle Gallinazo Period, there were no cities that would meet the criteria I have adopted for this work. There was, however, the dense population concentration characteristic of an advanced village stage.[7]

A city, considered as a further stage of development, and even today antepenultimate in the graded scale of population groupings, cannot develop spontaneously without a previous pattern of urbanization having existed in the region.[8] Our modern metropolitan and suburban areas represent quantitatively two scales of population groupings unknown in pre-Columbian America and in preindustrial societies in general. The process of development is different, even for preindustrial peoples, when planned or spontaneous colonization takes place in a new and uninhabited area. In this event, cities usually rise up within a few years without intervening sedentary or urbanized societies. Permanent colonization of new territories has frequently been the work of groups belonging to urban cultures, which tend to bring with them an already tested way of life. History is full of such cases, usually planned cities, or at least cities laid out in accordance with some basic principles of organization, since the subdivision of rural and urban land was the lure to attract settlers. We see examples of this process in Greece and Rome; in the intense urbanization which took place in northern Spain, the south of France and eastern Germany during the twelfth and thirteenth centuries; in the Spanish colonization of America; in the mushrooming railroad towns on the plains of the United States and Argentina, and, in recent years, in the expansion toward the interior of Brazil.

Similar movements took place in pre-Columbian America, among them the program of building cities from the foundations up with some having specialized functions, initiated by the Inca toward the end of the fifteenth century. The same may have occurred on the north coast of Peru in the fourteenth and possibly as early as the twelfth or thirteenth centuries when a number of regularly laid-out centers with similar characteristics emerged, coinciding with Chan Chan's growing power as the regional nucleus of cultural influence and political unity. In the two South American examples, we see how a civilization, heir to an ancient cultural tradition, utilized its surplus wealth to further the specialization and organization of its inhabitants, the authority of a powerful ruling class, and an economy and way of life that was, for its time and place, urban. In both cases, when these colonizing processes were taking place each state was already in existence and had both a capital and a not-in-considerable network of cities spread over sizeable portions of its territory.

The use of contemporary criteria and definitions to ascertain the size, density, population, and functions of a city which had been destroyed and abandoned centuries before, would be irrelevant if we did not try to relate them to the social and economic system which had produced that city. For this reason, the ten criteria I have chosen can be applied only to a specific society at a certain phase of its development and in a particular area. In the following chapters, I will try to demonstrate that an urban way of life had individual characteristics for each subarea and each epoch of pre-Columbian America.

I have chosen the ten criteria which stand the best chance of verification by using such information as we already have on Indian cultures of America, or which might be clarified by future investigations. They are classified according to a priority based on the possibilities I feel each offers for concentrated research. They are not exclusive. That is, certain cities, or supposed cities, can fulfill only some of the requirements, yet are considered urban because they more than satisfy the rest. I suggest that in pre-Columbian America a city was a human grouping with the following characteristics and functions:

1 - Large and highly populated for its time and place.
2 - A permanent settlement.
3 - Having a minimum density for its time and place.
4 - Having urban structures and layout, as indicated by recognizably urban streets and spaces.
5 - A place where people lived and worked.
6 - Having a minimum of specifically urban functions, such as a market and/or a political and administrative center and/or a military center and/or a religious center and/or a center of intellectual activity with the corresponding institutions.
7 - A hierarchical heterogeneity and differentiation of society. Residence of the ruling classes.
8 - A center of urban economy for its time and place, having a population which depended to some extent on the agricultural production of people who lived partially or totally outside the city

proper. Part of the labor force was involved in processing raw materials for a market larger than the city itself.

9 - A center of services for neighboring areas and the nucleus of a progressive pattern of urbanization and diffusion of technical advances.

10 - Having an urban way of life, as opposed to a rural or semirural life, for its time and place.

A COMPARISON OF THE CITIES OF INDIAN AMERICA WITH OTHER PRE-INDUSTRIAL CITIES

During the centuries preceding the Spanish Conquest, urbanization in America evolved with the resources indigenous to the continent, and in definite periods in specific areas which we can place in fairly precise chronological order. Therefore, any formal similarities these cities may have had with those of other continents in the same epoch, or in earlier or later periods, should not be seen as the result of extra-continental contacts.

Although this evolution was not constant, we must bear in mind that, in Mexico at least, in the wake of two invasions by nonurban peoples and the subsequent periods of adjustment, Indian civilizations embarked on new stages of development marked by greater complexity and accentuated urban characteristics. We can trace the following urbanistic process and characteristics in pre-Columbian America up to the beginning of the sixteenth century.

Indian America's stages of urbanization took place centuries, even millennia, after the fluvial civilizations of the Nile and Indus, in Mesopotamia, China and even in Europe, perhaps because the American cultures never attained the same technological level. One unproved explanation suggests that the level of knowledge brought in by the successive waves of Asiatic migrants in their travels across the Bering Straits was consistently inferior to that possessed by the more advanced groups established in the eastern Mediterranean region and in Mesopotamia. I am inclined to believe that there were also other reasons. Perhaps it was only toward the third or fourth millennium B.C. that there were concentrations in America large enough to find the solutions necessary to accelerate the technological process and secure the time and energy required to broaden their economies. We know that metallurgy appeared during the first millennium before the Christian era on the north coast of Peru (Willey,

1953), and reached the Oaxaca area and later the central Valley of Mexico in Mesoamerica several centuries later.[9] This dates metallurgy in America at between four and five millennia after it had been known in "the cradle of civilization." Copper and its uses, for example, were known in Palestine by the middle of the fifth millennium B.C. (Albright, 1954), but at the beginning of the Christian era it was employed only for agricultural tools and weapons by Mochica craftsmen on Peru's north coast (Mason, 1957), although it had already been in use for ornamental purposes since the period of Chavín expansion around 800 B.C. in the same region.

Monumental architecture appeared in Mesopotamia and later in Egypt (Frankfort, 1956) at least 2,500 years before the first known mounds in Mesoamerica and South America. The first attempts to keep some kind of records also began much later in America than in Asia and the north of Africa. The limitations of America's Indian civilizations in writing, transportation, and metallurgy are well known, but most important for subsequent urban development was the lag of 4,000 years before agriculture and its techniques made their appearance in America.

Technological differences between the cultures of the Old and New Worlds were sharpest during the centuries belonging to the Pre-Ceramic and Pre-Agricultural Periods in America, or from the fourth to the second millennium B.C. With a few centuries' difference, we find the Zacatenco culture in the central Valley of Mexico, where people lived in perishable dwellings and apparently lacked community or religious buildings, and Tell-el-Amarna, the beautiful city of Akhen-Aten on the banks of the Nile. Mohenjo-daro and Harappa, the two principal cities of the Harappá kingdom in the Indus Valley, were planned with a regular layout and boasted a considerable agricultural surplus and an economy that we can qualify as urban for their time. They belong to the same epoch as the small groupings of dwellings built of adobe, where the fishermen-gatherers lived in the Valleys of Peru's north and central coast during the third millennium B.C.[10] The Golden Age of Athens was already past when the first true cities made their appearance in America.

An urban way of life implies urban institutions and an important percentage of the population living and working in a nonrural environment; an economy based, at least in part, on the mass production of goods for market; heavy population density; and a marked social stratification. Such an urban life was known in the Valley of Mexico and possibly in some other areas of Mesoamerica only around the beginning of the Christian era. The same is true on the north and central coastal valleys of Peru—that is, 2,500 years later than in the Indus Valley and around 3,500 years after urban civilization in Mesopotamia. Between the sixth and fourth millennia B.C., the first sites were occupied more or less permanently in the central Valley of Mexico (Piña Chan, 1955) and possibly some in other areas of Mesoamerica. Only in the third millennium B.C. do we find the same preceramic and preagricultural level on the northern coast of Peru (Willey, 1957; Lanning, 1967). In both areas, we are dealing with limited groups which lived off gathering plants and hunting and, where possible, collecting shellfish and fishing. They may even have domesticated some animals, among these the dog. Around the beginning of the fourth millennium, plant cultivation became a small scale activity.

The first permanent villages appeared during the last half of the third millennium. This period's best known areas, though not the only ones, are the central plateau of Mexico and the north and central coast of Peru which developed the highest cultural levels of that time. But other groups with possibly a similar cultural level existed in other parts of South America and Mesoamerica such as the south coast of Peru and the northern coast of Chile, in still little-known sites on the Peruvian and Bolivian plateaus, on the central coast of the Gulf of Mexico, on the Yucatán Peninsula, and in the highlands of southern Mexico and Guatemala.

The first villages had few contacts with each other. They were actually small hamlets made up of a few dozen families at the most who lived in perishable housing and maintained a self-sufficient economy. They practiced an incipient agriculture, taking advantage of the swampy banks of lakes and rivers. An improved diet and a sedentary way of life, which replaced the uncertainties of gathering, fishing and the hunt, supported groupings of a size and density unknown until then.

Many of the original areas occupied by the first sedentary groups continued to be centers of life and technological evolution during the subsequent developmental stages of these Indian cultures. It is interesting to note that throughout the Spanish Colonial Period, the central Valley of Mexico, the Guatemala highlands, and the coast of Peru were the most densely urbanized areas of these three countries as they are today.

Toward the middle of the second millennium B.C., villages were already agricultural and pottery making had been introduced. The Formative, or Initial Period, in Mesoamerica and South America lasted until the end of the first millennium B.C. In Mesoamerica, it was represented by the Zacatenco culture, and later by the Ticomán, in the central Valley of Mexico; by the beginnings of the Olmec culture in San Lorenzo and later in La Venta, on the Gulf Coast; by the San José and Guadalupe phases and by the earliest occupation of Monte Albán, in the valley of Oaxaca; by the Arévalo and Las Charcas cultures in Kaminaljuyú in the highlands of Guatemala; by the Xe and Mamon cultures in the lowlands occupied by the Maya. In South America, we find it in the Guañape and Cupisnique cultures in the valleys of Peru's north coast, and by the appearance of monumental ceremonial centers in the Casma Valley, Ancón and elsewhere but principally in the Chavín expansion in the highlands and on the central and northern coast of Peru.

Throughout the last half of the second millennium and the first millennium B.C., villages grew larger, and the increase in population led to the adoption of maize as the dietary staple. Other agricultural products and fishing, meanwhile, took the role of supplements in an increasingly varied and abundant diet.[12] Also toward the middle of the second millennium or before, the earliest religious constructions were built. This may indicate the first marked influence of a ruling class.

In the same epoch, on the north coast of Peru, appeared a type of dwelling which consisted of a single, regularly shaped chamber. Although this model was repeated frequently in the same site, it did not represent a step toward urban planning, and we might think of it as an early example of unit housing. Pre-Christian times, however, saw at La Venta, an Olmec site on the swampy coast of Veracruz, the construction of a ceremonial center with a preplanned layout that was later imitated in varying forms in other Mesoamerican centers and in the Valley of Mexico in particular.

Increased food production was essential to the change in scale of human groupings. In this way, small sedentary establishments became villages. In a more advanced stage, especially after the Classic Period, canal irrigation on the Peruvian coast, *chinampa* farming on fertile, manmade plots, sometimes called "floating gardens," and pot irrigation and canal irrigation in the nuclear areas of Mexico allowed intensified cultivation in these regions. The more plentiful food supply encouraged concentrations of people in densities hitherto unknown (Armillas, 1951; Kosok, 1940; Palerm, 1954; West and Armillas, 1950). We can see that in America, as elsewhere in the world where urban cultures developed, some sort of intensified farming system preceded, and may have been a prerequisite for the great city stage. Clearing methods, leaving the land fallow, and a system of irrigation indicate different degrees of agricultural yield all over America, and therefore a new scale of human concentration and urbanization.[13] Large-scale intensive farming facilitated by irrigation, or the *chinampa* system, may have made possible the development of such great cities as Chan Chan and Cajamarquilla in South America as well as Tenochtitlán, Texcoco and, in a sense, Teotihuacán in Mesoamerica.[14] These five cities, like other less important ones which developed during the Classic and Post-Classic Periods on the coast of Peru and on Mexico's central plateau, were located in regions where irrigation and water control were indispensible, or at least of prime importance, to insure adequate food production for the relatively dense population.

The centuries between the first permanent villages and the emergence of the first cities produced a spontaneous pattern of ceremonial centers which served as a focus for religious and community activities in more or less extensive areas. In some cultures these acted as political, administrative, and scientific centers as well as markets. Cuicuilco is the oldest known ceremonial center in the central Valley of Mexico. Even earlier we find similar functions filled by San Lorenzo (Michael Coe, 1968) and by La Venta in the Olmec area (Drucker, Heizer and Squier, 1959) Monte Albán in Oaxaca, Uaxactún in the Petén, Kaminaljuyú in the Guatemala highlands (Shook and Proskouriakoff, 1956), Kotosh and Chavín de Huantar in the Peruvian highlands (Willey, 1951), and the settlements represented by the mounds discovered in the Virú and other river valleys on the north and central coast of Peru (Willey, 1953). There were undoubtedly other centers with like functions constructed in every region of Mesoamerica and South America already densely inhabited.

It is difficult to determine when the first cities, which conform to the criteria established for this book, appeared. It may have been during the last pre-Christian centuries or early in the Christian era. The addition of the Carbon 14 dating method to archeological techniques has allowed a significant revision of existing sequences. In a number of cases, the relative dates of the developmental stages of the principal Indian cultures in America have been pushed back in time. Even the concept of a ceremonial center, used and occupied sporadically yet not a true city, may have to be revised in keeping with future findings. This needed revision is sure to be facilitated by the current excavations in Oaxaca, Teotihuacán and on the coast of Peru, by the results of cartographic work and research in Tikal, Dzibilchaltún and other centers of Maya culture, and by broader studies of patterns of human occupation over more extensive areas.

The Urbanist Period in pre-Columbian America occurred at the zenith of those Indian cultures we call Classic or Florescent. These cultures progressed in a parallel manner while retaining a stylistic autonomy. Some basic cultural features were known both to the north and to the south of the Isthmus of Panamá, which suggests that frequent contacts and possibly the organized exchange of ideas and luxury goods between Mesoamerica and South America existed before the Pre-Classic Period. These contacts were maintained and almost certainly intensified during the Classic and Post-Classic centuries.

The principal Mesoamerican Classic cultures were those of Teotihuacán on Mexico's central plateau, the Olmec on the southern coast of Veracruz, the Totonac in the same area of the coast but to the north, the Zapotec in Oaxaca's highlands, and the Maya in Yucatán, the Petén lowlands, Chiapas, and the highlands of Guatemala. Their major cities were Teotihuacán and Azcapotzalco, La Venta, El Tajín, and Monte Albán, as well as Dzibilchaltún, Tikal, Uaxactún, Copán, Kaminaljuyú, and others. (Plate No. 1) Dispersion of Classic cultures in South America was more restricted, limited to the river valleys of the Peruvian coast and certain areas of the southern highlands. These are represented by the Mochica and Gallinazo cultures on the north coast and the Tiahuanaco in the southern highlands. The scale and population of cities in South America during this period was inferior to those in Mesoamerica.

To generalize, we might say that the development of a more elaborate, stratified society than that of the Pre-Classic Period coincided with the first sizeable urbanistic attempts in America, probably before the emergence of the first true cities. In all the urban cultures discussed, authority in political, administrative, military, and religious matters seems to have resided in a limited priesthood. The people themselves were the great mass of farmers who periodically abandoned their fields to take part in construction projects and occasional military activities. Artisans and merchants constituted a middle class, obviously urban but subordinate to the ruling group. Slavery existed in all Classic cultures.

I believe that urbanistic development was made possible by large-scale organization of the population in order to accomplish various public works programs, mainly irrigation, road building and religious and mili-

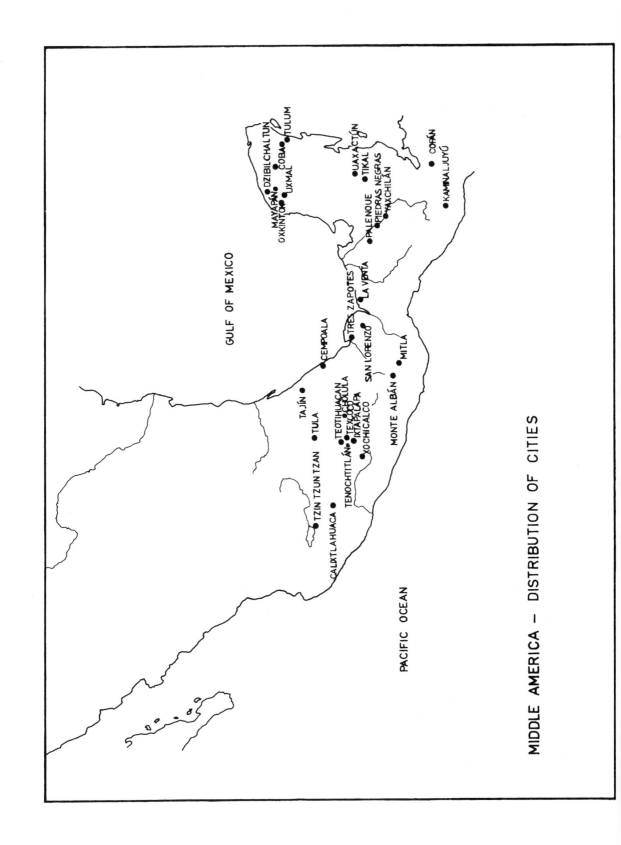

MIDDLE AMERICA – DISTRIBUTION OF CITIES

tary construction. We also find active participation of a growing artisan class in the economy during this period.

Only a small percentage of the population belonging to each culture concentrated in the cities. The majority of the inhabitants remained near their fields, tending to group together in small, self-sufficient villages, not much different from people who live in vast rural areas of Latin America today.

The zenith of Classic Indian cultures in America coincided with the declining centuries of urban life in Europe. When grass was growing in the cobbled streets of Rome, its people decimated by Barbarian invasions, Teotihuacán was a powerful center of cultural influence in Mesoamerica and, for its time, one of the largest cities in size and population in the world. The cultural regression which occurred early in the Middle Ages in Europe coincided with the flowering of the Maya civilization, one of the great scientific and artistic movements of history.

Archeology has yet to clarify whether some, or all, of the cities of Classic Indian cultures were capitals of a great state, or if we are dealing with independent city-states grouped into federations. For the Maya, this second possibility is probable (Morley, 1956; Thompson, 1959). Teotihuacán, on the other hand, appears to have been the capital of a state which controlled a good part of the central plateau of Mexico. The vast extent of the area occupied by the city, and the cultural relations between Teotihuacán and other smaller centers point to its regional predominance.

Mesoamerican Classic cultures were gradually overcome by seminomadic groups of warriors from northern Mexico who plunged the conquered cultures into their own Dark Ages. Perhaps its location decreed that Teotihuacán was the first to fall, around the eighth century A.D. Within two centuries at the most, the intensity of urban life had decreased in almost all Mesoamerica. Some of the cities were totally deserted, while others harbored only a reduced group of inhabitants. In South America, the diffusion of the Tiahuanacoid culture managed to maintain the characteristics of the Classic cultures for some time until the whole Peru-Bolivian area finally sank into a period of political decline and disintegration like that in Mesoamerica.

The great cities encountered by the Spaniards were relatively recent

1 *Middle America: Distribution of Cities.*

creations and, to a large extent, the result of the imperialistic policy undertaken by the two most important Post-Classic civilizations—the Aztec and the Inca.

The abandonment of Teotihuacán ushered in a cultural regression on the central plateau of Mexico. After the ninth century, a new people, the Toltecs, controlled the former Teotihuacán territory and founded Tula in the far north of the plateau. For two short centuries Tula was Teotihuacán's cultural heir, but ultimately it too was abandoned. Tula's prestige endured in the minor cities of the small states into which the central plateau was divided until a new tribe, the Tenochca or Aztecs, were able to take over the Toltec's cultural heritage, using this as a key factor in their imperialist designs. After 1325, Tenochtitlán was the Aztec capital. Other cities, occupied in their turn by tribes recently arrived in the center of Mexico, became rivals or allies of Tenochtitlán, especially Texcoco and Azcapotzalco, but none reached the size and population of the Aztec capital.

For unknown reasons, the principal Maya centers of the Petén were abandoned in the ninth and tenth centuries. While in the Petén and Chiapas, the characteristic semiurban life of the Maya was in almost total decline, other centers in Yucatán continued as repositories of the old culture. In the eleventh century, military groups of Mexican origin transformed Maya religion, its form of government and even its architecture. From a series of power struggles, the city of Mayapán emerged as the center of government over its rivals, Uxmal and Chichen Itzá. By the time the Spaniards arrived in Yucatán, Maya culture was in full decline.

In South America, urban life was born again in the valleys of Peru's north coast, where numerous small states were formed with urban centers as their capitals. After the twelfth century, the Chimú kingdom incorporated the north coastal states. Its foreign policy and methods of government were a forerunner of the organization and future conquests of the Inca dynasty. Chan Chan, the Chimú capital, was the first great city of South America, perhaps even larger and more densely populated than the Inca capital of Cuzco at its height, around 1500. Chan Chan and, to some extent, Cuzco in South America, as well as Tenochtitlán, Texcoco, and Cholula along with other Post-Classic Mesoamerican centers, were great cities for their time, not only in America but in the world. In addition to the great cities in the Aztec zone of influence in Mesoamerica and in the territory dominated by the Inca, there was a broad pattern of territorial occupation with urban centers of varied size serving a dense rural population that continued to live in its traditional villages.

The 300,000 inhabitants who, according to the conquistadors, lived in Tenochtitlán in 1519, had almost no parallel in Europe at the beginning of the sixteenth century.[15] Only Paris had an equally large population but certainly not London, Florence, Rome, Venice, the cities of the Hanseatic League, nor the Spanish cities. Constantinople's importance had declined after the tenth and eleventh centuries. Even the great culture of Cambodia, which had a population settlement pattern and semiurban characteristics not unlike those of the Maya, had fallen into stagnation in the twelfth century after great periods of building in the ninth and tenth centuries. China had, without doubt, the greatest population concentration in those times, and Marco Polo's testimony demonstrates that in the Far East, the city was a phenomenon determined by sociopolitical circumstances not too different from those which produced the cities of pre-Columbian America.

The majority of cities in America began as unplanned settlements. I do not believe that Teotihuacán and Tiahuanaco, for example, had a previous urban plan which included both the religious center and the housing neighborhoods. Native architects concentrated all their skill in the design of the ceremonial groups which formed part of those cities and centers following certain principles that seem to have had distinctive regional variations in each cultural area, though they may once have had a common origin. Urban planning in pre-Columbian America was, in other words, a succession of coherent decisions undertaken by highly placed members of the social order who sought to guide or correct the physical development of an urban center.[16]

Besides the ceremonial groups, parts of other districts of the city, especially the housing neighborhoods, may have been planned during the Classic or Urbanist Period, but urban planning as such was more systematic during the Post-Classic or Imperialist Periods, coinciding with the expansion of the Aztecs in Mesoamerica and of the Chimú and Inca in South America. Chan Chan and perhaps other cities of the north and central coast of Peru were planned, as were their citadels. They were built by the repetition of large urban features, standardized in form and layout. The Inca planned several small cities such as Ollantaytambo, for use as garrisons, depots or agricultural colonies and here, too, made repeated use of regularly shaped elements. In Mesoamerica, the succes-

— *NOTES ON PREFACE* —

1. RECENTLY WILLEY, ECKHOLM AND MILLON defined seven attributes which would establish the difference between "civilized," or urban, and "non-civilized" peoples. They are: monumental public architecture, great art styles, development of practical sciences and means of recording, population of relatively great size and density, differentiation of the population into a number of social classes, conservation of natural resources for public enterprise and extensive foreign trade (Willey, Eckholm and Millon, 1965). These seven attributes can be included among Childe's ten criteria. Notably absent are the invention and use of writing—which is particularly important in Childe's work but would not conform to the situation in the Mayan and Andean areas—and the formation of an "acting capital" based on a system of taxation of primary products.

2. Childe used ten criteria to distinguish the first cities from earlier or contemporaneous villages. They are as follows: 1) the size and population; 2) the emergence of specialists; 3) the formation of an "acting capital" based on a system of taxation of primary products; 4) the construction of buildings and public works on a scale unknown before; 5) the emergence of a "ruling class" made up of priests, civic, and military leaders and functionaries; 6) the invention and use of writing; 7) the beginnings of exact and predictive sciences such as mathematics, geometry, and astronomy, which made it possible to determine the tropical year and led to the creation of the calendar; 8) an art which produced conceptualized and refined styles; 9) the development of foreign trade centered around "luxury" items and prime materials such as metals; 10) an assured supply of raw materials to the artisans which enabled them to become exclusively dedicated specialists.
Childe devoted several of his major works to an analysis of the origins of urban life. You will find additional information in *What Happened in History* (Penguin, 1954), *New Light in the Most Ancient East* (Grove Press Inc., New York), *The Dawn of European Civilization* (London, 1950) and *Early Forms of Society* in Volume I of *A History of Technology* edited by Charles Singer *et al.* (Clarendon Press, 1954), as well as in *Man Makes Himself* (The Rationalist Press Association, Ltd., London, 1936).

3. Weber says that the different definitions of a city have one element in common: a city consists of a group of one or more dwellings, separated yet relatively concentrated. In general, although not necessarily, the houses of a city are built connected to each other, in our day often wall to wall (Weber, 1958).

4. The appearance of writing and a literary group has been considered significant by the majority of authors who have made studies of urban life. The term *literati* has been used by Toynbee, Childe and Redfield among others to distinguish the literate and educated group in each society. Further information on this theme can be found in *Man Makes Himself* by V. Gordon Childe (The Rationalist Press Association, Ltd., London, 1936), in *History Begins at Sumer* by Samuel Noah Kramer (Doubleday Anchor Books; New York, 1959) and in *"The Primitive World and its Transformations"* by Robert Redfield (Cornell University Press, Ithaca, 1953).

5. A list of definitions used in the estimation of "urban" population as nationally defined can be found in *Growth of the World's Urban and Rural Population, 1920-2000;* Department of Economic and Social Affair, Population Studies No. 44, Annex II, p. 81-84, United Nations, New York, 1969.

6. In recent years, researchers have begun using instruments that measure the resistance of the soil through its electric conductivity (Stirling, Ramey and Stirling Jr., 1960) and magnetic intensity (Black and Johnston, 1962).

7. Schaedel suggests that the term city should be tried for "entities of between 25,000-50,000, together with the other nominal sociological criteria (social differentiation, complex occupation specialization), and the adequate resolution of such problems as high density (let us say between 510,000 h/km^2) with systems of water supply, defense, drainage. and disposal of refuse and of the dead, food storage and internal and external intercommunication" (Schaedel, 1969).

8. I have adopted the spatial divisions proposed by Willey and Phillips; the site, the locality, the region, and the area. The site is the minimum operational unit of geographic space; the locality is a geographic space small enough to take on complete cultural homogeneity at all times; the region, because of its scale, offers the most favorable field for a detailed study of the relationship of culture and environment, and the area corresponds loosely to the ethnographer's cultural area and is usually divided into subareas to facilitate the study of significant cultural differences even within a sphere of cultural similarity (Willey and Phillips, 1958).

9. The limits of Mesoamerica at the beginning of the sixteenth century were: the arid lands of North America to the north, approximately fixed by a mobile line running from the Panuco River to the Lerma and Sinaloa Rivers; to the south, from the outlet of the Motagua River in Nicaragua to the Gulf of Nicoya (Kirchhoff, 1943; Piña Chan, 1960).

10. The centralized power, possibly backed by a dominant religious element, is apparent in Mohenjo-daro and Harappá, as seen in the common ground plan and citadel (Piggot, 1952). Plant cultivation only became important in the valleys of central Peru after 2500 B.C. based on a more extensive use of floodlands. Settlements were still small in size and population (Patterson, 1971).

11. Apparently pottery was known in northern and southern Colombia earlier than in Mexico, Central America or Peru (Lanning, 1967).

12. Maize remains dating from around 1500 B.C. were found at a site called Las Aldas on the north coast of Peru and another, named Culebras, where maize was first cultivated, on the central coast (Lanning, 1967). This maize had been cultivated by the inhabitants of villages which already had ceremonial buildings. These recent finds precede the Chavín Period on Peru's coast by seven or eight centuries. Findings at a site near Huarmey, on the north central coast of Peru, indicate that maize occurs in a preceramic context (Kelley and Bonavía, 1963).

13. An interesting discussion on farming systems and their influence on the development of communities is included in Flannery and others, 1967.

14. This point has been subject to endless debate. The investigations by Robert Adams might prove that, at least in the Near East, irrigation was not a prerequisite for the emergence of the city (Adams, 1960).

15. In my opinion, Tenochtitlán never reached such a large population. See the fifth chapter of this book.

16. For a more detailed analysis of the criteria used for defining a city in pre-Columbian America see Hardoy, 1968, p. 8-13.

·1

THE ORIGINS OF AMERICAN CIVILIZATIONS

"God the creator against God the destroyer, an eternal struggle that never ends. Forever forming and transforming the world, it dominates nature and determines man's existence."

PAUL WESTHEIM
(ARTE ANTIGUO DE MEXICO)

1

THE EVOLUTION of America's Indian civilizations ended abruptly as the first generation of Spanish conquistadors arrived on the mainland of the Continent.[1] We can only speculate as to their future had they not come to a premature end. As isolated phenomena of cultural development, Indian civilizations had not even reached, in many aspects, the technical level of the pre-Christian civilizations of Europe or the Near and Far East. We also have serious doubts as to how far they might have been able to progress since they had only an elementary knowledge of metals, a limited number of domesticated animals, did not utilize the wheel, and lacked a system of alphabetical writing.

During the middle of the sixteenth century, the initial thrust of the Spanish Conquest had spent itself, and the first stage of colonization had already begun. Over the ruins of Indian cities and villages, around the more protected bays of the coast or near the mouths of rivers, in the lower valleys and in the fertile plains of North and South America, the first European style cities appeared as the unmistakable stamp of a colonization intended to endure. A new society took the place of the old, promoting values unknown to the Indian cultures.

With the appearance of the viceroys and mayors, bishops and preachers, adventurers, gold seekers, and large landowners, came the first questions. Who were these unexpected persons with strange customs who lived in the forests, coasts, and highlands of this newly discovered world? How could they exist in contradiction of biblical tradition and scientific theories of the epoch? Were they, perhaps, human beings, and therefore descended from Adam? How was it possible that they had reached a level of civilization and built cities which, in many respects, surpassed those known by most of the colonizers in the Old World?

3

The first speculations about man's origins in America were not slow in coming. By 1590, Father Acosta had already affirmed, wisely as it later developed, that man came to America by crossing the cold regions.[2] From this first position sprang many theories suggesting Phoenicians, Canaanites, Carthaginians, Egyptians, Armenians, Greeks, Jews, Tartars, Vikings, and even a Chinese Buddhist monk as the first inhabitants of America.[3] Then there were those who, like Sarmiento de Gamboa in 1570, declared that in the year 1320 B.C. some Europeans who had settled in a section of the immense Atlantic island (Atlantis) remained isolated there as a result of a flood, the sixth, which submerged part of the island, "and thus the people in this part lost commerce and contact with those from Europe and Africa and other parts, so that they even lost memory of it. . . ." The survivors of Atlantis settled "the rich and most powerful kingdoms of Peru and neighboring provinces," and none other than Ulysses and the Greeks were the first to come "to the land of Yucatán and Campeche, land of New Spain, because the people of this land wear the Greek costume, head-dress and garment from the nation of Ulysses, and use many Greek words and have Greek letters" (Sarmiento de Gamboa, 1947).

The first methodical studies took place during the nineteenth century. The theory of the origin of American man, stated by Ameghino at the end of the preceding century was gradually abandoned for lack of evidences of human remains on the continent (McCown, 1950). Prehistoric studies in the Americas, particularly in North America, have made great strides in the last decades. However, we still are faced with a confusing and often contradictory picture. The ice sheets which marked the end of the last glacial period retreated about 20,000 years ago. In their wake, taking advantage of favorable geographic conditions, came the first Asiatic migrations to the American continent. This is the position generally accepted by archeologists, supported by the total absence of any skeletal remains which can be dated earlier than about 20,000 years ago. However, Stewart tells us that before that epoch, related types existed in east Asia (Stewart, 1960), and Sellard reports that in several sites in California, such as one on the island of Santa Rosa seventy kilometers off the west coast of the United States, as well as in another called Texas Street near San Diego, evidence of human presence has been found dating from 20,000 and 35,000 years ago respectively (Sellards, 1960).

The picture of American prehistory is a complex one and subject to endless speculation.[4] It is generally accepted that the majority of the original settlers of the American continent were Mongoloids who came across the Bering Straits.[5] These people must have been small groups formed by several families of hunters, fishermen, and gatherers who crossed Alaska following the animals that served as their food. The problems inherent in supplying food for sizeable groups had yet to be solved, and the clan, the small semifamilial nucleus, was the largest grouping that the environment could support. Lacking beasts of burden, they traveled slowly on foot, carrying their possessions with them. It would certainly have taken them several centuries to travel from one end of the continent to another.

About 8,500 years ago, Pre-Ceramic bands hunting horse and sloth reached the southern tip of the continent and temporarily occupied some caves on the coast of the Straits of Magellan. Traces of their passage have been found in California, Wyoming, Texas, New Mexico, and Nebraska in the United States; in northern Mexico and in the central Valley of Mexico; in the western chain of the Peruvian Andes; on the Bolivian Plateau; and in caves of the central mountains of Argentina. Their remains were sometimes found together with bones of the mastodons, mammoths, horses, bison and other huge animals they hunted for food.

Almost all the accessible regions of America must have been traveled, temporarily occupied, abandoned and reoccupied in an unending search for the most favorable environmental conditions. The first arrivals, who had taken advantage of periods of glacial retreat in the north of the continent, were pushed southward by new migrants. Along the longitudinal valleys of North America and the Pacific Coast, the first great exploration of the continent began. While the women gathered the vegetable foods and hunted the small game found near the caves and camps which served as their base, the men hunted and fished to obtain the protein food needed for survival. When they came across a natural port which offered the combination of abundant fish or shellfish and a source of fresh water, the group halted their travels and enjoyed a period of stable life which encouraged the development and refinement of their limited utensils. The many mounds with remains of shells, artifacts, and vegetable residue which have been found along the Pacific Coast bear witness to the stays of these groups.[6] Willey and Phillips emphasize that any theory about population dispersion in Mesoamerica and South America must assume the north to south movement of these groups and cultures of a stone age development (Willey and Phillips, 1958).

Some of the principal migration routes may have converged in the central Valley of Mexico. Once past the Isthmus of Tehuantepec, the migrating groups would probably choose the Pacific Coast for its possibilities of fishing and shellfish gathering. Topography determined the route, and environmental possibilities decided the length of stay. Climate and those products which nature generously offered, rather than the quality of the soil, were what attracted the more vigorous groups to the protected valleys of the American plateaus and the coastal areas where fish and shellfish were plentiful. Agriculture was still unknown and pottery useless to people always on the move. Industry was limited to chipping obsidian and other hard stone into crude tools and weapons with which to hunt the great herbivores for food.

While some groups remained, others continued toward the south, across the highlands of western South America as far as the plains. They must have then crossed Patagonia along the coast or over the mountains, living on guanaco, horse, and sloth meat until they came to Tierra del Fuego. Others probably traveled down the Pacific Coast in canoes, feeding on birds, fish and shellfish, tossed about by the rains and relentless winds that devastated the unfriendly terrain, to finally converge in the caves of the Straits or on the freezing islands of the far south (Bird, 1938). Other groups may have traveled eastward across the interminable sameness of the forest without coming across any geographic features which induced them to linger, until they came to the mountain ranges of eastern Brazil, only to then again head south. Thus ended the first great exploration of America, two hundred and fifty or three hundred generations ago.

The inherent advantages or disadvantages of certain environments gradually became factors encouraging either a sedentary pattern of life with cultural progress or a nomadic existence and stagnation. In the valleys of the highlands and small rivers, where some of the great American water systems originate, in coastal areas where a river opens into the sea, on the fertile and humid banks of lakes and rivers where vegetation never stops growing, America's first inhabitants found the resources and incentives they needed to develop the successive stages of a cultural progress which was to culminate in the great Indian civilizations. The central Valley and Gulf Coast of Mexico, the highlands of Oaxaca and Guatemala, the swampy areas of the Petén, the Peru-Bolivian highlands, and the river valleys of the Peruvian coast are of particular interest for this book, along with other sites of ancient and prolonged occupation. These are certainly not the only sites occupied by the stone age hunters of Mesoamerica and South America. On the contrary, the stone age sites seem to have been more numerous in temperate, open areas where game was abundant (Willey and Phillips, 1959). But in the central Valley of Mexico, in the north and central coastal valleys of Peru, and in some of the other areas mentioned, many of the principal events of the prehistoric and historic epochs of America transpired. Here some of the most important Indian cultures and later the *mestizaje,* or racial mixture, of Colonial life, developed.

Even today, when technical advances can manipulate topography and science is ever widening our possibilities of modifying environment, some of the sites where the preagricultural and preceramic cultures of America lived are still being occupied, now by the cities of a progressively industrial civilization.

Not all Indian societies of Mesoamerica and South America reached the urbanist stage. Those which achieved it did so in limited areas of particularly propitious regions. The area occupied by urban civilizations and their zones of influence was restricted in comparison to the immensity of the continent. Demographically, however, the percentage of the Indian population which it included was certainly greater than their nomadic and seminomadic counterparts. I do not mean that the majority of pre-Hispanic American civilizations lived in urban conditions. This was not the case. I only want to point out that the influence of an urban way of life, with the characteristics we have discussed, affected to some degree a considerable percentage of the population living in the areas studied in this book, distinguishing their manner of living from that of other areas. This cultural difference in living practiced by the principal civilizations and their peripheral areas was even more accentuated at the time of the Spanish Conquest, and the gap between the technological levels and subsistence of the inhabitants of one area as compared to another was widening long before the beginning of the Classic Period in Mesoamerica and South America.

On the other hand, with few exceptions, the inhabitants of the territories which today constitute Argentina, Uruguay and Paraguay, and those of east, central, and northwest Brazil never got beyond the level of hunters, fishermen, and gatherers who lived in limited groups in portable or perishable shelters. Other peoples in the interior of South America did not progress beyond a level in which agriculture alternated with a seminomadic life, banding together in groups which stayed only a few years in each place. When the soil became exhausted and game grew scarce, the group moved on to another bend in some river in Brazil, to a new place on the plains of Venezuela or Colombia, or to the east of Peru, Ecuador, or Bolivia. Certain communities reached an acceptable specialization, and in this case each tribe made the baskets, pottery or canoes they needed to exchange with other tribes. The village was the basic social unit, and its members were generally related by family ties (Bennett and Bird, 1949). Unending warfare, infertile soil which was periodically subjected to erosive clearing methods, and natural conditions beyond the scope of their meager technical resources prevented these people from increasing their numbers and developing an urban life.[7]

Temporary settlements arranged along a pathway or in a circle, small round huts scattered separately and without order, or a huge common house up to fifty meters long and ten meters high were the ultimate expressions of urban progress among these seminomadic groups. Lowie found that it was characteristic of several groups in this cultural area to live in a large communal house accommodating from twenty to seventy residents, as among the Yecuana and Guinan. The houses of the Tupari, next to the Guaporé River, are said to have lodged up to thirty-five families. Lowie describes a Tupinamba village as consisting of four to eight houses, each accommodating thirty to two hundred families. Often a single structure, or a pair of this type, accommodates the entire population, as in the villages along the Aiarí River (Lowie, 1948).

The Tupinamba villages represent one of the most evolved forms of settlement in those areas of South America that did not reach an urban stage. Their spacious communal dwellings, regular in plan and up to 150 meters long, were arranged around a civic-ceremonial plaza (Métraux, 1948). The villages were defended by a single or double palisade at times reinforced by trenches and stakes driven into the ground, as was also common among the Guaraní.

In the Antilles, only the Taino and the Caribes, among the four known aboriginal cultural groups, practiced rudimentary agriculture and lived in simple huts of logs and reeds. They had no cities, but were grouped into villages which they built on easy-to-defend, natural elevations (Pichardo Moya, 1958).

THE EARLY STAGES OF URBAN
EVOLUTION IN MESOAMERICA

Stone age man left traces of his passage in various sites scattered all over Mesoamerica. Remains of his artifacts, along with the fauna existing then, have been found in the basins of the rivers and lakes of the Mexican States of Baja California, Chihuahua, Tamaulipas, and Durango and in the caves of Nueva León, Cohuila, and Tamaulipas. Sites in the States of Guanajuato and Jalisco have yielded evidence of these Pre-Ceramic cultures of hunter-gatherers. Even to the south, near Mitla in the State of Oaxaca, and in Concepción in the State of Campeche, archeologists have found an important collection of stone artifacts fashioned by chipping (Aveleyra, 1960; Willey and Phillips, 1958; Piña Chan, 1955; Di Peso, 1963).

The central area of Mexico is the best known of the Pre-Ceramic areas in Mesoamerica and the desert valley of Tehuacán, some 150 miles south of Mexico City, the most intensively excavated (MacNeish, 1971). Remains found here indicate a hunting society culturally no different than its neighbors to the north and south. They shifted camps seasonally and were grouped in small bands. Although by 7200 B.C. the sources of food and technology had not changed much, an increase in population took place showing a growing dependency on plant collecting. By 5000 or 4000 B.C., camps were larger than during the earlier periods. Subsistence was probably easier although the selection of plants and game was unchanged. Wild maize, chili, and avocado were used, but the seasonal pattern of migration was very much the same as three, four, or five millennia before. By 1500 B.C., the people of the Tehuacán Valley were full-time agriculturists and lived in small villages.

Because of a combination of circumstances, it was in the central plateau of Mexico and on the not-too-distant central Gulf Coast that culture advanced (Plate No. 1, page 15). Its beginnings in the Archaic Period are uncertain, but probably earlier than Vaillant indicated (Vaillant, 1955). His sequence for the central Valley of Mexico is too close together, and the dates he proposes too recent. New dating techniques have pushed back the beginnings of the Archaic Period to 1500 B.C., (Ekholm, 1958) or even several centuries earlier (Krickeberg, 1961) (Plate No. 2).

2 *Chart of the Evolution of the Middle American and South American Cultures.*

EVOLUTION OF THE MIDDLE AMERICAN

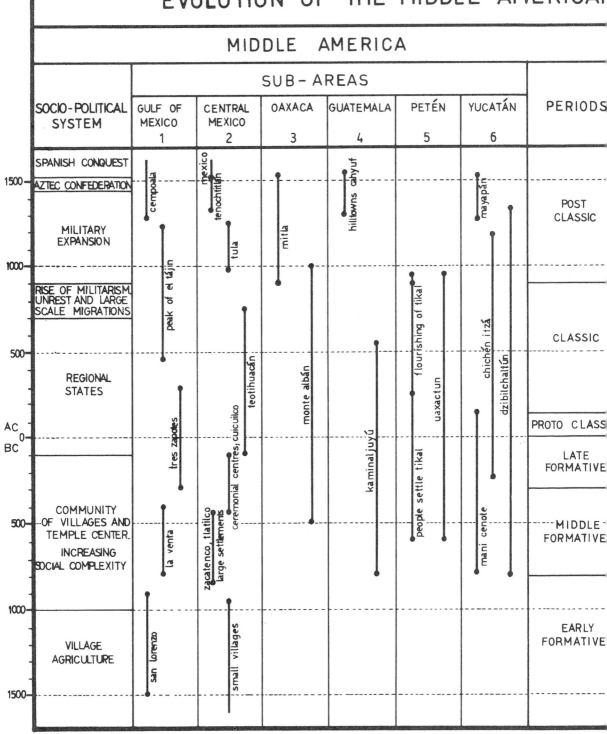

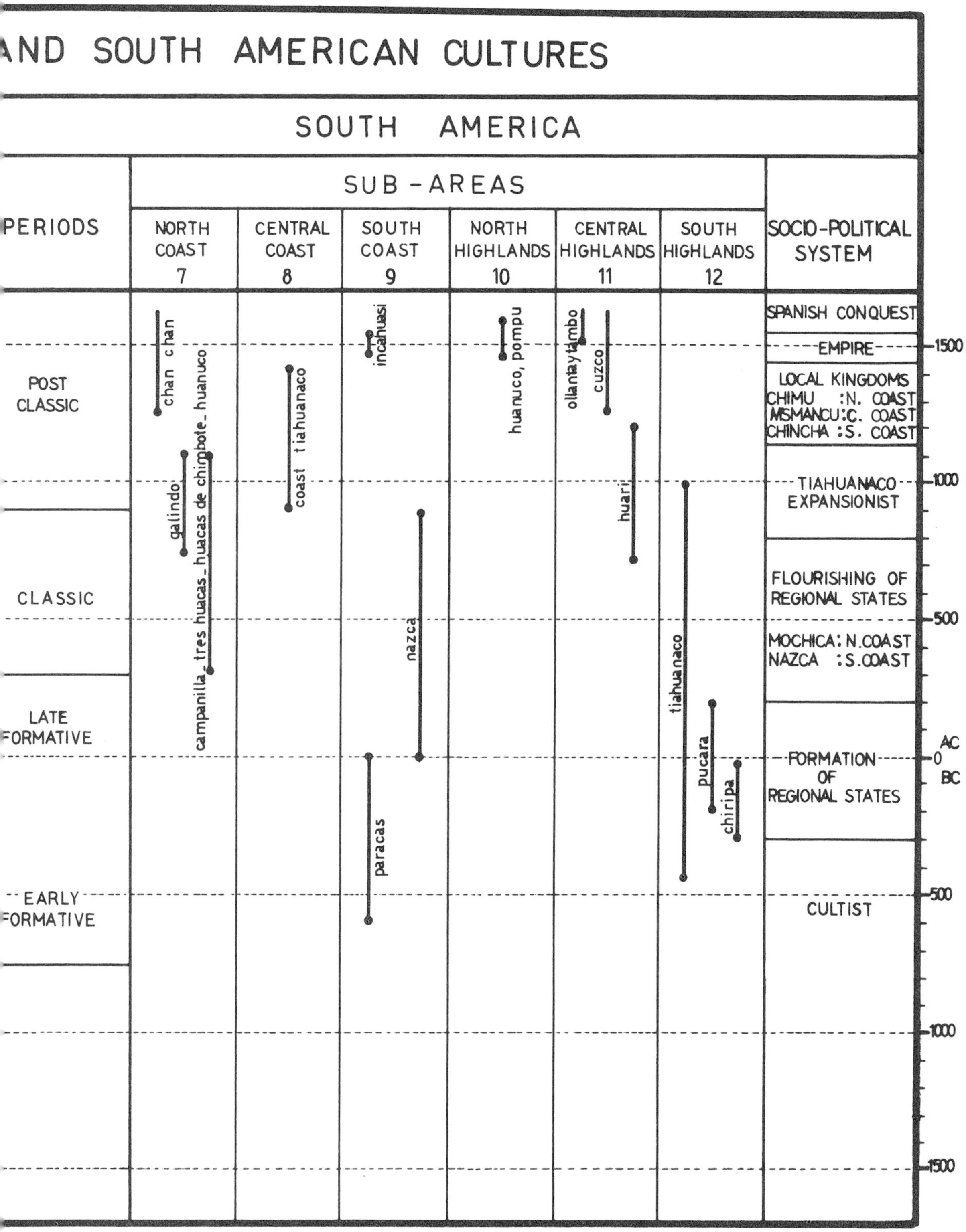
AND SOUTH AMERICAN CULTURES
SOUTH AMERICA
SUB - AREAS
PERIODS
NORTH COAST 7
CENTRAL COAST 8
SOUTH COAST 9
NORTH HIGHLANDS 10
CENTRAL HIGHLANDS 11
SOUTH HIGHLANDS 12
SOCIO-POLITICAL SYSTEM
POST CLASSIC
CLASSIC
LATE FORMATIVE
EARLY FORMATIVE
chan chan
galindo
campanilla_tres huacas_huacas de chimbote_huanuco
coast tiahuanaco
incahuasi
nazca
paracas
huanuco, pompu
ollantaytambo
cuzco
huari
tiahuanaco
pucara
chiripa
SPANISH CONQUEST
EMPIRE
LOCAL KINGDOMS
CHIMU :N. COAST
MSMANCU:C. COAST
CHINCHA :S. COAST
TIAHUANACO EXPANSIONIST
FLOURISHING OF REGIONAL STATES
MOCHICA: N.COAST
NAZCA :S.COAST
FORMATION OF REGIONAL STATES
CULTIST
1500
1000
500
AC
0
BC
500
1000
1500

Two successive cultures, which Vaillant calls Zacatenco and Ticomán, presumably originated in the west and east of the central Valley of Mexico respectively, where they predominated for a millenium and a half in an environment which was probably not much different from that of today. The members of the Zacatenco culture had already adopted a sedentary life, living in large and small villages of houses built of perishable materials and set out with no apparent plan. They still lacked a developed ceremonialism and knew nothing of stone architecture. In that epoch they were still democratic societies without social distinctions and political and military preoccupations (Bernal, 1955). Agriculture, which now included maize, squash, beans, chili, avocado, and other edible plants along with hunting and fishing, provided their diet. Tlatilco, near Tacuba and within the present metropolitan area of Mexico City, was one of the villages occupied by this culture, about 800 B.C., although El Arbolillo, a site on the western shore of Lake Texcoco, is considered chronologically older (Piña Chan, 1954; Vaillant, 1955; Coe, M., 1966).

Tlatilco's artists earned their culture and village an ever-growing fame. No one who has seen the clay figurines found at this site in 1936 can fail to be attracted by their engaging simplicity. The figurines provide an extensive gallery of men, women, and children with their dogs, tools, clothing, and adornments, which tell us much about their life and customs. We see women cradling children; women with babies on their backs or playing with dogs; players preparing for the ritual ball game; realistic animal figures; human figures with one or two heads, slits for eyes and often flattened skulls; dancers and acrobats; and, possibly for the first time in Mesoamerica, the representation of the fire god and the first magicians. This represents a naturalistic art cultivated by a people among whom the first specialized artists may not even have appeared.

We know little of the social structure of Tlatilco's inhabitants when they occupied that large and unplanned site. Some time later, other groups of the same culture occupied Zacatenco. El Arbolillo, Tlatilco and Zacatenco remained inhabited throughout several centuries. Then came the occupation of Atoto, Coatepec, Xaloztoc, Lomas de Becerra, Copilco, Azcapotzalco, Tetelpán, and perhaps other sites (Piña Chan, 1955) near the western shore of Lake Texcoco, which was shrinking continuously as the result of a prolonged drought. Most of these were small villages, inhabited by a few hundred people, that remained occupied during the entire evolution of the Ticomán culture without significant modifications.

During the Formative Period, the central plateau of Mexico was subject to outside influences. The Zacatenco culture of such long duration was finally superseded by the Ticomán culture which may have originated on Mexico's east coast.

During the last centuries of the Formative Period, the whole perimeter of Lake Texcoco's basin was becoming settled with growing villages. Chimalhuacán, Tlapacoya, Papaletla, and Tepetlaoztoc were Archaic sites on the eastern shore, the last two located inland in a fluvial basin. Other new villages were added to those already on the western shore, like Ticomán, a few kilometers from El Arbolillo; Cuicuilco; San Miguel Amantla; San Sebastián; and Cerro de Tepalcate, which was an inland site with dwellings of superior quality for its time laid out with care on artificial terraces. At some point in the Middle Formative Period, probably between 1000 and 500 B.C., the slopes of the valley of Teotihuacán were occupied with small rural communities. At the end of the pre-Christian era the Alluvial plain was favored.

The first polychrome pottery on the central plateau of Mexico belongs to the period of Ticomán culture. This suggests the emergence of an artisan class that could dispense, at least partially, with the agricultural work which still occupied the rest of the population. This first example of specialization may be connected with an increase of agricultural production in the Valley and the adoption of maize as the main crop. The appearance of certain social differences, perhaps intimated in the representations of Tlatilco's figurines, became quite evident in the final stages of the Formative Period, when the ruling priesthood appears to have controlled administrative as well as religious matters.

During this same period, the first temples were built. The temple at Cerro de Tepalcate was a simple, rectangular structure of perishable materials, with a slanted roof supported by a talus platform of stone and clay. It is the oldest known temple in central Mexico (Piña Chan, 1955).

The Pyramid of Cuicuilco also belongs to the Formative Period. We find the ruins of this immense structure near the modern University City in the Mexican capital. The pyramid, which may have stood up to twenty meters high, had a circular shape and was formed by four stepped bodies in talus form. The lower platform was covered by lava from the eruption of the Xitle volcano in pre-Christian times, which gives us the impression that the structure is too flat for its diameter and volume. Even so, its simple shape is imposing, and reconstruction attempts indicate that its builders were concerned with the proportions of their work. Its size is so great—the base diameter is about 135 meters—that we need to back away to take it all in at a glance. The stone and adobe structure, covered over with mud and painted red, was built in several stages, each perhaps representing a former temple, but always respecting its circular form. On the upper terrace stood a temple which was reached by ramps on the east and west sides of the pyramid. Various authors consider the Pyramid of Cuicuilco to be the first known example of monumental architecture (Kubler, 1961) or the first temple (Krickeberg, 1961) in central Mexico. I believe that the architectural conception of the Pyramid of Cuicuilco may have had antecedents outside the Valley of Mexico, although as a form it was not repeated often thereafter. In this Pre-Classic pyramid, we already see stepped bodies in talus form and the apparent disproportion between the immense volume of the base and the diminutive, often perishable temple structure which it supported on the upper platform. This incongruity of the size of the temple and the volume of the base is seen repeatedly throughout the evolution of Indian civilizations and may have been dictated by religious reasons.

The origin of this architectural form and the reasons behind it are less interesting for the purposes of this book than the verification of some facts confirming class divisions in Pre-Classic cultures in central Mexico. These facts are the authority of a ruling religious group, the emergence of specialists, and the organization of what would be called a large work force for that time and place. These laborers would have been dependent, at least part of the year, on the primary production of other sectors of the population working in the fields. We can even assume the beginnings of commerce, considering the existence of numerous villages which could have developed local specializations. All these factors herald the Urbanist Period.

Cuicuilco, Cerro de Tepalcate and perhaps other centers in the central Valley of Mexico may have been agricultural or semi-agricultural villages, but they possessed a temple and thereby earned the role of civic-ceremonial centers of regional influence.[8] Judging by the volume of the Pyramid of Cuicuilco and the work force needed for its construction, Cuicuilco may already have been a center with a considerable degree of self-sufficiency in religious and political matters, ranking high among the sedentary settlements of Mexico's central plateau during the Formative Period. This marks Cuicuilco as one of the first of a series of centers with increasingly varied and complex functions which includes, successively,

Teotihuacán, Azcapotzalco, Tula, Texcoco, and Tenochtitlán; each reflecting the changing political organization of central Mexico. While one or more centers stood out from the others, concentrating on increasingly urban functions, the majority of the villages kept their rural character while losing some of their original simple localism.

Two aspects of Cuicuilco would be interesting to investigate from an urban point of view. If it was really the Ticomán culture, perhaps originating on Mexico's Gulf Coast, that introduced the Olmec influence into the central Valley (Krickeberg, 1961), it would be important to inspect the surroundings of Cuicuilco's circular pyramid in detail, studying the arrangement and characteristics of the neighboring structures and the spaces left between them. At the same time, a deeper study of the pattern of the Olmec ceremonial centers of the Coast should be made. I believe that these two antecedents could help explain the astonishing maturity of the urban design of Teotihuacán, though this secret may lie buried within the limits of that center's occupied area itself, as we shall see in the next chapter.

The Pyramid of Cuicuilco may have been built a few centuries before the Christian era, but the site had been occupied even before then. At some point the Xitle volcano on the flank of Ajusco Mountain erupted, its lava covering part of the valley in a layer six to eight meters deep in some places and burying several Pre-Classic sites, some already abandoned, but others, like Cuicuilco, in full flower. During this time, about 100 kilometers northeast of Cuicuilco on the opposite side of Lake Texcoco, those conditions were in the making which would impel Teotihuacán to become the principal center on Mexico's central plateau throughout the next six or seven centuries. The zenith of Teotihuacán and the Classic cultures was also the period of the first true Mesoamerican cities.

Other areas of Mesoamerica passed through parallel stages, although none of them are as well known as the Valley of Mexico. Archaeologists have been able to determine certain technical as well as aesthetic similarities which link the various Formative cultures (Willey and Phillips, 1958). Perhaps the most outstanding characteristics of the Formative cultures were the stepped pyramidal bases for religious structures and the population growth in all cultural areas of Mesoamerica with its accompanying increase in size and number of existing villages. This established a pattern of urban and semiurban settlements that remained unchanged throughout the Classic Period. A final characteristic of the Formative cultures is seen in the gradual shift in importance of certain of these villages which grew into true civic-religious capitals, perhaps even political and administrative centers, during the Classic Period. Some of these capitals, already in gestation during the Late Formative Period, were the first in Mesoamerica and those which best represent the Classic cultures: Teotihuacán in the central Valley of Mexico; Monte Albán in the highlands of Oaxaca; Kaminaljuyú in Central Guatemala; El Tajín on the Gulf Coast; perhaps Uaxactún; and possibly other centers with origins yet to be established in the lowlands of Petén; Dzibilchaltún, its antiquity and Pre-Classic occupation recently proved, in Yucatán. Although these and other centers were linked with each other, they retained their own regional differences during the Pre-Classic Period. The common characteristics which set the Classic cultures apart were not yet widespread.

THE OLMEC CEREMONIAL CENTERS

Centuries before the emergence of the Classic cultures of Mesoamerica, a short, stocky people of corn farmers with mongoloid features who lived on Mexico's Gulf Coast began to exert a growing cultural influence on their neighbors in the southern lowlands and the Mexican plateau. For some authors, the Olmec is the mother of such other cultures as the Maya, Teotihuacán, Zapotec, and El Tajín (Jiménez Moreno, 1942), in other words what we consider the Classic cultures of Mesoamerica. Covarrubias stated[9] that the Olmec style is distantly yet tangibly connected with the oldest Teotihuacán art, with the Totonac (El Tajín) style, with the most ancient forms of Maya art, and with Zapotec objects which tend to be more Olmec the older they are (Jiménez Moreno, 1942). This position has also been supported by a new generation of Americanists (Coe, M., 1966). It would seem evident that Olmec culture spread widely throughout Mesoamerica and that its influence was felt several centuries before the Christian era. Some of the oldest known dates in Mesoamerica belong to the Olmec era, and one Olmec site, inhabited up to the end of the Classic Period, seems to have been already occupied in the Pre-Classic, coinciding in time with Tlatilco's occupation in the Valley of Mexico (Ekholm, 1958) and another, San Lorenzo, precedes it by several centuries (Coe, M., 1968).

Certain characteristics identified with the Classic cultures already existed among the Olmecs. We should first mention the appearance of a form of writing, and the calendar, since these usually precede the urbanist stage of a society (Krickeberg, 1961); but equally important was the cult of the jaguar, which Olmec art represented often and in all available materials—in jade and stone, in miniatures, in bas-relief, and in sculpture. The widespread jaguar cult was undoubtedly supported by a coercive priesthood already in authority which probably represents the first regional stratified state in Mesoamerica with influence over a vast area and population (Coe, M., 1968). The vast public projects of the Olmecs leave few other alternatives of administrative and political organization. The Olmecs also developed ceremonial architecture on a larger scale than had ever been known in Mesoamerica. The place of origin of the building materials and the site at La Venta where they were used is in itself an indication of an organized society which could call on a surplus work force for at least part of the year.[10]

The Olmecs excelled as sculptors and carvers of delicate jade miniatures, incised simply with faithful representations of human figures. Their monumental and realistic sculpture in stone, some of which are heads of superhuman proportions or half-kneeling human figures, constitute the best artistic synthesis that Mesoamerican art has produced. In the stone altars and stelae at San Lorenzo, La Venta, and Tres Zapotes, artists introduced the bas-relief technique which later spread over all Mesoamerica. We also know that a ball game was practiced by the Olmecs, using a ball of rubber, a substance plentiful in their land.[11]

Future excavations in known Olmec centers and in the area as a whole should provide us with much important information. Hot and humid, yet rich in those natural resources prized by pre-Columbian Indian cultures, such as cacao, rubber, brilliant feathers, jade, and certain precious metals, this low coastal area may have been the birthplace of the ideas which urged a good part of Mesoamerica toward its Classic stage.

The Olmec area provides valuable data for urbanists as well. In San Lorenzo, in Tres Zapotes, and in La Venta, we already see the regularly proportioned plazas outlined by rectangular platforms which were to become the model for the plazas built by all Classic cultures of Mesoamerica with the exception of the Maya.[12] Slightly modified versions of this plaza appear centuries later in some of Teotihuacán's groups and, with greater modifications, in Tula, El Tajín, and Xochicalco. Also from Tres Zapotes are the first structures in which we find the combination of a talus and vertical panel or *talud-tablero,* a feature characteristic of

Teotihuacán (Krickeberg, 1961) and subsequent architecture of the central Valley of Mexico up to the time of the Conquest.

Between 1200 and 900 B.C., a monumental complex was built in San Lorenzo on the top of an artificial plateau raised fifty meters above the seasonally flooded plain of the Coatzacoalcos and Chiquitos basins. It was formed by an axial sequence of three courts framed by low platforms with a small central pyramid of earth and clay (Coe, M., 1968).

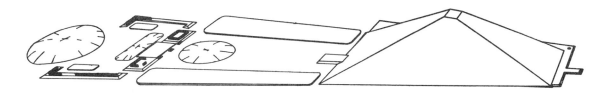

3 *La Venta: In La Venta's spatial arrangement we find some of the characteristics that lasted throughout two millennia in subsequent examples built in the central plateau of Mexico. La Venta may have been one of the first attempts in Mexico to establish a predetermined pattern in the grouping of structural complexes, utilizing a directional axis and a symmetrical layout. (Credit: Drucker, Ph; Heizer, R.F. and Squier, R.J.: "Excavations at La Venta, Tabasco, 1955"; S.I., B.A.E., Bulletin 170, Washington, D.C., 1959.)*

Centuries later in La Venta, a pyramid on a rectangular foundation was built, flanked to the east and west by regular shaped mounds and bounded at the far end of the plaza thus formed by a pair of platforms symmetrically placed along its main axis (Plate No. 3). These platforms, while narrowing the line of lateral mounds, formed an entrance to a second, smaller plaza, also rectangular and surrounded by a series of basalt columns. The longitudinal axes of both plazas were perpendicular. On the north side of the plaza, closing off the complex of the two plazas, was a structure which may have been of considerable size, under which tombs have been found. There seems to have been a deliberate intent to create a dynamic sequence between the two perpendicularly arranged enclosures. In the way that the plazas have been laid out to serve as atria for the pyramid, we see a predetermined order which may represent one of the first attempts at planned urban spaces in Mesoamerica.[13] This intentional arrangement is in contrast to the apparently disordered distribution of other structures surrounding La Venta's ceremonial center, such as several rectangular and circular mounds which may have been altars, the location of the stelae, columns, and the strange Olmec heads of gigantic proportions. However, in San Lorenzo, centuries before La Venta's ceremonial center was built, Coe found that monuments were frequently aligned.

The combination of a plaza surrounded by columns does not seem to have been repeated again in Mesoamerica. The position of La Venta's main pyramid in relation to the larger plaza and the location of the central mound is an early example of the known spatial organization adopted in Classic complexes, or at least that accepted by the builders of Teotihuacán during its first periods. An immature example though it may be, it already had the same features and organization of plazas which we see forming the immediate accesses to the Pyramid of the Sun and the Pyramid of the Moon at Teotihuacán. This composition may have been repeated in other smaller Classic centers built on level ground, but it was already greatly modified by the time Teotihuacán's inhabitants built the Citadel and when, centuries later, the Toltecs planned their city of Tula.

Orientation was important at San Lorenzo, as at La Venta. The north-south axis determined the alignment of the pyramid, the main structures and the symmetrically laid out mounds which outlined the two plazas.[14]

I do not believe that San Lorenzo, Tres Zapotes or La Venta were cities in the sense that Teotihuacán was to be centuries later. La Venta's site, a 500- to 600-hectare island surrounded by swamps, was unsuitable for permanent residence and may even have been chosen for a ceremonial center because of its isolation (Drucker, Heizer and Squier, 1959). Any dwellings which might have been built around these civic-ceremonial centers must have been simple huts, scattered at random. The local population probably lived in scattered villages closely related to the farms they tilled and were seasonally mobilized by the Olmec leaders, perhaps as a form of tribute, to undertake the construction of the élite centers, projects of water control, etc.

La Venta dates from Pre-Classic centuries, and radiocarbon dating shows that the group studied, known as Complex A, was built and utilized between approximately 800 and 400 B.C. (Drucker, Heizer and Squier, 1959), although the site may have been occupied earlier and was abandoned only when Teotihuacán's influence began to grow.

THE EARLY STAGES OF
URBAN EVOLUTION IN SOUTH AMERICA

The arid coastal valleys of Peru give us the best information today on Pre-Ceramic cultures of South America. As I plan to go into detail about the evolution of the cultures on one sector of the coast, in one valley, specifically, I will only name the principal stages of cultural evolution in South America and their dates (Plate No. 2, page 26).

The Pre-Ceramic Period on the coast is represented by a series of finds, some of which, like those of San Pedro de Chicama, may date from 6000 B.C. Pre-Ceramic man's dispersion along the coast during this early epoch seems to have been wide, since his presence has been confirmed in sites north of Ancón on the bank of the Chilca River and near the town of Lurín about 5200 B.C. (Patterson, 1971), in the Nazca Valley about 4000 B.C., as well as on the northern coast of Chile. However, recent excavations in a number of caves near Lake Lauricocha, around the source of the Marañón River, some 4,000 meters high, yielded the find of primitive stone utensils which have been dated between the eighth and sixth millennia B.C. and may even go back to the beginning of the ninth millennium. The seasonal camps of hunters of guanaco and deer have been found in the highlands of Peru and Bolivia and are dated as early as 7500 B.C. (Lanning, 1967).

Between the sixth and the middle of the second millennia B.C., a hunting-fishing-gathering population lived in the hills near the sea of the coastal valleys of Peru. Gathering wild foods led these people to the first deliberate plantings, probably after the middle of the third millennium B.C., which later evolved into agriculture. We find this first in the settled valleys of the north coast and later in those of the central and southern coasts. Ceramics were still unknown, maize had not yet become the basis of their diet, nor had they acclimated the llama which may have been domesticated some time before in the mountains. The coastal valleys were more humid than today and vegetation during the winter must have been plentiful for settlements of small size.

Toward the middle of the third millennium, these primitive South Americans lived in small villages, half submerged in the sandy coast not too far from the sea or near the floodlands. A more intense use of resources led to population growth and to permanent settlements of increasing size in most coastal valleys. Even though agriculture provided them with a reserve food supply, alternating rainy and dry years required them to seek other sources of food.[15] They became farmers and fishermen. They made nets in which cotton now replaced the earlier wild plant fibers, they cultivated gourds to make bottles and dishes, and they constructed reed rafts and carved tools of bone. Sedentary life undoubtedly encouraged the construction of temples, pyramids, cemeteries, and improved their technology.

The Pre-Ceramic Periods also witnessed a vast, confirmed population dispersion in the north, central, and southern mountains of Peru. Some zones, such as Huancayo-Jauja and Huancavelica in the central mountains, show evidence of Pre-Ceramic occupation (Lumbreras, 1960). According to Ibarro Grasso, Pre-Ceramic remains at Viscachani, in the Department of La Paz, Bolivia are extremely old, as are the finds made by Rex González at Pampa de Olaen in the Province of Córdoba, Argentina, which yielded lanceolate points belonging to a Pre-Ceramic culture called Ayampitín and dated 6000 B.C. (Rex González, 1962, 1963).

Around the beginning of the first millennium B.C., an artistic style spread along the north and central coast and into the northern mountain ranges of Peru which may have represented the zenith of a culture called Chavín, after its center of dispersion. The Chavín style, with local variations, is found in the art and architecture of a series of coastal valleys and highlands extending its influence to the south coast and possibly as far north as southern Ecuador. The Chavín style marks also the earliest of Pre-Columbian Peru's three cultural horizons and, as Rowe suggests, an expansion of trade (Rowe, 1963).

The centuries of the early horizon provided greater abundance, thanks to a burgeoning agriculture based partially on irrigation, and to the introduction of advanced techniques in crafts, especially metallurgy. As a result, the population in the coastal valleys increased, at least in the north and central sectors, which was reflected in new and larger villages and settlements.

The Early Intermediate Period (200 B.C.-600 A.D.) in Peru reached its known peak in the fluvial valleys of the coast, but, excepting the area around Lake Titicaca, a similar flowering has yet to be found either in the Peruvian highlands or in the other areas of South America where urban cultures developed. Not all the cultures of the Peruvian coast enjoyed the same abundance of resources during this period, nor did they reach the same level of urban life or undergo a similar demographic evolution nor specialize in the same crafts. In the north coastal valleys, such as those of the Chicama and Lambayeque, the Moche, Virú, and other rivers, the inhabitants constructed great irrigation works and had sizeable areas of land under cultivation (Schaedel, 1951 a, 1951 b; Willey, 1953). Even their villages seem to have been larger and more densely populated, the public works more ambitious, and the specialization of certain groups more evident than in the central and southern coastal valleys. Urban concentrations in the south possibly never reached the development characteristic of the Early Intermediate Period on the northern coast, but they were extensive and included stone foundations, plazas, and shrines. The sites of Pachacamac and Cajamarquilla in the central coast, which were to become important during and after the Middle Horizon, were already occupied (Rowe, 1963).

The reasons for these differences, which I have analyzed as far as our present knowledge permits in other chapters of this book, suggest the presence of a centralized society on the north coast ruled by a secular or ceremonial hierarchy. As this society became more stratified, a progressively urban way of life emerged along with increased dependency of the growing group of specialists on the primary production of the mass of the population.

All coastal cultures excelled in the production of textiles, ceramics, and metallurgy. Craftsmen in certain valleys were outstanding in their particular specialization. The Nazca culture, for example, on the southern coast of Peru, has usually been included among the Classic cultures because of the quality of its pottery and textiles (Willey and Phillips, 1958), yet, only recently we have found evidence that their inhabitants built true cities, the mark of all Classic cultures of Indian America. Members of the Mochica culture, which developed in the valleys surrounding the Moche River and neighboring valleys, were also skilled in ceramics but were outstanding in the art of working metals, a skill which seems to have been common to Middle Horizon cultures of this sector.

In recent years, archeologists have found evidence of true cities during the Early Intermediate Period in certain highland areas, especially those fronting the north, west, and south sides of Lake Titicaca. Pucará, north of Puno, and Tiahuanaco, on the south shore of the lake, were sites occupied during this Period, but their Urbanist stage is not as clearly defined as those centers on the northern coast.

The Middle Horizon lasted on the coast and in the highlands through the first millennium A.D. New stratigraphic studies, however, may push back the origins of this Horizon to an even earlier century. On the north coast, for example, the beginnings of the Gallinazo culture have been experimentally dated seventh century B.C., and the late stage of Mochica culture, also Classic, probably took place during the second century A.D. (Wauchope, 1954). This regression of the Middle Horizon on the coast coincides with the new dates obtained in Tiahuanaco, where the period of the great constructions, or Tiahuanaco II, presumably developed between the second and the fourth centuries of the Christian era.

PARALLELS BETWEEN INDIAN CULTURES

We can logically assume that the nomadic groups that traveled across America, from north to south, during the Continent's first thousand years of habitation, continued their migrations throughout the Archaic and up to the beginning of the Formative Period.[16] This may have lasted, with less intensity, into the Classic Period, since we find cultural similarities between the more advanced peoples of Mesoamerica and South America and obvious parallels in their stages of development. Could such similarities be due to these spontaneous migrations, the result of continuous organized exchange between north and south, or a combination of both?

Although distant and arduous, communications by land or sea were not impossible during the evolution of Indian cultures (Bennett, 1951) since there were no insurmountable barriers. Direct contacts between the cultures along maritime routes existed from the Formative Period (Coe, 1960), and we should not overlook possible indirect connections through less advanced, intermediate cultures in the northwest of South and Central America. Undoubtedly, such contacts took place as America's Indian cultures already had so many factors in common that it is impossible not to think in terms of a single formative base. Differences became accentuated, however, when the cultures reached the Classic Period, partly due to growing specialization, but also because of those geographic factors of the American Continent which made for isolation then, as in our day. This explains why the links between Mesoamerica and South America were never those of continuous, organized trade. Certainly, there was the barter of luxury items, which may even have been the incentive for long and dangerous journeys, but even more important for the development of America's urban cultures was the exchange of ideas and techniques which this brought about.

We are not certain where maize was acclimated, nor about the beginnings of the cultivation of cotton, peanuts, manioc, beans, pimiento, and other plants basic to Indian diet and industry since Pre-Classic times, but their diffusion and popularity is evident throughout pre-Columbian America. The potato, however, eaten regularly in South America, was almost unknown north of the Isthmus of Panamá, and the use of coca as a stimulant was rare in Central America and nonexistent in Mesoamerica. Cacao, used as currency as well as a drink, seems to have been limited to Mesoamerica and the Caribbean. Maguey was another plant of many uses but was cultivated mainly in certain areas of Mesoamerica. The South American cultures, on the other hand, utilized a greater variety of tubers. Agricultural methods were similar all over. The digging stick, sometimes reinforced with a metal tip, was used by the farmer in the Maya territory, the Mexican plateau, and in Peru to make a hole into which he dropped a few seeds. This system still exists in large sectors of these areas.

The Aztecs and the Maya had product transportation problems which they never really solved. The backs of porters were the only form of transport between the highlands and lowlands of Mesoamerica in places with no navigable rivers or lakes, which were scarce and, in any case, did not provide a continuous route. On the other hand, in the highland and coastal areas of South America where urban cultures did develop, the llama and alpaca were irreplaceable.[17] It seems significant that the maximum expansion of the Inca Empire coincided with the greatest known dispersion of these animals prior to the Conquest. The dog, the turkey, and the guinea pig were domesticated and used for food in both areas.

The Maya and Aztecs developed a system of writing which allowed them to solve difficult problems in chronology. Among the Peruvian cultures, the Inca *quipu,* a mnemonic device of knotted strings, was used to record information necessary for its complex governmental administration. The Mesoamerican cultures progressed beyond the stages of pictographic and ideographic writing. The Maya, for instance, perfected an ideographic system which was on the verge of developing phonetic characters (Morley, 1956).

The diffusion of paper in Mesoamerica was related to the evolution of writing. As early as several centuries before the Aztec expansion, paper was in use from Oaxaca to Yucatán, first for ceremonial and later for cultural purposes.[18] It was made from slices of bark beaten to the desired thickness, a technique which seems to have been known since the Formative Period. In Peru, neither the Inca nor their predecessors produced paper.

Peruvian cultures seem to have excelled in metallurgy and the manufacture of textiles. The Mixtec goldsmiths in the valleys of Oaxaca designed beautiful and intricate gold jewelry, but metallurgy seems to have originated in South America and was only known well in Mesoamerica after the beginning of the Christian era. Gold was used in ornaments by the Chimú in the Post-Classic and by the Mochica in the Classic Period, but the gold objects manufactured by the Chavín culture artists may possibly represent the oldest works of metallurgy in America (Mason, 1957). Many of the best examples of gold pieces came from the Indian cultures of Colombia and Panama, demonstrating the advantage of their geographic proximity to the more evolved peoples of the north and south.[19]

The development of religion in Mesoamerica and South America followed similar regional beginnings. In their early stages, these cultures may have worshipped visible phenomena, such as the sun, moon, rain, and animal life, which seemed mysterious and incomprehensible. As the cultures became more ritualized and the priesthood acquired authority, certain differences emerged.

The cult of the creator god was spread among all the superior cultures of America. He was called Quetzalcóatl in Tula and Tenochtitlán; Kukulcán among the Maya of Chichen Itzá and Mayapán; and in South America he was identified with Viracocha, possibly after the Middle Horizon. The cult of Viracocha reached such proportions during the reign of Pachacuti, the ninth Inca ruler, that some authors believe that these decisive years in the evolution of the Inca dynasty show a marked trend toward a monotheistic religion.

The Aztecs also evolved toward the worship of a single god, symbolized by Huitzilopochtli, the war god, who became "the symbol of imperial sovereignty" as the Mexica relentlessly extended their dominion (Padden, 1970). The Maya war god was a less bloodthirsty deity named Ik Chuah, and the Inca never developed the war god cult. Respect for the gods of conquered peoples was in the interest of unification and, therefore, common practice among the Inca and Aztecs. In all urban cultures of Indian America, sacrifice was customary. Whereas in Peru the offerings were limited to llamas and small animals with only an occasional human sacrifice, among the Post Classic civilizations of Mexico, and the Aztecs in particular, human sacrifice formed an integral part of religion.

Significant contrasts emerged as America's Indian cultures evolved and acquired their own individuality. In religion, these differences were important, as we can see in the Inca dynasty's development of a state religion revolving around the cult of the sun and moon or in the Aztec's enthronement of Huitzilopochtli, in which only members of the ruling class participated. The commoners retained their former fetishistic and animalistic cults, familial and local, which had long enjoyed popular acceptance among the ancestral family cells. These gods were respected by the people and integrated by the Inca into a large national pantheon. Such concepts did not develop in Mexico, however, where Aztec religion was an extension of man's recognition and fear of natural forces and his efforts to control them (Vaillant, 1955). Maya religion was based on worship of the celestial bodies and the process of time.

Despite these different focuses, some ritual manifestations had their parallels in a number of cultures. The ball game had a ceremonial character, yet it also served as popular entertainment. Its traces have been found from Arizona to Paraguay, with similar rules and few variations in the proportions and ground plans of the playing fields (Kidder II, 1940), but its popularity was greater in Mesoamerica than in South America.[20]

A parallel urbanistic process developed in similar stages in both Mesoamerica and South America. Ceremonial centers preceded cities in areas of urban culture but appeared much later than the first permanent villages inhabited by groups of early farmers. On the Peruvian coast, irrigation and more efficient methods of food production were fundamental to cultural progress toward an urbanist stage. It required a larger population concentration in a particular region while assuring the production surplus which allowed both demographic growth and the development of a group of specialists engaged in nonagricultural activities. Of course, conditions were more favorable in the Valley of Mexico than on the Gulf Coast and other areas of Mesoamerica where irrigation was not essential and was, in fact, less utilized during the Classic centuries.

The first true cities were contemporaneous with the Classic Period in Mesoamerica and the Middle Horizon in South America and with the increasing centralization of their governments. The authority of a ruling class over the general population was almost certainly entrenched before the first cities appeared. Cities emerged as a result of the political, economic, and administrative needs of that class and were made possible by the kind of centralized government they developed. At some stage of their evolution, the cultures of Indian America adopted urban planning or organization, but we know very little of the technical aspects of their construction. We do know that the Inca used models of projected buildings for this purpose, and Mesoamerica may have had a similar system or a workable form of plane surveying. In planning their cities, they followed a regular, though not checkerboard, outline.

Mesoamerican cities were generally the largest and most densely inhabited. Judged by the criteria used in this book, their economy and way of life was more urban than in South America. The fundamental difference between the cities of Mexico, Peru, and Bolivia, however, lies in their size and in the conception of their ceremonial centers. While monumentality was emphasized in the cities of Mexico's central plateau from Teotihuacán to Tenochtitlán, this characteristic was totally lacking in pre-Inca and Inca urban architecture, with the sole exception of Tiahuanaco.

Pre-Hispanic architecture of Mesoamerica and South America also exhibits similar forms and features. Builders in both areas utilized stepped structures as temple bases, although limited by regional availability of certain materials. Constructions were usually grouped, creating enclosed spaces where altars and commemorative stelae were placed. Sunken courtyards were common in both areas. One important detail is the lack of the true arch which imposed a severe restriction on the spatial possibilities of the architecture of each area. Both in Mesoamerica and South America, meander designs in stone or adobe adorned walls, and color was lavished on exterior and interior decorations. Recent discoveries near Tejupilco, in the State of Mexico, of stone slabs with simple, geometric bas-reliefs hitherto unknown in Mesoamerica, are similar to those previously found near Cuzco and the Chavín-style reliefs analyzed by Covarrubias near Placeres de Oro, in the State of Guerrero (Wicke and Bullington, 1960). This suggests an exchange of ideas and techniques as early as the Formative Period.

The similarities in the civilizations of Mesoamerica and South America are many and varied, and involve almost every sphere of cultural activity. We need only learn how these exchanges came about and by which routes.[21] The subject will undoubtedly be clarified by renewed research in the archeologically less well-known areas occupied by urban cultures.

and the coasts of Peru and Chile, did llama wool, sometimes mixed with cotton, offer a variation unknown in Mesoamerica.

Coca was consumed by the Inca, but its use was restricted to the ruling class of the Empire. It was brought from the warm valleys of intermediate altitude east of the Andes. Although accepted as a stimulant and narcotic from early times, its use spread among the commoners only after the Conquest. Coca's area of dispersion was mainly the Peru-Bolivian highlands, but its properties were also known north of the Isthmus of Panamá.

Tobacco may have originated in the Caribbean area. In any event, it was cultivated by the Maya and known by the Aztecs.

Each region probably had several varieties of a same species of domesticated plant, there having been over a hundred in all. The majority were food plants, but others were used in crafts, such as the cotton and maguey already discussed, indigo and the bark of certain trees which were used as dyes, and sisal, a fiber of many uses.

Hunting and fishing were resources utilized as circumstances permitted. Fishing was the dietary basis of the coastal peoples during the first stages of their evolution and may also have been so among the inhabitants of the lake basins. For the Inca, hunting was a royal sport, and a portion of the game was divided among the commoners, who cut the meat into strips and dried and salted it. Aztec kings even had their own hunting grounds. Among the Maya, the hunt was limited to the necessary, and the meat distributed to the inhabitants of the hunter's village (Thompson, 1959). The Inca and Aztec kings ate fish from the sea which was brought from the coast, thanks to the speed with which light cargoes could be transported in those nations; but only the more important members of the upper classes could enjoy it. Fattened dogs, turkeys, perhaps geese, ducks, quail (Vaillant, 1955), and lesser game, especially lake birds, could be found in Tenochtitlán's market, but price put these products out of reach of most people. In Peru, the guinea pig was domesticated and raised for its meat, as was the wild turkey among the Aztec and the Maya, who also kept bees in straw hives (Morley, 1956). The llama and alpaca, unknown in Mesoamerica, were mainstays of the pre-Inca and Inca economies and were raised not only to be used as beasts of burden or for their wool but also for their meat.

NOTES ON · 1

1. IN REALITY, THIS REPRESENTED the second generation of Spaniards in America. During the first three decades the Conquest only affected some of the principal Caribbean islands. Taking the capture of their respective capitals as marking the end of independent evolution of the greater Indian civilizations, we can say that the Aztec came to an end in 1521, the Cakchiquel in 1524, the Inca in 1533, what was left of the Yucatecan Maya in 1542 and the Chibcha in 1538. As dates, I have adopted the years in which Tenochtitlán, Iximché, and Cuzco were definitively taken and Mérida and Bogotá were founded.

2. Father José de Acosta was a Jesuit who lived in Peru for fifteen years during the second half of the sixteenth century. He wrote *Historia Natural y Moral de las Indias,* one of the most complete studies on the pre-Hispanic epoch. Born in 1540, he died in 1600.

3. A brief synthesis of these theories can be found in several works. The most available are: *Prehistoria de América* by Salvador Canals Frau (Canals Frau, 1950); *El Perú Prehispánico* by Hans Horkheimer (Horkheimer, 1950), and *Los orígenes del hombre americano* by Paul Rivet (Rivet, 1960).

4. In Osvaldo Menghin's prologue to the book by Augusto Cardich, *Los yacimientos de Lauricocha* (Cardich, 1960).

5. Haag states that the first men probably crossed the land-bridge along the Bering Straits before the Wisconsin Period, since during the glacial period mentioned, the oceans retreated enough to leave a passage several hundred kilometers wide between the two continents. If remains left by man's crossing have not been found, it is because the passage today is covered by a hundred meters of water and thirty meters of sediment. Haag also warns us that for this reason archeologists should not be surprised if, in the future, they discover evidence of man's passage in different parts of North America dating back 50,000 years or more (Haag, 1962).

6. Patterson presents a good analysis of food procurement systems on the coast of Peru (Patterson, 1971).

7. Among agricultural methods of pre-Hispanic America, the land-clearing system was probably the most widespread. It involves burning off the vegetation in a sector of the woods which has previously been cut and left

31

to dry. This system is still used in vast areas of Mexico and Central America and, of course, among the less developed tribes of the interior of South America.

8. Chang states that during the Late Formative Period, the groups of communities functioned ceremonially and perhaps politically. Each group was symbolized by a ceremonial center; the resident priests may have had political control over the resident members of satellite communities (Chang, 1960). In the Santa Maria phase in the Tehuacán Valley, which lasted between 900 and 200 B.C. and therefore is contemporary to Cuicuilco, "the settlement pattern reveals that the people lived in small wattle-and-daub houses in villages which were oriented around a single, large village having ceremonial structures" (MacNeish, 1971).

9. During the Round Table organized by the Mexican Anthropological Society in Tuxtla Gutiérrez in 1942.

10. Two types of rock were probably used in La Venta's construction, and, judging by the location of the nearest quarries, both were transported considerable distances to the ceremonial center. The volcanic type has been found sixty kilometers away and the metamorphic rock from the hills a hundred kilometers south of La Venta (Drucker, Heizer and Squier, 1959). Those used in San Lorenzo came from Cerro de Cintepec, more than a hundred kilometers to the northwest (Williams and Heizer, 1965).

11. The Olmecs were known as the "rubber people," their land frequently mentioned as an earthly paradise.

12. I believe that the difficult topography in areas where the majority of Maya Classic centers were located could have been one of the causes of this exception. In addition, Maya centers were always more complex and less regular in their spatial organization than Classic centers of the Gulf Coast and of Mexico's central plateau in general.

13. The base of La Venta's principal pyramid was a rectangle 420 feet (140 meters) on its north-south side and 240 feet (80 meters) on its east-west side. It was approximately 103 feet (34 meters) high (Drucker, Heizer and Squier, 1959).

14. Apart from Marquina, whose list of principal works appear in the bibliography, the orientation of Mesoamerican ceremonial centers has been analyzed by MacGowan (MacGowan, 1945).

15. Posner describes how, in certain years—traditionally every seven—the

32

tranquil way of life on the Peruvian coast is interrupted by an event which, at times, assumes catastrophic proportions. The Humboldt Current seems to disappear, and the temperature of the water on the surface rises rapidly. On land, frequent torrential rains are produced. In the sea, the fish die or go away, and the seabirds, too, must leave or starve to death. This event (probably caused by atmospheric conditions) is known by the name of El Niño (the child) because it appears shortly before Christmas (Posner, 1954).

16. In sites occupied by the Chavín culture on the north coast of Peru about 800 B.C., were found pottery shapes associated with figurines which closely resemble those found in sites belonging to the Tlatilco culture. Michael Coe writes that "this all sounds very much like the Spinden hypothesis which proposes a unified spread of Formative culture with maize and pottery, out of Mexico to the south, the harbinger of the civilizations which were to spring from this foundation" (Coe, M., 1966).

17. When the Spaniards arrived, the llama and the alpaca were unknown in the central highlands of Colombia where the Chibcha were living.

18. The Aztecs received 32,000 sheets of paper as yearly tribute from the region of Morelos (Molins Fábrega, 1956).

19. See the brief but detailed work by Stephan F. de Borhegyi (Borhegyi, 1959). It contains an excellent synthesis of the parallel traits between the cultures of Mesoamerica and Ecuador, discussing among others, the shapes, designs, and techniques of ceramics, as well as offering a broad bibliography.

20. The ball game was also practiced among nonurban cultures. One of the most important features in the settlements occupied by the Tainos and Caribes in what is now the Antilles, was the playing fields of this ritual game (Pichardo Moya, 1958).

21. Michael Coe calculates that a round-trip journey by sea between the north of Guatemala and the area of Guayas, on the Ecuadorian coast, would take approximately a year. Mesoamerican traders must have begun their journeys during the month of December, taking advantage of the north winds predominating during the dry season, and have started their return trip from Guayas in September when south winds prevail. They would have reached the north of Guatemala again in December of the following year (Coe, M., 1960).

22. Annual rainfall in the Valley of Tehuacán averages 500 millimeters a year but falls April through October (Mangelsdorf, MacNeish, Galinat, 1964).

·2

THE URBAN EVOLUTION OF TEOTIHUACÁN

" . . . the name Teotihuacán evokes the concept of human divinity and suggests that the city of the gods was none other than that place where the serpent miraculously learned to fly; where man elevated himself to heavenly status."

LAURETTE SÉJOURNÉ
(PENSAMINENTO Y RELGION EN EL MÉXICO ANTIGUO)

□ 2

DURING THE CONVENTION organized by the Mexican Anthropological
Society in Tuxtla Gutiérrez in 1942, an erroneous theory associating
Teotihuacán with the Toltecs was finally cleared up. For many years we
had realized that the origins of Teotihuacán's culture were to be found
outside the central plateau of Mexico. But it was only after deeper knowledge of the Olmec culture and its links with the development of Pre-Classic Mexican cultures had been gained, and after the identification of Tula
in the present State of Hidalgo as one of the Toltec centers, that we could
determine a more precise period of occupation for Teotihuacán. Over the
past twenty years, research done on the central plateau and the Gulf
Coast of Mexico by Armillas, Acosta, Bernal, Michael Coe, Drewitt,
Millon, Noguera, Sanders, Séjourné, as well as by teams from the National Institute of Anthropology and History of Mexico, and the University of Rochester, among others, have pushed back the chronology of
Teotihuacán's various periods of occupation. Also during these years, we
have developed a different image of the urban characteristics of a city. A
new chronology worked out by Millon (Millon, 1969) has replaced the
one by Vaillant which dates from the 1930's (Vaillant, 1955) and has
modified the one by Armillas which dates from the 1950's (Armillas,
1950, 1952). Finally, the surveys made by Millon (Millon, 1960, 1967,
1969) seem to prove definitely that Teotihuacán was a city and not merely a ceremonial center occupied by a small permanent population. Even
so, the final studies are still incomplete and excavations concentrated in
limited areas. We still have limited knowledge of the relations of Teotihuacán with adjacent regions (Parson, 1968c) and with the rest of Mesoamerica, as well as of its economic base and social structure.

This chapter will attempt to summarize Teotihuacán's urban evolution

37

based on archeological studies undertaken during this century.[1] As a guide, I have adopted Millon's chronology (Millon, 1969).

THE SITE

The easily accessible archeological zone of Teotihuacán is located fifty kilometers from Mexico City. It occupies an area of more than twenty-two square kilometers that includes the great ceremonial center, with the Avenue of the Dead as its axis. A substantial part of the area is occupied by small cultivated properties which, in general, have been in the hands of the same families for several generations. After overcoming the resistance of the present proprietors, researchers at Teotihuacán have been able to excavate some of the city's ancient residential districts, palaces, and secondary ceremonial centers literally from beneath the crops.

Teotihuacán was built on the floor of a valley of 500 square kilometers with a slight slope from northeast to southwest, an extension of the central Valley of Mexico, which it joins to the west. At an altitude which varies from 2,240 to 2,300 meters, it is completely surrounded from the north and south by mountains which rise up to 600 meters above the level of the archeological zone. Today it is an eroded valley with an annual rainfall of less than 550 millimeters, and because of frequent droughts irrigation is necessary to insure a harvest (Sanders, 1965). The main river is the San Juan which runs lengthwise down the valley, cutting through the present archeological zone and ancient urban residential area. Today some streams and wells supplement the water supply, but the climate may have been more humid when the city was inhabited. Prolonged occupation and cultivation of these lands may have provoked a gradual erosion that ultimately deforested the mountain sides.

Teotihuacán (from the Náhuatl word, *teotia,* to worship), the "place of deification" or "place of the gods," was not the name of the city during its centuries of occupation. During Colonial times, nothing was known about the history of this site, possibly the oldest of the great urban centers of the Americas. Even the Aztecs did not know who had built the two great pyramids which they named after the Sun and the Moon. At the time of Aztecs, Teotihuacán had been uninhabited for centuries, and they assumed that the architects of such massive constructions must have been the gods themselves, before man lived on earth. The Colonial chroniclers never committed the mistake of crediting the Toltecs with having built Teotihuacán. This was a modern error, later rectified after Acosta's excavations at Tula confirmed the chronological difference between the Teotihuacán and Toltec cultures (Acosta, 1942, 1956-1957).

To put Teotihuacán's urban evolution in order, I have used Millon's chronology, and the ten criteria adopted in this book's preface to define a city as a human grouping differentiated from a ceremonial center, a village, and rural areas. Various famous names in American archeology have been connected with the excavations and mappings of Teotihuacán. Among those outstanding in the decades prior to the second World War were Charnay; Batres, who reconstructed the Pyramid of the Sun at the beginning of this century; Gamio; Hrdlicka; Kroeber; Vaillant; and Linné.

THE PRE-CLASSIC OR LATE
FORMATIVE PERIOD (100 B.C.-1 A.D.)

Proto-Teotihuacán I-
Patlachique Phase

Teotihuacán was one of many sites on Mexico's central plateau occupied during the Pre-Classic Period, although we do not know exactly when or by whom.

The oldest remains within the boundaries of the classic city indicate the occupation of two large settlements toward the north and the west of the locale where, centuries later, the Pyramid of the Moon was built (Millon, 1957, 1960, 1966), and two smaller settlements to the northwest and south. They represent a movement of population to settle the plain, a change from previous tendencies to reside primarily on hill tops (Sanders, 1969). Preliminary excavation suggests an area of more than four square kilometers for the larger ones, yet these sectors have never been systematically explored (Millon, 1966). At present, the population of Teotihuacán during this phase is estimated at about 5,000 inhabitants, although it would appear to have been permanently occupied, witnessing great building activity and enjoying a certain technological level, as demonstrated in the size of the structures, its orientation, and the organization of temples (Millon, 1966).

As in other parts of Mesoamerica, it is possible that between the occupation of the Pre-Classic and the first Classic cities on Mexico's central plateau there may have been an intermediate period when many ceremonial centers were built. These were later occupied by the highest ranking members of a society which was growing increasingly stratified. The mounds found in Teotihuacán, both isolated and grouped, are situated in sectors apart from each other, leaving large, open areas in between. If we could prove that a good part of the larger settlements were left unbuilt, we would find the general density of these sectors to be lower than that of the principal villages of the same epoch. That is, the urbanistic process would not have resulted from densification of those sites already occupied during the late Pre-Classic, but from a gradually increasing population in the valley, concentrated around certain ceremonial centers which later took on the urban characteristics associated with Classic cities. The overall distribution of constructions in the large settlements of this phase must have reflected the semirural organization characteristic of the transition period from Late Pre-Classic to Classic. It would also be in accord with the political and administrative importance acquired by the priesthood during the same period. This settlement pattern would have encouraged greater population concentration in cities.

From their excavations in Ostoyohualco, a sector toward the northwest of the Classic city, archeologists have tried to determine the possible origin of Teotihuacán. Although no street plan has come to light, two plazas connected to religious buildings have been discovered. Plaza 1, or Tres Palos, is formed by the ruins of three mounds and one platform; its function seems to have been ceremonial (Cook, de Leonard, 1957). Million discovered a second, rectangular plaza about 1,500 meters north of the Pyramid of the Moon (Millon, 1957b). This is called Plaza 2, and the brief description we have of it indicates that it is bounded by fifteen mounds. It may have been in Plaza 2 that architectural groupings appeared for the first time in Teotihuacán, in this case a group of four mounds on a broad platform. This type of grouping was later used in the construction of the Citadel and other minor groups in the city. Since both plazas belong to the same period, we can logically suppose that these complexes, perhaps built to accommodate massive concentrations, and other complexes as yet undiscovered, might have been connected by thoroughfares or ceremonial highways.

We know little about Teotihuacán's Pre-Classic inhabitants. To judge by the volume of constructions found, the number of workers required to build them must have been considerable, although, as was customary around ceremonial centers, agricultural work would have taken up a good part of their time. Ceramics, often with negative decoration, wall paintings, and figurines with carefully defined features and details, all suggest the development of a specialized artisan class which must have lived, at least for prolonged periods, near the plazas and wherever building activity was most intense.

TEOTIHUACÁN I-
TZACUALLI PHASE (1-150 A.D.)

Why was such an important city built in this particular valley? What changed the tendency that had prevailed during the Early and Middle Formative Periods to choose sites close to the Gulf Coast or the central lakes of the Valley of Mexico, with the outstanding exception of Monte Albán (Cook, 1947)?

There was a time, perhaps contemporary with "Tepexpán man" or even earlier, when Teotihuacán's site was on the banks of Lake Texcoco. Its first occupation, however, came much later, and the perimeter of the lake system had shrunk during the long years of drought that affected the central plateau of Mexico. Even the use of man-made land mounds, called *chinampas,* characteristic of the banks of the lakes and rivers of Texcoco's lacustrine system since Pre-Classic centuries, did not develop in the sub-valley of Teotihuacán for topographical reasons. Therefore, a rural agricultural population could never have multiplied in Teotihuacán as it did fifteen centuries later in Tenochtitlán. In all probability, irrigation was limited in the territory immediately surrounding Teotihuacán from the first centuries of its evolution.[2] Even so, existing surface water sources must have always been insufficient to irrigate the land necessary to support a city which, at its apogee, reached 85,000 inhabitants and occupied an area of about 2,200 hectares. Of the valley's water systems, those of the Nahualco and San Marcos Rivers would have given poor returns in comparison to the effort entailed by their use and were probably only used in emergencies. Only the San Juan River seems to have been a worthwhile source, although we should not overlook the use of wells since there is proof of underground water in this and other valleys of Mexico's central plateau (Millon, 1957a).

Based on similar processes in other civilizations, Teotihuacán's period of self-sufficiency probably did not endure past the Late Pre-Classic Period. Perhaps during Teotihuacán I, when the great pyramids were built, but more likely during the middle period of Teotihuacán II, the city must have been an administrative, political, and religious center supported by tribute from a gradually expanding territory, the exact size and influence of which we have yet to learn. From this time on, the prestige of its crafts may have converted Teotihuacán into a center of production for goods of high quality, taking into consideration its time and place.

Gamio found that of the 10,500 hectares under cultivation in 1917, 9,500 were irrigated (Gamio, 1922). Let us suppose that this was the case toward the end of Teotihuacán I and the beginning of Teotihuacán II, and that the irrigated area needed to support an Indian family has not changed in over two thousand years. Let us also suppose that irrigation practices remain the same and that each family keeps part of its land under irrigation and allows the rest to lie fallow. Given these conditions, we would find that eighty-six hectares in this mixed system would be needed to support one hundred families, based on contemporary yearly harvests (Palerm, 1955). I have found no data on the percentages of any one particular crop as compared to another in this system of farming, but we can logically add an area of 30 per cent for each family to produce enough to pay tribute and barter for other products. We would then have a total area of 111.8 hectares for 100 families. In other words, if we adopt an irrigated area of 9,500 hectares, we would have 8,497 families of six members each, reaching a total population not greater than 50,982 persons for the entire valley of Teotihuacán. These figures seem too low in view of the huge constructions that were begun at the end of the Pre-Classic Period, even taking into account a system which allowed farmers to become builders during certain periods of the year, as possibly was the case among the Olmecs and the Maya. Furthermore, as I have pointed out, irrigation does not seem to have been essential to feed the urban population in the valley of Teotihuacán during its period of greatest occupation, as dependency on tribute probably increased.

We might consider another possibility. Seasonally, the inhabitants of other valleys, even in distant parts, might have come together to collaborate in building a religious and administrative center with which they maintained contacts of various kinds.

Both possibilities point to the existence of a centralized organization and a well-planned common effort, voluntary or not. Besides being a religious center at the end of this first period, Teotihuacán must have also been the administrative center and market place for a large territory.

Some authors (Mayer Oakes, 1960) believe that throughout its existence Teotihuacán was merely the ceremonial center of the valley as well as the residence of the élite or ruling priesthood, and that other sites of Teotihuacán culture, such as Azcapotzalco, Portezuelo and El Risco, linked to each other and to Teotihuacán by Lake Texcoco, constituted centers with different but complementary functions. We will now see how those characteristics which permit us to call it a city gradually appeared in Teotihuacán with functions and urban structures similar, in many respects, to those of our cities today.

Teotihuacán's urbanization and overall design probably took place concurrently with the growing power of the priests, who directed the city's activities, and the development of a class structure. These developments are detected in the emerging importance of religious buildings. I do not know if the authority of this priesthood evolved over a period of time or if a better organized, more highly cultured group came in from another part of the country and took power.

Toward the end of Teotihuacán I, we find a refinement in construction and decoration, showing improved craftsmanship and pointing to a wider division between the activities of the rural population and those of the decidedly urban group. Commerce may also have expanded during this period to reach its greatest development in the Classic Period. Tribute probably appeared as a reflection of the city's enlarging zone of influence. I believe that, in this same epoch, governmental centralization must have intensified, as it now became essential to insure distribution of food and other goods among those members of society who were so deeply engaged in various nonagricultural activities that all economic sectors of the city were affected.

Late in Teotihuacán I came the construction of the great pyramids (Millon, 1966, 1969), after careful calculation of the general orientation of the center as a whole. The arrangement of earlier ceremonial groups already points to the existence of a previously conceived plan for the finished complex, which only attained a monumental character with the development of the principal ceremonial center. The influence of the design of the Olmec centers, like La Venta, on Teotihuacán's overall plan and

4 *Teotihuacán: Archeological Map of the Northern and Northwestern Sections, State of Mexico, Mexico. (Credit: University of Rochester, Rochester, N.Y.)*

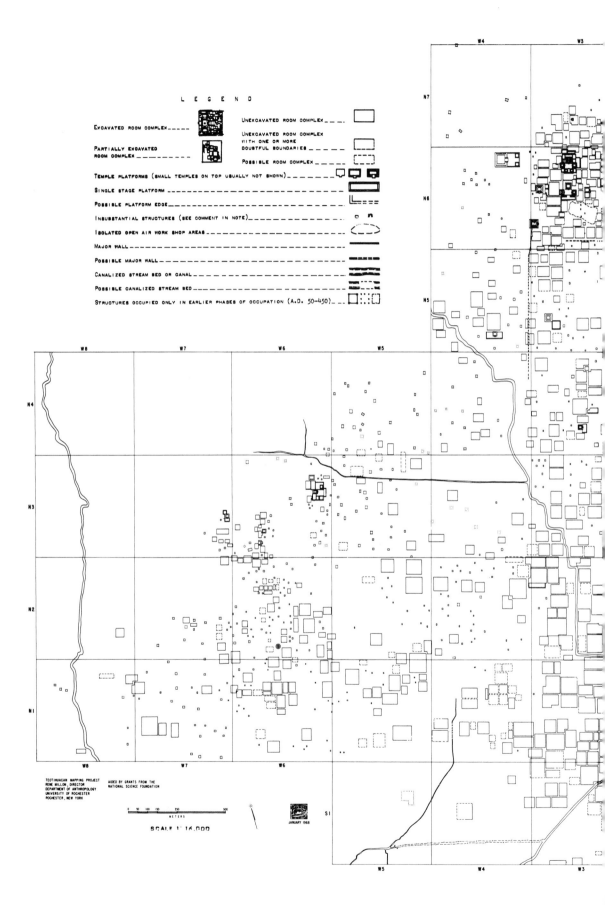

L E G E N D

Excavated room complex _____

Partially excavated room complex _____

Unexcavated room complex ____

Unexcavated room complex with one or more doubtful boundaries _____

Possible room complex _____

Temple platforms (small temples on top usually not shown) _____

Single stage platform _____

Possible platform edge_____

Insubstantial structures (see comment in note)_____

Isolated open air work shop areas _____

Major wall _____

Possible major wall _____

Canalized stream bed or canal _____

Possible canalized stream bed _____

Structures occupied only in earlier phases of occupation (A.D. 50-450) ___

TEOTIHUACAN MAPPING PROJECT
RENE MILLON, DIRECTOR
DEPARTMENT OF ANTHROPOLOGY
UNIVERSITY OF ROCHESTER
ROCHESTER, NEW YORK

AIDED BY GRANTS FROM THE
NATIONAL SCIENCE FOUNDATION

JANUARY 1968

0 50 100 150   250   500
METERS

SCALE 1:16,000

IMPORTANT NOTE: THIS MAP SHOULD BE USED WITH THE MAP OF THE NORTH CENTRAL ZONE ON WHICH
BUILDINGS IN THE CENTER OF THE CITY ARE IDENTIFIED. MOST OF THE TEMPLES AND OTHER BUIL-
DINGS ALONG THE "STREET OF THE DEAD" (THE NORTH-SOUTH AXIS OF THE CITY) HAVE BEEN AT
LEAST PARTLY RECONSTRUCTED. MOST OF THIS WAS DONE RECENTLY UNDER DR. IGNACIO BERNAL'S
DIRECTION AS PART OF THE PROYECTO TEOTIHUACÁN OF THE INSTITUTO NACIONAL DE ANTROPOLOGÍA
E HISTORIA OF MEXICO. WITH FEW EXCEPTIONS, MOST OF WHICH SHOULD BE EVIDENT, ALL OTHER
BUILDINGS, INCLUDING TEMPLES, SHOWN ON THIS MAP ARE "RECONSTRUCTIONS" BASED ON THE TEO-
TIHUACÁN MAPPING PROJECT SURVEY OF THE SURFACE REMAINS OF UNEXCAVATED BUILDINGS.
IN MOST CASES THE SPECIFIC LOCATION OF INSUBSTANTIAL STRUCTURES WITHIN THE SITES WHERE
WE BELIEVE THEY EXISTED IS ARBITRARY. MANY INSUBSTANTIAL STRUCTURES OF THE EARLIEST
TEOTIHUACÁN PHASES WHICH LIE OUTSIDE THE LIMITS OF THE LATER CITY ON THE NORTH AND
NORTHWEST ARE NOT SHOWN ON THIS MAP.
THE MAP SHOWS APPROXIMATELY 2/3 OF THE ANCIENT CITY (CA. 15 SQUARE KILOMETERS OR 6 SQUARE
MILES) CA. 500-700 A.D. (DURING MOST OF THE XOLALPAN AND METEPEC PHASES). THE TOTAL
AREA OF THE CITY AT THAT TIME WAS CA. 20 SQUARE KILOMETERS (CA. 8 SQUARE MILES).

TEOTIHUACAN
NORTHERN AND NORTHWESTERN SECTIONS
ESTADO DE MEXICO, MEXICO.
ARCHAEOLOGICAL MAP

its ceremonial center in particular, is an antecedent that should be investigated in further detail. We recognize cultural similarities between Olmec art and technology and examples from the same epoch found in sites on Mexico's central plateau such as Tlatilco (Drucker, Heizer and Squier, 1959), but we still do not know how profoundly a ceremonial complex such as La Venta, of minor architectural value yet built according to a definite previous plan, might have influenced the design of other central plateau centers, especially Teotihuacán. What seems certain is that about this time the city of Teotihuacán started to evolve according to a preconceived plan modified in the course of time. Both the north-south axis, or Avenue of the Dead, and the east-west axis were designed to provide the basic framework for the gridiron layout that is one of the main characteristics of Teotihuacán's urban plan.

In summary, over the Late Pre-Classic Period, Teotihuacán gradually acquired the physical characteristics and urban functions that reached their peak in the two following periods as a form of urban life developed, unique for that time in the central Valley of Mexico, perhaps even in Mesoamerica.

THE DESIGN AND CONSTRUCTION OF THE CEREMONIAL CENTER

A subject of continuous discussion and frequent discrepancy is the exact period of construction of the Pyramids of the Sun and the Moon, and the Citadel or Temple of Quetzalcóatl. Most archeologists agree that both pyramids were built during Teotihuacán I (Armillas, 1950; Millon, 1966b; Millon and Drewitt, 1961), and were finished by the end of that period (Bernal, 1959a). But the ceremonial center was only completed during Teotihuacán II and was subject to later modifications which may have affected the architecture of certain buildings but scarcely altered its general scale and outline. (Plate No. 4)

The Pyramids of the Sun and the Moon are the oldest monuments in the ceremonial center. Both structures are entirely artificial and were built in a single operation, as witnessed by the uniformity of their inner fill of red volcanic tufa and adobe blocks made of earth and rubble from around the area (Millon, 1957b). The substance of this fill and its date

5 *Teotihuacán: View of the Avenue of the Dead from the Pyramid of the Moon.*

6 *Teotihuacán: Pyramid of the Sun.*

7 *Teotihuacán: The Pyramid of the Moon at the end of the Avenue of the Dead, as seen from the Pyramid of the Sun.*

8 *Teotihuacán: The Citadel was a complex of platforms and temples surrounding the pyramid dedicated to Quetzalcóatl. Passing in front of the Citadel we see the far end of the Avenue of the Dead. The San Juan River is in the foreground. (Credit: Cia. Mexicana Aerofoto, S.A.)*

were studied in 1922 and 1933 by cutting two main tunnels and several lateral shafts (Pérez, 1935). In the summer of 1959 one of the tunnels was opened again, revealing the existence of at least one structure of stone of relatively small size used for ceremonial purposes (Millon and Drewitt, 1961). These excavations verified the existence of a culture connected with the Archaic cultures of the central Valley of Mexico, earlier than that of Teotihuacán I, or the Tzacualli Phase. Although the Tzacualli Phase culture may have imposed itself on the declining Archaic, continuing its evolution to the point of undertaking the construction of the pyramids, contrary opinions maintain that the arrival of new immigrants from the west of the Valley of Mexico precipitated a new population displacement, breaking continuity between the Tzacualli Phase and that of the pyramids' builders. In recent years the probable dates for the pyramids have been modified, and Millon places them in the first century B.C., or even earlier (Millon, 1960). This pushes back the dates set by Vaillant (Vaillant, 1955) at least six or seven centuries.[3]

The axis of the ceremonial center is the Avenue of the Dead, a broad thoroughfare forty-five meters wide and over two kilometers long, from the Citadel's main access to the Pyramid of the Moon, oriented with a 17 degree deviation east of north (Marquina, 1951). The Avenue was paved, and to accommodate thirty meters of uneven terrain between the higher northern end and the southern end, its builders constructed a series of terraces reached by stairways the same width as the Avenue itself (Plate No. 5).

The Pyramid of the Moon is a five-bodied structure forty-two meters high, standing on a rectangular platform 150 by 130 meters at the far north end of the Avenue of the Dead. The Pyramid of the Sun is possibly older, much larger and has different characteristics.[4] It was subsequently surrounded by a platform 350 meters on each side, with an axis perpendicular to that of the Avenue, and is oriented so that it faces the setting sun (I.N.A.H., 1959c). The pyramid's base is 215 by 215 meters, and its height, including the four talus bodies and a panel body in between the third and fourth taluses, was higher than the sixty-four meters we see today, since it now lacks the temple on its upper platform. (Plate No. 6)

Although both are truncated pyramids with stepped bodies, each structure has observable differences. In the Pyramid of the Moon, the base is not the same as that of the Pyramid of the Sun and it lacks the latter's surrounding platform. Instead, it has an important one-bodied anterior plaza of rectangular form next to the platform of the second talus where we find the great access stairway (Plate No. 7).

At the far south of the Avenue of the Dead, also built on its own east-west axis perpendicular to the main one, we find a huge ceremonial complex around the Temple of Quetzalcóatl (Plate No. 8). This complex, occupying an area of 400 meters on each side, is called the Citadel. It is accessible only from the west by a broad stairway built directly off the Avenue of the Dead.

The Citadel's construction is more finished than that of the pyramids. It exhibits the sober character, the use of symmetry in the whole and in secondary structures, and those decorative features which marked the culmination of Teotihuacán architecture, and were to be an influence in Tula, Tenayuca, Tenochtitlán, and Texcoco, that lasted until the arrival of the Spaniards. The Citadel is delimited by a perimetric platform three meters high with a width varying between 32.50 meters on the east side and sixty-five meters on the other sides. It supports fifteen pyramidal bases, three on the east and four on each of the other sides, and encloses a large sunken court in which the temple stood. Two stairways fronting the bases of the north and south sides lead up to the platform (Marquina, 1951 and Kubler, 1962).

This space has two well defined sectors: a rectangular court of more than two hectares next to the main access, where periodic ceremonies were held; and a back platform partially occupied by chambers built around patios, following the arrangement which was to evolve into the residential complexes characteristic of Teotihuacán II and III. The stepped Temple of Quetzalcóatl divides the two sectors on the Citadel's main east-west axis. In front of the temple, in the middle of the forecourt, stands a square altar-temple with a stairway on each side.

Upon entering the Citadel's sunken courtyard from the Avenue of the Dead by the only possible access, your first glance inevitably lights on a stepped structure of four bodies which has been partially reconstructed. This structure dates from Teotihuacán II and was built over an existing temple dedicated to Quetzalcóatl, in keeping with the practice among America's high Indian cultures of using a former building as the nucleus for the new one demanded by their religion. In this case, the nucleus, or Temple of Quetzalcóatl, had been a lavishly decorated, six-bodied, stepped pyramid. It dates from the beginning of Teotihuacán II, coinciding with the period when some of Teotihuacán's best works of architecture and sculpture were created.

I do not propose to undertake an analysis of pre-Hispanic architecture, as it has already been the subject of excellent studies (Marquina, 1951; Kubler, 1962; Robertson, 1963). I will only point out those aspects of Teotihuacán's architecture which had reached full maturity in the Temple of Quetzalcóatl and which subsequently exerted a great influence on religious structures of the Indian civilizations in the Valley of Mexico. These characteristics are: regularly shaped stone construction with an interior fill of *tezontle*, a porous material; a preference for truncated pyramidal masses of several bodies in taluses and vertical walls; vertical walls defined by panels of large, perfectly-joined stones, carved and painted over a stucco base; large wall sculptures, also painted, representing gods (in the Temple of Quetzalcóatl, we see Tlaloc, god of rain, and Quetzalcóatl, symbolized by a serpent); pyramids serving as temple bases and reached by a stairway with balustrades; and architecture of simple shapes and straight lines forming elementary geometric masses.

The Pyramids of the Sun and the Moon and the Citadel, or Temple of Quetzalcóatl, were the most important structures of Teotihuacán's ceremonial center, but not the only ones. The archeological zone itself is thickly covered by the partially reconstructed ruins of temples and terraces, palaces and various structural groups, built one over another in a senseless, interminable building process which stopped only when the city was destroyed and its inhabitants dispersed.

Teotihuacán's urban characteristics, like its agricultural features, were repeated throughout Mexico's central plateau until the Conquest. Modified as necessary for more intense use in a special area destined to be a ceremonial center, Teotihuacán's three basic urban design principles—axial arrangement of structures; symmetry of partial groups; and use of simple volumes, isolated or connected by platforms of lower height to determine urban spaces—reappear several centuries later in Tula, and again in Tenochtitlán, Tlatelolco, and Texcoco. Of equal significance was the adoption of two axes of some 6,000 meters in length, crossing in a point where the Citadel and the Great Compound were built, marking the administrative and possibly the commercial center of the city. This gigantic cross divided the city in four large quadrants, a physical organization we will find more than a millennium later in Tenochtitlán, and acted as a point of reference for the gridiron layout used in the residential districts.

In the design of Teotihuacán's ceremonial center, the principles I have mentioned are employed consistently. The main axis, oriented according to an ancient ritual concept, determined the general structural layout,[5] and a series of minor axes perpendicular to the principal one served as orientation for other symmetrical complexes, urbanistically isolated, yet linked by their complementary functions. Teotihuacán's ceremonial complex is laid out simply, without disruptive elements. It is a synthesis of Teotihuacán's aesthetic concepts during its centuries of splendor, tending toward geometric principles, which are also seen in its sculpture—the beautiful masks and stone figures—as well as in its architecture.

But where are the antecedents of these concepts? Is it possible that a plan with the monumentalism and classicism of Teotihuacán's ceremonial center might be the result of a civilization's first attempt at the art of urban design? This is hard to believe, even supposing that it represented the work of several generations and that the secondary axes and structural groups were introduced when the two main axes and the location of both pyramids, the Citadel, and the Avenue of the Dead were already determined. It seems certain that future excavations in the settlements of the Patlachique Phase could clarify at least part of this question, since it is here we find the regularly shaped patios outlined by various isolated structures, some even connected by platforms, which were to become common in later periods. We need not leave the central Valley of Mexico to find the antecedents of truncated pyramidal forms serving as temple bases. Furthermore, the use of superimposed platforms appears in a Pre-Classic building excavated in Cholula (Noguera, 1956). But where are the antecedents of the principles of urban planning? Perhaps among the Olmecs. In the ceremonial centers of this Gulf Coast culture we find, probably for the first time, many of the cultural aspects defining the Classic Period in Mesoamerica such as monumental sculpture, accentuated social stratification reflecting definite priestly leadership, writing, and technical and scientific advances (Bernal, 1959b). But as yet, archeology has provided us with no definite proofs.

The Pyramid of the Sun is the dominant visual element of the ceremonial center, but the Avenue of the Dead is the guiding principle of the plan. It is a true urban, spacious avenue, on which our line of vision is directed toward the Pyramid of the Moon or toward the San Juan River, depending on which direction we are heading, by a visually uninterrupted series of mounds, some only five meters high today, which were minor temples and palaces during the Classic Period. Confirming its character as an elongated, defined space, we notice as we walk along that we can see only the upper half of the Pyramid of the Sun. The base is hidden by the structures lining the Avenue. The Avenue of the Dead begins at its northern end in a regularly shaped plaza, really a forecourt of the Pyramid of the Moon, enclosed on four sides by six large mounds six or seven meters high, with a small central platform on the Avenue's axis. From the plaza, the only long view is toward the south along the Avenue of the Dead itself. The thirty-meter difference in elevation between both ends of the Avenue was adjusted by stairways, which created small semi-enclosed plazas at intervals, bounded at their ends by stairway-ramps and at the sides by the minor structures along the Avenue.

An inhabitant of Teotihuacán, walking up the Avenue of the Dead from the Citadel toward the Pyramid of the Moon in a south-north direction, would have enjoyed the changing views of the Pyramid of the Sun along his approach past a series of simple architectural sequences. At the far end, the Pyramid of the Moon would seem to vanish and reappear before his gaze as he emerged from the semi-enclosed feeling of the Avenue's level to the top of one of its stairway-ramps, only to descend again on the other side and continue his way along the Avenue.

Let us imagine the paved Avenue, the buildings bordering it stuccoed and painted, the richly adorned persons, the masks, ear ornaments, and beaded necklaces of jade, jadeite and other hard stones, the apparel and plumes, the headdresses representing animal heads, and the elaborate garments of the priests and ruling classes who moved along this great ceremonial highway. In contrast to such sumptuousness, we should think of the austerity of the linear landscape, so like the architecture of the temples, in order to realize the solemnity which must have attended a ceremonial procession in Teotihuacán.

The use of compositional axes set according to a predetermined orientation and the monumental effect of the large outlines of the whole; the symmetrical grouping of minor structures forming plazas, although the relation of the Pyramids to each other and to the Citadel was completely free; the variety in the arrangement of smaller buildings serving as atria or major structures, or joining small structures with related functions, always with simple compositional principles; the use of large connecting stairways and platforms between constructions and the use of simple, isolated structures to define open spaces; urban proportions in secondary groups within a complex of super-human scale, considering the technological level of this civilization; the absence of details in architectural works, except for sculpture and painting—all these elements characterized urban design in the ceremonial center of Teotihuacán. Many of them may have originated in cultures prior to that of Teotihuacán, but I believe that here they were used together for the first time in Mesoamerica. The result was a complex unequaled in magnitude and clarity of concept among the Indian civilizations of the American Continents.

THE EARLY CLASSIC PERIOD (150-250 A.D.)

Teotihuacán II-Miccaotli Phase

The majority of recent studies refer to Teotihuacán's second period as Classic (Caso, 1953; Ekholm, 1958; Willey and Phillips, 1958; Bernal, 1959a and 1959b; Millon, 1966b and 1969). Although the beginning and decline of the respective Classic Periods of the various Mesoamerican regions do not coincide in time (Bernal, 1959b), we can set the first seven or eight centuries of the Christian era as the culminating period of those cultures which had been developing since Pre-Classic times in the valleys of Oaxaca, the Guatemala highlands, Yucatán, the Petén, the Gulf Coast, and on the central plateau of Mexico.

The Classic Period began in Teotihuacán earlier than in other regions and presumably started its decline some centuries sooner. Classic Teotihuacán corresponds to Armillas' Periods II and III, between the first century B.C. and the seventh century A.D., and to Millon's Periods II, III and IV between 150 and 750 A.D.[6] The reasons for this early culmination might be found in the direct influence which an advanced culture, coming from outside the valley, could have had on the undeveloped Archaic cultures or their replacements. These new arrivals showed rapid adaptation and comprehension of the potential of an environment with an ecological balance rare in Mesoamerica, such as that of the central plateau of Mexico.

The Classic Period in Mesoamerica was characterized by population growth, the construction of large urban centers, improved agricultural practices, specialization of labor, the formation of states, and the general use of writing and the calendar, and by the great artistic styles which so well represented the developing trends toward symbolism in different regions. This led to the destruction of the stylistic unity which had prevailed in Mesoamerica up to the Classic Period.

From an urbanistic point of view, the Classic is the period when the first true cities appeared, establishing their definitive urban settlement patterns which they were to maintain for centuries without great modification. In some regions, as on Mexico's central plateau and in the valleys of Oaxaca, such patterns still exist. As these already well-differentiated cultures reached their peak, they also acquired a momentary equilibrium between their own demographic growth and the ecology of the region.

The Classic Period was also that of the large, planned civic and ceremonial complexes. With the exception of Teotihuacán, this urban planning may never have encompassed a whole Classic center, but the design of the ceremonial centers and even the layout of some of the known urban districts indicate that this epoch was one of the most significant in the evolution of Latin American cities. Given the cultural influence of Teotihuacán over a good area of Mesoamerica, it is intriguing that a gridiron base along two main axes has not been found in other classic centers of the central valley of Mexico. I also think it possible that for the first time the various ceremonial, administrative, artisan, and residential functions came together in a single site, and on a vast scale during this epoch.

The definitive pattern of Teotihuacán's ceremonial center may have been set at the end of its period I. During the centuries of its construction, the workmen totally or partially occupied the Pre-Classic districts and the districts near the Avenue of the Dead. Teotihuacán's pyramids and the Citadel are ambitious constructions for any culture. They take on the nature of super-human enterprises if we consider the technological level of their builders, who had no knowledge of iron and lacked beasts of burden. Based on the volume of completed works, it is estimated that the Pyramid of the Sun needed 3,000 full-time artisans, backed up by an equal number of laborers to prepare and haul the building materials. The priests, chiefs, and nobles in charge of directing the constructions, general civic affairs, and the ritual aspects connected with the cults which were worshipped in Teotihuacán, were estimated at another 2,500 persons. If we add a minimum number of dependents to these figures, we reach a total of 17,000 persons directly connected with the planning, direction, and construction of the Pyramid of the Sun and with the city's administration during the Classic Period. This figure might be increased if we include the high ranking members of the ruling group (Cook, 1947).

Let us assume that each of the larger structures was built separately and that 17,000 persons were connected with activities which we might call planning, administration, and execution of the city's public works. Based on the daily diet of 2,000 calories which sustains the average Mexican today, Cook calculated that 150,000 persons lived around Teotihuacán. More recent research has shown, however, that this figure almost doubles the estimated population of Teotihuacán at its peak (Millon, 1966). The city's population would have included the 17,000 already mentioned, a numerous group of farmers and artisans who produced food and consumer goods for the whole population, a certain number of warriors, merchants and their dependents, as well as minor groups.

Without fixing a date for the construction of the pyramids, another author, Mayer-Oakes, says that the size and purpose of Teotihuacán's architecture suggests that its construction and maintenance had greater support than could be provided locally (Mayer-Oakes, 1960). This is a possible explanation for the enormous volume of work accomplished in a relatively short period of time, as we have proof of the simultaneous occupation of various sites in the same valley, as well as in neighboring valleys, by groups of Teotihuacán culture during the Classic Period. However, as Teotihuacán grew in size and population, a parallel decline was taking place in the settlements of adjacent valleys (Parsons, 1968).

I have calculated the density of the residential district of Tlamimilolpa, east of the ceremonial center, at 300 persons per hectare, although I do not think this figure is characteristic of Teotihuacán's urban districts in the light of excavations undertaken to date. But let us suppose this was so, and that the 150,000 persons suggested by Cook actually did congregate in the city of Teotihuacán. We would then have a net area of 375 hectares exclusively occupied by residential areas with densities resembling those of Tlamimilolpa.

Although 300 persons per hectare is a density somewhat higher than those we find for Chan Chan[7] and Cuzco, and much higher than the densities for Mayapán, the Classic Maya centers, and possibly Tenochtitlán at its peak, it does not seem so high compared to other cities contemporaneous with Teotihuacán or older. The Mesopotamian cities of Ur, Eshumar, and Khafaje were two thousand years old before their urban densities varied from between 270 and 440 persons per hectare (Frankfort, 1950). Of course, the fluvial plains of Mesopotamia were more difficult to unify, which may explain the higher densities of its cities.

Despite the limited area excavated, archeologists have confirmed that the district of Tlamimilolpa had clearly urban and residential characteristics with few streets and apparently no open spaces or areas set aside for institutional buildings. According to modern percentages of utilization of urban land, the streets of a medium-sized city and the areas left vacant account for 30 per cent of its area. Applying this criterion in Teotihuacán, we would have to add 112.5 hectares to those which were exclusively residential. In addition, we have the archeological zone consisting of 200 hectares around the principal ceremonial center which is occupied by religious structures of different sizes, by the Avenue of the Dead, and by some palaces and plazas. The palaces found close to the ceremonial center represent an especially low residential density. In any case, approximately 150 of the 200 hectares were purely ceremonial.

Adding together the three general areas—the 375 hectare residential district, the area of 112.5 hectares for other uses, and the ceremonial center of 200 hectares—we obtain a total of 687.50 hectares for Teotihuacán. We break this down into a rough estimated density of 218 persons per hectare, still based on the supposition that all the city's housing areas had the same degree of concentration as Tlamimilolpa, which was evidently not the case. Millon and his team have defined an area of 2,250 hectares (22.5 square kilometers) which they consider as urban for the Early Classic Period, when Teotihuacán reached its maximum extension but still was far from reaching its maximum population. During the Miccaotli phase, the city had around 45,000 inhabitants or an overall density of twenty persons or 3.3 houses per hectare if the whole area considered as urban was occupied with a similar density. This is a very low average density indeed and could hardly be called urban even for that time and place. We might reasonably assume that large sectors of that total area either were not occupied simultaneously or, more likely, had been occupied and then were abandoned for reasons which are not clear. The existence of small agricultural lots within the area considered as urban would increase the density of the true urban districts. We can be reasonably sure that Teotihuacán's physical expansion had reached its maximum during Teotihuacán II, and that the occupation of the different districts did not continue throughout the city's entire evolution. For example, the lack of remains from Teotihuacán II in some Teotihuacán I districts points to their early abandonment. It is also possible that, for reasons yet unknown, the direction of the city's expansion changed during different periods. Consequently, the north and northwest sectors of the ceremonial center preferred during Teotihuacán I were replaced in importance by the central and southern sectors during Teotihuacán II.

Teotihuacán, like other classic centers in Mesoamerica, had no defensive walls. It had no limitations then for physical expansion, as had most cities in Europe and Asia at that time. Nor was the population of Teotihuacán forced to densify to obtain existing services such as water from conduits, fountains or wells, manpower and market places which, together with walls, were the major factors for densification in European and Asian cities. Even though Teotihuacán was built with one story structures, as shown by the palaces and blocks of apartments, it would be unreasonable to suppose that the whole population benefited from similar standards. It is possible then that Teotihuacán, like other unwalled preindustrial cities, had several districts with characteristics which physically and demographically could be called urban, leaving empty spaces unbuilt which became partially occupied in the city's later periods. In my opinion, the entire area considered urban never had true urban characteristics nor was it occupied simultaneously.

We may wonder whether the complex functions characteristic of a city were already being fulfilled during Teotihuacán II. In the first centuries of the Christian era, Teotihuacán was a city permanently occupied by a population that lived and worked there, sharing the responsibilities and the specializations belonging to an urban economy. Archeological finds of this period show that the city had a good number of painters, musicians, sculptors, laborers, and artisans dedicated to pottery, basketry, weaponry (although few examples have been found), and creating objects of obsidian which took the place of hard metals in the Teotihuacán culture (Spence, 1967). The precision of measurement in construction and the architectural styles, the general layout of the city and the existence of drainage systems indicate the work of well-trained engineers and surveyors. This group of technicians and artisans consumed the food and worked the raw materials which were imported or produced by the more numerous agricultural group, who probably lived in precarious settlements located in the neighboring valleys, and on the city's periphery (Sanders, 1969).

Everything points to the presence of a stratified society not unlike that of the Sumerians, Egyptians, or that of Tiahuanaco when it became necessary to undertake construction on such a large scale. Linné tells us that Teotihuacán society seems to have been strongly theocratic, with public life greatly influenced by religion (Linné, 1942). The upper classes ruled the population with an iron hand, organizing their large numbers with efficiency. Priests played a significant role in this well-differentiated society, while the importance of the warrior group seems to have grown through time (Million, 1966b, 1966c; Sanders, 1965).

Of all the housing groups found in Teotihuacán, the Viking Group, situated three hundred meters southwest of the Pyramid of the Sun toward the middle of the Avenue of the Dead, is the group most likely to have been built during Teotihuacán II (Armillas, 1950). It is earlier than Tlamimilolpa and Xolalpán, groups belonging to Teotihuacán III, but later than the pyramids. We can place it in the first or second century of our era, contemporaneous with the majority of minor structures bordering

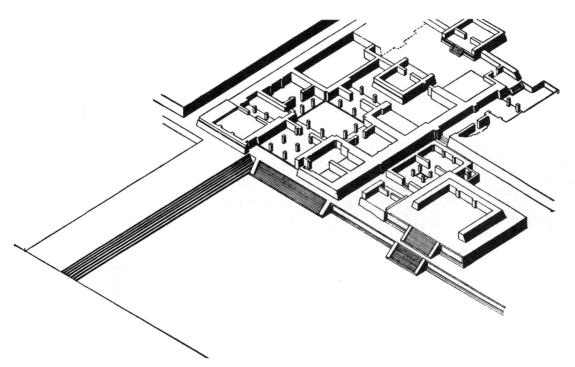

9 *Teotihuacán: The Viking Group. The ruins of this palace built during Teotihuacán: II were excavated by Armillas over twenty years ago. It consists of a series of chambers opening on to a central open patio with columns which can be reached through a covered hall. A broad stairway descends to join the Avenue of the Dead. (Credit: Armillas, Pedro:* Teotihuacán, Tula y los toltecas, *Runa, III-1 and 2, Buenos Aires, 1950.)*

the Avenue of the Dead, and perhaps with the Citadel. The Viking Group
seems to have served residential functions, judging from objects found
there.[8] The chambers are regularly shaped and surround interior columned patios (Plate No. 9). The general plan of this group is similar to
those of Xolalpán, Atetelco, Tetitla, Tepantitla, and Zacuala, complexes
which seem to have been palaces or residential groups housing Teotihuacán's upper classes. It does not resemble Tlamimilolpa with its more
urban layout and higher density. For that time in Mesoamerica, however,
the Viking Group had urban characteristics. We do not find palaces like
this, with a drainage system, bordered by streets, and exhibiting such
skillful techniques of composition and construction in the rural areas of
Mesoamerica. Even the use of columns to form porticos around regular
patios, and the appearance of columned vestibules are features which
were thereafter associated with the urban architecture of Teotihuacán
and of Mexico's central plateau in general, as we see in Tula. If these features spread beyond the central plateau, as far as Chichen Itzá and other
Maya centers of Yucatán, they were introduced by the influence of later
Mexican cultures.

During the Classic centuries, Teotihuacán seems to have been a safe
place to live. As in other Mesoamerican Classic cities and centers, investigators have found no traces of fortifications and few weapons (Linné,
1942). From those reproductions of frescoes I have seen, I only remember one having a military theme—that of a warrior holding a circular shield and a handful of arrows (Marquina, 1951). Were times so
peaceful, or had Teotihuacán reached the necessary power and prestige to
keep conflict away from its territory?[9]

Whether as the capital of a hereditary kingdom (Vaillant, 1955), or as
the center of a federation of small states united by cultural ties (Linné,
1942), or as a state associated with a religious cult, Teotihuacán was unquestionably the most important city in the spontaneous pattern of settlement and urban development that took place during the Classic Period in
the Basin of Mexico. Though unrivaled as an administrative capital,
market and interchange center, and as a place where utilitarian and
nonutilitarian items were produced for local as well as external consumption, its prestige was due more to its role as a Mecca for pilgrims even
from far beyond the Valley of Mexico. Thousands of "foreigners" were
possibly attracted to the city every year by these unusual characteristics.

The cult of Tlaloc, one of the most important in the city, is exemplified by the wall paintings decorating the various housing groups (Caso, 1942; Villagra, 1957). As the god of rain to the inhabitants of Teotihuacán and to all urban cultures of the time, Tlaloc's cult spread throughout Mesoamerica. Not only was it the most widespread cult, but it endured the longest. Venerated by the Maya who called him Chac, and centuries later by the Aztec, he is represented by a mask with circles around the eyes.

The principal god of the Classic pantheon, however, was Quetzalcóatl, whose naturalistic image as a feathered serpent can be seen in the Citadel at Teotihuacán, at Chichen Itzá, and at Uxmal where he was called Kukulcán, and in countless Maya and Náhuatl temples. Laurette Séjourné explains, "According to Quetzalcóatl, the end of life means passing beyond the limits of individual existence to participate in the transfiguration of nature in its entirety. This transformation takes place by the action (in Quetzalcóatl's era, it was called movement) which, releasing the spirituality enclosed in every earthly particle, frees matter from gravity and death." She then adds, "Teotihuacán was built to glorify this principle of redemption, and it is hard to conceive of a purer reflection of religious experience" (Séjourné, 1959). Quetzalcóatl was the god of life and fertility and the focus of Classic civilizations.

Teotihuacán's cultural features radiated over a vast area. The Classic Period in Mesoamerica saw the culmination of such centers as Monte Albán (Period IIIA) and Yucuñudahui in Oaxaca; El Tajín among the Totonacs of the central Gulf Coast; Cholula, in the State of Puebla; several sites belonging to the Tzakol culture in the central area of Maya culture; Kaminaljuyú in the valley of Guatemala; Pasión (Periods III-IV), in the Huastec zone; several sites in Michoacán and western Mexico, and the second and third phases of Teotihuacán (Armillas, 1950; Caso, 1953). Objects from Teotihuacán, carried by traders, have been found in such remote places in the south of Mesoamerica as Tikal and Kaminaljuyú in Guatemala; and to the north, in San Juan del Río in the State of Querétaro, as well as in Armería, Colima, and El Ixtepete in Jalisco (Piña Chan, 1960). Toward the end ot the Early Classic a Teotihuacán merchant colony was well established in Kaminaljuyú (Michels, 1969). All these centers were influenced by Teotihuacán while contributing their own cultural traits, whether through commerce or, as Linné suggests to explain the dispersion of ceramics and Teotihuacán artistic styles, by traveling artisans (Linné, 1956).[10] In each subarea or region of Mesoamerica, a local culture developed with its own artistic styles and characteristic writing system. Nevertheless, Teotihuacán was the foremost influence in the region of the central plateau of Mexico and was possibly also the first city to acquire importance outside its own region, thus making its influence felt in other areas such as Oaxaca and particularly Monte Albán during its Period III.

At the end of Teotihuacán II, the city had probably reached its maximum physical growth and completed the construction of its basic street pattern and its sound drainage system, both essential urban services. At that time, Teotihuacán had a population of about 45,000 inhabitants (Millon, 1966a).

THE CLASSIC PERIOD: (250-450 AND 450-650 A.D.)

Teotihuacán IIA, III and IIIA- Tlamimilolpa and Xolalpán Phases

During the last thirty years, several housing districts have been excavated in Teotihuacán, the majority of which belong to Periods IIA and III. By studying their location, and through a careful reconnaissance, it was possible to outline the area occupied by the city during the centuries of its maximum population. The transition years between Teotihuacán II and IIA mark the maximum residential expansion and a period of population growth. During the Tlamimilolpa Phase Teotihuacán extended over an area of 2,200 hectares, slightly less than during the previous Miccaotli Phase (Millon, 1966a).

We do not know which were the occupied sectors between the ceremonial center itself and the outer limits and, if inhabited, to what degree. Today, cultivated fields of maize and maguey have grown over the presumed urban area. In the excavations in separated sites within the limits of the archeological zone, investigators have found several palaces and housing districts which enable them to determine the more densely ur-

10 *Teotihuacán: Tlamimilolpa. Of all housing groups excavated to date in Teotihuacán, the district of Tlamimilolpa is the only one with truly urban characteristics. The dotted lines indicate the location of the drains that flowed into a main conduit which coincided with one of the narrow streets serving as access to the houses. The houses opened on to a central patio and the outer walls had no openings other than the entrance doorways. (Credit: Linné, S.: "Mexican Highland Cultures," The Ethnographical Museum of Sweden, Publication No. 7, Stockholm, 1942.)*

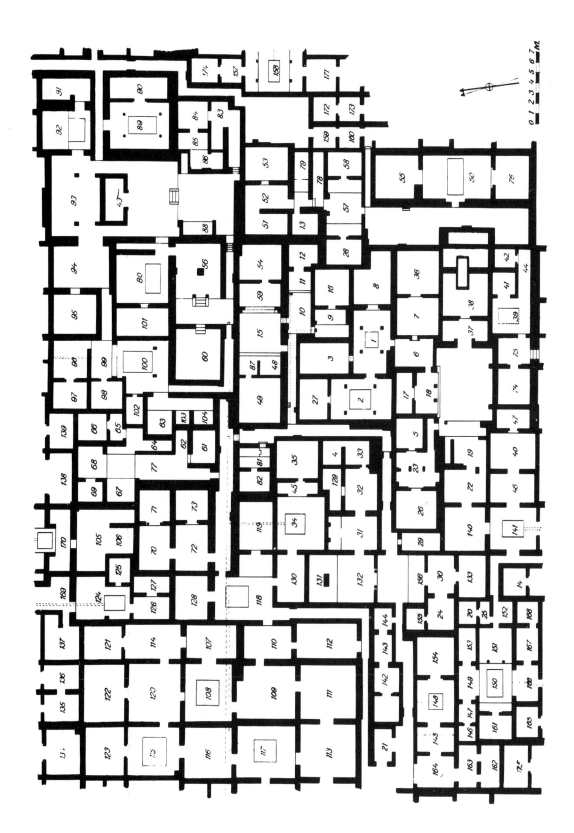

banized area of Teotihuacán and its peripheral districts, or suburbs, at some 2,200 hectares, four kilometers to the east and west of the Avenue of the Dead and three kilometers south and north of the east-west axis. In this area, the extensive principal ceremonial center was situated in a north-south direction, somewhat to the west of the center of the urbanized area. The external form of the urbanized area was quite irregular, showing a heavier concentration to the north of the east-west axis. The majority of the groups excavated, such as Tlamimilolpa, Xolalpán, Atetelco, Tepantitla, Tetitla, and Zacuala, belong to Teotihuacán IIA and III. Except for Tlamimilolpa, which may have had different functions, these groups were apparently the residences of the rich.

The district of Tlamimilolpa is situated 2,500 meters east of the Pyramid of the Sun. Linné dated it as belonging to 236 A.D., plus or minus sixty-five years, or approximately third century A.D. (Linné, 1956). The excavated area covers 3,500 square meters and contains 176 chambers of regular shape but varying size, as well as several forecourts and courtyards. The dwellings undoubtedly extended beyond the explored limits (Linné, 1942). Excavations also uncovered a previous residential occupation of the site, yet few variations in building techniques which seem to have remained unchanged for centuries. Houses were built of adobe or stone, the walls plastered in white stucco on which were painted realistic or religious motifs in red, blue or green; flat earthen roofs were supported by wooden beams which were, in turn, supported by the walls or columns or masonry pillars; white stuccoed floors were five to ten centimeters thick. (Plate No. 10)

Tlamimilolpa seems to have been a neighborhood of dwellings which was built up gradually, or as Linné says, a housing district with the characteristics of a small village, lacking the breadth and sophistication of Xolalpán or Zacuala (Plate No. 9). It was probably a neighborhood inhabited by minor functionaries, merchants or artisans. The existing maps and reports of the excavations do not allow us to outline the area occupied by each dwelling, and it is not likely we will ever be able to do so since the land has been returned to cultivation. An agreement between the archeologists and the land's proprietors required that the area be covered over again after it had been studied.

An alley, straight but so narrow that it hardly qualifies as a street (at one point its width is only sixty centimeters and at no point more than 1.10 meters), appears in the western section of the plan. After turning 90 degrees to the north, it enters a four-by-six-meter open space (No. 118 on the plan)[12] which could have been either a small plaza or a forecourt. Chambers 130, 45 and 35 and the patio (No. 34 on the plan) may have belonged to a single dwelling. Number 110 might have been the entrance to a house made up of several chambers. Number 128, and the semi-open space without a number on the east side of the small plaza in front of chamber 119, could have been commercial sectors. From here, the alley twists toward the east, stopping in a dead end fifteen meters further on.

Within the excavated area, we find a second alley as narrow as the first, with which it seems to have had a common origin. This alley also follows a general west-east direction, becoming wider at the entrances to the two dwellings (No. 156 and 132 on the plan), narrowing again, and then turning 90 degrees to the north to rejoin the first alley. In the plan, we see several shorter passageways with similar characteristics, which may have been the ends of these winding alleys.

Even for a culture without beasts of burden, the ratio between the width of pedestrian paths and the intense occupation of the terrain seems disproportionate. None of the alleys found can be considered a street connecting districts of the same neighborhood. I think they must have been mere paths of access to housing groups laid out in the cul-de-sac arrangement of a contemporary neighborhood. The chambers of the dwellings opened out on to interior courts and occasionally to the streets. Following an old Mexican tradition that still exists today, these dwellings lacked windows. Light and air entered through the street and patio doors and, in some cases, through the roofs. Some of the interior spaces, seventeen in all, were possibly courts (Nos. 115, 117, 108, 148, 150, 34, 141, 124, 170, 2, 1, 39, 100, 80, 50, 89, and 158 on the plan); others, twelve or fourteen in all, were entrances or forecourts (Nos. 156, 18, 77, 99, 9, 10, 45, and others); numbers 21, 128, and 119 seem to have been commercial, and I have already mentioned number 118 as an outside space. This leaves 140 probable chambers. Let us suppose that, judging by their size, proportions and location, half of these were used for sleeping and were occupied by an average of one and one half persons for each chamber. We would end up with a density of 105 persons in an area a bit over one-third of a hectare, or 300 persons per hectare.

The plan of Tlamimilolpa's excavated area shows some urban characteristics similar to those found in cities three millennia older than this site in the Valley of Mexico. Some of the districts in Ur, the city of the Chaldeans (Woolley, 1953) and of Mohenjo-daro, on the banks of the Indus River (Piggott, 1952), provide examples: the orderly pattern of the dwellings in relation to each other and to the rectilinear direction of the alleys; the narrowness of these alleys, even more pronounced than at Tlamimilolpa; the absence of windows in all rooms so that streets were defined by the smooth walls of the dwellings, broken only by doorways; the arrangement of chambers around a patio with some rooms opening out on to the street, presumably for commercial purposes. These are all urban structural features shared by three civilizations separated in time and cultural area of influence. Certainly, in Tlamimilolpa we have found no street which would allow the passage of four carts abreast as in Mohenjo-daro, nor were they functionally necessary, and none of the buildings excavated in Tlamimilolpa, Xolalpán and other districts of Teotihuacán had an upper floor like those in Ur. Evidently the narrow alleys found at Tlamimilolpa led to broader streets which in turn may have led to the main streets which formed the gridiron pattern discovered in recent years.

Xolalpán, situated a few hundred meters east of the Pyramid of the Sun, was also excavated by Linné (Linné, 1934). The complex was formed by a series of apartments with independent entrances arranged around a central open space, or rectangular patio, with an altar in its center and four platforms oriented to the cardinal points. From the patio, the platforms could be reached by stairways, flanked by balustrades on each of their four sides. The shapes of the chambers and open interior patios of the dwellings were regular, but of larger dimensions than those in Tlamimilolpa. We find the same type of construction and drainage systems in both zones. Obviously, Xolalpán was a neighborhood of better quality housing than Tlamimilolpa, yet not as good as others found in Teotihuacán. Linné suggests that it may have housed priests, wise men and artists or, perhaps on the contrary, it had purely secular uses. These are merely conjectures, however, since we have found nothing to indicate any specific use. If we suppose that it was a housing group, using the same formula as for Tlamimilolpa, we would calculate that 18 chambers of the 47 floor spaces found totally or partially in the 1,200 square meters of the excavated area were used for sleeping. This would give us a density of approximately 200 persons per hectare.

Archeologists have found the same layout of a square or rectangular central patio surrounded by regularly shaped chambers and porticos in other groups excavated in different parts of Teotihuacán, such as Tepantitla, Atetelco, Tetitla, and Zacuala. The dimensions of the floor spaces in these three groups are larger than those in Xolalpán and Tlamimilolpa. They seem to have been a product of the better times in the city's history and may have housed the ruling groups or Teotihuacán's nobility.

All the known housing groups were built with the same features—patios, porticos and chambers. Teotihuacán's architects knew how to use these to advantage by introducing varying levels, stairways, ponds, and columns as well as by the simple device of giving varied dimensions to spaces with similar functions.

The ruins of Tepantitla lie 500 meters east of the Pyramid of the Sun (Caso, 1942). The outstanding features here are the frescos depicting Tlaloc, a superior example of which is in the patio. This particular painting represents *Tlalocán,* the paradise in store for those chosen by Tlaloc, among whose numbers were drowned persons, those struck by lightning, and lepers (Armillas, 1950).

Ceramic finds at Atetelco, 1,500 meters southwest of the Pyramid of the Sun (Armillas, 1950), place it early in Teotihuacán III when the styles of the preceding period had not yet disappeared. It seems to have been abandoned while the city was still growing. Here, too, we find figures and personages connected with the cult of Tlaloc in decorations on the interior walls of the palace (Villagra, 1956-57).

Tetitla lies in the same southwest direction as Atetelco, but only 1,000 meters beyond the Pyramid of the Sun. Judging by the different levels of its construction, this site was occupied over a prolonged period of time.

The last palace to be excavated was Zacuala. In the same sector as Atetelco and Tetitla, but over 2,000 meters from the Pyramid of the Sun (Séjourné, 1959), it covered an area of about 4,000 square meters and consisted of rooms and porticos distributed around thirteen patios which were bounded by more porticos. The central patio, much larger than the others, included a temple which occupied its entire east side. The paintings in Zacuala are excellent; as at Tepantitla and Atetelco, figures representing abstract aspects of Teotihuacán's religion were drawn in yellow, dark blue, and turquoise over a brilliant red background.

In the course of its history, Teotihuacán underwent modifications, additions and even abandonment of some of its occupied districts. The ceremonial center was subject to continual building activity and never acquired a final form, although its original general outline was respected. During the Tlamimilolpa and Xolalpán Phases, Teotihuacán went through a process of densification for reasons which are not clear. Population grew to an estimated 65,000 inhabitants during the Tlamimilolpa Phase and to 85,000 during the Xolalpán Phase when it reached its peak. Simultaneously, the physical area of the city during the later phase was 10 per cent smaller than during the Miccaotli Phase, some three centuries before. Concentration was undoubtedly helped, both in the administrative and physical aspects, by a precise and functional street pattern which by these centuries covered most of the central districts of the city. Streets surrounded the housing blocks on their four sides. I do not know if the streets that formed the basic gridiron pattern had different widths, indicating their relative importance in the city plan. Except for the Avenue of the Dead and, to a lesser degree, for the east-west axis, urban vistas may have lacked importance in the city plan, in which case streets would probably have been little more than lines of communication to get from one place to another, rather than architectural devices to dramatize a building.

It is interesting to speculate about the land uses that prevailed in Teotihuacán during these centuries. The location of the ceremonial center had been defined for centuries and it was not changed. At the point where the Avenue of the Dead intersected with the east-west axis were the administrative and political districts, if indeed those were the functions of the Citadel facing the principal commercial area, and if such was the activity that took place in the Great Compound. Undoubtedly, other market areas must have existed in a city of such size and population. The location of the ruins of Tepantitla, Atetelco, Tetitla and Zacuala could mean that the most prestigious housing districts surrounded the Avenue of the Dead and extended toward the west and to the north of the west axis. In other words, the residential district where the members of Teotihuacán's hierarchy lived could have been the northwest area of the city. Most obsidian workshops were found to the east of the Avenue of the Dead or to the north of the Pyramid of the Moon (Spence, 1967). As the source of green and gray obsidian was located outside or inside the geographical limits of the valley but always to the east of the city, the northeast and southeast areas were a logical location for an activity which depended on the consumption of local as well as of external markets. Foreign pottery was found mainly concentrated in the northeast area (Millon, 1969). The east area then, confirming the lower quality of housing of Tlamimilolpa in relation to Tepantitla, Atetelco and other districts, could have been the location of the districts where artisans and nonspecialized workers lived.

During the Tlamimilolpa and Xolalpán phases, Teotihuacán reached its maximum political influence, possibly controlling, through direct occupation, a vast although physically unconnected geographical area. As Sanders points out, research suggests that Teotihuacán was a more militaristically political oriented culture than has been supposed (Sanders, 1965).

THE LATE-CLASSIC PERIOD

Teotihuacán IV-
Metepec Phase-650-750 A.D.

Toward the end of the seventh century (Bernal, 1959b), Teotihuacán culture began its decline, and about 750 A.D. the city was abandoned as a consequence of a catastrophe (Millon, 1966a). We know neither why nor exactly when. Perhaps in the causes of its desertion and eventual destruction, we might find the key to the city's true position among the cultures of the central plateau of Mexico. There is no doubt that the unending construction work was such a physical and economic burden on its inhabitants and tributary groups that the population might have nursed a growing rebellion which could have exploded in the overthrow of their traditional hierarchy (Bernal, 1959b). Or, perhaps in the seventh century A.D., or earlier, after invasion by some more vital, ambitious people, Teotihuacán was already semi-abandoned. But were there invasions in that epoch? And if so, why did the Classic Period continue through several centuries more in Oaxaca, the Petén, and Yucatán? Is it possible that Teotihuacán had weakened itself to the point of being unable to fend off attacks from half-savage tribes and was taken without a fight? If there was an invasion, would there not be traces of some sort of fortifications and defenses for archeologists to find? Earthquakes, droughts, floods, and soil erosion with resulting famine and plague[13]—all may be considered with equal validity as causes for Teotihuacán's abandonment. But, I believe that the rigid socio-economic structure evolved by Mesoamerican Classic cultures was the cause of its destruction. It may not have been the only reason, although it was certainly the one behind the disintegration of the Classic cultures of Mexico's central plateau before they were absorbed by other groups inferior in technology but with a vitality, flexibility, and fortitude forgotten among Classic societies, by then depleted by centuries of government geared to supporting a hierarchy which grew more oppressive as popular discontent increased.

After Teotihuacán's evacuation, some of its inhabitants may have taken refuge in San Miguel Amantla, Santiago Ahuizotla, and especially in Azcapotzalco, but the city was not totally abandoned. Between the end of Teotihuacán and the beginning of the Tula of the Toltecs, a period transpired about which little is known. Toltec culture reached its peak during the tenth and eleventh centuries, when Tula became the capital and most influential city on the central plateau of Mexico (Acosta, 1956-1957).

For its size and population, Teotihuacán marks one of the climactic periods of urban life in the Valley of Mexico. It was only in the fourteenth century that cities finally regained the prestige and power they had enjoyed during the Classic Period. In its design of classic simplicity and monumental scale, Teotihuacán was an architectural and urban model for subsequent developments in the region.

——— *NOTES ON · 2* ———

1. THE FIRST TEMPLES were excavated by Leopoldo Batres between 1905 and 1910.

2. Demographic pressure might have been one of the reasons for the introduction of hydraulic agriculture in the valley of Teotihuacán as early as 500 B.C., during the Cuanalán phase (Sanders, 1965).

3. It is interesting to compare these dates with those appearing in an article by Linné (Linné, 1956) which were derived from analysis by the carbon fourteen dating system of charcoal remains found in the Pyramid of the Sun during the tunneling work in 1933. Linné says that there was no doubt but that the charcoal came from the precursors of the Teotihuacán culture. He gives the probable dates, 2484 plus or minus 500 years, and 1915 plus or minus 200 years, that is, anywhere from 978 B.C. to 22 A.D., and from 237 to 637 A.D. Such divergent dates are of little use to us and differ from other kinds of archeological evidence.

4. Piña Chan believes that the Pyramid of the Sun was built at the beginning of Teotihuacán II (100-250 A.D.) during a period of coexistence of two cultures, one of them highly esoteric which introduced abstract art and developed an intellectualized cult to the god of water (jaguar-serpent) and which seems to have come from the Gulf Coast. These people imposed themselves on the already established agricultural groups and activated the cultural evolution of this great ceremonial center (Piña Chan, 1960). The Pyramid of the Sun was probably one of the earliest, if not the earliest, monumental structure built at Teotihuacán (Millon and Drewitt, 1961).

5. The majority of Mesoamerican centers were built with some deviation in the north-south axis. Laurette Séjourné comments, "In keeping with Náhuatl cosmology, it is the solar monument which dictates the orientation of all the others. This orientation offers an interesting peculiarity in that the west-east axis, representing the trajectory of the drama of incarnation and liberation adopted all over Mesoamerica, is modified 17 degrees to the north. After careful investigation, the architect Ignacio Marquina finally discovered that this distortion was caused because the pyramid faced toward the point where the sun is hidden the day it passes directly overhead" (Séjourné, 1947). See *Arquitectura prehispánica* by Ignacio Marquina (Marquina, 1951).

6. Ekholm thinks that the Pre-Classic Period in Teotihuacán came to an end around 300 B.C., or at the moment of transition from Teotihuacán I to Teotihuacán II (Eckholm, 1958). Piña Chan dates this transition at 100 A.D. (Piña Chan, 1960).

7. This is considering the total area occupied by Chan Chan, except the citadels, as independent housing units. See Chapter XI of this book.

8. Armillas comments, "We assume this to have been its function (residential) from the room distributions and from the discovery there of several grinding stones (*metates*)" (Armillas, 1950).

9. The hypothesis that the Archaic and Classic Periods were peaceful and that wars were frequent during the Post-Classic is questioned by Palerm (Palerm, 1954).

10. While Michael Coe speculates that "it would have been greatly in the interest of an armed *pochteca* (merchant) group to have seized the Petén so as to control the commerce originating in the Maya jungles" (Michael Coe, 1966b), Millon says: "We don't know if there were (in Teotihuacán) groups of merchants resembling the *pochteca* nor how long distance trade was organized" (Millon, 1966b).

11. For an excellent sequence of maps of Teotihuacán during its different Periods and phases see Millon, 1966a.

12. The measurements are those which I took from Linné's plan (Linné, 1942) and are, therefore, approximate.

13. Some authors think that the expansion of the cult of Tlaloc reflected the existence of a prolonged, gradual drought, brought on by cutting down the trees (Olivé and Barba, 1957). These authors also claim, with reason, that it is hard to accept the theory of soil depletion since the decline of the Classic cultures took place several centuries apart. A progressive and simultaneous impoverishment of the land in both forest and highland areas of Mesoamerica is scarcely credible.

·3

MESOAMERICAN CITIES AFTER THE FALL OF TEOTIHUACÁN

"Tlaloc, who makes things grow, god of lightening and of rain, is the most important deity of this group and one of the oldest worshipped by man in Mexico and Central America. The Maya called him Chac; the Totonacs spoke of him as Tajín; the Mixtecs named him Tzahui, and the Zapotecs, Cocijo. Throughout Mexico and Central America, his cult is lost in antiquity."

ALFONSO CASO
(EL PUEBLO DEL SOL)

□ 3

THE FALL OF TEOTIHUACÁN marked the end of the Classic cultures in Mesoamerica.[1] On the central plateau of Mexico, this event heralded the beginning of more than two centuries of cultural regression, political disintegration, the emergence of new cults, and the momentary eclipse of urban life—momentary in that it had not disappeared, but had only lost the brilliance of former centuries.[2] People lived in less nucleated groupings as if a process of ruralization became the prevailing tendency.[3] In the cities, the monumental scale, proportions, and handsome architectural detail of construction vanished. Artistically, this was a period without unity, a mixture of shapes and motifs from Teotihuacán combined with those introduced by weaker and less developed cultures.

No city, during those centuries, could have hoped to inherit the position of capital of the Valley of Mexico which Teotihuacán had held for so long. Perhaps the population in the cities declined after the seventh century, as indicated by Teotihuacán during the Metepec Phase, and this instability imposed the need for more modest proportions. Some of these centers, parallel in evolution to Teotihuacán and important in their own right, managed to stay free of the oppression of the invading tribes and emerged as the dominant cities in the era following Teotihuacán's decline. Azcapotzalco was one of these. A continuously inhabited center since before the beginnings of the Teotihuacán culture, it became the main refuge of Teotihuacán's citizens after the final abandonment of that city. We know little about the real importance of Azcapotzalco during the Classic centuries since its present archeological area is located beneath the northwest section of Mexico City. However, its occupation seems to have begun in the middle of the Pre-Classic or Formative Period (Piña Chan, 1955), that is, in the fourth or fifth centuries B.C., as indicat-

77

ed by the small carved Archaic heads found around the site. It continued to be inhabited during the Late Formative, at a time when a large population increase had resulted in the formation of new centers of permanent occupation on Mexico's central plateau, among them Teotihuacán.

Azcapotzalco was unquestionably an extensive and active commercial city during the Classic Period. Its location, on a central peninsula on the western shore of Lake Texcoco, facilitated contacts with the entire lake basin and the territories of central Mexico. I know of no references to its layout and general urban structure, although excavations indicate that its architecture did not reach the monumental proportions nor technical and artistic quality of Teotihuacán. When Teotihuacán was abandoned, Azcapotzalco became the center of its declining culture. Favored by a geographic location which kept it safe from direct attack during the tumultuous centuries following the fall of Teotihuacán, Azcapotzalco endured up to the time of Aztec expansion in the fifteenth century.

Azcapotzalco was not, of course, the only city of Teotihuacán culture on the central plateau during the first Post-Classic centuries. Portezuelo, on the southeast shore of Lake Texcoco, also seems to have been a residential and religious center of considerable size, with functions and hierarchies similar to those of Azcapotzalco. Defined as a kind of provincial center during the Classic Period, its expansion took place after the collapse of Teotihuacán (Parsons, 1968). El Risco, which was first occupied in the Classic Period, must also have existed during this epoch, although with different functions (Mayer-Oakes, 1960). About seventy kilometers west of Azcapotzalco was Calixtlahuaca, another center with its origins back in the Classic Period, which became the capital of the Matlatzinca culture (I.N.A.H., 1960).

Xochicalco, in the State of Morelos, was still another of those cities which were occupied and developed at the same time as Teotihuacán. Its ruins lie on the western edge of Mexico's central plateau. Because of its importance as an apparent bond between the cultures of the central plateau and those that developed in other regions of Mesoamerica, it will be analyzed separately.

Also in the western part of the Valley of Mexico were Malinalco, Cuernavaca, and Tepoztlán, which probably had Pre-Classic origins. Cholula, in the south of the Valley, and one of the oldest inhabited sites of Mesoamerica, was also one of the most important religious centers of the central plateau's Indian cultures. Its history has lasted into the twentieth century.

THE TOLTECS OF TULA

At the beginning of the tenth century, the Tolteca-Chichimeca, a semi-barbaric northern tribe, invaded and proceeded to dominate the center of Mexico for almost two centuries (Bernal, 1959b). Led by their chieftain, Mixcóatl, they settled in Culhuacán, a strategic site in the Valley of Mexico, where they founded their first capital.[4] From Culhuacán, Mixcóatl initiated several campaigns, and it was probably there that he was assassinated by one of his officials who had usurped the throne. Soon after his death, his son, Ce Acatl Topiltzin, was born and went on to take the name of Quetzalcóatl when he became a priest of that god.[5] After a childhood spent in exile, Topiltzin-Quetzalcóatl was finally recognized by his father's supporters, who·helped him return to his family's domains, overthrow the usurper, and eventually claim the throne as king of the Toltecs (Bernal, 1959b).

The first important act of Topiltzin-Quetzalcóatl's government was to move the capital. This decision led to the creation of Tula at the end of the tenth century; probably in 980.[6] During the nineteen years of Topiltzin-Quetzalcóatl's rule, Tula achieved considerable size and prestige as the capital of an empire that included a great part of the territory which had been under the direct influence of Teotihuacán centuries before. It also became the center of the cult of Quetzalcóatl, which that king naturally attempted to impose on his people.

The urbanistic concept of Tula was new in the Valley of Mexico, although Teotihuacán influence can be seen in its architecture and in the general design of its isolated groups. On the whole, Tula lacks the monumentalism and classicism which characterized Teotihuacán.

The existing plan covers only the central zone, which surrounds and includes the main plaza. Excavation and reconstruction work has been concentrated in this area (Acosta, 1942, 1956-1957, 1961).[7] There are other important ruins, however, some distance from the city. On a hilltop, six kilometers to the southeast, we find a Toltec palace of fifteen rooms arranged around patios (Marquina, 1951), and to the north of the plaza, archeologists have explored and reconstructed a circular structure with two rectangular additions called "The Corral" (I.N.A.H., 1957b). The foundations of numerous other dwellings appear scattered over a wide area.

Eighty years ago, Charnay explored a group of chambers of obvious Toltec occupation a short distance southwest of Tula's center. The group's principal feature was a large, slightly trapezoidal courtyard, somewhat less than twenty-five meters on each side, onto which the different rooms opened. The entrance to the palace was through a vestibule which faced a rectangular room of approximately eight by four meters, referred to as the "reception hall." The ground plans show the palace to have been a household; the large, open spaces within its walls could have been used for domestic animals. Charnay found a similar complex northwest of the principal ceremonial center, but we have yet to find even the remains of neighborhoods such as Tlamimilolpa, nor religious structures as large as those of Teotihuacán, nor a hierarchical street arrangement like the one developed centuries before in Teotihuacán and centuries later in Tenochtitlán.

Despite a relatively brief occupation of only two hundred years, Tula grew to a considerable size. We know it extended from the Cerro del Tesoro, or "Treasure Hill," to beyond the Tula River, which runs along the south, west and a portion of the north sides of the city's center, but we have no available data as to its total area or population. We know it was occupied permanently during its two centuries of existence and that its population lived and worked there, as indicated by evidences of continuous building activity. Besides being a market, it was the political and military capital of a state and the religious center of the cult of Quetzalcóatl. Tula lacked the urban characteristics of Teotihuacán. We have found no street system in the Toltec capital, and it is doubtful if one existed since, with the exception of the structures in the central plaza and the monuments mentioned, we find only indications of a dense agricultural population surrounding these groups (Ruz Lhuillier, 1945). The palaces and possible secondary ceremonial centers dependent on the central one are too few and unimportant to allow us to think in terms of a street system connecting them. Tula may have been a city by tenth and eleventh century standards on the central plateau of Mexico, but compared to Teotihuacán, it represented a step backward.

Tula was built over much more irregular terrain than Teotihuacán, which may have discouraged a similar monumentalism in construction, although I do not think this was the whole reason. Perhaps we should try to establish a relationship between the cultural level reached by the Toltecs and the design of their city. Topiltzin-Quetzalcóatl is known to have brought artists and artisans to Tula from more evolved cultures (Bernal, 1959), among them, the survivors of Teotihuacán. In spite of this, the general cultural level of the rest of the central plateau during the tenth and eleventh centuries was lower than it had been during the Classic centuries.[8] Time and other factors were against refinement and maturity being reached in Tula's architecture. Perhaps the traditions of Teotihuacán had been largely forgotten. Topiltzin-Quetzalcóatl may have imposed such an intense building tempo on his capital that the artists, lacking fresh models, based their work on half-forgotten traditions. Influenced by the stylistic trends introduced into the Valley of Mexico after the demise

11 *Tula: General view from the Central Plaza facing the Great Vestibule at the base of the Pyramid of Quetzalcóatl with its Atlantean figures that once supported the temple. (Credit: Hardoy.)*

of Teotihuacán, the artists naturally accepted and blended new concepts which, given Tula's brief occupancy, they had no time to refine with already matured forms. It is not surprising, therefore, that Tula's urbanism and architecture seem those of a provincial capital when we compare them with Teotihuacán.

The limited data we have on the structure of Toltec society point to the existence of a military aristocracy, united around the cult of Tezcatlipoca, a rival god of Quetzalcóatl, that governed a people who never adjusted to the transition from an agricultural economy to a socially and economically urban one. Part of the agricultural population may have lived within the limits of the city itself, where their proximity to the center made them part of the city's daily scene.

In spite of a greater dependency on agriculture than had existed in Teotihuacán, Toltec society maintained specialized artisans. Except for the ruling minority and the crafts groups who lived around the center, I do not believe that the way of life of the majority of Tula's inhabitants was much different from that of thousands of subordinate groups who were concentrated near centers not too far removed from the capital.

We can appreciate the skill of Tula's potters in the collection of *pulque* cups, bowls, censers, braziers, vessels, perfumers, pipes, figures, and cylindrical jars on display in the local museum. Toltec artists also excelled in monumental sculpture and relief work. The Atlantean figures, supporting the roof of the temple of Tlahuizcalpantecuhtli, built on the upper platform of the Pyramid of Quetzalcóatl (Plate No. 11), exhibit rigid architectural as well as sculptural features. These statues have been described as realistic, massive, powerful, and monumental works, yet they manage to give us a synthesis of the details of a Toltec warrior's attire. The *Chac-Mool* statues, also realistic representations of human figures, were abstract in detail since these reclining sculptures were made to support ceremonial objects on their abdomens and, therefore, were simplified to mere suggestions of principal physical and decorative features.

Toltec art reached its height in the relief work on such architectural elements as pillars, columns and especially banquettes, panels, and walls. The Toltecs combined horizontal panels, decorated with realistic jaguars, coyotes, eagles, warriors, and various other personages, with meanders and abstract designs, and they employed the simple artifice of repeating colors on a red background according to the part of the body or type of adornment. We find, for example, cerulean blue for feathers and adornments of jade or turquoise; yellow ochre for feathers, weapons and jewels; pink ochre for skin; white for eyes, fangs, bones and cotton garments; and black to outline the motifs and make them stand out (Acosta, 1956-1957). Toltec architecture acquired new contrasts and patterns, becoming one of the finest expressions of artistic integration among America's Indian cultures.

Tula's architecture, like that of Teotihuacán, revolved around two main types of construction: huge, isolated, pyramidal structures and extensive, single-storied apartment units or "palaces." Even so, the concepts and building techniques in Tula were inferior to those of Teotihuacán and offered few innovations. The architects of Tula's pyramids limited themselves to repetitions of a series of stepped bodies in the Teotihuacán *talud-tablero* style, with the vertical panels greater than the talus sections. In their palaces, the Toltecs continued the Teotihuacán tradition of arranging chambers around a regular, rectangular patio limited by porticos. This could be explained by the haste with which they finished the principal structures, but even then, it is hard to understand such lack of interest in the treatment of details on the part of the Toltec builders.

Nevertheless, in some Toltec structures, we find totally new form and function, as in the *coatepantli,* or "Serpent Wall," built to outline a special area. Centuries later, this type of wall acquired great importance in other centers in the Valley of Mexico, such as Tenayuca and Tenochtitlán. Colonnaded vestibules, too, assumed a different form in Tula. In Teotihuacán, such structures had been utilized only as porticos to emphasize the transition between a court and the chambers of a palace. In Tula, though they may have been used for this purpose as well, vestibules took on an urban dimension for the first time by appearing as intermediate elements between an exterior space, the plaza, and the main buildings of the city.

Bounded naturally by steep drops to the south and west, the principal ceremonial center of Tula was built on a treeless hill, which had been artificially leveled to resemble a broad platform, extending toward the northwest and falling away gently to the east. Today cultivated fields stretch beyond a broad hollow where the Tula River flows through tree-lined banks.

Tula was not walled, and the military strategy of that time was probably not a factor in selecting its site since the high, steep hill to the west of the center would have offered a more favorable defensive location. De-

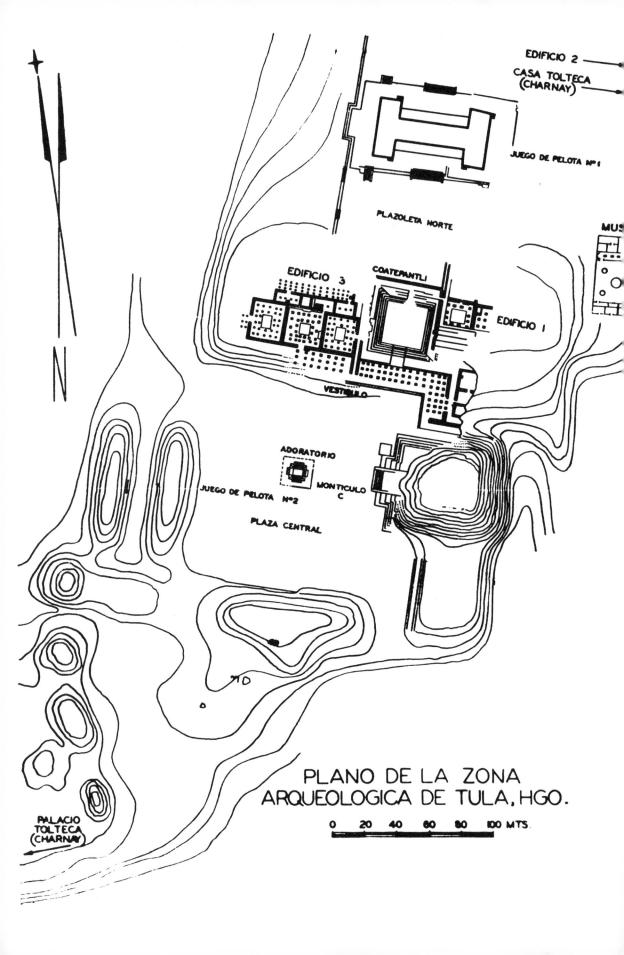

EDIFICIO 2

CASA TOLTECA
(CHARNAY)

JUEGO DE PELOTA N°1

PLAZOLETA NORTE

MUS

EDIFICIO 3

COATEPANTLI

EDIFICIO I

VESTIBULO

ADORATORIO

MONTICULO
C

JUEGO DE PELOTA N°2

PLAZA CENTRAL

PALACIO
TOLTECA
(CHARNAY)

PLANO DE LA ZONA
ARQUEOLOGICA DE TULA, HGO.

0   20   40   60   80   100 MTS.

spite Tula's geographic position during the tenth and eleventh centuries on the frontier between the urban cultures of the Valley of Mexico and the barbarian groups to the north, the prestige of its government and the power of its alliances must have been defense enough, as had been the case in Teotihuacán several centuries earlier.

Tula's center was formed by two plazas, the Central Plaza which extended toward the southeast, and the North Plaza, separated from the other by the main structures of the city (Plate No. 12). The Central Plaza was a wide, almost square space, closed to the north by the Great Vestibule with its columns elevated above the level of the Plaza, hiding the base of the Pyramid of Quetzalcóatl and the Burnt Palace. On the east, the Plaza was closed by a second pyramid, similar to the first though larger, which projected into the Plaza itself. The northwest, southwest, and southeast corners of the Plaza were open. Between the Ball Court, which formed the western side, and a rectangular platform to the south, was a passage opening to a kind of balcony overlooking the valley where the Spaniards began to build Colonial Tula in the sixteenth century. Between the southern platform and the platforms beside the east pyramid, was a second passageway.

The Central Plaza, 120 meters wide, was lower than the North Plaza and the colonnaded vestibule which were built at almost the same level. In the center of the Plaza stood a small, square structure about as tall as a man, with stairways on all four sides. It may have been an altar of the type found in the Toltec constructions at Chichen Itzá (I.N.A.H., 1957b). Seen from the altar, or from the southwest corner looking northwest, the Plaza seems an enclosed space. This impression is heightened by the sturdy foundation forming the platform base of the Great Vestibule which, even in its ruined state, still provides the fundamental visual element connecting the two pyramids and relating them to the Burnt Palace to the west as well as to other, as yet partially unexcavated, structures to the east. The Vestibule, formed by fifty-four pillars placed in three rows of columns, is one of the most significant original features of the center. It leads from the Plaza to the access stairway which, in turn, leads to the upper platform of the Pyramid of Quetzalcóatl where the Temple of Tlahuizcalpantecuhtli[9] stood, supported by its Atlantean figures.

We find innovations in urban design in Tula unknown in Teotihuacán. Plazas in Teotihuacán were generally spaces bounded by isolated struc-

12 *Tula: General plan.*

tures, grouped according to rigid symmetrical principles in the composition and axial arrangement of the complex. In Tula, on the other hand, urban spaces were only partially determined by isolated structures. For the first time among the great complexes of the central plateau of Mexico we find an emphasis on the visual continuity of structures and free balance of volumes.

A premeditated, though not necessarily symmetrical, order is evident in Tula. The principal complex, as in Teotihuacán, is oriented with a deviation of 17 degrees from the astronomical north (Acosta, 1956-1957), and despite smaller overall proportions, it has the vitality of a work intended to last.

The architects of Mexico's central plateau, unlike those who planned the great Classic Maya centers in the Usumacinta River Valley, did not utilize differences in elevation to enhance the architecture and visual perspectives of their buildings. The architects of Teotihuacán were able to take advantage of a site which lent itself admirably to a design of Classic monumentality. Perhaps the territorial limitations of Tula's site account for the innovations contributed by the Toltec architects and their reason for not copying more closely the urban design principles used by a culture which they admired. Tula's topography certainly must have been a basic factor in situating the groups, which are few in number and limited in size. No attempt was made to employ monumental principles.

In contrast to the Central Plaza, the North Plaza gives the impression of being undefined, almost unfinished. It serves more as a wide passageway between a second ball court, larger than the first, and the *coatepantli*.

The ruins of the Burnt Palace, one of the most remarkable structures of the city, lie west of the Pyramid of Quetzalcóatl. We find traces of three almost square halls, side by side, each with a similar portico arrangement around a regular patio. Each hall had a separate entrance and was surrounded by a wall. The center hall was the only one having direct access from the Central Plaza, which makes us think that it may have been used for some civic functions since religious ceremonies took place in the temples (Acosta, 1961). This long complex forms part of the division between the two plazas as well as the northern boundary of the Central Plaza. The low, elongated proportions of the Burnt Palace enhance the height and simple forms of the two pyramids.[10]

Less than twenty years after establishing himself in Tula, Topiltzin-Quetzalcóatl abandoned the city he had founded as his capital. This move came as the culmination of several years of conflict between the supporters of the monotheistic religion which Topiltzin-Quetzalcóatl had tried to impose, and the adherents to the cult of Tezcatlipoca, the preferred deity of the military. The triumph of this faction forced the abdication of the king. Topiltzin-Quetzalcóatl left Tula around 987 A.D., accompanied by a small group of the faithful (Bernal, 1956b). The first stage of his exile took him to Cholula, then on to Coatzacoalcos, a coastal town on the Gulf of Mexico. From there, after giving his promise to return, he finally headed for Yucatán.[11]

With the help of his followers, Quetzalcóatl, or Kukulcán as the Maya called him, managed to impose his cult and establish it in various centers of Yucatán. The principal one was Chichen Itzá, where Maya structures were gradually replaced by architectural forms and features similar to those of Tula, and the ancient Maya pantheon ceded to Quetzalcóatl-Kukulcán.

Quetzalcóatl's departure from the Valley of Mexico and his vow to return, together with his bearded face and white skin, proved to be fundamental factors in the subsequent conquest of the Aztec empire and of Mexico itself by Cortés.[12]

Having defeated Quetzalcóatl, the militaristic group in Tula turned to expansion of the Empire. The last king of Tula and the Toltecs, Ce Coatl Huemac, ruled for sixty years. The first decades of his reign brought prosperity to the Toltecs, but in 1168, Huemac was forced to leave Tula following a number of years of continuous social crisis, made more acute by hunger and invasions resulting from a long period of drought in all central Mexico.

The Toltec war, about 1000 A.D., was the first in a series which continued for a period of five centuries in the heart of Mexico's central plateau. Perhaps the departure of Huemac, and his suicide or assassination in 1174, marked the end of the Toltec Empire of Tula. Some Toltec groups later settled in various sites of the Valley, and, by the middle of the thirteenth century, Culhuacán, Xico, and Chapultepec had become centers of Toltec culture in a territory dominated by the recently arrived Chichimecs. In 1224, Tula was finally sacked and burned by invaders from the north. It was totally abandoned fifty dark years later.

Tula's urbanistic importance lies in its intermediate position in time between Teotihuacán and Tenochtitlán. The principles of urban design adopted from Teotihuacán were applied on a much smaller scale, over a different topography, and underwent logical modifications, as reflected in the design of Tula's Central Plaza.

Tenochtitlán's builders profited from this example. Let us not forget that Toltec prestige lasted several centuries after the fall of Tula, and it was of political importance to the Aztecs to lay claim to its cultural heritage. For the inhabitants of the central plateau, the Toltecs, even in decline, continued to be the great artists and craftsmen, magicians, insuperable poets, and scientists. Toltec culture, the chronicle of its kings, and the legend of its capital were frequently cited in pre-Hispanic and later historical sources.

The Toltecs of Tula were the last to successfully oppose the invasions of the nomadic peoples from the north. Toltec defeat allowed the Chichimecs to enter the central Valley of Mexico and come into contact with the urban cultures which had developed since the fall of the Classic cities. Thus began a period of disunity in the twelfth century, characterized by the formation of many states, small in size and limited in individual power.

LA QUEMADA AND CHALCHIHUITES

Farmers from Central Mexico moved to the present State of Zacatecas during the centuries of apogee of the Toltec culture and settled what was considered a frontier between the urban civilizations to the south and Chichimec country to the north. The Chichimecs were at that time semi-nomadic hunters constituting a collection of tribes with large populations and some knowledge of farming. The ruins of two well-known settlements, La Quemada and Chalchihuites, lie in the modern State of Zacatecas, 450 and 550 kilometers, respectively, northwest of Tula as the crow flies. In contrast to the Classic cities, defense was the primary consideration in the selection of these two sites. The architecture of both settlements shows interesting similarities with the architecture of Tula (Kubler, 1962). In both cases, the inhabitants chose isolated, easily defended hills which they made more secure by a system of walls.

La Quemada became one of the most formidable examples of fortifications in Mesoamerica, with walls three meters wide and sloping sides ten meters high. Its finished shape was that of a long, narrow fortress, with a minimum extension of 1,300 meters in a north-south direction and a width which varied from 80 meters in the central neck to 350 in the broad northern esplanade. Access was via the southwest corner, along a causeway thirty meters wide which led up to the south group of structures in the lower part of the fortress inside its defense system. This group,

formed primarily by broad terraces, had few structures. Ascending northward, almost at the center of the city, was a second complex of several
large courts partially surrounded by chambers. The third and principal
level was at the top of the hill. It was formed by irregular terraces, regular patios and chambers, some quite large, joined together by galleries
and stairways to accommodate the unevenness of the terrain. The north
sector of the fortress was essentially a vast platform, with almost no
structures, but strongly fortified (I.N.A.H., 1960b).

La Quemada's defensive walls were of uncut stone slabs while the
chamber walls were made of stone and adobe. Utilitarian and lacking artistic details, the complex was built by a culture intermediate to the advanced civilizations of the south and the nomad tribes from the north of
Mexico. Its purpose was to serve as a refuge for the neighboring population and perhaps even as a ceremonial center. Its housing groups may
have extended down the slopes of the hill, but we have found no remains
of the modest structures made of perishable materials that these people
would have built.

A hundred kilometers north of La Quemada lie the ruins of Chalchihuites, another fortified site built on a low, yet easily defended hill. La
Quemada and Chalchihuites were alike in their frequent use of terraces
and stairways and their broad rectangular chambers with heavy interior
columns that held up the roof beams. The zenith of both La Quemada
and Chalchihuites probably coincided with the centuries of Toltec dominion. We speculate that the partial abandonment of both centers occurred
in the twelfth century when, for unknown reasons, their inhabitants
joined or were destroyed by the nomadic Chichimec hordes that disrupted
the urban cultures of central Mexico and destroyed the dynasty of Tula's
kings.

XOCHICALCO

During Teotihuacán's final centuries and later, during the period of
Toltec expansion, Xochicalco was one of the most important cities in the
central highlands. Ceramic remains do not show direct influence from
Teotihuacán, but we do find indications of ancient contacts between Xochicalco and the Maya centers and, later, during the Classic centuries,
with the inhabitants of Monte Albán. Perhaps it was only after the beginning of the decline of the Teotihuacán culture in the seventh century
A.D., that Xochicalco began to flower, coinciding with one of the great

periods in the history of Monte Albán and of the Maya culture. There is an undeniable connection between the architectural styles of Xochicalco and Tula, which suggests the relationship of its inhabitants to Toltec cultural evolution. The only traces of Aztec pottery found in Xochicalco lay near the surface, indicating that the city had perhaps already been abandoned before the founding of Tenochtitlán at the beginning of the fourteenth century. We conclude, then, that after a previous occupation of unknown duration, but probably begun in the centuries just before the Christian era and lasting throughout the different stages of Teotihuacán's evolution, Xochicalco acted as a transition between the southern Mesoamerican Classic civilizations and the semibarbaric cultures of Mexico's central plateau during the interregnum between Teotihuacán and Tula. It was during the seventh, eighth or possibly during the tenth and eleventh centuries, the last of Toltec glory, that Xochicalco reached its peak.

Some connection between the architecture of Xochicalco and that of the Maya is apparent in form and decoration. We can compare the dimension, ground plan, and playing field of Xochicalco's ball court to the various courts found in Copán, Cobá, Piedras Negras, Yaxchilán, Río Bec, and other Classic Maya sites (Noguera, 1945; I.N.A.H., 1960c). No structure resembling a ball court was found in Teotihuacán, where they seemed to have been unknown, and yet one was built in Tula three centuries later. Tula's most important ball court is almost identical to that of Xochicalco, which might well indicate a direct cultural contact (Marquina, 1951).

Xochicalco's principal monument, located in the main plaza of the city, was an almost square foundation, decorated with magnificent reliefs depicting Quetzalcóatl. Topping this base, we find a slanting cornice, an architectural detail which crops up again in various Maya Puuc-style structures at Uxmal, Chichen Itzá, Labná, and other centers in Yucatán prior to the Toltec invasion,[12] as well as in some buildings of Monte Albán[13] and in the Pyramid of the Niches in the complex called El Tajín Chico at El Tajín. I can not recall seeing this detail repeated in Tula, nor do I believe evidence of it has appeared in the reconstruction work done there. We find it, surprisingly, in simplified form in a clay model of what appears to be an Aztec temple found at the Toltec capital (I.N.A.H., 1957b). When the Toltecs occupied Chichen Itzá, however, this type of inverted cornice was introduced to top the temple built on the upper platform of El Castillo, a pyramid of the style developed in central Mexico.

There is an undeniable connection between the Maya reliefs and those found on the principal monument of Xochicalco, as well as in the system of numerals based on bars and dots used by both cultures. The very plan of Xochicalco's ceremonial center is reminiscent of Maya centers in its superb use of terraces and spatial sequences ascending to the principal plaza. Locating the important constructions on elevations around the hill occupied by the main groups was also a common technique in such Maya centers as Piedras Negras (Plate No. 13) and Yaxchilán (Plate No. 14), as was joining the different sectors of the city by wide causeways.

It would be hard to find two locations more dissimilar than those of Teotihuacán and Xochicalco, but even so, there seems to have been a predetermined idea in the choice of each site in keeping with the tradition of each culture. Xochicalco, like Teotihuacán in its time, was both the most important city of a culture and a regionally important religious center dedicated to the cult of Quetzalcóatl as its principal monument testifies. It was in neighboring Tepoztlán, or nearby, that the mother of Ce Acatl Topiltzin had hidden to give birth to the future Toltec leader. It was also from here that Topiltzin, converted to the principles of Quetzalcóatl's cult, left to reconquer the kingdom of his father and to found Tula (Bernal, 1959b).

Xochicalco's site was not chosen for its defensive possibilities, and the city was never really fortified. Its survival through one of the most chaotic periods in the history of central Mexico was due, as in other Classic and Post-Classic centers, to its prestige and power, in addition to its geographic position out of the path of the barbarian tribes as they entered and occupied the Valley of Mexico during the Post-Classic centuries.

The region of Morelos around Xochicalco is mountainous with broad valleys. Though semiarid, its soil is capable of supporting moderate agriculture. The city developed on an irregularly contoured hill, over 1,000 meters long in a north-south direction, eventually spreading over other elevations around it (Plate No. 15). The hillsides around the acropolis, or upper terrace, were totally transformed by the hand of man. Today, from the main plaza on the summit, we have an uninterrupted view southwest to the valley and north to where the lights of Cuernavaca glow above the background of mountains that ring the central Valley of Mexico. To the west of the plaza, a narrow river runs through a steep-sided valley.

Xochicalco was inhabited permanently over a prolonged period by a population that depended for subsistence on the production of the neighboring valleys and perhaps also on tribute. In Xochicalco, as in other Mesoamerican Classic centers, a large percentage of its population must

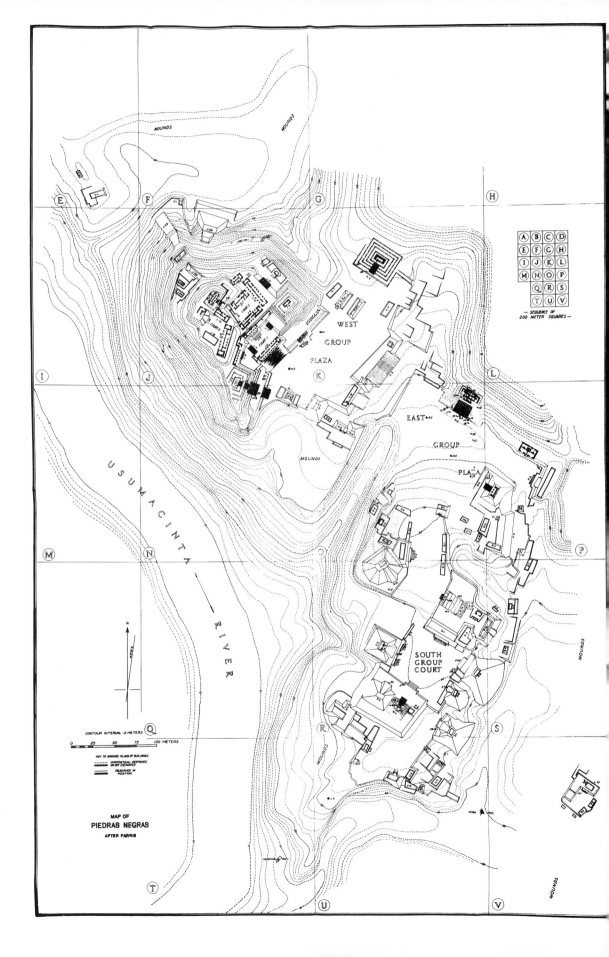

MAP OF
PIEDRAS NEGRAS
AFTER PARRIS

CONTOUR INTERVAL - 2 METERS

0   25   50   75   100 METERS

KEY TO GROUND PLANS OF BUILDINGS

- - - - HYPOTHETICAL - DESTROYED
        OR NOT EXCAVATED

———— OBSERVED IN
        POSITION

WEST GROUP PLAZA

EAST GROUP PLAZA

SOUTH GROUP COURT

USUMACINTA RIVER

- SEQUENCE OF
  200 METER SQUARES -

A	B	C	D
E	F	G	H
I	J	K	L
M	N	O	P
Q	R	S
T	U	V

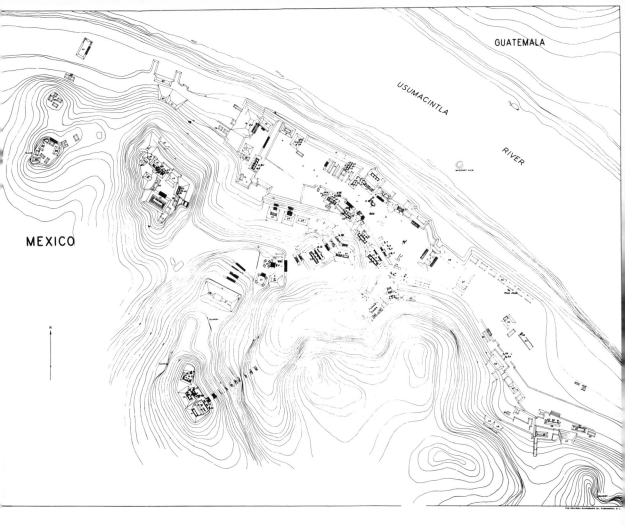

GUATEMALA

USUMACINTLA

RIVER

MEXICO

14 *Yaxchilán: Credit: Morley, Sylvanus: "The Inscriptions of Petén,"
Carnegie Institution of Washington, No. 437, Washington, D.C., 1937-
38.)*

13 *Piedras Negras: (Credit: Morley, Sylvanus: "The Inscriptions of
Petén," Carnegie Institution of Washington, No. 437, Washington, D.C.,
1937-38.)*

15 *Xochicalco: Aerial View of site. (Credit: Cia. Mexicana Aerofoto, S.A.)*

have subsisted exclusively on agriculture and lived in the city's outskirts which spread across the hillsides.

The city appears to have been quite extensive (Plate No. 16). The only fortified sector of Xochicalco[14] is found on La Bodega hill to the northeast, the highest point in the complex. The sector of La Malinche, to the southwest, possibly served as a housing area for the ruling group as well as for certain ceremonial functions. Farther west, on a lower level, was another housing sector called El Temazcal. Between these principal groups were a number of terraces supporting other housing groups, spreading out in all directions to form an urban zone estimated at about 100 hectares (Sanders, 1952).

The main access to the city was from the south (B, in Plate No. 16) along a steep, paved thoroughfare. About 500 meters from this south entrance, past several vacant terraces on the left and a series of buildings on the right, the main thoroughfare was joined by an almost perpendicular, descending secondary axis. Along this route were arranged the structures covering La Malinche hill.

The La Malinche group was the lowest in the central sector of the city, at twenty-five meters below the principal plaza and fifteen meters below the juncture of the two axes. The axis of this group was a wide twenty-meter causeway which descended in a westerly direction, bordered on its north side by a series of pillars and to the south by a large palace built on different levels that probably housed the chiefs or priests (I.N.A.H., 1960c). Today, the name La Malinche refers to a badly deteriorated rectangular pyramid (R, in Plate No. 16) about ten meters high, still one of the largest structures of the city, which terminates the causeway to the west. The most important construction of this group was the splendidly proportioned Ball Court[15] which, with its platforms and taluses, occupied an area of 4,500 square meters. The outer wall of the south talus and the access stairway to the spectators' platform bordered the roadway. From the Ball Court's access stairway to the juncture of the two causeways, a stairway led up the steep bank to the main paved road.

If we climb northward from this crossroad, we come to a terrace where a group of four, still unexcavated, platforms form a small plaza bounded to the north by the retaining wall of another platform built on an upper level. A rectangular based pyramid set on this new level closes off the view of the causeway leading to the upper platform. Continuing up to the top of the hill and the main plaza, we must turn left and then right, until we come to another small plaza, outlined by low walls like the others.

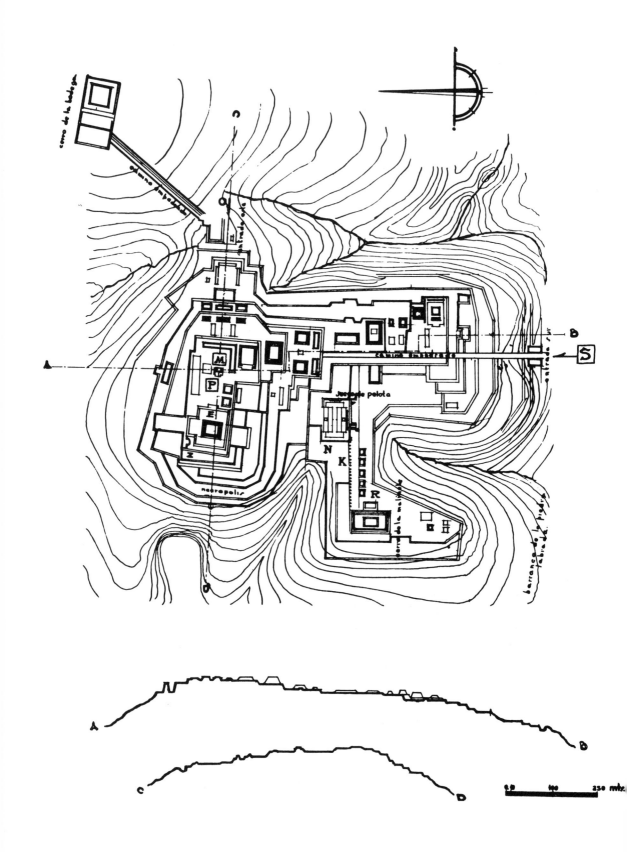

From this vantage point, we have an excellent view westward across the valley and the La Malinche structural group on the hill below.

The small plaza served as an antechamber to the main plaza where the series of open spatial sequences came to an end. It was a basic element in Xochicalco's general design as it not only directed pedestrian traffic, but its deep and elongated shape led toward the principal plaza and the temple of Quetzalcóatl, the most important building in the city.

The main plaza (P, in Plate No. 16) measured about 15,000 square meters. As was usual with other platforms in Xochicalco, it was outlined by a low wall that also served as a balcony. All structures found within the plaza are isolated. This is characteristic of Xochicalco since its architects did not use columned vestibules and broad stairways, as in Tula, to help define the urban spaces they were creating.

Xochicalco's main plaza was built on the upper terrace of the hill, bounded on the west by a rectangular pyramid built on a large platform (E, in Plate No. 16). Behind the pyramid and the balcony of its platform, a series of terraces descended on various levels, following the abrupt angle of the hillside. Within the limits of the main plaza, as determined by the platform-balcony, lie the ruins of several isolated structures with square or rectangular foundations that define the space in which the Temple of the Plumed Serpent (Quetzalcóatl) was built (M, on the plan 16). The platform of this monument, some 400 square meters in area, rose 4.33 meters above the level of the plaza and was topped by a second body.[16] The interior fill of the construction was made with earth and rock covered with dressed stone. Access to the principal platform was by a broad stairway flanked by balustrades facing pyramid E.

The Temple of the Plumed Serpent was built during the Classic Period (Bernal, 1959b) and is famous for the stylized relief work decorating its various bodies.[17] In these carvings on the base, we see Quetzalcóatl depicted as a series of serpents with crowns of feathers on their heads and whose undulating bodies form a continuous meander (I.N.A.H., 1960c). Between the undulations of the serpents' bodies on the principal base, seen both in the frieze and in the panel, as well as on the walls of the upper structure, there is a series of seated persons. Their posture, the position of

16 *Xochicalco: Plan of the ceremonial center of Xochicalco. Letter M indicates the location of the structure dedicated to Quetzalcóatl, standing on the highest plaza of the complex. Letter N marks the ball court about twenty-five meters beneath the plaza. (Credit: Marquina, Ignacio: "Arquitectura prehispánica," I.N.A.H., Mexico, 1951. Plan by Tirado.)*

their hands, and their receding foreheads are markedly similar to Maya figures.

Xochicalco's main plaza is different from those analyzed so far, and we find features here unknown elsewhere in the central plateau of Mexico. Its architects made skillful use of the topography. When faced with the steep ascent to the main plaza, they utilized the sides of the hills to introduce changing visual sequences. Almost all the buildings were set back from the edges of their platform bases, creating a balcony effect that offered an exceptional view of other sectors of the city and surrounding valleys.

I believe that Xochicalco was the first example in central Mexico where the use of partial axes in organizing structural groups gave rise to total freedom in general composition. This sense of urban spatial organization, involving the use of short, limited vistas while closing off the external spaces, so common among the Maya, did not appear again on Mexico's central plateau, at least in a city of any importance.

Quetzalcóatl's temple is situated in the center of the main plaza as the pivot between this and the small plaza-antechamber. All lines of vision converge on this structure from any angle of the main plaza; its massiveness breaks up the space into various sectors, diminishing the impression of the plaza's vast size. This was not the case in Teotihuacán, where precision in the general lines of design and perfect symmetry of partial groups were fundamental. Nor do we find this in Tula where, in spite of greater informality of composition, the temple was so small in relation to the total plaza area that the space maintained its unity.

In the freedom with which Xochicalco's structures were related to each other and in the way its large and small plazas were linked, we find principles foreign to the Classic tradition in the central plateau of Mexico, but similar to those employed by Zapotec and Mayan architects in the construction of Classic centers built over rugged terrain.[18] Xochicalco's main plaza was paved and seems to have been completed in successive stages. Location of the different structures shows that the architects subordinated new works to the general composition of the whole. The entire center of Xochicalco must have grown up in this manner, without a previous plan, accommodating new groups to those already there.

Another feature links Xochicalco's design with that of the Maya and Zapotec. A man, walking toward the main plaza across the spatial sequences we have discussed, never confronted the principal buildings face on until he came up to them. An example of this is seen in the first glimpse we have of the Temple of Quetzalcóatl and Pyramid E as we enter the main plaza from the small plaza, or in the location of Pyramid R in relation to the western road in the La Malinche group.

Xochicalco is one of the best examples of urban design in central Mexico during the centuries after Teotihuacán and before Tenochtitlán, for its overall scale, excellent use of varying levels in determining urban spaces and linking them together, and for the splendid visual expanses achieved by leaving free the edges of the platforms that outline the plazas. Xochicalco may have lacked a general plan to guide its urban growth, although the broken topography of the site would have limited its applicability, but we can appreciate the inventiveness and creativity of its builders in the design of its central religious sector.

THE COASTAL CITIES OF THE GULF OF MEXICO

During the Pre-Classic centuries the Gulf Coast cities, and those of Mexico's central plateau, maintained cultural and commercial ties. These were intensified at the beginning of the Classic Period when Teotihuacán became the political, religious and stylistic center of a vast territory.

From Teotihuacán to the north coast of the State of Veracruz is less than 300 kilometers, but the rugged terrain and steep mountain passes must have discouraged frequent contact. The plateau and the coast are so different climatically that they constitute distinct geographic regions. The coastal plain is tropical, humid, and warm, and the low hills covered with dense vegetation. It does not have the characteristics of a region likely to produce such an advanced culture as the Totonac. Even the appropriate environmental conditions found all over the high valleys of central Mexico and Oaxaca are lacking. It was only at the beginning of this century that the petroleum industry began to contribute to the region's development. During the last of the Classic and beginning of the Post-Classic Periods, when El Tajín and other Totonac centers such as Misantla and Yohualichán reached their peak, agriculture and trade must have been the only sources of livelihood for the population, as they became throughout Colonial times.

EL TAJÍN

The first inhabitants of El Tajín were the forebearers of the historic Totonacs, perhaps the Pipil (Bernal, 1959b).[19] The Totonacs occupied an extensive area. They built their cities, El Tajín certainly, during Teotihuacán's last centuries. According to the periods proposed by García Payón (I.N.A.H., 1957a), El Tajín's stages of development would correspond chronologically to those established for Xochicalco on the opposite slope of Mexico's central plateau. The apogee of both sites probably occurred some centuries after those of other Mexican Classic centers such as Teotihuacán.

Ceramics from El Tajín's first epoch indicate that during the fifth century, if not earlier, its inhabitants had contacts with Teotihuacán.[20] In spite of the Totonacs, relations with the most sophisticated Classic cultures, El Tajín retained its own characteristics, developing an individual architecture with features unique among Mesoamerican cultures. Some of their outstanding original stone sculptures are the mysterious objects connected with the ritual ball game—*palmas, hachas* ("axes") and the carved *yugos* or "yokes" of basalt or andesite.[21] This high point of Totonac art occurred during El Tajín's second epoch and lasted through its third. The presence of such architectural details as the frequently used inverted cornice, the roof of inclined planes found over the entrance of one of the buildings, and some of the decorative motifs suggests that the Totonacs were also in contact with the Yucatecan Maya, particularly during the flowering of the Maya Puuc style.

El Tajín and Xochicalco both seem to have been abandoned between the twelfth and thirteenth centuries. For the second time in the space of a few centuries, the civilizing influence of the great urban centers disappeared from Mexico's central plateau and its zones of immediate contact, leaving their advanced cultures to be dominated once again by the semi-barbaric tribes from the north. Only at the end of the fourteenth century, when Texcoco and Tenochtitlán finally imposed their supremacy, did the cities once more begin to establish their centralizing policy and acquire the physical characteristics and the cultural and material riches which so surprised the Spaniards.

El Tajín was the principal Classic and Post-Classic city of the Gulf Coast[22] (Plate No. 17). It occupied an extensive area of rolling terrain over which numerous structural groups were scattered with no apparent order.[23] Much of El Tajín is still unexcavated, and the majority of the mounds have yet to be studied. Reconstruction work has been concentrated on the buildings of the group known as El Tajín Chico and the famous Pyramid of the Niches.

El Tajín's ceremonial center was built on three levels, taking advantage of a flat area and a hill, surrounded on the east and southeast by two streams. The oldest structures are those on the lower level, the flat south sector near the confluence of the streams. Beneath the Pyramid of the Niches, a Period II structure, lay a single-bodied pyramid. This early pyramid, discovered by tunneling, probably dates from El Tajín's Period I (Marquina, 1951). In the future, we may find other Pre-Classic structures, but for the present, we can only determine that the center grew in a north-south direction and that the empty spaces left between stuctural groups from the first epoch were gradually filled in by the addition of new groups. We still do not know where the entrances to the center were, nor does the observable relation between groups of mounds provide us with clues.

El Tajín's low sector appears to be the result of unplanned growth of groups arranged in an orderly manner around regular plazas. Once the lower level was filled with buildings, the architects had to resort to terracing the sides of a neighboring hill to the north of the original locale. Later, they had to construct even more terraces, to accommodate the group of structures around the Building of the Columns, the largest complex at El Tajín. This carelessly constructed building (I.N.A.H., 1957a) may have belonged to El Tajín's third period, contemporaneous with the El Tajín Chico group on the middle level which is thought to have been built at the same time as Tula (Marquina, 1951).

The lowest level was occupied by religious structures, the main group consisting of three platforms of different heights and the Pyramid of the Niches to the west. The plaza formed by these four masses was almost rectangular, although the axes of the structures on either side did not face each other and were not parallel. The Pyramid of the Niches represents the high point of Totonac architecture and presents one of the most outstanding examples of religious construction among Mesoamerican Indian cultures. By the use of simple, repeated architectural features, such as thick stone cornices slanted outward and deep niches separated by vertical panels and inclined planes, the architects achieved a rhythmic series of horizontals and verticals which the setting sun dramatized in a play of light and shadow.[24] The Pyramid formed in six stepped bodies, square and with a single stairway, was topped by an upper platform supporting a temple, the seventh body of the building.

The south sector of the ceremonial center was made up of over thirty structures. With the exception of the Pyramid of the Niches, they were all rectangular and arranged, in general, at right angles around three main

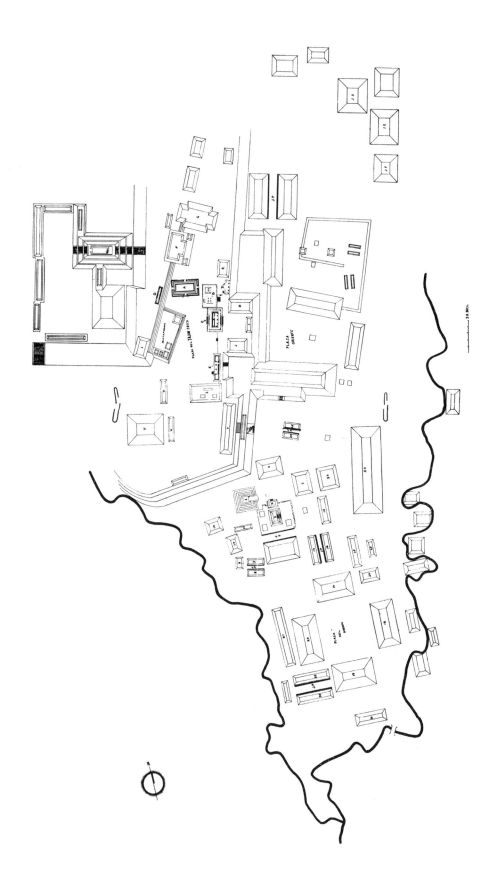

plazas and a series of undefined spaces. The Plaza del Arroyo, bounded by four isolated mounds laid out symmetrically, was the largest, but it probably did not have the civic and ceremonial importance of the plaza of the Pyramid of the Niches. Apparently all structures in the south sector served religious functions, and several ball courts of different sizes have been found among these ruins. The general lack of compositional order and the use of isolated volumes to define plazas and external spaces, are, so far, the principal characteristics of the south group.

The central group was built at an intermediate height on an artificially leveled hill. This group has been called El Tajín Chico. Its main buildings (A, B and C in Plate No. 17) served civil functions. These three structures are of a later date than the Pyramid of the Niches and form the north and eastern sides of a trapezoidal plaza located about fifteen meters above the level of the main plaza of the south group.[25]

El Tajín Chico's plaza opens toward the southwest and is bordered to the west by the taluses along the hill where the Building of the Columns was constructed. This building, the largest in the city, was originally a pyramid of four bodies topped by a rectangular temple of proportions similar to the base. Today, the pyramid sits on a vast floor which extends westward, forming a platform half enclosed by various unexplored mounds. The platform and its plaza, lying about twenty-five meters above the level of the plaza of the Pyramid of the Niches, constitutes the third level of the civic and ceremonial center of El Tajín. The original height of the Building of the Columns was twenty-four meters above the platform (Marquina, 1951). From here, today's visitor is offered an excellent view of this surprising complex of mounds, extending in all directions like so many small hills covered over by dense tropical growth.

There is no doubt but that the general design of the El Tajín center had links with those of the Maya in the way the platforms, esplanades, and stairways unite the structures of the intermediate and upper levels. We also find similarity in the plans of El Tajín Chico's civil structures and in the apparent informality of the exterior spaces in this group. The curious appendage which bounds the East Plaza to the south, for instance, and which is nothing more than the artificial modification of a natural elevation so as to utilize it as a structural base, also appears in a number of

17 *El Tajín: This plan shows the central section of this principal Classic and Post-Classic center of the Gulf Coast of Mexico. (Credit: "Guía oficial de El Tajín," I.N.A.H., Mexico.)*

Maya centers. Even in the southern group, with its right-angled organization of buildings around plazas, we find similarities with such Maya centers as Yaxhá where the overall composition is also haphazard and structural groups were arranged at right angles around plazas of varying sizes and shapes.

THE CITIES IN THE
VALLEYS OF OAXACA

The fertile valleys of the State of Oaxaca have been inhabited since pre-Christian times, possibly coeval with the Archaic cultures in Mexico's central plateau. Almost all of Oaxaca is mountainous, eroded, and unsuited for cultivation, but the fertile valleys in the central section enjoy a favorable subtropical, frost-free climate, and their breadth encouraged a densely settled population that reached its Urbanist stage and cultural peak at the same time as other Classic cultures in Mesoamerica. The region was also rich in gold and copper resources. In the Etla, Tlacolula, and Zimatlán Valleys, the Zapotec culture came to flower. Even today, Zapotec descendents cultivate the land of their ancestors and maintain their thousand-year-old community spirit when it is necessary to tackle works for the public good or merely to help the needy (Mendieta y Núñez, 1949).

The Zapotecs of Oaxaca's central valleys were valiant farmers and merchants who for years resisted the attempts of the Aztecs, and later the Spaniards, to conquer them. Their cultural level was not much different from that of the peoples of Mexico's central plateau. Maize, beans, tomatoes, and chili peppers, with some game and fish, provided their daily diet. They planted their fields with the *coa*, or digging stick, and burned the brush to clear the cultivable land. Pot irrigation and canal irrigation were also used since the Formative centuries (Flannery, Kirby, Kirk and Williams, 1967). They were one of the first Mesoamerican peoples to work in metals, a technique they learned from the south; they excelled in creating copper pieces and, later, in *repoussé* work and fashioning gold and silver jewelry.[26]

In all Mesoamerica, the level of scientific achievement of the Zapotecs was surpassed only by that of the Maya. Their calendar was the *tonalpohualli*, or ritual calendar of 260 days, but they apparently were familiar with the solar calendar (Krickeberg, 1961), and they used hieroglyphic writing, both sciences of pre-Christian origin. In this, as in their architecture, their recording of numbers in dots and bars, and in their sculptural representations of human figures, they approached Maya culture.

Recent research directed by Kent Flannery in the Etla Valley revealed an early village farming period (1500-600 B.C.) coinciding with the San Lorenzo and La Venta periods in the Olmec region, with evidence of considerable water control, material wealth, status differentiation, and contacts with other regions of Mesoamerica (Flannery, Kirby, Kirk and Williams, 1967). During the last centuries of the Middle Formative (around 600 B.C.), villages of close to forty hectares with ceremonial centers were frequent, possibly as a consequence of increased centralization of power and its extension over neighboring valleys. By the Late Formative (around 300 B.C.), the size of San José Mogote in the Etla Valley, had reached 200 hectares, showing elaborate houses built around courtyards.[27]

From Formative days, Oaxaca's geographic location placed it in the direct path of commercial and cultural contacts between the peoples from the north and east of Mesoamerica and those from Chiapas, the Pacific Coast, and the Guatemalan highlands. It is no surprise that we find in Oaxaca the ancient tradition of working hard stones. This technique was possibly learned from the Olmecs, the best lapidaries of Mesoamerica. During the Formative centuries, the Olmec influence could be seen in the bas-reliefs of figures with rounded bodies and thick lips, drawn in a single line. We find many such designs in the Building of the *Danzantes,* or "dancers," belonging to Monte Albán's first period of occupation, about 600-200 B.C.

During the centuries when the Classic cultures flowered, the influence of Teotihuacán was felt in all the cities of Mesoamerica. Monte Albán, during its third period and truly Zapotec epoch (150-850 A.D.), was no exception. Monte Albán IV, (850-1150 A.D.), was contemporaneous with Toltec expansion, and Monte Albán V, (1150-1500 A.D.), or its period of Mixtec occupation, coincided with the development of the Aztec empire. Contrary to what occurred in the Classic Period, Mixtec cultural influence was strongly felt in the Valley of Mexico during the Post-Classic centuries (Eckholm, 1958).

Apparently Zapotec government was never concentrated in a single individual. In a state where religion regulated games, sports, and warfare (Caso, 1942), Zapotec theocracy was centralized in the hereditary authority of a high priest. The monarch, despite his high rank and political strength as a representative of the military groups, probably never exceeded the high priest's authority, although at some point he may have taken this privilege.

MONTE ALBÁN

The origins of Monte Albán go back to pre-Christian times. This extensive Zapotec metropolis is located on a chain of hills a few kilometers from Oaxaca. The first capital of this culture was not Monte Albán, but Teotitlán del Valle, in the Tlacolula Valley. The people who established Teotitlán del Valle, and centuries later Monte Albán and Zaachila, possessed an advanced culture comparable to their contemporaries in the central highlands. They also introduced into the high valleys of Oaxaca the cult of Cocijo, god of lightning and rain.

Between the sixth and second centuries B.C., the transformation of the hills on which Monte Albán was built must have been under way, and during the first period of the city's occupation, its magnificent plaza almost 400 meters above the valley had probably begun to take shape (Plate No. 18). During the last centuries of the Middle Formative, it may not have been an important settlement; a religious center, perhaps, which left us a small structure covered over by later buildings, along with the beautiful stelae and the decorated base of this first architectural effort of Monte Albán's oldest inhabitants. The largest settlements were probably located in the valleys near the agricultural fields.

Whereas Monte Albán I was stylistically related to the Olmecs, the ceramics of the second period are typical of cultures of the same epoch in Guatemala (I.N.A.H., 1957c). During Monte Albán II (200 B.C.-200 A.D.), several important architectural works were added to the extensive platform on which its Great Plaza stood (Plate No. 19). Among these was Mound X, to the north of the Plaza, a simple structure formed by a rectangular chamber and a vestibule flanked by two columns, which was subsequently covered over by a construction of the Classic Period. Mound J (Plate No. 19), another structure belonging to Monte Albán II, is one of the strangest buildings in Mesoamerica. It was built on a small elevation in the middle of the Plaza[28] and is thought to have been an astronomical observatory (Caso, 1942). What commands our attention is its off-center position on a none-too-precise north-south axis of the complex, and its curious pointed end, which makes it the only irregularly shaped building of the pre-columbian epoch (Westheim, 1950).

18 *Monte Albán: Aerial view. The ruins are located on a hilltop near the modern city of Oaxaca. (Credit: Cia. Mexicana Aerofoto, S.A.)*

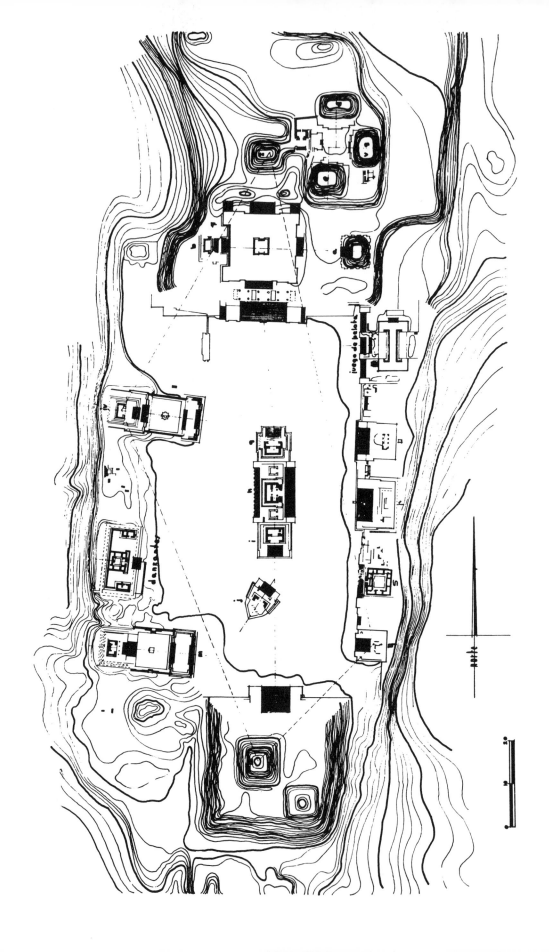

juego de pelota

danzantes

After a transition period during which Monte Albán was subject to influences from Mexico's central plateau, the Zapotec culture reached its peak in the centuries beginning the Christian era. During the first millennium A.D. Monte Albán was unquestionably one of the centers of greatest cultural and political influence of Mesoamerica. Its many tombs, and the variety of objects exhibited in different museums, attest to its size[29] and population (Caso, 1942). In those centuries, the building of the city was completed and existing structures were superposed by new ones, exhibiting the full maturity of Zapotec architecture. The result is Monte Albán's Great Plaza, one of the most splendid civic spaces created by man, and certainly the most beautiful in Mesoamerica (Plate No. 20).

What makes Monte Albán's Great Plaza so beautiful? Not just its location atop an elongated hill with steep sides, nor the apparent informality in the arrangement of its different structures set along the edges of the hilltop. A visitor, walking over Monte Albán's ruins carefully, would observe that the Plaza is an enclosed space with virtually no view of the valleys which surround the hill on three sides. The impression of enclosure and completion is heightened by looking from the top of the pyramid on the South Platform toward the large court of the complex on the North Platform. Topographical limitations forbid extension of the Plaza, but the overwhelming spatial scale and unity of its simple architectural works of stone with geometrically decorated panels need no additions. Its important feature is its negation of topography and natural environment; temples and palaces set a framework in which each new building sacrificed its individuality for the unity of the whole. Compare the arrangement of Monte Albán's Plaza with Xochicalco's platforms, especially the upper platform where the use of balconies and changing vistas direct the gaze toward the valley below.

In the center of Monte Albán's Great Plaza stood four structures: a group of three temples joined laterally (g,h,i, in Plate No. 18), built during the Classic centuries, and the Observatory, Building J, from the Pre-Classic Period. For today's visitor, the remains of this complex might seem of secondary importance, but for the Zapotec who came to the

19 *Monte Albán: Plan of the plaza of Monte Albán. The enclosed space has no view of the valleys surrounding it on the east, south, and west. This same visual impression still exists. (Credit: Marquina, Ignacio: "Arquitectura prehispánica," I.N.A.H., Mexico, 1951. According to a reconstruction by Alfonso Caso.)*

20 *Monte Albán: A reconstruction of Monte Albán's plaza in a south-north direction. In the foreground we see the principal pyramid. Classic Zapotec architecture featured simple volumes upon which the sunlight*

cast sharp contrasts of light and shadow. (Credit: Marquina, Ignacio:
"Arquitectura prehispánica," I.N.A.H., Mexico, 1951. Drawing by Sala-
zar.)

Plaza to witness or take part in a religious or civic ceremony, it was this structural group that organized the main area into its four sectors. The enormous Plaza, 300 meters in a north-south direction by 200 meters from east to west, might seem broken up when seen from the ground, but not so from the overall view to be had from either of the two platforms which closed off the artificial hilltop plateau at its north and southern ends.

When Monte Albán was occupied, the buildings were painted but never as profusely decorated with sculptures and relief work as Mayan or central Mexican constructions. The sun shining on the simple architectural volumes, the accentuated shadows at dusk in contrast to the luminosity of the taluses at the buildings' bases, and the geometric line of shadow projecting the relief of a panel on a wall were highlights of Zapotec architecture.[30]

Only one palace (S, in Plate No. 19) was located on the Plaza, standing beside a group of unexplored chambers on the west side near the Building of the *Danzantes* and Building IV. Like the palaces built on Mexico's central plateau during the Classic centuries, it was completely closed to the outside except for a single doorway leading out to the Plaza. Based on the same principle was a complicated group of buildings to the north of the Plaza, built around a broad, sunken court with a central temple. On the platforms bordering the Plaza on the east and west sides, archeologists have found ruins of several temples in apparently parallel lines.

The main axis of the majority of these structures has a pronounced deviation from an exact east-west orientation. In its freedom of conception, Monte Albán's Plaza is closer to the Maya civic-ceremonial complexes than to the monumental, rigid impression which guided the urban design of Mexico's central plateau cultures. Monte Albán and Xochicalco represent two transitional examples in the urban art practiced by the Maya and that of the Teotihuacán culture and its heirs.

The city extended in all directions. Southeast of the Plaza, around the South Platform and down past a depression, we come to a ceremonial group arranged around a court, known as 7 Venado, or "Seven Deer." From this secondary group, we see the structures on the eastern side of the principal center as an actual extension of the hill itself.

The residential sector of Monte Albán stretched northward, over a series of hills of varying heights constituting a continuation of the hill where the Great Plaza was built. It is here, to the north of the Plaza, where archeologists have found most of the tombs containing riches—testimony to the burials of high ranking personages. On the valley slopes, on the terraces in the depressions between hills, and in neighboring valleys, Monte Albán's inhabitants built their modest houses, scattered with no order other than that imposed by the terrain.

After the flowering of the Classic cultures, Monte Albán began to decline. Mitla and ancient Zaachila took over its functions as religious center and capital, respectively (Caso, 1942). Yet Monte Albán was still inhabited, at least partially, up to the time of the Spanish Conquest. During its periods IV and V (850-1150 and 1150-1500 A.D.), a different people, the Mixtecs, took possession of the city and controlled the neighboring valleys. Mixtec predominance was important in that sector of Oaxaca during the years of strife with the Aztecs when, allied with the Zapotecs, these valley peoples managed to keep the expansionist ambitions of the lords of Tenochtitlán at bay for some time.

MITLA

The ruins of Mitla lie scattered over twenty hectares on both sides of the Mitla River, which cuts across the archeological zone from east to west. A town grew up around these ruins during Colonial times, and today its three thousand inhabitants live in simple adobe houses among the remains of pre-Hispanic structures.

Over the slightly rolling terrain, Mitla's ancient inhabitants built five structural groups (Plate No. 21). Two of these are of a style common all over Mesoamerica from La Venta to Tenochtitlán, that is, the regularly shaped plaza surrounded by rectangular platforms, with a pyramid on one side. The other three groups, also the best known, are the Arroyo Complex, the Group of the Columns, and the Catholic Church Group. Each of these three complexes is formed by two courtyards surrounded by platforms which support simple, elongated, one-storied buildings. On the north platform of the main patio of each of these groups, Mitla's architects erected a structure which led to a small patio, surrounded in turn by four chambers. It was in such chambers in the Group of the Columns that the *Xigana,* or High Priest, lived (Caso, 1942).

In addition to its role as sacred city, Mitla was also the cemetery of kings and principal priests. It retained its importance as a necropolis, religious and, perhaps, political capital from the eleventh century, coinciding with period IV at Monte Albán, up to the conquest of Oaxaca by the Spaniards under Francisco de Orozco in 1521.

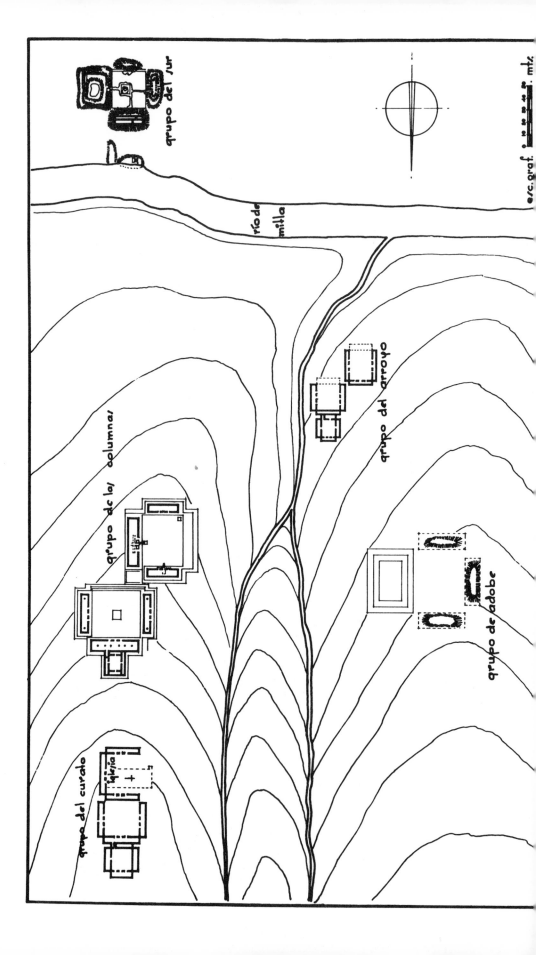

grupo del sur

grupo del curato

grupo de los columnas

grupo del arroyo

grupo de adobe

río de mitla

esc. graf.

iglesia

Mitla does not have the urbanistic importance of the great Post-Classic cities of Mesoamerica. We might even wonder whether it really was a city since its sacred character would have eliminated it as a residential area for the common man. The arrangement of the five known groups is ordered, with an exact north-south orientation in the three palace complexes and east to west in the two pyramidal groups. We do not know what the unused spaces remaining between the groups were used for but, since no buildings of any importance seem to have existed in the intermediate area, we might suppose they were occupied by the precarious housing of those serving the High Priest and the temples.

Mitla's interest lies in the decoration of its temples and palaces. As in other Mesoamerican structures, its walls of rock and mud were covered over by stone slabs. In Mitla, the curious exterior walls, leaning outward and supported on a high base, were formed from bottom to top by a talus, three panels, and a cornice.[31] The panels were decorated with meanders of inlaid, small, cut stones that fit together so perfectly that they also offered structural value. There were many such designs, forming horizontal borders around the exteriors of the buildings or decorating the interiors of the dark rooms where Mitla's priests lived. As in Monte Albán, light and shadow were architectural elements, but in Mitla, the pure beauty of a wall bathed in light was sacrificed in favor of a wealth of decoration and exaggerated ornamentation. Only from a distance do the elaborate façades take on unity when the pointillism of their panels appears in contrast to the smooth surfaces of the borders surrounding them, producing a horizontal sweep, undulating and geometric, which provides the principal visual value of the individual structures.

Neither Mitla nor Monte Albán were fortified. Monte Albán, like Teotihuacán, El Tajín, and the Maya centers, reached its peak during the Classic centuries, when the prestige of the great theocratic cultures, their far-flung territorial influence and the precarious maneuverability of enemy armies may have sufficed to dissuade would-be attackers. Mitla, renowned as a religious center, could count on protection from the fortresses that the Zapotecs and Mixtecs built on strategically located hilltops and could also rely on the allied armed protection of the two peoples that lived there.

21 *Mitla: The ruins of Mitla lie south of Oaxaca in southern Mexico. Mitla is famous for the decoration of its temples and palaces with their walls covered by panels formed by small stones inlaid in a Greek meander design. The best examples of this is seen in the Group of the Columns and the Catholic Church Group. (Credit: Marquina, Ignacio: "Arquitectura prehispánica," I.N.A.H., Mexico, 1951. According to a reconstruction by Holmes.)*

1. I WILL DISCUSS the Maya culture separately and so have excluded a study of its centers in this chapter.

2. Considering that Teotihuacán fell in 750 A.D. (Millon, 1966c) and Tula became the Toltec capital by decision of Topiltzin, born in 935 or 947 A.D. (Coe, M., 1966a), who was forced to leave the city about 987 A.D., slightly more than two centuries might have elapsed between the abandonment of the great Classic center and the establishment of Tula.

3. Parsons is very clear about this trend. After the fall of Teotihuacán, he writes, "large segments of the highly concentrated urban population of the old Classic center relocated themselves in sparsely populated areas, and a broad, largely unoccupied zone in the central part of the Texcoco Region is suggestive of a political buffer zone separating the spheres of influence of two new centers, Tula to the north and Cholula to the south" (Parsons, 1968). Sanders estimated that the population in the Teotihuacán Valley during the Mazapán phase (950-1150 A.D.) "was no more than 20-25 per cent that of 1519," which was close to the population of the entire Valley at its peak (Sanders, 1965).

4. Culhuacán was situated on a peninsula at the south of Lake Texcoco, within the present metropolitan area of Mexico City. The site probably lay somewhat to the east of an imaginary straight line from the city's center out to Xochimilco.

5. According to the chroniclers, the mother of Ce Acatl Topiltzin was called Chimalmán and was a native of the present State of Morelos. There the future Toltec king was born, in a place not far from Tepoztlán where the cult of Quetzalcóatl was worshipped.

6. "Tula was built in the center of a region which was predominantly Otomí" (Rattray, 1966) and according to legends, Mixcóatl had to fight the Otomí in order to consolidate his control over the center of Mexico. Jiménez Moreno believes that the Otomí were responsible for the fall of Teotihuacán (Jiménez Moreno, 1966). In all events the Otomí people were an important political and cultural force in Central Mexico during the Coyotlatelco phase of the Early Post-Classic Period (750-950 A.D.).

7. The Annals of the National Institute of Anthropology and History periodically publish the results of Acosta's work in Tula. The excellent maps and photographs included in some of these reports are of great value to the urbanist. The last report published discusses the twelfth season of explorations, from July 23 to December 31, 1956 (Acosta, 1961).

8. One author says that Topiltzin-Quetzalcóatl brought to Tula a group of artists and craftsmen called *nonoalcas,* which means deaf or mute persons or simply those who can not speak correctly. Perhaps this refers to a people who spoke a different language. These new arrivals worshipped Quetzalcóatl, which leads us to suppose that they were descendents of the inhabitants of Teotihuacán (Peterson, 1959). Jiménez Moreno confirms the origin of the *nonoalcas* as coming from Teotihuacán but places their arrival at Tula at an earlier date (Jiménez Moreno, 1966).

9. Tlahuizcalpantecuhtli is "the morning star" of the Aztecs. Tula's temple was given this name because of the relief work decorating its columns (Marquina, 1951; Krickeberg, 1961).

10. Acosta says, referring to the Burnt Palace, that it would not be at all surprising if this were the palace of the last king of Tula, Ce Coatl Huemac, whose tragic figure marked the twilight of the Toltec empire (Acosta, 1961).

11. Quetzalcóatl predicted his return for the same day of the year as his departure. By a strange coincidence, the news of the arrival of Cortés and his men reached Moctezuma, the superstitious Aztec king, when that very month was drawing near.

12. The importance of Quetzalcóatl's legend in the collapse of the Aztec Empire and in the behavior of Moctezuma II is well presented by Padden (Padden, 1970).

13. We see examples on the bases of the lateral structures of the Building of the *Danzantes* and on the upper cornice of Mitla's Group of the Columns.

14. In Vaillant's opinion, Xochicalco was fortified by a wide gully at its points of easiest access (Vaillant, 1955). Noguera stated that Xochicalco was a sacred city as well as a fortress (Noguera, 1945).

15. Built on a flat section of La Malinche hill, against the bottom of the artificially modified sides of the principal hill, the location and proportions of Xochicalco's Ball Court make it one of the handsomest I have seen. It has an H shape, with the central bar elongated. The outside dimension is sixty-nine meters east to west.

16. "The platform profiles are designed to carry across great distances. They consist of the familiar talus and panel augmented by a cornice of upward-slanting section" (Kubler, 1962). At Tula the panel is a narrow element in comparison to the importance of the talus and the cornice.

17. An excellent description of this building appears in the *Guide to the Archeological Zones of the State of Morelos* published by Mexico's National Institute of Anthropology and History (I.N.A.H., 1960c). Its author, Eduardo Noguera, is one of the Mexican scholars who has worked intensely in Xochicalco.

18. Compare Xochicalco's layout (Plate No. 16, pg. 76) with those of Piedras Negras (Plate No. 13, pg. 75), Yaxchilán (Plate No. 14, pg. 75). Do not try to compare the general composition so much as to make note of the use of partial groups and other features.

19. There are now some 136,000 Totonacs in northern and central Veracruz (Wolf, 1959) occupying the lowland plains where the Classic Veracruz Civilization flourished. There has been some doubt that the Totonacs were the builders of El Tajín and other classic centers on the Gulf Coast (Coe, M., 1966).

20. Ekholm presents a chronological table in which he puts Tajín I in the same epoch as Teotihuacán II, and Tajín II contemporaneously with Teotihuacán III and Monte Albán III; Tajín III is indicated as prior to Teotihuacán IV (Ekholm, 1958).

21. *Palmas* are strange, prismatic-shaped objects on which the features of persons, animals, and plants are carved. *Hachas* are representations of thin heads and, occasionally, human forms. *Yugos* are highly decorated replicas of ballplayers' U-shaped protective belts.

22. Tlaloc, the god of rain, was called "Tajín" by the Totonacs. We believe that the Pyramid of the Niches was dedicated to his cult (Krickeberg, 1961; Peterson, 1959).

23. Unexcavated mounds, completely covered by tropical vegetation, are scattered on the sides of the hills and in the depressions over an area of about 1,000 hectares (I.N.A.H., 1957a).

24. The construction of the niches is unusual. Each niche is formed by two small side walls of stone slabs which support a slab projecting forward to form its roof. The interior of the niche was painted dark red and its framework, blue. A detailed description of the Pyramid of the Niches may be found in *Arquitectura prehispánica* by Ignacio Marquina (Marquina, 1951) and in the *Official Guide of El Tajín* published by the National Institute of Anthropology and History (I.N.A.H., 1957d). The text in the Guide is by José Garciá Payón.

118

25. The estimate of the difference in levels between the plaza of El Tajín Chico and the plaza of the Pyramid of the Niches is my own. I know of no altimetric mapping of the ruins, and the only reference in the *Official Guide of El Tajín* is confusing.

26. Gold and silver work in Mesoamerica reached its peak during the Mixtec period of Monte Albán, or Monte Albán V. Objects found in Tomb Seven at Monte Albán testify to the fantasy of the goldsmiths of that region; diadems, brooches, tobacco boxes in the shape of small gourds, bracelets, pectorals, tweezers, and elaborate necklaces with pendants shaped like bells or pears can be seen near a magnificent rock crystal goblet and carvings in jadeite and obsidian in the Museum of Oaxaca.

27. Information furnished by Kent Flannery in a lecture given at the Department of Anthropology of Yale University January 23rd, 1970.

28. See the plan of Mound J in *Arte antiguo de México* by Paul Westheim (Westheim, 1950).

29. Only a limited part of Monte Albán has been explored, but the ruins are spread over forty square kilometers (I.N.A.H., 1957c).

30. The longitudinal direction of the plaza is indicated by the north-south axis with small deviation. This means that the north and south sides alternately received the light at sunrise and sunset.

31. See an excellent detail of the Group of the Columns and read the description of it in *Arquitectura Prehispánica* by Ignacio Marquina (Marquina, 1951).

·4

THE AZTECS

Fear not, my heart:
There on the battlefield, I long to die by an obsidian blade!
Our hearts yearn only for death in war!
Oh, you already in battle:
I long for death by an obsidian blade.
Our hearts yearn only for death in war.

Stanza from Small Songs in *"La casa del Canto,"* taken from POESÍA PRE-COLOMBINA; selection by MIGUEL ANGEL ASTURIAS.

□ 4

THE CULHUA, MEXICA, TENOCHCA, OR AZTECS, came from the north-west outer regions of Mexico's central plateau, judging by the stages of their migration. Aztecs records mention that in the year 1168 they began their long wanderings in search of lands where they could settle perma-nently.[1] Three hundred and fifty years later, the territory annexed by the Aztecs included thirty-eight tributary provinces and several dependent states. Their borders stretched northward along the Pacific Coast to the Gulf of Mexico at approximately 22 degrees north latitude and as far south as Tehuantepec, keeping a weak control over southern Oaxaca and south-ern Chiapas to the present Mexico-Guatemala frontier, where they estab-lished the important fifteenth century commercial center of Xoconusco.[2] The Aztecs tried repeatedly to expand toward the north and north-west, but never succeeded in overcoming the Chichimec *señorío*, or do-minion, of Meztitlán. About 1475, the Tarascans defeated the Aztec army under King Axayácatl, fixing a northwestern frontier which thereafter re-mained unchanged. This left the capital in a progressively off-center loca-tion as the Aztec zone of influence expanded southward and eastward. Throughout their history the Aztec armies tried without success to con-quer another Chichimec state, the *señorío* of Tlaxcala, which remained hostile to Tenochtitlán and, favored by its central location, played an im-portant role in its fall.

The Aztecs never organized into a united empire as did the Inca. Perhaps they never even tried to do so, although governmental central-ization was stressed after Ahuizotl became king in 1486 and especially during the reign of Moctezuma II, his successor. After a conquest, the Aztecs imposed a tribute on the defeated people, and assigned land for the benefit of their own lords, but still permitted the subjected group to keep some political and administrative autonomy and to worship their

123

own gods. The amount of tribute exacted varied according to the needs of the Aztecs and the economic potential of the conquered people.[3]

Aztec conquests always had religious or economic motives. We will discuss the complex religious motivation later in detail, but the economic reasons are readily understood. We need only remember that in the principal cities of the Aztecs and their allies lived an artisan group who were in constant need of raw materials for the manufacture of consumer goods which were later traded among the Aztecs themselves or exchanged for products from their neighbors and tribute-paying subjects. The agricultural production of the allies was often insufficient for their population's needs. Equally important was the development of a quasi-feudal system with an increasing demand for agricultural land and serfs for the benefit of a growing nobility. Last but not least was the need for slaves to be sacrificed to the gods as state and religion merged into one unified system.

In the last years of their brief history, the Aztec nation included more than 300 vassal tribes which never amalgamated into a political or administrative entity. The language spoken by the Aztecs and their near neighbors was Náhuatl, but the Otomí, Huaxtecs, Totonacs, Mixtecs, Zapotecs, and Matlaltecs, to name only a few of the partially or totally subjugated groups, conserved their own languages, cultures, and gods. Even within the relatively loose limits of the Aztec state, a number of peoples maintained a precarious independence: the Tlaxcaltecs in the very heart of the empire whose capital was only a few hours march from Cholula; the domain of Meztitlán, northwest of the Valley of Mexico;[4] the Yopi on the Pacific Coast, and the Chinantecs[5] from the mountainous region north of Oaxaca (Soustelle, 1956).

The Aztecs were only one of a number of semi-nomadic groups that invaded Mexico's central plateau after the twelfth century, provoking the disintegration of the Toltec empire and the fall of Tula. At the beginning of the thirteenth century, guided by their god Huitzilopochtli, the Aztecs established themselves in the area around Tula. They did nothing without consulting Huitzilopochtli, who told them where to settle, how to plant seeds and harvest the crops, and later advised the scouts as to which directions they should take in search of new lands where the people could prepare the next stage in their slow peregrination.

In 1215 the Aztecs arrived in the center of the Valley of Mexico. The thirteenth century passed as they avoided encounters with those peoples already established in the Valley who were stronger than themselves. They absorbed the more advanced culture of their occasional neighbors, especially those of Culhuacán,[6] learning the value of agriculture, the calendar, and stone architecture, while developing their own reputation as brave and cruel warriors.

At the beginning of the fourteenth century, they settled in Chapultepec. The years that followed were tragic and full of unrest. Finally, expelled from Chapultepec by a coalition formed by the Tepanecs who lived in Azcapotzalco, and the inhabitants of Culhuacán, the Aztecs took refuge on a small, swampy island in Lake Texcoco. Always defeated; provoking fights which they despaired of winning; hardening body and spirit in adversity; obeying unfailingly the instructions of Huitzilopochtli, who appeared to them whenever circumstances required, the Aztecs reached the end of their long journey.

In 1325, on the rocks of the small island which served as their refuge, the Aztecs erected the temple around which the city of Tenochtitlán grew. Two years later one of the Aztec tribes settled in Tlatelolco, an even smaller island separated from Tenochtitlán by a narrow channel. Here ended their migration. Throughout their travels they had maintained a democratic, egalitarian social structure in which only the four *tlamacazques,* or bearers of Huitzilopochtli, were eminent. These four men were also the war chiefs, sole authorities and probably the priests (Moreno, 1962).

Tenochtitlán's site enjoyed defensive, political, and commercial advantages (Bernal, 1959b). In addition, the island's geographic location enabled the Aztecs to come into contact with the lake peoples, especially those on the western shore. During the early years of Tenochtitlán, the Aztec's political weakness made them dependent on more powerful neighboring states.

In the second half of the fourteenth century, the inhabitants of the central Valley of Mexico lived under continuous warfare. Once the hegemony established by the Chichimecs from their capital, Tenayuca, had been destroyed, the small states bordering Lake Texcoco engaged in conflict with each other and with neighboring states.[7] Taking advantage of these fights, the Tepanecs of Azcapotzalco, guided by their king, Tezozómoc,[8] gained control of the whole central part of the Valley, and finally, in 1418, took Texcoco. The Aztecs participated in these wars as mercenaries, fighting for the Tepanecs under the command of King

Tezozómoc. In 1367, they captured Culhuacán, where the Toltec's descendants lived, and in 1371 they took Tenayuca, the ancient Chichimec capital.

Eventually, the Aztecs decided to elect their own king. The Tlatelolco group asked the Tepanecs to send them a governor, while the Tenochtitlán Aztecs received a Culhuacán prince named Acamapichtli as their first king in 1376. The first political step taken by the Aztecs of Tenochtitlán could not have been more astute since the choice of a representative of the Toltec succession was fundamental to their prestige. By this move, they became heirs to the culture of great artisans and artists.

Less than one hundred and fifty years passed between the beginning of the Aztec dynasty and its disappearance. This period saw the reign of nine monarchs. The reigns of the first three kings, Acamapichtli, 1376 to 1396, Huitzilihuitl between 1396 and 1414, and Chimalpopoca from 1414 to 1427, were obscure.[9] Through matrimonial alliances with the Tepanecs, the first Aztec kings retained a measure of independence, but upon the death of their king Tezozómoc, in 1426, Matlatzin, his son, immediately entered into conflict with the lords of Tenochtitlán, Tacuba, and the exiles from Texcoco. This war precipitated the defeat of the Tepanecs, clearing the way for the Aztecs and their new allies to gain control of central Mexico.

The fourth king of Tenochtitlán was Itzcóatl, a son of Acamapichtli, whose reign lasted from 1427 to 1440. During his first years on the throne, Itzcóatl participated in the war against the Tepanecs and in the capture of Azcapotzalco, an event which allowed the exiled Chichimec king, Nezahualcóyotl, to return to Texcoco.

From then on, Tenochtitlán, Tlatelolco, and Tacuba, or Tlacopán, joined in a Triple Alliance, formalized in 1434, the purpose of which was to conquer and exact tribute from other tribes.[10] When the time came to divide the titles of the conquered territories, Itzcóatl adopted that of "Lord of Culhuacán," thereby shutting out all other pretenders to Toltec succession.

During Itzcóatl's reign, the Aztecs and their allies began to expand, using the political and military tactics which had won success for Tezozómoc. They subjugated Coyoacán, Chalco, and Xochimilco, and penetrated far to the southeast, which permitted the allies to control a number of centers outside of the Valley of Mexico.

Itzcóatl's successor was his nephew, Moctezuma I, who ruled from 1440 to 1469 and is considered to be the most important of the Aztec kings. He expanded the frontiers of the empire to the coast of the Gulf of Mexico where he captured Cempoala and other Totonac centers, southward, establishing Aztec authority in Oaxaca, and on toward the southwest (Kelley and Palerm, 1952). The conquest of the Totonacs was vital to the allies as it allowed them to control the most productive maize-growing area in all Mexico, thereby assuring food for their people during periods of drought and hunger.

Moctezuma I introduced the "Flower Wars" among the Aztecs, a custom which had been in existence for almost a century under the Tepanecs. The object was to test the courage of the opposing powers in battle, and to secure the captives needed for the religious sacrifices practiced among the civilizations of the central Valley of Mexico at that time. The "Flower Wars" were never wars of conquest. The time and place of combat were agreed upon by both sides, and the warriors tried to make sure to take a prisoner whose capture would bring them prestige. The motivation of Aztec society was glory, by which its members earned honor and riches.

Moctezuma I also changed the appearance of the Aztec capital. With the aid of Nezahualcóyotl, king of Texcoco, he built an aqueduct to bring water from Chapultepec as well as a dike to the east of the city to serve as flood protection and to separate the saline from the fresh waters of the lake. In Chalco, near Tenochtitlán, an artistic center had developed where potters kept in contact with the Mixtecs and the inhabitants of Puebla (Marquina, 1951). Moctezuma I brought architects from Chalco to his capital to undertake the first great constructions in stone.

Axayácatl, also a descendent of Acamapichtli, succeeded his father, Moctezuma I, and governed between 1469 and 1481. His conquests took him as far south as Oaxaca and the Isthmus of Tehuantepec and northward to fight against the Matlatzinca whose principal city, Calixtlahuaca, he finally conquered in 1475. A year later, he took the cities of Coatepec, Malacatepec, and Malinalco in the present state of Mexico. He had much less success, however, in the war he undertook against the Tarascans, who defeated the Aztecs and preserved the independence of their cities, Tzintzúntzan and Ihuatzio, among others, up to the time of the Spanish Conquest. Axayácatl's greatest triumph was in forcing the incorporation of Tlatelolco, Tenochtitlán's ally and sister city from the days of their difficult beginnings on the small islands in Lake Texcoco.[12]

Reaction against Aztec ambition was the cause of frequent revolts in the tributary cities and states, necessitating the establishment of garrisons in these areas. The responsibility for this vigilence fell to Tizoc, Ax-ayácatl's younger brother, who reigned briefly from 1481 to 1486. His reign was regarded as a failure by his collaborators and various sources indicate that he was poisoned (Duran, 1951). Tizoc continued the work on Tenochtitlán's Great Temple, or Templo Mayor, which had begun under his predecessor.

Ahuízotl, another son of Moctezuma I and brother of the two previous kings, completed the conquest of southern Mexico up to the Guatemalan frontier, where he established the commercial center of Xoconusco.

At the end of the fifteenth century, Tenochtitlán was an extensive city and an important commercial center, so densely populated that a second aqueduct had to be built. The inauguration of the Templo Mayor, during Ahuízotl's reign, gave an almost definitive aspect to Tenochtitlán's cere-monial center.

Politically, Tenochtitlán was already the great power of Mesoamerica. While Aztec merchants traveled the trade routes, transacting business and paving the way for new conquests, the warriors and governors exer-cised their dominion by exacting tribute and gathering the designated quotas of prisoners to be sacrificed to the many gods of the Aztec pantheon.[13] In this society, already divided into classes, the last kings of Tenochtitlán accentuated their power and gradually took on the at-tributes of gods, establishing the basis for a hereditary nobility.

Before he assumed power, Moctezuma II, the last Aztec king, had been an accomplished and valiant warrior and devoted priest. However, during his reign, which lasted from 1502 to 1520, he became a tyrant, preoccupied with suppressing the revolts provoked by his policies and those of his predecessors. He began to brood about superstitions and prophecies and finally became a weak and vacillating man, helpless in the face of the Spanish threat. A member of the royal lineage, he was Ax-ayácatl's son and the nephew of both Tizoc and Ahuízotl. His end and that of his kingdom are too well known to bear repetition.

There were two other royal names whose brief reigns were no more than nominal in a territory already dominated by superstition and Span-iards. Cuitlahuac succeeded his brother, Moctezuma II, only to die of mumps four months later. Finally came Cuauhtémoc, the Mexican hero and cousin to the previous kings, who directed his people's resistance against the Spaniards and who ended his days in 1524, hanged by order of Cortés.

AZTEC SOCIETY

We see a dramatic transformation of Aztec society, from the uncertain tribal days when its members had sought the promised land, to the last stage of its evolution when it was already converted into an aristocratic and imperialistic state, feared and hated by almost all the peoples of Mesoamerica.

The seeds of class division in Aztec society may have been implicit in the four priests who carried the god, Huitzilopochtli, during their peregrinations, acting as interpreters of his orders and wishes. The Aztec state's true structure, however, was not really seen until much later when, as a group paying tribute to Azcapotzalco, they began to gain prestige among the other peoples who lived on the shores of Lake Texcoco. But only when Itzcóatl assumed power, and Tenochtitlán acquired political and economic importance beyond the limits of Mexico's central Valley, was Aztec centralism accentuated in the figure of the king, to the point where the last ruler, Moctezuma II, embodied absolute temporal and spiritual power.

THE RULING CLASSES

Although the social organization of the Aztec tribes was completely democratic in theory (Vaillant, 1955), and each king was elected by the members of a Council which also theoretically represented the Councils of all the tribes, the situation ultimately changed in favor of an aristocratic monarchy.

The Aztec tribes were established before they ever arrived in the central Valley of Mexico. These tribes were based on clans, or *calpulli,* each made up of several families, with twenty clans forming a tribe. Each clan elected its Council, which in turn designated one of its most respected members as representative to the Tribal Council. Through the Tribal Council, each of the tribes making up the Aztec confederation regulated its affairs. Each Tribal Council appointed a representative to the High Council, and the High Council elected four of its members to choose the future king.

The importance of the High Council as an advisory body, responsible for the election of the Aztec royal succession, is understandable. The composition of the Council ultimately began to change, and Ahuízotl and

Moctezuma II were elected by a Council representing only the firmly entrenched ruling class.

Prescott tells us that the Aztec monarchy could be considered elective. However, the choice always went to a descendent of Acamapichtli, the Toltec prince who originated the dynasty. In this way, the Aztecs reaffirmed their pretensions as cultural heirs of the Toltecs. Whether by chance or intuition on the part of the electors, or perhaps because all potential candidates received the appropriate training, the fact remains that almost all the elected monarchs had been outstanding military leaders during their predecessor's reign and, without exception, enlarged their domains during their own.

The Aztec custom of succession was totally different from that practiced in Texcoco, where one of the sons of the king's legitimate wife was elected, subject to approval by a council of the principal lords who could refuse the legitimate successor and appoint another if they felt that the former was unfit to govern.[14]

The descriptions of Cortés and Bernal Díaz del Castillo give us excellent pictures of the hierarchical differences between the emperor and the noblemen nearest him which existed during the last years of the empire. Bernal Díaz del Castillo devoted a chapter to analyzing the appearance and character of Moctezuma II and describing the luxury and pleasures he enjoyed: "the aviary and zoo," "the gardens of fragrant flowers and trees," "dancers and tumblers," his meals of "thirty kinds of dishes," the humble garments worn by great lords in his presence, and a guard of "two hundred noblemen." The chronicler does not forget to mention that the Aztec king had "lords' daughters as women friends, although he had two great *caciques'* daughters as legitimate wives" (Díaz de Castillo, 1955).

The paragraph which best describes the submission of Moctezuma's subjects to their ruler is the following: "They did not turn their backs to him on taking their leave, but with face and eyes cast down in his direction, they did not turn around until they had left the chamber." Motolinia enlarges on this: "All his vassals, great and small, respected and feared him, for he was cruel and harsh in punishment" (Motolinia, 1941). The Aztec king was called *Tlatoani* ("He Who Speaks"), and also *Tlacatecuhtli* ("Chief of the Warriors"), symbolizing his absolute power in administrative and military matters. Toward the end of the empire, both these functions were filled by Moctezuma II since the King was also the High Priest.

During the rule of Moctezuma II, the apex of the pyramidal structure of this increasingly stratified society was the emperor, a figure of semi-divine attributes who wielded absolute power. These characteristics approach the type of absolute monarchy which existed among the Inca, yet differ from the government adopted by the Classic Maya, who were grouped into small states administered by hereditary members of a family.

In the last decades of the Aztec state, the ruling class was firmly established. It was responsible for directing military, judicial, and administrative affairs, and, with its duties and titles, it held special rank in the hierarchy. The members of this class, called *tecuhtli,* or lords, were designated by the monarch or by the councils of the important cities.

After the reign of Moctezuma I, the man closest to the king was the *cihuacóatl,* a sort of Grand Vizier, whose multiple administrative and religious responsibilities included acting as supreme judge and even taking his monarch's place when the king was away from Tenochtitlán (Soustelle, 1955). The first *cihuacóatl* was Tlacaélel, a half brother of Moctezuma I, who was the great reformer of Aztec society and created an hereditary lineage parallel to that of the king.[15] In fact, the king's relatives were gradually occupying the most important positions in Aztec society to the point of becoming the real advisory body to the throne.[16]

In the rank just below that of the *cihuacóatl* were the four men whose combined duties were roughly equivalent to chiefs of the troops supplied by the four districts which formed Tenochtitlán. It was from these four that the successor to the empire was chosen.[17] One of the four was the *Tlacateccatl,* who was the commander of the armies of Tenochtitlán and of the Triple Alliance. Several Aztec kings held this position before they were elected by the Council.

The sons of the *tecuhtli,* or nobles, were generally educated in the *calmecac,* a school where they lived for the better part of their training period. Sahagún tells us that they were taught good habits, doctrines, exercises, and led an austere and chaste life. No effrontery, reproach nor disrespect was tolerated toward any customs practiced by the ministers of the gods. The young men learned to speak well, use correct forms of address, and behave respectfully. They were taught "all the verses of the songs," "Indian astrology and the interpretation of dreams and the count of the years" (Sahagún, 1943). Discipline in the *calmecac* was rigorous and included fasts, midnight prayers, and vows, which, if not fulfilled, were punished with due severity.[18] The *calmecac* was supported by the community, and all such tasks as cleaning, cooking, and construction were the responsibility of the young members of this institution.

The emperor chose his principal functionaries, religious and military leaders, from among the students of the *calmecac*. This established a differentiation from birth between the sons of the nobles and the commoners' sons (*macehualli*) who went to the *telpochcalli,* or ward schools. Such a division strengthened and promoted the Aztec ruling group which occupied the high posts in Aztec bureaucracy, one of the largest and most influential groups ever to exist among American Indian cultures. However, particularly able boys of commoner families were accepted to the *calmecac.*

Below the ranks of the Aztec king's councillors and closest relatives, the administration was made up of three main groups: the *tlacochtecuhtli,* who were the highest ranking provincial functionaries as well as the military and administrative governors of cities and provinces; the *calpixque,* who wielded great power and were in charge of collecting tribute, planning and supervising public works and making sure that the land was duly cultivated, especially when its harvest was destined for a tax payment; and a group of lesser functionaries who assisted the *calpixque,* kept accounts of all that was done and managed various provincial affairs.

Next in the hierarchy came the judges, a group carefully selected by the king from among the elderly and experienced who had earned popular acclaim.

I would like to interject a brief explanation here about the village chiefs and ward chiefs. I mentioned that these members of the ruling class were appointed by the monarch or by the cities, but as the Aztec state moved toward an aristocratic monarchy, a radical change took place in the system, and the position of ward chief ultimately became hereditary, offering the descendents greater opportunities and privileges.

The chiefs of each *calpulli* or, as it had come to mean, ward,[19] were elected by the inhabitants of the wards from among their members, but the position had to be confirmed by the emperor who, in addition, appointed a supervisor from the central government. These chiefs were called *calpulle* (*calpullec* in plural), and their duty was to administer justice, organize religious life and administer the lands of the *calpulli,* or *calpulalli,* and divide the produce.[20]

The village chiefs, like the *calpullec,* did not belong to any particular lineage. Their functions and privileges were similar to those of the *calpullec,* and they were supported by the group under their jurisdiction. To a certain extent, the village chiefs were also military chiefs and acted as intermediaries between the people and the highest judicial and administrative rank of the Aztec state.

War and the priesthood, activities which might coincide during youth as they were the only paths toward prestige, honors and riches, were the life goals of every Aztec. For the Aztecs, the purpose of war was to gain economic advantage and capture prisoners. Positions and titles were earned on the field of battle according to the number of prisoners taken by each warrior. A man's failure as a warrior meant having to renounce his aspirations and content himself with the poor, obscure life of the *macehualli,* or commoner. Success in war, on the other hand, allowed him to hope for successive honors, to participate in councils of war, to obtain a ranking place in ceremonial life and to be included in the division of material rewards. Free land and labor were the benefits received by these newcomers to the aristocracy formed by the *pipiltin* or lords.

All Aztec men took part in war at some point in their lives.[21] It is significant that several emperors were chiefs of the army, or *tlacateccatl,* during their predecessor's reign. Westheim rightly says that Aztec warriors were soldiers of God charged with nourishing Huitzilopochtli by the sacrifice of war prisoners (Westheim, 1950). This explains the importance of military orders such as the Jaguar Knights and especially the Eagle Knights, whose house, or *cuacuauhtinchan,* was, at the same time, a school for warriors and the Ministry of War (Alcocer, 1935).

The priesthood was open to both men and women, the priests being called *tlamacazqui* and the priestesses, *cihuatlamacazqui.* Some authors state that only the *pilli,* sons of nobles by birth, and merchants' sons could enter the priesthood, but other authors maintain that members of the humble classes could also aspire to it. The priests studied in the *calmecac* until they reached twenty years of age, after which they served in the wards or were consecrated as assistants to a cult. Few ascended to the title of *tlenamacac,* among whom one of the electors of the future monarch could be found, nor did many come to be members of the high ecclesiastic hierarchy.

The cults of Huitzilopochtli and Tlaloc were the most important in the Aztec religion. Twin temples in their honor crowned the top of the Great Pyramid of Tenochtitlán. Two High Priests of equal rank were consecrated to the cults of these two supreme gods of the Aztec pantheon. The High Priests were called *Quetzalcóatl-Totec-Tlamacazqui* and *Quetzalcóatl-Tlaloc-Tlamacazqui,* respectively.

The gods possessed property from which they extracted tribute, besides receiving frequent large donations. These gods were administered by high-ranking priests on a lower plane than that of the two High Priests. Important in this hierarchy was the priest in charge of supervising education in the *calmecacs* and managing all religious affairs in the provinces and capital. This priest was called the *mexicatl teohuatzin*. He had two assistants, the *huitznahuac teohuatzin,* a sort of undersecretary of religion, and the *tepan teohuatzin,* whose functions might parallel those of an undersecretary of education.

THE MERCHANTS

In the last century before the Spanish Conquest, there emerged a group of growing economic and military importance whose members and their heirs had obtained almost the same privileges as the *pilli,* or nobles. These were the *pochteca,*[22] the merchants who engaged in long distance trade and exchange with the most distant peoples and regions (Chapman, 1957). Probably the merchants originated as an intermediate group between the *pipiltin* and the *macehualli,* the nobles and the commoners. In time, furthered by Aztec political and military expansion and favored by their contacts with the *pipiltin,* especially with the king and ruling class for whom the merchants supplied luxuries their land did not produce, the *pochteca* of Tenochtitlán, Tlatelolco and the cities of the confederation became a real and affluent middle class.[23]

The *pochteca* tended to remain apart from the rest of Aztec society, maintaining a solidarity within their own group. Their directive positions were hereditary; they lived in separate wards, appointed their own judges and possessed their own gods,[24] rites, and festivals (Chapman, 1957).

Organized commerce arrived relatively late in the evolution of Indian economic activities. It contributed to urbanistic development and the formation of a typically urban class and economy, but probably did not affect the vast rural population which lived off the land in traditional self-sufficiency.

Each of the principal cities of the Aztecs and their allies had its group of organized merchants. Those of Tlatelolco were considered most able and influential; Cholula's merchants specialized in jewels; those in Texcoco dealt in certain kinds of pottery, and Azcapotzalco controlled the profitable slave trade. There were also other centers, far from the great capitals of the state, whose merchants were highly respected by the *poch-*

teca from the center of Mexico. One such group was made up of the merchants of Tochtepec, in Oaxaca, who were favored because of the strategic location of that city between the markets of Mexico's central plateau and the rebellious groups in the south.

The *pochteca* acted as spies and even special envoys from the Aztec kings during the period of expansion.[25] We should bear in mind that the provocative attitude these merchants frequently assumed was due to well-laid plans which served the Aztec rulers as pretexts for launching their campaigns (Krickeberg, 1961). The presence of these Aztec merchants in a foreign territory was generally regarded as an augury of an impending conquest by other Indian peoples. Naturally, the reaction was violent and only precipitated matters.

Although the benefits derived from commerce were replaced by tribute once the chosen province or city was conquered, the *pochteca* also knew how to take advantage of the new situation, thanks to their financial connections with the artisan groups. In this respect, they constituted a quasi-military group, aware of the dangers involved in the double mission which motivated their travels and of the risks of long journeys across territories constantly in a state of alert.

There were several classes of merchants (Chapman, 1957):

1. The *pochtecatlatoque,* or retired merchants, who served as advisers and still maintained a financial interest in commercial expeditions. This group probably produced the judges.

2. The slave traders, whose centers of operation were in some of the large cities, but who kept purchasing bases in the furthermost cities.

3. The *teucunenenque,* or merchants in the exclusive service of the king or nobles.

4. The *naualoztomeca*, or merchant-spies. They constituted a military group with specialized training in languages, disguises and techniques not unlike contemporary spies.

There seems to have also been a fifth group which is not clearly defined.

As currency did not exist in Mesoamerica, barter was the accepted form of exchange. Cacao beans, as well as gold dust and hammered copper knives, were often used as currency (Vaillant, 1955).

Commerce was the basis of the economy in two or three regions of Mesoamerica, and some centers, favored by geographic location and political circumstances, grew into "ports of trade." Coatzalcoalco, Cimatán, Zinacantán and most of all Xicalango, on the Gulf of Mexico, west of the Laguna de los Términos, and Xoconusco, north of Guatemala on the Pacific, were cities with special districts occupied by Aztec merchants with their employees and warehouses. In these centers the *pochteca* met with their colleagues from the Mayan areas of Yucatán and Central America.

THE LEARNED MEN

We find them in all principal towns as a group dedicated to the study of the ancient religion of the Toltecs (Portilla, 1963) and of other pre-Aztec cultures. They were called *tlamatinime* and their role was praised by Sahagún who compared them with medical doctors (Sahagún, 1946). "The *tlamatinime* preserved, in contrast with the popular cult of Huitzilopochtli, the war god, the ancient belief in one god who was beyond all celestial floors" (Portilla, 1963).

THE DOCTORS

Other groups of Aztec society were organized in guilds, subdivided according to specialities. One such guild was composed of medical men, an hereditary profession passed down from father to son.

Aztec doctors excelled in the treatment of fractures, cranial trephining and puncturing, gout, dysentery, blennorrhea, jaundice, internal congestions, tumors, dislocations, and other ills. Their medical lore included potions and poultices made from medicinal herbs which the *pochteca* imported from other lands.

In some advanced Mesoamerican cultures, specialists emerged such as the surgeon who cut with obsidian blades and sewed with hair, the bloodletters who used leeches and lancets, the midwife, the general practitioner who cured with poultices and whose figure we see in the Florentine Codex, and, finally, the herbalist who selected and catalogued medicinal herbs (Vargas Castelazo, 1954-1955).

Like other guilds, the Aztec doctors had their own gods, some of which were already part of the Aztec pantheon. Among these were Quetzalcóatl who was invoked for sterility in women; Tlaltecuhtli, the god of sick children; and Xochiquetzal, the goddess of childbirth.

THE ARTISANS

Aztec artisans already constituted a large group with their own particular gods and institutions. All the great cities had districts of artisans who had inherited the position and specialty of their parents after a long apprenticeship which began in childhood. In the Florentine Codex we see the figure of a goldsmith and that of an artist making feather adornments, as well as representations of less esteemed craftsmen.

The Aztecs knew metallurgy, but did not excel in artistic techniques for working metals, as this craft was foreign to their lands. It was probably in the eleventh century that metallurgy came to the Valley of Mexico (Vaillant, 1955). The craft seems to have originated in some part of Peru or Ecuador, and to have been transmitted via Central America and Oaxaca where it was known as early as the eighth century. The great goldsmiths of the early Aztec period in the Valley of Mexico were Mixtec groups who had settled in Texcoco in the fourteenth century. These Mixtecs, famous throughout the major Mesoamerican centers, came from the almost inaccessible valleys north of Oaxaca.

In Mexico City's Museum of Anthropology, we find an excellent modern reproduction of the quetzal plume headdress of Moctezuma II. The original, now in the Vienna Museum, was sent to Charles V by Cortés. The quetzal is the national bird of Guatemala, and its feathers were one of the luxury items which Aztec traders brought to Tenochtitlán. The colored feathers of quetzal, heron, parrot, and other birds were used to make mosaics and mantles, to decorate the warriors' shields, and to make adornments which served as the leaders' insignia. The inhabitants of Amantla were, during one epoch at least, the great specialists in this unique art (Soustelle, 1956).

Coral, obsidian, shells, pyrite, jade, and turquoise were used to decorate wooden, stone or bone artifacts or to manufacture masks, shields, mirrors, jars, vases, and other special pieces of great artistic value. The workers in this craft, as well as those working with feathers and gold, formed privileged groups among Aztec artisans as they created almost all the adornments of the privileged classes, of the king and of the religious images (Krickeberg, 1961).

The Aztec potters covered the whole range of shapes and decorations for ritual and utilitarian purposes, demonstrating manual skill and sensitivity. Work in wood, obsidian tools, articles from the weavers and basket makers are all examples of hand crafts which have endured to our time.

Architects and sculptors were eminent among Aztec artists. Monumental Aztec sculpture is represented in museums by many pieces of complex symbolism. Many works were saved from Spanish destruction and can be seen today in the patios and halls of Mexico City's Museum. Coatlícue, goddess of the earth, is a massive figure whose faintly suggested human form stands on two claws. Her body is covered with fragmented adornments without apparent artistic relationship, yet she gives an extraordinary impression of unity, force, and vitality. The Sun Stone or "Aztec Calendar," the Stone of Tizoc, the gigantic vase in the shape of an ocelot, are all well known works of the final monumentalistic period of Aztec art and have been analyzed by specialists in diverse works (Westheim, 1950). I must also offer a word of admiration for the head of the Eagle Knight. In this piece, we find the supernatural and surrealistic elements which characterize Aztec art replaced by a realism and dignity comparable to what we might find in a Medieval masterpiece. It is a true symbol of those values which the Aztecs hoped to find in a man.[25]

THE PEOPLE

The Aztec commoners were not slaves. The gulf separating them from the ruling class in the way of opportunities, privileges, and rewards, however, became gradually more apparent as Aztec society moved toward an aristocratic monarchy. The development of the large estates during the last decades of the empire might have been a symptom, reflecting the social step backward provoked by the combination of rapid Aztec expansion and the ensuing obligatory rewards needed to maintain an imperialist policy.

Although the tribe was still important as a social and military unit, as we see in the urban territorial division of Tenochtitlán, let us remember that the power of its representatives declined perceptibly during the last reigns to the point of being almost nonexistent at the time of the election of Moctezuma II.

How far would Aztec society have evolved if the state could have continued its territorial expansion? What would have been the symptoms of this change? What would this evolution have meant to the Aztec people? The Aztec state certainly could not have broadened upon and consolidated its rapid conquests without having first established a strong centralized government. Even the manner of succession to the throne would have had to adapt to the new circumstances, requiring the certitude of a continuity which the Aztec state theoretically lacked. But the main question is whether the *calpulli,* the basic cell of Aztec society, would have had enough force to resist the growing expansion and ambition of the ruling class, inasmuch as the clan had lost its political strength, retaining only its usefulness as a productive and military unit. The second question is, how would the state have reacted, if there had been no Spanish invasion, in the face of the continuous resistance that its policy of vassalage aroused among the conquered peoples?

The difference between the noble, or *pipiltin,* and the man of the people, or *macehualli,* begins with his relationship with the soil. The first is an absentee owner who draws an income from his land that is worked with labor that belongs to no clan. The second man is theoretically a proprietor, since his parcel of land will be inherited by his descendents as long as he keeps cultivating it personally and his line continues, but he has received the parcel according to the pro rata division which the *calpulli* has fixed for the lands allotted by the tribe. Therefore, the *macehualli* worked directly on the land he had received or operated collectively according to the type of work to be done. A third group was also linked to the land—the serfs, who were limited to working others' lands (Kirchhoff, 1954-55). The *pipiltin* and *macehualli* made up the two great social classes of Aztec Mexico. The merchants, artisans and other specialists occupied an intermediate position, and the serfs and slaves were at the bottom of the scale.

The *calpulli* assured the common man his food, housing, clothing, tools, and a life with his peers. During their first years in the Valley of Mexico, the economic base of the *calpulli* was agriculture. The produce was shared among the members and any surplus was stored. As Aztec society continued its policy of conquest and new tribes were incorporated, the specialization of some of the *calpulli* emerged to the point where they dominated a particular craft.

The diets of the *pilli* and *macehualli* differed substantially in variety and quantity. The thirty cooked dishes which were presented daily to Moctezuma II, and the frugal diet of maize, beans and chili peppers which the commoners ate day after day, morning and night, exemplified the distance between a demigod and a humble citizen. The preparation and presentation of the meals was another symbol of the accentuated class difference which existed toward the end. The meals of Moctezuma

II remind us of those of European royalty of the same epoch with their profusion of servants, musicians, and attendants. The meal of the common man was a brief, silent affair, eaten while the men squatted at a distance from the women.

Cacao, flavored with honey or vanilla, was too expensive to be enjoyed by any but the wealthy. The noble ate fish fresh from the sea. The commoner had to content himself with the fish found in the Valley's many swamps and lakes so as to vary his monotonous diet without cost. He also ate frogs, tadpoles, and the larvae and eggs of water insects. But the dietary basis of lord and commoner was the same—maize. This grain was prepared in many ways. The most common maize dishes were six or seven kinds of tortillas and tamales, in soups or toasted, or made into a paste which was diluted with water, fermented and later drunk as a beverage. The Aztecs also consumed several kinds of beans, squashes, prickly pears, and sweet potatoes. Onions and tabasco peppers, tomatoes, pumpkin seeds and the ever-present chili peppers served as seasoning. Their diet was supplemented by fruits such as pineapples, which were brought from the coast, Indian figs, plums, avocados, and mamey.

Meat consumption among the commoners was low, as it is today, but roast and cooked meat formed part of the daily diet of the king and the ruling class. The Aztecs domesticated few animals, certainly no beasts of burden. They raised turkeys, a special kind of dove, quail and a particular breed of small dog which was fattened for food. In the markets, game from the hunt was sold. Deer, rabbit, hare, tapir, and otter were available, but these were expensive and increasingly hard to get as the population grew in the Valley during the years the Aztec state was at its height (Dávalos Hurtado, 1954-55). All these foodstuffs were sold in the daily markets of Tenochtitlán, Texcoco, Cholula, and the larger cities, and in markets held on fixed days of the month in the smaller cities (Sanders, 1952). Aztec markets were well organized and even had special judges and inspectors who controlled the price lists, the quality of the merchandise and accuracy of measurements.

Tenochtitlán was essentially a consumer city, since the agricultural production within the island's limits, although some did exist, must have been quite small. At all hours of the day canoes swarmed through the city's canals, piled high with the most varied products for market. They could be seen tied up in the special port on the eastern side of the island after their trip across the lake. Numerous porters took the place of beasts of burden, carrying their loads along the causeways to the city, singly or as part of a *pochteca* caravan.

The abundance and variety of foodstuffs to be found in the major Indian cities astonished the Spaniards, who have left us with excellent descriptions (Díaz del Castillo, 1955; Sahagún, 1943; Cortés, 1961). These foods represented "the almost unbelievable richness and fertility of the land called New Spain" (Motolinia, 1941). In spite of Motolinia's lavish descriptions, however, the Indian farmer fought hard to make his meager lot produce in a land where large areas could yield an adequate crop only if irrigated. In his lot the *macehualli* grew maize, beans and squashes by primitive methods. The limited efficiency of the digging stick, which also served as a plow, together with the scant use of fertilizers and infrequent rotation of crops, made it necessary to work the land even harder to produce a crop.

During the reign of Moctezuma II, Tenochtitlán must have been a sizeable city. The chroniclers credit it with 60,000 hearths, a figure accepted by Vaillant (Vaillant, 1955). On this basis, we can calculate that 300,000 inhabitants lived in Tenochtitlán around 1520. This figure is accepted by Cook and Simpson for the twin cities of Tenochtitlán and Tlatelolco. These same authors believe that by the end of the empire another 400,000 persons lived in the area of Texcoco, Huexotla and Atenco, to which we should add the 100,000 residents of Chalco (Cook and Simpson, 1948).

I find these figures for Tenochtitlán-Tlatelolco rather high, but at least they give us an idea of the kind of society the Spaniards must have found on their arrival in the center of Mexico and provide a reference to cities of considerable size, even by European standards of that time. Let us not forget that, besides the great urban centers located on or near the lake, there must have been many other smaller cities and villages inhabited by several hundreds of people, and possibly even thousands. Motolinia had the opportunity to travel over the territory of Mexico a few years after the Conquest, and he tells us that the mountainous area surrounding the central valley was well populated and that there were more than forty medium-to large-sized towns, with others, not much smaller, subject to them (Motolinia, 1941).

These large urban populations which, for the most part, possessed modest resources, consumed food that few of them produced. They lived on the provisions which they could acquire in the markets by bartering their crafts or in exchange for professional services or by payment with cacao beans if they were lucky enough to have any. Agricultural products came from the banks of Lakes Chalco and Xochimilco where the shallow depth permitted cultivation in *chinampas,* the rich, man-made land mounds reclaimed from the waters.[26] Even in our day, a good part of the fresh vegetables eaten in Mexico City come from these areas.

The lake system facilitated direct and rapid communication by water between the different cities in the central Valley of Mexico. This mode of transportation lasted throughout the Colonial Period and up until regular roads took their place. Even at the beginning of this century, the long, narrow canoes paddled up the Viga Canal carrying greens and flowers for the city markets (Wolf, 1959).

The *macehualli* constituted the largest group in Aztec society and formed the basis of the *calpulli.* Life was modest but not without possibilities since war and the priesthood offered youths an opportunity to distinguish themselves. Even in the final years of the Aztec state, when the ruling class took over the more important posts, valor in combat earned social elevation and rewards.

A member of the *macehualli* cultivated the land allotted to him, sent his sons to the ward school and participated with his family in the festivities and tasks of his community.[27] For him, belonging to the *calpulli* was a guarantee of security as well as an obligation, since he had to pay a tax, serve in the army and do his share of community work. Expulsion from the *calpulli* meant falling into the isolated position of the *tlalmoitl,* or serfs, who worked the land of others but retained their liberty and their obligations to society. Twenty *calpulli* together formed a tribe which had its own arsenal, used special ensigns and coordinated the instruction of new members.

At the bottom of the social scale were the slaves, a large group made up of prisoners of war who had been pardoned in exchange for their special skills, and the commoners who worked as slaves in exchange for food, housing and clothing after hunger or other circumstances had reduced them to a state of total indigence. Certain criminals could also be condemned to slavery. However, justice was severe, and the death penalty was frequent for offenders who, in today's society, would receive a light sentence. Even the slaves had privileges, however, and slavery did not involve their families since the sons of slaves were born free. Aztec slaves could marry, own property and even possess slaves themselves.

Some authors believe the Aztec population was in decline when Cortés and his men landed in 1519. This might have been caused by an ecological imbalance in the Valley of Mexico which would have led to abuses on the part of powerful groups to the detriment of the weak. Demographic decline could also have been the result of the continuous sacrifice of so many persons in their full virility.

Spinden believed that the population of Mexico's central plateau began to decline after the Toltec era, that is, after the tenth and eleventh centuries (Spinden, 1928). Since we have no trustworthy demographic figures from the Indian period, we must turn to the reports of the Spanish chroniclers, even those a generation later than the conquistadors, with their unanimous astonishment over the intense human occupation of the Valley of Mexico and numerous references to the cities they found in their travels. Then, the figure of eleven million persons for the center of Mexico in the year 1519 does not seem strange (Cook and Simpson, 1948). For the chroniclers' descriptions, read Cortés, Bernal Díaz del Castillo, Motolinia, Oviedo, and Sahagún, among others.

The territory presently included in the Federal District of Mexico is an intricate urban area formed by part of the central basin and its surroundings, which, four and one-half centuries ago, must have been a vast complex of cities gathered around the lake. These cities were inhabited by a society whose political evolution and geographic location encouraged the development of an urban, consumer economy, and transformation of imported raw materials as never before in Indian America.

From an urban point of view, the great cities of the central basin of Mexico in 1500 were unique specimens in America. No Indian cities belonging to other civilizations had a physical aspect, social structure and economy which came as close to the accepted contemporary criteria that define a city.

The Aztecs of Tenochtitlán and their immediate neighbors constituted a progressively urban group. The city was already something more than a mere physical environment that made a new way of life possible. It had become the symbol of the centralism imposed by the last Aztec kings. Tenochtitlán's institutions were urban, just as its nucleus, the aristocracy or ruling class of the new society, was urban.

Cortés immediately understood this transformation as an advanced urbanistic process and insisted, after the Conquest, that the former inhabitants repopulate the Aztec capital. Decimated by the Spanish siege during the tragic months of 1520, their city leveled in an attempt to destroy their past, Tenochtitlán's survivors nevertheless formed the basis of the new city and the *mestizo* society which grew up in the most prosperous Spanish colony in America. Mexico City had a political and economic reason to be rebuilt, and for the same motive, the viceroys and bishops made it the seat of their governments.

NOTES ON · 4

1. PADDEN GIVES 1168 as the date of Tula's fall to the barbarians (Padden, 1970).

2. To reach the cacao-producing center of Xoconusco, the *pochteca,* or Aztec merchants, had to cross the valleys of Oaxaca. Xoconusco was conquered by the Aztecs around 1486, at the beginning of Ahuízotl's reign; apparently the southern frontier of the empire did not extend much farther. Nevertheless, the Aztecs never succeeded in completely dominating the alliance of Oaxaca's Zapotecs and Mixtecs. Ahuízotl only acquired the right of passage across the center of Oaxaca, which privilege had to be defended by several small forts and the Cuilapa fortress.

3. "In essence, the Mexica remained little more than a band of pirates, sallying forth from their great city to loot and plunder and to submit vast areas to tribute payment without altering the social constitution of their victims" (Wolf, 1959).

4. The inhabitants of Tlaxcala and Meztitlán were part Náhuatl and part Otomí.

5. The Chinantecs were a warrior people feared by the Aztecs. Their hatred of the lords of Tenochtitlán impelled them, like the Tlaxcaltecs, to become allies of Cortés.

6. The Culhua were the inhabitants of Culhuacán, an important city to the south of Lake Texcoco. After the abandonment of Tula in the middle of the thirteenth century, one of the Toltec groups established itself here.

7. About 1350, the more powerful states in the basin of Lake Texcoco were: the Chichimecs of the south, who had recently established a new capital in Texcoco where they came into contact with a Mixtec group. This fusion produced the most civilized people and city of the last Pre-Columbian years; the Chichimecs of the north, who lived around Tepetlaoztoc; the Tepanecs, whose capital was Azcapotzalco; the Otomí, who lived to the north of the lake and whose capital, Xaltocán, was also built on an island in Lake Texcoco; the Acolhua tribe of Coatlínchan, a city near Texcoco.

8. Tezozómoc was king of the Tepanecs after 1346. He was a great general, an able politician, and a cruel ruler. During his reign, Azcapotzalco was the most important city in the Valley and imposed a hegemony in the center of Mexico such as it had not known since the Toltec centuries. The

145

Tepanec confederation fell apart in the hands of Tezozómoc's descendents.

9. Huitzilihuitl was the son of Acamapichtli and the father of Chimalpopoca. He married a daughter of Tezozómoc, the king of Azcapotzalco.

10. Moreno describes the Alliance as a simple war pact for the purposes of offense and defense. This pact included the right of partition of conquered lands and tributes imposed on the defeated nations. In the event of an attack on any of the three allied nations, the other two were obliged to come to its aid (Moreno, 1962). Tlacopán was always a junior partner.

11. Padden suggests that the Flower Wars originated during the reign of Moctezuma I at the initiative of Tlacáelel (Padden, 1970).

12. Although the Aztecs of Tenochtitlán used a domestic problem as a pretext for its war with Tlatelolco, the real reason may have been a desire to possess the prosperous rival market, the most important commercial center in the central Valley of Mexico.

13. It is possible that by the time the Spaniards arrived the Aztec state might already have been reaching the limits permitted by its political and administrative organization and the technological level of its culture. They were restrained to the north by warrior peoples whose level of life and production did not make them a tempting conquest. The only possible expansion was southward, across the Isthmus of Tehuantepec, toward the prosperous Guatemala highlands and the rich coasts and tropical forests abounding in cacao, quetzal feathers and other articles highly prized among the Aztecs.

14. In practice, sons succeeded fathers on the throne of Texcoco for two hundred years. The Chichimec dynasty of Texcoco began with Xolotl, the great chief who invaded the central plateau of Mexico in the first half of the thirteenth century when the power of Tula and the Toltecs had crumbled. Quinatzin, who governed from 1318 to 1377, was the great-grandson of Xolotl. Quinatzin began to build the city of Texcoco around 1327. He was succeeded by his son, Techolatlalltzin, who reigned between 1377 and 1408 and was in turn succeeded by his son, Ixtlilxochitl, who ruled from 1409 to 1418. Between 1418 and 1433, the throne of Texcoco was in the power of Tezozómoc, king of Azcapotzalco, and of Maxtla, his son and successor, but in 1433 it was recovered by Nezahualcóyotl, son of Ixtlilxochitl, who then reigned from 1433 to 1472. His son, Nezahualpilli, succeeded him and ruled from 1472 to 1516. After this date, the power of Tenochtitlán and the Aztec lords was great enough to impose a government of their choosing on Texcoco. Moctezuma II installed his nephew

Cacama, but had him imprisoned in 1519 at Cortés' orders when he became a leader of the resistance, and replaced him with Coanacoch.

15. The Cihuacóatl of Ahuízotl was Tlacaélel's son. (Van Zantwijk, 1963). Tlacaélel died in 1496 during Ahuízotl's reign (Padden, 1970).

16. During the last years of Moctezuma's II reign, his nephew Cacama was king of Texcoco, another nephew was king of Coyoacán, one of his brothers was king of Ixtapalapa and one of his relatives was king of Toluca.

17. While Soustelle mentions four great military dignitaries who were the principal councillors of the emperor (Soustelle, 1955), Krickeberg appears to establish a difference between the two officials of high rank, who were generally near-relations of the king and his presumed heirs, and the two high dignitaries of equal rank belonging to the numerous group of Aztec nobles (Krickeberg, 1961).

18. The *calmecac* was really a combination of monastery and preparatory school in which religious education predominated. Young men remained in the *calmecac* about ten years.

19. The *calpulli* was the basis of the Aztec socio-economic system. It originated from the collectively organized consanguineous group around a totem animal. When the Aztecs settled in Tenochtitlán and Tlatelolco, the *calpulli* identified itself with its ward. On a local level, it still kept a good part of its former socioeconomic structure, although it began to lose its influence in civil and military decision making, as we have seen. The structure and function of the *calpulli* are the subject of periodic debates.

20. Moreno tells us that the real estate of the *calpulli* could be characterized as communal property, the hereditary right of a family, a right limited exclusively to those families belonging to the *calpulli* since time immemorial. The hereditary right of succession to the lands of the *calpulli* was dependent on the obligation to cultivate the lands. Whoever failed in this obligation for two consecutive years was dispossessed of his parcel (Moreno, 1962).

21. On certain occasions military service was compulsory. Krickeberg tells us that this measure was put into practice during the battles with the Spaniards (Krickeberg, 1961).

22. *Pochteca* means coming from Pochtlán. One of the Aztec *calpulli* that settled in Tlatelolco received this name (Krickeberg, 1961). Commercially, Tlatelolco was always more important than Tenochtitlán.

147

23. Krickeberg states that the Aztec merchants were also bankers and money lenders. I have not explored this aspect of Aztec economy, but I think it is worth while to study in detail the possible relationship between the rise of the *pochteca* and their connection with the urbanistic process.

24. The god of the merchants was called Yacatecutli. The fifteenth month, or *Panquetzaliztli,* was dedicated in his honor.

25. When a *pochteca* died in one of these missions he was honored as a warrior (Krickeberg, 1961).

26. Cultivation in *chinampas* permits permanently high yields and several harvests per year, but it is only feasible in marshes or shallow, fresh-water lakes (Armillas and West, 1950). To achieve greater efficiency, the *chinampas,* like the irrigated lots, tend to be given regular shapes as intensity of cultivation increases. I think this is one of the possible explanations for the regular outline of the *chinampas* adopted by the Aztec cities bordering the lake. The regular scheme allowed optimum utilization of water and a more efficient irrigation and transportation system. *Chinampas* are large platforms heaped with mud and anchored to the shore or the lake bottom by the roots of trees. The mud is rich, and crops were usually planted from shoots to save time. For a description of the system of construction of a *chinampa* see Moriarty, 1968; Armillas and West, 1950; and Wolf, 1959.

27. Almost every ward or *calpulli* had a school, or *telpochcalli,* generally located in connection with the temple. Each youth received a varied education, which included religion, ethics, history, music, and essentially the art of war. Sons learned the trades of their fathers who served as their teachers (Peterson, 1961). Education was compulsory for all children (Portilla, 1963).

TENOCHTITLÁN

"The life of a city is concentrated in three places; in every city the same. One is the house of the gods, another the market and the third is the emperor's palace."

ALEONSO REYES
(VISIÓN DE ANAHUAC)

□ 5

THE THIRTEENTH, FOURTEENTH AND FIFTEENTH CENTURIES witnessed a period of intense urbanization in the central Valley of Mexico that reached its peak by the year 1500.[1] During these three centuries, some of the ancient urban centers which had their origins in the Formative and Classic Periods, such as Azcapotzalco and Coatlínchan, flowered. As a consequence of the formation of new states, new cities appeared. Among these, Tenochtitlán, Tlatelolco, and Texcoco were the most important.

Other important cities in the Valley of Mexico were Tenayuca, to the northwest of Tenochtitlán, the first capital of Xólotl, chief of the Chichimecs, probably established at the end of the twelfth or beginning of the thirteenth century; Coyoacán, to the south, a Tepanec city and one of the first conquests made by the Aztecs during the reign of Itzcóatl; Tlacopán (today's Tacuba), to the west, the junior member of the Triple Alliance; Culhuacán, to the south, the residence of one of the Toltec groups after the fall of Tula who became the symbol of Toltec culture; Xico, to the southeast, and Chapultepec, to the west, both Toltec centers; Xaltocán, Cuauhtitlán and Xoloc, to the north; and Huexotla and Chimalhuacán, to the east.

Tenochtitlán was unique among Post-Classic American cities for various reasons. Probably no other city in South America or Mesoamerica during these centuries possessed such a huge population or covered such an extensive area, and, as we shall see, no pre-Hispanic city of this continent, with the possible exception of Teotihuacán at its apogee, acquired such definitely urban characteristics and functions as the Aztec capital.

When the kingdom of Moctezuma II was at its height, around 1510, Tenochtitlán was one of the most populated cities in the world. The most

151

important centers in Europe during the fifteenth century were Paris, Florence, Milan, Venice, and certain commercial cities of the Hanseatic League. In all of them, as in lesser cities, the lingering ravages of the Great Plague of 1348, and its successors in 1365, 1390, and 1462, resulted in shrinking markets and substantial modifications in population distribution, not only in Europe, but in other parts of the world commercially linked with these European centers. Because of high urban density, the plagues' effects were felt more intensely in the cities than in the countryside. Florence lost almost half its 135,000 inhabitants in a short period of time, and, despite cultural and commercial preeminence, it took centuries for the population to reach its former level. In 1470, Florence numbered only 70,000 persons. Milan, the city which Leonardo tried to decentralize in an attempt to minimize the plagues' consequences, had fewer houses in the year 1500 than were found by a traveler at the end of the thirteenth century.[2] All of Italy was hit by major plagues in these years, as well as by lesser ones in between. The effect on the commercial cities in the central and northern sections of the peninsula was such that, at the time of America's discovery, these cities lacked the industrial and commercial force they had enjoyed during the thirteenth and the first half of the fourteenth centuries.

At the beginning of the sixteenth century, Venice's splendor had already faded, and by the year 1510, scarcely 50,000 people lived in Rome. The period of the popes, who were builders and patrons of the arts and who made the Vatican and its city the cultural and artistic nucleus of Italian baroque, had only recently begun.

By the fifteenth century, 100,000 inhabitants were left in Constantinople (Hackett, 1950). It was only after the sixteenth century, as a consequence of the establishment of London, Paris, and Lisbon as capitals of their respective monarchies, that these cities began to grow—a vast difference from urbanization in fifteenth century Spain, in the splendorous years of Al-Andalus, when Córdoba counted 600 mosques and 900 baths for the inhabitants of its 200,000 houses.

The astonishment of Cortés' men was understandable when, from the mountain peaks surrounding Mexico's Central Valley, they looked down upon colored and white pyramids rising from the middle of a tranquil lagoon, the ceremonial center of a city of a dimension unknown to them.

The majority of these men had probably never seen cities other than the reduced towns of Castille and Extremadura, their Medieval characteristics preserved well into the sixteenth century. Nor had they ever, in all probability, walked through streets other than the narrow, crowded alleys of Andalusia's Islamic cities. Their contact with regularly laid out towns was limited to nights spent in military encampments, such as Santa Fe, or in some small and orderly frontier town. Even their initial contact with America's Indians had shown them nothing but modest villages of huts built of branches and logs.

Although we must accept the Spaniards' figures and descriptions with some scepticism and expect errors to be unavoidable due to the difficulty of accurate appraisal combined with the forgivably human desire to exaggerate the value and importance of what they had seen, Tenochtitlán and its neighbor and rival, Texcoco, must have provided an unequaled spectacle. In the middle of a fertile valley, shadowed by dark groves of cedar and oak, the Spaniards saw white villages scattered along the winding shore of a vast lake, with Texcoco standing out among them, and Tenochtitlán spread out on an island in the lake itself.

THE POPULATION OF TENOCHTITLÁN

It is not easy to determine the population of Tenochtitlán. We have the calculations of the first conquistadors and chroniclers, favored with direct observation of the city before its destruction, but without commenting on the chroniclers' possible reasons for exaggeration, I know from my own experience how hard it is to estimate with a glance the population of any large city. The estimation becomes still harder when the city's inhabitants, like those of Tenochtitlán, are accustomed to living away from home a good part of the time, traveling from one market to another, roaming through the plazas, or simply passing back and forth through the gates of the city.

Many modern authors have offered their calculations, based on often arbitrary interpretation of the chroniclers' writings and approximations of the composition of an Indian family group at the time of the Conquest. Recent research based on archival sources dating from the Colonial Period have served to bring together information not used before and to offer a more real and serious picture of the population of Tenochtitlán (Callnek, 1968, 1969).

First of all, I feel I must emphasize again that Tenochtitlán was a large city for its time, both in population and area. Let us look at some commentaries. Cortés writes briefly in the second of his *Cartas de Relación* to Charles I of Spain: "The city is as large as Seville and Córdoba"

(Cortés, 1961). Rather than making a direct comparison with these Spanish cities, I think the conquistador, who had never left Spain until his voyage to the West Indies in 1504, meant to say that he believed the city was unrivaled among those with which he was familiar. Then, referring to Tlatelolco's market place which occupied a good part of that city, he adds, ". . . every day there are over sixty thousand souls buying and selling; here they have every kind of merchandise to be found anywhere in the world . . ." The chronicler of Mexico's conquest, Bernal Díaz del Castillo, marveled at the crowds in the market: ". . . some buying and others selling, so that the murmur and buzzing of voices and words could be heard a league away. We have among us soldiers who have been in many parts of the world, in Constantinople and in all of Italy and Rome, and they say that never have they seen a plaza so well laid out and of such good order and size filled with so many people . . ." (Díaz del Castillo, 1955). Once again we find a questionable comparison with those cities which the chronicler and his companions had admired, but which, at the beginning of the sixteenth century, no longer enjoyed their former splendor. At the time of the Conquest, most of them were undoubtedly inferior in population and size to Tenochtitlán.

Attendance at a market, however, whether in the years of the Conquest or today, is not the soundest basis on which to calculate an Indian city's population. At best it can only suggest the commercial importance of a particular center and its radius of influence. It was, and still is, the custom among people in small cities and villages to travel long distances to gather at certain markets on fixed days. Tlatelolco's market, the most famous in Mexico at the time, had been incorporated within Tenochtitlán's limits by the end of the fifteenth century and must have attracted many people from other areas. Motolinia, who arrived in Mexico less than five years after Cortés, had similar impressions: ". . . and I still state and affirm that I doubt if there is anything as opulent as Tenochtitlán; and so full of people . . ." (Motolinia, 1941).

Estimates of Tenochtitlán's population vary, but most of them are based on the premise that the city contained 60,000 houses or residences, in other words, some 300,000 inhabitants. For the most part, ancient and modern authors agree on this figure. Among the former, we have Pedro Mártir, López de Gomara, and Herrera. One modern author, Prescott, limits himself to saying that no contemporary writer estimates the population at less than 60,000 houses, which by ordinary accounting rules would make 300,000 people. He later adds, perhaps influenced by Herrera's *Historia,* that if a dwelling frequently contained several families, as has been suggested, the number would be considerably greater. Vaillant, who based his ideas mainly on the narratives of the *Conquistador Anónimo*, tells us that Tenochtitlán reportedly had 60,000 hearths or households (Vaillant, 1955). When the German scientist, Humboldt, visited Mexico at the beginning of the nineteenth century, he calculated that the population of Tenochtitlán must have been three times the population of Mexico City, which at that time had 137,000 inhabitants. According to his figuring, the Aztec capital would have had 411,000 citizens.

Although the figures of 60,000 houses and 300,000 inhabitants may be widely accepted, there are a number of dissenters. Torquemada, in his *Monarquía Indiana* writes of 120,000 houses each having three to ten residents. If we consider the term "resident" to mean the head of a household, as it was interpreted at that time, rather than taking each resident as a separate inhabitant, we come up with a much larger total. A recent calculation is presented by Soustelle who, while acknowledging his procedure to be arbitrary, has fixed the population of Tenochtitlán-Tlatelolco at 80,000 to 100,000 households, each containing seven persons. The French author concludes: "Let us say that this population was certainly greater than 500,000 persons and probably less than 1,000,000" (Soustelle, 1950).

I always had reservations about the population figure of 300,000 for Tenochtitlán-Tlatelco, although I realize how difficult it must have been for the conquistadors and chroniclers to estimate the city and its inhabitants accurately. I do, however, want to call attention to one point. Until recently it was assumed that the twin cities, Tenochtitlán-Tlatelolco, were built on neighboring islands the combined surface of which were estimated at seven and one-half square kilometers, or some 750 hectares (Toussaint, Gómez de Orozco and Fernández, 1938). These authors based their estimate on the previous reconstructions of Orozco y Berra (Plate No. 25, page 121) and of Batres and Alcocer. According to a post-Cortesian plan of the area drawn on maguey paper by Fernández himself, a broad section of the city bordering Tlatelolco's market was built on land retrieved from the lake by the system of man-made islands called *chinampas*. By adding on to these islands, the Aztecs gradually joined and expanded the rocky, once separated, islands where Tenochtitlán and Tlatelolco had been established in the years 1325 and 1327 respectively. (Plate No. 24, page 120).

Taking the area shown on the maguey paper map as an average example of population density, we would reach the following conclusions. The plan represents a surface of approximately 242,000 square meters, or some 24 hectares, in which up to 400 plots are located with their respective dwellings (Toussaint, Gómez de Orozco and Fernández, 1938). Calculating, as has been done in previous surveys, that each Indian family consisted of five members, we would have 2,000 persons occupying an area of 24 hectares, or in other words, a density of 83.3 inhabitants per hectare, 120 square meters per person or 600 square meters per family. And supposing, though evidently this was not the case, that this density of 83.3 inhabitants per hectare held true throughout the entire city, we would then end up with a figure of 62,475 citizens living in the 750 hectares occupied by the twin cities Tenochtitlán-Tlatelolco at the time of Moctezuma II. This gives us a population of slightly more than one-fifth of that generally accepted by Spanish chroniclers and modern writers.

To try to determine what portion of the city was built on *chinampas*, I will have to take a circuitous route.

The map attributed to Cortés (Plate No. 22, page 118) is the oldest piece of cartography we have of Tenochtitlán, but as it lacks graphic scale and was drawn with total disregard for visual scale, we find a distorted representation of the city which is not easy to interpret. One possible reason for this is that the map may have been drawn during Cortés' first stay in the Aztec capital which lasted from his entry into the city in November of 1519 up to the moment of his precipitous departure for the coast to confront the forces of Pánfilo Narváez in May, 1520 (Toussaint, Gómez de Orozco and Fernández, 1938). If this was the case, I think we are dealing with a map meant for purposes of illustration in the reports Cortés sent his king. It is not unlikely that he might have wanted to emphasize the magnificent and astounding ceremonial center of Tenochtitlán, the neighboring palaces and the religious and commercial center of Tlatelolco, rather than the modest adobe houses and rustic huts built on reclaimed land which would have accounted for the majority of the city's buildings. It was common cartographic practice during the sixteenth century to draw attention to the more important features of a city plan in this manner.

Studying this map closely, I was surprised by the wealth of detail lavished on those urban elements having a military significance. Not only do we see Fort Xoloc on the south causeway, the canoe port to the east of the city, and the neighboring cities around the lake's edge, but we have detailed plotting of canals and the cuts which sectioned off the causeways with their footbridges, the aqueduct coming in from Chapultepec, and a group of minor constructions difficult to interpret. All these features may have had strategic importance to Cortés, or perhaps he had already envisioned the difficulties which might arise from the capture and defense of Tenochtitlán, should it ever come to that. And indeed, this was exactly what did happen in the final climactic battle between the Spaniards and the Aztecs.

When Cortés left for the coast, he had no reason to imagine the events which were to erupt a few days after his departure, thanks to the cruel and thoroughly undiplomatic attitude of Alvarado, whom the conquistador had entrusted with city affairs until his return. Between June 30, 1520, when the Spaniards were driven out of Tenochtitlán, and August 13, 1521, when, following a seventy-five day siege, the Aztec resistance was overcome and the city passed definitively into Spanish hands, Cortés' sole objective had been to conquer the city. The map may well have been made in the months that passed between abandonment of the center and the 30th of October, 1520, when Cortés finished his second report which was not dispatched until March 5, 1521 due to bad weather and three successive shipwrecks (Cortés, 1961).

In any event, the map certainly was sent to Spain before May 15, 1522, since Cortés refers to it in his third report, written on that date while he was living in Coyoacán.[3] If this map was drawn during the thirteen and one-half months of the war between the Aztecs and the Spaniards, we are seeing a reconstruction based on the recollections of the Conquistador and his men and on data supplied by his collaborators and Indian spies.

Whether it was intended as a military map or merely an illustrative plan, the most important elements of the city are made to stand out. We see clearly the Great Teocalli or ceremonial center of Tenochtitlán with its plaza and neighboring palaces, as well as the Teocalli and structures forming the center of Tlatelolco. Together, these occupied a surface on the map equivalent to three-fifths of the total area of the city, or some 450 hectares of the 750 estimated for Tenochtitlán-Tlatelolco. In reality, the Great Teocalli took up a square scarcely more than 400 meters in area, or 17.6 hectares.

In the center of Tenochtitlán, around the Great Teocalli, was a district composed of large palaces owned by nobles and lords and housing sizeable retinues of servants. These palaces, generally rectangular in form, were built on solid ground, with spacious patios and gardens. The palace of Axayácatl, who reigned between 1469 and 1481, covered approximately 14,000 square meters; the residence of the Cihuacóatl, second to the king in the hierarchy, took up some 8,500 square meters and the lands where Moctezuma II built his palace, or "New Houses," covered an area almost three times as great.

A number of priests, novices and their servants resided inside the precinct of the Great Teocalli.[4] The majority lived in the *calmecac,* or school, and in the temples where they served the various deities. It is difficult to determine with any precision the number of nobles, priests, warriors, novices, and servants who might have lived more or less permanently in this central sector of the city. In spite of the land occupied by temples, as well as that left vacant, the sector must certainly have been thickly inhabited since the palaces were planned to house a large number of permanent residents and guests.[5] There was undoubtedly a similar concentration around the Teocalli of Tlatelolco, although smaller in size and population.

From descriptions of their density, plan, construction, and functions and from some archeological evidence, we can assume that these city centers were the exclusively urban districts of the Aztec capital, and that they were inhabited by the ruling class. They may have extended farther than is shown on the map, especially along the causeways leading in to the center, but I doubt that they would have occupied an area much larger than that of the original islands on which the twin cities had been established. "A little islet, almost a swamp, with some rocks standing out from it, surrounded by reeds, in Lake Texcoco," writes one author, referring to the site where the Aztecs built their capital (Bernal, 1959b).

According to studies, the waters surrounding the original island of Tenochtitlán, what we could call solid ground, came up to the present-day Calle de la Corregidora (the former Calle de la Acequia) which bounds today's Palacio Nacional on the south; on the west, to the Palacio de Minería; on the east, almost to the line of the Spanish drawing made in 1521; and in the north, to the district of Santa Catarina Mártir (Galindo y Villa, 1955). In other words, there were approximately 130 hectares of solid ground. The remainder of the 750 hectares, with the exception of some 60 hectares of solid ground belonging to the island of Tlatelolco, were made up of the *chinampas* constructed in the lake.[6] Some of these were probably relatively recent suburbs of fishermen and gardeners whose numbers I have already mentioned. Other *chinampas,* however, built earlier and sufficiently established as to be practically the same as solid ground, probably supported wards of artisans, merchants, and lower ranking administrators in the hierarchy. These would have been districts of moderate social standing which were becoming progressively urbanized by Aztec standards. Unfortunately, I can add no information about the general density of these neighborhoods where "middle class" Aztec society lived, but I assume that the districts built on solid ground inhabited by the ruling class and the districts of older *chinampas* which surrounded them, had a higher density than the districts of *chinampas* around the periphery.

Recent research, only partially published, modify different aspects of the picture I have presented and introduce new light about the urban characteristics of Tenochtitlán. The reasoning, however, is substantially the same. The maguey plan would not represent the area of Tlatelolco attributed by Toussaint, Fernández and Gómez de Orozco, but part of Tenochtitlán or perhaps an area on the main land.[7] Independent of its location, the maguey plan is important because it provides an illustration of the characteristics of a *chinampa* area such as its regular layout, the symmetrical shape of each site, the alternating pattern of streets and canals, and the location of each house in the lot. (Callnek, 1969) These characteristics appeared in a *chinampa* area documented by Callnek south of the Tlacopán or east-west causeway. The maguey plan illustrates a *chinampa* area where most lots were of almost similar size. This was not the case, as the cultivated area on each lot varied between a maximum of 850 square meters and a minimum of 100 square meters with cultivated sites between 100 and 400 square meters representing the majority (Callnek, 1969).

Most *chinampa* lots in districts considered as urban or suburban had two clearly defined areas: the *chinampa* itself or cultivated land and a section where the house was built. The proportions between these two areas in each lot are not clear and surely present a great variety of possibilities. I assume that in the *chinampa* lots located nearer the center of the city the proportion of cultivated land was lower than in suburban lots. An average of some 500 square meters per *chinampa* lot would represent twenty families or one hundred persons per hectare in the *chinampa* areas; increasing the average lot to 600 square meters the density declines to 16.6 families or eighty-three persons per hectare.[8] However, *chinampa* areas were not entirely built of *chinampa* lots as streets and canals were essential for transportation and there may also have been areas dedicated to undefined uses. These uses could have required at least 10 per cent of the total surface thereby reducing the density in a similar percentage. This would yield densities of 90 or 74.3 persons per hectare. Furthermore, it has been indicated that the total urban area of Tenochtitlán-Tlatelolco was not less than 1,200 hectares (Callnek, 1968) and possibly even 1,500 hectares and that 40 per cent of this surface, or between 480 and 600 hectares, were solid ground, the rest being formed by *chinampas.*[9] Taking the lower estimate, we would find a city of 480 hectares built on solid ground and 720 hectares of *chinampas.* The population, then, could have reached 67,800 or to 53,784 persons, depending on which density we accept, in the *chinampa* districts and an additional number of inhabitants living in the districts built on solid ground. We have little or no evidence on which to estimate the densities in the latter districts. Most of the central districts of Tenochtitlán and Tlatelolco were built with one story houses and palaces. Surfaces dedicated to public use such as squares, temples, institutional buildings, etc., were unusually large for that epoch. Causeways, streets and canals also represented a substantial percentage of urban land use in the central districts. All together they could have occupied around thirty per cent of these districts or 144 hectares, leaving 336 hectares for housing. Even accepting a net residential density of 300 hectares, like the one I suggested for Tlamimilolpa, the artisan neighborhood in Teotihuacán, we would have a population of 100,800 persons living in the central *barrios,* or districts of Tenochtitlán-Tlatelolco and a total population of 165,600 or 154,584 inhabitants depending on the density of the *chinampa* areas. Such a residential density was quite high by pre-Columbian standards although Tenochtitlán-Tlatelolco, because of their location on two major islands and a number of smaller ones, must have faced unusual problems in physical expansion and their planners undoubtedly considered densification in the *barrios* built on solid ground as a necessary practice.

To return to the population figure of 62,475 previously calculated; I am inclined to think it too low, since the chroniclers' descriptions and the points I have raised indicate that a considerable percentage of Tenochtitlán and Tlatelolco were truly urban and, therefore, more densely populated than the man-made land areas. Although the figure of 165,600 or 154,584 persons may be excessive it is not as extreme as that of the 300,000 persons generally accepted. Still, if we accept the death toll of

22 *Plan of Tenochtitlán attributed to Cortés. This frequently reproduced plan first appeared in the Atlas by Benedetto Bordone, edited in Venice in 1528. Bordone's copy is a simplification of the one attributed to Cortés. (Credit:* Libro di Benedetto Bordone nel quale si ragiona de tutta l'isole del mondo con li loro nomi antichi y moderni, *Venice, 1528.)*

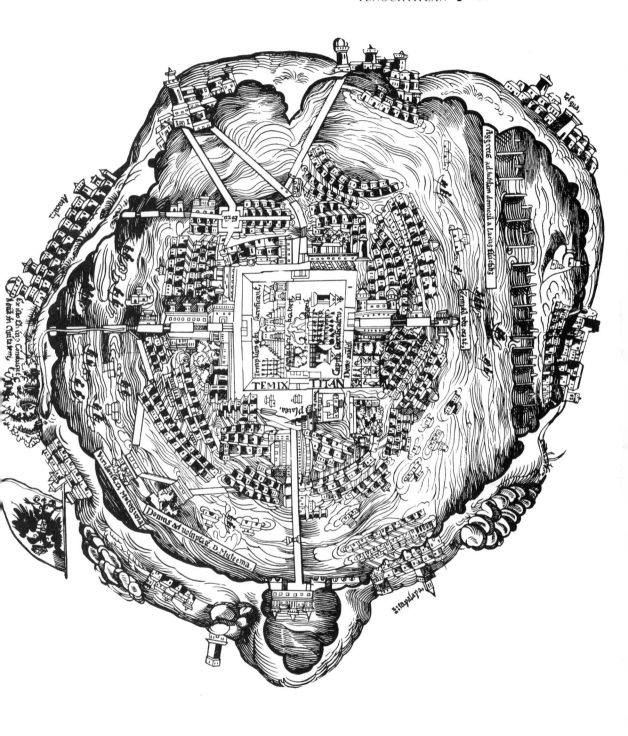

150,000 Indians from the Spaniards' siege of Tenochtitlán, as Clavijero states in approximate agreement with the Mexican historian Nicolás de León,[10] we can logically presume that a good part of the dead belonged to groups from allied or subjugated cities who came to help defend the capital.

MAPS OF TENOCHTITLÁN

The Cortés map is fundamental to knowledge of the general outlines of the city (Plate No. 22). Besides our doubts about the date it was actually drawn, we cannot even be certain of its author. It is usually agreed, however, that if it was not drawn by Cortés himself, it was made by one of his sea pilots or "surveyors," or by some conquistador who knew how to draw (Toussaint, Gómez de Orozco and Fernández, 1938). If the map was really drawn after June of 1520 in order to plot strategy for the siege, we could not exclude from its possible authors the geometrician Alonso García Bravo who had arrived on the Mexican coast a few months earlier with Pánfilo de Narváez and whom Cortés had commissioned to lay out plans for the Colonial city.

This map is the oldest we have of Tenochtitlán and the most ancient known plan of an American city.[12] It was first published in Nuremberg in 1524 to illustrate the Latin edition of Cortés' second and third reports to the king. An Italian edition of these letters was printed in the same year and successive Spanish editions soon after, all of which omitted the map (Toussaint, Gómez de Orozco and Fernández, 1938). Cortés' second report was published separately in Seville at the end of 1522, but in this, too, the map was left out. Since then, it has been reproduced frequently, if not always accurately.

The map shows the city of Tenochtitlán as almost circular, with the Great Teocalli, or Templo Mayor, in its center. The causeways uniting the city with the mainland stand out clearly. The author has rounded out Lake Texcoco, placing Tenochtitlán in its center, equidistant from the other cities and towns along the shore. However, Tenochtitlán was not, in actuality, situated in the middle of the lake, but in a gulflike extension at its southwest corner. This extension stretched towards the south where it joined the waters of Lake Texcoco, Lake Xochimilco, and Lake Chalco (Plate No. 23).

Tenochtitlán and Tlatelolco were built on islands relatively close to the shore to which they were connected by causeways to the north, west, and

23 *Central Valley of Mexico's lacustrine system with its surrounding cities. Tenochtitlán was built on a small island not far from the western shore of Lake Texcoco, which allowed the Aztec capital to be joined to solid ground by three causeways. (Credit: Peterson, Frederick:* Ancient Mexico, *George Allen and Unwin, Ltd., London, 1959.)*

south. Cortés comments that "This great city of Temixtitán is founded in a lagoon, and from Dry Land to the body of that city, by whatever way you may choose to enter, is two leagues" (Cortés, 1961). This was a miscalculation on Cortés' part since from the west and north the mainland was about three and four kilometers away, while it was, in fact, a scant two leagues, or almost nine kilometers, by the southern causeway. As Cortés entered the city by the southern causeway from Ixtapalapa, his mistake is understandable.

The distance to the eastern shore of the lake was much farther. Because of this, the Aztecs established a port for canoes, which permitted traffic of people and products to and from the cities, among them Texcoco, about twenty-four kilometers away in a straight line, and Chimalhuacán. These two cities are shown on the Cortés map. Starting from the east and moving clockwise, the other cities are: Ixtapalapa and Churubusco, next to Lake Xochimilco, and Coyoacán to the south; Tacubaya, the woods and spring of Chapultepec, and Tacuba to the west; Azcapotzalco and Tepeyac to the north[13] (Toussaint, Gómez de Orozco and Fernández, 1938).

Cortés, or the map's author, called the city Temixtitán, the name he used in his *Cartas de Relación* (Cortés, 1961). The chronicler Díaz del Castillo always refers to the "City of Mexico" (Díaz del Castillo, 1955), but in his *Historia Verdadero*, he, too, modifies and simplifies the spelling of cities, gods, persons, and everything with Indian names. This map formed a part of the many collections of plans and marine maps published in Europe from the sixteenth century on.

The first atlas to include a reproduction of the Cortés map was that of Benedetto Bordone, published in Venice in 1528, and entitled, *Libro di Benedetto Bordone. Nel quale si ragiona de tutta l'isole del mondo con li lor nomi antichi y moderni.* In reality, he used a simplified copy of the map.[14] Furthermore, through an engraving error, north is located at the left of the map and not at the right as it was in the original plan. Bordone's map adds nothing to our knowledge of the city at the time of the Conquest.

In the map of Tenochtitlán included in the third volume of the work, *Delle Navigationi et Viaggi* by Giovanni Battista Ramusio,[15] published in Venice in 1556 a year after his death, the erroneous angle of Bordone's map was not corrected. Geographically, Ramusio's map is more like Bordone's version, from which it was probably copied, than the original assumed to be by Cortés. The Cortés map certainly must have been consulted, however, as its influence is seen in the drawing of the zoological garden, or "House of the Animals," which formed part of Moctezuma's palace and which appears in Bordone's map as a garden placed slightly to the south of its actual location. Ramusio's map differed from those made previously in that it provided an accurate representation of the lake system. Under the name Lago Dulce, he introduced Lake Zumpango and Lake Xaltocán and their islets north of Lake Texcoco into the cartography of the central basin of the Valley of Mexico. But once again, the city was placed in the middle of Lake Texcoco and covered almost its entire surface.

Many variants of these three maps—Bordone's, Ramusio's and the one Cortés is reputed to have made—have subsequently appeared. They provide the only graphic evidence we have today of the Aztec capital as it was seen by the Spaniards for the first time, although, beginning with the color plan which formed part of the *Islario General* of Alonso de Santa Cruz in the middle of the sixteenth century, extensive mapping of the city of Mexico took place during the Colonial period (Carrera Stampa, 1949; Toussaint, Gómez de Orozco and Fernández, 1938).

No maps of Tenochtitlán drawn by Indian map makers have survived to our day. There is reason to believe they existed, however, and that they probably served as a guide to the city's development during its expansion.

The next most important map for an urban study of the Aztec capital is the one drawn on maguey paper now in the National Museum of Mexico (Plate No. 24). It is a partial plan, showing a district of *chinampas* which for many years was believed to be located north of the city, a few hundred meters east of the center of Tlatelolco. Even if the location on the plan was erroneous the plan itself retains its usefulness for the reasons explained before.[16] This map was apparently drawn after the Conquest, possibly between the years 1557 and 1563, during the government of Don Cristóbal de Guzmán whose person is represented in the drawing (Toussaint, Gómez de Orozco and Fernández, 1938). Another author suggests that the map may have been started a generation before and finished during these years, as he found variations in the drawing which led him to suspect the intervention of a second hand[17] (Lenz, 1949).

The maguey paper map is of immense value, since it helps us to rebuild the urban structure of an important sector of Tenochtitlán and study the *chinampas* which constituted the most extensive part of the city. Each lot is shown represented by a cultivated section and a figure to symbolize a house. The lots are regular, almost square in shape, with canals and footpaths on alternate sides crossing each other at right angles. The only ir-

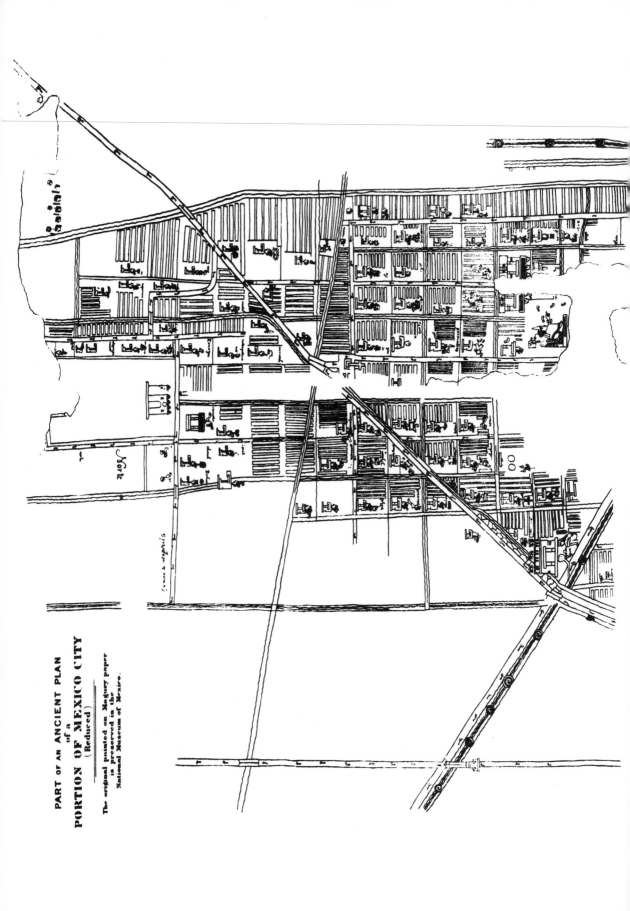

PART OF AN ANCIENT PLAN
of a
PORTION OF MEXICO CITY
(Reduced)

The original painted on Maguey paper
is preserved in the
National Museum of Mexico.

24 *Plan of Tenochtitlán on maguey paper. The original is in the National Museum of Mexico. Reproduced here is a sector of Tenochtitlán to the north of the Great Teocalli and southeast of the market of Tlatelolco. We see a* chinampa *district. Observe how the canals, indicated by three parallel lines, alternate with the streets, represented by footprints between a double line. The size and shape of each lot can also be distinguished. (Credit: Maudsley, Alfred: "The Valley of Mexico," Geographical Journal, Vol. XLVIII, July, 1916.)*

regular lots are those cut by causeways and canals which diagonally cross the sector appearing in the map. Tenochtitlán was constantly being enlarged by the addition of these *chinampas.*

I believe we can take the sector represented in the plan as an example of the prevailing system of land subdivision used by the Aztecs, their neighbors in the lake shore cities, and possibly by those of their predecessors in similar geographical circumstances. There are two reasons for my theory that the other Indian cities built along the lake may have had a systematic arrangement similar to that of Tenochtitlán. First, constructing *chinampas* was expensive, so they were destined to produce fresh vegetables or flowers with as high a yield as possible; sharp angles were eliminated as unproductive.[18] Secondly, thousands of canoes of all sizes, carrying people and produce, came to market every day from the smaller towns and *chinampas* around the principal cities. The chronicler Herrara says, "There are in Mexico, only to supply the City and bring and take people, almost fifty thousand (canoes)" (Herrera, 1945). Although Herrera's estimate seems grossly exaggerated, we can imagine the traffic problems which would have occurred if this massive circulation of porters and canoes were not regulated by a system of straight, orderly pathways and canals.

We have some reconstructions of the general outline of Tenochtitlán. One is the incomplete map that Orozco y Berra made at the end of the last century showing the city as it must have been during the reign of Moctezuma II[19] (Plate No. 25). According to this reconstruction, after the islands of Tenochtitlán and Tlatelolco were united by filling in the canal which had separated them, they and their respective *chinampa* districts formed a single, trapezoidal island of irregular outline. This new island was wider at the south end, where it measured some 3,600 meters, than at the north, where it was only 2,100 meters. It was even narrower in the center. Its main axis was north-south and may have been as much as 4,200 meters long; the east-west axis was probably about 3,750 meters, and the perimeter of the island would not have exceeded fourteen kilometers, comprising the generally accepted area of 750 hectares. Small islands toward the west served to support the two causeways from Tacuba and its branch to Chapultepec. The water immediately surrounding Tenochtitlán was

25 *Mexico City, prior to 1519. Plan of Tenochtitlán, as it was in the time of Moctezuma, after a restoration by Orozco y Berra. The market (24) and the temple (23) of Tlatelolco were originally separated by a natural canal from the Great Teocalli or Templo Mayor (5) of Tenochtitlán. The plan suggests how Tenochtitlán must have been a few years after the arrival of Cortés. (Credit: Library of Congress, Washington, D.C.)*

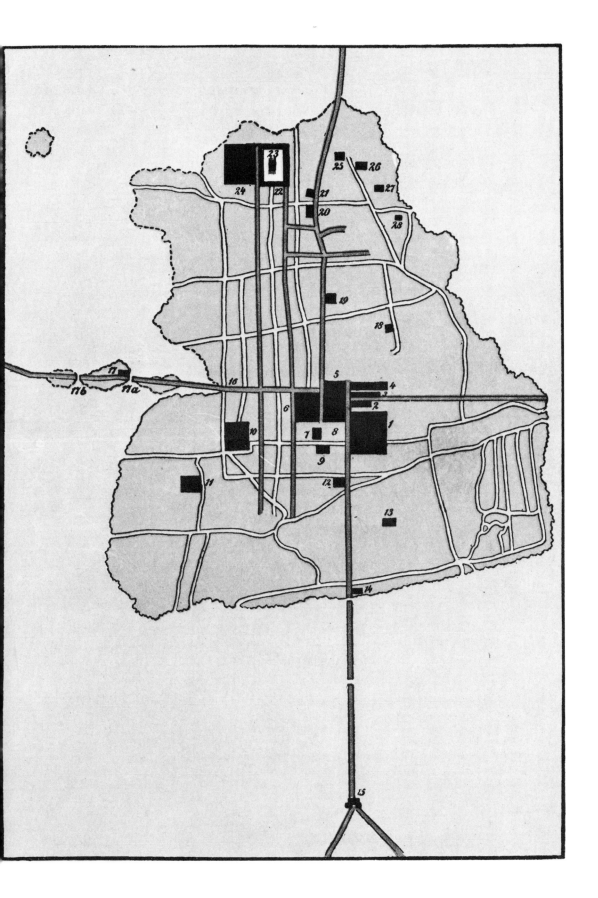

shallow, and if the Conquest had not interfered, the city might have ultimately been joined to the mainland to the west by the *chinampas*.

In a recent reconstruction by Callnek "the boundaries of the city have been determined by compiling references to points said to have been located at the limits of continuous habitation. The eastern and southern boundaries are probably accurate; those to the north and west may require substantial future revision. The total area shown here is approximately twelve square kilometers, exclusive of (the island) Nonoalco, the limits of which cannot be accurately reconstructed" (Callnek, 1969). The general outline of Tenochtitlán-Tlatelolco, according to Callnek's reconstruction, was irregular but wider in the center, where it reached 3,500 meters, narrowing to the south and north. The main axis was north-south with a total length of about 5,000 meters[20] (Callnek, 1969).

THE ORIGIN OF THE CITY

The legend of Tenochtitlán's founding and the reasons for choosing its particular site are well known. The original location strongly dictated the general shape of the city, its plan and its stages of development.

Durán, an early Spanish writer tells us: "They (the Aztecs) came seeking and looking for a place which was suitable for building a seat; and going about in this manner from place to place among the reeds and grasses, they found a most beautiful spring, in which fountain they saw marvelous things greatly to be admired. This the wise men and priests had forecast to the people by order of Huitzilopochtli, their god" (Durán, 1939). The Aztecs had reached Chapultepec, but they had not yet finished their long wanderings.

One night, according to legend, Huitzilopochtli, the humming bird god of the Aztecs and of war, appeared in a dream to Cuauhtloquetzqui, a priest who, in accordance with tradition, guided his people's peregrinations. The God told the priest to lead his tribe to a place where a cactus plant was growing from the buried heart of Copil, a nephew of an Aztec deity. He added that on the cactus the priest would see an eagle. This place was to be called Tenochtitlán, and here the Aztecs should build "the city which will be queen and lady of all the others of the earth and where we will receive all other kings and lords and to which they will come as to one supreme among all the others" (Durán, 1939).

In the middle of the lagoon, on a small island, the Aztecs found their promised land. They built a simple shelter with sticks, mud and grasses to serve as Huitzilopochtli's sanctuary, and soon the first huts began to rise around it (Alcocer, 1935). The site had unquestionable advantages to compensate for its aridity and lack of good water.

In the fourteenth century, the central basin of Mexico was formed by five lakes which joined each other during Aztec times and far into the Colonial period. With its 23,000 hectares, Lake Texcoco was the most central and largest of the five, offering abundant fishing, hunting along its shore and encouraging cultivation on *chinampas* in the shallow waters along its banks and in other parts of the lake. The hospitable environment in the central Valley of Mexico attracted successive cultures over several thousand years, so that by the time the Aztecs arrived, they found a dense population already living in the cities and villages scattered along the shoreline.

We usually accept as fact that Tenochtitlán was founded in 1325 by the Aztecs who sought refuge on the islands in the lake after powerful neighboring tribes drove them from Chapultepec's woods and spring. The Aztecs were still few in number and, lacking allies, were powerless. A few years later, either in 1327 or 1337, another Aztec group founded Tlatelolco on a small adjacent island.

The beginnings were hard. In addition to precarious relations with other tribes, the Aztecs had to work unceasingly to obtain a minimum subsistence.[21] For a century they waited for their moment. Finally, during the reign of Itzcóatl (1428-1440), and subsequently under Moctezuma I (1440-1469), the Aztecs achieved preeminence in the Valley thanks to their alliance with the lords of Texcoco. From then on, Tenochtitlán grew and became rich as the power and prestige of its inhabitants increased. In a few years, they were sending military expeditions to Puebla, Veracruz and the neighboring states.

Moctezuma I strove to improve living conditions in the city. He ordered a double aqueduct built to connect the island with the spring in Chapultepec. "The Mexicans brought this water through two very thick conduits made of tightly packed Earth as strong as stone, using only one of the two conduits at a time. When one was dirty and slimy, the Water was run through the other, and in this way the Water ran clearer than crystal. The whole City drank from this spring, and they filled all the Reservoirs and Founts, which many of the principal Houses had, and certain wooden conduits through which the water ran to the irrigation ditches. Many Indians collected Water in their Canoes to sell to others; and this was their trade for which they paid a tax to their King" (Herrera, 1945). Moctezuma's kingdom existed at the same time as that of Nezahualcóyotl in Texcoco, and the two kings agreed to build a dike fifteen kilometers long between Atzacoalco and Ixtapalapa to protect the water near the capital from Lake Texcoco's highly saline waters.

The features of the city seen by the Spaniards had begun to take shape during the reign of Moctezuma I. The temple already occupied the symbolic center of Tenochtitlán, and here, too, began the two main streets which cut the city into four sectors. Construction of the immense pyramid which served as a base for the twin temples of Huitzilopochtli and Tlalòc was begun by Tizocicatzin, or simply Tizoc, who reigned between 1481 and 1486. The temple was consecrated by Ahuízotl, Tizoc's brother and successor, in 1487, the first year of his reign. The event was marked by impressive celebrations attended by all the heads of allied or subjugated tribes. In honor of Huitzilopochtli, there was a mass sacrifice of thousands of prisoners and slaves especially acquired for this purpose.

THE LAYOUT OF THE CITY

Seen against the tranquil surface of the lagoon, and backed by a distant circle of snowy mountain peaks shrouded in clouds through which rose Popocatépetl and its smaller neighbor, Iztaccíhuatl, the city at the beginning of the fifteenth century must have appeared as a level expanse, trees sprinkled along its canals and muddy banks extending in all directions.

A century later, Tenochtitlán, or at least its center, had changed radically (Plate No. 26). In the middle of what had once been the principal island, now the precinct of the Great Teocalli, rose the pyramidal mass of the Templo Mayor, thirty meters high and attracting all eyes. Beyond it, Tlatelolco's recently completed temple could be seen.[22] All over the city minor pyramids marked the centers of the twenty wards into which the Aztec capital was divided. The general impression was one of a city which had gradually acquired a workable, if incomplete, urban plan. From maps, archeological excavations in various sectors of the present day city, lucky finds unearthed during construction of modern public works, and the chronicles and histories of the sixteenth century, we can envision a city laid out in rather rudimentary form. But it was certainly a city where a general layout and a traffic system was emerging to satisfy the needs of a large population and a traffic consisting entirely of pedestrians and canoes.

The reports of the first Spaniards who came upon the city agree. Cortés, describing it in the second of his *Cartas de Relación* says, "Its streets, that is the principal ones, are very wide and very straight, and these and all the rest, are made half of earth and the other half of water, on which they travel in their canoes. All the streets have openings at intervals through which water passes from one side to another, and over all these openings, some being very wide, they have bridges of very wide and long beams, so well made and sturdy that ten horsemen side by side might pass" (Cortés, 1961).

The Conquistador Anónimo also remembers, "the beautiful and wide streets" characteristic of Tenochtitlán and of "all the other towns which we have said are on this lake, in that part having sweet water." Lack of any references to secondary streets does not alter my impression that the plan of the major part of the city was regular, or becoming increasingly regular, canals alternating with paths or roads of earth built on embankments. This would have been essential in order to make maximum use of land which was scarce and difficult to wrest from the lake. We must also remember that in a society in which the head of each family was responsible to his clan for the productivity of the parcel of land allotted him, the *chinampas* would have been subject to logical and equitable distribution.

Tenochtitlán's plan is not always precise, either in its larger layouts or in the details of the outlines of its better built districts. This was probably due more to a lack of adequate instruments for measuring, or disinterest in greater precision, than to a disregard for a scheme which would have offered the inhabitants maximum advantage of the scarce available land.

Architecture of the Indian civilizations of Mesoamerica generally lacked the precision of measurement seen in Egyptian architecture. In spite of outstanding mathematical and astronomical knowledge, the Indian civilizations could not overcome the absence of stable materials with which they could repeat certain measurements exactly. Axial compositions, however, were common in Mesoamerica, and Indian architects excelled in designing large structural groupings to be built on flat land. These gradually gave rise to building complexes of an urban character, laid out with unquestionable symmetry and precision. Even in those ceremonial centers constructed on the uneven terrain of Chiapas and the Petén, Maya architects employed quadrangles to set out groups of temples and principal buildings. Use of partial axes was common in these groups of structures as well as large axes of composition in relating the variety of structures forming a ceremonial center to each other. Tikal is a

26 *Diego Rivero's work in the National Palace of Mexico City. This idealized reconstruction of Tenochtitlán gives an approximate idea of the physical characteristics of the Aztec capital. It is interesting to note the relative importance of the pyramidal volumes of the temples over the*

city's other structures. The Great Teocalli stands in the center. To its right we see the large open space where Tenochtitlán's market was held. The large avenue leading up to the Teocalli is the causeway from Tlaco-pán or Tacuba. (Credit: I.N.A.H. photographic archives, Mexico.)

clear example of this principle as are Nakum, Yaxhá, Naranjo, and other less important ceremonial centers.

We can see the culmination of this type of design in Tulum where, on a site removed from their decaying ceremonial centers, the Maya adopted what I believe was their first deliberate urban plan.

All cultures dependent for subsistence and economic development, from their early evolution, on intensive cultivation of land requiring drainage and irrigation, have quickly learned the importance of a regular layout which permits maximum profit from this land. The first known urban planning on a large scale appeared in the Middle and Near East among the cultures that had developed in river valleys. Certainly in America, the logical evolution of various cultures as they adapted to environmental conditions elicited solutions similar to those evolved by the river cultures of India, the Indus and Mesopotamia thousands of years before.

Tenochtitlán was no exception. A spontaneous but ordered plan emerged in all the new districts that were continually being added to the city, and the Aztecs probably repartitioned and redistributed sectors in the peripheral areas which were periodically devastated by floods. This, I believe, explains the unceasing rearrangement of the original layout, which was probably more disorderly than the one the Spaniards saw. And this, too, I feel, was how the districts of Tenochtitlán were connected, following the general outlines imposed both by the causeways, which determined the two main axes of the city's orientation, and by the regular base of the central precinct occupied by the temples. We are not dealing with a precise gridiron as we find in Greek or Roman cities, nor even a regular plan such as the Inca developed in some of their new settlements. Instead we see a pattern adopted progressively as extensions were added to the city.

Tenochtitlán had two principal routes or axes which crossed near the geographical center at a point at the base of the Templo Mayor's stairway. These two streets, converging on the solid ground of the original island, were continuations of the causeways which served the dual purpose of crossing the lake and avoiding the swampy *chinampa* areas. The causeways not only connected the city with the mainland towns but also acted as dikes to contain floods.

One of the axes crossed the city from north to south, and in turn was divided into north and south sections. The largest section, running south from the Sacred Precinct to Ixtapalapa, was the route by which Cortés and his men entered Tenochtitlán. It was formed by two branch roads, originating at the cities of Ixtapalapa and Coyoacán, which joined into a single road about two kilometers from the coast. From the juncture of the roads to the southern bank of the island was about six and one-half kilometers, eight in all to the center of the city.[23] The causeway to Ixtapalapa was built around the year 1429 by order of King Itzcóatl (Galindo y Villa, 1955).

The causeway to Tepeyac started at the Sacred Precinct and ran north. It was not as straight as the first one and crossed the city to the east of Tlatelolco's market. At approximately two kilometers from its point of origin, it veered northeast, passing through the last *chinampa* districts near the shore, and crossed over the lake to the city of Tepeyac, a distance of some four kilometers. Another causeway connected Tlatelolco with points on the shore to the northwest.

The two most important causeways ran from the center of Tlatelolco and Tenochtitlán westward to Tlacopán. The latter was formed by two branch roads, one which started at Chapultepec and the second at Tlacopán. Both converged at about 2,500 meters from the shoreline, near the island of Mazatzintanalco.[24] It was along this causeway that the aqueduct to bring fresh water from Chapultepec's spring to Tenochtitlán was built.

These three causeways were fundamental in determining the plan of the later Spanish city. In fact, the modern streets of República Argentina and Seminario coincide with the north-south axis of the Aztec city, and the Calle de Tacuba with the western causeway. A fourth short causeway went from the center of the city to the eastern shore of the island where it came to an end at the canoe port.

These causeways captured the attention of the Spanish. Cortés tells us that the city "has four entrances, all man-made causeways, as wide as two lance lengths" (Cortés, 1961). Díaz del Castillo adds that on the way to Tenochtitlán from Ixtapalapa "we went on the causeway before us, which is eight paces wide, and goes so straight to the City of Mexico that it seems to me that it turns hardly at all" (Díaz del Castillo, 1955).[25]

All of the causeways were defended by openings, cutting across them from one side to another, which could only be crossed by drawbridges. These openings also served to regulate the water level in the fresh water lake created artificially between the shore and the north-south causeway. The causeway to Ixtapalapa probably had only one opening, formed by the irrigation canal bounding Moctezuma's New Houses and Tenochtitlán's main plaza to the south. It was, however, defended by "a bulwark of stone . . . with two towers on the sides" (Herrera, 1945). It was next to these "little towers," as Bernal Díaz del Castillo calls them (actually the Fort Xoloc shown in Cortés' map) that the Spanish conquistador had, in November 1519, his first meeting with the Aztec king.

The two main axes determined the direction of the city's major streets and canals. According to Orozco y Berra's reconstruction, the center of Tlatelolco and the western causeway from Tlacopán joined a few meters to the west of the Great Teocalli of Tenochtitlán via two streets which ran parallel to the north-south axis or causeway from Tepeyac. Tenochtitlán had few streets but canals crossed it in all directions, especially on the outskirts of the city. In the center and in the older, more densely populated districts, streets of packed earth alternated with canals in an apparently intentional, parallel arrangement.

We may wonder if Tenochtitlán reflected the urban life that was beginning to develop on the central plateau of Mexico, whether the Aztec capital's plan and urban elements were repeated in the smaller towns of the Valley, or whether Tenochtitlán was an exception because of its location, size, rapid development, and political importance. Aside from the conditions imposed by Tenochtitlán's very location, we have reason to believe that the Aztecs were beginning to develop principles of general city planning in order to achieve an efficient urban organization. I consider this possibility based on the words of a well-known Mexican historian: "When a site was chosen to build a town, two crossing lines were drawn, one pointing north to south and the other from east to west. Where these lines crossed, a quadrangular space was reserved, and was enclosed by walls, leaving four gateways at each of the four cardinal points. Each of the four principal streets led up to these gateways. These streets were laid out in as straight a line as possible." He later added, "In the center of the court a truncated pyramid was constructed, its western side reserved for the principal stairway" (Alcocer, 1935).

Motolinia has left us a detailed description of Indian cities: "These temples are called teocallis, and we find all over this land, that in the best part of town, they made a large, square courtyard; in the large towns there is an arrow's shot from corner to corner, and in smaller towns the courtyards are smaller. They enclosed this court with a wall, and many of these were topped with merlons; their doors opened on to the principal streets and thoroughfares which were made to end at the courtyard. To further honor their temples, they laid out their roads in a very straight line, from one to two leagues, which was impressive to see from the height of the main temple, since from all the smaller settlements and districts, these very straight roads came up to the court of the teocallis." Later he says, "In the large teocallis they had two altars, and in the others, only one, and every altar had its offerings. . . . In front of these altars they left a large space, where they performed their sacrifices. . . ." After referring to the height of the teocallis in Mexico and Tezcoco (Texcoco), Motolinia explains the characteristics of the secondary commercial centers of the big cities. "In the same courtyards of the principal towns were twelve or fifteen other very large teocallis, some bigger than others, but not too near the principal one. Some had their fronts and steps facing others, some faced east, others south, and in each of these was only one altar with its chapel. Each one had its chambers or apartments for those Tlamacazques or ministers, who were many, and for those who served to bring water and firewood; because in front of all these altars were braziers which burned all night long, and there were also fires in the chambers. They kept all those teocallis very white, burnished and clean, and in some there were little gardens with flowers and trees" (Motolinia, 1941).

The Aztec capital was not the only one which deserved to be called a city. Even by today's standards, Texcoco, Cholula, Coyoacán and many others would be considered true cities. They had the physical characteristics, sufficient size and population and were, for their time and place, active centers for processing raw materials and markets of influence and attraction. Carlos I of Spain was told: "And they call this city Tezcuco (Texcoco), and it must have at least thirty thousand *vecinos*. They have here, My Lord, marvelous houses and mosques, and large well-built chapels. There are very big markets. . . ." (Cortés, 1961). If we interpret thirty thousand *vecinos* to mean that number of heads of families, Texcoco may have had about a hundred and fifty thousand inhabitants in 1520.

A few kilometers away, as Cortés relates, were the cities of Acurumán and Otumpa with three to four thousand *vecinos* each, or between fifteen and twenty thousand inhabitants. These cities were not unique. The chronicler Herrera attributes six thousand houses to Coyoacán, five thousand to Hiucilopuchco, and four thousand to Mexicaltcingo (Herrera, 1945). Next to the lake was Ixtapalapa, governed by a brother of Moctezuma II, a city of between twelve and fifteen thousand *vecinos* or some sixty or seventy-five thousand inhabitants who lived "half of them on water and the other half on dry land" (Cortés, 1961). Considering its location, we can assume that *chinampa* districts with their rectilinear systems of canals and streets existed in this city as well as in the other riparian towns.

Cortés considered Tlaxcala, the capital of his allies, as being larger, more powerful and having a greater population than Granada at the time of its conquest by the Catholic Kings in 1492, and having a market where "every day there are thirty thousand souls or more buying and selling" (Cortés, 1961).

On entering Cholula, the Spaniards found streets and rooftops filled with people anxious to see the "men like us" and the horses (Díaz del Castillo, 1955). Herrera says of Cholula, "It was a very populous city in a beautiful plain, with twenty thousand Houses, and an equal number outside, in what they called farms, with many Towers on the Temples, which were beautiful to see, and according to what they say, these were as many as the Year has Days" (Herrera, 1945).

Cortés' reports, Díaz del Castillo's chronicles and the writings of the first chroniclers and historians of the Indies abound with phrases of admiration for the quality of the houses, the size of the temples, the well laid out buildings, the variety and order in the markets, the cleanliness of the streets, abundance of foodstuffs, and the excellence of services. All these are praises to a disciplined, responsible society which gradually enacted programs and laws to achieve an efficient urban arrangement. Aztec architects probably drew up their ideas and schematic designs in a presentation similar to the one we see in the maguey paper plan, using clay models to show ornamental details. We can be almost certain that they at least had a hand in planning and directing the construction of their cities.

A complex of buildings with the magnitude and proportion of the one the Spaniards encountered in the center of Tenochtitlán is not the result of chance. The street, "wide, straight and very beautiful, with Houses along both sides of the one by which the Spaniards entered" (Herrera, 1945), could only be part of a preconceived urban plan, at least in its general outlines. But, it is difficult to judge the degree of perfection the Aztecs reached in urban planning. We would have to study the chroniclers and the codices in much greater detail and verify descriptions of other Indian cities which kept their original appearance for a longer period than did the capital.

Nothing remains of Tenochtitlán. The city was almost completely destroyed in the seige preceding the final conquest. During the battle, the

Spaniards filled in canals with the rubble of houses to provide firm footing for the horsemen. After the war, the temples and palaces were pulled down and replaced by the churches and houses of the Colonial Period. But the main outlines of the Aztec city were respected, and on this base rose the gridiron of Colonial Mexico City which we still see today. Not only has the city plan survived the intervening centuries, but the same religious, administrative, and civic importance of certain areas of Tenochtitlán's center has been maintained, the buildings replaced by their modern counterparts: the Colonial plaza over the Aztec market, the Cathedral built on top of the Templo Mayor, and the National Palace covering the New Houses of Moctezuma II.

Perhaps we will someday be able to reconstruct the original plans of Texcoco and Cholula, of Ixtapalapa and Tacuba, cities which the Aztecs encountered, redesigned and remodeled in keeping with their own concept of city planning. Only then can we learn about the urban structure of those cities covered over by five centuries of building.

As a hypothesis, I suggest that urban planning in Mexico's central plateau at the beginning of the sixteenth century had declined in comparison with that of the Classic Period and was once again in an experimental elementary stage. Builders relied on general schematic layouts, conforming to accepted principles, by which they determined the direction of a causeway, the broadened area of a ceremonial center, or the site of a market. Details of urban planning developed in relation to architecture, and architecture was only to be found in the city's principal and secondary ceremonial centers, in palaces and in the houses of more urbanized districts.

In Tenochtitlán and the riparian towns around Lake Texcoco, the *chinampa* system imposed an urban scheme of regular lines. I do not believe that this would have occurred in inland cities where *chinampa* cultivation was impossible and the irrigated areas scarce. Herrera tells us that in Tlaxcala "the town was divided into wards, small stretches without order, unlike our custom, and within a stone's throw are many Houses together, and among them many twisting alleys. . . ." (Herrera, 1945).

Anyone unfamiliar with an Aztec city would have found it impossible to identify Tenochtitlán's simple shoreline districts or the miserable huts of inland cities with the enormous, costly religious structures or the spacious palaces of the nobility. The structure of Aztec society and its hierarchical differentiations dictated the arrangement of the city's zones. This is confirmed by the few chroniclers' reports we have, which refer, albeit briefly, to the difference in size, quality, and materials existing between the houses of the nobles and those of the general population.

THE DISTRICTS OF TENOCHTITLÁN

Tenochtitlán and Tlatelolco were founded by two different Aztec groups, and coexisted for a hundred and fifty years as two separate cities, politically and physically. Political union was completed in 1473 after Tenochtitlán conquered its neighbor in a swift and bloody war. Physical union was accomplished by inhabitants of both cities who filled in the narrow canal separating them with *chinampas*. Tenochtitlán and Tlatelolco were thus united into one island, but their temples and market squares still marked their respective centers. After 1473 Tlatelolco was ruled by a representative of Tenochtitlán and condemned to pay a heavy tribute.

When the causeways entering the city were completed, Tenochtitlán-Tlatelolco was divided into four main quarters, possibly different administrative divisions, with the Templo Mayor in the center. The sector northwest of the city's center was called Cuepopán, to the northeast was Aztalco, the southeast sector was known as Teopán, and the southwest sector was named Moyotlán. They correspond to the present districts of Santa María la Redonda, and to the colonial districts of San Pablo, San Sebastián and San Juan Bautista respectively (Portilla, 1963).

Each of these four quarters included a number of the already existing wards or *barrios*, probably corresponding to a *calpulli*, each with its temples, market places, premises, precincts, and structures for services common to the clan. Each clan maintained a public school, or *telpochcalli,* for the education of its youth (Vaillant, 1955). Possibly each ward also had a council chamber, where the older men of the clan gathered, and an armory, since the organization of the Aztec army reflected the political organization which, in turn, was manifested by its distribution in the various districts of the city. Caso tells us that wards, besides being territorial divisions, were the place of residence of the old clans which played such an important role in the social and political life of the Aztecs (Caso, 1956). Twenty wards in all are usually mentioned, which would have corresponded to the same number of original clans,[27] but it is possible that the larger wards were subdivided into smaller ones.

The central sectors of Tenochtitlán were built on the solid ground of the original island and must have been the most thickly built-up part of the city. The only free spaces were the plazas and areas surrounding the temples and important buildings. But despite its density of low buildings, closely packed over most of the area, the city as a whole must have given an impression of greenery and coolness, with trees and flowers growing in its courtyards.

Aztec gardens astonished the Spaniards. I suppose the concept of public parks or gardens as we know them did not exist in Tenochtitlán, but almost all its inhabitants, from great lords down to the humblest members of Aztec society, grew flowers in their houses. Cortés describes one of these gardens in the palace of the Governor of Ixtapalapa:[28] "In many rooms there are very fresh high and low gardens, with many trees and fragrant flowers; also well-made tanks of fresh water, which have stairways to the bottom. Next to the house, there is a very large garden and over it a gallery with beautiful corridors and chambers, and in this garden is a large, square tank of fresh water which has walls of attractive cut stone. Around it is a platform of very good brick, so wide that four abreast can walk on it. It is four hundred paces each side, or one thousand six hundred in all. On another part of the platform, toward the garden, is a grillwork of cane, and behind this, all the groves and fragrant plants. There are many fish in the tank and many birds such as wild duck, widgeon and other species of waterfowl; so many are they that they often almost cover the water" (Cortés, 1961).

The lords of Tenochtitlán and Texcoco, and also the Governors of the neighboring Tarascan territories, owned pleasure gardens outside the cities. The pleasure garden of Nezahualcóyotl, the great king of Texcoco in the fifteenth century, dominated the lake from a hilltop (Nuttall, 1925). Besides the palace he built next to the Teocalli in the center of the city, Moctezuma II had "a smaller house, where he had a very beautiful garden with galleries which opened out on to it, and the marbles and floor stone of these were of jasper and very well worked" (Cortés, 1961).[29] This garden had tanks of both fresh and salty water— remember that the waters of Lake Texcoco were brackish—with birds brought from different regions by men dedicated exclusively to this work. The palace provided guest rooms and quarters where the king kept "men, women and children, white from birth in face and body and hair and eyebrows and eyelashes," in other words, albinos. He also kept hunchbacks and other deformed persons who were regarded as extraordinary phenomena of nature. Moctezuma's zoological park aroused the interest of the Spaniards who had never seen pumas, jaguars, wolves, foxes, wild cats, and such other exotic animals before.

Canoes circulated daily about Tenochtitlán's waterways, loaded with flowers for market or to be taken to the Sacred Precinct where they were used in ceremonies. Even today, we consider the variety and color of the floral bouquets as one of the main attractions in Mexico's local fairs. The Aztecs used a special word to refer to a rich man's garden and another for the garden of the commoner, but an innate love for flowers and pride in their orchards and gardens were traits shared by all levels of society.

Most of the houses in the older neighborhoods were one-storied structures, although those of officials and chiefs were more spacious, some even having two floors.[30] In both cases, the buildings were simple, clean and well ventilated. The main rooms opened out on to a patio where family festivities were held to the music of wind and percussion instruments. In the better class of houses in this group, the service and slave quarters were placed out of the way. Houses usually had a regular floor plan and were windowless, with doors providing the only ventilation. To avoid the danger of floods, they were built on platforms. Roofs were constructed of beams which were then covered with a layer of mortar. Floors were cement, painted red and highly polished (Vaillant, 1955).

Furniture was simple and sparse. Mats covered the floors where large, braided straw pillows lay scattered about to provide seating. Mats also served as beds, curtains or to cover openings. There was a hearth in the kitchen for the preparation of food, and no house lacked a stone *metate* to grind the meal for *tortillas* which were then molded into flat, rounded shapes with the palms of the hands.

Houses had two entrances, the main one that opened out onto the street, and a second one on the canal side that was used to unload provisions, or by anyone arriving by canoe.

In the center of the city, along the main streets near the Templo Mayor, stood the palaces of the ruling class, chiefs and governors, a few minor temples, and some of the more important public and institutional buildings, such as the headquarters of the Eagle Knights[31] and the "House of Song," or *cuicacalli,* where dancing, singing, and music were taught.[32]

The larger the palace, the better was its construction and decoration. Each of the Aztec emperors, like the Inca, followed the custom of building his own palace. I do not know if this was an ancient practice, but we know for certain that at least three of the last four Aztec kings, Axayácatl, Ahuízotl, and Moctezuma II occupied different palaces. Royal princes, too, owned palaces of considerable size in the center of the city.

Northwest of the Great Teocalli, or Templo Mayor, stood the palace which Cuauhtémoc inherited from his father and in which he probably lived during the reign of his cousin, Moctezuma II. To the southwest was the palace of the Cihuacóatl, chief adviser to the reigning monarch.

Moctezuma II built his palace, also called the New Houses, to the east of Tenochtitlán's central plaza and southeast of the Great Teocalli, on the site where the National Palace or Government House of Mexico City stands today. The palace occupied a broad, rectangular area in which a series of one- and two-storied buildings were arranged around square or rectangular courts. Moctezuma II rarely left his palace which was equipped to serve as seat of government as well as residence and place of diversion for the king, his family, numerous relatives and guests. Offices for governmental and judicial administration were on the main floor. The upper story held the chambers of the king and rooms for important guests. About 600 lords and other notables awaited the king's orders daily from sunrise on, "and their servants and persons who accompanied them swelled into two or three large courtyards" (Cortés, 1961).

The size and complex layout of the Aztec palaces were fascinating to the Spaniards. They were built severely and without pretension. The floors were of well-polished wood, and mirrors of burnished stone hung on the adobe walls which were overlaid with brilliant stucco ornamentation. The Aztecs spread jaguar skins on the floors and placed low, square stools and rush benches around for seating. To warm the large halls, they used braziers which burned bark and aromatic gums.

In the humble straw and reed huts of the *chinampa* districts on the city's periphery, in closer contact with the lake than with the city itself, lived the families of fishermen, gardeners and the poorer workers.[33] Lake Texcoco and the smaller lakes which formed the lacustrine system of the central basin of Mexico have all but dried up with the passing centuries. However, in the outskirts of Mexico City we can still find areas of *chinampas*, or "floating gardens," which give us an idea of what the humbler districts of the Aztec capital might have been like.

All noise and movement produced by a large and active population, such as Tenochtitlán's, was concentrated in the markets and within the houses themselves. On the streets and canals, it was an orderly, silent populace that went about its business.

The majority of the most pressing urban problems in those days had been solved. Plentiful fresh water arrived from Chapultepec to a loading zone where it was received by canoes commissioned to peddle it throughout the city. By street and canal, porters and canoes delivered foodstuffs and building materials. Trash was thrown into the canals for the water to carry away, and public latrines provided sanitary facilities. Even the city's defense was assured by the very location of the island, and by fortifications and the cuts in the causeways with built-in drawbridges.

THE MARKETS OF TENOCHTITLÁN

Descriptions of Tlatelolco's market[34] left by Cortés and Díaz del Castillo point out some fundamental characteristics of Aztec society.[35] They give the impression that not only for its population, size, density, plan, and architecture was the Aztec capital a great city, but also for its economy, services and the specialization of its inhabitants.

The tourist who visits Mexico City today is invariably drawn to its markets. Some of these are famous enough to attract organized tours. Depending on the city, the tradition of its market and its zone of influence, these popular gatherings take place every day, or on special days of the week, today as they did four hundred and fifty years ago.

Unlike the cities, few smaller towns can organize a daily market. Even today, a significant percentage of Mexicans live off the land and maintain a self-sufficient familial economy, coming to market only to exchange their surplus products for articles they do not produce themselves. An exclusively agricultural population cannot support a daily market. If the market has enough patrons to warrant increasing its days of operation, a large enough sector of the population must be earning its livelihood from nonagricultural activities to serve as consumers of the market's produce.

A city, on the other hand, is characterized by its daily markets where employees, artisans and other specialized groups come to fill their needs. Tenochtitlán, Tlatelolco, Texcoco, Cholula, and the main cities of the Aztec federation fall into this category. A large portion of the population depended for its foodstuffs on the agricultural production from the areas bordering each city. The *chinampas,* forming some of the peripheral districts of Tenochtitlán and of the lake shore cities, supplied only a fraction of the daily consumption. The rest came from the rural villages.

For its time and place, Tenochtitlán was a specialized center with a sizeable concentration of artisan activity. Raw materials were brought to the markets of Tenochtitlán-Tlatelolco to be transformed by their craftsmen into articles of worth: crude gold, silver, copper, shell, and hard stones for the jewelers; wood for carving; brilliant feathers for Aztec artists; lime, adobe and stone for the masons; and medicinal herbs for the herbist to classify. Each day hairdressers came to market looking for clients, and set up their stalls "where they wash and trim heads." Here, too, were apothecaries who "sell prepared medicines, drinkable as well as unguents and poultices"; porters hoping to be hired; proprietors of houses "where they serve food and drink for a price"; those who "sell colors for painters," or "many kinds of cotton yarn of all colors, in their skeins," or "deer hides with and without hair, white and dyed different colors." The land's various products were assigned places in organized streets and sectors so that the vendors were easily found by the buyers and the market inspector's work was facilitated. Game was located in one street; fruit and vegetables in another; fish which was sold both "fresh and salted, raw and cooked in another; and further away were cooked eggs." There was sugar-cane syrup and bee's honey, mats for all purposes, clay braziers, pottery, earthenware jars, charcoal, and wood. Corn was sold as grain or in dough and cakes prepared with fish or fowl. "They sell everything by count and measure," says Cortés. Payment was by barter or in cacao beans after consulting price lists hung in conspicuous places. To arbitrate disputes and administer justice "in this great plaza, there is a very good house like a tribunal. Ten or twelve persons sit here, acting as judges and passing sentence on all cases and things which happen in this market, and ordering wrongdoers to be punished. In this market, there are persons who continually go about among the people looking at what is sold and the means used to measure it, and a false measure has been known to be broken" (Cortés, 1961).

Tlatelolco's market was the largest and best supplied in the city as well as in the whole Aztec empire.[36] It was not the only one in the city, nor was it the only one operating daily. Next to Tenochtitlán's Great Teocalli was another important market, situated in the enclosure of the city's main plaza, surrounded by the palaces of the nobles. The Colonial plaza later occupied the same space, and today, with altered proportions, it is called Plaza de la Constitución. There may have been other markets which served the people living in the various neighborhoods (Sanders, 1952), perhaps set up in the plazas adjoining the temples of each ward.

Like an Arabian bazaar or a Medieval fair, Tlatelolco's market provided the Aztecs with diversion and exchange of news. It was a place where they could amuse themselves for hours watching the thousands of passers-by, taking in the colors, noises, and odors of one of the most amazing human spectacles of Indian America.

27 *Reconstruction of the Great Teocalli or Templo Mayor of Tenochtitlán done by Ignacio Marquina. The circular pyramid in the center of the complex served as a base for the Temple of Quetzalcóatl; facing it stands the largest pyramid crowned by the temples dedicated to Huitzilopochtli and Tlaloc; to the left of the model is the* calmecac *or school, in*

the right foreground is the Temple of the Sun; the ball court lies between these two structures. The causeway from Tlacopán or Tacuba ends at the gateway located in the center of the enclosing wall seen in the left foreground. (Credit: I.N.A.H. photographic archives, Mexico.)

THE CENTER OF TENOCHTITLÁN

At the intersection of the two causeways, or main axes, stood the Great Teocalli, marking the center of the city. Thanks to the efforts and patient research of the Mexican architect Ignacio Marquina, it has been possible to construct a good-sized model of the Templo Mayor and study the urban and architectural characteristics of its composition as it was when the Spaniards arrived[37] (Plate No. 27).

The Templo Mayor of the Aztec capital was made up of a group of structures which occupied a square area of about four hundred and twenty meters, surrounded by a wall two and one-half meters high. This wall, or *coatepantli,* also called the "Serpent Wall" for its exterior decoration featuring hundreds of plumed serpents, outlined the Sacred Precinct (Plate No. 28). The Precinct had three gateways which marked the starting points of the principal causeways. Only the eastern wall was completely closed.[38] Inside the Precinct stood eighteen single structures and principal complexes as well as other smaller ones. The Great Pyramid stood out above all the rest. On its upper platform, at a height of some 30 meters, sat the twin temples consecrated to Huitzilopochtli, god of war and deity most venerated by the Aztecs, and to Tlaloc, the rain god.[39] All the rest of the structural complex revolved around the Great Pyramid.

From a study of the model, we see a complex of monumental proportions with an axis of symmetry which was not always respected in detail. This east-west axis was determined by the main façade of the Templo Mayor. Each of the single buildings or complexes had its own individual axis. Only one of the smaller, but important, structures—the platform, or table, of Huitzilopochtli—seems to have had two axes.

Between the structures and their bases were pedestrian areas where the public could walk, or linger to witness the ceremonies performed in the temples on the uppermost platforms of the pyramids, high above the level of the Plaza. We cannot know whether these open areas constituted thoroughfares or plazas. They were broad, quite similar to each other, and served to set off the individual architecture of each building as well as to permit traffic around the structures that filled the Sacred Precinct. With the exception of the street that connected the north and south gates of the Great Teocalli, running in front of the Great Temple-Pyramid, the other spaces were undefined and broken up by platforms supporting and elevating the larger structures.

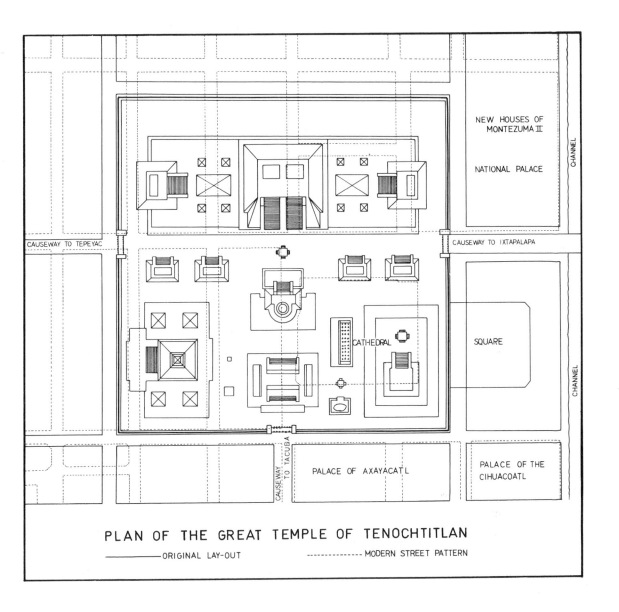

NEW HOUSES OF
MONTEZUMA II

NATIONAL PALACE

CHANNEL

CAUSEWAY TO TEPEYAC

CAUSEWAY TO IXTAPALAPA

CATHEDRAL

SQUARE

CHANNEL

CAUSEWAY TO TACUBA

PALACE OF AXAYACATL

PALACE OF THE
CIHUACOATL

PLAN OF THE GREAT TEMPLE OF TENOCHTITLAN

——————————ORIGINAL LAY-OUT   -------------- MODERN STREET PATTERN

28 Plan of the Templo Mayor of Tenochtitlán drawn up by Marquina for
his reconstruction seen in Plate 27. Today's block-shaped outline of this
central sector of Mexico City is indicated by fine lines. Numbers 1 and 2
point to the twin temples topping the Templo Mayor; number 8 is the
Temple of Quetzalcóatl, 18 is the calmecac, *13 is the ball court. Numbers*
23, 24, and 25 mark the three access gateways to the Templo Mayor. The
Temple of the Sun is number 15, and 7 is the table of Huitzilopochtli.
(Credit: Marquina, Ignacio: "Arquitectura prehispánica," I.N.A.H.,
Mexico, 1951.)

Temples topped pyramidal structures on square or rectangular foundations. The Temple of Quetzalcóatl was an exception, having the circular foundation common in buildings dedicated to this god. Other structures might be described as adjuncts, such as the *calmecac*, or school, the ball court, or *tlachtli*, and the buildings around the Temple of the Sun. These were of one story and regular shape, supported by their respective platforms. The bases, gigantic pedestals for the pyramids and special buildings, were always painted white, their colored friezes standing out in contrast.

Trees and all other vegetation were excluded from the Sacred Precinct with the exception of the *Tentlalpán*, a small fenced grove of maguey and other plants which was the site of an annual ceremony simulating a hunt; the tree of *Xocotl-Huetzi*, a branchless timber planted yearly during the festivals of the tenth month; and the *Tozpalatl*, a small temple of great importance to the Aztecs since it had been built around the spring which existed on the site where the first temple had been founded. These were kept for their symbolic rather than landscaping value (Marquina, 1960).

The people of Tenochtitlán, as well as visitors from other cities, freely entered the Sacred Precinct to witness religious ceremonies which they watched standing, or to participate in processions. The Great Teocalli did not attract crowds because of its renown as a civic or commercial center, but rather because the Aztec religious calendar was so full of ceremonies, many of which lasted several days or even weeks, that a large number of people must have passed through its gates every day, and at all hours, to gather before one of its altars.

Priests, novices, and servants of the various temples lived within the Precinct. Some lived in the *calmecac* in rooms arranged around a square central court about forty-five meters on each side or around four smaller courts each about eighteen meters wide. Others may have lived inside the precinct of the Temple of the Sun, in rooms to the north, south and west of the platform that served as a base for this complex. And we can not discard the possibility that, at least temporarily, a number of priests and servants of a particular cult lived in some of the temples.

Let me reconstruct the sensations experienced by a person arriving for a ceremony through the northern gateway and finding himself standing in front of the Templo Mayor.[40] Walking along the Tepeyac causeway, he would have seen from afar the twin temples of the Great Pyramid rising above the flat rooftops of the houses on either side of him, Tlaloc's blue temple in the foreground and behind it the sanctuary of Huitzilopochtli, painted red. To the right of these rose the conical straw roof of Quetzal-cóatl's Temple and the tops of some lesser temples. Looking far away to the south, he might notice the jagged, snow-covered peaks and volcanos that encircle the central Valley of Mexico. At the end of the causeway, the visitor would encounter the canal which surrounded the Sacred Precinct.

The northern gateway was marked by an entrance hall, a kind of vestibule formed by a double row of eight columns, giving a feeling of transition between the city and the Precinct.[41] On each side of the door stretched the smooth merlon-topped wall, the heads of intertwined feathered serpents decorating its base. Once inside, the visitor's glance would fall on the polished surface of a perfectly level paved floor from which rose the simple, geometric shapes of temples and platforms. The ceremony he had come to see was about to take place right in front of him, a few hundred steps away, and some people had already arrived. The impassive silhouettes were outlined against the back of the opposite gateway, the *cuauhquiahuc* or "Eagle Gate," to the south, formed by a double colonnade marked by two solid pillars supporting a simple entablature decorated in its center and frieze with emblems of the military Orders of the Eagle and Jaguar Knights.

There were only 200 meters between the northern gate and the axis of the Great Temple-Pyramid. The visitor would cross over on a street bordered on his immediate left by the Great Pyramid's platform and on the right by two pyramids, each of which had two bodies and supported similar rectangular temples. The first of these, the *coateocalli*, was dedicated to the gods of the conquered countries. The second was the Temple of Cihuacóatl, goddess of the Xochimilco tribe. Walking past the long platform of the Great Pyramid toward the opposite gateway, the visitor might think he was seeing the same sight over again when he looked at two other pyramids supporting two more temples with rectangular bases. The first of these was dedicated to Chicomocóatl, goddess of vegetation, the second, to Xochiquetzalli, goddess of painters and weavers. Once past all four of these temples, the visitor would have crossed most of the Sacred Precinct.

Past the *coateocalli* and the Temple of Cihuacóatl, the street widened in front of the Templo Mayor. Here stood the Temple of Quetzalcóatl, with its circular foundation and conical crest. This was one of the most unusual structures in the Sacred Precinct, if not in the entire city. It was supported by a broad base and consisted of four stepped bodies. The rectangular pyramidal base was not, in itself, extraordinary. What captured the visitor's attention was the temple on the upper platform, circular in form with a straw roof, conch-shaped merlons, and an impressive entrance marked by the gaping fangs of a gigantic serpent.[41] From this temple, at sunrise and sunset of each day, a priest on the upper platform beat "an enormous drum which was heard all over the city and which was the signal to begin and end all business and work of the day" (Alcocer, 1935).

On the axis of the Great Pyramid and Quetzalcóatl's Temple, also the main axis of the entire ceremonial group, the visitor would notice a small platform on a square base with four symmetrically placed stairways. This was the table of Huitzilopochtli. Standing around it were a group of people staring up at the top of the double stairway of the Templo Mayor. There, on the terrace, some thirty meters high, lay a man, his body arched over a stone, arms and legs immobilized by four priests, ready to be sacrificed to the Aztec god.

Coming in by the western gate on the causeway from Tacuba was quite different. The visitor faced the Great Pyramid on its axis before even coming into the Sacred Precinct, and as he walked toward the complex of buildings, it seemed to open up as he drew nearer. He passed through a gateway structurally similar to the other two, with a pair of feathered serpent heads sculpted in stone on each of the side pillars, and found himself in front of the colonnaded entrance to a single-story construction. This was the *tlachtli*, or ball court, a structure completely closed on two sides. On the south end, the colonnade concealed a long narrow court from which a stairway of twenty steps led to the upper platform of the ball court. A similar stairway on the northern side permitted direct access from the level of the plaza.

The ball court and the Temple of Quetzalcóatl blocked the visitor's way to the Great Pyramid. On the left, the serene façade of the *calmecac* would steer him toward the base of the pyramid, passing quickly by the *Tentlalpán*, or grove, then by a symmetrical platform with steps on four sides and then a second grove. As he walked, the visitor noticed the imposing circular pyramid and temple of Quetzalcóatl with its elegant conical roof. At last he entered the north-south street and, crossing the line of temples, he came up to the foot of the Great Pyramid's stairway where he joined the other people who had already arrived to witness the ceremony.

In the southwest corner of the Precinct stood four structures. One of these, a well-proportioned pyramid of four bodies, was the second tallest in the entire complex. This pyramid was part of a group dedicated to the Sun, one of the most important cults in the Aztec religion. It was in front of the access stairway to the temple that one of the most curious customs of this people took place—the gladiatorial sacrifice.

The Great Pyramid was the most important structure in the Sacred Precinct. The line along its front and long platform-base, as well as two other symmetrically placed temples, follows the street line of today's Calle República de Argentina and its prolongation, Seminario. The pyramid's axis, also the east-west axis of the Sacred Precinct itself, lay a few meters north of the modern street, República de Guatemala.

The Great Pyramid, as the Spaniards saw it, had been completed during the reign of Ahuízotl, but four smaller structures had previously stood on the same site. According to calculations, the Great Pyramid's base measured 100 meters in the north-south direction and 80 east to west. The base rested on an immense platform about five meters high which supported two other twin pyramids of four sections each, topped with similar temples, one of these dedicated to Tezcatlicopa, the universal god. These temples, symmetrically placed on the Great Pyramid, were reached by a pair of forecourts. In the Great Pyramid we find proportions and shapes similar to those in earlier constructions in such other cities as Texcoco and Tlatelolco, the Pyramid of Tenayuca apparently having served as a model for them all. In the Great Teocalli of Tenochtitlán, certain architectural principles were also repeated, such as the double stairway flanked by ramps, the break in the ramps at a certain height, construction in stepped bodies—four in the pyramid of the Aztec capital—and the masterful use of stone.

Tenochtitlán was, in synthesis, one of the most truly urban of all the cities of pre-Columbian America's civilizations. It was the religious and cultural capital of a great people, the political center of a developing state and the military center of an army which undertook and successfully carried out many daring conquests. Furthermore, Tenochtitlán was a commercial center which developed the most important markets in Mesoamerica at that time. Attracted by the goods made by skillful artisans and the prospect of a large concentration of potential customers, merchants from distant regions flocked to these markets.

Tenochtitlán's growth was vertiginous. I can think of no city in the pre-industrial world which reached such a vast size and population in so short a time as did the Aztec capital. A hundred years after its founding, already well into the fifteenth century, it was still a group of miserable huts inhabited by mercenaries. Less than a century later, after a cycle in which tribute and direct conquest gave it a prestige and wealth unequaled in Mesoamerica, Tenochtitlán had already been destroyed and replaced by a new urban concept which the conquered Aztec people themselves were forced to construct.

Why did Tenochtitlán fall and why did the Aztec state collapse? Not from lack of courage, certainly, nor lack of faith in their way of life and religion. We will undoubtedly never know. I believe that the Aztec weakness lay in the complexity of its government and in the demands of its religion. The arrival of the Spaniards elicited a variety of reactions among the subjugated peoples as well as among the Aztec's enemies. Some favored the Aztecs, but more often they did not. Cortés had only to exploit the resentments of whole groups and lead them against the common enemy.

Tenochtitlán was the capital of a nation which was approaching its territorial peak, although it is difficult to speculate how much farther it might have gone. I am inclined to think that not even its rulers knew. Perhaps the capital might have followed the evolution of the state: new inhabitants would have required new *chinampas*, the old *chinampa* districts would have become more urbanized, new temples would have replaced old ones and others would have sprung up in the new neighborhoods.

There were few regions of any economic or strategic importance left for the Aztecs to conquer. They could only tighten their control over the already conquered territory and increase its productivity. Perhaps their next move would have been to devote time and effort to technology, which could have moved the Mesoamerican peoples out of the years of stagnation following the Classic centuries. They might have pondered on the dangers of a religion which called for the sacrifice of their best subjects, or they might have revised the form of absolute government adopted by their last kings. But could the Aztecs have accomplished this? Or did they, as is suspected of the Maya, unknowingly carry within their very culture the seeds of its own destruction? Would there have been another barbarian invasion in central Mexico, another interregnum during which the cities would have been places of savagery and disorder? We will never know; we can only speculate.

For good or bad, the arrival of the Spaniards introduced a new concept of things. On the altar of a new religion, Mesoamerica's temples were destroyed; in the interest of a new culture, Indian books and documents were burned; in honor of a new form of government, the Aztec leaders were slaughtered.

1. In reality, the urbanization in the central Valley of Mexico, which took place in the thirteenth, fourteenth and fifteenth centuries, represents the third urbanistic period for this region. The first lasted through the Classic centuries and ended about the eighth century A.D. with the fall of Teotihuacán. The second coincided with the rise of Toltec influence in Mexico's central plateau. The third and most important from an urban point of view, though we can not be sure it coincided with maximum demographic development, belongs to the period of Aztec expansion. During the Colonial centuries, the population of the center of Mexico was less than it had been in pre-Hispanic times.

2. See the description of Milan in 1288 in *The Medieval Town* by J.H. Mundy and Peter Riesenberg; D. Van Nostrand Co., Inc., New York, 1958.

3. While the ruins of Tenochtitlán were being cleared and the new Colonial capital built, Cortés lived in Coyoacán, a city on the lake to the south. A section of the southern causeway connecting the lake shore to Tenochtitlán began at Coyoacán.

4. See Plates No. 27 and 28 which show the excellent study by Marquina of *The Templo Mayor of México* (Marquina, 1960). Estimated measurements of the area are mine and, of course, approximate.

5. Kings and lords of friendly, as well as enemy states, were invited to witness and participate in the celebrations that took place in Tenochtitlán when a new king was crowned. A successful military campaign, the inauguration of a temple, a state funeral, and religious occasions were all pretexts to invite foreign kings and lords. Inevitably a mass sacrifice was the high point in these celebrations.

6. The islands of Tenochtitlán and Tlatelolco were located at the southwestern end of Lake Texcoco. The lake around the islands, but especially to the south and west, was shallow, facilitating the construction of *chinampas* as well as the causeways that connected the islands with the shore of the lake and the dikes that protected the city from periodic floods (Moriarty, 1968).

7. Personal communication of Dr. Edward Callnek.

8. In a personal communication, Dr. Callnek suggested that the average total size of a *chinampa* lot could have been between 500 and 600 square meters.

9. Personal communication of Dr. Edward Callnek.

10. A reference taken from the work of Angel Rosenblat, *La Población in-dígena y el mestizaje en América* (The Indian population and racial mixture in America) (Rosenblat, 1954).

11. According to early chroniclers 240,000 defenders died in the siege while only 60,000 survived (Padden, 1970).

12. We have to wait until 1541 for the next oldest plan of an American city to reach us. This is a plan of Nombre de Dios kept in the Archivo de Indias in Seville. The plan was reproduced in the collection of colonial plans published in Madrid in 1951 (I.E.A.L., 1951). Two small imaginary reproductions of Tenochtitlán, of iconographic value only, were included in two ancient world maps exhibited in the galleries of the Vatican Museum: the "Grande Planisferio" by Girolamo Verrazzano, Rome, 1529 and the "Planisferio Anónimo," possibly of Italian origin, dated circa 1530.

13. See the map attributed to Cortés (Plate No. 22).

14. The map appeared on page X, Book One, of the first edition of Bordone's Atlas (Bordone, 1528).

15. Of the three volumes of Ramusio's collection, the third is the only one dealing with America (Ramusio, 1556).

16. The plan on maguey paper does not match with the areas covered by housing in the district east of the center of Tlatelolco and north of the center of Tenochtitlán. If the interpretation of the glyphs included in the map is correct, it would show an area expropriated from Azcapotzalco (Personal communication of Dr. Edward Callnek).

17. The original map could have been a copy, with some changes, of a map made prior to the Conquest, or drawn again from a manuscript of the period immediately after the Conquest (Lenz, 1949).

18. Study the new land reclaimed from the sea by the Dutch, and you will have a contemporary example of this immutable law.

19. See Plate No. 25.

20. See figure No. 1 in Edward Callnek's *Subsistence agriculture and the urban development of Tenochtitlán* (Callnek, 1969).

21. The first work of any size I am familiar with is a precarious aqueduct which united Chapultepec with Tenochtitlán. It was built by order of Chimalpopoca, third king of the Aztec dynasty.

22. The Aztecs of Tenochtitlán conquered Tlatelolco in 1478, destroying its Great Temple. A generation later, they began to rebuild it, and it was finished a few years before the arrival of the Spaniards (Peterson, 1959).

23. The causeway from Ixtapalapa had two lateral canals eight to ten meters wide. Its highest point rose 1.30 meters above lake level, and its width varied between fifteen and twenty meters. The causeway was not paved; its surface was made with a mixture of volcanic material and tamped earth (González Rul and Mooser, 1962).

24. See figure No. 1 in Callnek, 1969.

25. The measurements which Bernal Díaz del Castillo mentions are notably smaller than those cited by González Rul and Mooser (see note 23). On the other hand, Galindo y Villa gives larger measurements: thirty *varas* wide and two *varas* high above water level (25.98 by 1.72 meters) (Galindo y Villa, 1955).

26. Evidently we are witnessing in Tenochtitlán and in other cities in Central Mexico a revival of Teotihuacán's principles of urban planning, such as the use of two main axes, the construction of a plaza or market area at the crossing point and a regular layout.

27. The names of the twenty wards were probably: Tzapotla, Huehuecalco, Tecpanealtitlán, Cihuatleocaltitlán, Yopico, Teocaltitlán, Tlaxilpam, Tequicaltitlán, Atlampa, Tlacacomoco, Amanalco, Tepetitlán, Atizapán, Xihuitongo, Tequixquiapán, Necaltitlán, Xoloco, Chichimecapán, Copolco and Tezcatzonco (Moreno, 1962).

28. The governor of Ixtapalapa was Cuitlahuac, a brother of Moctezuma II.

29. The pleasure house of Moctezuma II was situated on two small islands southwest of Tenochtitlán. A pair of causeways connected the islands with the city and other causeways joined them to each other.

30. I have come across references to a work on Aztec dwellings which I was not able to consult. It is a study made by the architect Francisco M. Rodríguez called *La habitación privada de los aztecas en el siglo XVI* (Aztec private houses in the sixteenth century).

31. The Order of the Eagles represented the principal Aztec military group, formed by their bravest warriors. The buildings belonging to the Order housed a school where the sons of the members of the nobility were trained in handling arms and the techniques of war.

32. Singing and dancing were two art forms much appreciated by the Aztecs. According to Alcocer, "there were public dances in the temple courtyards dedicated to the gods, dances in the palace courtyard for the king's entertainment and dances in the *Cuicacalli* where this art was taught to the youth" (Alcocer, 1935). For a complete survey of pre-Columbian music, songs and dances see Marti, 1961.

33. Only in rather exceptional cases was a *chinampa* lot large enough to support an individual, much less a whole family (Callnek, 1969). The conclusion is that the unskilled workers living in the *chinampa* lots worked as porters or in construction jobs, or in the markets. Some probably were part-time or full-time artisans.

34. The pre-Hispanic market was located where the Plaza de Santiago stands today. The church of Santiago is built on the site of Tlatelolco's temple.

35. Padden suggests that Díaz del Castillo described the view of the city from atop the pyramid of Tenochtitlán and not of Tlatelolco. See his note 3 in chapter IX (Padden, 1970).

36. When Tlatelolco was captured in 1473 by Tenochtitlán a heavy sales tax was imposed on all transactions that took place there.

37. The model is exhibited in the Mexican Museum of Ethnography which is situated precisely over one of the corners of the Great Pyramid of Tenochtitlán.

38. Some authors mention a fourth gateway located at the east side, which must have been much smaller than the other three. Alcocer calls it the Huiznahuac Gateway (Alcocer, 1935).

39. The height of the upper platform has been calculated by the number of steps in the central stairway. In general, the chroniclers give a figure which varies between 113 (Torquemada) and 120 or 130 steps (Durán), but all agree that there were more than 100. It is generally accepted that the two temples had a height of seventeen to eighteen meters. Therefore, the Great Pyramid must have had a total height of forty-seven to forty-eight meters.

40. I have made this reconstruction based on the reports from the time of the Conquest and on general data, but mostly on the excellent reconstructions of Marquina and the analysis of his model of the Templo Mayor.

41. The historian López de Gomara described it as follows: "And among them (the temples) was one round one; the entrance of which was through a doorway made like the mouth of a serpent, and diabolically painted."

·6

THE MAYA

"They sleep. Everything sleeps. All is suspended, all empty, motionless and silent."

Fragment from the episode, "La CREACIÓN," from the POPUL-VAH

□ 6

THE CLASSIC PERIOD in Mesoamerica lasted six or seven centuries, dating from the third century of the Christian era (Plate No. 2, page 26). Even though we are unable to fix an exact parallel in time, we can assume that the series of regional characteristics which marked the flowering of Mesoamerica's Indian civilizations developed approximately during the same period. These centuries of constant population growth gave rise to an intense interchange of ideas and luxury goods which favored the diffusion of paper, writing and those arts and sciences in which the pre-Hispanic Indians were outstanding. This was also the period of increased social stratification and differentiation which we call urbanistic. Its principal protagonists were the inhabitants of Teotihuacán, the Zapotec of Monte Albán, the Olmec of La Venta and Tres Zapotes, the Totonac of El Tajín, and the Maya of the Petén and Yucatán. Perhaps none of these cultures, with the exception of Teotihuacán, ever became an imperial state, but they apparently settled for common traditions, sharing their technical advances and language and worshipping the same pantheon.

At some point in the prolonged Classic Period, other Mesoamerican cultures also reached a considerable level of development, such as those which developed in Calixtlahuaca[1] and in the west of Morelos, as well as other urban groups, perhaps subordinate to the simultaneous force of the more advanced civilizations. Among these peoples, the Maya attained an artistic and scientific level and a social structure which distinguished them from all others.

Technical and aesthetic progress crystallized during the Classic Period, and a way of life spread which was a significant advance over that of the Pre-Classic or Formative Period. Throughout the Formative Period, we find great similarities in the style and manufacturing techniques of ce-

205

ramics, as these developed in the different cultures, but no proof of regional markets and settlements of the size that developed during the Classic Period (Sanders and Price, 1968). What is more, the Formative cultures coincided in erecting the first religious structures supported by a pyramidal base, in evolving the beginnings of a social stratification, and in the dissemination of clay figurines throughout their communities where household gods were still worshipped. It is also probable that all cultural sub-areas of Mesoamerica exhibited similarities in dress and diet, which never varied much thereafter, even to the decorations, materials, and techniques used to produce them.

The various cultures gradually developed distinguishing characteristics. We do not know the exact epoch in which certain features began to differentiate one culture from another, but it is possible that some of these traits already existed in the Formative Period. We have examples of this in the Maya manner of burying their dead, a characteristic retained throughout their history, in their custom of skull deformation, and the naturalistic representation of certain physical features such as the nose sculpted on their clay figurines (Thompson, 1959).

The Maya Formative Period in the Southern Area (Pacific Coast) is usually thought to have lasted more than 1600 years, from 1500 B.C. to 150 A.D. (Coe, M., 1966b), but its origins are hard to date and are not as old as in the Central Area (the Petén) and in the Northern Area (Yucatán) (Plate No. 2, page 26). Mayanists usually agree that this period ended when the Maya began to use the Long Count Calendar, construct their first great ceremonial centers, erect the first stelae with sculpted hieroglyphs, introduce new architectural forms and techniques such as the "false" or corbel vault, and manufacture polychrome ceramics. These characteristics, which marked the beginning of the Maya Classic Period (Thompson, 1950), had already been in existence for some centuries when the Maya recorded the oldest known dates of their calendar on a series of stelae. On Stela 29, recently discovered in Tikal, the oldest known date of the Petén was recorded, corresponding to about 292 A.D. or even two hundred and sixty years earlier, depending on which correlation you use (Coe, W., 1959b; Shook, 1960). Stela 29 is twenty-eight years older than the famous Leiden Plate, dated 320 A.D., which shows a similarity in style, and thirty-six years older than Stela 9 at Uaxactún, which dates from 328 A.D. (Shook, 1960).[2] This leads us to think that the Classic Period began in the lowlands of northern Guatemala before the third century A.D.

It is most possible that future discoveries may push back the beginnings of Classic Maya culture. Current investigations in Dzibilchaltún, an extensive site on the outskirts of Mérida, have already thrown new light on the Formative Period in the Yucatán Peninsula, and the director of the excavations there believes that the correlation between the European and Maya calendars will eventually be set at a time several centuries earlier than the present chronology (Andrews, 1961). In addition, we have proof that hieroglyphic writing was already known by other Mesoamerican cultures before the Classic Maya had occupied Tikal and other centers of the Petén, and that the inhabitants of the ancient site of Kaminaljuyú, near the present capital of Guatemala, among other groups, constructed stone monuments long before the erection of Stela 29 in Tikal (Shook, 1960).

We must also consider the results of Harvard University's archeological excavations at the site of Altar de Sacrificios, a long occupied ceremonial center located in the western Petén near the confluence of the Salinas and Pasión Rivers some 130 kilometers southwest of Tikal.[3] The inhabitants of Altar de Sacrificios had already built a ceremonial center by 500 B.C. and used the corbel vault during the first millennium prior to the Christian era. The site of Tikal was already inhabited by 600 B.C. or even earlier, its people trading for obsidian, quartzite, and stingray spines with neighboring regions (Coe, W., 1965).

The Formative Period seems to have developed concurrently in the highlands of Guatemala, the Yucatán Peninsula and, judging by excavations, at Altar de Sacrificios, Tikal, and Uaxactún in the Petén lowlands (Willey, 1965a, 1966; Coe, W., 1965; Coe, M., 1966b). We know that the people in the Guatemala highlands had possessed Maya cultural features and characteristics since the Formative Period, although we can not be sure that they were the settlers of the Petén.[4] Perhaps the origins of Classic Maya culture are to be found in La Venta, Tres Zapotes or other Olmec centers, or in the region of Chiapas (Thompson, J.E., 1959), geographically located between the Zapotec culture and Maya territory (Plate No. 1, page 15). Nor can we discard the possibility that the ties between the Maya area and the rest of Mesoamerica were stronger than has been thought, and admit that other Mesoamerican civilizations provided the stimuli necessary for the flowering of the Maya culture. These stimuli were then taken to the Petén where they reached their apogee after 300 A.D.

By this I do not mean to imply that the Petén was uninhabited during the Formative Period. Structure E-VII-sub at Uaxactún is a valuable piece of evidence that Maya groups lived in the Petén lowlands during the Chicanel Phase (350 B.C.-150 A.D.) of the Formative Period. They built their houses on platforms and had already adopted, in their religious structures, the pyramidal shape on a regular base with profusely decorated stairways. All these characteristics were repeated and modified during the Classic centuries, but they do not, in themselves, provide sufficient proof that Uaxactún had been the center of a radiation of Classic culture. Therefore, the hypothesis maintained for fifteen or twenty years by Morley (Morley, 1956) should be revised since it seems unwarranted to assert that Maya culture originated in the Petén based only on the fact that it was this particular region which yielded some of the oldest examples of hieroglyphic writing and roofs with angular arches—two principal Classic Maya features. Let us not forget that, until a few years ago, studies of the Maya Formative Period were almost completely limited to the Petén area.

The Formative Period in Yucatán was much more important and lasted longer than is generally thought. We had known about the existence of a numerous agricultural population grouped around water holes or *cenotes*, but since no remains of ceremonial architecture was found, it was thought that the cultural level of these people was not high. Pottery, too, discovered in sites where, centuries later, some of the Classic centers were built, showed little variety in form and design, as seen in pots and bowls decorated with simple grooves and geometric incisions. At Río Bec, Edzná, Santa Rosa Xtampak, El Palmar, and other sites in Campeche, remains of ceramics have been found and dated as early as the Middle (600-300 B.C.) and Late Formative (300 B.C.-150 A.D.) (Piña Chan, 1970). It was only in the 1959-1960 season of excavations in Dzibilchaltún that archeologists found a structure built entirely in the Formative or even Pre-Formative occupations of the site (Andrews, 1961). At Dzibilchaltún, Structure 450, as they called it, was formed by four superimposed structures. Six periods of occupation could be determined in its phases. The most recent building phase was added at the same time as those belonging to two other structures at Dzibilchaltún which had already been dated 310 B.C. by the radiocarbon method. We have yet to learn the dates of the first and oldest construction stages of Structure 450.

One significant factor stands out. In its final phase, Structure 450 consisted of a raised pyramidal base which supported a temple. The base rested on a trapezoidal foundation and was reached by a stairway flanked by two projecting terraces. The stairway faced a broad rectangular plaza with its axis slightly off-center. The plaza measured about twenty-eight meters wide by thirty-eight long and was enclosed on three sides by a wall more than one meter wide and one or two meters tall. The fourth side, facing the base, was formed by three rectangular platforms. The wall seems to have existed since one of the earliest construction phases of the complex and was subsequently rebuilt during some of the later phases found in Structure 450 (Andrews, 1961).

In other words, since several centuries before the Christian era, the Maya cultures of Yucatán laid out their temples with plazas which, when surrounded by walls, took on the characteristics of a semienclosed precinct.[5] This arrangement was later to become prevalent in areas influenced by Maya culture in and outside of the Yucatán Peninsula, even in such removed sites as Bonampak, Quiriguá, Kucikán, Nakum, and many others.[6]

I think that it was architectural beginnings such as these which gave rise to the acropolis arrangement we find later in such principal Classic ceremonial centers as Copán and Cobá (Plates Nos. 29 and 30). With the data we have, it is difficult to determine exactly when urban design began among the Maya, but I was surprised to find a relation between temple and walled plaza at such an early time.

The art of urban design is quite different from urban planning, which is essentially a technique, or from architecture, sculpture, painting, and the lesser arts. Only those civilizations which have reached a certain artistic level and civic consciousness, be it popular or aristocratic, are concerned with urban design. It is a leisurely art, planned for the future, and its results are not immediately enjoyed. According to one famous Mayanist, Maya society was ruled by moderation, discipline, and dignity (Thompson, J.E., 1959), and I think perhaps for this reason they consciously raised urban design to a level rarely reached in the history of civilization. Detailed study of their prevailing principles may offer us deeper knowledge of other aspects of their cultural development.

The Formative Period came to an end in the Guatemala highlands in the second or third century of the Christian era (Shook and Proskouria-

30 *Coßa: Plan of the ruins. (Credit: Thompson, J.E., Pollock, H.E.D. and Charlot, J., "A preliminary study of the ruins of Cobá-Quintana Roo, Mexico," Carnegie Institution of Washington, No. 424, Washington, D.C., 1932.)*

29 *Copán: The Acropolis. (Credit: Proskouriakoff, Tatiana: "An album of Maya architecture," Carnegie Institution of Washington, No. 550, Washington, D.C., 1946.)*

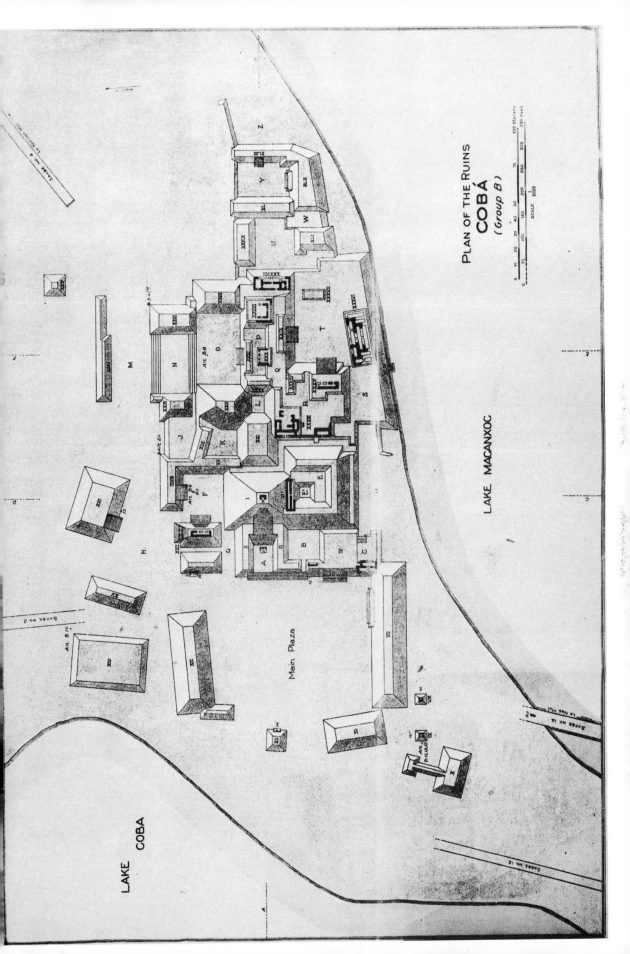

PLAN OF THE RUINS
COBÁ
(Group B)

LAKE MACANXOC

LAKE COBA

Main Plaza

koff, 1956; Smith, 1955). In this region, the Formative was a period of continuous evolution which culminated, during the centuries immediately prior to the Christian era, in events similar to those which pushed the other major Mesoamerican cultures forward to their Classic stage. The transition from Formative to Classic in the highlands of central Guatemala was reflected in an increase in the numbers of principal centers of cultural influence and in a change towards agglutination around the nuclear centers.

Toward the end of the pre-Christian or the beginning of the Christian era, the Petén was well populated by groups possessing some of the characteristics which later distinguished the Maya from other Classic cultures. For unknown reasons, the center of influence of Classic Maya culture shifted toward the present Department of Petén in northern Guatemala, and toward the neighboring territories of British Honduras and the Mexican provinces of Chiapas and Quintana Roo. It was in this inhospitable environment that Maya culture came to flower.[7]

The rolling ground of the Petén is covered by a thick tropical forest of mahogany, ceiba, cedar, palm, and sapodilla trees.[8] The northern Petén is low, lacking both rivers and lakes. There is ample farmland but the soil is thin and wood clearance must have demanded continuous efforts. Prolonged periods of drought alternate with months of intense rains which flood the depressions or *bajos* and encourage moss to cover the stones of the buildings and trunks of trees.

To control nature and exploit its resources has been a constant challenge to mankind. To achieve this goal, man has felt compelled to determine the social and economic structure which best adapts to his needs and possibilities. The first urban cultures in Asia and northern Africa reached their peak favored by the comparative advantages of the rich river valleys of the Nile and Indus, and in Mesopotamia and China. Fertile land and irrigation permitted intensive agriculture and assured harvests, thereby encouraging population groupings previously unknown in size and density. As a result of the obvious advantages these waterways offered for transportation, the peoples living up and down the valleys established cultural ties. Merchants were not long in reaching the sea to brave the dangers of travel to other lands, and so promote the interchange of ideas, products, and people. This commercial activity gave rise to groups of specialists such as artists and artisans as well as the traders themselves.

Theoretically, nothing like this could have occurred in the Petén. It was an isolated region when the territory became the center of Maya culture. During Formative centuries, Mesoamerican overland and commercial routes were probably more to the south, along the Pacific escarpment toward Kaminaljuyú, or northward from the central Valley of Mexico toward the Olmec centers, and around the shores of the Laguna de los Términos up to the centers of Campeche and Yucatán. Certainly water trade routes existed along the coasts of the Gulf of Mexico and the Pacific. But there was no incentive which could possibly have tempted merchant or colonizer to undertake the long, dangerous journey through the trackless forests of the Petén. Easy wealth was not to be found there, and the land was thin and difficult to work. In order to plant a section of land, the Maya farmer had first to clear giant trees and to protect the subsequent harvest from animals, blight, unexpected drought, and the inexorable invasion of weeds.

The Petén has not changed fundamentally in two thousand years. The sapodilla tree grows today as it did centuries ago when its wood was used for lintels in temples and palaces.[9] The climate, flora, and fauna have not undergone any major changes, according to the studies of the zoologists, ornithologists, botanists, and other specialists collaborating with the team from the University of Pennsylvania which is in Tikal studying the causes underlying the rise and subsequent decline of Classic Maya culture in the Petén.

Were the occupants of Tikal, Uaxactún, Altar de Sacrificios, Seibal, Holmul, and other Formative centers of the Petén the descendants of a group, physically akin to the Maya but weak, subjugated, and obliged to take refuge in such an unpropitious region? And could they, nevertheless, create those conditions necessary to receive, adopt, and spread the ideas which are recognized as the characteristics of a civilization and had been developed centuries before, under more favorable environmental and cultural conditions by the urban cultures of the Nile and Indus, Mesopotamia and China? Or was this the voluntary migration of an "élite" which, with the cooperation of the settlers already living in the region, undertook to colonize a territory with no apparent possibilities? Were these groups driven out for religious or political motives? Could a period of warfare have caused a population displacement even though nowhere in the Formative centers of Guatemala's highlands, in Yucatán, nor for that matter in any of the Early Classic centers of the whole Mayan area, do we find man-made fortifications?[10] Perhaps, as Thompson cautiously suggests, the forefathers of the Maya arrived during the Formative period in small groups, accompanied by other peoples of about the same physical appearance, at the lands which were later to be their definitive habitat (Thompson, J.E., 1959).

POLITICAL ORGANIZATION

The Post-Classic urban cultures of Mesoamerica and South America are distinguished by their tendency toward organizations of vast political units with imperialist and military characteristics. The Inca and the Aztecs, at their zenith a few decades before the arrival of the Spaniards, were examples of centralized governments which, backed up by military machines, based their rapid and surprising success on politico-administrative organizations, superior for their time and place. They were further helped by their unprejudiced ability to absorb what other subjugated cultures had achieved before their annexation. Even the technical limitations of the Inca and Aztecs go unnoticed in the face of the dimensions of their undertakings.

We have no such complete knowledge of the kind of political organizations which predominated among the Classic cultures. They seem to have developed under quite different conditions. Although it is true that each of them reached a cultural identity permitting us to distinguish what was specifically influenced by Teotihuacán, what was Olmec, Zapotec or Maya, this is not conclusive proof that these cultures were backed up by centralized governments with dominion over an extensive territory. The Maya may have been a nation with a strong central authority and a class society, or they may have been composed of a loose confederation of small, freely integrated, independent territories. It is this second possibility which was generally accepted until recent years, and for this reason, the subjugated territories, subordinate to the principal ceremonial centers, have often been compared to the Greek city-states after the eighth century A.D., as well as to the Italian free cities of the twelfth to fifteenth centuries and the commercial cities of the Hanseatic League (Morley, 1956; Thompson, J.E., 1959). Recent research has shown that the second possibility was partially wrong and that the lowland Maya were probably ruled, since Early Classic times by a theocratic élite (Coe, W., 1965) with influence over a not well-defined territory.

The Classic Maya may have been united by the same language—different from that spoken by the other Mesoamerican civilizations—and linked by a common religion based on a cult of time in its diverse manifestations that was never equaled elsewhere in the world, neither before nor after that epoch (Morley, 1956). Also, the Maya maintained the same traditions and shared technical and artistic advances. Among the latter, we find art and architecture in stone based on similar principles of construction and aesthetics, although the quality of the materials used would necessarily impose certain regional and even local differences.

I think, however, there is a more basic difference between the Maya form of government and its analogy in Greece. The triumph of the Greek city-state lay in the kind of government it attempted and in the ideals of its inhabitants, even though putting these into actual practice was not always successful. Similar principles were not in effect among the Maya, judging by what we know about their social structure during the Classic Period. Pericles described the ideal city as a free city with a government of the people and by the people; having a Parliament, Municipal Council and Courts which bring together all free citizens; a society in which merit receives recognition, and everyone participates in public life because he wishes to, and no one is excluded; a people who achieve physical and mental balance, who love beauty and keep their tastes simple, who can confront risks conscious of the dangers and who create no differences between farmer and city-dweller because everyone enjoys intellectual contemplation (Glover, 1953).

Was it, perhaps, ideals such as these which moved Maya farmers to rebel against the ruling class on more than one occasion, as the many destroyed effigies of persons—but not gods—attest? Was that social unrest, apparently restrained for centuries, the factor which directly or indirectly precipitated the decline of the Maya centers? Perhaps, most likely of all, was it simply a matter of a revolt growing out of the people's general discontent in the face of the labor required by the endless religious construction ordered by an ever more tyrannical hierarchy, anxious to appease the gods and solicit better harvests? Or will we discover some day that at the bottom of everything was the honest desire of the people to retain the cult of their ancestral gods, like Chac, the simple god of rain, and the other gods of nature who were being pushed out by malevolent and bloodthirsty foreign gods?

The Greek city-state was a way of life adapted to the special geographical characteristics of the area which produced the stages of Hellenic political and social transformation. Territorially, the Greek city-state occupied a limited area—a valley, or at most, neighboring valleys, with exact geographical boundaries, where physical environment favored the development of a community group with shared interests and problems. The Greek city-state of its time was supported by historic and economic factors. It later became the mode of living best adapted to the Hellenic concept of a Democracy which sought to maintain equitable balance in population and productivity.

Plato's ideal city-state required the necessary number of inhabitants to defend it in case of danger, yet never so many that the people could not personally know their political candidates. Greek statesmen held that the relation between population and the productive possibilities of the territory was an essential condition for economic and political equilibrium. A city-state should be large enough to be a self-sufficient unit, but the number of its inhabitants must not be so great as to impede the work of governing. In synthesis, the Greek city-state was an experiment in a communal way of life with regional and local shadings, but which, for political, cultural, economic, and moral reasons, retained its identity even outside the Hellenic territory itself.

If the Maya, independently of their internal political and social structure, were organized in separate political units, circumstances may have arisen to determine a way of life suited to their needs and adapted to the possibilities of the environment where they developed their particular form of civilization. The forest encouraged dispersion rather than urban concentration, but we should not overlook the possibility that the idea, even the socio-political structure favoring the formation of independent territorial units, may have been brought in from other regions. It might have come from the Guatemalan highlands, where even today the valleys promote isolation and self-sufficiency in population groups; or it may have come from Yucatán, where localized and scarce sources of available water gave rise to a concentrated community life; or from lowland Tabasco, where slash and burn agriculture had been practiced for a long time.

Geographically, the Petén is the exact opposite of central Guatemala and central Mexico. Agriculture in the forest, unlike that in a river valley or on a delta, does not require the participation of large groups; rather, it is on a family scale. There were no economic or geographic reasons, nor do we know of any historical antecedents, which might have favored the existence of city-states among the Maya. I have already pointed out that, politically and socially, the Maya seemed to have preferred a different kind of organization. It is possible, however, that each political unit of the Maya may have had jurisdiction over a specific territory and maintained the necessary ecological balance by periodic colonization.

Considering its stratified social hierarchy and hereditary form of government, some of the centers may have acquired preeminence over others: Copán, as the intellectual center of Classic culture; Tikal and Chichen Itzá, as religious centers and Meccas for pilgrims; Palenque and Yaxchilán, to a lesser degree, as artistic centers, and so forth. In all Maya territory, however, we find no capital which acted as seat of a centralized government controlling an extensive area, until the time of Mayapán in the Yucatán Peninsula when the culture was already in full decadence. The larger Classic centers, moreover, are not thought to have exerted pressure on the smaller ones other than that entailed by their greater prestige, and then, it would have been on a cultural rather than a political plane.

Each Maya political unit was probably marked by a ceremonial and community center and would have included other minor centers subordinate to the main one. Hamlets and clusters of houses were spread between these centers. We have yet to learn if two or more centers of primary importance and relative proximity, such as Tikal and Uaxactún, belonged to the same or to different political units.

THE RULING CLASSES

Each Maya political unit was probably directed by a single chief called *halach uinic*[11] who was succeeded by his eldest son. This was a hereditary position generally limited to a single family, since custom decreed that brothers act as regents and even successors if the *halach uinic* died leaving minor children or no direct heir. Only when the ruling family lacked male members, did the principal members of the state elect a competent successor (Landa, 1938). These observations of Bishop Landa reflect the situation existing in Yucatán at the time of the Spanish Conquest, but it is not clear if they are applicable to the Maya states during the Classic Period. Probably not, as Yucatán had been ruled for centuries by a hereditary élite of Mexican origin.

The *halach uinic* had broad powers (Morley, 1956), and his responsibilities were not only civil but religious and military as well. His every act was circumscribed by an elaborate ceremony, and his complex, ornamented garments must have proved burdensome during the long hours he had to spend fulfilling his multiple duties. Basing his decisions on prior proof of the candidate's capabilities, the *halach uinic* selected the town heads, or *batabs,* and those men who were to occupy other administrative posts. He was also responsible for political decisions, but in this case he relied on an advisory group made up of the head priests, specially appointed advisers and other chiefs.

The relatives and descendents of the *halach uinic* and the magistrates and chiefs he appointed constituted a nobility which retained its privileges until after the Spanish Conquest. Important administrative and ceremonial positions descended from father to son or to a near relative. Only in the event of war or an internal revolt did some affairs become subject to the decisions of the military chief (Morley, 1956). This chief was elected every three years from among the members of the lesser nobility who filled the subalternate ranks of the army.

All we know of the classic Maya is based on archeological evidence and on the translation of Maya hieroglyphs. The situation existing in the Petén between 300 and 900 A.D. is far from clear. However, we can assume that Maya civilization was not uniform although a uniform system of recording and communication was used (Willey, 1966). Differences between the architecture and pottery in the Petén and Yucatán during the Classic Period are easy to detect.

Priests must have had great prestige in this society. Not without reason are temples, platforms, and other structures connected with their religion the finest, as well as the largest examples of Mayan architecture. The priesthood could be attained only after a novitiate period which the candidates entered as boys. Novices lived together for long periods, receiving special instruction, and participating in frequent ceremonies. There was probably a distinction made between ordinary priests and those occupying the most important positions in the hierarchy.

The High Priest's was also a hereditary position; at least this was the custom at the time of Yucatán's conquest, according to Bishop Landa. Perhaps to keep these positions closed to other candidates, the members of the highest ecclesiastical hierarchy made sure to pass on their knowledge to their descendents. The high clergy enjoyed special educational opportunities and made up an intellectual élite which, with good reason, distinguished the Maya from other cultures in pre-Columbian America.

For the first time in the history of mankind, a system of numeration was conceived, based on the position of number symbols, which involved the concept and use of the mathematical quantity "zero" (Morley, 1956). Maya chronological calculations form a progression based on the determination of a fixed date. They also developed two parallel calendars. The sacred one, called *tzolkin,* with 260 days divided into twenty months of thirteen days each, would have been the one used by the people. A second calendar, or *haab,* consisting of eighteen months of twenty days each and a short month of five days, made up the Maya civil year of 365 days. Both calendars coincide in the initial date of the year once every 52 *haabs* —in other words, once each 18,980 days.

The Maya also developed ideographic writing, generally used to record their astronomical chronologies and observations but not the important historical events of their civilization. Their knowledge of astronomy permitted them to correct the duration of the solar year with an even closer approximation—1/10,000 part of one day—than that reached by the Gregorian modification which was adopted a thousand to fifteen hundred years after the Maya (Morley, 1956).

The activities of this intellectual élite constitute one of the most important and least known scientific movements in the history of civilization. The results of their investigations benefited the entire Maya society since we can suppose that the scientist-priests concentrated in the different ceremonial centers met from time to time to exchange ideas and unify standards which could then be adopted by all the communities (Redfield, 1958).

Although we primarily attribute the scientific advances of the Maya civilization to the priestly class, their range of interest and influence was undoubtedly broader. They surely brought their presence and knowledge to bear on those arts and techniques in which the Maya excelled, and they probably had more effect in this sphere than they have received credit for.

In the European society of great Gothic cathedrals, priests were responsible for many of the more notable architectural works. As part of the small educated group in medieval society, they influenced music, literature, painting, and sculpture. When not planning and designing, we find them promoting and maintaining cultural traditions.[12] It was a period of intense community pride which, elevated by religious faith, gave rise to an essentially anonymous artistic movement, although some medieval artists did succeed in standing out as individuals as their signatures, marks and other kinds of identification will attest.[13]

In Mayan art, anonymity seems to have predominated. If we find images of persons, apparently members of the ruling class, preserved in painting and bas-relief, I think this was not because of their military prowess or their scientific or artistic contributions, but rather for their identification with the process of time—that is, with an event or a cycle marked by the erection of a stela. Who, for example, was the personage depicted on the Red Stela of Tikal who so enraged the people at one point in history that they defaced his image? In an art showing occasional scenes of daily life and the representation of apparently important historical events, the protagonists remain impersonal.[14]

What was the contribution of the priestly class in all this? I think there can be no doubt that they participated in deciding the location and even the size of the structures and monuments, and therefore their form, since they were used as astronomical observatories for the detailed study of the solar year. We see examples of this in the arrangement of the structures forming Group E at Uaxactún (the location of Pyramid E-VII in relation to Temples E-I, E-II and E-III); the architectural characteristics of the Caracol, or observatory, at Chichen Itzá; and in other cases where a special interest in the placement of the stelae in a particular location within the ceremonial center is indicated.

Another fact which leads me to believe that the priesthood participated in some of the arts in which the Maya were outstanding, as well as in the general planning of the ceremonial center, is the repetition of certain patterns in bas-relief sculpture seen to advantage in the glyphs decorating the stelae. Since these underwent few variations in the same epoch and within the same ceremonial center, it suggests that the models were passed down from father to son. We can be almost sure that certain centers stood out above others in their own particular specialities, owing to a geographic location which put them in the path of influences from other lands. The inhabitants of these centers gradually refined their special skills and passed their techniques on from one generation to the next. The Piedras Negras artists excelled in stone sculpture, those in Tikal were unrivaled as woodcarvers, and Palenque artisans were unique among the Maya for their use of stucco (Morley, 1956). I question, however, if the art of urban design can be transmitted so easily.

Mayan architects used topography to set off groups of buildings forming a ceremonial center. Hills were transformed by the use of terraces, streams channeled to serve utilitarian and aesthetic purposes, and artificial reservoirs for water storage incorporated into the overall design. Because of the difficulty of working with a variety of such large elements, the orderliness of the architectural masses of a Maya ceremonial center, achieved by the use of axes of composition for individual groups and often by skillful use of general axes for the entire ceremonial complex, is particularly noteworthy.

The proportions of the structures and the technical problems which their erection must have entailed, could only have been worked out by specialists with mathematical and mechanical knowledge. The results point to the active participation of persons with highly specialized training. We can not consider these constructions the creations of artists and artisans exclusively, no matter how skillful and precise the work of their basalt or diorite chisels, their hair or feather brushes, their delicate tools of obsidian or bone used to carve jade miniatures. Such men would have lacked the knowledge and even the interest necessary to evolve architectural complexes of such an outstanding spatial quality. Furthermore, they would have lacked the prestige and power to mobilize the human resources needed to build them. It is for this reason that I believe the priestly class must have played an active role in the planning and directing of the architectural work and in the arranging of the groups of buildings which formed the ceremonial centers. Their influence in the other arts is harder to substantiate, but undoubtedly many of the designs painted or sculpted by skillful Mayan artists and artisans were following conceptions of the priests and perhaps were even directly guided by them.

The influence of this group may have been decisive in the formation of plans and calculations for engineering works, especially in laying out and constructing the regional roads and causeways which linked the groups of buildings in the ceremonial centers, as well as in building water storage reservoirs, drainage operations, moving large masses of earth and in engineering the corbeled interior vaults of the temples and palaces.

Recent writers are inclined to accept that Maya leadership was theocratic and priestly and that Maya society became more stratified towards the Late Classic (Willey and Bullard, 1965; Coe, W., 1965; Haviland, 1967). Burials discovered at Tikal show striking differences in their conception as well as in their location. By the Late Formative, after centuries of continuous occupancy of the same area, the people of Tikal witnessed the consolidation of an élite with superior power and control over the farmers. The élite were buried in the Acropolis, carefully bundled and surrounded by pottery. Commoners were often buried below the floors of their houses. Stature has also been used to prove social differences in Tikal and the development of an hereditary élite, height being affected by the diet (Haviland, 1967). Wall paintings, relief sculptures, and drawings also point to a class structure where élite and commoners are distinctly represented, with serfs and slaves, probably prisoners of war, forming the lower groups.

THE MERCHANTS

Between the agricultural population and the ruling classes, a significant middle group existed, made up of artists, artisans, musicians and such skilled workmen as stonecutters, potters, carpenters, and weavers. Because of its specialized nature, this work must have required full-time dedication, particularly in times of feverish construction. The members of this group probably lived on a daily wage paid in specie.

In a strata slightly above this group, but still below that of the ruling class, were the merchants. Most of the data we have about them is limited to Yucatán about the time of the Spanish Conquest. During these declining centuries of Maya society, the merchant was apparently much more closely identified with his political chiefs than was the Aztec merchant (Chapman, 1957). Bishop Landa, in his classic *Relación*, provides us with proof that even the ruling classes were interested in commercial activities. He mentions that a member of the Cocom family, which at one point governed in Mayapán and later had their headquarters in Sotuta, fifty-five kilometers east-southeast of Chichen Itzá, was away trading outside the territory when the Xiúes, the principal family of Maní, formerly from Uxmal, fell upon his city in his absence, and slaughtered his whole family. The provincial lords of Calkini and Acalán also engaged in trade (Piña Chan, 1970).

Maya merchants traveled from Yucatán's centers to Xicalango, an important city on the western shore of the Laguna de los Términos in the swampy delta formed by the Grijalva River where it empties into the Gulf of Mexico. They also journeyed southeast, where there were two important commercial centers: Nito in Guatemala, and Naco in Honduras

(Méndez, 1959). The region around Nito, near Lake Izabal's outlet into the Bay of Honduras, and Naco, between the Motagua and Chamelcon Rivers, which was inland but not far from the coast, was an important producer of cacao, the Mesoamerican Indian's currency. Considering the difficulties of overland travel across the Peninsula of Yucatán, it is quite possible that a good deal of the traffic followed the coast, where the important markets of Cozumel, Champotón, Ecab, Bacalar, Polé and others sprang up.

In Xicalango, Maya merchants came in contact with their Aztec colleagues. They brought with them slaves and salt, a trade partly controlled by a foremost Yucatecan family, the Cheles; as well as honey; flint, both unworked or already made into utensils; and cotton cloth—an ordinary item on the Peninsula but highly prized elsewhere (Chapman, 1957). They also brought wax, honey, coral, and henequen from Yucatán, cacao from Chiapas and Tabasco; obsidian and alabaster from Honduras, and feathers from Guatemala (Piña Chan, 1970).

The Maya of the end of the fifteenth and the first decades of the sixteenth centuries lacked the imperialistic pretensions of the Aztecs, so the Yucatecan merchants never became infiltration agents of the state. Their mission was as peaceable as allowed by the confused political circumstances in Yucatán during the years prior to the Spanish Conquest. Trade and the traders did not emerge from the changing political and social structure nor from a need to reactivate the economy through a large-scale exchange of products. They developed as a logical consequence of the most efficient utilization of the production of three huge geographic zones, each having its own characteristics and resources.

Regular trade and the merchants themselves, as a specialized and outstanding group in Maya society, existed during the Classic and perhaps even the Formative Periods (Thompson, 1959). In a room of Structure I at Bonampak, we see paintings of merchants belonging to the Classic Period. Their apparel indicates no particular rank, and the wares they exhibit, such as pelts and fans made of feathers, are those in which that region must have specialized. But the necklaces they offer for sale seem to be of jade, a hard stone imported from the Olmec territory, 300 kilometers distance from Bonampak through forests and over mountains, or from the mountains north of Zacapa, in Guatemala (Thompson, J.E., 1959). Classic Mayan artists earned fine reputations and good prices by carving this demanding stone and reexporting their work.

Kaminaljuyú seems to have been an important stop on the Classic trade routes. At this site, archeologists found many three-legged vessels with covers, molded in a Teotihuacán shape and painted and stuccoed in designs characteristic of that center. Toward the end of the Early Classic Period, about 500 A.D., Kaminaljuyú probably was a merchant colony of Teotihuacán (Michels, 1969). Other vessels found here point less definitely to connections between Kaminaljuyú and the territories of the south and with Monte Albán and El Tajín (Kidder, Jennings and Shook, 1946).

Trade was not limited to the principal centers. Even smaller centers must have been subject to influences of every kind. Along the Usumacinta River and its tributaries, especially along the Pasión River and its offshoots, an important traffic of persons and goods must have flowed between the Petén and central Guatemala as far as the rich strategic coast occupied by the Olmec cities (Coe, W., 1959a). This traffic was surely a primordial factor in the artistic flowering of such outstanding Classic centers as Palenque, Piedras Negras, Yaxchilán, and others still relatively unknown.

Perhaps the most conclusive proof of the intensity of commercial activity which characterized Mesoamerica before the coming of the imperialist states was the extraordinary diffusion of two types of pottery. One of these, Plumbate Ware, was widely disseminated during the eleventh and twelfth centuries. The large iron content of the clay and a high firing temperature gave Plumbate pottery a special hardness and uniform leaden color (Méndez, 1959) which made it a prized utilitarian and decorative article throughout Mesoamerica. The other pottery came in two varieties: Fine Orange and Thin Orange Ware; the latter already known during the Classic Period (Thompson, J.E., 1959).

THE PEOPLE

The Maya people were farmers. The produce of the earth formed the basis of their diet. With the production from his *milpa*, or maize field, the farmer fed his family and paid his share of the tribute which supported the specialized artisans and the ruling class concentrated around the ceremonial centers. Each farmer was a member of a community. The community owned the land and paid the tribute to the groups living in the ceremonial centers, upon which there must have been some kind of dependence. The farmer worked his assigned section of land and accepted this tribute payment as just another of his community's responsibilities.

All over Mesoamerica, from pre-Columbian times up to today, a *milpa* refers to a parcel of land, cleared of weeds, where the farmer plants his crops. The *milpa* of the Maya farmer was generally made of the thin soil of the forest which yielded less the more it was cultivated. This made it imperative to rotate the *milpas* every two or three years and finally to let them lie fallow for periods up to four times that long. If the Maya farmer did not have the use of a *milpa* large enough to encompass this system of crop rotation, he would have to alternate his annual farming in widely separated plots of land. As the result of this system, population density in the agricultural areas was necessarily low.

Let us suppose that conditions in the Mayan area have hardly changed in fifteen hundred years, which is not unlikely, and that agriculture is the same today as it was a thousand or more years ago during the Classic Period. The spring rains fall in May in Yucatán and the Petén, and the Maya farmer must await them with his *milpa* ready to be planted in maize. The actual planting will have to wait several weeks until the ground, hardened by months of drought, receives enough moisture. The dry months last from January to May, and the farmer utilizes this time to burn the trees and brush which he has cut down during the wet season. Once the maize is planted, the farmer waits five months before it is ready to harvest. This work begins in November and takes four or five months. Taking advantage of these waiting months, the farmer works his *milpa,* weeding it frequently if the terrain has been planted the year before since in certain areas the weeds tend to grow thicker on land which has been used for one or two seasons.[15] The harvested maize is then stored, generally still on the cob, in cribs built on wooden posts and roofed over with palm leaves (Morley, 1956).

What conclusions can we draw at this point? The primary one for this study is that the Maya farmer's life was closely tied to his *milpa*. In the middle of his parcel of land, he had a modest hut where he kept tools and even slept during the most active seasons in the fields. His permanent dwelling was near those of the other farmers, in small settlements or simply groups of huts which might be a few hundred meters apart or separated by several kilometers. This settlement pattern of rural Maya dwellings was determined by the characteristics of the land, and by the methods used in preparing the fields and in the cultivation and rotation of the crops. It is interesting to note that lack of metal tools such as axes and machetes obliged the Classic farmers, limited to using fire and stone tools, to work twice as hard as their present-day counterparts to clear a parcel of land. On the other hand, since other chores, such as building fences to protect the crops from domestic animals, were not necessary, we can surmise that the time needed to plant and harvest the same size plot of land has not changed (Hester, 1952-53).

Assuming environmental conditions similar to what we find today, the distribution of the agricultural population throughout the territory occupied by Classic Maya culture, at least in the Petén, was determined by the necessity of letting the land lie fallow four years after one harvest or seven years after two successive harvests from the same parcel (Cowgill, 1960). This system, in spite of its obvious disadvantages, was the only feasible one in the tropical forest for a people lacking draft animals and plows.

The second conclusion we reach is that the Maya farmer had a good deal of free time to spend in other work. The diet of the Maya has not changed much in ten centuries, and so today, as in the Classic Period, they grow the major part of their foodstuffs. Between 75 per cent and 85 per cent of what the modern Maya farmer eats is maize. Other foods are *frijoles,*[16] or kidney beans, chili peppers, honey, fruit, squashes, and edible tubers (Morley, 1956). Chocolate was not an ordinary drink among the common people, although it was for the ruling class. Hunting deer, wild turkey and ocelot supplied a pleasant change in an essentially vegetarian diet.

Some forty years ago, investigators calculated that a Maya family of five consumed an average of 3,000 pounds of maize a year in addition to the other food supplements we have mentioned (Ricketson and Ricketson, 1937). Today, as possibly during the Classic Period, a maize harvest in the Petén yields 1,425 pounds per acre the first year of cultivation and 1,010 pounds the second. It has also been observed that the yield of emergency crops planted in swampy areas and high places during years of drought or disproportionate rains show small variation in their average (Cowgill, 1960). With this data, we can calculate that a Maya farm family of five needed less than three acres—approximately 1.35 hectares—to feed itself.[17]

Let us revise the calculated figure of three acres to include the percentage paid in tribute. If the land's fallow period was equivalent to four times that of its period under cultivation, each *milpa* would have between twelve and fifteen acres—5.4 to 6.7 hectares—perhaps less. The farmer would cultivate a fifth of this area annually, or between 2.4 and 3 acres, which would take him about two weeks to prepare, one or two days more to shed the grain, another couple of weeks to sow, and ten days to harvest. To these forty days, we should add those devoted to maintaining the field during the growing period, storing the harvest and other minor chores (Morley, 1956). In approximately two months, the Maya farmer of the Classic Period produced the quantity of food necessary to feed himself and his family, as well as his share of the community tribute payment. Certainly he would spend part of the remaining time in some kind of hand craft or in making and repairing his tools, which included the *xul*, a sharpened stick used to make holes in the earth; the *chim*, or fiber bag, used to carry the seed; and his bow and arrows. He might also help build a house for a couple whose wedding was approaching—an undertaking in which the whole community joined. The majority of his free time, however, would be spent in constructing the temples, palaces and other buildings which formed the ceremonial centers, or in excavating and re-covering the water storage reservoirs, or in clearing woodland and hauling stone needed to construct the causeways or *sacbe* which connected one principal complex with another.

Organized into crews, the farmers were taken to the quarries to bring out the rock and cut the blocks used in all major construction. They then had to transport this stone, using log rollers, hard wooden levers, and fiber ropes, to the construction site. Some of the men watched over the lime kilns, while specialized artisans on scaffolding worked on a frieze or carved the specified designs on a stela, and the Maya farmer-workman built trestles and inclined ramps of earth and tree trunks, pulled on the ropes and pushed the heavy blocks into place.

This work was never ending. Year after year, generation after generation, the Maya paid tribute to their gods and to the system imposed upon them in this manner. Ceremonial centers grew larger, a new pyramid was built over an old one, a new group of buildings appeared in a forest clearing, and every twenty years a new stela was erected. With humility and devotion, probably mixed with fear, the people respected the decisions of those who interpreted the will of the gods, of those supposed to have the power to intercede for a better harvest or to put an end to a period of drought. In the feverish building mania the priesthood imposed on the people, there must have been something more than a simple desire to continue religious and aesthetic building projects. This pressure was undoubtedly a means to dominate the population, to establish a social differentiation and to demonstrate who held the power by playing on the Maya farmer's fear of nature's uncontrollable phenomena.

Slaves were at the lowest level of Maya society and surely already existed during the Classic Period. The condition of slavery was passed down from generation to generation. Yet, in a communal society traditionally honorable and respectful, in which each member willingly shared in misfortune and abundance alike, there must have been few commoners who would have wanted to harm their fellow man.[18] Perhaps slavery was the punishment inflicted on anyone committing a serious offense, most likely against a member of the ruling class. The majority of slaves, however, were prisoners of war or foreigners bought from traders. The destiny of these slaves was uncertain, and many must have ended their days as sacrificial victims of some religious ceremony or accompanying their deceased masters to the tomb to serve them in the next life.

Maya society was divided into distinct classes, which was reflected in the location of their respective clusters of dwellings around the complex of temples and plazas forming the ceremonial center.[19] The ruling class probably lived in the palaces and in the districts close by the principal structures of each center. Nevertheless, despite the difference in rank and location, there were no major variations in the type of houses of the two extremes of Maya class structure, the nobility and the commoner. Only the palaces represent a different approach to domestic architecture and they seem neither numerous nor large enough to house the élite groups living in each center.

The Maya farmer built his house near the field he worked; therefore, away from the ceremonial centers. Isolated, or grouped together with similar houses, its character has changed little since the height of Maya culture. After the farmer had picked out the site and cleared away the brush, he assembled the materials needed with the help of family and friends. He invariably built his house on some small elevation of the ground and supported it on a platform of earth and rock somewhat wider than the area to be roofed over, although he might on occasion omit the platform if the terrain was high and flat enough. These platforms sometimes served two, three or even four houses each (Bullard, 1953, 1954, 1960; Wauchope, 1938; Haviland, 1965; Willey and Bullard, 1965).

The farmer built his floor of well-packed earth which he sometimes covered over with a thin layer of mortar. Four holes were then sunk in the earth floor to hold the forked wooden posts which supported the roof beams. Roofs were thatched with palm, their slant varying with the region up to as much as 60 degrees in some areas of Yucatán (Wauchope, 1938). The farmer raised his walls using poles daubed with mud to stop up the gaps.

Contrary to what was once supposed, Maya houses were not all alike. We are beginning to realize that the differences between them were significant from an historic as well as economic and social point of view. Structurally speaking, however, the Maya had few possible forms to choose from, given the building materials at their disposal (Wauchope, 1940).

Two basic floor plans eventually emerged, one square and the other rectangular, depending on regional custom. In the rectangular house, the builders usually rounded the corners or built the narrow ends into an arch shape. There were no openings other than the two doorways, one on each of the two long walls.

A house destined for a single family, which rarely consisted of less than five members, measured forty square meters or less, according to the individual plan. The hearth, made of three stones, stood in one corner. In the opposite corner, at times separated by a partition, sleeping hammocks hung from the beams. The only other furnishings were a bench or two and the simple pottery pieces used in preparing food.

The Maya farmer spent the day away from home. His wife, on the other hand, was busy from before dawn with household activities: grinding maize, cooking, arranging her utensils, and cleaning the modest home where she had lived since the day of her marriage, where she had borne her children, and where she would stay until she died.

Near the main plazas of the ceremonial centers, archeologists have found unusual buildings which, for lack of a better word, we call "palaces." These palaces seem to have been more common in the centers of Yucatán and Campeche (Thompson, 1959) than in the Petén and the Usumacinta River Valley. However, they have also appeared in such important centers of Yucatán, as Uxmal, Chichen Itzá, and Dzibilchaltún and in smaller centers like Sayil, Labná and Kabah, as well as in Tikal, Palenque and other places removed from Yucatán (Plates No. 31 and 32).

The palaces which have been found are invariably built of stone, and their floor plans reflect the serious technical limitations of the volumetric

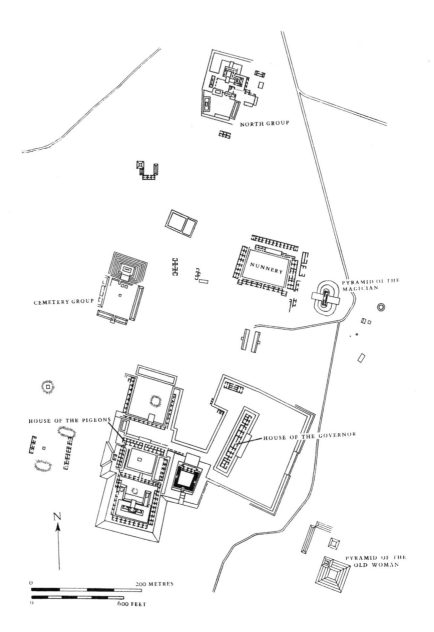

NORTH GROUP

NUNNERY

PYRAMID OF THE MAGICIAN

CEMETERY GROUP

HOUSE OF THE PIGEONS

HOUSE OF THE GOVERNOR

N

PYRAMID OF THE OLD WOMAN

0   200 METRES

0   600 FEET

31 *Uxmal: Plan. (Credit:* Guía Oficial de Uxmal, *I.N.A.H., Mexico, 1956.)*

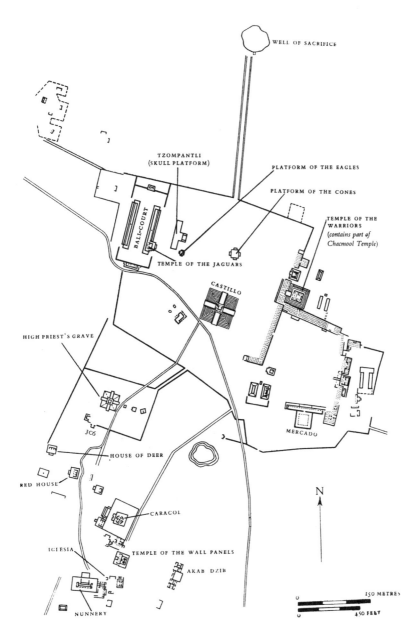

WELL OF SACRIFICE

TZOMPANTLI
(SKULL PLATFORM)

PLATFORM OF THE EAGLES

PLATFORM OF THE CONES

TEMPLE OF THE
WARRIORS
(contains part of
Chacmool Temple)

BALL-COURT

TEMPLE OF THE JAGUARS

CASTILLO

HIGH PRIEST'S GRAVE

3C6

MERCADO

HOUSE OF DEER

RED HOUSE

N

CARACOL

IGLESIA

TEMPLE OF THE WALL PANELS

AKAB DZIB

NUNNERY

150 METRES

450 FEET

32 *Chichen Itzá: Plan. 1) Sacred* cenote, *2) Ball Court, 3) Skull Platform, 4) Platform of Jaguars and Eagles, 5) Venus Platform, 6) The Castillo (castle), 7) Temple of the Warriors, 8) The Market, 9) Steam Bath,
10) Cenote and Temple of Xtoloc, 11) The Ossuary, 12) The Red House,
13) The House of the Deer, 14) The Caracol (snail), 15) Temple of the
Sculptured Panels, 16) The Nunnery and Annex, 17), The Church, 18)
The Akab-Dzib ("place of obscure writing"). (Credit:* Guía Oficial de
Chichen Itzá, *I.N.A.H., Mexico, 1955.)*

Mayan architecture. Their interest lies in the way these masses were presented within the general design of the ceremonial center and in the beautiful composition of the façades which were formed by two main horizontal tiers. The lower tier was usually left as a smooth surface and belonged to that part of the building we might call functional. In contrast, the upper tier, often wider, was always lavishly decorated with geometric designs and naturalistic abstractions. It served as covering for the masonry and fill used to form the interior arch, and at the same time, topped the building as a decorative and imposing crest (Plate No. 33).

In the architectural use of space, a Maya structure lacks interest. The interiors are elongated and dark, monotonously alike. It is surprising that a culture which reached such a high scientific level in some fields should have been unable to free itself from the spatial limitations imposed by its unevolved building technique. The corbel vault of overlapping rows of projecting stones permitted only restricted light. Interior space was narrow, for instance: two-and-one-half meters wide in the Palace at Sayil; less than three meters in the small building called "Chinchachob," or Red House, belonging to the Maya period at Chichen Itzá; two-and-one-half meters in some rooms of the Nunnery and Annex, also at Chichen Itzá; one-and-one-half meters in the Castillo at Meco, in Quintana Roo; and two meters in the Palace of the Stuccos in Acanceh (Marquina, 1951). Palaces were frequently formed by an arrangement of these long rectangular rooms several chambers deep.[20]

The deficient structural technique that characterized Mayan architecture in stone did not produce an atmosphere suitable for prolonged occupation. Not only were the rooms narrow and dark, but they were inconveniently proportioned and uncomfortably damp during long periods of the year when their porous stones became impregnated with moisture. It is difficult to believe that these palaces were permanent residences, but it is also difficult to determine other uses for them.[21] It is possible that much of the nobility and priesthood lived in houses not much different from those of the farming population. We find the ruins of house platforms among the groups of temples making up ceremonial centers, or not far from them, and the only difference between the houses of members of the ruling class and those of the commoner seems to have been in the greater size and better construction of the houses nearest the center.

33 *Palenque: Photograph showing roof-crests. (Credit: Hardoy, 1961.)*

This generally accepted opinion may change when detailed studies are made of the specific functions served by certain of the ceremonial centers' structures. The recently mapped center of Tikal and its surrounding area shows that the greatest density of structures was around the main plaza (Plates No. 43 and 44, pages 181 and 184). From their size and characteristics, we think that many of these buildings must have been used as dwellings.[22]

THE DECLINE OF THE CLASSIC CULTURE

The causes underlying the abandonment of the Classic centers of the Petén and Usumacinta Valley have been the object of much speculation. Doubts live on, and theories come and go without providing us with conclusive proofs which either uphold or discredit them.[23]

During the last two or three centuries of the Classic Period, the people of this region produced the masterpieces of Mayan art. Maya sculpture reached its zenith in the three great ceremonial centers of the Usumacinta Valley between 692 and 795, a century of superb sculpture work, first in Palenque, then in Yaxchilán a generation later, and finally in Piedras Negras, where the art of sculpture reached its greatest splendor. Along with this artistic growth, new ceremonial centers were being built, existing ones enlarged and the number of palaces increased. During these centuries, the zone of Maya cultural influence probably reached its maximum range and the territory its greatest densification.

During the first years of the ninth century A.D., some of the ceremonial centers began to be abandoned. This exodus must have occurred gradually, started, perhaps, by the priests and nobility, and it involved not only the centers of the Petén and southern Guatemala, but also those located in the Usumacinta Valley, in Quintana Roo and in some parts of Yucatán.

While the Maya centers realized their last and greatest creative effort, the other Classic cultures in northern Mesoamerica were already in decline. At some undetermined point in its development, the Classic Period was upset by invasions of semi-nomadic peoples and warriors coming from the territories north of the central plateau of Mexico. These peoples must have directly or indirectly provoked Teotihuacán's destruction. In the wake of the invasions followed a dim and little-known period during which urban life throughout Mesoamerica continued its downward path.

The Maya ceremonial centers occupied during the Classic Period, however, were far from the scene of these invasions, and to have been affected by them, their decline must have already been in progress.

At the end of the tenth century, the Yucatán Peninsula was invaded by a Mexican group who ultimately imposed a different style of life from the old one. It was an invasion of "ideas," transmitted by a Toltec élite who took over after the Classic Period. But was Altar de Sacrificios occupied by a similar group? Was the Usumacinta Basin and, therefore, assuredly all the Petén, invaded by warlike Mexican people?[24] And were those invaders the descendants of advanced Classic cultures from central Mexico, pushed out of their cities by even more warlike peoples from the north? Or was it simply the seminomadic groups who had finished off the Classic cultures in northern Mesoamerica and then continued their conquests down to Maya territory?

What were the real causes behind the decline of the Maya? Was it sudden? The result of invasion? Did the invaders take advantage of a material and moral decline which had already begun among the Maya? The theory held up to a few years ago was that, toward the end of the Classic Period, there was a population explosion in the Petén Maya centers, as well as in those of the Guatemala highlands, such as Kaminaljuyú, and in the Valley of Mexico, including Teotihuacán (Willey and Phillips, 1958). Since the Maya clung to their traditional farming system without introducing technological improvements, erosion of their fields would have become critical and meant repeated harvest failures. Hunger and discouragement could have led to a progressive exodus.[25]

Change of climate, earthquakes, epidemics, and invasions have also been suggested as possible causes for the abandonment of the Classic centers. But the climates of the Petén and Yucatán do not appear to have undergone significant variations (Thompson, 1959); we have no proof that the Petén was subject to earthquakes (Morley, 1956);[26] the majority of illnesses which affect the present-day inhabitants are of European importation; and, with the exception of some centers like Benque Viejo in British Honduras, we have yet to find evidences of massive and violent invasions (Mac Kie, 1961).

It is also possible that erosion, brought about by faulty farming methods, filled in the lakes and reservoirs, reducing the availability of water and turning the area into the swampland that constitutes a large part of the Petén territory today (Cooke, 1931). Nevertheless, even if this had been the case, it could only have provoked a partial exodus since it seems unlikely that the water supply needed for such a dispersed population as the Maya would have been reduced to this extreme (Bullard, 1960). How would we explain that Kaminaljuyú, with a totally opposite environment, was also abandoned at the end of the Classic Period (Shook and Pros-kouriakoff, 1956)? And how could we account for the evacuation of the important centers in the Usumacinta Valley which were located near permanent sources of water?

In several of the Classic centers in the process of excavation at the present time, archeologists have found sculptures which show unmistakable signs of having been intentionally broken. The remarkable part about this is that, while the stelae or panels or thrones themselves remain intact, the effigies on them have been removed as though by violent blows. Some of the most famous works of Maya sculpture show the results of this apparently premeditated desire to get rid of the likeness of some personage. These defacements are found all over the Classic area, in Tikal as in Piedras Negras, and have been interpreted to be the result of a social revolution, originating in one or more as yet undetermined centers, which gradually spread over the whole Classic territory, putting an end to the old social structure.[27]

Once the priests and members of the nobility had been exiled or assassinated, the Maya farmer-worker would have been incapable of establishing a different order (Thompson, 1959). As a result, while part of the population moved to other regions, reduced groups of people would have remained near their fields or around the ceremonial centers, pitiful remnants of a culture which would never again rise to such heights. This persuasive possibility bears relation to events which occurred centuries before on Mexico's central plateau, where a social revolt is thought to have caused Teotihuacán's downfall (Bernal, 1959b).

If this actually was the case, then what were the causes motivating the revolution? Were they material, rising out of the growing scarcity of food? Were they spiritual, provoked by a religious transformation? Or was it a logical reaction of a people, weary of living in the semislavery the ruling class had imposed on them for so many centuries? Any of these alternatives, or others which may come to light in the future, lead to the same end. What we must not overlook is that, by its very social structure, Maya culture nourished the seeds of its own decline.

At the end of the ninth century, only three ceremonial centers continued to erect the stelae by which the Maya commemorated the passing of the centuries.[28] One of these was Uaxactún and another Tikal. It had been from these centers that Maya culture had begun to radiate six or seven centuries before.

NOTES ON · 6

1. BETWEEN THE FOURTH AND EIGHTH CENTURIES A.D., the inhabitants of Calixtlahuaca were strongly influenced by Teotihuacán. Considering the importance of some of the structures of this period, the zone of Calixtlahuaca must have already been densely occupied and its inhabitants enjoying a relatively high level of culture.

2. These are the oldest known dates in the Maya lowlands. However the inscription on Stela I found at El Baul, a late Formative site between Kaminaljuyú and the Pacific Coast, has been dated 36 A.D. Long Count dates from pre-Christian years have been recorded in Chiapa del Corzo, a late Formative site in the Grijalva Valley, and in Tres Zapotes, the Formative site in Veracruz (Coe, M., 1966).

3. The Salinas and Pasión Rivers are part of the Usumacinta River system, the natural communication route between the lowlands of the Gulf of Mexico and the forests of Chiapas and the Petén.

4. The excavations at Altar de Sacrificios have not completely clarified the origin of the Maya in the Petén. Mention has been made of the inhabitants of Guatemala and of the highlands of Chiapas as the probable ancestors of the first occupants of Altar de Sacrificios.

5. Consult the plan and the section of Structure 450 at Dzibilchaltún in the excavation director's report for 1959-1960 (Andrews, 1961).

6. The spatial arrangement of the plaza in front of Structure 450 at Dzibilchaltún was characteristic of the Olmec, as we have seen in a previous chapter. However, at La Venta, the complex was more elaborate and monumental and evinced signs of having been constructed according to a previous conception in which the use of an axis was emphasized. On the other hand, it is not equally clear that there was any previous concept in the group at Dzibilchaltún.

7. Good farmland, hardwoods, and abundance of flint and limestone may have been the main attractions of the Petén (Coe, W., 1965).

8. A recent historical study has permitted classification of more than two thousand species from the Tikal zone in the heart of the Petén (Lundell, 1961).

9. The sap of the sapodilla tree produces chicle, used in making chewing gum.

238

10. Earthworks have been discovered at 10 kilometers south and 4,5 kilometers north of the Great Plaza of Tikal. Their function is not clear but they could have been used as defenses (Puleston and Callender, 1967).

11. Literally translated, the term "halach uinic" means "true man."

12. The most notable example was Abbot Suger who promoted the construction of the Abbey of Saint Denis, a few kilometers from Paris. Benedictine monks from Cluny also wielded great influence. A monk of Canterbury took charge of the construction of his Cathedral when the planner and director of the work, William of Sens, had to retire as a result of a serious accident. Several abbots were responsible for directing the work on the Cathedral of St. Albans during the thirteenth century. The list is long and, with rare exceptions, it can only be catalogued after the thirteenth century.

13. According to Pevsner, each one of the Gothic cathedrals had its author, but in the first centuries of the Middle Ages the names of these authors had no importance, however immortal their works may have seemed. They were content to be laborers, working for a cause greater than their own fame (*Esquema de la arquitectura europea;* Nikolaus Pevsner; Ediciones Infinito, Buenos Aires, 1957).

14. Thompson says that the thousand or more Maya monuments discovered with glyphic texts were only used to record the passage of time and provide data on the gods and the necessary rituals (Thompson, 1959).

15. Recent experiments show that, at least in certain zones of Maya territory, for example around Lake Petén, weeds do not multiply after the first harvest (Cowgill, 1960).

16. Lacking meat, *frijoles* supplied necessary protein in the daily diet.

17. At present, each family of five persons requires two hectares of land in the San José area, on the banks of Lake Petén Itzá. Conditions in the Tikal area are today quite similar (Reina, 1967).

18. In villages and settlements, justice was administered by the oldest members of the community (Thompson, 1959).

19. "A political structure is implied by this ascending order of settlement units with minor leadership in the minor centers and greater power and authority residing in the major centers" (Willey and Bullard, 1965).

239

20. In Tikal, several palaces have been discovered near the Great Plaza and in the central districts.

21. Some authors are inclined to think that the palaces were used for administrative functions (Coe, W., 1962).

22. Some of the principal groups of buildings which form part of the center of Tikal must have been used as dwellings. These are the group which formed the southern boundary of the Great Plaza, the structures grouped around two immense courts to the left of Temple V, the groups located to the east of Temple V and the group of ruins we find about two hundred meters from the Madeira Reservoir (See Plate No. 44).

23. One of the main objectives of the University of Pennsylvania's present excavation program is to discover the causes for Maya decline in the Petén Lowlands (Coe, W., 1965).

24. According to the results of excavations in Altar de Sacrificios by the Harvard Foundation, the center was invaded by a non-Maya people, presumably Mexican, towards the end of the tenth century or perhaps even later, a fact which might have initiated the decline of Maya civilization in this region (Willey, 1966). In reports I have consulted on the University of Pennsylvania's studies in Tikal (see Coe, 1959b, 1962; Shook, 1958a, 1958b and 1960; Carr and Hazard, 1961; etc.), I have not run across any data which either supports or refutes the possible invasion of Tikal by non-Maya groups.

25. The progressive erosion of the fields is demonstrated in the profiles of the soil made during the Tikal excavations, in which only thin layers appear in the upper soil strata. Apparently the Maya farmer was well advanced as a practitioner but not as a scientist (Lundell, 1961).

26. For a more recent, dissenting opinion, see Mac Kie, 1961.

27. The social and political system which existed in Tikal during the Classic Period ended not later than the year 900 A.D. (Coe, W., 1965).

28. Stela II of Tikal was probably erected in 869 A.D. (Coe, W., 1965).

240

·7

DID THE MAYA BUILD CITIES?

"Skill and an inexhaustible patience had taught them to transcend the limitations of their neolithic technique; they were free to do whatever they liked with their material."

ALDOUS HUXLEY
(BEYOND THE MEXICO BAY)

□ 7

FROM GUATEMALA CITY to the ruins of Tikal takes an hour and a half by plane. A regular flight transports cargo, passengers and tourists from the most populated centers of the Republic to the lonely camps in the Petén.

A few minutes after takeoff, the landscape changes abruptly. The Guatemala highlands, with their lofty peaks and cultivated valleys, give way to flat, interminable jungle as far as you can see, interrupted only by a cut in the vegetation indicating a river. An hour's flight takes you to Lake Petén Itzá, with its three or four villages, and Flores, capital of the isolated Department of Petén, built on an island near the bank. Further north lie Tikal and Uaxactún.

Between the massed treetops, only a few trails and some cultivated fields near the lake are discernible. From time to time, a large greenish blot appears, indicating a swamp. Nothing on the ground moves. No one lives here, and no one traverses the forest.

More than one thousand years have passed since the Petén was almost totally abandoned by members of one of the most advanced civilizations in pre-Columbian America. During the intervening years, nothing has altered the existence of the reduced agricultural groups which remain tied to their worn-out maize fields.

Four years after the conquest of Mexico, Cortés and an army of one hundred forty Spanish soldiers, with three thousand Indian auxiliaries, crossed the Petén jungle (Cortés, 1961). At that time, the territory was occupied by the Itzá, a group that never reached the cultural level of the former inhabitants. Only at the end of the seventeenth century were the Itzá conquered and Tayasal, their principal city, built on an island off the banks of Lake Petén Itzá, captured by the Spaniards.[1] With this, the Colonial Period began in the Petén lowlands, a century and a half after its beginnings in Yucatán and in the highland area of volcanos and lakes where Alvarado founded Santiago de los Caballeros, the first capital of Guatemala.

During Colonial times, the Petén forest remained isolated. Some ruins, perhaps Tikal and Yaxchilán among them, were visited by missionaries and Spanish soldiers, but their arrival was due more to chance than to any particular interest in the region. Only at the end of the eighteenth century were there reports of finding the ruins of Palenque, a discovery which led to the explorations by del Río, a Spanish soldier, and Waldeck, a French adventurer, in the first decades of the nineteenth century. Years later, journeys by Stephens and Catherwood and the publication of their books contributed much to our knowledge of Maya ruins.[2] Stephens' clear text and the excellent drawings by Catherwood still provide us with a valuable source of reference.

Toward the end of the century, Alfred Maudslay traveled extensively over Maya territory (Maudslay, 1902). Some of his maps of Maya ruins represent a pioneer effort. The works of Maler, Seler and Tozzer appeared in the last years of the nineteenth and the first part of the twentieth centuries. The first half of this century knew in Morley, and later in Thompson, two of the most outstanding Mayanists in an ever-increasing group. The sheer number of specialists working today in Tikal, Altar de Sacrificios, Dzibilchaltún, Palenque, Kaminaljuyú and lesser centers, shows the level of interest on the part of private American institutions and the Mexican government in unveiling the many mysteries that still shroud the ruins of these centers of a brilliant civilization and in knowing the marvels of its art.

Before the research and reconstruction by the University of Pennsylvania in 1956 made it necessary to clear a part of the jungle for an airstrip, it was extremely difficult to get to Tikal. Today, while your two-engine plane is flying over the field, you can catch glimpses through a dense mass of cedar, mahogany, ceiba, sapodilla, palm, and other tropical trees, of the remains of the most extensive center occupied by the Maya during the Classic Period. Thirty meters or more above the highest tree-tops rise the imposing, yellowish roof-crests of the temples, some already cleared of the vegetation which hid them until recently (Plate No. 34).

Hours later, as you walk along open paths in perpetual shade, beneath trees and lianas which shut out the sun, starving the weeds into stunted growth; as you pass a few meters away from the unrecognizable ruins of

34 *Tikal: Aerial view of Great Plaza. (Credit: The University Museum, University of Pennsylvania.)*

an ancient temple or "palace" overgrown with roots, trees, vines, and grasses; when you become aware of the great distance between the remains of one group of ruins from another; while you endure the humidity, the heat, the flies, ants, mosquitoes, and millions of other insects; and as you see how wood rots in the torrential rains that last from May to January, you may well ask yourself—was Tikal really a city? Why did the Maya choose this inhospitable place right in the middle of a tropical forest? What forces impelled them to develop a civilization which apparently kept an unchanged political structure and socioeconomic organization for centuries, yet one that reached a level in the arts and sciences unequalled by any other Indians of pre-Columbian America and, indeed, by few preindustrial cultures?

Did the Maya build cities? Were Tikal and Palenque, Dzibilchaltún, Chichen Itzá and Uxmal, Copán and Cobá, Yaxchilán and Piedras Negras, cities? They do not seem to have been, in the light of present day knowledge and if we compare them with the formal contemporary criteria specialists use to define a city. For the purposes of this work, however, we must temper the usual standards of urbanism by considering the functions a center served in its region and in a certain period of its history. Perhaps, after all, Maya centers were true cities (Plates No. 43, 33, 42, 32, 31, 29, 30, 14, 13).

Let us imagine a fifth or sixth century merchant from Teotihuacán visiting some of the centers we have mentioned, to trade articles made in the central Valley of Mexico for products from the tropical forest. He would have found it difficult to apply the term "city" to the harmonious temple complex he found built around a plaza in the middle of the swampy Petén forests, its dwellings scattered about in clearings made by cultivated fields. For this merchant, the concept of a city implied an orderly plan, avenues bordered by temples and palaces or simple streets and alleys lined by houses with common dividing walls, with population densities that differed sharply from those in the *milpas* and in the cultivated plots near the more central city neighborhoods.

Nothing he saw in Tikal bore any relation to his idea of a city. Where were the streets, the rows of houses and the density typical of a city? As soon as the visitor became familiar with the various activities in Tikal, however, he would have realized at once that he was dealing with a center unlike any others he had encountered on his trip through the jungle. He would have noticed an unusual architectural scale, numerous and impressive palaces and a detail and harmony in the wooden lintels and in the stone friezes which pointed to the hand of superb artists. The number of stelae was greater than usual, and the ceremonies were more elaborate and witnessed by greater numbers of people. Every few days, merchants and travelers would arrive, bringing products from such remote places as the Pacific coast or the central Valley of Mexico. As he wandered through the plazas, mounted the temples or strolled toward the palaces, the visiting merchant would see people who appeared different in their manner, clothing, and in the adornments worn on their heads. These were members of the ruling class which governed the destinies of the rest of Tikal's inhabitants. Tikal filled almost every prerequisite generally accepted to differentiate a city from a village (Childe, 1950), but the Maya are an exception, and we must analyze them according to criteria other than those of increased technological advances and complexity (Redfield, 1958). More pertinent for this society are such criteria as the adoption of a particular form and structure for their centers; their utilization of values and elements in Tikal, Uaxactún, and other centers that differed from those of the villages and rural areas occupied by members of the same society; their introduction into these centers of certain economic and political functions that did not necessarily reflect a complex society, but rather one in which the members shared an accepted way of life unlike that in the neighboring *milpas*.

Maya society gradually acquired an aristocracy which reached its height in the Classic Period. Served by a specialized group, set apart from the rural farming population, yet probably not in the extreme theocratic position of the central Mexican societies during the same centuries, Maya aristocracy almost totally closed its doors to new members.

Its specialized minority is one proof that, at the beginning of the Classic Period, Maya society had passed beyond the village stage and was entering that of the city. We find further proof in the dependency of these urban groups on the primary production of people who lived outside the central complex of temples and palaces. There emerged both a producing group and a ruling class, "literati," as some authors call them (Redfield, 1958). But whether Maya centers had artists and artisans who created works and products for purposes other than merely satisfying local needs is hard to tell. There must have been artists totally dedicated to their craft, and possibly some of these were so outstanding that they were invited to other centers, where they promoted the regional stylistic variations we see in Maya art. But did some craftsmen form a group that worked exclusively on goods for market? Did Maya centers really develop workshops to transform raw materials into products, some destined for export, others for local use? Were the raw materials used in these workshops extracted by members of the community other than the craftsmen who created the actual goods?

In my opinion, the answers to these questions could provide us with a clear distinction between the village and city economies of that time. Basing my judgment on the known radius of dispersion of some of their products, I believe this separation into primary and secondary activities existed in Tenochtitlán and in Teotihuacán as well. On the other hand, it may have been unusual for the specialized Mayan artists and crafstmen, paid by the ruling class with tribute exacted from the rural population, to have stopped work on the friezes of the temples and palaces, on stelae and altars, on fitting the stone blocks or painting frescos, in order to devote themselves to manufacturing goods for local and foreign markets. Once his daily chores were done, the farmer, away in the countryside, would help his wife weave the cloth that waited in the loom, or he might mold clay with agile fingers or make and repair his tools, dispensing altogether with the manufactured products of the craftsmen.

Maya ceremonial centers undoubtedly were used for civic purposes in addition to their religious and commercial functions. That social and economic activities appropriate to a city took place in a community center, however, does not justify designating its immediate zone of influence as a city or an urban area. The known distribution pattern of ceremonial centers in a specific region of Maya territory—in this case an area of 2,200 square kilometers in the north of the Department of Petén—exemplifies how close together the Classic centers were built.

In 1958, Bullard, a Harvard University archeologist, traveled over this slightly rolling, densely wooded area, with vast swamps that today cover up to 30 per cent of the explored area. The ruins of twelve major ceremonial centers of the Classic Period are found here—among them Tikal, Uaxactún, Naranjo, Holmul, Yaxhá, and Nakum (Bullard, 1960). If these twelve centers were evenly distributed over the 2,200 square kilometers of explored territory, each center would have a zone of influence of 183.3 square kilometers. However, a ceremonial center of such importance was not limited to the great plaza, the acropolis, and the temples, nor to the palaces and other surrounding buildings.[3] Tikal's central section, for example, measures two kilometers each side, if we take as limits the North Group, Temple IV to the west, the Temple of the Inscriptions to the southeast, and the group of structures around Temple V to the south. We have been unable to determine the limits of the smaller groups which radiate out into the jungle.[4]

There are 1,300 meters between the ruins of Group E and those of Group A at Uaxactún, and 1,500 between those of Group C and Group F of this same center (Plate No. 35). Here, too, smaller groups spread out from a central point. In other words, smaller ceremonial centers were interspersed between large ones, but we cannot tell, when trying to identify them and establish some sort of urban scale in the territory, if these were city centers or village centers.

Major and minor centers differed mainly in size, but also in that the principal centers contained ball courts and palaces as well as stelae and altars which were often carved. Also, major centers were composed of several structural groups instead of one (Bullard, 1960), which suggests that a center's function may have depended on its size. Major ceremonial centers were generally located so as to be easily accessible, preferably on an elevation. Bullard, in his journey, found so many house ruins that his first hasty impression was that they were practically everywhere. Groups of two, three or four houses around a raised courtyard were built on a platform which was rarely over one meter high. In some cases, up to twelve buildings were spread over six hectares, situated according to the water supply and cultivable lands. Bullard reported that the size of a village might suggest that it was occupied by a consanguineous group (Bullard, 1960).

There seems to have been some relation between the distribution of villages and clusters of houses and the location of the minor ceremonial centers. Bullard suggests that each minor religious and civic center, formed by one or more pyramids and some secondary buildings grouped around a plaza, served from fifty to one hundred dwellings in what we might call zones.[5] The minor center's area of influence spread out over approximately one square kilometer until it encountered a similar zone from a neighboring center. This indicates a population density of about fifty to one hundred houses per square kilometer, or one to two hectares per dwelling. Such a density agrees with that found in Barton Ramie, a Classic site near the Belize River in British Honduras (Willey, Bullard and Glass, 1955). Here, too, 250 house ruins were recorded in an area of

MAP OF UAXACTUN

AFTER BLOM AND ANDREWS, 1924
WITH EXCAVATIONS BY
RICKETSON AND SMITH, 1931

one square mile (256 hectares) around a single religious structure (Willey, 1956a). Even if we assume that many of the platforms discovered were occupied by two or three dwellings, the total density must have been low.[6]

Willey suggests that the coincidence of mounds of ceremonial centers in the groups of housing mounds constituting a village, strengthens our impression that there was a relatively dispersed ritual and religious life associated with religious buildings similar to those in the principal ceremonial centers (Willey, 1956a). Minor centers were subordinate to the major ceremonial centers, which acted as the directing nuclei of much larger districts of at least a hundred square kilometers. In the Petén, at the time of the Classic Maya culture, the population was distributed in a density of approximately one dwelling, let us say five or six persons, per hectare, seldom more. The distribution of house ruins shows a stereotyped layout, and buildings are invariably located so as to take advantage of topography. From the low-density settlement pattern and total lack of a street system, we conclude that both major and minor ceremonial centers, with their surrounding dwellings, failed to constitute cities and villages by modern definitions.[7]

The two studies I have mentioned corroborate those undertaken by the Carnegie Institution of Washington over a quarter of a century ago, in which archeologists tried to establish the size of a population dependent on a ceremonial center (Ricketson and Ricketson, 1937). Through painstaking mapping of the ruins within a specific cross-shaped area, starting at the principal ceremonial center of Uaxactún, archeologists calculated a population density for the center's zone of influence at 271 inhabitants per square mile, or scarcely more than one person per hectare. Determined by a hypothetical percentage of housing occupation, these densities should be accepted with caution, but at least they confirm the absence of concentrations with urban densities among the Petén's Classic Maya.

Even around Tikal, the most important Classic center in the Petén, densities were probably not much greater. Calculations of the number of possible house ruins found in four sectors of one square kilometer, each one located at a corner of the mapped area around Tikal (Carr and Hazard, 1961), give us the following results: in the sector at the northwest corner, 63 dwellings or a density of 315 inhabitants per square kilometer (at five persons to a house); the sector at the northeast corner, 124 dwell-

35 *Uaxactún: Plan. (Credit: Ricketson and Smith, 1931; after Blom and Amsden, 1924.)*

ings or 620 inhabitants per square kilometer; the southwest corner, 65 dwellings or 325 inhabitants per square kilometer; and the southeast corner, 137 dwellings or 685 inhabitants per square kilometer. The average density, if all houses were occupied at the same time, would have been 486.2 persons per square kilometer or 4.86 per hectare. However, if we calculate on the basis of 25 per cent simultaneous occupation of housing, as did the Ricketsons, the density is hardly greater than 20 per cent of that found at Uaxactún.

We could accept that most houses were occupied at the same time, as once houses were built, they were occupied continuously up to the time of their final abandonment, although with frequent alterations (Haviland, 1969) and we might also increase the average family size to 5.6 people, as Haviland does. Even so, we would have densities between six and seven persons per hectare or six hundred to seven hundred per square kilometer (Haviland 1965, 1969).

In the immediate environs of Tikal's Great Plaza and around the Palace Reservoir, population densities were higher than those we have been discussing—considerably higher if current research proves that the palaces had residential functions. The concentration of population seems to have decreased noticeably a few hundred meters away from the center, since the four sectors under study begin only 1,300 meters in a straight line from the Plaza. Except in the immediate vicinity of a major center, a similarly low density probably prevailed throughout the territory, topography permitting. A superficial exploration, however, shows that all ceramic remains found near possible housing sites belong to the Late-Classic Period, which fact suggests almost simultaneous occupation.

Willey tried all three logical Maya grouping possibilities (Willey, 1956b). The first is that the ceremonial center was surrounded by dwellings so close together that there was no room to plant anything between them. The second postulates that there were no dwellings at all in the ceremonial center and that the houses of the population supporting it were scattered over a wide adjacent area. Willey's third possibility is the one which he and his collaborators formed in their study of the Belize River Valley (Willey, Bullard and Glass, 1955). He sums it up by reporting that there was no appreciable population concentrated around the ceremonial center, but the inhabitants supporting it lived in the neighboring countryside in small hamlets or villages rather than in isolated dwellings. His concluding suggestion is that we might also think in terms of two combinations of these three possibilities (Willey, 1956b).

The Maya way of life has changed little during the ten centuries that have passed since the abandonment of the Classic centers. The rural character of its civilization still exists among today's inhabitants of Yucatán and Guatemala who derive most of their livelihood from agriculture. Nor has the ancient settlement pattern of the population suffered significant changes. The former ceremonial center has been replaced, at times superposed, by a complex consisting of the Christian church, public buildings laid out around a plaza, and a few dwellings. Many of these are unoccupied during the better part of the year since they belong to farmers who only periodically leave their fields to meet in town for religious festivities and to go to market. A few houses belong to merchants and craftsmen. The present function of such a settlement is similar to that of the ancient ceremonial centers, as the bulk of today's Maya population still lives in the countryside.

There are various categories of centers, today as a millennium ago. In Guatemala, the difference between them lies in the relative importance of their markets and in the degree of permanence with which merchants and craftsmen occupy their houses. Colonial times introduced a city plan laid out in squares, which may have simplified the practical needs of subdivision in large cities, but which had and still has today a purely theoretical value in villages.

Layout alone does not determine whether a grouping of persons and structures constitutes a city—it is the sum total of many factors. Primary among these is function. Today, as in the Colonial Period and perhaps even during the Maya apogee in these lands, many villages might be considered urban based on their particular layout and type of buildings. However, they may lack the density, permanence of occupation, continuous presence of a diversified laboring group, and the manufacturing economy which would allow us to call them cities.

The prevailing Classic Maya scheme was apparently one composed of a predominantly rural population scattered in small settlements which depended on civic-ceremonial centers of varying importance. To those studies I have already cited, I must add that of de Borhegyi who, on the basis of recorded population movements, concludes that the lack of known massive displacements leads us to believe that modern towns were built either on or near the sites of existing pre-Columbian establishments (de Borhegyi, 1956).

Vogt has been doing research in the southern Mexican State of Chiapas where descendents of the Maya currently live. In his preliminary report on Zinacantán, Vogt suggests that the basic pattern of groupings was that of a ceremonial center surrounded by scattered villages in an arrangement not unlike that of Zinacantán today. He admits being tempted to interpret Zinacantán as a principal ceremonial center, the outlying hamlets as minor ceremonial centers and the groups around the water holes as villages (Vogt, 1959).[8]

The Maya did not always live in such dispersion. The settlement pattern, and its relation to those Maya centers I have analyzed, is the arrangement that probably prevailed during that culture's height in the Petén lowlands, Chiapas and the Usumacinta basin. This same form was no longer maintained, however, at the time of the reoccupation of these Classic sites, several centuries after their abandonment and just before the final Spanish Conquest. We can not even be sure that these were the population patterns and densities existing in Yucatán during the Classic Period, although we know they were definitely not those in use during the time of power of the League of Mayapán. Perhaps the settlement pattern of Maya territory changed according to the sociopolitical character of each great period in its history.

In the Petén, the Classic Period was probably relatively peaceful, the only disturbance of the large ceremonial centers' tranquil existence seems to have been a few local revolts provoked by popular resistance to certain individuals. Classic centers lacked defenses, although this does not necessarily mean that the Maya were unaware of the dangers inherent in the ambition of their neighbors beyond the forest. On the contrary, the location of some principal centers in remote and inaccessible sites suggests that military factors may well have been taken into consideration.

The Maya evidently had confrontations with their neighbors, but we know nothing about the extent of their military operations nor the kinds of external threats they had to meet. In the frescos at Bonampak, and in many of the reliefs, we see groups of prisoners and scenes of battles which indicate that warfare was certainly not unknown in Classic Maya life. We can only wonder whether the scenes represent events which took place within Maya territory or somewhere else. Perhaps united Maya power and prestige were enough to discourage more than one army; or it may have been their isolation that kept them away from the encroachment of the cultures from the Valley of Mexico and Oaxaca. Of course, warfare may have involved only combat in the open country, so that the aggressors never laid siege to the settlements.[9]

Whatever the reasons for the apparent security of the Maya, it vanished with the abandonment of the Classic centers. Post-Classic centers in still-isolated regions like the Petén were quite different at the time when the first Spanish conquistadors and missionaries visited them in the sixteenth century. The Itzá's capital, Tayasal, may have been established after the abandonment of Chichen Itzá around 1200 by part of the Itzá family. It was not only built on an island reachable only by canoe at the time Cortés saw it early in 1525, but was equipped with trenches and fortifications when Martín de Ursúa, Governor of Yucatán, captured it in 1697 (Morley, 1956). Built on several small islands in Lake Yaxhá was a Post-Classic town called Topoxté. The exigencies of its site required it to adopt a density and character totally different from those which had prevailed in the same zone during the Classic Period (Bullard, 1960).

Defense seems to have been an important factor in urban location for the Post-Classic sites in the Guatemalan highlands. Once Maya hegemony had disappeared, perhaps toward the middle of the tenth century, Guatemala's highlands were invaded by Mexican groups, mainly the Quiché. This invasion may have been as peaceable as that accomplished by similar groups in Yucatán during the same years, but we know definitely that when Quiché predominance decreased, local chiefs began warring. ring.

Ceremonial centers in this region of beautiful lakes and volcanos, valleys and deep ravines readily lent themselves as natural fortresses. Cahyup, in the modern Department of Baja Verapas; Mixco Viejo in Chimaltenango; Pantzac, Chutixtiox and Chutinamit in the Department of Quiché, were, without exception, located in inaccessible places. None of these centers seems to have served as a permanent residence except for a limited group of priests and chiefs. In general, these sites filled the double function of religious center and place of refuge for the agricultural population living in the surrounding hillsides and valleys.

Cahyup (Plate No. 36) was built on an almost perpendicular hill, strategically dominating the valley two hundred meters below (Smith, 1955). The site, accessible only from the west by a narrow stairway up the hillside, lacked natural water resources. The total surface area of the principal group, built on the highest point of the hill, was 250 by 150 meters. Chutixtiox was built on the summit of a hill over one hundred meters above

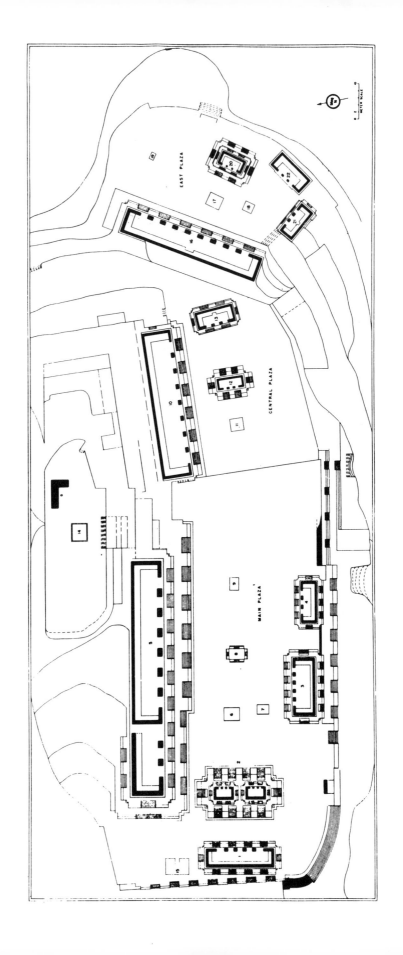

36 *Cahyup: Plan. Cahyup was a Post-Classic ceremonial center in the Department of Baja Verapas, Guatemala. It was built on a naturally defended site in accordance with the tendency prevailing during this period in the highlands of Guatemala and in other areas of Maya culture. (Credit: Smith, A. Ledyard: "Archaeological Reconnaissance in Central Guatemala," Carnegie Institution of Washington, No. 608, Washington, D.C., 1955.)*

37 *Chutixtiox: Department of Quiche. This Post-Classic ceremonial center was built on a hilltop, probably for defensive considerations. (Credit: Smith, A. Ledyard, "Archaeological Reconnaissance in Central Guatemala," Carnegie Institution of Washington, No. 608, Washington, D.C., 1955. After a reconstruction by Tatiana Proskiouriakoff.)*

the Río Negro, which curved around all sides of the site except the northwest (Plate No. 37). Ledyard Smith, who visited more than sixty centers in Guatemala, describes Mixco Viejo as having practically impregnable natural defenses. Not all these sites were initially constructed with defense in mind, however; some, like Taculen, must have added fortifications later. Iximché, the capital of the Cakchiquel, was built on a fortified plateau surrounded by ravines (Guillemin, 1967).

Of all Maya territory, Yucatán endured the most wars. It is not surprising, therefore, to find that several Yucatecan cities, which were built or rebuilt during the Post-Classic Period, have extensive and often elaborate defense systems.

Bishop Diego de Landa's description of this territory in his *Relación* is one of the few existing records from the first years of Colonial times: "Before the Spaniards conquered this country, the natives lived grouped together in cities in a most civilized manner . . . in the middle of the city were the temples with their beautiful rooms, and around the temples were the houses of the lords and priests and then those of the most important people. Next came the houses of the richer citizens and those of persons held in greatest esteem, and on the periphery were the houses of the lower class" (Landa, 1938). We cannot be certain that Bishop Landa's report gives us an accurate picture of life in Yucatán and other parts of Maya territory during the Classic Period, but his description seems to confirm the existence of the hierarchical social structure that shows up in the population's urban distribution pattern. In the Temple of the Warriors at Chichen Itzá, we find frescos painted during or after the eleventh century that depict Maya villages. We can see the crowded, disorderly pattern of a coastal town (Plate No. 38) and Maya city at the time of the invasion. The structures and urban features that Landa reports, the plazas and temples, palaces and whitewashed houses, are those cited by Bullard in his article to exemplify the quasi-urban mode of life which probably existed centuries earlier in the Petén.

38 *Chichen Itzá: This fresco in the Temple of the Warriors at Chichen Itzá depicts a fishing town on the Yucatán coast. Note the characteristic shape of the Mayan houses and the inclusion of trees in the residential area. (Credit: Morris, Earl H., Charlot, J. and Morris, Ann A., "The Temple of the Warriors at Chichen Itzá, Yucatan," Carnegie Institution of Washington, No. 406, Washington, D.C., 1931.)*

MAYAPÁN

At the end of the tenth century, Toltec groups from Central Mexico invaded Maya territory. This powerful militarist group introduced new cults and artistic concepts among Yucatán's Maya. Chichen Itzá was made the capital of a vast united kingdom. Mexican hegemony lasted for two centuries. Once its influence weakened, various family chiefs in the principal centers entered into prolonged conflict. Mayapán and the Cocom, an Itzá lineage, emerged triumphant. Their rivals, the Itzá of Chichen Itzá, abandoned the sacred city sometime around the end of the thirteenth century and never returned. The Kiú, who ruled in ancient Uxmal, finally took refuge in the city of Maní.

Mayapán's destiny seems to have been foreseen when it was founded by the Itzá leader, Quetzalcóatl-Kukulcán, in the last third of the thirteenth century. Kukulcán surrounded it with walls and made it the political center of the country, as the unwalled city of Chichen Itzá was the religious center (Krickeberg, 1961). Mayapán remained the principal city of Yucatán during the Post-Classic Period. Its ruins are located about forty kilometers south of the present city of Mérida and approximately the same distance from Chichen Itzá and Uxmal. The land around them is flat, without much vegetation.[10] Although the site of Mayapán seems to have been occupied before Kukulcán's arrival, we find no building remains from this earlier epoch (Proskouriakoff, 1954).

The ruins of Mayapán were surveyed and studied by a team from the Carnegie Institute of Washington (Jones, 1953; Bullard, 1953-1954; Shook, 1952). The city was enclosed by a stone wall nine kilometers around and rarely more than two meters high (Plate No. 39). The wall was widest at the base and two-and-one-half meters thick on the average, widening to four and even six meters in some places. It was cut by twelve gateways, seven large and five small (Shook, 1952) and followed the lightly rolling terrain of the area. This wall gave Mayapán an oval shape, somewhat pointed at the northeastern end. The intramural area today measures 4.2 square kilometers (420 hectares), the farthest points being 3,200 meters from east to west and 2,000 from north to south (Jones, 1953). Within this area, archeologists have found the remains of 2,500 different structures, almost all of them dwellings.[11] If we hold to the average of five persons to a house, as in the calculations for Tikal and Uaxactún, and assume that all houses were occupied at the same time, Mayapán would have had a maximum of 17,500 inhabitants at its apogee, between the middle of the thirteenth and the middle of the fifteenth centuries.[12]

In Mayapán, a house-group generally consisted of two or three associated structures, usually laid out in a rectangular form and set on a common terrace (Bullard, 1954). If one family had lived in each house-group, the total might have shrunk to 1,750 or even 1,158 family groups, and the number of inhabitants might have varied between 8,750 and 5,830 persons. However, in Mayapán, we find up to five or six structures on the same platform. Perhaps consanguineous groups lived here together. Still, the size and shape of the structures indicate that a good many of them may have served as dwellings for two or more separate, though related, families.

If the 420 hectares were occupied by 8,750 persons, the density would have been about 20.8 persons per hectare, but if the total population were only 5,830, overall density would decrease to 13.8 persons per hectare, which seems a rather low figure. Of course, if each of the 3,500 dwellings housed a five-member family, the density could have reached 41.6 persons per hectare.[13] Whatever the exact figure may have been, Mayapán's general density was probably not greater than thirty persons, or six dwellings, per hectare. This density is significantly lower than that in some districts of Teotihuacán, such as Tlamimilolpa, and of Tenochtitlán toward the end of the fifteenth century. It is more like the population of a contemporary suburb quite far out from the city proper.

The distribution pattern of Mayapán's ruins shows that the population density decreased from the center of the city outward toward its periphery, marked by the wall. In Sector R of the plan (Jones, 1953), next to the main ceremonial center we find probably more than fifty inhabitants per hectare, and Sector Q, which includes the ceremonial center itself, had an even higher density. Density declined to some twenty inhabitants per hectare in Sector I, on the periphery, falling off sharply in the zones outside the wall. Availability of water was also a factor in densification, since we find greater numbers of houses in the neighborhoods around the nineteen *cenotes* located in the intramural area.

Unlike Bullard's findings in the Petén and those of Willey and his collaborators in Belize, Mayapán's housing pattern did not follow a scheme in which each family lived next to, or near, its fields. Two factors seem to have prevented this. If one person needed 0.35 of a hectare to feed him-

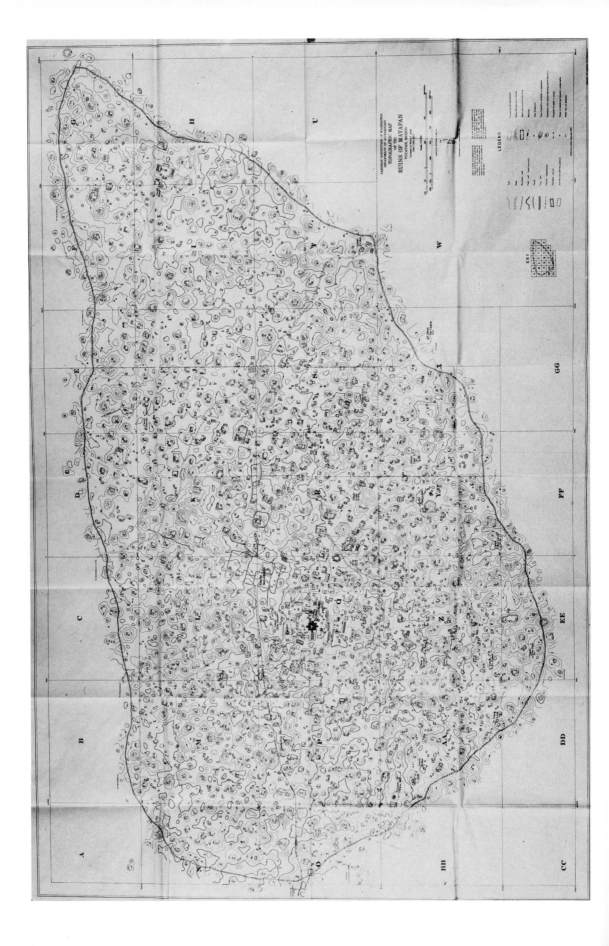

CARNEGIE INSTITUTION OF WASHINGTON
DEPARTMENT OF ARCHAEOLOGY
TOPOGRAPHIC MAP
OF THE
RUINS OF MAYAPAN
YUCATAN, MEXICO

LEGEND

self, according to O.G. and E.B. Ricketson, and assuming that 17,500 persons lived in the city, Mayapán's population would have required up to 6,125 hectares in yearly production to sustain itself.[14] A high percentage of the land around the city was difficult, if not impossible, to cultivate, and certainly Mayapán proper was built on rocky ground. In any event, their method of clearing the land obliged the Maya to leave sizable areas fallow. We would have to multiply the area mentioned by six, giving 36,750 hectares, or a square of about nineteen kilometers each side, to include the amount of land necessary to feed the population concentrated in the city. Mayapán's inhabitants could not possibly have lived near their fields as in the Classic centers.

The only possible explanation for the different way of life adopted in Yucatán during the Post-Classic centuries is that it resulted from the turbulent times prevailing throughout the last periods of Maya civilization. In view of this unrest, Mayapán's wall was more than justified. Krickeberg points out that the country was ruled by a warrior class, which was more interested in a concentration of population in various fortified sites than in rural groups scattered over a broad territory, that came together in the great religious centers only during the periodic celebrations (Krickeberg, 1961). If this were the case, it still does not explain why Mayapán permitted such a low population density spread out over the urban zone, making it necessary to build a long protective wall, both costly and hard to defend. Perhaps Mayapán was a true capital where only the ruling classes, chiefs of subjugated states, certain groups of merchants and artisans, and a large servant group resided, while the bulk of the population lived and worked around their fields at a distance from the city, in the ancient settlement pattern of their ancestors.

The mass production of incense burners and images, probably under the supervision of specialists dedicated exclusively to this work, was the result of an artistic decline and an abrupt change in religion that moved toward a personal worship without the intervention of priests (Proskouriakoff, 1954).

39 *Mayapán: Mayapán was the principal center in Yucatán during the Post-Classic Period. Note the surrounding wall and the location of the main ceremonial group (square Q on the plan). Each square is 500 meters each side. Houses have been indicated by outlined squares or rectangles. (Credit: Jones, Morris R.: "Map of the ruins of Mayapán," Carnegie Institution of Washington, No. 606, Washington, D.C., 1953.)*

In themselves, these factors do not prove that Mayapán had an urban economy, but they do corroborate the existence of a preeminent and ever-growing military ruling class, maintained by the production of the surrounding lands and by tribute collected from subjugated cities. Another explanation for the wall is that it surrounded the administrative area (Jones, 1953).

Mayapán lacked a city plan. Groups of houses were constructed to take advantage of natural elevations, and the people moved about on pathways in the free spaces left between platforms. Toward the north and center of the city, we find the remains of a short roadway, or *sacbe*, about a hundred meters long, that seems to lead nowhere. A second roadway of at least four hundred meters linked two structural groups of undefined function to the east of the main ceremonial center. The ruins of the principal center occupy an area of approximately four to five hectares in the west central half of the city. The center was built next to a *cenote*, and its main structure was a pyramid-temple dedicated to Kukulcán. Although a classic example of Toltec architecture, this building lacked the artistic merit of other similar structures belonging to a later period, such as the Castillo at Chichen Itzá. Only the higher building density and perhaps the superior size and quality of construction of the dwellings around the principal center confirm its civic and religious importance, marking it as the residence of the ruling class.

Mayapán contained other less important religious centers, scattered without any particular design within the intramural area, though most often found near the *cenotes*. I have tried to ascertain whether or not neighborhoods grew up around *cenotes* and religious buildings, but have found no salient features in the urban arrangement to indicate their possible boundaries.

In Mayapán, we find almost all the features that had formerly appeared in the Classic centers. The only innovation was the greater population concentration in densities probably unknown before in Maya territory, but the spatial treatment of Mayapán's ceremonial centers was inferior to that of the Classic Period.

Mayapán represents a late Maya stage, but, I think, an initial step in this civilization's evolution toward life in a progressively urban environment, even though we must assume that it presents a poor picture of urban life. Mayapán was the capital of a state in a period of cultural decline. Its development, like the development of the Maya Post-Classic

Period, coincided with the emergence of strongly centralized governments. Mayapán was probably a market town as well as the military center and residence of a warrior aristocracy. Foreign soldiers enjoyed great prestige here and belonged to the group which controlled Yucatán politically during a good part of the Post-Classic Period. The priesthood seems to have already lost its power. Class distinctions had become sharper, though this is not emphasized in the type of housing or urban structures found.

Economics did not, apparently, foster the beginnings of the Post-Classic Period in Yucatán since the basic economy continued to be the same type of agriculture as in the Classic centers, that is, spread out and with little or no irrigation. The reasons behind increasing urbanism had to be political and military. These factors, too, can push a society toward a way of life considered urban for its particular time and region.

Other Post-Classic cities in Yucatán had characteristics similar to those in Mayapán, though on a smaller scale. Chacchob, for example, also had an oval shape with a main axis of five hundred meters and was surrounded by a stone wall four to five meters wide by two meters high (Pollock and Stromsvik, 1953). The wall was built like that of Mayapán, formed by an interior ledge where the defenders could stand, protected by a higher exterior parapet. The intramural area was about fifteen hectares, from which rose the ruins of the broad Castillo, off-center with respect to the total plan. Chacchob, like Mayapán, shows no evidence of urban planning.

TULUM

On the eastern coast of Yucatán lie the remains of the walled city of Tulum. Its modern name, meaning "wall" or "fortification," replaces the original name of Zama. Of all Maya centers, Tulum is the one which, by its shape and layout, most approximates our image of a small city (Plate No. 40).

Tulum's beginnings go back to the Maya Classic Period. Its oldest inscription dates from 564 A.D. (Krickeberg, 1961), but, as a result of successive superpositions, we have only its final plan left from some time in the Post-Classic Period.

In the architecture of the Castillo, the most imposing structure at Tulum, we find such Mexican features as the two serpent-shaped columns

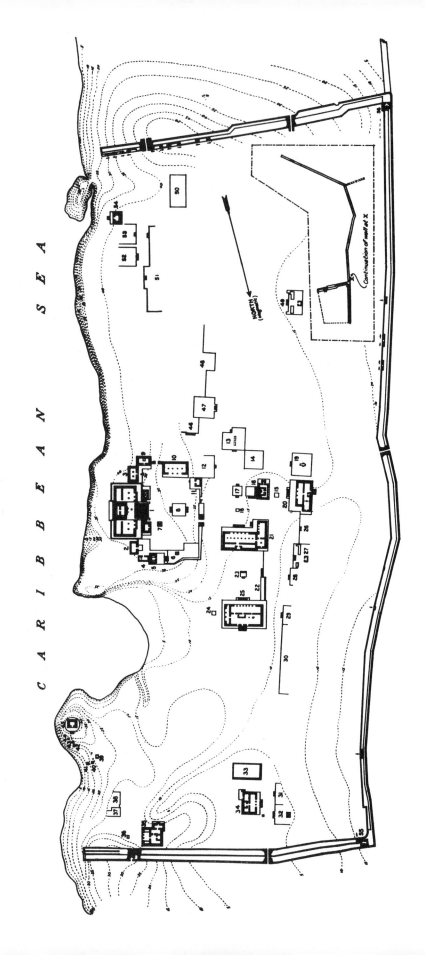

of the sanctuary doors and the figure of the Diving God. Paintings of the same origin in the Temple of the Frescos, like others in the city, are symbolic rather than realistic, similar to the Maya codices and strongly reminiscent of the Mexicans' painted manuscripts (I.N.A.H., 1959d). This suggests that the urban layout we see today was set definitively during the period of Mexican influence in Yucatán.

Tulum must have been a sprawling city, extending far beyond its walls. It probably was the city seen by Grijalva's Spaniards in 1518 which they compared to Seville (Lothrop, 1924).[15] Molded between the sea and the city wall, Tulum took on a rectangular form. Its boundaries were the ten-meter escarpment to the east, and the wall, over five meters wide and between three and five meters high, that enclosed the other three sides. The intramural area was 380 by 170 meters, with the longest side parallel to the coast. The wall was unquestionably built for defense and, from details found, it appears to have been better maintained than that of Mayapán.

A sizable percentage of Tulum's intramural zone was occupied by palaces and temples and the Castillo, a complex formed by several structures surrounding a closed rectangular court. The Castillo was the city's highest structure, and its massive form is still visible from far out to sea (Plate No. 41). Housing enclosures also formed part of this principal complex.

In Tulum, perhaps for the first time among Maya cities, we see two—possibly three—streets with clearly recognizable urban characteristics bordered by palaces, residences, and other minor structures. The two open gateways in the north wall, farthest from the coast, match the two in the southern side so exactly that we can draw an almost straight line between them without touching a building. We find an obvious intentional alignment of structures along this street, which runs the length of

40 *Tulum: Tulum was a Maya-fortified center on the east coast of Yucatán occupied during the Classic and Post-Classic Periods. For the first time among the Maya we find evidence of an urban layout and the existence of rectilinear streets bordered by temples and "palaces," as evidenced by the lines connecting the gateways on opposite sides of the wall or gateways in relation to the buildings. In the center of the plan facing the coast stands the Castillo, an elaborate religious complex which may possibly have been used for residential purposes. (Credit: Lothrop, Samuel K.: "Tulum. An archaeological study of the east coast of Yucatán," Carnegie Institution of Washington, No. 335, Washington, D.C., 1924.)*

41 *Tulum: Aerial view from the sea. In the foreground stands the Castillo. Note the isolation of this site. Defense towers can still be seen in the angles of the wall. (Credit: The University Museum, University of Pennsylvania.)*

the city. Near the south gateway, at the sea side, stands a series of buildings facing each other, forming what seems to have been a section of a shorter road parallel to the first one. A third street, running parallel between the other two, passes in front of the Castillo's main entrance. These streets indicate a sense of urban order in Tulum not found in other Maya cities. Judging from their characteristics, we can assume that the streets were laid out first and that the buildings which later filled the intramural zone were situated accordingly.

There is nothing to indicate that the density and housing pattern in Tulum differed from those found in other Maya cities, since the three streets mentioned affect only its walled part. Perhaps the ruling class and their servants lived inside the wall. However, taking into account the preponderance of palaces over religious structures, we can not discard the theory that Tulum may have been the refuge of some lord, who exacted tribute from the settlers of the surrounding territory during the Anarchic Period in which Yucatán lived after the decline of Mayapán. We do know that there were several minor temples about a hundred meters from the area subsequently walled, but we can not be sure whether they were still in use when the feudal years began in Tulum.

Local wars and the needs of defense forced many Maya centers, inhabited at the time of the Conquest, to fortify themselves. Some principal centers like Chichen Itzá were never walled, even during the years of greatest political unrest among the lords of Yucatán, and some groups, too reduced in number to undertake the construction of a wall, relocated in easily defended sites. The ruins of Xelhá are similar to those of Tulum (Marquina, 1951), which suggests the same Post-Classic origin. They lie on a peninsula with a neck 125 meters wide, fortified and completely enclosed by a wall three meters high. This wall was equipped with an unusual bastion which projected out over the line of defense, protecting the access of the single gateway (Lothrop, 1924). Champotón, in Campeche, had trenches and stone fortifications, and Ichpaatún, a few kilometers from the modern city of Chetumal in the southwest of Quintana Roo, was also walled (Armillas, 1948).

DZIBILCHALTÚN

Excavations in Dzibilchaltún, fifteen kilometers north of Mérida, by the National Geographic Society and the University of Tulane, and the work begun by the University of Pennsylvania in Tikal in 1958, could substantially modify the substance of this chapter, when the final conclusions of many years of work are published.

These excavations have thrown light on the development of a pre-Columbian culture in the north Mayan area and its relation to the environment and ecology, as well as on the origins, development and reasons for the abandonment of Classic centers in the Petén. These studies also indicate that the density and population of Dzibilchaltún and Tikal were greater than had been assumed up to a few years ago. If such were the case in these two centers, it could also have been true in Copán, Chichen Itzá, Uxmal, Cobá, and in the districts bordering the principal ceremonial centers.

According to the director's report, a number of facts have emerged from the excavation program at Dzibilchaltún. The north Mayan area was not only densely inhabited during the existence of the Petén centers, but it was covered by a network of massive architectural complexes which was at least as extensive, if not more so, than any we know in the south. This implies an equally advanced level of sociopolitical organization, apparently of a theocratic nature. When the Petén's cities were abandoned, their population may have migrated to Yucatán. In this case, they would have come as refugees, rather than as bearers of culture, to an area which, centuries earlier, had become their cultural equal or superior. Dzibilchaltún, among several other Yucatecan centers, seems to have survived the disintegration of its neighbors to the south (Andrews, 1961). Andrews also adds that finds made there of pottery, artifacts, and architecture indicate that this astonishing city was settled between 2000 and 1000 B.C., possibly even earlier. Its culture developed in the area itself and flourished throughout the Classic Period, when the city may have been the largest in the New World (Andrews, 1959).

Dzibilchaltún's archeological remains extend over almost fifty square kilometers, which are presently being carefully studied (Plate No. 42). In the center of this area, covering some ten square kilometers, was the main ceremonial site (Andrews, 1960). The first reports indicate a dense occupation of the whole area and a settlement pattern which ranks it as a principal ceremonial center to which other religious centers, of different size and category, were subordinate.

We do not know if Dzibilchaltún's settlement pattern changed or even if it had an urban layout and density. Although archeologists found only a few permanent structures, a good percentage of which probably belonged to the Formative Period, the director of excavations suggests that there were possibly 10,000 to 15,000 dwellings in Dzibilchaltún at its apex (Andrews, 1959). These dwellings may have been occupied by 50,000 to 75,000 persons, which, in an area fifty square kilometers in size, produces a density of ten to fifteen inhabitants, or two to three dwellings per hectare. This density may even have been doubled in some districts of the city, if we consider Dzibilchaltún's exceptionally large area designated for "public" uses. I have been unable to find out if those fifty square kilome-

42 *Dzibilchaliún: Partial reconstruction. (Credit: I.N.A.H., Mexico.)*

ters represent the limit of the archeological remains, or if they were adopted arbitrarily, with the actual ruins stretching out interminably as they do around Tikal. Nor could I verify whether the density of occupation of the ruins bears any relation to the distribution pattern of the ceremonial centers, becoming intensified in their immediate area and diminishing with greater distance from these centers.

Ceremonial groups were connected by causeways. A published map of Dzibilchaltún shows the existence of a monumental axis of some 2.100 meters in length. Smaller axes developed as branches from the main trunk.

Not only did the extent and occupation of Dzibilchaltún's zone of influence come as a surprise, but so did the antiquity of the site itself and its prolonged occupation during the Formative, Classic and Post-Classic Periods in Yucatán. Under its old name of Holtún Chable, the city was still an important religious center at least until the end of the period just prior to the Conquest.

Like Teotihuacán and other important centers of human concentration in Mesoamerica, Dzibilchaltún was probably only partially occupied during its different phases, that is, the entire area was not inhabited at the same time. Certain important architectural groups—the terrace of the Seven Dolls for example—seem to have been occupied in the early periods, only to be abandoned later during the Florescent Period, when all efforts were concentrated on building a new complex a few hundred meters away from the older one (Andrews, 1961). From the Late-Formative Period, or, chronologically, during the last pre-Christian centuries, Dzibilchaltún must have been a well-populated center which had already developed an architecture using pyramidal forms and had adopted the acropolis system for grouping complexes.

During the flowering of such famous Yucatecan centers as Chichen Itzá and Uxmal, Dzibilchaltún's hierarchy survived the abandonment of the great Classic centers, and Mayapán emerged as the nucleus of political life in the north of the peninsula.

TIKAL

The University of Pennsylvania researchers had different problems to confront than those encountered in Dzibilchaltún by the Tulane University team. Until a few years ago, Tikal was almost totally isolated.[16] The forest covered the smaller ruins, and many of the taller temples were, and still are, crowned by the tops of trees where their roots have dug into the stone sides of the pyramids.

In Tikal, researchers faced the huge undertaking of securing a water supply, building a permanent camp and opening pedestrian pathways and tracks for jeeps and tractors, transporting provisions, vehicles and personnel by air, and the never-ending clearing of the vegetation.[17] The jungle needs only a few days to reclaim what has cost weeks and months of back-breaking work to clear. The annual rainfall makes the continuous repair of roads imperative.

Tikal's fascination is unique, and excavations of the area have broadened our knowledge of Classic Maya culture in the Petén. The reconstruction of some of the temples, clearing the Great Plaza, setting various stelae and altars back into place, and opening several palaces have restored Maya architecture to the splendor and beauty which marked one of the culminating artistic periods of America's Indian civilizations.

One of the most important contributions made by the University of Pennsylvania in Tikal has been mapping the area around the principal ceremonial center (Plate No. 43). After several seasons of careful surveying and measuring, the first plan showing the occupation of a Maya center was completed.[18] To determine the occupation of Tikal's immediate surrounding area, the team arbitrarily selected a square, four kilometers on each side, with the central plaza in the middle. In almost the entire area, archeologists found conditions similar to those observed by Bullard in his travels, which are discussed in the previous chapter (Bullard, 1960). Here, too, house ruins are away from the low zones and are grouped around small patios built on platforms raised just above ground level. Temples and palaces are scattered among the dwellings, forming groups dependent on the principal center (Shook, 1958b). I chose at random a sector of one square kilometer in the southeast corner of the map that contained 137 small ruins and a rectangular structure 60 by 50 meters. These surrounded a court on three sides, leaving the northwest side open. If the 137 ruins were dwellings, only six, or 4.4 per cent of the total, were single structures. One group of five ruins and another of six were found, but 117, or eighty-five per cent of the total, were connected in groups of two, three, and four, of equal size.

Following the same procedure, I found the remains of isolated structures in 13.8 per cent of the ruins recorded in a sector of one square kilometer in the southwest corner, 13.7 per cent in the sector at the northeast corner, and 16 per cent in the sector at the northwest corner. On the other hand, only one ruin out of the 112 recorded in a central sector one-fourth of a square kilometer, belongs to an isolated building. In this case, we are dealing with one of the sectors of highest density which includes

43 *Tikal: Plan of the ruins. (Credit: See 44.)*

44 *Tikal: Plan of the Great Plaza (detail). (Credit: Carr, R.F. and Hazard, J.E., "Tikal Report No. 11, Map of the ruins of Tikal, El Petén, Guatemala," The University Museum, University of Pennsylvania, Philadelphia, 1961.)*

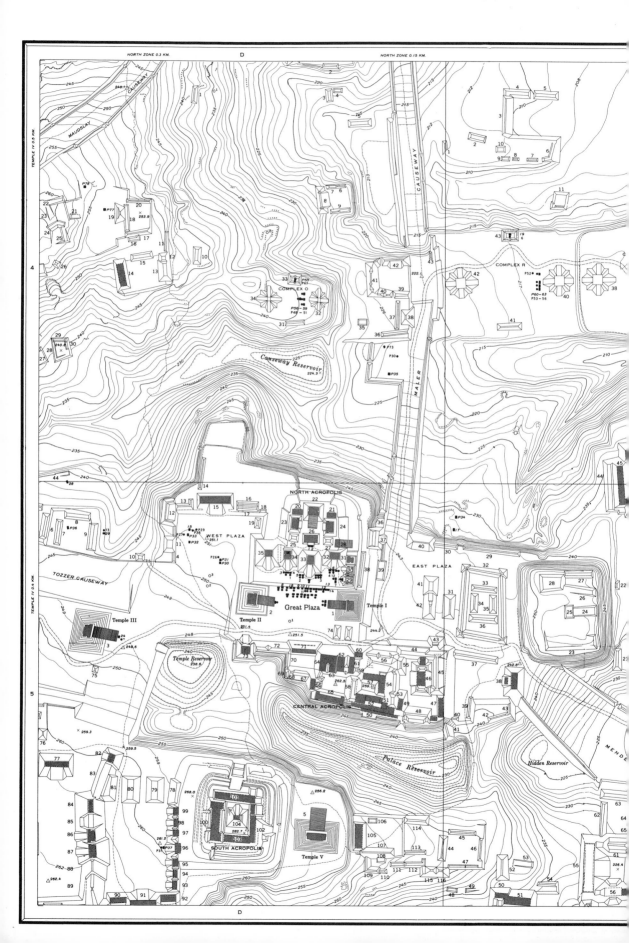

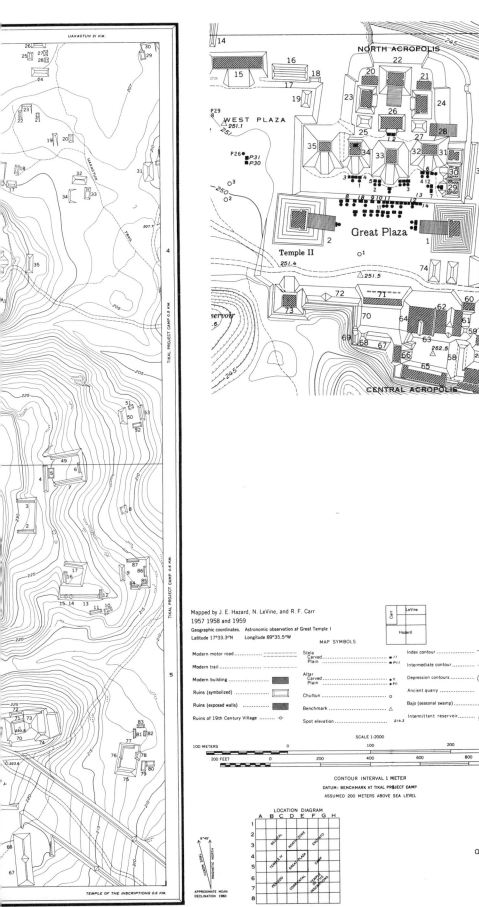

GREAT PLAZA
1959

other groups, palaces perhaps, not considered in the calculation. About ten per cent of the ruins situated in other central sectors were isolated.[19]

The groups of ruins tend to be more numerous in the central sectors than on the periphery and are usually more complex in form, but there do not seem to be any differences in size between them, regardless of whether the structures are grouped or isolated. Based on their numbers and internal arrangement, we assume the ruins of the central sectors to have been palaces.

Tikal's builders chose a pronounced elevation in the land for their principal group. The structures comprising this group are set out within an irregular rectangle of about 500 by 1,000 meters in the middle of the raised area. Other centers were connected with the main one by wide causeways which adapted themselves to the uneven topography.

The north group, 800 meters from the main plaza by the Maler Causeway, is the most complex. Here we find two principal pyramids, a quadrangle, and a complex consisting of two minor pyramids and other structures. The ground falls away abruptly to the north of this group. Similarly, between the north and central groups, the causeway drops thirty meters, but later regains its former height since the Great Plaza and the terrace base for the complexes in the north are almost on the same level. Situated between these north and central groups was one of Tikal's most important reservoirs for water storage.

About 650 meters west of the Great Plaza, by the Tozzer Causeway, stands Temple IV.[20] This imposing structure is a stepped pyramid on a rectangular base, eighty by fifty-five meters. As was the custom among Indian cultures, the top platform supported a temple, its soaring roof-crest making it one of the highest points around. Temple IV is connected to the north group by the Maudslay Causeway. From the Great Plaza, we go down the Méndez Causeway, in a southwesterly direction, to the Temple of the Inscriptions, standing alone some 1,300 meters away.

A structural group totally unrelated to those we have mentioned, about 1,400 meters southwest of the Great Plaza, also has a short causeway. Its purpose was evidently the same as that of the other three—to heighten an important building both in aspect and access. Two individual and almost symmetrical complexes, each formed by two pyramids and two minor structures, are situated halfway between the north and central groups, at the bend of the Maler Causeway.

The central group represents one of the most extraordinary architectural concepts to be found. Despite accelerated reconstruction work it was still difficult, some years ago, to discern the layout of the group of temples and other structures surrounding the Great Plaza which marks the center of Tikal. The Plaza itself, a magnificent semi-enclosed rectangular expanse, about eighty-two meters from east to west by sixty-five in the north-south direction is bounded to the east by Temple I, or the Temple of the Giant Jaguar, and to the west by Temple II, or the Temple of the Masks. Each temple stands on a stepped pyramid, rising to a total height of forty-seven and forty-three meters, respectively, above the level of the Plaza. The North Acropolis, fronting the Great Plaza on this side, consists of sixteen pyramidal structures of different heights resting on a wide floor raised above the Plaza's level (Plate No. 44). The Central Acropolis constitutes the south side of the Plaza. This complex was built about ten meters higher than the level of the Plaza and is made up of thirty-one structures, mainly of a palace type, arranged around five principal courtyards and some smaller ones. Most of these structures were built during the Late Classic Period, between 650 A.D. and 900 A.D. (W. Coe, 1965). Today the Great Plaza is partially overgrown by trees, but during its centuries as the center of religious ceremonies its floor was a paved expanse, broken only by a series of stelae with their altars. The majority of these were erected against the magnificent stairway leading to the floor of the North Acropolis where other stelae stood.

The Plaza must have had several accesses, but the main ones seem to have been at the southeast and southwest corners, entering from the smaller East and West Plazas respectively. These two plazas probably served as huge vestibules for the Great Plaza. The Méndez and Maler Causeways opened into the East Plaza, and the West Plaza was entered by the Tozzer Causeway.

The Great Plaza's impression of being enclosed was heightened by the volume and verticality of the structures surrounding it. Only at the southwest corner was there a direct line of vision outward, toward the West Plaza and Temple III. A view from the top of the surrounding temples or from the edge of the Central Acropolis would have shown an immense amphitheater capable of holding several times the number of people living in the ceremonial center.

The apparent symmetry of the arrangement deceived the first surveyors of Tikal. After the plan made by Tozzer and Merwin, the authors of subsequently published maps believed that the more important groups and temples were, individually and collectively, arranged in accordance with various compositional axes. Nothing is farther from the truth. Everything in Tikal seems to display a subtle disregard for exactitude, as though the architects were concerned only with achieving the effect of a grouping and disdained such rigid impositions as careful measurements, matching lines and secondary axes subordinate to principal ones. If this was their intention, they were successful. The Great Plaza of Tikal and its subordinate plazas and structural groups provide a splendid example of balance and skillful use of topography to create simple effects and changing vistas in whatever direction you walk. The weight of the composition is the result of visual stability achieved by compact bases connected by immense floors. The pyramidal shapes accentuate the bulk of these bases, reinforcing the impression that the Great Plaza is closed in from the eyes of the passer-by.

As we know, density diminished from the Great Plaza outward toward the periphery of the mapped area, but not even in the most thickly inhabited sectors do we find concentrations with the character and density we might consider urban. The highest density was concentrated south of the Great Plaza where the different palaces surrounding the Palace Reservoir may have been the only examples of large collective dwellings in Tikal. Other structural groups, such as the complex formed by the two large courtyards north of the Madeira Reservoir and west of Temple V, the complex near Hidden Reservoir at the northern end of the Méndez Causeway, and the buildings located to the east of the Madeira Reservoir may have been, totally or in part, the residence for Tikal's ruling class. While I can add nothing as to the number of dwellings or inhabitants, this group, together with the complexes surrounding the Palace Reservoir to the north and south, undoubtedly had the highest population concentration within relatively limited areas. These complexes were also expressions of an architecture which could be considered urban because of its volume, materials, and functions, as opposed to the ordinary dwellings of perishable materials built on platforms. But, even if each one of these complexes served as housing for a sizeable population—an unlikely event in view of the spatial characteristics of Mayan architecture—the distances between complexes were considerable and left a high percentage of the central group's area either without construction or occupied by buildings of a religious nature.

Aside from the palace groups, the highest density in Tikal is found in a sector southeast of the central group (Square E-6), occupied by many dwellings grouped in the typical Maya manner. In this area of 25 hectares, 112 ruins are recorded, the majority concentrated in groups of three and four. According to the criteria we used before, this would indicate a density of 560 inhabitants in 25 hectares, or 22.4 persons per hectare, assuming simultaneous occupation. The possible occupants of what may have been two palaces in the north of the square are not included in this calculation. On the other hand, the 25 hectares have no *bajos,* or natural depressions, and may have been more densely covered by dwellings, the platforms of which have not been found.

A similar calculation on a seventy-five-hectare area (Squares C-4, D-4 and E-4), located north of the central group and adjacent to it, exhibits a density of only seven inhabitants per hectare. Of course, the terrain in this sector is broken and partially occupied by religious structures, but such a low density is not in keeping with its central position.

It seems as though there were no operative rule of housing distribution in Tikal other than that imposed by topography and access to water. We find the greatest concentration of palaces and temples around three sources of water: the Temple, Palace, and Hidden Reservoirs, the second of which was perhaps the most important.[21] This relation between housing concentration and reservoirs does not seem to have existed in the centers nearer the periphery. Another interesting discovery was the connection of *chultuns,* or subterranean chambers, with domestic architecture (Puleston, 1965).[22]

As in all Classic Maya centers, the population traveled about on footpaths. The causeways, though well built, did not constitute real urban thoroughfares. They served to connect religious structural groups and facilitate massive pilgrimages rather than improve the mobility of the people. In the way they spanned large suburban areas, the causeways are more like some of the Roman roads than ordinary streets bordered by buildings. Mayan architects probably used these causeways to dramatize the approach to the temples and principal complexes, and in Tikal, we invariably find a temple at the end of one of these elongated perspectives.

I should like to point out two characteristics of Maya centers, as I believe them to be preplanned, confirming the exceptional sensitivity of their architects in dealing with massive complexes. One is the use of nonaxial perspectives, unlike architectural practice in Mexico's central plateau during the same centuries. The other is the knowledgeable use of topography to emphasize the isolated structural masses and accentuate their size. Tikal's architecture displays a monumental character totally different from that created by the Olmecs, by the builders of Teotihuacán and, centuries later, by the Aztecs. We see examples of this in the access to Temple IV from the Great Plaza along the Tozzer Causeway's gentle ramp, and in the Maler Causeway's sharp ascent toward the north group where our line of vision is blocked by a pyramid, as well as in the pronounced descent from the Great Plaza to the Temple of the Inscriptions.

DID THE MAYA BUILD CITIES?

We can not be sure of the number of people who lived in Dzibilchaltún, Tikal, and other Maya centers prior to Mayapán's dominion in Yucatán and the abandonment of the Petén's Classic sites.

Morley supports the urban character of Maya centers with the reservation that Maya centers of population were not as concentrated, as tightly compressed into compact blocks, as are our modern cities and towns. On the contrary, they were dispersed over extensive outskirts, inhabited more loosely, and scattered in a series of small farms. They were more like suburbs than concentrated urban areas. Morely also points out that the religious and public buildings were not lined up along streets as in our cities, but formed groups around plazas and courtyards (Morley, 1956).

Shook and Proskouriakoff favor a settlement pattern in which nuclei with religious and civic buildings, permanently inhabited by small groups, served a dispersed rural population (Shook and Proskouriakoff, 1956). Other authors disagree, basing their opinions on physical appearance and the modern concept of the functions of a city. Thompson, one of the great contemporary Mayanists, observes that the word "city" is applied frequently, and perhaps inappropriately, to Maya ruins. He stresses that there is ample reason to believe that they were never inhabited towns but merely religious centers. The population, living in small groups scattered in the surrounding countryside, would come to these centers for religious ceremonies or certain civil functions, such as the appointment of chiefs and tribunals of justice, and perhaps to hold markets every five to thirteen days (Thompson, 1945). Thompson's position subsequently became that of other authorities (Thompson, 1959; Terner, 1951; Willey and Phillips, 1958; Redfield, 1958). Some authors call Maya centers urban without further explanation (Hester, 1951-1952), and Stephens in the last century also called them cities (Stephens, 1841).

Now that the initial results of the research in Tikal are known, and barring any conflicting data from Dzibilchaltún or some as yet undiscovered site, one fact seems confirmed: the Maya of the Classic Period lived in a less concentrated manner than other Indian cultures in America. There was no street system between dwellings, although wide causeways interconnected the principal groups within the ceremonial center. During the Post-Classic Period, the Classic pattern was intensified as the population grouped together in sites which may have been determined by political and military needs. Despite greater densification, the houses in Mayapán and other centers occupied during the Post-Classic centuries never outlined urban spaces so as to form streets and plazas.

We have already seen one exception—Tulum. Its urban evolution would have to be studied in detail to determine the reasons for the appearance of an urban form and layout so uncharacteristic of Maya civilization in any stage of its development.

Most authors agree that the Maya, even at their apogee, never congregated in cities, despite their cultural readiness to move beyond the sedentary to the urbanist stage (Childe, 1950). In explanation of what seems to be a cultural lag, I am inclined to think that the Maya had no need to build cities. The labor entailed in building and then inhabiting them would undoubtedly have been disproportionate to the limited benefits they could provide. In the Petén lowlands, the adopted settlement pattern around civic-ceremonial centers and reservoirs is better suited to the environment, to the *bajos* and the jungle, to the Maya technological level and economy, than the construction and maintenance of vast urban areas. The decentralized pattern also ties in with the difficulties of transporting agricultural produce. In addition, there were no military, commercial, or administrative reasons that might have impelled the Maya to concentrate in cities, as occurred in other civilizations. We have seen that defense was not a consideration in the election of Classic sites and only became a factor during their decline. Only at the end of their history, and then almost certainly through foreign influences, did the Maya support a political entity which required a capital.

Commerce underwent an intense development among the Classic and Post-Classic Maya in the Petén, Chiapas, and Guatemala. They became exporters of materials of vegetable origin such as indigo, liquidambar, resins and dyes in general, cacao which was cultivated on Guatemala's

Gulf Coast, and animal products such as feathers and pelts (Méndez, 1959). They imported items selected for beauty and rarity, such as jade, obsidian and hematite, certain dyes from the Guatemala highlands, and marine products from the Pacific and Atlantic Coasts (Shook, 1958a). In Maya centers, these materials were transformed into religious offerings or were used as adornments by the ruling class. They were not a medium of exchange and were probably utilized only in the territory around their point of manufacture, giving rise to the regional stylistic differences we have mentioned. I have found no reference indicating that the Maya manufactured articles for export, as was done in other eras with ceramic pieces made in Teotihuacán and Cholula and with the famous feather mosaics from some of the Aztec cities.

Besides economic reasons, there are others that might have influenced the low density of Maya population. The dispersion of water sources in the Petén lowlands and the long seasons of drought characteristic of that region obliged the Maya to construct huge reservoirs. We find many of these around the large centers. Tikal has seven (Shook, 1948b) with an actual capacity of 154,310 cubic meters (Carr and Hazard, 1961). Several wells, which may have served a limited number of families, have also been found near some of the housing complexes. Rain water was drained from the floors of plazas and patios into these pools in an effort to conserve every drop of the precious liquid, since in Tikal and Uaxactún, at least, there are few permanent lakes and almost all rivers and streams lack a continuous flow. As we find no evidence of a significant change in climate from Classic times to our day, we can assume that the water supply must have presented a serious problem for the ruling group. It is no wonder that house ruins and those of some ceremonial centers are found near the *bajos* (Bullard, 1960). The reservoirs and artificial water holes the Maya constructed as a solution to the long rainless seasons point up the limitations that the Petén's environment imposed on a dense concentration in any one site. We have found no remains of aqueducts, so common near permanent water sources in the cities of other American civilizations, that might have indicated resources nonexistent today. There were undoubtedly no such sources.

One of the objectives of the University of Pennsylvania in Tikal is to find out the reasons why the Pre-Classic Maya spontaneously chose or accepted the Petén forest as a habitat, and to determine which factors permitted the development of an advanced civilization in such an inhospitable environment, so unlike the areas where other important civilizations flowered. The answers to these two questions are sure to clarify some of the reasons why the Maya adopted their particular density and settlement pattern. They certainly knew how to utilize to the maximum an environment we consider unfavorable and not naturally adapted to an urban way of life. Apparently, as there was no need for large concentrations, the Maya adopted the life best suited to their needs.

Conditions prevailing in the Petén and in Yucatán during the Classic Period had a certain similarity. The Yucatán Peninsula almost completely lacks surface water sources. The prime factor in choice of location for Pre-Classic, Classic and Post-Classic centers was that of proximity to the *cenotes*. Even in those centers we call urban, such as Mayapán, the most densely populated intramural sectors were concentrated around these sources of water. *Cenotes,* sometimes modified to increase their utility, filled the function in Yucatán that the reservoirs and water holes did in the Petén. Since it was difficult to draw water out of them, and many had a limited capacity, this, too, discouraged a high population density.

Other reasons, mainly political and military, impelled the Post-Classic Maya toward their Urbanist stage. During these centuries, there was marked Mexican influence in the most varied aspects of Maya life, leading to a change in the power structure. Although they never reached the great city stage, as did the Aztecs in the Valley of Mexico and the inhabitants of the Chimú Empire on the north coast of Peru, the Maya were apparently on the road to urbanism.[23]

Perhaps the Yucatecan Maya might have come nearer true city building if the calamities in the years just before and after the Spanish Conquest had not halted them. Before the start of their decline, the Maya of Yucatán had established a net of semi-urban nuclei which, had circumstances permitted, might have produced some center of greater importance than the rest which would then have gone on to develop into a great city.

Perhaps the Classic Maya never wanted the city as their chosen mode of life, at least as the Aztec and the inhabitants of Teotihuacán knew it. For the Maya farmer who worked in his *milpa* in a forest clearing near a minor ceremonial center, a visit to Tikal or Copán, Chichen Itzá, or Dzibilchaltún may have meant going to the city, meeting new people, witnessing a religious ceremony, or watching artists at their unfamiliar work of carving a stela or a frieze or painting a wall. Perhaps the Maya, like the Greeks, felt it necessary to limit the number of persons who lived around a center so that all men could know and understand each other, reinforcing their concept of life in which, as Thompson observes, moderation and dignity prevailed.

NOTES ON · 7

1. PROBABLY THE ITZÁ were of non-Mayan origin (Reina, 1961). Tayasal was captured by Martin de Ursúa on March 13, 1697.

2. The first trip was made between 1839 and 1840. The main sites visited by Stephens and Catherwood were Quiriguá, Copán, and Palenque (Stephens, 1841). In their last trip, between 1841 and 1842, they visited a number of centers in Yucatán, among them Uxmal, Edzná, Labná, Kabah, Chichen Itzá, and Tulum, a town to which they came by sea (Stephens, 1841).

3. Judging from their design, Maya ceremonial centers can be classified into two main groups. Those which we might call centralized complexes are formed around an acropolis, like Cobá and Copán (Plates No. 30 and 29). The decentralized centers are grouped around a plaza or a series of plazas. The great majority of centers belong to this second group, including Tikal, Palenque, Uaxactún, Piedras Negras, Yaxchilán, etc. (Plates No. 43, 33, 35, 13, 14).

4. In the introduction to his monograph which includes the map of Tikal, Shook describes how, in 1956, he made a general survey of several kilometers to the north, south, east, and west of the known groups of ruins, trying to determine the limits of the ancient city. He found no recognizable boundaries. House ruins and those of small groups of temples and palaces were scattered in all directions throughout the mapped area of 3.5 square miles (Carr and Hazard, 1961). A more recent survey showed that the north and south limits of the site lie beyond the limits of the site map (Haviland, 1965).

5. Bullard included schematic plans of several smaller centers in his article. The center called La Flor consisted of a rectangular platform 70 by 50 meters, in the western half of which stood a single pyramidal structure. Dos Aguadas and El Venado were of the acropolis type, several square or rectangular pyramidal buildings on a platform. Yaxhá was somewhat larger and was formed by the ruins of seventeen pyramidal structures of different sizes, grouped around a main plaza and a secondary court, over an area of about 13,000 square meters (Bullard, 1960).

6. Densities at Dzibilchaltún during the Classic Period were much higher. Andrews reported one thousand structures per square kilometer in an area of some fifty square kilometers (Andrews, 1960). Densities at Post-Classic sites in Yucatán, such as Mayapán and Tulum, were also higher

than in the classic sites in the Petén. Post-Classic densities in the Petén, as in Tepoxté, a small cluster of houses on an island in Lake Yaxhá, were also much higher than Classic densities in the same region (Bullard, 1960; Willey and Bullard, 1965).

7. Reread the contemporary criteria used by the Bureau of Statistics and the Bureau of the Census to define an urban area, as discussed in the preface to this book.

8. Vogt admits that functioning ceremonial centers would require permanent personnel but that personnel for the lesser positions were recruited from the surrounding clusters of houses (Vogt, 1964).

9. We find, throughout millennia of urban history, that defensive walls inevitably correlate with high urban densities in the walled districts. Besides building costs there is a basic defensive strategy involved in concentration, such as the mobilization of soldiers from one side of the wall to another combined with the reduction of weak defensive points. The main objective of the defenders was to resist as long as possible, forcing the attackers to retire due to lack of supplies, frustration, internal disagreements, etc.

10. The Yucatán Peninsula is flat and covered by limestone formations. There are no rivers above ground, and the only sources of water are water holes and *cenotes*. See Chapter XXII, pages 234-240 of *Geografía de América* by Jorge C. Tamayo (Tamayo, 1952).

11. Almost all of Mayapán's four square kilometers are suitable for construction, and the difference in elevation between any sectors of the city is never more than five or six meters. The areas included between elevations of twenty-four and twenty-five meters usually have a lower building density, whereas it is rare to find lots above elevation thirty that have no buildings.

   Tikal's terrain is much more irregular. Almost all buildings in the principal center were built above elevation 250, and some structures, such as Temple IV, above elevation 260. Fourteen per cent of Tikal's mapped area is low and subject to flooding in the rainy season. The *bajos* are usually found below elevation 190, but because of their relation to the drainage of each sector, *bajos* appear even in higher elevations (Carr and Hazard, 1961). Forty-three per cent of the cross-shaped area 365 meters wide and 1,000 meters long, studied by the Ricketsons in Uaxactún, was in *bajos* (Ricketson and Ricketson, 1937).

12. The ruins found in Mayapán were the remains of platforms on which the

Maya had built their dwellings.

13. This figure may be low. A Maya family in Yucatán today consists of only 3.7 children, even though women marry young and the birth rate is high (Morley, 1956). Infant mortality, according to Morley, reaches seventy per cent before the age of five.

14. The Ricketsons calculated 0.7 of an acre per person, which is slightly less than 0.35 of a hectare. I have adopted this figure to facilitate calculation, since the difference hardly affects the total area.

15. Juan de Grijalva continued the exploration of the coast of Yucatán begun in 1517 by Francisco Fernández de Córdoba. He subsequently lived for a time in Mexico, and took part in the conquest of Nicaragua, where he died in 1527. Grijalva was born in Cuella, Spain, in 1440.

16. Read Thompson's impressions of his visit to Tikal, more than thirty years ago, in the prologue of his *The Rise and Fall of Maya Civilization* (Thompson, 1959).

17. The greater part of the working seasons of 1956 and 1957 were dedicated to these tasks (Shook, 1958b).

18. The map of Mayapán is earlier and its cartographic technique is similar to that used in Tikal. Jones did the field work in Mayapán during the years 1949 and 1951 (Jones, 1958). In both cases, a square 500 meters each side was adopted.

19. The sixteen kilometers mapped were divided into sixty-four squares of five-hundred meters each side to facilitate recording of the existing structures. Therefore, each square included an area of 250,000 square meters of 25 hectares. Constructions which may have been superposed by those seen on the surface today were not recorded.

20. The schematic plan by Tozzer and Merwin made in 1910 was the main cartographic work on Tikal in existence until the recent work of the University of Pennsylvania. In the 1910 plan, we clearly see the symmetry with which structural groups and isolated buildings were laid out. The plan was later modified by the findings of other scholars, to become the excellent map we see today.

21. The combined capacity of the three reservoirs mentioned has been calculated at 68,440 cubic meters, constituting 44.3 per cent of the total capacity of the reservoirs and water holes recorded on the plan, the total capacity of which must have been 154,310 cubic meters (Carr and Hazard, 1961).

22. The functions of *chultuns* are not clear. They were probably used for the storage of food (Puleston, 1965).

23. Sjoberg tells us that as a society widens its political control, its economic base broadens at the same time (Sjoberg, 1960). His argument is correct in reference to the Aztec State in Mesoamerica and the Chimú and Inca Empires in South America, but it does not exactly apply to the one and only imperialistic attempt in Maya territory, as represented by the expansion and influence of Mayapán. Politically, the influence of the lords of Mayapán might have grown past the limits known in a Maya state, but the scarce potential of the territory they controlled prevented great diversification in the economy.

Proof of mass production has been found in Mayapán (Proskouriakoff, 1954), and indications that commerce had developed on the peninsula (Méndez, 1959), but technological deficiencies added to environmental limitations must have been difficult obstacles to overcome. Nevertheless, I believe that Yucatán's political structure during the Post-Classic centuries was on the way to reflecting a different, more accentuated urban settlement pattern in its population centers.

▪8

THE FIRST STAGES OF URBAN EVOLUTION IN SOUTH AMERICA

". . . next to this town of Chabin is a large building of notable grandeur, made of very well cut stone. It was the Shrine or Sanctuary, one of the most famous that the pagans have, like Rome or Jerusalem is to us. The Indians come here to make offerings and sacrifices, because the devil in this place tells them many prophecies, and so they come from all over the kingdom. Below the ground there are great chambers and lodgings, so many that some say they continue under the river which passes by the Shrine or Old Sanctuary."

ANTONIO VÁZQUEZ DE ESPINOSA
(COMPENDIUM AND DESCRIPCIÓN DE LAS
INDIAS OCCIDENTALES)

·8

NOWHERE IN SOUTH AMERICA has there been such a prolonged and detailed local sequence as in the Virú Valley.[1] It lasted throughout five thousand years or more from the Pre-Agricultural and Pre-Ceramic Periods, through the Urbanist and Imperialist stages into the sixteenth century, when the valley was finally occupied by the Spaniards.

Taking the local sequence of the Virú Valley as representative of the north coast of Peru, I have tried to determine how urban civilizations developed in the six principal Andean cultural areas of South America, a territory which includes a good part of the modern Republics of Peru and Bolivia. Three of these areas are coastal; three are highland (Bennett and Bird, 1949) (Plate No. 45).

Although recent research has made necessary a different regional subdivision, I decided to use the six traditional areas because of its simplicity (Plate No. 2, page 26). Lumbreras, for instance, divides the north highlands into three subsections, which he calls Cajamarca, Huaras-Chavín and Huánuco, and includes a fourth highland area, the Titicaca *altiplano* (Lumbreras, 1969). In his division, the central highlands correspond to the basin of the Mantaro river and the southern highlands to the basin of the Urubamba river, in other words to the areas where Huari and Cuzco, respectively, were located. Lanning concentrates on fifteen archeological regions: one in the *montaña,* seven in the highlands and seven on the coast (Lanning, 1967). His main difference from Lumbreras is the division of the Titicaca *altiplano* into a northern Titicaca basin (the Peruvian *altiplano*) and a southern Titicaca basin (the Bolivian *altiplano*), but then he divides the three traditional coastal areas into seven: the Far North, which was outside Bennett and Bird's subdivision, the North and North Central Coast, the Central and South Central Coast, the South Coast

291

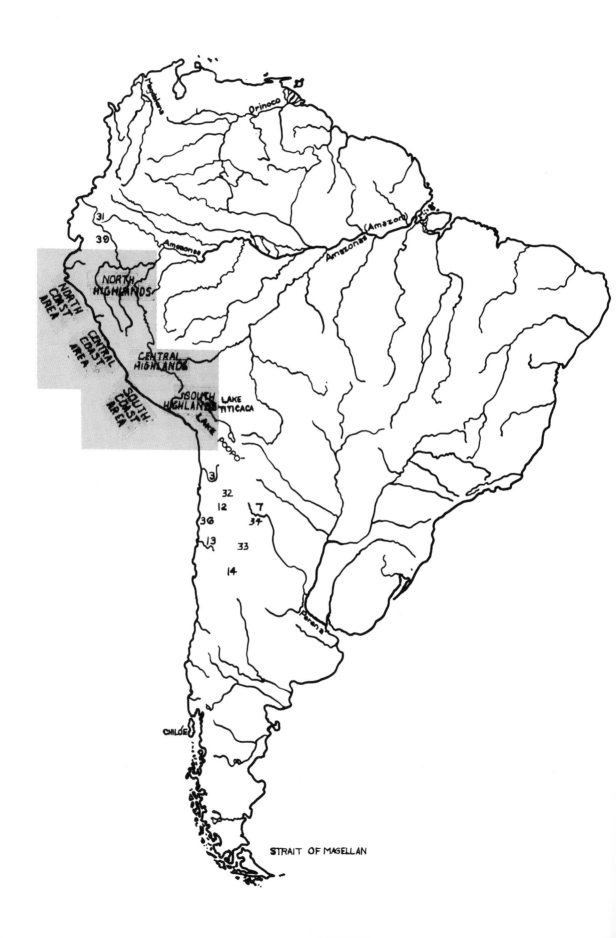

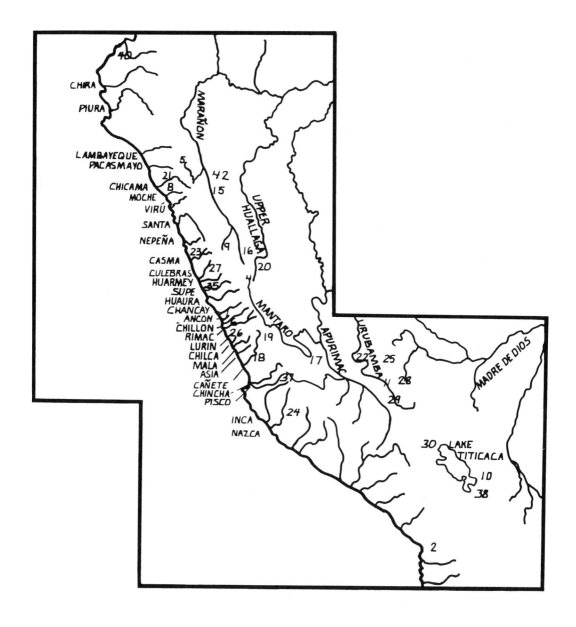

45 and 45a *Map of South America showing major highland and west coastal sites.*

and the Far South (Lanning, 1967). To use the subdivisions proposed by Lumbreras or by Lanning would have meant incorporating in the text a greater refinement of archeological data than I have at my disposal.

The fluvial valley of the Virú River formed part of the cultural area of the north sector of the coastal desert of Peru, which runs from the Leche to the Casma River, between 7 degrees and 9 degrees 30 seconds south latitude. The Chicama, Moche, and Virú valleys had been the principal centers of human occupation in this sector since Pre-Agricultural times.

The central coast region comprises the area between the valleys of the Huarmey and Lurín Rivers, 10 degrees to 12 degrees 20 minutes south latitude. Other important valleys of this sector are those of the Supe, Chancay, Ancón, and Rímac Rivers.

The cultural area of the south coast is located between 13 and 15 degrees south latitude. In this region, the Pisco, Ica, and Nazca River Valleys were the most densely occupied.

Each of the three cultural areas of the highlands was formed by groups of valleys with different geographical and cultural importance. The northern area of the Peruvian highlands extends northward from Cajamarca to include the zones of Huaráz and Callejón de Huaylas as well as Chavín de Huantar. In the middle of the intervening region are the basin of the Mantaro River and the valleys around Cuzco. The southern highland area includes the zone of Puno to the north of Lake Titicaca and the Bolivian Plateau to the south.

In the highland valleys and the irrigated sectors of the Peruvian coast, a succession of cultures culminated in a relatively intense Urbanist stage. Although it was inevitable that individual characteristics emerge in each of the six areas as a result of varying abilities to take advantage of different environmental resources, we should, nevertheless, make note of certain parallels in time and in the development of techniques which some of the areas learned to manage better than others. These six zones were the only regions large enough to allow any kind of pre-Columbian development (Bennett and Bird, 1949), and are grouped together for their archeological similarities.

Except during the interludes brought on by the three pan-Peruvian horizons,[2] metallurgy, textiles and especially the pottery of these coastal and highland areas acquired distinct forms, designs and workmanship, dependent upon the availability of different materials and prolonged cultural heritage. The groups living in each of the six areas maintained ties with each other from the early stages of their evolution, stimulating the adoption of similar techniques and shared knowledge. The importance of these contacts is even greater if we consider that, in spite of geographical semi-isolation, they led to the later stages of this Andean cultural evolution.[3]

Of the common technical knowledge used with varying degrees of success, we find irrigation and intensive agriculture, rotation of crops, the development of certain farming implements, and use of terraces for cultivation. Domestication of the llama, alpaca and other animals and the consumption of maize, coca, various kinds of beans, tomatoes, squash, potatoes, and other plants were common to most areas. Although we find it difficult to ascertain which area used a specific technique for the first time or where the plants composing the South American Indian diet were first domesticated, we can trace their rapid diffusion throughout the coastal and highland areas. Geographic isolation was not an insurmountable barrier, but it did encourage a certain localism.

These six areas have another peculiarity in common—each of them is formed by several intensely populated mountain or coastal valleys constituting geographic and economic units with a high degree of self-sufficiency. This independence was achieved in valleys which were seldom over 2,000 square kilometers in size.

The Chicama Valley, the largest on the north coast, is only 4,200 square kilometers. The Virú, despite continuous, intense occupation throughout almost five millennia, is only 900 square kilometers. The irrigated area of each valley, however, is much less and actually amounts to only 30,000 and 5,000 hectares respectively (Strong and Evans, 1952). The majority of the highland valleys are smaller, with limited useable soil, which made it essential to build farming terraces and other community works to increase production. Even today we can still find some of these characteristics, especially in the highland valleys.

The three pan-Peruvian horizons encompassed a territory which grew progressively larger with each of them. They bear no relation to one another, and we can not be sure that the Inca were even aware of the two movements that had gone before.

The Chavín, Tiahuanacoid and Inca expansions had different characteristics and were initiated by factors which are difficult to determine, but were certainly not similar. Each of the three movements, in its time, established a clear and vigorous stylistic unity. Even the towns peripheral to the territory of most intense influence did not escape the effects. The rapid Tiahuanacoid expansion was supported, as was the Inca expansion centuries later, by an efficient politico-administrative organization in the service of a military cause (Bennett, 1953; Lanning, 1967; Lumbreras, 1969). Chavín expansion, on the other hand, does not seem to have been backed up by force.

It has proved easier to determine stratigraphic sequences on the coast than in the highlands. Even so, there are few coastal valleys where these have been satisfactorily established. It is mainly on the coast itself, especially in the north and south sectors, where archeologists have worked most intensely and with greatest success, since the predominately dry climate favors the preservation of textiles, wooden pieces, plant remains, and artifacts in general.

New techniques even allow an analysis of the diet of the Pre-Ceramic inhabitants who lived in the Chicama Valley (Callen and Cameron, 1960). Unfortunately, we cannot count on the same variety of remains in the highlands or the mountains, where only stone tools, metal or bone artifacts and pottery fragments have escaped the ravages of climate. We have little hope of recovering many clues about the first human settlements in these highland areas, much less of determining a detailed local sequence such as was possible in the Virú Valley. I have, therefore, adopted the sequence established for the Virú as a general base of comparison, to establish a parallel which might aid our understanding of the urbanistic process in the Peruvian and Bolivian territory occupied by Indian cultures. The valleys of the northernmost Peruvian coast above the Leche River, such as the Piura, Chira, and Tumbes Rivers, are less known archeologically, so I have excluded them from this study.

THE PRE-CERAMIC AND PRE-AGRICULTURAL PERIOD

The Virú Valley is an oasis in the desert which covers the entire coast of Peru.[4] Except for its smaller size, it does not differ much from the other north coast valleys. The Virú, like the neighboring valleys of the Moche, Lambayeque, Chicama, Leche, and Chiclayo Rivers, was apparently more favorable for human habitation than the central and south coastal valleys. This explains why settlements in the north coast are older. The difference rests mainly in the northern sector's more regular system of rivers, since water constitutes the principal source of life and is, therefore, the vital factor in human densification. More than forty rivers flow into the Pacific Ocean from the Cordillera, their importance diminishing the farther south they are located.[5]

Sauer points out that the weak formations of the coastal plains allowed the strong currents of the Andean rivers to widen the floors of the Chiclayo, Moche, Chira, and other rivers, creating the broadest and most valuable stretches of the Peruvian coast (Sauer, 1950a). The first spurs of the Andes run parallel to the Pacific Coast, at times only a few kilometers away, forming a narrow coastal strip. The climate is dry, the nights cool, tempered by the Humboldt Current, and the average temperature is 18.8 degrees.

The Virú River runs through a deep canyon in a southwesterly direction toward the coastal plain, where it meanders and finally empties into the ocean south of a small peninsula, the only projecting land in a long stretch of sandy coast. Its continuous, easily controlled current has provided irrigation since ancient times. Before entering the plain, its waters are joined by those of the Huacapongo, a tributary which also runs through a canyon down from the Cordillera.

Today, coastal people still subsist on fish,[6] shellfish and the guano-producing seabirds, but the turkey, rabbit, quail, and deer have almost vanished from the valleys. Vegetation is scarce and, except in certain areas under actual irrigation, planted with cotton, maize, sugar cane, and other similar crops, all is desert. This desert stretches from valley to valley, along more than 2,300 kilometers of coast.

In 1946, the Institute of Andean Research undertook a study of prolonged human adaptation in a small area (Willey and Ford, 1949). The study was planned with the collaboration of eight groups of specialists who were to tackle related aspects of the project. The Virú Valley was the sample site ultimately chosen, and researchers worked there during the better part of 1946, some continuing their work until 1948.[7]

The team studied the Pre-Ceramic Period on the north coast of Peru, dating the occupied sites by a surface examination (Ford, 1949; in Willey and Ford, 1949) and establishing a stratigraphy of the initial prehistoric and final periods of occupation (Strong and Evans, 1952). They studied the period of most intense human occupation in greater detail (Bennett, 1950) at the same time examining the present day geography, ethnology, and sociology of the valley. They studied 315 sites in all, amounting to approximately 25 per cent of the known prehistoric area (Willey, 1953). In choosing the sites, the team considered all sectors of the valley, finally selecting the larger ones and those representative of different types of occupation.

The periods of occupation of the archeological sites have been established from ceramic samples, although the Carbon 14 dating method has given us some data. Primarily by the study of pottery remains, researchers have established several archeological periods, some broken down into subperiods. Any prehistoric finds discovered with ceramic samples of a particular period were considered to belong to that period.

My personal interest lies in analyzing the settlement pattern of those sites which display a certain permanency of occupation in their successive stages of cultural development in the valley. The most logical method is that employed by Willey (Willey, 1953), which involved taking the great cultural periods of the Virú Valley's prehistory and analyzing the location and characteristics of each. To enable me to discuss possible parallels, I must introduce pertinent information and conclusions drawn from other earlier or similar studies, using the sequence established in the Virú Valley as typical of the north coast valleys, and as a basis for comparison for analysis of urban evolution in the other cultural areas of Peru and Bolivia.

Although the Virú Valley has yielded no remains that indicate the presence of a hunting people from a preagricultural epoch (Strong and Evans, 1952), we suspect their existence, since Bird and Larco Hoyle have found traces of hunting groups north of the Chicama Valley, only eighty kilometers to the north of the Virú, and pressure-flaked objects have been discovered in the desert between the Virú and Moche Valleys (Bird, 1952). These groups would have been the first to settle in the Virú Valley with any permanence, possibly in the third millennia B.C. or even earlier, and their remains would constitute the oldest proof of permanent occupancy to date in the Valley.[8]

The findings at Huaca Prieta, at the mouth of the Chicama Valley, are of a fishing-gathering people, living in semi-subterranean rooms and numbering a few hundred persons, who cultivated cotton and gourds and possessed some domesticated plants such as squash, beans, aji peppers, and edible roots as well as a protoneolithic technology. They made baskets, mats, and nets from vegetable fibers, and stone knives and scrapers by pressure-flaking. This period, called Cerro Prieto in the Virú, ended about 2,000 B.C., if the few dates available from the radiocarbon method are correct (Wauchope, 1954), or even earlier.

We should not overlook the possibility that other Pre-Ceramic cultures, having the same technological level as those in the Chicama and Virú Valleys, may have settled at the same time, or even earlier, in the

Supe, Pacasmayo (Willey, 1953) and other north coast valleys.

The remains of small Cerro Prieto Period semi-subterranean rooms have been found in the Virú Valley. Rectangular in shape, about three by four meters in size and built with hand-made adobe bricks, these dwellings lie in three groups north of the river within a five hundred meter radius. They are not far from the ocean, located near a point on the coast where a rocky peninsula forms a small bay, offering plentiful fish and shellfish. The Cerro Prieto people apparently needed neither religious structures nor defenses, and we have found no evidence of irrigation nor of works which suggest any organized labor force.

The choice of sites for these three groups of dwellings and for Huaca Prieta reflects the degree of cultural development of their inhabitants. Cerro Prieto society's main concern was subsistence. Its choice of site, therefore, was based on the resources offered by the immediate environment and whether these could be readily utilized, at least for a period of time.[9] The need to think in terms of the gradual development of a site and the subsequent problems entailed had not yet arisen. In the location of a relatively permanent center of human habitation in an isolated cultural environment, the prime factor would have been its possibilities for supporting life—in this case, coastal fishing, water supply, and plant gathering along the river banks.[10]

Most Late Pre-Ceramic settlements in the coast were located near the shore. Evidences show the existence of not less than thirty sedentary villages dating from 2500 B.C. to 2000 B.C. (Lanning, 1967). Culchas and Las Haldas, both located in the north-central section of the coast were the largest and most impressive sites of this period. They probably reflect the densest concentration of population of any coastal valley during the Pre-Ceramic centuries.

Culebras was built on the top of a hill which was artificially leveled with terraces. The hill was near a source of fresh water, the Culebras River, and the seashore. The semi-subterranean rooms were built with stone blocks and paved with clay. Seafood was an essential part of the diet but the few hundred families that lived in Culebras could also depend on a large variety of cultivated plants and on the meat of guinea pigs which were specially raised (Lanning, 1967).

Engel suggests that Las Haldas had a population of 1500 to 2000 persons, enough to support a ceremonial center (Engel, 1970). The most important construction at Las Haldas is a 465 meter long complex of squares and buildings organized according to a northeast-southwest axis.

Houses surround this ceremonial group built on a dry *pampa,* or plain near the sea shore. However, the largest known ceremonial complex of the Late Pre-Ceramic times was found in the Chillón Valley, just north of Lima. Called Chiquitanta, it covers a surface of about 50 hectares. This probably was the most important farming community of the valley which by then was comparatively well settled with farmers. Lanning has estimated the population of Chiquitanta at 1000 persons or more (Lanning, 1967). Other sites on the central and south coast are not so large nor do they show the variety of buildings of the three above mentioned settlements. We have no such exact data about the highlands but it is possible that research will bring to light villages with a technology far more advanced than we suspect.

THE FORMATIVE PERIOD
(1500-200 B.C.)

We find a cultural continuity between the Cerro Prieto people and those at the beginning of the Formative stage, which was marked in the Virú Valley by the Guañape Period, lasting from 1200 B.C. to 400 B.C. (Willey, 1953), or, if we choose a more recent chronology, from 1500 to 200 B.C. (Lumbreras, 1969). According to Wauchope, the oldest ceramics found in the valley belong to the Guañape period and were probably made about 1200 B.C. (Wauchope, 1954). This pottery was black to red in color, undecorated, of uneven firing, and falls into the period accepted by Willey for the appearance of ceramics in the valley. Its sequence would place it in the Early Guañape, the first of this period's three subdivisions in the Virú Valley. The long span of the Formative Period corresponds to Rowe's Initial Period (1400 B.C.) and Early Horizon (700 to 600 B.C.), and Lanning's similar sequence (Rowe 1963; Lanning 1967).

During the first Formative centuries, there may have been links between the inhabitants of neighboring valleys, but considering the self-sufficient economy of each valley, and perhaps village, where even today we can still see great political and social hegemony, it is hard to believe that the reasons for such contacts were commercial. There were few cultural innovations during the Early Guañape Period except for the appearance of pottery. Building techniques were unchanged, dwellings were still clustered together without order forming complexes of irregular shapes as new chambers were added. One of the Pre-Ceramic sites from the earlier Cerro Prieto Period was still inhabited, but we find no evidence of an increase in population over that of the Pre-Ceramic centuries, and we assume the diet continued to be based on products from the sea.

During the Middle Guañape Period, maize and manioc or yuca had already been added to the agricultural products of the valley. The introduction of maize had a noteworthy effect on the settlement pattern of the population and the structure of society. Demographic growth, as yet unnoticeable in the Middle Guañape, seems to have taken place during the Late Guañape Period. It was reflected not only in the appearance of a greater number of sites, but also in their location in new sectors of the valley. As the population learned to consolidate their traditional dietary base, supplied up to then almost exclusively by fish, shellfish and some plants, they moved inland from the coast toward the interior of the valley. Some settled near the river banks, others on the hillsides of the middle valley, although still not too far from the river. Toward the end of the Guañape Period, a few sites even appeared in the upper valley where the canyon of the Virú River enters the coastal plain.

During the Middle Guañape, two entirely new urbanistic aspects emerged. For the first time in the valley we find structures with specialized functions, such as a cemetery and an apparently communal building, the temple, of simple, rectangular architecture, serving as a center for several communities.[12] This suggests the appearance and gradual predominance of a directing group, probably the priesthood. In the late Guañape, a new type of village developed, now built entirely above ground and formed by detached dwellings of one, two or even six rooms, scattered without plan over an area of about three hectares.[13] Rectangular or square rooms ranging in size from two to twenty meters predominated in these dwellings, which were built of stone and mortar or adobe with sloping roofs of cane and clay. A few structures of rounded or irregular shape were also found here.

During the Middle Guañape Period, we also find the emergence of a society in which some of the members had acquired a certain specialization, this contributing to the establishment of a social hierarchy. The pottery from this period includes pieces decorated with fine and coarse incisions as well as shapes and motifs similar to those of the Chavín-Cupisnique style, the oldest we know on the coast (Bennett, 1946). There may have been some work in gold at this time, also influenced by Chavín art style which (between 900 and 800 B.C.) spread all over the coast from north of Piura to south of Paracas.

The lack of any remains of large-scale civic works such as terraces, irrigation canals, roads or fortifications, which would necessarily involve the mobilization of a sizeable work force, indicates that politico-administrative centralization did not yet exist in the valley.

Willey's concept of the locality as a factor in the location of communities is suggested by the clustering of several villages around the temple, or capital as he calls it (Willey, 1953). However, we find the concept of a site is even more frequent.[14] The appearance of maize and with it a more intense agriculture in the middle and upper valley next to the river allowed the Middle and Late Guañape peoples gradually to give up fishing as a means of feeding themselves.[15] As a result, the proximity of cultivable fields began to determine the location of new communities produced by urbanistic expansion toward the interior of the valley after the Middle Guañape Period. Construction of the first temple must have come after some of these agricultural settlements had already been established, but once it was built, new communities grouped around it. We find the concept of a locality already present, but not as yet the important factor determining the choice of location of agricultural communities which it was to become. The concept of a site seems to have been a more powerful influence in choosing a place to settle while the valley's growing population evolved toward the self-sufficient, independent city, coinciding with the early stages of cultural development of a society such as that in the Virú Valley. In the light of present-day knowledge, this sequence holds true, chronologically and stylistically, for the north coast valleys of Peru, with minor local variations.

A survey of the central and south coast river valleys has helped to locate many Pre-Ceramic and Pre-Agricultural sites in the valleys of the Nepeña and Culebras Rivers, in Puerto Supe and the Bay of Salinas, in the Seco and Chillón River Valleys, and in sites included today in metropolitan Lima, such as Playa Grande, near Cerro San Pedro, and Zig Zag in Chorillos (Engel, 1957).

On the south coast, archeologists have found huge mounds of shells left by agricultural groups not far from where the Ica and Grande Rivers empty into the Ica and Nazca Valleys. Recent excavations also indicate the existence of sedentary groups that lived off fish, game, and wild plants in a sector of the southern coast known as the Otuma shell-heaps, a few kilometers south of the desertlike Paracas Peninsula. Carbon 14 methods date the site's occupation as far back as 1750 B.C. (Engel, 1957; Harth Terré, 1960). Like the sites of the Pre-Ceramic and Early Formative periods in the Virú and other north coast valleys, all the sites studied in the central and south coastal sectors are a short distance from the sea and almost always near the river that gives each valley its name. Judging by the remains found in the Otuma shell-heaps, the diet of the south coast Pre-Ceramic inhabitants was based on fish and shellfish, especially mussels, as well as on such agricultural derivatives as wild seeds. Bird, seal, whale, and dolphin meat were probably rare treats (Engel, 1957).

Although all this evidence points to the prolonged occupation of some of the south coast sites, we still know little about the degree of permanence and cultural level of their inhabitants. The cultural peak in the south coast valleys seems to have come later than in the valleys of the north coast, perhaps between the Chavín and Tiahuanaco Periods.

During the Early Formative stages the coast witnessed a series of technological changes, such as the introduction of pottery, which was less important to the standard of living of a growing population than the incorporation of manioc and peanuts, the extensive use of the llama and a wider use of maize. Settlement patterns on the coast, as I have mentioned for the Virú Valley, did not experience great changes in location although they appeared in increasing numbers. Sedentary life, now possible thanks to better agricultural practices, expanded throughout the coast. The concentration of population made possible the construction of monumental temples of a size unknown until then, such as La Florida, near Lima. Hacha, in the Acarí River Valley, is a large irregular settlement covering an area of about sixteen hectares. The location of this Early Formative village on the south coast, where no trace of maize has been found, is more than twenty kilometers from the seashore (Rowe, 1963).

The most important temple built in the highlands during the Early Formative was Kotosh, near the source of the Huallaga River. The first temple in Kotosh was built during Late Pre-Ceramic times and the whole ceremonial center precedes the spread of Chávin influence. As in La Florida, no housing has been found in the vicinity of the temple. This pattern, characteristic of the Early Formative on the coast as well as in the highlands, was based on the nuclear role of a temple supported by an agricultural population living in villages located close to the fields.

The volume of work demanded by such unusual constructions for that time and those regions must have required a centralized organization at least on a microregional scale not very different from the one that existed among the Olmecs almost at the same time. Before Chavín, then, some sort of political organization existed on the coast and in some points in the highlands indicating a class stratification. But still we are far from having cities. Settlements were small in size and in population. Although larger in number than during the Pre-Ceramic years, their people had developed only a self-sufficient economy, apparently with little or no surpluses and few products to exchange. In Kotosh we find, for the first time, the work of a sculptor, but probably not yet a full-time specialist. Pottery and cloth were produced for local consumption. In any event, the size and volume of the constructions found at Chavín were not repeated elsewhere. The villages inhabited during the Middle Formative Period were not significantly larger than those of the Early Formative nor do they show improvements in building techniques.

At the beginning of the chapter, I mentioned that environmental problems complicated the finding of Pre-Ceramic remains in the highlands. Even so, Pre-Ceramic sites have been found in the central mountain range, south of the Department of Huancavelica, and in Huancayo Jauja (Lumbreras, 1960a).

We know of three sites in the southern highlands prior to the earliest occupation of Tiahuanaco, located not far from the place where that great culture of the south highlands flourished centuries later. Oaluyu, near Puno, and Chanapata and Marcavalle, near Cuzco, are Early Formative settlements where quite similar ceramic styles have been found (Rowe, 1963; Lumbreras, 1969). In the course of my research, however, I found few references to Early Formative Period finds in these areas.

THE MIDDLE FORMATIVE PERIOD

The Chavín Culture

At the beginning of the first millennium B.C., a gradual expansion of an artistic style took place which introduced new cultural refinements foreign to those that developed earlier on the coast and in the highlands. This style has been called Chavín. We are only recently beginning to learn about its origins, characteristics, area of expansion, and the reasons for its decline. Chronologically, the Chavín art style lasted longer in some areas than in others, and its influence does not seem to have been uniform throughout its territory of presumed influence.

Some Peruvianists believed the Chavín expansion was that of a kingdom which extended along the coast and into the highlands, comparable to the Inca Empire in its zone of influence, cultural unity, and indigenous nature (Carrión-Cachot, 1948). We find no evidence indicating an imperialistic expansion striving for the political unity of a vast territory which, at any rate, seems doubtful, but we have enough proof to affirm that from approximately the tenth to the sixth centuries B.C., Chavín art style influence was felt from the valleys of the north coast, or perhaps even farther north, to the Ica Valley and over the north and central highlands.

We are not certain as to the place of origin of this culture, but at its height, the main center of its influence seems to have been Chavín de Huantar, a site on the banks of two tributaries of the Puschca River, at an altitude of 3180 meters, and about 104 kilometers southeast of the present city of Huaráz.[16] Many ceremonial centers of Chavín culture have been found near other tributaries of the Marañón as well as in such north coast valleys as the Jequetepeque, Chicama, Chancay, Moche, and Virú[17]; in the Nepeña, Sechín, and Supe River Valleys on the central coast and on the Bay of Ancón; and even on the Paracas Peninsula on the south coast.

According to known finds, the most important ceremonial centers must have been as follows: Ancón, where pottery fragments similar to those at Chavín de Huantar were found; Cerro Blanco and Punkurí in the Nepeña Valley; Pallka, Moxeque and perhaps Cerro Sechín in the Casma Valley, and Kuntur Wasi a few kilometers west of Cajamarca. Attempted reconstructions of the temple at Moxeque show a strange similarity to certain temples built several centuries later in some Maya centers, especially those at Uaxactún and Piedras Negras, both in the use of superimposed platforms with rounded corners and in the construction of twin sanctuaries, sunken courtyards, and stairways.[18]

Chavín de Huantar was built in a protected valley with agricultural land sufficient for only a small population. It is interesting to note that the size of the temple is not so large that its construction would have required a sizeable work force, yet it must have been built by a group larger than could be supported by the resources of the valley. Nevertheless, the ruins are impressive despite their deteriorated state. It is then logical to assume that the construction of Chavín required the efforts of many more people than those that could have been supported by the production of the valley.

For many years it was believed that Chavín was not a village, much less a city. The visible remains are only those of the temple, or Castillo, which undoubtedly served a considerable population as a center for pilgrimages. This presented the possibility that the inhabitants of a vast region took advantage of these periodic pilgrimages to bring in necessary building materials and perhaps do the heavy stone work (Bennett and Bird, 1949). Afterward, specialized artisans and artists could have completed the works according to a general plan which may have been drawn up by the priests of the cult.

However, the remains of a settlement of, perhaps, up to fifty hectares lie underneath the modern village, and remains of smaller settlements have been found not far from the temple (Rowe, 1963). It is not clear if the settlements were contemporaneous to the years of construction of the temple, or how a settlement of such size was supported. If Chavín art style spread as a result of conquest, tribute probably was a source of basic supplies as well as of goods that could be traded, taking advantage of the excellent geographical situation. Militarism sooner or later requires a "capital" which becomes the political and administrative center of the controlled territory. I am inclined to believe that those were the key functions of Chavín, as I doubt that peaceful religious proselytization could bring such deep and rapid changes over such a vast and heterogenous territory, given the technological level of Middle Formative cultures in Peru.

The stone architecture of Chavín de Huantar is massive and its dominating direction is horizontal. The foundations of the complex cover an area of about five to six hectares. The bodies of the four principal structures are simple and geometric, built in alternate courses of thick and thin, elongated sandstone or basalt blocks. These structures rest on terraces which form a broad, square sunken plaza at the southeast corner of the complex, a U-shaped temple to the west and two pyramids, one to the north and the second to the southwest. In the center of the plaza an obelisk was found.[19] Inside the structures we find galleries and dim rooms which could only have served as lodging for small groups, and temporarily at that. Each major structure has a bilateral symmetry of its own but the complex as a whole does not follow a main axis.

The exterior walls of the temple form a continuous surface without openings. We can still see traces of incised friezes and strange carved heads tenoned into the masonry. These heads are typical of the Chavín style, presenting a curious gallery of human and feline personages with rounded features, wide noses and bulging eyes, the deep carving emphasizing the physiognomy that makes each head a distinct personality. They are several times larger than life, and may represent gods. Bas-reliefs of incised friezes adorn the cornices and some of the principal stone works. Decorative motifs are alike in theme, and closely related to the Chavín religion.[20]

Sculpture in stone did not enjoy as wide a dispersion as did the motifs on pottery, found in regions far removed from Chavín de Huantar. Some principal themes of Chavín ornamentation were the hermaphroditic dragon symbolizing the supreme divinity, the jaguar and birds (hawks, eagles or condors) which were agents of this divinity, the serpent, the river fish, the cayman, human heads, and feline heads with human features. Most of these figures were of animals foreign to the site of Chavín de Huantar but which lived in the not-too-distant eastern forests where the religion and its art is thought to have originated.[21]

On Peru's north coast and in the Virú Valley specifically, Chavín expansion coincided with the introduction of maize in the Middle Guañape Period or sometime between the ninth and the sixth centuries.[22] I do not know if there is any relation between these two events, or whether they represent isolated incidents, but urbanistically, both have great importance. In the first place, as maize took over as the basic food of the coastal economy, a demographic growth followed. Its effects are seen not so much in the Middle and Late Guañape, as in the beginnings of the Early Intermediate Period, called Puerto Moorin in the Virú. This is not surprising, as the adaptation of maize to the coastal environmental conditions and the work necessary to intensify its cultivation must have taken time. In the second place, the temple or community building acquired new importance, becoming an attraction which drew new agricultural villages around it. Chavín influence seems to have encouraged a different settlement pattern from that existing earlier, marked by the appearance of specialized structures such as temples and, for the first time, filling functions other than housing. These characteristics are seen in the Virú Valley toward the end of the Formative Period. The coastal villages of Chavín influence were larger in size and population than any we know up to that time, but they still lacked any sort of planned layout. It was not a period of cities, judging by the characteristics of the permanent groupings we have found, nor would this be expected, given the assumed economy and the size of the coastal valleys.

About the fifth century B.C. the influence of the Chavín style and the feline cult declined in almost all regions. Chavín art style disappeared in some areas but in others it evolved toward new regional styles with their own designs and techniques.

THE LATE FORMATIVE PERIOD

In the Virú Valley as well as in other valleys of the north coast, an ex-perimental stage with profound regional characteristics emerged shortly after the Chavín Horizon had vanished. Its manifestation in the Virú, called Puerto Moorin, immediately preceded the valley's 'Golden Age.' New techniques developed, and their influence on the valley's economy, presaging the Florescent Period to come, earned this period the name Ex-perimental (Mason, 1957).

We have seen how a more abundant and varied diet, in which maize played a predominant role, led to demographic growth in the valley. This population increase is reflected in the number of sites we have found belonging to the Late Formative Period. Of the 315 sites studied by the Institute of Andean Research teams, perhaps 83 are from the Puerto Moorin phase, between 400 B.C. and the beginnings of the Christian era. Only eighteen of these sites date from the previous Early and Middle Formative Periods, which lasted from the fifteenth to the fifth centuries B.C.

During the Late Formative Period, a number of irrigation ditches and roads were built in the Virú, which undoubtedly influenced agricultural methods and the distribution of produce. Their size suggests that they were constructed by a large and well-organized work force. The combina-tion of these civil engineering works and demographic pressure resulted in cultivation over wider areas and the subsequent introduction of such new plants as the cucumber and several kinds of beans. We cannot be certain, however, that major irrigation systems existed in the valley dur-ing the Late Formative.

Let us see the influence of these events on choices of location for popu-lation groupings in the valley during the Late Formative Period and on the appearance of the first planned settlements. We have found indica-tions suggesting that one of the first attempts at a centralized government occurred in the Virú Valley, or part of it, in the centuries around the Christian era (Willey, 1953). This attempt may have been backed by mili-tary groups, producing a growing class differentiation which created an improvised ruling élite or nobility, composed of the military and the priesthood. Much more evident is the tension that developed among the different groups in separate sectors of the Virú and between the valley's inhabitants and their neighbors in other valleys, as the appearance of walls and other fortifications testifies.

Demographic growth, the fear of war, and new techniques of intense farming required the displacement of a large segment of the population, whether for irrigation works, channeling and controlling the river or for flood prevention in the middle valley. This led to the settlement of the valley's interior and the almost total abandonment, except for one site, of the villages near the ocean.

Coincident with the beginning of the Puerto Moorin phase was the first large concentration of permanently inhabited sites along several kilometers of the north bank of the Huacapongo River before it joins the Virú. The sites in the Huacapongo Basin rested on the sides of the mountains, seeking protection from attack and flooding in these heights and freeing wider strips of valley land for cultivation.

These sites lack carefully laid out ground plans and are formed by clusters of rooms of such disparate sizes that they seem to have been used for many different purposes. Some sites were densely populated, whereas in others the dispersion characteristic of the Early and Middle Formative Periods still remained. We can see that the Late Formative Period introduced not only a change in location of sites within the valley, but innovation in their layout. The village of separated dwellings of different sizes set out without plan, which probably predominated during the Early and Middle Formative Periods, had been partially replaced by a concentrated village of irregular plan, occupying a smaller yet more densely populated area. The concentrated village, formed by some twenty-five chambers, in general regularly shaped and haphazardly assembled, constituted an intermediate step toward the emergence of compound villages.[23] One example of the compound village may belong to earlier centuries, but I think its influence was fundamental in the form and layout of urban complexes in the following periods. This was a regularly shaped, walled compound, about 29 by 18 meters, which does not seem to have been enclosed for defensive purposes. Inside, fifteen rooms and courtyards of different sizes and shapes are situated at random. Willey states that, as a whole, the community was preconceived, having a certain finished form as defined by the exterior wall or enclosure, most often rectangular in outline (Willey, 1953). I think that this example must have represented one of the first attempts in the Virú Valley to provide a housing group with a predetermined form. Rejecting the role of the wall as a defense, its function could only have been related to the socioeconomic structure prevailing in the valley at that time.[24]

During the Late Formative Period, we see the introduction of fortified centers as places of refuge. The most representative of these is Cerro Bitín, belonging to the third or second century B.C. It sits on an isolated hilltop on the coastal plain, about 290 meters above sea level. The redoubt was an elongated oval, measuring four hundred meters in an east-west direction and one hundred meters north to south. The site lent itself naturally to defense or protection, and its effectiveness was enhanced by an exterior stone wall that faithfully followed the contours of the highest elevations.[25] Inside the enclosure, archeologists found three small pyramidal platforms that must have served as temple bases, and about twenty-five house ruins. The temples and wall suggests their double function, defensive and ceremonial, but we have no indication whether or not this center served as a permanent residence other than for a limited garrison. Cerro Bitín was surrounded by a ring of villages in a radius of about two to five kilometers. This new settlement pattern of a sector of the valley's population suggests mutual dependence between the place of refuge and the villages, in war as in peace.

Fortifications in other coeval sites were designed to protect the valley, or some part of it. One such site, located in the middle valley, is similar in layout to Cerro Bitín and must have served the same purpose. Other sites were easier to defend against outside attack, being simple platforms situated strategically on the sides of the Las Lomas, Sarique, and other hills of the upper valley, at the point where the Virú River's basin narrows before it flows out onto the coastal plain.[26]

Also from the Late Formative Period come the first pyramidal structures of earth, stone, and adobe, which probably served as bases for religious or community buildings. In general, these had flat, rectangular tops which were reached by ramps. As we shall see, the use of ramps becomes more common in the periods that follow.

During the four centuries prior to the Christian era, the Virú Valley saw an evolution toward political centralization which led to the construction of irrigation ditches and roads that permitted better utilization of the valley's resources. As productivity increased, so did the population, spurring on technological evolution.[27] The first complex of dwellings with a preplanned urban form sprang from the uncertain relations of the centralized administration with other valleys. Its choice of location was influenced by the same political, technical, and strategic conditions that had produced it in the first place.

The new villages of the Late Formative Period disassociated themselves from the site and its limitations. They were located in relation to other existing villages, obeying the need to control the entrance to the upper valley as well as to obtain maximum use of the river before it was lost in its meanderings down the middle and lower valley. The new villages grew up near work areas, since now the subsistence of the valley's entire population probably depended on a collective effort. The gradual domination that its inhabitants gained over nature allowed them to achieve some small economic advance and exert a measure of control over their means of survival.

The indispensable organization and specialization demanded by these activities worked toward making a more heterogeneous society. Some priests and professional military men probably took over as the ruling class and may have constituted the kernel of a nobility which, with the groups of specialized artisans, depended on the great mass of farmers for food. The farmers constituted the largest population group and also provided the manpower needed for the public works that benefited the community as a whole.

By the end of the Late Formative Period, the emergence of the city seems a certainty. The necessary prerequisites had been fulfilled, and specialization in the inhabited sites had been accentuated to the point where these communities had become mutually dependent.

The fortress-religious center occupied an important position in the new settlement pattern. It served a sector of the valley as defense, but as a religious center its influence was probably felt over an even wider zone, perhaps throughout the valley. The fortress was built on a hilltop for strategic reasons, and the villages formed a circle around it. Some villages may have existed before the fortress was built, but the final overall layout must have come later.

In the Virú, the Puerto Moorin phase was related to the Salinar Culture in the Chicama Valley on Peru's north coast. Larco Hoyle has studied the Salinar Culture, and he describes it as having both limited geographical dispersion and political dominion. This culture emerged before the great organized regimes and constituted a chronologically important stage between the Cupisnique (Guañape or Formative in the Virú) and

Mochica (Gallinazo or Classic in the Virú) Cultures (Larco Hoyle, 1946). Compared to what we find in the Puerto Moorin phase of the Virú Valley, the limited area of dispersion of a coastal culture such as the Salinar indicates that each of the north coast valleys still formed a politically isolated unit.

The Salinar Culture, like that which developed contemporaneously in the Virú Valley, shows great technological advances over the Middle Formative or Cupisnique Periods in the Chicama Valley. Firing techniques for pottery were improved, producing a more even color, and molds may have been used for the first time. Crudely made gold objects and ornaments appeared, some examples demonstrating that the people of this culture knew the technique of soldering.

The most significant characteristic of the Late Formative is the beginning of the regional diversification of ancient Peruvian cultures, a process that reached its full maturity during the following period. Experimentation with new technologies, settlement patterns, crafts and art styles are seen throughout the coast and the highlands. Pucará and perhaps Chiripa, in the northern and eastern Titicaca Basin respectively, were Late Formative settlements. The size of the residential area of Pucará and of its public buildings and the variety of economic activities that probably took place there suggest a settlement of urban characteristics unprecedented in the southern highlands. Higher densities and larger settlements developed in the valleys of the southern coast showing a stronger dependency on agricultural production than before. Villages and small towns were moved to the interior of the valleys in close relation with the flat areas that could be easily irrigated and harvested.

THE EARLY INTERMEDIATE PERIOD
(100-600 A.D.)

Development of the Regional Cultures

The Virú Valley attained its Golden Age coincident with the first eight centuries of the Christian era. This was unquestionably the period of its greatest recorded flowering (Willey, 1953; Mason, 1957). The irrigated and cultivated area covered 40 per cent more surface than it does today and has been calculated to have been more than 9,800 hectares. Never had the valley produced so much food nor possessed such a superior road system over which to transport it. Maize was perfectly adapted by then, and was cultivated throughout the valley. Squash, cucumbers, frijol and other beans, chili peppers, and various fruits, while not new to the valley, fed a population which reached the greatest development known in the valley up to our time. Fish, shellfish, and game from the hunt rounded out a more abundant diet than ever before. No new plants were introduced during these centuries, but the valley was self-supporting as far as food was concerned. This same situation probably prevailed in the other valleys all along the coast.

Ceramic sequences indicate that the Gallinazo pottery showed stylistic similarities with pre-Mochica and Mochica work in the neighboring valleys. Obviously, some kind of contact existed between these valleys, continuing the interchange begun in the Formative Period.[28]

During these centuries, the inhabitants of the Virú Valley undertook extensive public utility works which raised the general standard of living. The problem of irrigation was met by ambitious civil engineering projects based on the principle of one main canal feeding branches where needed. Toward the middle of this period sunken fields were built for the first time (Willey, 1953; Parsons, 1969). Sunken fields are large excavated sections of the sandy valley soil, deep enough to reach the moist subsoil near the water table. These were probably used to grow the *totora* reeds, used for rafts, as well as certain food products.[29] Defense works were the most extensive known up to that time.

Despite lack of real proof, we can consider two political alternatives for the Virú: a centralized state which dominated the whole valley, or a confederation of small entities, each controlling its own sector, which would have been the continuation of a process probably begun during the Late Formative Period. Either way, relations within the valley were apparently peaceful, and the dangers of war could only have come from outside the area. In spite of the political centralization, we find no indication of a major site or capital where the valley's administration might have been concentrated.

Whatever the political organization of the Virú Valley may have been, it is important to remember that the valley formed a cultural unit, as witnessed by the homogeneity of ceramic styles, the individual settlement pattern of each inhabited site, the architecture and even the shape of adobe bricks used in different sectors of the valley—all elements predating the Early Intermediate Period. Weaving was highly developed, either in cotton, llama wool or a combination of both. Bird found examples of weaving in different sites in the valley, the great majority belonging to the Gallinazo phase. The technique of tapestry was used for the first time in the valley as well as that of twilled or crossed weaving, infrequent in other areas of Peru (Bird, 1952). Metallurgy, too, reached a high level of development with the introduction of new methods which permitted making tools and arms out of copper.

A population increase over that of earlier stages was reflected in the greater number of sites found for this period. Ninety-four Early Intermediate sites were recorded in this survey, an increase of 13 per cent over the previous period. During the early centuries of this Period, the Virú's inhabitants continued to use the sites from the Late Formative, but centuries later, for reasons unknown, there was an expansion toward the interior of the valley and the Huacapongo Basin. In the final stages of the Early Intermediate Period and during the Middle Horizon, the Virú Valley reached its maximum population with already occupied sites becoming even more densely populated. During the valley's heyday, partial occupation of the Huacapongo Basin and the entrance to the coastal plain near the juncture of both rivers continued. New groups grew up in the middle valley on both banks of the river, producing a dense occupation of an extensive site called the Gallinazo group (Bennett, 1950), located not far from the coast, or from the site utilized by the primitive inhabitants of the valley during the Pre-Ceramic and the first centuries of the Formative Period.

Agricultural production and defense seem to have been the main factors in the choice of locale for the new villages. Although we find isolated pyramidal mounds with a distinct religious character in the different sectors of the Virú, religion alone does not appear to have been the reason for the concentrations of people situated around the structures. These mounds have been found over almost the entire valley; they are massive structures of a volume previously unknown and could only have been built through the efforts of a vast body of well-organized and directed workmen. However, if defense and agricultural production were really the main concerns of the Virú Valley's ruling group during its Golden Age, this would explain the choice of the strategic gorges and arable, irrigable plains of the middle and lower valley as locations for the new villages.

For the first time in the Virú, the upper, middle and lower sectors of the valley were occupied simultaneously. In the upper valley, we find several villages situated around four fortifications which closed off the gorge giving access to the coastal plain. The large San Juan *huaca,* supported by a base connected to other platforms, must have served as the principal temple of the upper valley. We can deduce that the main duties of the inhabitants were not only to defend the access to the plain, but to keep the all-important irrigation canals free of sediment.

The reasons for the location of settlements underwent a considerable evolution during the centuries following the Experimental and throughout the Early Intermediate Period. The valley as a whole gradually assumed importance as a geographic unit, receptive to a progressive plan of production based on a program of public works. New settlements were located in accordance with this general idea. I believe this to be valid proof of the existence of an effective political and administrative organization that controlled the valley's available resources.

There was no parallel urban evolution of such importance. New urban forms did not emerge, though we find innovations in the types of dwellings. None of the settlements or villages of the Gallinazo phase can be called a city, despite their urban character of high density and the honeycomb living arrangements of the inhabitants. The sites we have found were fortifications, religious or community centers, cemeteries and villages. No new type of structure had been added to those of the previous period.

The farming villages, formed by aggregation or superimposition of new chambers, grew haphazardly without plan or layout, tending to group together near the irrigated fields. For the first time in the valley, however, concentrations of several thousands of persons clustered in a series of villages only a few kilometers apart. The Huaca Gallinazo, a concentration of this type, is one of the valley's largest Early Intermediate sites, occupying an area of 200 by 400 meters (Willey, 1953; Bennett, 1950). It apparently grew up around a central pyramidal mound and was formed by a series of platforms and smaller mounds, chambers and burials. The chambers were small, 2.25 by 1.85 meters on the average, grouped into apartments. They were entered by the roof, as lateral doorways appear only toward the end of the Period. In Huaca Gallinazo, we do not find rooms grouped around a patio or clustered in a honeycomb arrangement.[30] Construction methods, however, were characteristic of the Period, using mold-made adobe bricks, some sites yielding walls of Cyclopean masonry.

Cities, as defined by the criteria used in this work, did not exist in the Early Intermediate Period, but undoubtedly some of the sites housed permanent groupings of a size and functional complexity to distinguish them from the simple agricultural villages scattered near cultivated areas in every sector of the valley. I am inclined to dismiss these semi-agricultural centers as true cities because of their size, lack of overall plan, and urban spaces. In addition, we have no proof that they were used either as administration or military centers or markets, or even contained an important segment of the population. This stage is a curious intermediate one, urban in its density, its various specialized public buildings at the same site, its technological and stylistic development, and even the existence of systems of representational ideographic 'writing.' However, it lacks several of the other attributes I have analyzed in the Preface to this work, that constitute an urban way of life according to my criteria. Urban planning had not yet made an appearance and only came into being centuries later during the Chimú Period in the Virú and other valleys of the north coast.

The Early Intermediate Period came to an end between the sixth and seventh centuries A.D. in the Virú Valley. It was followed by a period of unquestionable Mochica influence which had already been felt before the close of the Early Intermediate Period. This new Period is called Huancaco in the Virú and lasted to the end of the first millennium A.D. We find no important modifications in the valley where some previous sites were still generally occupied.

The Mochica Culture originated on the north coast of Peru, rather than in the Virú Valley itself, though its influence there may have been more than only stylistic. With the Chicama and Moche River Valleys as its center of dispersion, its influence spread northward as far as the Jequetepeque Valley and southward through the Virú and Chao, as far as the Nepeña River Valley (Larco Hoyle, 1946), but it never had much effect in the highlands. It was a military expansion, probably initiated toward the sixth century by some of the lords who dominated the Chicama and Moche Valleys. The existence of a single chief with semidivine attributes is attested by innumerable representations on pottery showing him as a doctor, farmer, musician, hunter, judge and so on.

The life of this society of farmers, warriors, and builders has been faithfully recorded in their pottery, in which we find the most unexpected vignettes, naturalistically drawn in minute detail. We see figures, painted or in relief, whose individual portraits stand out. There are also reproductions of surgical operations, acts of justice, religious scenes, battles, sexual acts, treatment of illnesses, sacrifice of prisoners, figures of gods, fishing and hunting scenes, etc. Depicting the human face seems to have been the principal theme of this essentially naturalistic art which contrasts with the symbolism of Chavín art.[31]

Directed by a centralized and seemingly efficient government in which the military chiefs and priests were embodied in the same person, a stratified and specialized society developed which planned and executed some of the most extensive civil engineering works in any American Indian culture. To irrigate the Chicama Valley, a canal seventy kilometers long was built which benefited the neighboring Moche Valley as well (Kosok, 1965).[32] The ruins of the aqueduct at Ascope, also in the Chicama Valley, still spans hills and crosses part of the valley in a section 1,400 meters long; other aqueducts were built in the Santa Valley (Larco Hoyle, 1946; Mason, 1957). These works indicate a significant dependence on an agriculture enriched by the addition of new plants and fruits, such as the potato, sweet potato, lupin, oca, pineapple, prickly pear, chirimoya, papaya, and granadilla. With the plants already introduced in this sector of the coast during the preceding periods, especially the Late Formative, these new ones complete the list of principal agricultural products at the time of the arrival of the Spaniards (Bennett and Bird, 1949).

The Mochica were great builders of roads which, in some cases, were almost ten meters wide. This society's structure is best represented by their fortifications and huge *huacas*, or temples, built in the Moche Valley, a few kilometers from the modern city of Trujillo, and in other territories under their control. The two great *huacas* of the Moche Valley are presently found on the edge of the irrigated area and are visible from far away. These huge adobe pyramids are called Huaca del Sol, partially surrounded by cultivated fields, and the Huaca de la Luna, smaller but still massive in volume, about a hundred meters away from the other temple. Even today, the Huaca del Sol is the largest adobe structure in Peru despite its deplorable state of preservation. A temple crowning its upper platform made it still taller. Scholars have estimated that 130,000,000 adobe bricks were needed to build it (Mason, 1957). The bricks were made in molds, as were ceramics, and there may have been a special crafts group dedicated to turning out these basic building materials.

Using the sites studied in the Virú Valley as a guide, we find no new urbanistic changes either in the location of the villages or in their internal arrangements. Groups of rectangular chambers were still built around temples, giving no indication of even a partial urban plan. On the other hand, dwellings formed by several rooms around a courtyard became more frequent. This courtyard, which seems to have been first used on the coast during the Early Intermediate Period, became an important element in spatial organization when the great cities came to be built.

Mochica architects continued to use the traditional wood-beamed gabled roofs, which were then covered with a cane and clay mixture. To finish the adobe walls of their buildings, they used stucco and mud plaster, decorating them with frescos.[33]

Along the coast and in some highland valleys, a similar process took place, perhaps abetted by frequent contacts with the coastal valleys. The regional differences we find indicate that some cultures specialized in particular techniques and may have had different social and economic organizations, but these do not necessarily reflect the advancement of any one culture over the others. Certain techniques were common to all three coastal areas, such as monumental adobe religious architecture, defense and irrigation works showing a high degree of organization, and the development of similar agricultural methods and skilled craftsmanship.

Whereas the Mochica of the north coast were outstanding in the manufacture and decoration of pottery, the Paracas craftsmen of the southern coast excelled since the Late Formative Period in the manufacture of embroidered cloth of cotton and wool, harmoniously combining the colors they used to make figures of animalistic deities stand out against the plain backgrounds.

Some south coastal valleys show signs of a much slower and less complete urbanistic evolution than that which I have described on the north coast. On the Paracas Peninsula, which seems to have been the center of cultural dispersion on the south coast during the Late Formative Period, we find the remains of extensive settlements of semisubterranean dwellings (Harth Terré, 1960; Engel, 1966). The Paracas culture gave rise to the Nazca, which occupied the sites of its predecessor and then spread over the Ica and Nazca Valleys. This culture produced neither great public works nor monumental pyramidal structures such as those found in the northern valleys or even in the Lurín Valley on the central coast, where the famous temple of Pachacamac was built in the same epoch. No remains of Nazca cities have been found, only small villages with adobe houses. We have no evidence of centralized governments controlling one or more valleys, and everything seems to indicate that during the Classic Period on the coast, Nazca society was in an early, democratic stage of its evolution.

For reasons that are still unclear, one of Indian America's most interesting artisan movements flourished in these south coastal valleys. Using figures of birds, felines, and fish, Nazca artists decorated vessels of simple rounded shape, or plates, flaring bowls, flasks, and the typical jars with stirrup-spouted handles. Colors were soft, with reds, grays, browns, and blacks predominating on red and white backgrounds. Nazca artisans were also skillful weavers, and their textiles in wool and cotton are magnificent examples of the techniques of embroidery, brocade, and tapestry in Peru. On the other hand, metallurgy was not well developed and gold was the only metal known.

The ruins of several large settlements from the Early Intermediate Periods have been found in the Nazca and in the Acarí Valley. Cahuachi is an extended site in the Nazca Valley formed by residential areas, public buildings and plazas (Rowe, 1963). It has been suggested that Cahuachi was a regional capital. If this were one of its functions, little evidence of a centralized government controlling one or more valleys has been found on the southern coast. Militarism on the south coast apparently did not have the imperialist objectives of contemporaneous north coast cultures. The Nazca was a culture of farmers but also of hunters and fishermen (Lumbreras, 1969).

The monumental quality of the north coast's great *huacas* may have a parallel on the south coast in the curious man-made lines that cross the arid plain stretching along both sides of the Palpa Valley. Several years ago I had the opportunity to fly over these prodigious figures which seem engraved on the bare ground by a giant chisel. It is hard to imagine the meaning of these geometric and naturalistic forms laid out over an area measuring hundreds or thousands of meters. The finished effect was certainly invisible to their authors. We see in these figures reproductions of the more frequent decorative pottery motifs, as well as parallel lines which at times become confused with the route of the Pan American Highway. Other lines cross each other, form spirals or outline areas which, from the air, show perfect regularity.

Economic pressure provoked by a growing population and the expansionist policy adopted by some of the north coast cultures was undoubtedly the cause of wars which, in turn, promoted a military group and accentuated class divisions. At the same time, a new art style called Tiahuanacoid emerged from its center of radiation in the south highland area and unforseeably spread throughout the coast and all the principal highland valleys. The influence of the Tiahuanacoid culture and its art was so thorough, despite its brief duration, that it could only have been put into effect with the backing and pressure of military groups. Tiahuanacoid influence on the coast signals the decline of the regional developments which made up the most brilliant artistic period in Peru's Indian history. These cultures were the Mochica, occupying several principal north coast valleys from the Jequetepeque to the Nepeña; the little-known Lambayeque culture farther north in the Chancay and Leche Valleys; the Lima culture on the central coast; and the Nazca culture on the south coast.

NOTES ON · 8

1. WILLEY AND PHILLIPS DESCRIBE a local sequence in its purest form as being a series of components found in a single site in a vertical stratigraphic succession. In such a sequence, the area involved is small enough to allow the supposition that differences between the components reflect differences in time (Willey and Phillips, 1958). In various sites in the Virú Valley, as we will see in this and subsequent chapters, no cultural differences appear in the same stratigraphic level. Furthermore, the Virú and other fluvial valleys along the north coast of Peru show so many cultural similarities that we can establish a regional sequence.

   The reader will find it useful to read Chapters 1 and 2 in *Method and Theory in American Archaeology*, by Gordon R. Willey and Philip Phillips (Willey and Phillips, 1958). Chapter 1, in particular, contains an excellent explanation of the archeological concepts most often used.

2. In order of appearance, the three pan-Peruvian Horizons are those promoted by the spread of the Chavín, Tiahuanacoid and Inca cultures.

3. Research increasingly confirms the existence of frequent contacts between the inhabitants of different ecological zones of Peru during the Formative Period, before the Tiahuanacoid Horizon (Murra, 1962). In a personal communication, Dr. Duccio Bonavía mentioned that organized contacts between different ecological areas were intensified during the Late or Inca Horizon.

4. Tamayo describes a strip of lowlands between the Cordillera of the Andes and the Pacific Ocean, extending along the shore from parallel 1 to 27 degrees south latitude. This region of morphological desert forms enjoys particularly low rainfall. It is cut transversely by small oases along the banks of those few rivers which run down from the Andean watershed and manage to cross this arid desert (Tamayo, 1952). The western desert of South America includes the south of Ecuador, the whole Peruvian coast and the north of Chile. See note 15 of Chapter 1 of this book.

5. Today, this coast is Peru's principal productive area. Cotton and sugar cane are first in importance, then come rice and other foods. The petroleum industry and refining are major activities in the far north of the coast around the city of Talara. The main industrial centers are also located on the coast. Of the coastal rivers, each of which constitutes an independent system, only about ten have a continuous flow all year long.

6. Peru is one of the major fishing powers of the world.

7. An interesting description of the preparation of basic material for the Virú Valley Project can be found in Willey and Ford, 1949.

8. Cultivated plants have been found in Huaca Prieta, a Pre-Ceramic site in the Chicama River Valley, as a result of a rudimentary type of agriculture (Bird, 1952). Different authors place Huaca Prieta in the Archaic Period, between 2500 and 1600 B.C. (Lumbreras, 1969) which corresponds to Lanning's Pre-Ceramic VI, between 2500 and 1800 to 1500 B.C. (Lanning, 1967).

9. See note 8 of the Preface.

10. The character of the coastal desert gave rise to localism among the peoples living in the valleys. Hunting was probably limited to each valley itself and only fishing might have occasioned trips to the nearby shores of neighboring valleys. We can easily picture a society in which men lived their lives without knowing any environment other than that of the small coastal valley where they were born.

11. Maize was cultivated on the north central coast at the beginning of the second millenium B.C., as shown by evidence found in the Culchas and Huarmey River Valleys. Maize appeared earlier than ceramics on the coast (Kelley and Bonavía, 1963).

12. The temple is known as Templo de las Llamas and was built with stones on top of Cerro Prieto (Strong and Evans, 1952).

13. This refers to sites V-83 and V-85 in Willey's classification (Willey, 1953). According to Willey, the two sites seem to have formed a single community of twenty-five to thirty dwellings and around seventy chambers.

14. For a definition of these concepts, see note 8 of the Preface.

15. The emergence of some communities in the upper Virú Valley during these centuries has been pointed out as a possible attempt to take advantage of the floodable areas next to the river for more extensive farming (Collier, 1955).

16. The reader and the tourist will find it of great value to go through the pages of the *Guía de Chavín* prepared by the Peruvian archeologist Luís Lumbreras (Lumbreras, 1970). The ruins are two hundred meters from the modern village of Chavín.

17. In the Virú Valley, the Chavín Horizon coincided with the Middle Gua-

322

ñape Period. During those centuries appeared the first specialized construction such as a community or ceremonial building and a cemetery.

18. Compare the reconstruction of the Temple of Moxeque done by Pedro Rojas and reproduced in Rebeca Carrión-Cachot's article (Carrión-Cachot, 1948) with Tatiana Proskouriakoff's reconstructions of the Maya centers (Proskouriakoff, 1946; Smith, 1955).

19. This is called Tello's obelisk.

20. Chavín art has been the theme of several important monographs (Rowe, 1962, 1967; Lumbreras, Chapter III, 1969; Tello, 1960; Willey, 1951).

21. The theory that the Chavín style originated in the forest was advanced by Tello, who was the first to study this culture in detail and attempt to classify it. According to Larco Hoyle, the Chavín style originated on the coast.

22. North coast Chavín style is called Cupisnique, coinciding with early Supe and Ancón styles on the central coast. On the south coast, the Chavín is associated with Paracas Cavernas, or early Paracas style.

23. "The compound village," as Willey calls it, is characteristic of the Virú Valley during the Middle Horizon, which corresponds to Tiahuanacoid expansion.

24. A walled residential site, about 160 by 170 meters, located in the upper Casma Valley, also has the symmetrical form of concentrated villages on the north central coast during the Late Formative Period. The distribution of rooms, passages, courtyards, and doorways in the interior do not reveal a planned layout (Donald Thompson, 1964).

25. Cerro Bitín's defensive wall was built between the elevations of 275 and 285 meters approximately.

26. Apparently Chanquillo was a Late Formative fortress built on top of a hill and located in the south central part of the Casma Valley where two branches of the river join. The three concentric walls also followed the contours of the terrain (Donald Thompson, 1964). Lumbreras suggests that Chanquillo was a ceremonial group (Lumbreras, 1969). According to a radiocarbon date, Chanquillo was already occupied by the middle of the fourth century B.C.

27. During the Late Formative Period, almost all the crafts known in the Virú Valley developed. Metallurgy, which had appeared on the north coast with the Chavín influence, made great forward strides.

28. Commerce between the valleys must have existed, made possible by the use of reed boats. Even though we find no indication of the existence of commercial relations between valleys during the Formative and Experimental Periods, transportation of produce could easily have taken place by water. Distances between valleys are so short that, with favorable currents and winds, a boat could cover them in a day or even a few hours. We do not know, however, what sort of merchandise would have been transported from one valley to another. Similar ecological conditions in all north and central coast valleys would have produced the same good and bad years throughout the whole region, so we can scarcely think in terms of important amounts of cargo being transported from valley to valley because of extreme need. However, the interchange of ideas was intense, and we cannot discard the possibility of occasional contacts by land since relations with the highlands were frequent.

29. Parsons defines three basic types: a) Salt evaporating beds; b) agricultural fields and c) beds for planting marsh reeds (Parsons, 1969).

30. Groups of regularly shaped rooms around a courtyard was the arrangement most often used after the Early Intermediate centuries. As we shall see in Chapters 12 and 13 of this book, this layout was used by the Inca. I have not been able to verify whether it originated during the Early Intermediate centuries on the coast or if it was known from previous centuries. Its spread was an undeniable contribution, since it adapts perfectly to the coastal environment.

31. Rowe calls Chavín art "basically representational." Its meaning "is obscured by the conventions which govern the Chavín style and, in many cases, by the fact that representational details are not expressed literally but in a figurative or metaphorical fashion" (Rowe, 1967).

32. The purpose of the canal was to irrigate the Moche Valley, but having its origin in the Chicama Valley it was used to irrigate the latter Valley as well (Kosok, 1965).

33. Mural paintings were found in 1951 in Pañamarca, where we find a structure formed by one pyramid and several courtyards in the middle part of the Nepeña Valley. The polychrome figures represent warriors, priests, and attendants (Schaedel, 1951b). Mural paintings have been found in several sites along the coast, especially sites in the Lambayeque, Chillón, Chancay, Nepeña, and Moche Valleys (Bonavía, 1961).

·9

TIAHUANACO AND THE URBANISTIC PERIOD

"Tiahuanaco, where the buildings were sumptuous and superb . . ."

ANTONIO VÁZQUEZ DE ESPINOSA
(COMPENDIUM AND DESCRIPCION DE LAS
INDIAS OCCIDENTALES)

9

LAKE TITICACA HAS BEEN DRYING UP gradually for centuries. I find this neither particularly alarming nor see it as proof of a possible climatic change from that which existed fifteen or twenty centuries ago. The view of the lake from the road bordering its western and southern shore is one of nature's marvels.

The land is arid. Along the road, Indian couples try to plant in the hardened, depleted soil, using methods that have not changed in over a millennium: one step forward, press down on the stirrup of the digging stick sinking it into the earth; another step, a new thrust; the wife follows, dropping seeds in the holes. With luck these will germinate. With more luck, they may produce a meager potato harvest. Here and there flocks of llamas graze, and every so often we see a pair of oxen hitched to a wooden plow.

The fish in the lake are growing scarce, and even the *totora* reeds, still used in making the fishermen's rafts, are harder to find in recent years. There is almost no vegetation and trees no longer cover the hills. The cold is biting, the work arduous and food scarce. The only compensation seems to be the view of the lake, immense, brilliant blue and enclosed to the east by snow capped peaks.

The lake level has dropped thirty-four meters since the time when the first great South American city was built near its shore, over 3,800 meters above sea level. Even today, it would still be one of the highest cities in the world.

Among the great archeological sites of America, Tiahuanaco is one of the least known.[1] Up until recently there had been no large-scale excavations, and the only maps of the ruins that I have found are incomplete. Despite their generality, such maps show a relatively limited area considering the vast surface covered by the city (Posnansky, 1904, 1945; Bennett, 1934).[2] A more recent map, important as a document to understand the urban design of the central part of the city, lacks scale but includes part of the ceremonial center (Ibarro Grasso, 1955).[3]

In the light of present-day knowledge, it is difficult to understand why a city would have been situated in such an inhospitable environment. Considering that today the ruins of Tiahuanaco lie twenty kilometers from the shore, the lake itself would not have been the main reason for choosing the site. We have to assume that the *puna,* or high plain, was rich in grasslands and had enough fertile soil to encourage a culture of shepherds and farmers to settle in the most propitious sections of the lake basin, or that the early inhabitants of Tiahuanaco recognized the commercial potentialities of a site located not far from the warmer valleys to the east (Parsons, 1968).

Tiahuanaco's location must have had features in common with those of other Pre-Classic settlements, as well as with Classic cities in the basins of Mexico's lacustrine system. If this is so, other groups, like those which occupied the site of Tiahuanaco before the epoch of large stone constructions, must have established settlements during the Pre-Classic Period at different points along the lake shore, taking advantage of easy contact by land and water. The known area of dispersion of the early Tiahuanaco style, however, is small and virtually limited to the southern part of the lake, as evidenced by ceramic remains belonging to this period which have been found only in Tiahuanaco itself and on the island of Titicaca, about seventy-five kilometers to the north (Bennett, 1946b). If the site had been chosen because it was thought to be sacred and later became a ceremonial center, it would indicate that this sector, though farthest from the known highland areas during the Formative Period, was already visited frequently. We know, as was mentioned in the previous chapter, of several formative sites in the western part of the lake not far from Puno.

We have then two possible explanations of the origin of Tiahuanaco. Its inhabitants may have come from regions farther south of the lake, as yet little known archeologically. Or, perhaps, they were shepherds, farmers, and fishermen who had gathered at Tiahuanaco's site or close to it and came to form a ring around the lake, where they gradually accepted the religious, if not political leadership, of some god worshipped in Tiahuanaco. Geographically, it is difficult to explain Tiahuanaco's location if not as a result of a previous settlement from regions south of Titicaca or as a consequence of gradual occupation around the lake basin during the Formative Period.[4] Recent work by the Center for Archeological

Studies at Tiwanaku have broadened our knowledge of the Formative Period in this site. Ponce Sanginés describes the culture as appearing suddenly, already formed and vigorous from its very beginnings, which suggests that its origins were not local, but foreign (Ponce Sanginés, 1961a).

This first epoch of Tiahuanaco was contemporaneous with the Puerto Moorin and Salinar cultures on the north coast of Peru going back to the final centuries of the last millennium B.C. It was represented by an agricultural society that knew the uses of copper, silver, and gold, and that undertook public works such as roads. A good part of their diet was based on *chuño*, or dehydrated potato (Ponce Sanginés, 1961c). We know nothing about houses from this first epoch, but assume they existed, based on the finding of a ceramic whistle modeled in the form of a characteristic Tiahuanaco style dwelling with a high gabled roof.[5]

Tiahuanaco I was contemporaneous with Chiripa. The Chiripa culture takes its name from a site located near the lake shore where the climate is milder. Chiripa was a small settlement formed by adobe houses built with double walls (Bennett, 1936). The technological level and ceramic style of both sites was similar.

Lake Poopo is located in a drier environment some 250 kilometers southeast of Lake Titicaca. A culture of farmers and shepherds built their small villages to the north and northeast of Lake Poopo, probably during the Middle Formative. The Wankarani Culture predates Chiripa and Tiahuanaco. In their use of copper we see a precursor of the technology of Tiahuanaco (Ponce Sanginés, 1970).

Carbon 14 dating indicates a greater age than that usually recognized for Classic Tiahuanaco. Archeologists have discarded as groundless Posnansky's position that the city is ten or twelve thousand years old. Some authors state that the third century of the Christian era corresponds to the Classic epoch, or flowering of Tiahuanaco culture (Ponce Sanginés, 1961c; Wauchope, 1954), coinciding with the peak of Mochica culture on the north coast and the Nazca to the south.

TIAHUANACO

The ruins of Tiahuanaco lie in a long valley, bounded by two parallel rows of hills. The remains of the civic and religious center cover an area of about 1,000 meters from east to west by 450 meters north to south. Built within this rectangle stood the structures forming the center of the city during its apogee. The archeological zone is bounded to the south by the old English railroad tracks which connect La Paz with the lake port of Guaqui. To the north of the zone, a road runs parallel to the railroad.

The area covered by the city was undoubtedly much larger. Two recent rough estimates suggest an urban area of about 240 hectares (Parsons, 1968) or a minimum of 300 hectares but more probably 420 hectares (Ponce Sanginés, 1969b). As the residential districts were built with adobe, more careful surveys than those permitted by surface examination or the available aerial photographs should be undertaken before an area of such vast human agglomeration can be defined. What is unquestionable is that Tiahuanaco was the largest known city in the southern highlands during the Early Intermediate Period, between 100 and 600 A.D.

In Posnansky's old map, which is the one reproduced by the majority of authors who followed him in studying these ruins, the ceremonial center appears as an unplanned grouping of isolated structures of considerable size and complexity which seem to have been built in different stages. Posnansky insisted that there were two epochs within the Early Intermediate Period, distinguished by different building techniques and materials—soft sandstone in the first epoch and volcanic rock in the second. Orientation of the structures must have varied with each of these epochs (Posnansky, 1945). There is nothing in Posnansky's map to suggest the existence of a culture that had reached the necessary level to plan and build large constructions with a view to the finished whole.

The facts seem to have been otherwise. A partial map of the ruins not only indicates that the spatial relation between the two main structures, the Akapana and the Kalasasaya, was not haphazard, but that we see before us one of the great examples of urban planning of Indian America (Plate No. 46). Let us hope for the publication of a more detailed map of the ruins that shows the location of streets and secondary structural groups.

I believe that Tiahuanaco was the first large planned complex in South America. Although it lacks the monumentality and detail of design of

46 *Tiahuanaco: Plan of the central part. Number 1 indicates the Akapana, number 4 marks the location of the Kalasasaya, number 11 points to the Puma-Punku. Tiahuanaco may have been the first planned complex in South America. (Credit: Ibarra Grasso, D.E.; Mesa, J. and Gisbert, T.: "Reconstrucción de Taypicala (Tiahuanaco)," Cuadernos Americanos, Vol. XIV, Mexico, 1955.)*

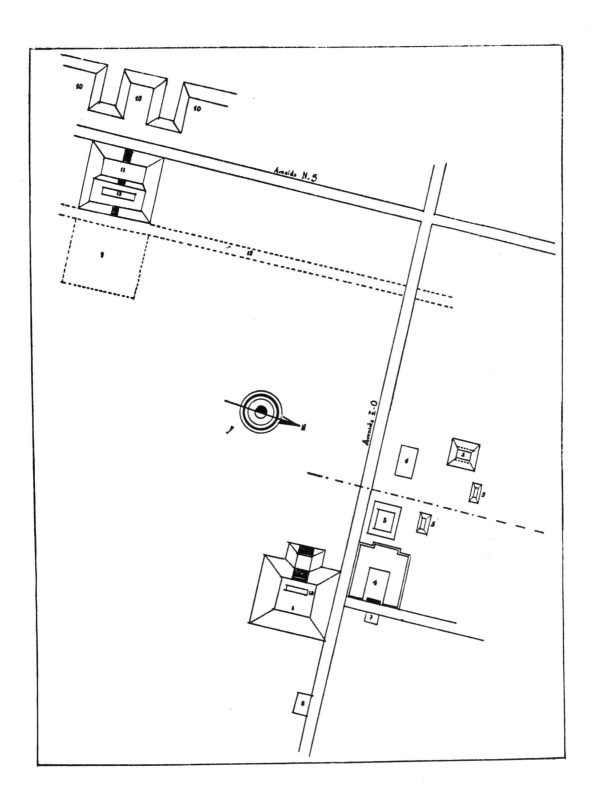

Teotihuacán, it shares a marked similarity with that center in its use of such determining features as the rectilinear direction of the composition and in the orientation to the cardinal points.

The above mentioned partial map shows two major compositional axes rigidly oriented to the four cardinal points. However, no visible or archeological evidence has been found to prove that such axes were intentionally designed (Ponce Sanginés, 1969b).

Certain architectural features appear in both Tiahuanaco and Teotihuacán: the regular ground plan and massive effect of the buildings; utilization of pyramidal platforms as bases for religious constructions; drainage canals; great stairways, and the use of stone as a building material. In Tiahuanaco, however, we have not yet found the proportioned urban spaces of Teotihuacán, such as the atrium-plaza in front of the Pyramid of the Moon, nor are the avenues visually limited and enriched by urban sequences like the Avenue of the Dead. Tiahuanaco's builders did not employ the monumental perspective which we find in Teotihuacán on a scale unequalled before or since in America, in fact setting the compositional axis of the entire ceremonial center. All the elements that enhance the urban design of any complex appear in Tiahuanaco in a less evolved, more primitive form. Sculpture, for example, revolved around one type (Bennett, 1934). It took on a feeling of superhuman dimension in the proportions of human figures represented over seven meters high.[6] This was monolithic sculpture which in its rigidity and synthesis of details of garments and physical features, was even simpler than Tula's Atlantean figures which it resembles, although Tiahuanaco's works were stelae and not pillars like those in the Toltec capital.

The principal constructions of the ceremonial center of Tiahuanaco seem to have been built entirely between 150 and 370 A.D. We know little about these people who built the great works in stone, or about their way of life. Since we have no proof of a significant change in climate compared to what we find today, and since in 1500 years no important technological innovations have been introduced into the primitive highland economy, we can surmise that the inhabitants of the Classic Period had a diet and general level of life not much different from the people today.[7]

Epoch III, to which the large square temple called Kalasasaya (Plate No. 47) belongs, as well as the small sunken temple (Plate No. 48) and possibly the Akapana Pyramid, goes back to the first centuries A.D. and it is characterized by the use of red sandstone. During Epoch IV (370-720 A.D.) builders used andesite in the construction of several enclosures and in the modifications made on existing structures. This is the epoch of large anthropomorphic sculpture (Ponce Sanginés, 1961c; Millé and Ponce Sanginés, 1968).

It has been suggested that Classic Tiahuanaco served only as a ceremonial center that attracted pilgrims from a wide territory. If this were true, the site of Tiahuanaco must have housed only priests and resident artists in charge of working the basalt and sandstone that pilgrims hauled from several kilometers away. However, it is doubtful that the pilgrims could have been organized to transport such weights as were used in the construction of Tiahuanaco. At present, we have insufficient knowledge to substantiate this theory of pilgrimages, and I know of no evidence proving that Tiahuanaco was not a true city, fulfilling, among other functions, that of a ceremonial center. As I indicate in the chapter on Teotihuacán, and from studies now in progress in some Classic Maya centers, we see that the idea of a system of pilgrimages has been used carelessly and applied to periods later than when it probably occurred. It is undeniable that Tiahuanaco was a sizeable urban center for its time and place, and that it was permanently inhabited for several centuries, but until a more thorough survey of its surrounding area is made, we cannot calculate its density and population.[8] I have been unable to determine whether Tiahuanaco was a politico-administrative capital, a regional market, a military center, or the center of cultural diffusion during the Early Intermediate Period and the Middle Horizon. The house ruins discovered up to now are still insufficient to confirm the permanent residence of a stratified society having urban institutions.

There is evidence to suggest that Tiahuanaco was the residence of a governing élite which took over Chiripa during Epoch III (Ponce Sanginés, 1970). Furthermore, the power and planning sense of such élite are apparent in Tiahuanaco. If this were not so, works on such a scale, using materials brought from considerable distances, could not have been carried out, nor would there have been any point in the monumental effect produced by the design of the ceremonial center (Hardoy, 1968).

The main structure of the ceremonial center of Tiahuanaco is the Akapana, a truncated pyramid 15 meters high with a base measuring 180 by 140 meters. The Akapana seems to have had surprising similarities to the Pyramid of the Moon in Teotihuacán. We see the likeness both in its

47 *Tiahuanaco: Entrance to Kalasasaya as seen from the sunken temple. (Credit: Hardoy.)*

48 *Tiahuanaco: View of the small sunken temple from the Akapana. (Credit: Hardoy.)*

plan and general form, such as the location of a projecting body on the main axis and the placement of stairways. Of course, the Akapana is built on a more modest scale than the Mexican pyramid,[9] but here too the upper platform yielded the remains of structures, perhaps temples.

Facing the Akapana stand the remains of a rectangular platform, 126 by 117 meters, with a sunken courtyard, reached by passing through a monolithic gateway and down six narrow steps. Near the northwest corner is a doorway, known as the Gateway of the Sun, a unique feature in pre-Hispanic architecture and the most popular monument at Tiahuanaco. Constructed from a single block of hard stone, it was lavishly carved with the typical designs of this culture. This north group is called the Kalasasaya, and certain of its features, such as the sunken courtyard, the perimetric platform and the stairway on the main axis of the group remind me of the Citadel at Teotihuacán. Opposite the Kalasasaya was a small sunken temple of almost square form.

Facing each other, at some 700 meters to the southwest of the Kalasasaya, lie the ruins of a curious platform notched at regular intervals, and those of a square pyramidal construction called Puma-Punku, six meters high and formed by two main platforms. Well dressed and fitted stone blocks were used in all these structures.

Excavations in Tiahuanaco begun a few years ago by the Center for Archaeological Studies at Tiwanaku are the most extensive to date, and their findings may clarify the functions of this center during the Middle Horizon of South American cultures. Up to the present, few housing remains have come to light: some house foundations from Epoch II, nothing from Epoch III, and from the following Period, only the Palace of Kheri-kala with its rooms aligned around a patio.[10]

The dispersion of Middle Horizon Tiahuanaco style was limited to a geographic area which included northern Chile, the south of Peru perhaps as far as Cuzco, the far southern valleys of the coast, and the highlands of north and central Bolivia. In the highlands and mainly on the Peruvian coast north of the Ocaña Valley, archeologists have found a quantity of ceramics with shapes and designs reminiscent of the style of Middle Horizon Tiahuanaco. Very little is known of the expansion of this style. We know that it was quick, lasted a brief span of time and that Tiahuanaco was its diffusion center.[11]

During the Middle Horizon, probably after the seventh century, the coast and highlands experienced the expansion of the Huari culture. Both of these separate expansions took place almost at the same time. The expansion of the Huari style was backed by military groups that swiftly ended the regional isolation that had characterized the Early Intermediate Period (Lanning, 1967).

The diffusion center of this style was the city of Wari, or Huari (Mason, 1957), situated twenty-five kilometers north of the present city of Ayacucho. Huari is one of the most extensive known urban areas of the pre-Inca periods in the central highlands, but as yet has been little studied by archeologists. It was known by the first conquistadors and is mentioned in Cieza de León's *Chronicle*.[12] Three North American archeologists who visited Huari briefly in 1946 reported that the area covered by the ruins, as seen from the highway across the valley, measures at least 3,600 meters north to south and possibly the same distance east to west (Rowe, Collier and Willey, 1950).

The schematic mapping of Huari done by Bennett (Bennett, 1953) shows an oval area surrounded on almost every side by ravines with its main axis running east. The mapped zone is much smaller than the area mentioned above, about 1,600 meters in each direction (Plate No. 49).

Although we have no real proof of a previous general plan of the city, we find regularity in the disposition of the fieldstone walls up to twelve meters high, the plazas and streets and in the structural forms. Houses too were regular in shape and had few windows.[13] Despite its position as the hub of cultural dispersion, Huari may have been a city that emerged gradually and reached its apogee about 900 A.D. coinciding with the first imperial expansion of the culture that made that city its capital. Two centuries later Huari was abandoned, reflecting the decadence of the military-religious structure which had once brought it to prominence.

Huari's importance lies in the possibility that it may have been the center of diffusion of those principles of urban planning and housing design which spread throughout the highlands and coast of Peru during and after the Middle Horizon. It seems clear that diffusion of a Tiahuanacoid style did not represent a more advanced stage in the evolution of Tiahuanaco culture which it resembled in sculpture and stone construction.

The centuries of the Tiahuanacoid expansion, between 800 and 1100 A.D., saw great political and social upheavals. The technological level typical of the Early Intermediate Period was maintained during this period, although interest in new aesthetic forms appears to have declined. At the start of its diffusion, the impact of the Tiahuanacoid style was more intense on the coast, only to fade gradually and to permit the reap-

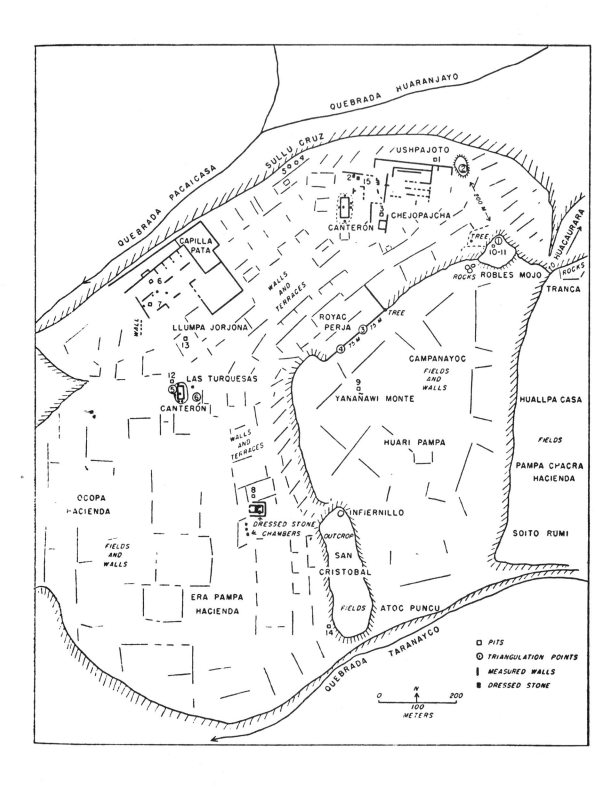

pearance of local styles. This influence of the Tiahuanacoid style was short-lived.

With the Middle Horizon came the first true cities and the adoption of an urban way of life in South America. We have already discussed the numerous centers constructed during the first millennium A.D. in the Valley of Mexico, the valleys of Oaxaca, the Central Gulf Coast and the Mayan area. Many of these were dedicated to specialized economic activities, depended on intensive rural production, and were inhabited by rigidly structured societies. Teotihuacán, Monte Albán, El Tajín, and the Classic Maya centers of the Petén and Yucatán are examples of this progressive urbanistic trend.

The excavations I have mentioned in the six cultural areas of Peru and Bolivia do not permit a similarly precise plotting of the transition from large village to city. Furthermore, the radiocarbon dates do not always coincide with the already established sequences in some of the principal archeological areas. Most authors agree that the Gallinazo culture precedes the Mochica diffusion on the north coast, that the Mochica predates the epoch of Tiahuanacoid influence on the coast, and that the Middle Horizon, in the archeological areas of South America included in this work, ended in the earlier part of the second millennium A.D. The Classic Period in Mesoamerica seems to have been almost contemporaneous with the Middle Horizon in South America.

The Late Middle Horizon and the beginnings of the Late Intermediate Period in South America were characterized by the appearance of cities with temples and religious constructions of an importance unknown until then, a superior level of life and the flowering of certain techniques such as stone architecture and such arts as sculpture. From an urban point of view, the most significant aspects emerging in those centuries were the progressive regularity in the layout of new cities and a decrease in their

49 *Huari: Plan. Huari was a pre-Inca center in the Peruvian highlands north of the modern city of Ayacucho. Because of its intermediate position between the decline of the Classic Period in Tiahuanaco and the emergence of the great cities on the north coast of Peru, Huari seems to have been one of the key sites in Peru's urban development during the centuries immediately following the Inca expansion. (Credit: Bennet, Wendell C.: "Excavations at Wari, Ayacucho, Peru," Publications in Anthropology, No. 49, Yale University Press, New Haven, 1953.)*

general density, although urban population was growing and the urban centers were increasing in size.

The large villages composed of numerous houses crowded together in a limited area with almost no passageways or intermediate streets, which were typical of the Middle Intermediate Period in the Virú Valley and the north coast sector, were replaced early in the Middle Horizon by large, rectangularly shaped enclosures (Schaedel, 1951; Willey, 1953). This change in urban form represented a growing trend toward larger, if fewer, groupings.

The upheavals of the first centuries of the Middle Horizon shook the localism in which the coastal and highland cultures had wrapped themselves. First came the Mochica domination in the north coastal valleys, but it soon disappeared, apparently routed by the expansion of the Tihuanacoid style. Tihuanacoid influence did not last long either, at least on the coast, where powerful kingdoms again emerged after the twelfth or thirteenth centuries.

During the period of Tiahuanacoid expansion, a new urban form was introduced in the north coastal valleys. This was the walled enclosure with a regular ground plan which could be adapted to different urban scales (Hardoy, 1968). Its origin is unknown, though Willey believes the idea to be ancient, having been established in other areas of Peru before it was brought to the coast by the Tiahuanacoid invasion (Willey, 1953). I have found no reference to this new form of grouping in periods prior to the coastal Tiahuanaco, except for a regularly shaped enclosure outlining an irregular agglomeration of dwellings discovered in the Virú Valley, that coincides with remains from the Late Formative Period.

The walled enclosure represents a totally different stage from the previous ones and is, in some ways, unexpected in the evolution of human groupings of South America's urban cultures. In the Virú and in other north coast valleys, archeologists have been able to trace the stages of evolution from semi-subterranean villages near the ocean to unplanned inland settlements, then several villages linked to a fortified hill that served as refuge and sanctuary, followed by the appearance of the great constructions, perhaps palaces, which served as sanctuary and housing, and finally the walled enclosures.

The regular walled enclosure represented an element of order and limitation in the disorderly general layout of the coastal villages by imposing a system of pathways and rectilinear spaces, along which a series of similar contiguous chambers were arranged. Ruins of such walled enclosures have been found, in the Virú Valley at least, on the coastal plain and in places easily accessible from all parts of the valley. We may wonder whether the choice of locale was not the result of new administrative requirements for the government of a new and different ruling group.

The Tiahuanacoid Period on the coast is called Tomaval in the Virú Valley. It is characterized by an efficient system of irrigation canals and by the walled enclosures we have mentioned. A broad, straight road about ten meters wide, partially bounded by walls of stone or adobe, that crossed the lower Virú Valley in a southeast-northwest direction, was probably built during this period, completing the existing network of local roads (Willey, 1953). This road may have connected the Virú with the neighboring valleys.

Although the Tiahuanacoid expansion produced serious unrest, its epoch saw an increase in commercial contacts among the coastal valleys and between the coast and the highlands. All this was reflected in further changes in the urban settlement patterns of the valleys along the coast. In the Virú, the same sector of the north bank of the Huacapongo continued to be occupied as it had been for over a thousand years since the Formative Period. The majority of inhabited sites were still irregularly laid out villages, but with larger houses. They were situated in the upper valley for the same reasons of defense and control of irrigation sources that had been responsible for their location centuries earlier. At the same time, cultivation of the lower valley was resumed. This simultaneous occupation of the entire valley demonstrates that the population remained at least at the same level as in the Early Intermediate Period. Based on the irrigated area, Willey calculated conservatively that a total of 25,000 persons lived in the valley.

Only in the settlements in the lower and middle valley do we find the system of walled enclosures, regularly shaped and of varying size, which contained small pyramidal mounds that may have had religious significance. The villages scattered over the level areas of the valley may have depended on four or five principal enclosures for all activities other than production and residence.

PIKILLACTA

The Huari empire developed a system of administrative and storage centers, a precursor of the organization of the Inca empire. About thirty kilometers southeast of Cuzco lie the ruins of an administrative town

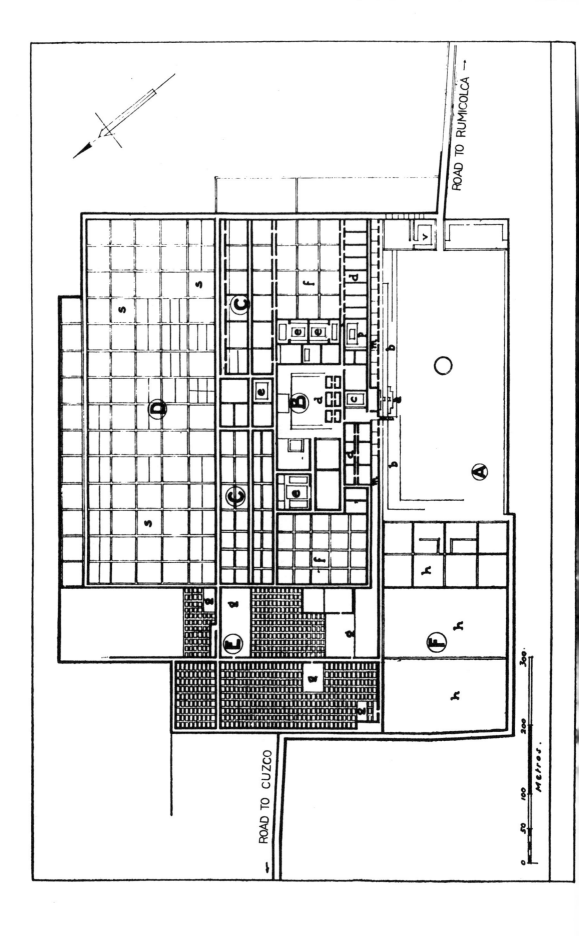

called Pikillacta. This center is almost square in shape, with its main axis 770 meters long at 45 degrees toward the northwest, and its shorter axis of 680 meters perpendicular to the first (Plate No. 50). The whole area, including housing sectors, plazas and districts of storehouses covered about fifty hectares. The ruins can be seen on both sides of a gentle depression in the Huatanay River Valley, resting against the now eroded spurs of a chain of mountains. In that sector of the valley, terrace farming is still common and the land around Pikillacta may have formed part of an agricultural zone that supplied the non-farming population living in centers of that type. The production of the zone was also stored as reserves for bad years.

The regularity of its layout and separation of zones according to function can still be seen in its ground plan. The streets crossed at right angles and their orientation was determined by the outer walls. The only access to the city was by a road that crossed it from west to east. Running through a narrow corridor bordered by two high, parallel stone walls, the road opened out into a large rectangular plaza of almost eight hectares with ritual platforms on the north and west sides.

All produce came to this plaza on the backs of Indian porters or llamas, to be distributed to silos or on special drying floors about forty meters each side, located along two streets running from the northwest corner and eastern half of the plaza, respectively. The droves of llamas were led to spacious corrals at the southwest corner of town. Along the peripheral street, produce was brought to deep, rectangular silos in the western sector of the city. Secondary streets led to the smaller drying floors surrounding a zone of sheds and housing.

Pikillacta's population must have consisted of several hundred persons, administrators and porters and llama drivers in the main. It may also have housed a small, permanent garrison or guard. The housing zone lay north of the plaza, forming an orderly district of rectangular chambers of different sizes, complete with special storehouses and reservoirs. This

50 *Pikillacta: Pikillacta was an Inca station thirty kilometers southeast of Cuzco, apparently used as a storage center for the agricultural products harvested around the area. Letter B indicates the civic plaza, surrounded by housing. Letter A marks the location of the grounds where provisions were loaded and unloaded for storage on the drying floors (D) and in the silos (District E). (Credit: Harth Terré, Emilio: "Pikillacta, ciudad de pósitos y bastimentos del imperio incaico," Revista del Museo e Instituto Arqueológico, Universidad del Cuzco, Cuzco, 1959.)*

housing sector had its own square plaza with characteristic platforms on three sides.

Pikillacta's plan is exceptionally well defined and adapted to its role as a regional administrative center. Even the width of the streets suited their function. The great plaza, off-center in the overall plan, was the heart of commercial life, whereas civic and religious activities were concentrated in the square plaza of the housing district.

MARCA HUAMACHUCO

In the northern highlands, population groupings were less concentrated than on the coast, perhaps because the potentially habitable areas were more numerous and not as restricted in size as in the river valleys. In certain especially propitious highland valleys, large population concentrations formed the nucleus of sizeable cities.

Some valleys, occupied since the Formative Period, were continually inhabited up to the Tihuanacoid expansion by groups not clearly identified. North highland settlers prior to Tihuanacoid dominion may have lived in fortified hilltop towns from which they descended to the agricultural terraces and the valleys below, but no ruins have been found of true cities from the Formative and the first centuries of the Early Intermediate Period.

Before the Tihuanacoid culture became the dominant force in the north and central highlands, as well as on the coast, the most important north highland center seems to have been Marca Huamachuco, one of the largest fortified cities of the pre-Inca period (McCown, 1945). At an elevation of 3,750 meters, the ruins are located two kilometers west of Huamachuco, the present regional center. McCown believes that Marca Huamachuco's settlers dominated their neighbors to become the center of local culture, outstanding for its engineering skills, its important agricultural contributions, and the precision of its stonework. However, its inhabitants never developed a quality of pottery, basketry, or gold and silver work to compare with that of the coastal cultures. Marca Huama-

51 *Marca Huamachuco: Plan of the pre-Inca ruins of Marca Huamachuco in the northern highlands of Peru. The wall that surrounds the Cerro del Castillo closely follows the uneven terrain, incorporating the site's topography in a manner similar to that found in other examples in the Peruvian highlands. (Credit: McCown, Theodore: "Preincaic Huamachuco," University of California Press, Berkeley and Los Angeles, 1954.)*

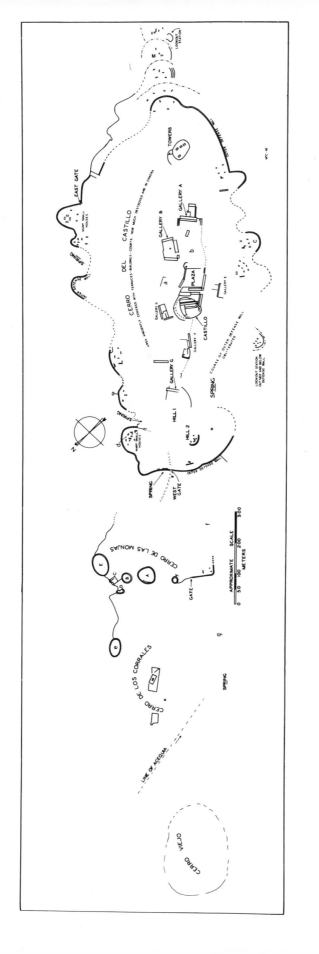

chuco was partially abandoned toward the last century of the first millennium. The causes are not clear but it seems to have been at the time of the first military expansion of the Huari culture.

Marca Huamachuco's population has been calculated at a few thousand inhabitants; certainly an insufficient number for the job of building the city with its fortifications, temples, and housing (McCown, 1945). Marca Huamachuco's urban form is totally different from the contemporaneous coastal cities (Plate No. 51). and I question the degree to which we can even consider it representative of other small urban centers of the highlands. It seems to me a large-scaled example of those elements which, grouped together, formed the walled towns in an epoch prior to Huari invasion of the region.

According to McCown's diagram, Marca Huamachuco was a fortress 3,500 meters long, built on a mountain top. The summit is relatively flat, with low elevations rising from it which were used to support smaller structures. The city itself was bounded by a low oval-shaped double wall that surrounded one of the elevations known as Cerro del Castillo. The main axis of the walled zone was about 1,300 meters long in a northwest-southeast direction, and the shorter axis of some 675 meters followed a northeast-southwest orientation. Calculation of the interior area is complicated by the wall's pronounced irregularities, but it may have been more than fifty hectares.

The intramural area was entirely filled with buildings and plazas resting on terraces, but the deteriorated state of the complex makes it hard to map. In other parts of the city, the remains of towers, platforms, and other defensive structures have been found. Almost in the center of the oval lie the ruins of a structural group called El Castillo surrounded by a curved wall and facing a trapezoidal plaza, the largest construction in the city. McCown describes El Castillo as one of the outstanding examples of the adaptation of a city plan to the contours of the land, typical of all structures in every sector of Marca Huamachuco (McCown, 1945). As we shall see in the following chapters, accommodating structures and urban features to the terrain was a characteristic of the highland peoples.

The builders of Marca Huamachuco skillfully utilized the differences in elevation and agricultural terraces to strengthen the city's defense system. On the elevations to the northwest of the mountain top, the inhabitants built other fortified complexes to defend the access to the city from that direction.

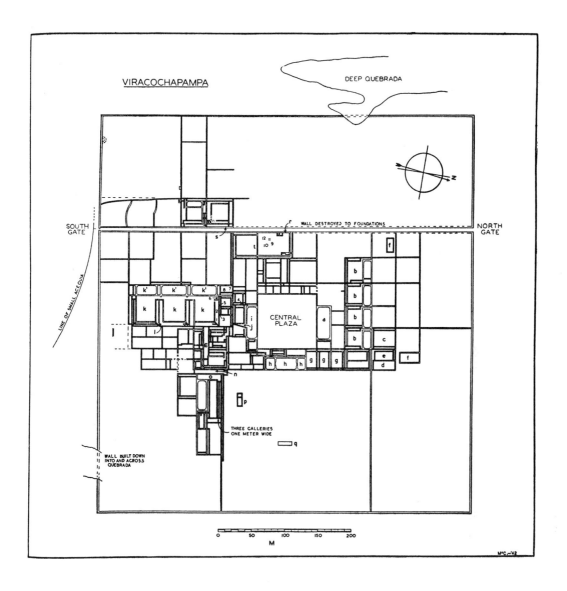

52 *Viracochapampa: Viracochapampa was an important Inca station between Cajabamba and Cajamarca. Groups of houses stood around the central plaza. The major part of the intramural area had no buildings and may have been used for corrals. (Credit: McCown, Theodore: "Preincaic Huamachucho," University of California Press, Berkeley and Los Angeles, 1954.)*

In other highland valleys, there may have been many villages, some quite large, but no true cities. If we consider that before the tenth century the north highland cultures were neither heavily populated nor important political entities, the absence of cities is explained.

VIRACOCHAPAMPA

About three kilometers north of Huamachuco, near the ruins of the pre-Inca city of Marca Huamachuco, lie the remains of Viracochapampa (Plate No. 52). Lumbreras suggests that Viracochapampa may have been a prestigious provincial capital in the northern highlands (Lumbreras, 1969). Like Pikillacta, urbanistically and architecturally Viracochapampa resembles Huari. It was probably built at about the same time Marca Huamachuco was abandoned (Lanning, 1967).

Viracochapampa had an almost square ground plan (McCown, 1945). Its long sides of 580 meters were oriented in an east-west direction with a slight deviation to the west; the short sides measured 565 meters and were perpendicular to the others. The overall scheme was orthogonal, and within the layout the streets also crossed at right angles. Pikillacta's street system, however, was more efficient, and seems to have been more directly related to the specific uses attributed to each district, than that of Viracochapampa. Nevertheless, in both cases streets were little more than corridors between blind stone walls, functionally adequate for the circulation of the townspeople as well as cargo transported by llamas and porters. Viracochapampa's housing district occupied the center of the city, surrounding a sunken plaza about eighty-five meters each side. This plaza marked the approximate center of the intramural area. We find similarities in the type of houses in both centers. Viracochapampa, however, lacked the wide spaces which have been called grain storehouses in Pikillacta. Pikillacta's general layout and features are enough like Viracochapampa so that they almost seem copied, which adds weight to the likelihood of their similar origins.

Viracochapampa's total area was approximately 32 1/2 hectares. The ground plan was divided into two sectors by a main street broader than the others that ran from north to south. It connected what seem to have been the only two entrances to the walled enclosure and divided the city into two rectangular zones: a western sector, with little construction, occupying 2/7 of the total area, or 9 1/2 hectares; and an east sector, taking up the remaining 5/7 of the area, where the bulk of the population

52 *Cajamarquilla: Aerial view. (Credit: Servicio Aerofotografico Nacional, Lima, Peru.)*

probably lived. The scheme of the large sector was more complex, but retained the orthogonal layout.

In the central part of the city, we find several groups formed by housing complexes surrounding small plazas. Around the periphery, the predominant vacant areas enclosed by characteristic stone walls may have been corrals or cultivated lots.

CAJAMARQUILLA

Pachacamac and Cajamarquilla were probably the largest and most densely populated cities of the central coast during the Middle Horizon. Pachacamac had such an important area of influence that some authors believe that it might have been the capital of an independent state or at least a center with a great degree of independence (Menzel, 1964). I know of no general map of the ruins of Cajamarquilla but we do have an old partial plan of a sector of the city (Squier, 1877). The area outlined by Squier comprises a rectangle of about six hectares—an insignificant percentage of the city's size at its height.

Cajamarquilla was built on the northern shore of the middle Rimac Valley. An aerial view confirms its large size despite the destruction to which the ruins have been subjected (Plate No. 53). The city was formed by a great number of houses of one, two, or more rooms built with adobe. These had high, windowless walls that outlined the narrow alleys which usually terminated in an open area or against another wall. Despite the regularity of its housing pattern, Cajamarquilla lacked the urban organization of the northern cities during the Late Intermediate Period. The Peruvian researcher, Alberto Giesecke, calculated that Cajamarquilla had ten thousand house ruins, which would normally yield a population figure of fifty thousand to sixty thousand persons (Giesecke, 1939). Although the chambers were generally more spacious than those of Chan Chan in later centuries, the density of the housing sectors must have been about the same.

PACHACAMAC

The most important site on the central coast during the Middle Horizon was the shrine of Pachacamac in the Lurín River Valley, a few kilometers south of Lima. Today, the Pan-American Highway cuts through its ruins, leaving the larger part to the southwest between the road and the coast (Plate No. 54).

54 *Pachacamac: Aerial view of the ruins of Pachacamac, the principal center for pilgrimages on the coast of Peru from pre-Inca times. The shrine to the Sun was located at the top and left of the photograph, next to the modern irrigated area. The straight line to the right marks the Pan American Highway. (Credit: Collection of The American Geographical Society of New York, New York.)*

Pachacamac's main building was a stepped pyramidal structure high on a hilltop. The tall vertical planes of the temple's terraces are visible from afar, altering the sides of the hill so that they seem to be part of the structure itself. The sector between the hill and the modern Pan-American Highway was almost completely built up, but today sand has covered a good part of the ruins and at first glance only a few are visible. An aerial photograph shows us a series of constructions—temples, perhaps, and palaces and housing groups—surrounded by regular walls. Intermingled with these are several unbuilt areas which may have been irrigated fields. It is hard to find any pattern in the ruins; what appear to be lines of transit, presumably bordered by walls at one time in keeping with coastal custom, do not follow the characteristic order of the northern cities during the following period.

Pachacamac had been a ceremonial center since the Early Intermediate Period and enjoyed continuous prestige until the Inca Horizon.

Once the direct influence and perhaps the control imposed by the culture represented by the Tiahuanacoid style had disappeared, the coastal valleys were free to settle their own affairs. Demographic pressures in valleys of limited productive capacity undoubtedly provoked conflicts. These struggles between villages may have reached such a degree that one group felt it necessary to ally itself with other groups within the valley and ultimately with groups outside the valley. From such alliances came larger political entities which extended beyond the limits of a single valley and in time grew into powerful kingdoms with dominion over vast territories. Unlike the Inca centuries later, these kingdoms never attained the simultaneous control of both the coast and the highlands.

The period of coastal empires was also that of the great planned cities. Despite the wide diffusion and acceptance of urban life which, for the first time, seems to have been the essential characteristic of those cultures in the six main archeological areas of Peru and Bolivia, the largest, best laid out cities were built on the coast.

The coastal valleys were, and still are, the most hospitable to human life, and a dense population concentrated in them during the Late Intermediate Period. It was not a period of outstanding artistic expression but it was remarkable in its technological innovations. The standardized ceramics point to a utilitarian mass production. Metallurgy developed to a high degree, with the use of copper and bronze to make knives, needles, points for digging sticks, and other tools.

During the Late Intermediate Period, social differences became emphasized. People sought protection, or were obliged to live in the large population concentrations in the middle or lower valley. Well organized, they built cities, fortifications, roads and other public works with speed and to last. They traded much of their freedom for strict civil and military rule. Once security became routine, civic consciousness and pride in their culture declined.

We can not even be sure that mass production indicated an advance in the material level of life of the Virú Valley's population since as the Late Intermediate Period continued, the number of sites and inhabitants diminished. It may have been that this decline was limited to the Virú and a few other valleys, possibly caused by political factors.

In the middle of the Late Intermediate Period, the Chimú Empire took power in the valleys of the north coast, and came to control a considerable territory. The Empire's capital was established in the Moche Valley, a few kilometers north of the Virú. The riches of the coast converged here, and people from the neighboring valleys may have come to share in building the great structures of Chan Chan and other cities in the valleys north of the Moche. The ruins of Chan Chan, among others, provide us with a perfect example of the high level of civilization reached in the north coastal valleys during the centuries of dominion by the lords of the Chimú Empire.

1. IN OCTOBER OF 1957, a group of Bolivian archeologists under the direction of Carlos Ponce Sanginés renewed the excavation. The Center for Archeological Studies was established at Tiwanaku, and a regional museum organized (Ponce Sanginés, 1961a). The results of the excavations are being released (Ponce Sanginés, 1969a, 1969b, 1970).

2. Dr. Ponce Sanginés informed me in a letter that a general map of the ruins is in the making.

3. A topographic map and an aerial photograph of the region surrounding the archeological area of Tiahuanaco can be found in Ponce Sanginés, 1969a, 1969b, and 1969c. Good illustrations showing architectural aspects of Tiahuanaco are included in Gasparini, 1962.

4. Carbon 14 dating has established that other sites in the Titicaca Basin, such as Chiripa in the Department of La Paz, Bolivia, predate Tiahuanaco's first epoch (Ponce Sanginés, 1961a, 1961c).

5. This data can be included thanks to a letter from Dr. Ponce Sanginés dated June 1, 1962.

6. The largest known Tiahuanaco sculpture, standing 7.30 meters high, was found by Bennett in 1932. The head alone is 1.90 meters, and the work can be best described as a monolithic pillar (Bennett, 1934). At present, it stands on view in front of the city stadium in La Paz.

7. The eastern side of Lake Titicaca is in the Department of La Paz in Bolivia, and its west side is in the Department of Puno in Peru. In 1950, the density of the Department of La Paz was 7.08 inhabitants per square kilometer, a figure which included the capital of the Republic and its 320,000 estimated inhabitants. If we exclude the city of La Paz, we would have a territorial density of barely 4.6 persons per square kilometer. In 1954, the approximate density of the Department of Puno was somewhat less than twelve inhabitants per square kilometer. The Bolivian figures are from the census of August, 1950, and the official Peruvian estimates from that of December 31, 1954.

8. Assuming that the density of Middle Horizon Tiahuanaco was comparable to the one suggested for the urban core of Teotihuacán during its apogee, Parsons suggests a rough estimate of about 20,000 inhabitants as a maximum (Parsons, 1968).

354

9. Although the base of the Akapana is 20 per cent larger than that of the Pyramid of the Moon, the volume of the latter is at least twice as great. The volume of the Pyramid of the Sun at Teotihuacán is roughly four times greater than that of the Pyramid of the Moon and nine times greater than that of the Akapana Pyramid.

10. According to Dr. Ponce Sanginés, the enclosure of Kheri-kala, excavated in 1958, is typical of Epoch IV, or the Classic Period. Kheri-kala was a rectangular building with four wings or halls arranged around a central open courtyard. The foundations are of polished squared stone on which rose a double wall of adobe. The chambers in each wing connected with each other and were probably roofed in the projecting false arch construction. Handsomely carved pillars of gray andesite appear only at the corners of the building. Ashlar stones from other structures were reused in the foundations (Ponce Sanginés, 1961c).

11. Menzel suggests that the dispersion of the Tiahuanaco style did not involve military conquest and that it was a religious movement probably initiated by missionaries (Menzel, 1969).

12. In Chapter 87 of his *Chronicle*, Cieza de León describes Huari as located on the outskirts of the ruins of the city of Huamanga (Ayacucho) founded by Pizarro in 1539. "The largest river is called Vinaque, where there are large and ancient buildings in such a ruinous condition that it bespeaks a great age indeed. When the local Indians are asked who built this antiquity, they reply that the builders were other bearded white men like ourselves, who came to live in these parts long before the Inca reigned. And from this and other ancient buildings in this kingdom, it seems to me that they do not look like those which the Inca built, because this building was square and those of the Inca were long and narrow" (Cieza de León, 1945).

13. The best published description of Huari was written by Lumbreras (Lumbreras, 1969).

·10

THE CHIMÚ KINGDOM

"Some Indians tell that in ancient times, before the Inca held dominion, a powerful lord lived in the valley. He was called Chimo, like the name of the valley today, and he performed great deeds, won many battles and built buildings which, though very old, seem once to have been something important."

PEDRO CIEZA DE LEÓN
(LA CRÓNICA DEL PERÚ)

□ 10

THE LATE INTERMEDIATE PERIOD
(1000-1476 A.D.)

BETWEEN THE 1370's AND THE 1470's the Chimú kingdom controlled the valleys of Peru's north coast and threatened to expand into the adjacent central valleys. As a result of military conquests and alliances, the kingdom extended from 5 to 11 degrees south latitude and across 700 kilometers of desert and irrigated valleys, yet it never penetrated the highlands.[1] Aware of the weakness of their eastern frontier, the Chimú lords made pacts with a small highland kingdom which controlled the area around Cajamarca.

The Chimú originated much in government and technology which was later adopted by the Inca. Perhaps their greatest innovation was an efficient administration, despite inadequate systems of writing and rapid counting. Along technical lines, they instituted programs of public works and mass production of goods. Their political techniques included the organization of an intricate network of cultural and economic relations with other peoples, who were allowed a certain autonomy yet required to pay the tribute needed to maintain and develop the Empire. Like the Mochica before them and the Inca after, the Chimú lacked means of transport other than llamas and porters, and their technology was as limited as that of the other Indian cultures of America which reached the Urbanist stage.

In any event, Chimú culture must have seemed astonishingly advanced to the highland peoples. Behind their achievements was the organized effort of a large population, directed and controlled by an aristocratic minority which had established the succession to the throne from among its members (Rowe, 1948). Considering the known characteristics of this so-

359

55 *Chan Chan: Chan Chan's ruins lie on the margin of the irrigated zone of the Moche River Valley on Peru's north coast, but when the city was the capital of the Chimú kingdom, the cultivated fields extended much further. Note the similar orientation of the large walled precincts and the rectilinear urban layout. (Credit: Collection of The American Geographical Society of New York, New York.)*

ciety, I am inclined to believe that it was here, for the first time in South America, that we find an experiment in administrative and economic planning, even though the Inca are usually credited with originating and applying this type of government in the continent.

Around 1460, during the reign of the Inca Pachacuti, a great warrior king, the armies of Cuzco reached the region of Cajamarca after having dominated the Peruvian highlands on the way. This new region conquered, the Inca army, under the leadership of Pachacuti's son, Topa Inca Yupanqui, continued on to the coast where, after a brief struggle, the last Chimú king, Minchançamán, was forced to surrender. Minchançamán was taken back to Cuzco, leaving his son, Chumuncaur, to rule on the coast as an Inca puppet. In this political manoeuver, as in many other aspects of war and peace, we see that the Inca had learned from the Chimú.

CHAN CHAN

The city of Chan Chan, in the Moche River Valley, was the capital of the Chimú kingdom. Perhaps for political, administrative, economic and technical reasons, the Chimú placed particular emphasis on cities. Chan Chan's ruins lie at the edge of the irrigated zone of the valley on a broad plain that descends gently toward the sea, about five kilometers north of Trujillo, a city founded by Pizarro in 1535 (Plate No. 55).

The desert has invaded Chan Chan. Each year the wind, the occasional but intense rains, the crops and the grave robbers add to its devastation. Nothing worth mentioning has been done to avoid its destruction, and only recently has methodical exploration begun. Sometimes small groups of tourists drive around its high adobe walls, walk through its citadels or climb its temple platforms. To them, the ruins must seem shapeless masses of adobe, difficult to identify and even harder to imagine in their former urban appearance.

From the top of Chan Chan's highest temple-mound, called Huaca del Obispo, or Bishop Huaca, at the northeast end of the designated archeological zone which includes the city's central sector, you can see the desert, the planted fields, the extensive boundary walls, and the formidable ramparts which once outlined the citadels. In the foreground you see isolated hills, and beyond them the great bluish range that encloses the coastal desert strip along the ocean. The Andes rise in the distance.

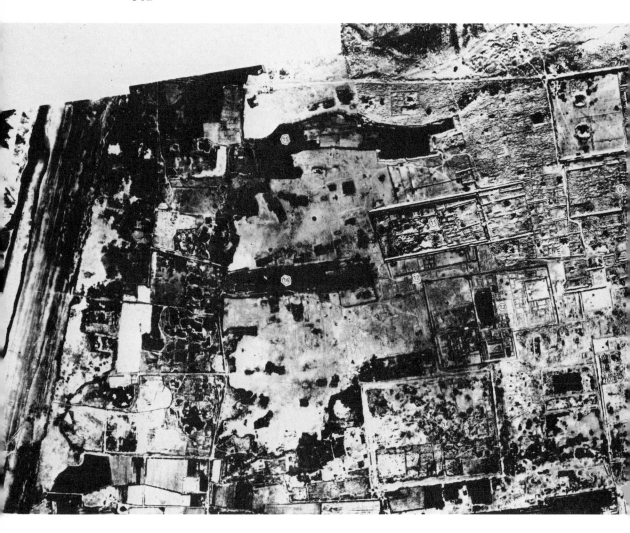

56 *Chan Chan: Aerial view of the archeological area.*
1—Bishop or Hope Huaca
2—O'Donovan or The Nuns Group
3—Arabesque Hallor Gran Chimú Group
4—Velarde Group
5—Forgotten Huaca
6—Bandelier Group
7—Toledo or Llomayocgoan Huaca
8—Municipal Council or Labyrinth Group
9—Tello Group

10—*Uhle Group*
11—*Rivero or Second Palace Group*
12—*Misa Huaca*
13—*Tschudi or First Palace Group*
14—*Chayhuac Group*
15—*Great Wachake (artificially dug cultivated land)*
16—*Small Wachake*
17—*Ruins of the Colonial chapel of San Jose*
(Credit: Servicio Aerofotográfico Nacional, Lima, Peru.)

To the southwest, you can glimpse the sea, and on quiet days its sound is heard in the citadels. Cultivated fields lie to the east of the city, reaching up to the Huaca del Obispo, surrounding it and even penetrating its ancient walls. As evening falls, the land and the ruins turn reddish in the setting sun, and silence takes over the dead city.

In its days of glory, Chan Chan must have held thousands of people moving about between the broad cultivated and wooded areas, in and around the citadels, cleaning the irrigation canals which assured the subsistence of the valley's inhabitants, working the fields and building religious and civic constructions.

Today, as we walk along the esplanades between the citadels, our line of vision is contained by the high walls. Above these, forming a broad semi-circle to the north and east, rise the ruined masses of four large adobe mounds. These bear the names of Huaca del Obispo, or Temple of the Bishop; Huaca de las Conchas, Temple of the Shells; Tres Huacas, Three Temples, and Huaca del Higo, Temple of the Fig.[2] Between the citadels, about 300 meters south of the highway joining Trujillo to Huanchaco, are the remains of a fifth temple, Huaca del Olvido, or the Forgotten Huaca (Plate No. 56).

Chan Chan's physical characteristics and plan were totally different from any pre-Columbian city of Mesoamerica. In Mesoamerica, the center in the majority of cities was marked by a building or a group of buildings, the size and location of which indicated the degree of dominion that the particular religion or minority group held over the population. This was a common practice among the first urban cultures of the Near East and the Mediterranean area, and centuries later among the cities of Medieval Europe and Spanish Colonial America. Such was not the case, however, in Chan Chan. Time has eroded the walls which are still its main attraction. The only features that rise above the horizon line of these walls are the *huacas*. They are distributed in different locations over the central area but they do not mark the city center. No structure in the citadel area seems to have imposed its authority over the surrounding area as did the Babylonian and Assyrian ziggurats, the Maya and Aztec temples and the Gothic and Spanish-American cathedrals, each in its age.

Chan Chan may well have been the most extensive planned city of South America before the Spanish Conquest. Its origin, at least that of the urban structure we see today, probably coincides with early Chimú expansion, during or after the time of the political consolidation of the Moche Valley. The construction of Chan Chan, however, was probably begun during the period of Tiahuanacoid influence on the coast as indicated by ceramic finds in styles characteristic of that culture (Willey, 1953).

Chan Chan's ruins cover an estimated area of between twenty square kilometers (Mason, 1957) and at least fifteen square kilometers (Lanning, 1967).[3] Although the archeological zone is smaller than this, it still probably exceeds the true urban districts of the ancient city. The archeological or central zone forms a rectangle approximately four kilometers from north to south by one-and-a-half kilometers east to west.[4] Like the city, it is oriented northeast-southwest with a deviation of 19 degrees east of north, corresponding roughly to the position of the setting sun at the winter solstice (Miró Quesada, 1957). The city's general axis slants almost 45 degrees from the coastline of the Pacific Ocean (Plate No. 57).

Of the ten or more citadels or compounds, sometimes called "wards" or "groups" in other works, all but one respected the city's orientation. These complexes were generally elongated rectangles but some were almost square. It is quite possible that they were not built at the same time but added gradually, assembled as pieces of a larger whole. Although a general rectilinear layout is evident, the citadels do not show any street pattern in the spaces between them. There was no checkerboard arrangement in the central area, nor was there any one dominant avenue or street. The density seems to have been high, the streets narrow and the urban land intensely occupied. Inside the walls of the citadels, however, there were streets which connected at right angles, but here too, none seems to have been more important than the rest, and we find no checkerboard pattern or attempt to create vistas. Chan Chan's greatness lies in its scale and in certain of its construction features.

The spaces formed between the citadels appear today as great empty lots. They do not seem to have been planned districts or urban areas but rather intermediate zones without specific purpose. Walking across the zones outside the citadels, however, you can see a number of ridges in the sand in a more or less linear pattern. Aerial photographs are more explicit. In these we clearly see the outlines of housing groups, including plazas and reservoirs, with some order and regularity although never as well laid out as those inside the citadels (Plate No. 55 and 56). I find two possible explanations for this. The first is that the citadels were built as individual units, following the general orientation of the city. Subsequently, after the inner area of the citadels was filled, Chan Chan's inhabitants began to fill up the exterior spaces left between them. The second and more likely possibility is the opposite. Following an arrangement similar to that in the great Classic villages of the north coast, a gradual occupation of a large area took place with no general plan and without the introduction of wide avenues or vistas. The result was based on the addition of simple, regular elements, built for various uses, such as housing groups, plazas, public grounds, temples, and reservoirs. Later, massive walls were introduced into this arrangement to demarcate those areas intended for special uses or groups. This developed the rectangular walled compounds characteristic of the Urbanist or Late Intermediate Period on the north coast of Peru. After the special area was outlined by walls, its interior was gradually organized into the rectilinear, orderly pattern we observe today. This second possibility would answer the hypothesis that Chan Chan was begun during the period of Tiahuanacoid influence on the coast and was later enlarged during the Chimú Period (Bennett, 1946b). Furthermore, the differences in housing qualities and in the intensity of land uses would reveal that, at least partially, the lower classes lived in the intermediate zones while the élite lived inside the citadels.[5]

Why were the walls built? Why was the city organized into separate wards, or citadels, and why did these apparently have no useable entrances? Did these complexes contain groups which, for political, social, or economic reasons, were obliged or wished to remain isolated from each other? Various explanations have been given. In 1877, Squier wrote that the population was separated for municipal and social reasons, although he himself admitted that there must have been other, simpler ways of achieving such isolation besides creating a number of fortresses

57 *Chan Chan: General plan of Chan Chan's citadels. The principal axis of the majority of the walled precincts is 19° east of north. Number 21 marks the Huaca del Obispo (Bishop Huaca). The following citadels are numbered on this plan:*
2—Gran Chimú
3—Bandelier
4—Uhle
6—Tschudi
8—Labyrinth
(Credit: Miró Quesada, Luis: "Chan Chan, estudio de habilitación urbanística," O.N.P.U., Lima, 1957.)

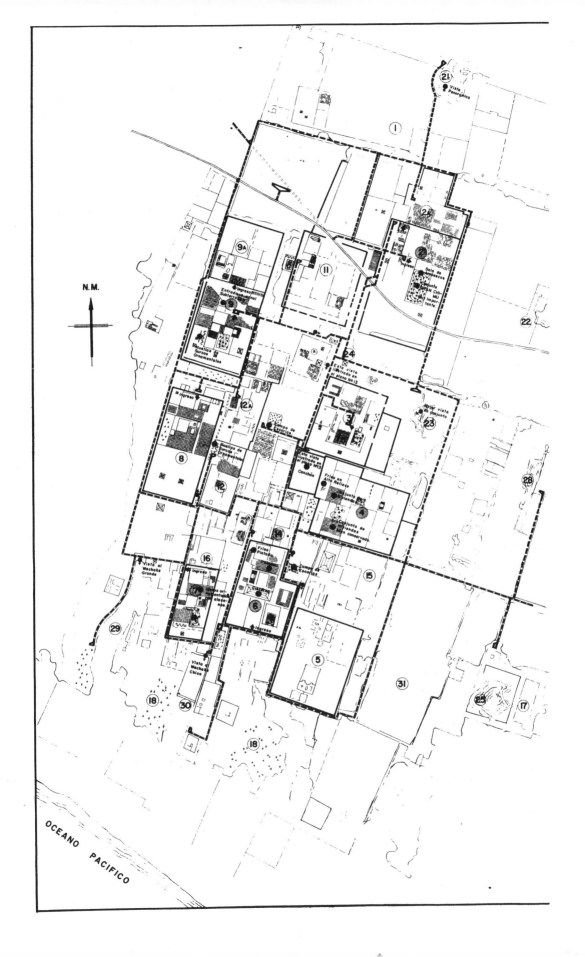

(Squier, 1877). Horkheimer also supported the theory that the walls were built to control the free movement of the population. Bennett, on the other hand, believed that the citadels may have represented subdivisions of Chimú society, perhaps clans (Bennett, 1946b). Mason leaned toward the second hypothesis, adding that each citadel may have been the domain of a sub-chief (Mason, 1957). This is essentially the same opinion that Harth Terré expressed to me, when he suggested that a citadel was the precinct of a chieftain and his closest servitors. It has also been proposed that the citadels served as centers for groups of specialized artisans (Miró Quesada, 1957, Horkheimer, 1944) or as market centers acting as redistribution points or as centers of manufacture (West, 1970).

I have come across no data confirming any of these theories. However, since we find the same urban features such as streets, plazas, dwellings and walls repeated in each citadel, noting their similar uses and groupings, we can surmise that each precinct housed a homogeneous social group, the members of which belonged to the same level of Chimú society. The importance of storage space, the number of walk-in-wells, the careful street pattern and the quality of architecture are indicative that the citadels were the residential quarters of Chan Chan's élite groups (Day, 1970).

The need for self-defense on the part of certain groups within the same city is not without parallel in other periods of urban history, for instance during the Middle Ages in Europe. In these cases, however, the protective wall was built to insure the security of some ethnic minorities. It was also common for medieval cities to grow by the addition of new neighborhoods to the initial fortified nucleus. This enabled the city's fortifications to retain a unity and continuity of outline which evidently was absent in Chan Chan. Later in this chapter, we will discuss the parallels between some of Chan Chan's urban aspects and those of certain Chinese cities. For the moment, let us examine another possibility.

Scholars have learned that, for political and administrative reasons, the Inca attempted to gather the chiefs of conquered peoples in Cuzco. Since apparently this was originally a Chimú idea, it might account for the citadels with their segregationist character.

We cannot easily determine a general density for the city on the basis of the population of the citadels and the probable number of chambers in each which might have been used for housing. However, Adolfo Bandelier, a scholar of the ancient cultures of Peru and Bolivia who worked at the beginning of this century, made a calculation that roughly thirty-five thousand persons lived in Chan Chan. Middendorf, who published one work on Peru and another on the Mochica and Chimú languages at the end of the past century, estimated a population of one hundred thousand. In recent years, Miró Quesada calculated that somewhere around sixteen thousand persons lived in the eleven citadels (Miró Quesada, 1957). Judging by the number of chambers apparently used for housing and the possible number of persons occupying each room, he concluded that 2,800 persons could have lived simultaneously in the largest citadel, Gran Chimú.[16] Similar population estimates for the other citadels yield the following results: 2,200 persons for Labyrinth, 2,100 for Velarde, 1,700 for Squier, 1,700 for Tello, 1,400 for Chayhuac, 1,100 for Tschudi, 900 for Uhle, 900 for Rivero, 700 for Bandelier, 300 for Section A and 150 for Section B. This makes a total of 15,950 inhabitants, excluding those occupying the outer zones of the citadels and the peripheral areas of the city. Considering Chan Chan's area, we must assume the overall population to have been much larger than that calculated for the citadels.[7]

The small size of many chambers inside the citadels makes it doubtful that all of them could be used as permanent housing. Storage has been suggested as a possible function for these rooms (West, 1970; Day, 1970). The density of the citadels would have been lower than that of the spaces between them, with a total population of about ten thousand persons or less (West, 1970). West estimated a population density of ninety persons per hectare for the metropolitan core which covered an area of approximately 750 hectares; the total population would reach, then, about 67,500 persons (West, 1970). Assuming a lower density for the rest of the site, the total population of Chan Chan during its apogee was not far from one hundred thousand persons.

I have included plans and aerial views for five of the citadels; Tschudi, Bandelier, Uhle, Rivero, and Labyrinth. By studying these specific plans and verifying the characteristics of the other citadels on an overall plan, we can make certain generalizations regarding Chan Chan's urban features. (Plate No. 58, 59, 60, 61, 62).

Three of the five citadels mentioned are rectangular in shape with their main axes oriented north-south, following the direction of the city as a whole. Of these three rectangles, Labyrinth and Rivero show a proportion of about 2:1, while in Bandelier the proportions are approximately 1.25:1 Tschudi is shaped like an elongated letter L, but still respects the general orientation. With the exception of Uhle, the only departure from this orientation, the four other citadels seem to have been constructed in a single building period and in their final form, showing no evidence of the addition of subsequent districts.[8]

In all five citadels we find the ground uses repeated in varying degrees of intensity.[9] These uses seem to have been similar: housing zones around so-called plazas; walk-in-wells, also known locally with the name of *pukios*, used now for intensive cultivation but employed by the inhabitants of the citadels as water reservoirs; temples in the housing sectors; small rooms, probably used for storage; *canchones* and so forth. Only the percentage of the land used in these ways varied with each citadel.

Gran Chimú citadel seems to have been the largest, but I do not believe any plan has been made of it as yet. Nor have I found plans of the remaining citadels, which I understand have yet to be mapped.

Of the five citadels compared and reproduced in this book, Uhle was the largest, covering an area of about 196,300 square meters, or 19.6 hectares. The smallest citadel was Rivero with approximately 72,000 square meters. A comparison of the areas of these five precincts with the number of inhabitants which Miró Quesada attributed to them (Miró Quesada, 1957) appears contradictory. For example, he figures the largest, Uhle, and Rivero, the smallest, had the same number of inhabitants, whereas Tschudi, with an area 12 per cent less than Bandelier, was occupied by a population 55 per cent greater.

The value of calculating a citadel's population by the number of possible chambers is questionable. Even if we could determine the housing area in each citadel with exactitude, we have no way of knowing if all these chambers served as permanent lodgings or whether they were partially used for religious purposes, as storerooms, etc. Considering the limited dimensions of most of the chambers which, in Labyrinth, are usually two by three meters and are four meters fifty by five in Tschudi, it is hard to conceive of whole families living in them.

Based on what I could observe at first glance during a short visit in

58 *Chan Chan: Tschudi Citadel. Number 6 on the general plan. This plan provides us with an excellent example of ground use in the interior of a citadel. The walk-in-well, or* pukio, *is the largest among those examples studied. Note the relation between the two plazas (dotted) and the location of the surrounding housing districts. (Credit: Miró Quesada, Luis: "Chan Chan, estudio de habilitación urbanística," O.N.P.U., Lima, 1957.)*

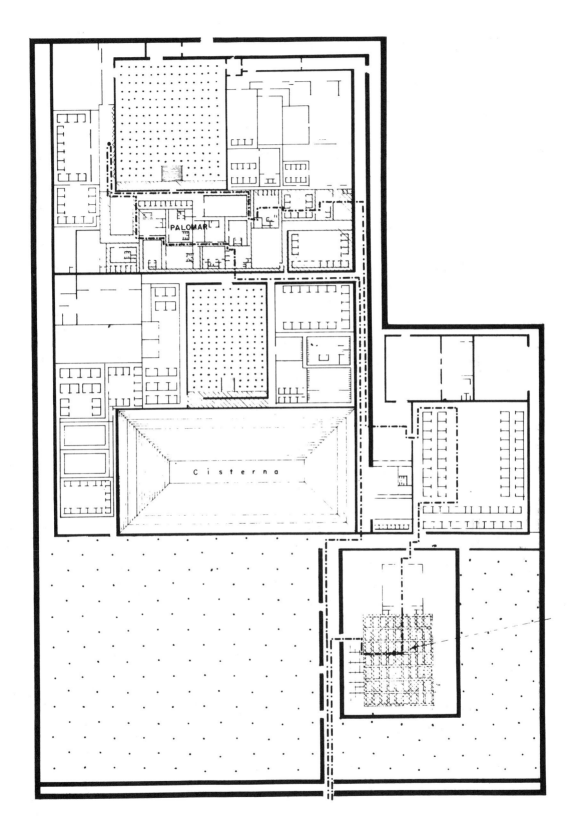

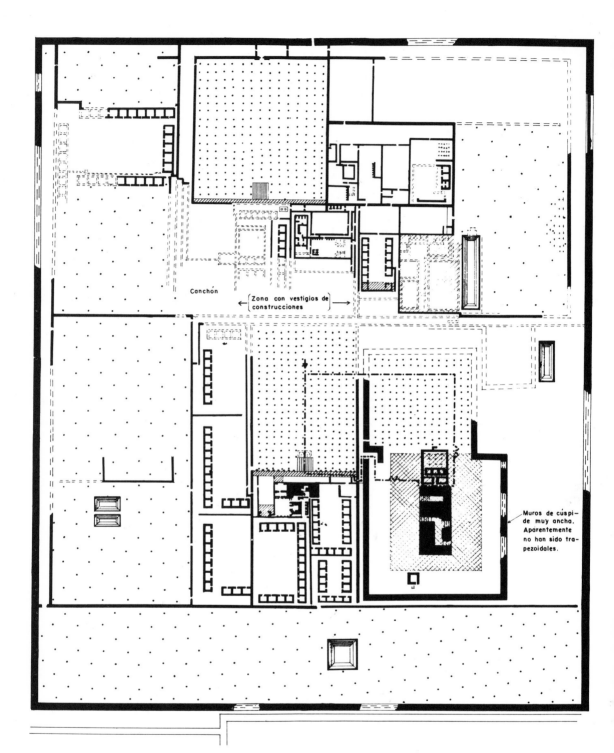

Canchón

Zona con vestigios de
construcciones

Muros de cúspi-
de muy ancha.
Aparentemente
no han sido tra-
pezoidales.

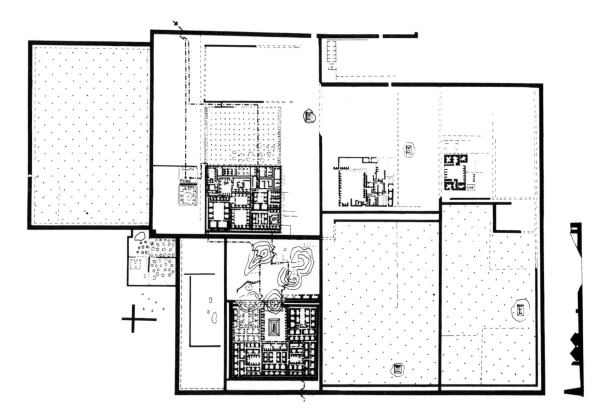

60 *Chan Chan: Uhle Citadel. Number 4 on the general plan. Note the additions that seem to have been added to the original nuclei indicated by housing groups. (Credit: Miró Quesada, Luis: "Chan Chan, estudio de habilitación urbanística," O.N.P.U., Lima, 1957.)*

59 *Chan Chan: Bandelier Citadel. Number 3 on the general plan. This citadel may have been the least densely populated of the five examples analyzed in this work. It also may have had the largest area of* canchones *or unbuilt spaces. (Credit: Miró Quesada, Luis: "Chan Chan, estudio de habilitación urbanística," O.N.P.U., Lima, 1957.)*

61 *Chan Chan: Rivero Citadel. Not shown on general plan. Aerial view. The wall system of this citadel is one of the best preserved. (Credit: Collection of The American Geographical Society of New York, New York.)*

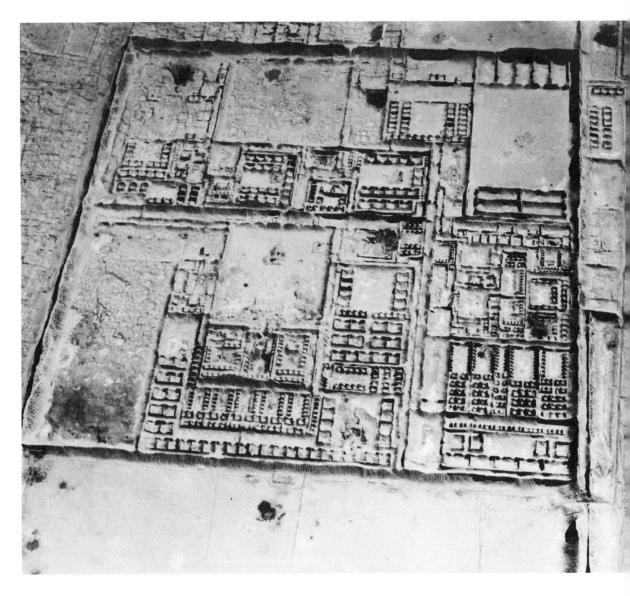

62 *Chan Chan: Labyrinth Citadel. Number 8 on the general plan. Despite the ravages of erosion, the rectilinear layout remains clear. (Credit: Collection of The American Geographical Society of New York, New York.)*

1960, I maintain that the citadels show no significant construction variations, which would indicate that they were all built and probably occupied simultaneously.

The percentage apparently intended for housing varied according to the citadel, with 13.3 per cent of Uhle's total area and 28.4 per cent of Tschudi representing the highest percentages.[10] Still, we must not overlook the possibility that other areas of the citadels for which we know no specific use might also have been destined for housing.

According to the total area of each citadel and the population estimated by Miró Quesada, I have made rough calculations which oscillate between 45 inhabitants per hectare in Uhle and 148 inhabitants per hectare in Labyrinth, and an approximate 112.4 persons per hectare for the five citadels together. The density would soar if we considered only those sectors designated as apparent housing areas. This would bring Labyrinth to 590 inhabitants per hectare, Rivero to 580, and Bandelier, probably the lowest in density, to 308. The overall density of the residential sectors of all five citadels would rise to 486.7 persons per hectare.

On the whole, the *canchones,* or unbuilt areas, constituted the most extensive use of the citadels' land. These areas could have been used as gardens or for farming, as has been suggested, although superficial burial grounds have been found. Walk-in-wells are frequently located inside or on the periphery of these areas. Low platforms which could have supported dwellings were also found in these open areas (Day, 1970). *Canchones* made up 35.9 per cent of the combined areas of the five citadels while 20.9 per cent was dedicated to housing.

We have noted the variations in the percentages of population as compared to housing areas. There is a similar variance regarding the *canchones.* In Labyrinth, estimated at having 2,200 inhabitants, 73,175 square meters were given over to *canchones*, or 49.2 per cent of the citadel's total area, while in Rivero with its assumed population of 900 persons, *canchones* accounted for only 7,000 square meters, or 9.6 per cent of the citadel. Accordingly, the respective maximum areas of cultivation per person would have been 33.2 square meters in Labyrinth and 7.7 square meters in Rivero. Even with irrigation and the continual use of fertilizers, a limited area like this would have proved inadequate to feed the population of any one of the citadels. The cultivated fields, if indeed they were such, could only have served in emergencies or for special crops.

The *canchones* could have been used as areas where porters and llamas unloaded goods and cargos brought to be stored in the citadels. However, each citadel had no more than one or two accesses and these were located in the housing sectors and not as a direct communication between the *canchones* and the outside.

Let us suppose that the reservoirs, the large cuts with terraced interior borders, were actually used for water storage as has been suggested, rather than as *pukíos* or cultivated plots, so common in the north coastal valleys even before the Late Intermediate Period.[11] The size of the reservoirs varies greatly and bears no apparent relation to the possible population of each citadel or to the field areas irrigated by them. Labyrinth, for example, with twice the population and more than double the open area of Tschudi, had a reservoir area equivalent to one fifth of the latter, and in Uhle, the largest of the five citadels, only 0.1 per cent of the total area was used for reservoirs.

Such variations in the size and importance of the open areas in the different citadels is hard to explain. Although the basic construction of the citadels seems to belong to the same epoch, Chan Chan itself was built over a span of years. It was a city formed of several independent units built by groups of people we know nothing about for purposes equally unclear. We can only surmise that those groups and functions must have been similar or complementary, giving rise to a series of urban units which fitted together perfectly according to a previous urban plan.

A reserve of cultivable land within city walls was a practice maintained in various epochs among a number of cultures throughout the world. Some European cities of lesser importance dating from Medieval times that remained aloof from the rapid demographic growth and territorial expansion brought on by the Industrial Revolution still keep small farms within their walls. These reserve areas had proved invaluable during the Medieval and Renaissance centuries as a means to absorb increased population, house refugees and grow food for the city's inhabitants when they were faced with a long seige.

Since we cannot clarify the function of the citadels and the walls, we can only wonder if at Chan Chan, like in the Medieval cities, *canchones* were intended as reserve areas. I do, however, suggest that since land use was similar in all of Chan Chan's citadels, the difference in intensity of this use may indicate progressive stages of development with the older precincts having less area in fields.

The plazas of Chan Chan's citadels were square or rectangular platforms, generally located in the housing districts, and slightly raised above street level. They were usually surrounded by a wall. Their main access was a ramp from a higher platform located to one side from which the most important personages of the citadel probably witnessed public events. In four out of the five citadels—Uhle is the exception—the access ramps to the plazas followed a north-south axis in accordance with the overall orientation of the city. In these four cases, the platforms were oriented to the north, which may indicate the location of the main structural group in each citadel. In Uhle, the one plaza we have found had the same orientation as the citadel itself, east to west, which is perpendicular to that of the city. The other four citadels had two plazas each. In these, the larger plazas were situated near the northern rampart and were square. The second plaza, always found toward the center of the citadel, was smaller and rectangular in shape. Compared individually, the largest of all the square plazas among the citadels seems to have belonged to Bandelier and was some seventy meters on each side. Also in Bandelier, we find vestiges of what may have been a third plaza linked to a curious complex which was surrounded by a wide internal wall. This wall delimited a precinct which may have held some religious significance. Bandelier's three plazas covered an area of approximately 15,100 square meters, or 12 per cent of the citadel's total surface, whereas Uhle's single plaza occupied only 3,000 square meters, or 3 per cent of its surface.

The plazas appear to have been utilized for civic and ceremonial purposes. We can, however, almost exclude the possibility of their use for markets, considering the difficulties involved in gaining access to them.

Chan Chan's high inner and outer adobe walls are today, as they must have been when the citadels were occupied, its most characteristic feature. We can still see something of the trapezoidal shape, broad of base and narrowing toward the top yet wide enough to walk along.[12] We could speculate endlessly on the function of the walls. Our first reaction is that the outer walls were intended as fortifications. But if this were the case, then why were they so important in Rivero, where we find sections of three parallel walls eight and ten meters high with narrow corridors between, and so simple in Uhle and Labyrinth? Furthermore, the area of walls and outer corridors (or fortifications if this hypothesis is correct) occupied 20,150 square meters, or 27.6 per cent of Rivero's total area, and only 6,560 square meters or 4.4 per cent of Labyrinth. The outer walls do not differ much in construction, all being made of rectangular adobe bricks of varying sizes, occasionally with foundations of uncut stone.

The almost total lack of entrances to the citadels is surprising. In Labyrinth and Bandelier, they appear to have been nonexistent. The accesses which admit us today do not seem to have been meant for that purpose originally. On the other hand, there are well-defined entrances on the north side and northwest corner of Rivero, on the north and south sides of Tschudi and on Uhle's north side. In the five citadels I have mentioned, the interiors are reached by passing through an outer perimetric corridor, and past a second wall. This double protection of the entrance gateways, and a recently discovered observation hole facing Rivero's northwest access, suggest that the walls were indeed meant for defense or for some sort of control. Except for Tschudi's southern gateway, the accesses to each citadel were connected to its housing district.

Generally, the inner walls are narrower and lower than the outer ones, except in Rivero where one wall that cuts the citadel in two is as wide as the exterior ramparts, and in Uhle where we find several interior walls the same width as the outer ones. In this case, the inner walls may represent the limits of the citadel in a previous stage with its subsequent additions. The function of the inner walls seems to have been to designate areas in which different activities took place as well as to direct the movement of the citadel's population. The same building techniques were used for both inner and outer walls.

In the five citadels we have analyzed, no true streets have been found, nor can we see any order of importance in type and function among the narrow alleys and rectilinear corridors which always meet at right angles. The builders of the citadels were not in search of vistas, and we find nothing in the relation of the plazas to suggest a desire to create urban sequences. The plan of the citadels was simple and utilitarian, following a layout common to all in its repetition of the same features.

The straw roofs slanting to one or both sides, which were supported by *algarrobo* wood beams, have long since disintegrated. The thick walls of the chambers have been washed and eroded by the wind and the rains, giving Chan Chan a totally different appearance today. Even so, we can still see the rectilinear pattern of its plan based on the repetition of an organizing element such as the arrangement of rooms of equal size in single or parallel rows of up to eleven units, often around a small plaza.

The citadels used only a small fraction of the central area of Chan Chan and probably less than one per cent of the city's estimated total area. Much of the central area was occupied by housing units of essentially two types: irregular multiple units and small enclosure units (West, 1970). The difference in their quality and density of occupation reveals the different socio-economic status of their inhabitants. The former housing units could have been inhabited by the manual workers, the latter, by the lower members of Chan Chan's administrative group (Day, 1970).

PARALLELS BETWEEN THE DESIGN OF CHAN CHAN AND CHINESE CITIES OF THE SAME EPOCH

We find an interesting similarity in urban plans and even in the elements utilized in their design between the Chimú cities of Peru's northern coast and Chinese cities of the same epoch.

In China's cities and even in some of its small communities, as in Chan Chan, the dominant architectural feature was the wall—simple, high and powerful—marking a clear differentiation between the city and the country (Siren, 1924). This contrast between urban and rural life in China (Gutkind, 1946) undoubtedly existed in Chimú society as well. In both cases, the wall symbolized the abrupt physical and cultural separation of city and country. Visually, the horizontal lines and vertical planes of Chan Chan's citadels with their earth-colored adobe walls dominated the coastal plain of the Moche Valley. A parallel is pointed out by Willets who tells us that in a Chinese city nothing superseded the importance of the walls, so that from the outside only the walls themselves could be seen (Willets, 1958). The typical city of northern China was built on a plain, as was Chan Chan. Obviously, defense considerations did not dictate the choice of site. The reasons governing the location of Chinese cities, however, seem to have been more administrative and political, related to the gradual centralization of power during the T'ang Dynasty, in the seventh, eighth and ninth centuries A.D. which was the culmination of a process dating back to pre-Christian times.

Both the Chinese cities and those of the Chimú were hubs of a centralized administration with a high level of technology for their respective times and places in history. The emergence of some cities over others in each area was the result of the administrative needs of each of these empires. The origin of such centers of government goes back to the time when they filled the role of strategically placed city-markets, serving territories dedicated to intensive agriculture.

The layout of Chinese cities and Chimú citadels was rectangular. The preference for this urban shape must have come about as the result of centuries of experience in problems of land subdivision on the part of both cultures. Perhaps the similar disposition of land use we see in Chan Chan's citadels and in the Chinese cities was merely repetition of a custom, following principles already in use, without further concern for detail. There is an undeniable similarity in the rectilinear patterns devoid of curves utilized by both cultures, and in their system of streets meeting at right angles yet never forming a checkerboard arrangement.

In an abstract sense, Chinese and Chimú city plans are really diagrams, and we cannot fail to admire the simple beauty to be found in the arrangement of the various parts within the city as a whole. The uncluttered urban layout, the limiting walls and the repetition of land use in some of the cities analyzed, suggest that each culture relied on prearranged guiding principles which were applied to all new or remodeled cities. The flexibility in the urban plans of Chan Chan or some city in China grew out of the repetition of small, equal and individual elements, such as Chan Chan's chambers and the dwellings in a Chinese city.

Architecturally, we can hardly compare the row of cells which served as housing in Chan Chan with the houses built around plant-filled patios found in a Chinese city. Furthermore, the principal street in a Chinese city was a clear, dominant feature that crossed the interior walled districts and served as an organizing feature for the whole city. We find no such street in Chan Chan in the arrangement of spaces between citadels.

Dwellings, in both cases, formed a compact network, leaving large intramural areas free. In Chinese cities these probably were used to harbor refugees or for farming (Gutkind, 1946). Willets suggests that in this way, small population increases could be accommodated without adding on to the city's general size or altering its plan (Willets, 1958). Such spaces may have been put to similar uses in Chan Chan.

In the Chinese and Chimú cities, as in those of South America's urban cultures in general, there were no buildings of architectural importance and volume great enough to dominate the city itself. That is, no building overshadowed the urban profile as did the Maya and Aztec pyramids and the medieval cathedrals marking the center of the city. Chan Chan's major constructions were the *huacas*, or temple-mounds, which were only rarely built inside the citadels, and which apparently seldom rose above the top line of the enclosing walls. A principal *huaca* like Obispo was located outside the city proper. We have found neither large palaces nor other constructions occupying sizeable areas in Chan Chan. Among the Chinese cities, of course, we find examples like the Palace of the Great Khan in Peking, which has excited the admiration of all travelers from Marco Polo's time down to today. Even this palace lacked an upper storey, and its impression of great length was created by its supporting base (Marco Polo, 1958). The palace's architectural wealth lies in its structural materials and in the magnificent sequences of planned spaces around the approaches to the palace proper. The city of Peking had been in existence for twenty centuries when it was rebuilt at the end of the tenth century A.D. (Hackett, 1950), and since that time, its urban plan has been considered unique for its clarity and symbolism.

More than with Peking or other large Chinese urban centers in those centuries, we should compare the Chimú cities with China's simple provincial cities, removed from the splendor of the oriental court and financially unable to undertake ambitious works and unnecessary additions to their urban areas. Adobe and wood were basic limitations to the aspirations of Chimú builders. Their cities show quality in detail, such as the arabesques which once covered the walls of various chambers in Chan Chan.[13] Similarly, even in a simple Chinese city, sculpted gateways demonstrate the inhabitants' civic pride in embellishing such conspicuous urban features.

The blind walls of the dwellings, forming continuous planes interrupted only by occasional doorways, were the principal visual and directing features of the streets of Chan Chan as well as those of Chinese cities. These streets were really corridors with the sole function of channeling transit. In both cultures, it was the custom to divide the city's interior districts by secondary walls, often no less formidable than those on the exterior.

Chinese and Chimú cities grew by the construction of whole new districts, which in due time were walled, rather than by adding on to those districts already in existence. In the esplanades between the outer walls of Chan Chan's citadels, there were dense housing areas. Certainly the city had large suburbs. Marco Polo says of Peking, the Khanbalik of his tale, "In this city there is such a multitude of houses and of people, both within the walls and without that no one could count their number. Actually, there are more people outside the walls in the suburbs than in the city itself. There is a suburb outside every gate, such that each one touches the neighboring suburbs on either side. They extend in length for three or four miles" (Marco Polo, 1958). In Peking, the walls established a line of demarcation between elements that Chinese society considered desirable and undesirable—the city's inhabitants and outsiders. The quarters of prostitution and even inns where travelers stayed were outside the walls. Unfortunately, very little is known about the activities of the people who settled the neighborhoods outside Chan Chan's citadels.

There are other similarities. Although both Chan Chan and the Chinese cities were formed by grouping isolated units, their north-south orientation served as an organizing element. In China, especially in Peking, Willets finds explicit symbolism in the fact that important buildings, whether administrative or private, faced toward the south (Willets, 1958). The north-south axis determined the direction of the principal avenue in Chinese cities and, in Peking, it led across the Chinese City and the Tartar City to the Forbidden and Imperial Cities.

Did Chan Chan have gardens like those in the Chinese cities, or houses with the same sense of periodic renovation? There is no doubt that the Chimú culture was far from the technical and cultural level of the Sung, Yuan and the first century of the Ming Dynasties, which correspond loosely to the rise and fall of the lords of Chan Chan. Any comparison between the two cultures can only be made with an understanding of this difference, basing our judgement on architectural forms and features as well as urban plans. Although structural elements were sometimes the same and the architectural principles seem alike, we find a key difference in their execution and in the scale and treatment of detail. On one hand, we have the dawning urban form used by a culture fettered by technical limitations, and on the other, the maturity of this same form, molded by one of the most advanced peoples of their time.

Perhaps the secret behind the use of similar principles lies in a factor as simple and fundamental to urban development as that of land ownership. Land in Chinese cities could not be privately owned or traded (Willets, 1958); even the right to work a parcel of rural land depended on the efficient utilization of it, rather than legal possession (Hackett, 1950). The lords of Chan Chan controlled land and water and through them the agricultural economy and social organization. For the coastal people of Peru during the Late Formative Period, water was life (Kosok, 1965). Without large scale irrigation projects the north coastal valleys could not have supported the number of people who lived there. Irrigation requires careful land subdivision to minimize building and conservation costs and to maximize the efficiency of water. Such objectives are generally found in

63 *Paramonga: Aerial view of the fortress of Paramonga, one of the·best examples of pre-Inca or Inca military engineering on the central coast of Peru. It is remarkable for its system of bastions built on elevations surrounding the central Nucleus. (Credit: Servicio Aerofotográfico Nacional, Lima, Peru.)*

relation to regular farming plots and urban forms.

I have made this digression from the general subject of this book merely to present the possibility of a new theme of study and perhaps to open
the door to further speculations on the relation between urban form and
the structure of the society that built it. But let us get back to pre-Columbian Peru.

THE EARLY FORMATIVE PERIOD
ON THE COAST

The Chimú Empire stretched southward to the Supe River Valley or
even further south. The fortress of Paramonga was built to the north, in
the Fortaleza River Valley, either by the Chimú as fortification for the
Empire's southern frontier or, more likely, by the peoples of the central
valleys as their northern frontier.[15] The Fortaleza Valley's population
lived close together near the sea next to the La Horca hill which was
probably used for religious activities as well as for defense (Giesecke,
1939). Reconstructed a few years ago, the present day fortress is located
on a hill partially surrounded by other mounds and cultivated fields several kilometers from the coast[16] (Plate No. 63).

Paramonga is one of the best examples of pre-Inca or Inca architecture
on the coast to survive into the twentieth century. The site was occupied
by the Inca who built the external structure we see today. The ground
plan adapts itself perfectly to the irregular contours of the hilltop, with
bastions at the four corners. Two of these bastions extend north and
westward to neighboring elevations, to prevent enemy occupation of these
vantage points which would have placed the defenders in jeopardy.

Perhaps our first reaction is to compare this system of bastions with
that of a European city of the sixteenth to the eighteenth centuries, when
the spreading use of gunpowder necessitated considerable modifications
in military engineering. Unlike European engineers, however, the builders
of Paramonga did not advance their bastions toward the enemy in order
to protect the central zone of the construction from long-range cannon
fire, as Indian warfare was carried on without gunpowder. Indian military strategy was simpler. Among the Inca, for example, the attack was
headed by the foot soldiers, followed by the archers and men with missile
arms such as slings and bolas. Lances and javelins were thrown by the attackers while the defenders held up a strong protective cloth to shield
their men from the rain of projectiles. As among almost all urban peo-

ples, soldiers protected their bodies with shields as well as thick quilted cotton armor and metal breastplates. For Paramonga's defenders, certain to be outnumbered by their assailants, the goal was to avoid being hit by these projectiles by keeping the enemy at a distance, taking advantage of their higher elevation or by occupying any possible strategic site themselves.[17]

From the point of view of military engineering, Paramonga was a simple and effective solution. It consisted of three platforms. The upper one, on which some possible house ruins have been found, rose nineteen meters above the plain. The contours of the middle platform were similar to those of the upper. Connected to the middle platform by a ramp, the lower platform, largest of the three, formed part of the main bastions. If we exclude the bastions, the nucleus of the fortress becomes a rectangle 110 meters north to south by 50 meters from east to west. The main entrance was located to the south, as close as possible to the river, a fact that could be used as additional proof that the defenders anticipated attacks from the north.

Paramonga provided a formidable obstacle to direct attack. It was only taken after a prolonged seige by the armies of the Inca Emperor Pachacuti, who advanced from the north after capturing Chan Chan.

The expansion of the Chimú kingdom had significant repercussions on the settlement pattern of the urban population in dominated territories. In some north coast valleys, population reached its maximum while in the Virú the number of occupied sites declined. As the population of the Virú diminished, the remaining inhabitants concentrated in centers formed by great, regularly shaped enclosures similar to those found elsewhere on the north coast. These were generally located in the flat sectors of the middle valley or near the coast.[18] Some sites in the upper valley, near the Huacapongo basin, remained inhabited during the period of Chimú occupation, called La Plata in the Virú, lasting from 1300 B.C. to the Inca occupation, around 1470.

We find many of the urban and architectural elements seen in Chan Chan incorporated into the design of the principal cities of the north coast. Chan Chan, the capital of the north coast, was not its only important city. Continuing northward, we come first to the Jequetepeque River Valley and the cities of Pacatnamú and Farfán, then the valley of the Leche River where we find Purgatorio, and finally to Apurlé, in the small valley of the Motupe River.[19] Next to Chan Chan, these four Chimú cities were the largest on the north coast and have been described as urban centers of the élite in consideration of the role they played in the Empire (Schaedel, 1951a). All belong to the Chimú Period, having been built between the thirteenth and fifteenth centuries A.D.

The ruins of Pacatnamú are located on a plateau bordered by the seashore to the north and the irrigated fields to the south. A natural ditch and a parallel wall defended the city to the east. To the west of the site were most of the adobe pyramids. A large citadel in the central part of the built-up area and smaller compounds show that urbanist trends were quite similar along the north coast during the apogee of the Chimú kingdom (Kosok, 1965). The ruins of Farfán are located far from the seashore to the north of the lower valley.

According to Schaedel, the ruins of Purgatorio (Plate No. 64) consist of a number of closely connected pyramids and walled groups spread around three sides of a natural hill. A large cemetary occupies the remaining area. On the upper sides and top of the hill are remnants of walls, small platforms and chambers which seem to have been observatories (Schaedel, 1951a, 1951c). Purgatorio lacked Chan Chan's size and orderly layout, but we still find the high walls characteristic of north coast construction. Similarly, most of the other élite urban centers were also built around hills. They differ from Chan Chan in the sites selected, their smaller scale, lack of a general order and in the trapezoidal form of the walled redoubts. At Cerro Purgatorio, for example, the only redoubt or citadel discernible in an aerial photograph is an elongated trapezoid. Its interior is divided by walls, and its lack of free space suggests that it was at least as densely occupied as Chan Chan's citadels. Scattered in a semi-circle around the hill lie the remains of other structural groups and smaller redoubts.

Schaedel describes Apurlé as a broad, spacious urban site with its principal structures grouped at the base of a natural hill, the Cerro Apurlé. Additional water, to supplement the Motupe River and to supply the city, was brought by two channels from the Leche River, some forty kilometers north (Kosok, 1965). We can still see traces of the broad avenues and irrigation canals that ran up to these buildings (Schaedel, 1951a).

The north coast formed part of a centralized administration, but each valley probably enjoyed home rule subordinate to the central government. Each valley also had one or more urban centers of varying importance, depending on the number of its inhabitants, and must have been

agriculturally self-sufficient. The primitive means of transport would not have made it feasible to bring food from one valley to another, except in emergencies. Trade existed, but most likely in the form of barter of luxury items.

Chan Chan, Pacatnamú and Farfán, Purgatorio, and Apurlé, were the administrative centers for their respective valleys. Each of these cities held a ruling group, specialized artisans and served as a market place. There were other settlements in these valleys which, from their location in the narrow upper sections, suggest occupation by military groups responsible for defending the valley's access, for instance Chicamita in the Chicama Valley, and Galindo in the Moche. In each valley, villages of farmers grew up around the cultivable fields. Some of these, such as Chiquitoy Viejo in the Chicama Valley, seem to have been planned (Schaedel, 1951a).

The élite urban centers of the north coast emerged when the agricultural population of the valleys reached a size and level of cultural development that permitted diversification of their activities. For the first time on the Peruvian coast, a balance between rural and urban activities seems to have appeared. This balance, however, was not reflected in the government or in the structure of society, since power was concentrated in an urban minority. In this respect, the walls of Chan Chan and Cerro Purgatorio symbolize the difference between the urban minority and the rural masses, the administrative élite and the farmers. The great cities appearing later in the same epoch on a scale new to this region coincided with the Chimú Period and it was from these cities that the orders came that transformed the north coast into a great kingdom.

The Chancay culture's zone of influence developed in the central coast valleys of the Chancay, Chillón and Rímac Rivers. Both the Chimú and the Chancay cultures emerged during the same epoch, and except for some stylistic differences, their way of life and technological level were similar. Pisquillo Chico and Lumbra in the Chancay Valley and Zapallan in the Chillón Valley were the principal urban centers of this culture

64 *Purgatorio: The town of Tucume on Cerro Purgatorio was one of the most densely populated of Peru's north coast before the arrival of the Spaniards. This aerial view clearly shows the city's organization into walled groups similar to those of Chan Chan. (Credit: Collection of The American Geographical Society of New York, New York.)*

(Lumbreras, 1967). Rectangular compounds built with plain adobe walls and large cemetaries were two aspects of this culture that retained a certain cultural independence even during the apogee of the Chimú. We find proof of this in the ceramic style called Chancay black-on-white, which developed on the central coast as a departure from the ceramic styles predominant at that time among the Inca and the Chimú. We do not know the political system that ruled the three river valleys mentioned above during the Late Intermediate Period. In the 1470s the Inca invaded the valleys of the Mala, Omas, Cañete, Topará, San Juan or Chincha, Pisco, Ica, Acarí, and Yauca Rivers, which together formed the territory of the Ica-Chincha culture. This regional culture, probably an independent state with regional influence, emerged at the same time as the Chimú and controlled a sector of the coast that stretched from the Omas Valley, one hundred kilometers south of Lima, to the smaller coastal valleys of southern Peru (Plate No. 45, page 191).

For reasons as yet unclear, during the Late Intermediate Period collective efforts in the north were directed toward construction of great urban centers and community works, whereas the southern peoples never undertook such ambitious building programs. Even the adobe architecture in the south did not reach the monumental character of that in the north and central valleys. One possible explanation for this is that the south coastal valleys were smaller than those in the north, with a proportionately lower population. Although the southern cultures evolved to the Urbanist stage, political instability may have obliged them to minimize construction of cities in favor of small defensive forts in such strategic places as Chancari, on the side of Cerro Tembladera in the Cañete River Valley.

In pre-Columbian America, the majority of the great cities were built by confederations or kingdoms or empires which were large, powerful, and stable. On the other hand, the hilltop fortifications were built either in defense of these empires, or by small states in an uncertain stage of their growth.

During the centuries preceding the Inca invasion, the valleys of the Cañete, Chincha, Pisco, Ica, Nazca, Acarí, and Yauca Rivers constituted a predominantly rural zone with different artistic styles, that never contained a large population. Menzel suggests that the social and political organization changed from valley to valley. While a central administration probably existed in the Chincha and Ica, evidence of a centralized government with control over the entire valley has been found in the

Pisco, Nazca, and Acarí Valleys (Menzel, 1959). The system of government may be reflected in the construction of small cities in some valleys during the Late Intermediate Period.

The most important center representative of this period on the south coast is Tambo de Mora, in the Chincha River Valley. La Centinela, a pyramidal complex in Tambo de Mora, is one of the most extensive building sites on the coast below Lima. The urban structure and architecture of Tambo de Mora are characteristic of the principal south coastal centers of that epoch. While never enjoying the importance of the north coast cities, Tambo de Mora was built like them in a dense complex of pyramids, platforms, housing groups, and free spaces delimited by adobe walls. Today, irrigated fields have split the ruins of the site and crops are beginning to cover the archeological remains, but we can still see the orderly, rectilinear pattern of the walls and the regular ground plans of the pyramidal bases and plots of land. Ica Vieja was the most important center in the Ica Valley during the Late Intermediate Period. No urban centers or large villages have been found in the Pisco, Nazca, and Acarí Valleys.

Despite the difference in scale and variety of architecture found even in neighboring valleys of the same kingdom, all the cities along the coast, throughout three or four centuries prior to the Inca invasion, shared many common characteristics, due primarily to the generalized use of adobe. As the only construction material readily produced all over the coastal area, it gave rise to similar building techniques.

If we compare known forms and features belonging to the Late Intermediate Period, the Peruvian coast between 6 degrees and 15 degrees south latitude presents great urbanistic unity. The main difference, perhaps reflecting varying degrees of population concentration or even lower stages of cultural development as we head southward, lies in the decreasing scale of the centers, their smaller structures, the gradual loss of urban order, and the diminished quality of urban elements.

1. THE CHILLÓN RIVER VALLEY, a few kilometers north of Lima is usually set as the southern boundary of the Chimú Empire. In the majority of works on the subject, authors refer to the fortress of Paramonga in the Fortaleza River Valley, 196 kilometers north of Lima, as part of the Empire. For divergent opinions on this theme, see: Giesecke, 1939; Rowe, 1948; Mason, 1957; Stumer, 1938; and Lumbreras, 1969.

2. The Huaca del Obispo is the highest, 50 meters high, approximately, and the largest, about 190 meters square (West, 1970).

3. West, who made an extensive survey of habitation patterns in Chan Chan in 1964, estimated that the size of the site is a little over 14 square kilometers (West, 1970) or 1400 hectares.

4. West calls this area the metropolitan core and estimates its area as 7.5 square kilometers approximately (West, 1970).

5. Complexes with larger houses, gardens, courtyards, etc., were also found in the intermediate zones, showing a building technology superior to the smaller units which frequently were irregularly laid out (West, 1970).

6. The citadels' names are all contemporary.

7. Another author proposes a population in the vicinity of ten thousand people for the citadels (West, 1970).

8. After Chan Chan fell to the armies of Topa Inca Yupanqui, the city was almost totally abandoned. Some dwellings were built afterwards inside the citadels but no remains showing an Inca occupation of the city have been found (Day, 1970).

9. An approximate calculation of land use in the five citadels, based on analysis of their respective plans and aerial photographs, shows the following results:

An approximate calculation of land use in the five citadels, based on analysis of their respective plans and aerial photographs, shows the following results:

	reservoirs		*canchones* (cultivable plots)		plazas		external walls perimetric corridors	
	m²	%	m²	%	m²	%	m²	%
Tschudi	9,580	9.2	30,180	27.4	7,040	6.3	11,730	10.6

	reservoirs		canchones (cultivable plots)		plazas		external walls perimetric corridors	
	m²	%	m²	%	m²	%	m²	%
Labyrinth	2,030	1.3	73,175	49.2	8,477	6.0	6,550	4.0
Uhle	225	0.1	74,850	38.4	6,000	3.0	11,800	5.6
Rivero	785	1.0	7,000	9.6	8,500	11.6	20,150	27.6
Bandelier	560	0.4	49,500	39.6	15,100	12.0	11,000	8.8
Totals	13,180	2.1	234,705	35.9	45,115	6.9	61,230	9.3

huacas	huacas (shrines)		without known use internal corridors		housing or similar uses		total area	
	m²	%	m²	%	m²	%	m²	%
Tschudi	2,000	1.7	17,700	16.4	31,220	28.4	109,450	100.0
Labyrinth	—	—	21,000	14.1	37,270	25.0	148,500	100.0
Uhle	—	—	77,245	39.6	26,180	13.3	196,300	100.0
Rivero	—	—	20,875	28.6	15,440	21.6	72,750	100.0
Bandelier	3,650	2.8	22,490	18.0	22,700	18.4	125,000	100.0
Totals	5,650	0.9	159,310	24.5	132,810	20.9	652,000	100.0

10. All my estimates are based on the study of the plans and have not been verified by a field survey. To my knowledge, published literature on Chan Chan does not deal with land use percentages inside the citadels.

11. For a discussion of the role of *pukios* see Parsons, 1968, Rowe, 1969; and Day, 1970.

12. The walls are about three meters thick at the base and about one meter at the top (West, 1970).

13. Of those arabesques we find preserved, the most interesting are in the Gran Chimú citadel.

14. Many of the irregular multiple units and small enclosure units located outside the citadels of Chan Chan had gardens which probably were symbols of status (West, 1970).

15. Stumer's opinion is the opposite of that of the three authors mentioned in Note 1 of this chapter. He states that we have ample evidence that Paramonga was not the Chimú's southern foothold, but was the northernmost bastion of the central coast peoples who were wary of the Chimú's expansionist potential. Stumer bases his position on three factors: 1) The bastions were facing north, in the direction of possible Chimú attack; 2) The fortress was built on the north side of the Fortaleza River, as though defending its waters (to the north, the nearest water was from the Huarmey River, some distance away); 3) Archeological evidence shows that the Fortaleza-Pativilca-Supe complex had great agricultural importance for the central coast cultures (Stumer, 1958). In relation to Stumer's point 1, an aerial photograph shows plainly enough that the bastions were built following elevations in the terrain. The largest elevation does, in fact, face toward the north (see Plate No. 63).

16. Lanning, like other authors before him, suggests that Paramonga was probably a temple (Lanning, 1967). If it was a temple its builders selected a strange and costly structural form to support it. The Chimú occupation of Paramonga was mentioned by several chroniclers and it is also substantiated by archeological discoveries (Kosok, 1965).

17. In March 1967 Dr. Duccio Bonavía, the Peruvian archeologist, and I made a short visit to Paramonga. We climbed the low hills to the north near the site and found the ruins of walls approximately following the highest levels. I don't recall any report of these walls, nor do I remember reports of any excavation made in the areas now planted with sugar cane to the east of the fortress or in the low mounds which look like islands in the middle of the plantation fields. Perhaps Paramonga was part of a defensive complex and not an isolated fortress, if such was its main function.

18. The decline in the Virú Valley's population may have been the result of some relocation program of the Chimú Empire (Willey, 1953), such as the *mitimaes* system used by the lords of Chan Chan, whereby people were transferred *en masse* to other areas to forestall rebellion.

19. Pacatnamú and Farfán were about 100 kilometers north of Chan Chan in a direct line, Purgatorio was 180, and Apurlé 200 kilometers, approximately.

·11

THE INCA

Oh, Mother Earth, keep your son the Inca quiet and peaceful upon you!

Inca prayer taken from *Ritos y Fábulas
de los Incas* by CRISTOBAL DE MOLINA

□ 11

THE INCA EMPIRE, OR TAWANTISUYU, was the second and last of the pan-Peruvian movements and the one which encompassed the largest territory. In its final and culminating stage of development, the Empire extended over more than a million-and-a-half square kilometers. From north to south, its indefinite frontiers spread over a small sector of southern Colombia, the highlands and lowlands of Ecuador, the highlands and desert coast of Peru, the Bolivian Plateau, northwest Argentina and the whole arid north as well as the fertile lands of Chile down to the Maule River at 36 degrees south latitude. That is, a territory stretching over 4,100 kilometers along the Pacific Ocean, widening to 800 kilometers in Bolivia, and at Lake Junín in Peru narrowing to less than 200 kilometers. It comprised two principal geographic zones: the mountains, or highlands, where the Empire originated and the Inca launched their first expansionist policies; and the coast, tropical, swampy and humid in Ecuador and a parched desert in Peru and Chile. The Inca never managed to dominate the forest area. They tried, attracted by its resources, but met with no success (Compare Plate No. 65, page 253, with Plate No. 45, page 191).

The Inca Empire was one of the most extensive and best administered in the history of pre-industrial civilizations.[1] It had its origins in the early part of the thirteenth century A.D., in Cuzco, at an altitude of almost 4,000 meters. From here it grew, and within 100 years, between 1430 and 1524, the Inca had conquered and controlled all the territory of their Empire. Its population has been estimated at six million persons (Rowe, 1946).

Politically, the Tawantisuyu was divided into four quarters, or *suyu,* with Cuzco, the capital, in the center.[2] The southwest quarter was called Cuntisuyu, the eastern one Antisuyu, the northwest quarter Chinchasuyu

397

and the Collasuyu quarter included the territories to the southeast and south. As we shall see later, this politico-geographical division was represented in the structure of the Empire's governing Council. The four quarters were divided into provinces which corresponded to the native states (Rowe, 1946).

The Inca Empire's expansion has some points in common with the evolution of the Roman Empire. In reality, almost all imperialistic movements have pronounced similarities. Valcárcel comments that the people of Cuzco, like men of any nation that leans toward expansion and imperialism, believed themselves to be a chosen group entrusted with a God-given mission—to impose the cult of the Sun throughout the world (Valcárcel, 1925). Was not Rome's main objective to spread the *Pax Romana* over the known world? Neither Cuzco nor Rome could plead demographic pressure, and all too soon the noble motives they had invoked upon incorporating the first territories and peoples fell into oblivion before the conquerors' lust for wealth and power.

Springing from such modest origins that untangling history from legend becomes a puzzle, Cuzco and Rome slowly consolidated their regional positions until fortuitous circumstances led them to mix in external affairs, seeking through alliances and conquest the incorporation of the territories they had chosen to annex. The eighth Inca emperor, Hatun Tupac, planned the first conquests and permanent dominion over peoples of non-Inca origin (Mason, 1957) early in the fifteenth century A.D., more than two centuries after the legendary birth of the Inca dynasty.[3] In the middle of the fourth century B.C., four hundred years after the founding of Rome, the Romans controlled the Campania as a result of the first Samnite war, in which they participated at the invitation of the people of Capua.[4] The inhabitants of southern Italy soon realized the imperialist intentions of the Romans, who devoted their economy's best resources, their political skill and inventiveness to this "Providential mission", backed by their growing military power.

These long-term imperialistic programs gradually unfolded. The unplanned development of the first stages of the Roman and Inca Empires was soon replaced by an overall plan on the broadest scale that resources and circumstances allowed in their respective times and places, even to including the most seemingly superfluous details. The expansions of Cuzco and Rome were supported by efficient administrations and a store of technical knowledge superior to that of the conquered peoples. Conquests were carefully planned and preceded by the undercover work of spies and intensive propaganda campaigns. Their human resources absorbed and natural resources weighed, the conquered peoples were gradually assimilated into the common effort.

Once a territory was taken, public works and legislation multiplied. New canals, granaries, roads and cities, new laws and administrative methods assured the incorporated people of better production, a more efficient distribution of increasingly plentiful goods, and a security and order which they had never known before. With such considerate treatment, the conquered peoples acquired a superior economic level, but the quality of their arts and their creativity diminished as the production of utilitarian objects, well made yet poorly copied in repetitive designs, increased.

The subjugated peoples introduced their cultures to the conqueror. Inca ideas on administration, urban planning, science, architecture, and art may have been influenced by the coastal peoples, especially the Chimú, even before they were incorporated into the Empire. We find a similar process in Rome's dealings with the Greeks, as the conqueror absorbed the teachings of the conquered, applying them on a much larger scale. Aqueducts, roads, bridges, storehouses, cultivation terraces, and city walls emerged in apparently unexpected places. Large population groups were moved to serve the political and economic designs of both empires, and depot-cities, garrison-cities, and colony-cities sprang up throughout the area. Today we can still detect the spread and influence of the *Pax Romana* in the ruins of a triumphal arch at Volubilis in the Moroccan desert; the theater of Italica near Seville; in the public baths of a town in northern England that once formed part of the Roman wall or in the colonnade of some Syrian city. If you fly in a small plane over the last spurs of the Andes, or travel along the roads where the messengers of the Inca emperor ran five hundred years ago, you will understand the magnitude of the accomplishments of the last Indian rulers of Peru in the space of three generations.

THE HISTORY OF THE
THIRTEEN INCA EMPERORS[5]

Cuzco was the capital of the Inca from their beginnings and the point of departure in their expansion.[6] The origins of Cuzco, like those of the

Empire, are so confused that we can only interpret them by drawing conclusions from legends that have come down to us through the accounts of writers who either participated in the Conquest or arrived soon after. We must then confirm these legends through archeological research.[7]

Researchers usually agree that the Inca dynasty began around 1200 A.D. (Rowe, 1946; Mason, 1957) and that its founder was Manco Capac. Legends about this founding father are contradictory but, whether legend or history, let us summarize the information. One of the legends tells us that Manco Capac and Mama Occlo were created on an island in Lake Titicaca by the Sun in order to civilize mankind. Bearing a golden staff, the couple set forth in search of a site where they could sink this rod into the ground with ease, which would be a sign to them to settle in that place. When they came to Cuzco, they established themselves and launched their divine mission.

According to the most accepted legend, Manco Capac set out from Paccarictampu, a site only forty kilometers southwest of Cuzco.[8] From that moment, under the name of Ayar Manco, Manco Capac's legend becomes confused with that of the four Ayar brothers.[9] In the legend, the four brothers represent four tribes. Ayar Manco stood for the Maska, Ayar Auka for the Chillka, Ayar Uchu for the Tampu, and the Mara were represented by Ayar Cachi (Valcárcel, 1939). Their immediate origin must have been in the region of the Apurimac River Valley or around the shores of Lake Titicaca. The four Ayar brothers, strong and courageous, went in search of lands suitable for cultivation and carried with them seeds such as maize, quinoa, and the potato. From Paccarictampu the brothers began their slow wanderings which ultimately brought them to the Huatanay River Valley where they founded Cuzco.[10] Before their departure, the four brothers had been named Incas, or Lords, by order of the god Viracocha.

Legend tells us that near Paccarictampu was a hill called Tampu-Tocco, having three natural openings through which the four brothers and their symbolic sister-wives passed as they embarked on their pilgrimage. The four couples guided their respective *ayllus* to the valley of Cuzco, where primitive tribes had been living peaceably since remote times. To the east of the present city's center, in the neighborhood known as San Blas, lived the Walla, the first people to have occupied the valley; to the north, in the modern neighborhood of Santa Clara, lived the Antasaya;

the Sawasiray lived to the south, in present-day Santo Domingo; the Allkawisa were the last to arrive and settled between the Sawasiray and the present Plaza de Armas (Valcárcel, 1939).[11]

During the years of wandering, Sinchi Roca was born of the union of Ayar Manco and Mama Occlo, and went on to become the second of the Inca rulers. In the course of their travels, Ayar Cachi was walled up in a cave and Ayar Uchu turned to stone. These events symbolize the branching off of the Mara, who settled near Urubamba, and the Tampu, who continued on as far as Ollantaytambo. Both settlements are a few kilometers northwest of Cuzco.

Ayar Manco and his sisters finally came to the valley of Cuzco which they decided to invade and dominate. The Walla fled before the new arrivals, and the other peoples of the valley were ultimately absorbed. The Maska, led by Ayar Manco (or Manco Capac) triumphed over the Chillka, symbolized by Ayar Auka (from *auka,* enemy), and became masters of a strip of land located between the Huatanay and Tuyumayo Rivers, where Manco succeeded in driving into the ground the golden staff entrusted to him by the god Viracocha. He immediately built a temple upon a rock, calling it Inticancha and dedicating it to the Sun. The migration had ended, and the city of Cuzco was founded symbolically. Manco Capac had established the Inca dynasty and assured the royal succession which was to rule over the development of the Empire for more than three hundred years.

During the thirteenth and fourteenth centuries, seven other Inca emperors followed Manco Capac to the throne. Although it is equally hard to untangle history from legend for this period, archeology has confirmed that Inca territorial dominion did not extend much farther than the outskirts of Cuzco.

These eight rulers present a varied gallery of strong and weak characters, some war-loving, others men of peace. Manco Capac's son, Sinchi Roca, and in turn his son, Lloque Yupanqui, were peaceable rulers. Not so, Mayta Capac, fourth in the dynasty and Lloque Yupanqui's son to whom Garcilaso attributes important conquests. Still, it seems that only during the reigns of the fifth Inca, Capac Yupanqui, and his son, Inca Roca, sixth in the lineage, that the frontiers were extended, though this may have been limited to the Cuzco Valley.[12]

The seventh Inca was Yahuar Huacac, a man lacking the vigor of his forefathers. On the other hand, his son, Hatun Tupac Inca, better known as Viracocha Inca, was the first true imperialist of the dynasty.

Inca history leaves legend, and begins to be passed down with the reign of the ninth Inca, Pachacuti, the most representative of the dynasty.[13] In 1438, this son of Viracocha Inca seized the throne which should have been his brother's.[14] Pachacuti spent much of his old age in organizing the administration, planning the enlargement of the capital and programs of public works and land reclamation to benefit his people. Pachacuti's greatest fame, however, is as a military leader. When he came to the throne, the Inca dominated only the immediate surroundings of Cuzco and were scarcely an important military power. Only a few years earlier, the Chanca, a neighboring people and ancestral enemy, were on the point of capturing Cuzco and so ending the dynasty. Newly inspired by their leader, the Inca embarked on a series of brilliant campaigns and conquests that was to make them masters of a vast empire.

The Empire was mainly the work of Pachacuti and his son, Topa Inca Yupanqui. The central highlands, the north highland sector up to Quito, the north, central, and south coast valleys and the southern territories were captured in that order. This rounded out almost the whole incorporated area mentioned at the beginning of this chapter.

The eleventh Inca, Huayna Capac, added little new territory. The northern and southern frontiers remained more or less fixed by the presence of less civilized, warlike tribes, who still lived on a pre-urban level and whose incorporation would have entailed serious inconveniences for the mechanics of Inca administration. The enormous distances, lack of real inducements and the climate must also have influenced Huayna Capac's decision to slow down the tempo of conquest. Huayna Capac's rule, between 1493 and 1527, coincided with the height of the Inca Empire's splendor and territorial extension.

Shortly before his death, Huayna Capac decided to divide his empire, perhaps because he felt that a territory so vast was hard to govern, or perhaps because he wanted to promote his preferred son, Atahuallpa, without destroying the traditional system of succession which favored the eldest son of the queen, in this case, Huascar. It is also possible that Huascar, whom his father had not seen in years, might have been put aside altogether, and that Ninan Cuyoche, another of Huayna Capac's legitimate sons who had strong backing, would have been designated heir. At any rate, Ninan Cuyoche died before he could be invested and his place was taken by Atahuallpa, who had the support of Huayna Capac's army. Whatever the facts were, Huayna Capac's decision proved a political error which, after his death, unleashed a civil war between Atahuallpa and Huascar and their respective followers.

The struggle lasted until the arrival of the Spaniards in 1532 and was so bloody that it brought about a visible decrease in the population (Kubler, 1946) as well as in the Empire's productivity. This decline was furthered in the following decades by the wars between the Spaniards and the Inca and, even later, by the system of mining and agricultural exploitation which characterized Colonial economy.

Atahuallpa's army, led by two brilliant generals, Quisquis and Challcuchima, overcame the forces of Huascar who was taken captive. While prisoner of the Spaniards, Atahuallpa ordered Huascar killed, only to be garroted himself by order of Pizarro in Cajamarca in August of 1533 (Prescott; Row, 1946; Mason, 1957).

The great Empire was immobilized by the death of The Inca, the supreme ruler who had held all powers and made all decisions. Resistance against the Spanish invader continued for several years, always strongest around the outskirts of the ancient capital, in the mountains of the Cordillera Vilcanota and the valleys of the Urubamba River. The vast territory gradually fell under Spanish dominion. In time, Spanish land-grants and serfdom created huge estates, destroying the Inca system of land ownership and mobilizing the members of the ancestral Indian socio-economic units into a new work force. Tribute demands forced Indian communities to grow different crops. Eventually the way of life changed, since the natural right of self-determination in community matters, a privilege even under the centralized Inca government, was replaced by various forms of slavery.

In 1571, the last of a series of pretenders to the Inca throne, some self-proclaimed, others puppets of the conquerors, was beheaded in Cuzco. On the surface, the Empire appeared the same. The great majority of the Indians practiced their old religion or adapted and incorporated the new faith. Their manner of dressing and their language scarcely changed. In the villages, they still worked the fields without modifying their traditional farming methods.

In the new cities of Lima, Arequipa, Trujillo and others lost in the immensity of the land, Spanish customs flourished. The countryside, however, remained Indian. The change was internal, brought about by the economic and political pressures of the Conquest and Colonial rule, as well as by the destruction of the moral values of a race which was not offered any real new values to replace their old. The change was also seen in a people decimated by the brutal labor in mines and fields imposed by the conquerors.

ORGANIZATION OF THE INCA EMPIRE

Rigid in administration, imprecise in its rule of succession, harsh in the application of its laws, unjust in its social structure and imperialistic in its foreign policy, the Inca government nevertheless respected the social and economic structure of the people they incorporated into the empire and assured its members full satisfaction of their material needs. The variety and scope of the governmental programs still astonish us, yet they did not infringe on the freedom of communities to decide their own affairs as long as they fulfilled their obligations as subjects.[15]

The despotic Inca Empire exemplifies a well-organized, centralized state in its clear governmental objectives, coordination of even the smallest administrative activities, its emphasis on maximum utilization of human, material, and natural resources and in its skillful and widespread use of statistics which defied limited means of recording.[16] Such a system of government was undoubtedly responsible for the level of material life under Inca rule.

Inca economy was essentially agrarian. Therefore, the government's best efforts were devoted to augmenting agricultural production and assuring distribution and conservation of the surplus. As a territory, the Inca Empire was self-sufficient. Although the state maintained periodic commercial ties along the Pacific Coast,[17] and eventually with the peoples occupying the territories peripheral to the Empire, these contacts in no way affected the satisfaction of the Inca people's basic needs. Commerce was limited to an exchange of products destined only for the ruling class.

As long as man has farmed in the highlands, the land's usefulness has been limited. Most valleys are narrow. These valleys and well-oriented hillsides were, and still are, the most productive farmland, though subject to flooding and quick erosion by the rains that last from December to March, coinciding with the maize harvest. Good farmland is limited.

I have discussed agricultural production and methods on the coast in previous chapters. The coastal valleys were clearly more favorable for the harvests needed by the Empire's dense highland population. Distance and a difference in altitude of 4,000 meters, however, proved insurmountable obstacles to a people who lacked draft animals, relying solely on the frail backs of llamas and Indian porters for the transportation of their produce.[18] These handicaps imposed a regional agricultural self-sufficiency, despite the variety of products cultivated within the Empire as a whole. In the highlands, dehydrated potato, or *chuño*, constituted the popular dietary staple, supplemented by a stew of oca, quinoa, or lupin and only occasionally a piece of *charqui*, meat cut into strips and dried. Dogs, ducks, guinea pigs, llamas, and alpacas were raised for their meat or wool. On the coast, fish and shellfish could be added to an otherwise predominantly vegetarian diet of maize,[19] frijol beans, tomatoes, squashes, peanuts, potatoes, and other plants. In the intermediate altitudes, maize and some of the other coastal produce were cultivated.

Consumption of coca, a stimulant used to combat the effects of dietary deficiencies among the highland Indians, was prohibited during the Empire, apparently reserved for the ruling class. *Chicha,* a beer made from maize or the *molle* tree was a popularly consumed fermented beverage.

Such was the diet of a population which has been calculated in such disparate figures that the accurate tally for the Empire must lie somewhere between three and sixteen million persons. Means estimated the population at between sixteen and thirty-two million (Means, 1931). Tello, Mariategui and other Peruvian writers calculated it at ten million at least. Baudin estimated it at between eleven and twelve million (Baudin, 1958). Rowe, basing his conclusion on the number of tribute-paying persons and their families in the census of 1571 by order of Viceroy Toledo, as well as on a possible decrease from four to one after the start of the civil war between Atahuallpa and Huascar, reached an approximate population figure of six million for the year 1525 (Rowe, 1946). This figure is seconded by Kubler (Kubler, 1946), whereas Steward has estimated three and a half million persons (Steward, 1949), excluding the areas of Ecuador and Chile that belonged to the Empire.[20] Using a depopulation ratio between 20 and 25 to 1 from a date of nadir around 1650, Dobyns estimated that the population of the Andean civilizations was between 30 and 37.5 million people at the end of the fifteenth century (Dobyns, 1966). We can assume that, at its height, the Empire's entire population was organized to participate in agricultural efforts, in the construction of public works and in war.

THE ADMINISTRATION

Not without reason is the Inca government admired for its administrative and economic organization and public works programs. In setting up these programs, we see the influence of a ruling group, perhaps the Council of the four nonhereditary members directed by the emperor. In addition, there was a large body of well-trained and coordinated administrators and technicians who analyzed problems and estimated needs, who directed and executed public works and saw that these were maintained, and who generally administered the government of the Empire.

In the early days of the Empire, the administrative group may have been formed by the best qualified members of the imperial *ayllu*, or kin group, but as the Empire expanded, its needs probably became so many and varied that descendents of subjugated chiefs, even commoners of exceptional merit and ability, were invited to join the governmental bureaucracy.[21]

Members of the imperial *ayllu* and the sons of the *curacas,* or subsidary chiefs, and sons of conquered chiefs received special training in a school called the *Yachahuasi,* located behind Pachacuti's palace in Cuzco. The term of instruction lasted four years, during which time the students learned the Quechua language, religion, history, and the use of the *quipu,* a recording device of knotted strings. The curriculum emphasized a knowledge of subjects useful to the governing group in solving the problems presented by the organization of such a heterogeneous empire, faced with the political and economic factors of participating members from many different conquered peoples. As complementary studies, students were taught some astronomy, cartography, and the use of measuring instruments. The teachers were the *amautas,* or wise men, whose broad knowledge equipped them to handle the most varied legal, technical, cultural, and religious problems. The Inca commoner received no training whatsoever.

Until a few years ago, scholars generally agreed that each member of the administration formed part of the Empire's pyramidal government structure. The emperor was at the top, then the Governing Council, the provincial governors, and lastly the *curacas*, whose posts were hereditary. The *curacas* were in charge of sectors of the population, or taxpayers, grouped decimally in fractions of ten thousand, five thousand, one thousand, five hundred, and one hundred families. The Hono Koraka was the chief of ten thousand families; the Piega Waranga Koraka chief of five thousand families; the Waranga of one thousand families; the Picoa Pacaka Koraka of five hundred, and Pacaka Koraka of one hundred families. In actual practice, however, the land-owning aristocracy seems to have prevailed, which maintained a totally static land-tenure system (Moore, 1958). The confiscation of the communities' land was a frequent practice. The Inca kept some land for himself and distributed the rest among his favorites (Métraux, 1970).

There were also specialized functionaries who lived in Cuzco and the provincial centers. The use of the *quipu*, for example, was the charge of the *Quipucamuyu* while conservation of tradition fell to the historians. Other important activities were similarly allotted to appropriate persons or groups.

All events in the Empire were recorded. Clay relief models represented conquered countries and *quipus* recorded population movements, the production of any particular province, the amount of grain in public storehouses and the number of llamas in a certain sector of the territory—in short, everything pertaining to the administration of the Empire. Messages were relayed by *quipus*, giving an account of the armed strength and numbers of a rebel group. Garcilaso writes, "The placement of the knots showed one, ten, one hundred, one thousand, ten thousand, and rarely, if ever, a hundred thousand, as each people kept their own count and each metropolis that of its district, and their numbers never surpassed a hundred thousand." He goes on to say, "In the upper part of the strings was the largest number, ten thousand, and lower down was one thousand, and so on down to one" (Garcilaso, 1943).

Such a complex governmental structure had to be based on great individual responsibility and strong collective spirit. If this attitude was found lacking, severe penalties were imposed. The law was unwritten, of course, but the mass of the people as well as members of the ruling class were fully aware of tradition. Traitors, adulterers, and thieves merited the death penalty. Long-term imprisonment seems to have been nonexistent. Lesser crimes were punished with exile, work in the coca plantations, torture, or loss of position. Perhaps the best proof of the quality of justice operating at that time is the fact that the functionary who permitted the condition of want to exist was punished equally with the thief who committed the crime. In extreme cases, the whole *ayllu* was penalized for the fault of one of its members. Mason tells us that crime was rare. The static nature of society did not encourage criminal acts, and such rigid application of the law tended to prevent them (Mason, 1957).

PUBLIC WORKS

As we shall see in the next chapter, urban planning was not customary among the Inca, although it was employed occasionally. On the other hand, in some aspects of territorial planning they reached heights unequalled in Indian or Colonial America, rare even among earlier, parallel civilizations in Europe and Asia. Of all the Inca's public works, their system of roads is today the most spectacular and best known (Von Hagen, 1958).

Two parallel roads, running north to south, one in the highlands and the other on the coast, formed the backbone of the Inca Empire's communications system (Plate No. 65). Perpendicular roads connected these two at various strategic points. Secondary arteries joined Cuzco and Arequipa, Jauja and Pachacamac, and Cajamarca and Chan Chan. All major cities of the Empire were included in this network. Quito, Huancapampa, Cajamarca, Huánuco, Juaja, Vilcas, Cuzco, and Ayavire were joined by the highland road (Rowe, 1946), and Túmbez, Chan Chan, Pachacamac, and the valley where the Spaniards founded Arequipa were connected by the road along the coast. From Cuzco, a road ran toward Lake Titicaca and Charcas, crossed the northwest of Argentina and Mendoza and went as far as the central valley of Chile (Strube, 1963). Since the Inca Empire was economically self-sufficient with an agricultural basis and regional distribution that did not justify trade, we can only assume that these roads were built for reasons other than commerce.[22]

Kosok suggests that the roads of the Inca as well as those of the preceding kingdoms and empires were built and maintained as an expression of the power of the state, to send troops, supplies and administrators from the capital into the conquered countries to bring back prisoners, booty and tribute (Kosok, 1952, 1965). Roads were constructed by local

65 *Inca Empire at its maximum is seen in the shaded area. Black lines indicate the road system of the Empire, one of the most spectacular public works undertaken by America's pre-Columbian cultures. The two major parallel roads are connected by secondary roads to join the most important centers. (Credit: Plan by the author, following those included by Victor von Hagen in* Los Caminos del Sol, *Hermes, Buenos Aires, 1958, and* Realm of the Incas, *A Mentor Book, New York, 1959.)*

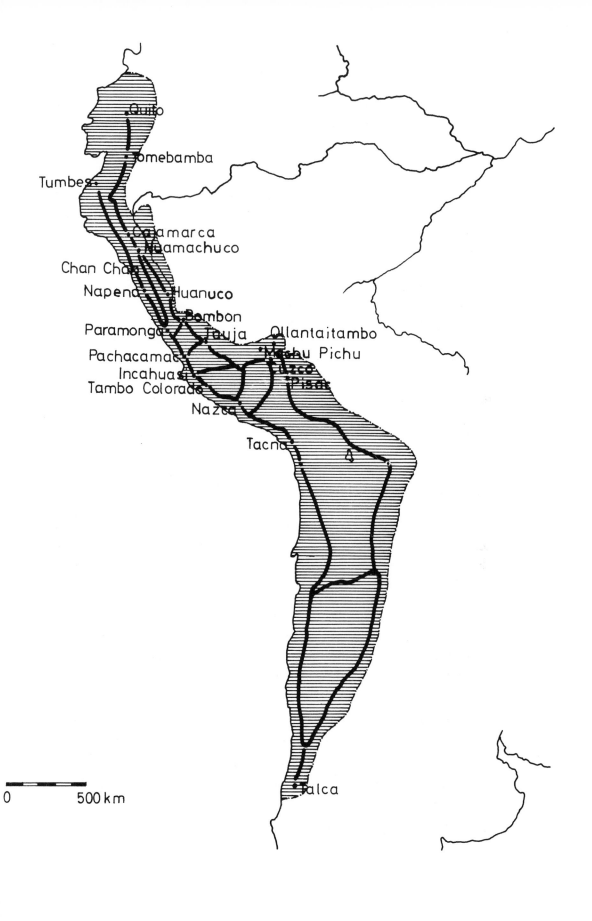

Quito

Tomebamba

Tumbes

Cajamarca
Huamachuco

Chan Chan

Napena
Huanuco

Bombon

Paramonga
Tauja
Ollantaitambo

Pachacamac
Machu Pichu

Incahuasi
Cuzco
Pisac

Tambo Colorado

Nazca

Tacna

Talca

0   500 km

work forces fulfilling their obligation under the *mita*, or obligatory work service, at the direction of government functionaries.

Roads were laid out as straight as topography allowed. On the coast, roads consisted generally of a leveled surface and were bordered by two stone or adobe walls one meter high. Highways were usually eight but never less than four or five meters wide. The highway to Chan Chan, in the Moche Valley, however, measured twenty-four meters (Kosok, 1952).

The terrain dictated the width and type of road. When crossing zones where flooding might occur, the roadbed was raised. In some places, it was bordered by two parallel canals, with adjacent cultivated fields and protective walls, perhaps to discourage the drifting coastal sands.

In the highlands, roads were narrower, and in some rugged passes they measured no more than one meter wide. Drastic changes in elevation required continuous stairways, even tunneling (Fejos, 1944). A highland road frequently followed the line of the highest peaks. This was desirable for military purposes to avoid ambush, and for technical reasons, to avoid having to cross wide canyons and their rivers. Inca engineering, like Aztec and Maya, had severe limitations, and their technology never solved the problem of bridging wide spans.

One of the conquistadors reported, "The mountain road is something to behold. In truth, we have never seen such beautiful roads in the Christian world over terrain so rough, and the greater part is paved. All the streams have stone or wooden bridges. Over one large river, broad and with a great flow of water which we crossed twice, we found bridges made of network, marvelous to see. We crossed the horses over them. Each passage has two bridges; one where the common people cross, the other used by the lord of the land or his captains. This latter is always kept closed and Indians guard it. These Indians collect a toll from those who cross" (Pizarro, 1953). I should point out that this duplication of bridges was not common, but did, in fact, exist in certain instances.[23]

Hanging bridges were complete with parapets and floors of tightly braided lianas or rushes; supporting cables were firmly fixed at both ends to solid masonry piers. The caretaker lived in a hut not far from the bridge.

Some roads had milestones set approximately 7,500 meters apart, or a league and a half, which was the *topo,* or unit, used by the Inca to measure distance (Rowe, 1946). In certain areas, *tambos*, or rest houses, were built at intervals of one day's journey, offering refuge to travelers.

The provisioning of the *tambos* as well as the construction of the roads leading to them, were the responsibility of the local inhabitants. This maintainance was part of the *mita*, or work tax, that the people owed the state.

The road system permitted rapid movement of troops and functionaries and even the transfer of entire peoples. It also provided a communications system of an efficiency unknown in Europe during the same epoch. Messages were transmitted verbally or by handing over a *quipu* from one runner to another, all of whom had been trained from infancy for speed and endurance. These runners, or *chasquis*, were stationed in post-houses located every quarter of a league, waiting for the relay messenger's arrival. Running ahead to intercept him, the fresh runner took the *quipu* or memorized the verbal message, and ran on to the next station. This method assured the rapid communication of news and orders at a speed of approximately 240 kilometers a day.

COLONIZATION PROGRAMS

Once a people had been conquered, the Inca emperor turned his immediate attention to two objectives: first to avoid rebellion, and second to organize the people and assure the self-sufficiency of the dominated region and incorporate it into the Empire. This gave rise to a complex program of relocation involving entire peoples. Mason comments that the resulting population mixture turned the Empire into a giant melting pot, on its way to becoming a homogeneous and unified nation, which was the precise purpose of the program (Mason, 1957).

The relocation programs were apparently begun about the middle of the fifteenth century, when the Empire's extension made it necessary to adopt security measures. Inca rulers were able politicians and never tried to eradicate the cultural values of the peoples they conquered. Although they imposed their language and worship of the Sun in new temples built for this cult, they did not forbid incorporated groups to retain their own religion and speak their native language.

Studying the needs and potentials of the conquered peoples and their administrative organization, the Inca tried to rectify any deficiencies in that system, so as to insure the Empire's new members material satisfaction which, in turn, led to conformity and acceptance of the conquerors' political and socio-economic structure.

Inca administrators and technicians arrived on the heels of the soldiers and diplomats. A governor was immediately appointed who, as in the case of Chan Chan, may have been a member of the existing reigning family. Next a provincial capital was established, almost always in an existing city. A tribute was levied and a service tax imposed. The chief of the defeated people was invited to live in Cuzco permanently, or at least for a prolonged visit. The invitation could not be refused. Even in war, the Inca tried to insure that the body of the army, largely made up of recruits from the subjugated peoples, was led by their own captains (Garcilaso, 1943), and only the commanders belonged to the regular Inca army.

To insure peace and self-sufficiency in a new territory, the Inca brought in colonists of proven experience from other provinces, to set an example and implement production. The regions vacated by these colonists were, in turn, occupied by groups taken from other territories recently incorporated by the Empire. Colonists were called *mitma-kona*, or simply *mitimaes*. They did not mingle with the old inhabitants, but rather constituted a loyal military garrison. In the event of an uprising anywhere in the Empire, rebellious groups were transferred at once.

There were also other reasons for population exchanges. When the Emperor wished to extend the land under cultivation so as to increase productivity, he sent colonies of Indians from developed to underdeveloped regions. He also sent colonists selected from the most loyal and valiant tribes to the frontier, where they performed the work of farmer and soldier as well as supplying the labor force needed to work the fields and to build the fortifications and public works planned for those areas. Work for the emperor was a compulsory service for which the communities received no compensation (Métraux, 1970).

Rowe reminds us that the Inca colonization programs have not yet been studied thoroughly. He adds that, in many provinces at the time of the Spanish Conquest, the number of *mitimaes* surpassed that of the indigenous population (Rowe, 1946).

GOVERNMENT

Inca government took the form of a hereditary monarchy. The throne was handed down by the emperor to one of his sons, who then assumed the title. From the time the dynasty began with Manco Capac until the end of the Empire in 1533, thirteen Incas succeeded to the throne. This number includes Huascar and Atahuallpa, sons of Huayna Capac and protagonists of the civil war which so devastated the Empire. The first five Incas in the royal lineage, besides being legitimate, firstborn sons, apparently were the most able among the numerous descendents of their respective fathers.[24] Only the seventh Inca, Yahuar Huacac, seems to have been favored by his father, Inca Roca, over the logical heir.[25]

The eighth Inca, Hatun Tupac Inca, or Viracocha Inca, was the third and youngest son of Yahuar Huacac.[26] The ninth member of the dynasty, the Inca Pachacuti, deposed his half-brother to take the throne, and the last Inca, Atahuallpa, was the son of a secondary wife. We see by this list that after the reign of Inca Roca, sixth in the lineage, the heir seems to have been chosen by the reigning Inca from among the sons of his legitimate wife, the *coya* who, in accordance with a custom imposed in the later generations, was his eldest sister. A daughter could not inherit the throne. There appears to have been no explicit law which established the right of succession of any one particular member of the imperial family.[27]

As the future ruler was chosen during the lifetime of the reigning Inca, it was customary for father and son to share the responsibilities of governing for a time. If he was old enough, the heir apparent was appointed chief of the armies, since his courage and ability were above question or he would not have been elected to succeed his father. It was as commanders-in-chief of the armies of their respective fathers that history associates the conquests of Viracocha Inca and his son Pachacuti, of Pachacuti and Topa Inca, and Topa Inca and Huayna Capac.

The system was not without its flaws, the most serious being the possibility that the Inca might die without naming his successor. Fortunately for the Empire, such an eventuality did not occur. Nevertheless, the civil war which facilitated the Spanish Conquest resulted from Huayna Capac's disregard of the law accepted since the time of Inca Roca, which had established that the kingdom be inherited by a son of the *coya*, or queen.

We can not question the ability, valor and energy of the majority of the Inca rulers, especially the three who made the history of the Empire during its years of expansion—Pachacuti, Topa Inca, and Huayna Capac.[28] These qualities were backed up by a prodigious activity which involved organizing the administration, directing development, passing laws, planning wars of conquest, and traveling throughout the Empire on lengthy tours of inspection.

The Inca ruler was believed to be the Son of the Sun, with divine right to the throne. To his people he was an infallible demigod whose decision was never challenged. The degree of benevolence or despotism reached in each Inca's reign depended entirely on the character and inclinations of the ruler. For the most part, The Inca did not abuse his power but respected the traditional rights of the communities. Paternalism has even been ascribed to some emperors. Atahuallpa, however, who seems to have been a popular leader during the war with Huascar, became transformed by his rapid success into a spoiled, vain, and cruel monarch (Mason, 1957), not to mention superstitious. One witness describes the last Inca: "He did not spit on the ground. When he cleared his throat, a woman put out her hand and he spat into it. Every hair that fell from his head onto his clothing was taken up and eaten by the women. The reasons he did this are well known; he spat because of his grandeur, and because he greatly feared sorcery, he ordered his hairs eaten to prevent them from being bewitched" (Ruiz de Arce, 1953). Even high ranking officials and members of the royal family approached The Inca humbly, bearing a burden on their shoulders and removing their footwear.

The day of his coronation, The Inca married his eldest sister who became his legitimate wife, the *coya*, but he kept an unlimited number of concubines. During the reign of an Inca, his family and descendents constituted the principal aristocracy of the Empire, forming their own *ayllu*.

At the death of The Inca, his son and successor inherited the throne and all it symbolized but not his father's worldly goods, which remained in the hands of the members of the dead ruler's *ayllu*. The new Inca founded his own *ayllu* which attained the same importance and privileges as the preceding one. Imperial *ayllus* remained as consanguineous groups, and their members formed part of an ever more numerous aristocracy, in turn absorbed by the increasing administrative, political, and military needs of a dynamic empire in full flower. Baudin reports that in Cuzco at the beginning of the sixteenth century, there were eleven imperial *ayllus* (Baudin, 1955).

Having finished their four years of training and passed a series of tests to demonstrate their strength, courage, skill, and technical ability, the young members of Cuzco's nobility and the sons of governors and administrators were received by The Inca. As a symbol of their rank, he awarded them heavy earplugs, which earned them the name of *Orejones*, or Big-ears, from the Spanish conquistadors.

The development of this social class provoked fundamental changes in the system of land tenure. Some authors believe that the Inca Empire was moving toward private ownership and inheritance of land and away from agrarian collectivism (García, 1959). Even some of the first chroniclers observed this transformation which was interrupted by the arrival of Pizarro and his men. Cieza de León mentions that a number of *Orejones* owned lands in the valley of Cuzco and passed them down to their children. Betanzos cites the partition of lands among the Empire's ruling group ordered by the Inca Pachauti.[29]

THE LAND

The last of the Inca rulers may have found themselves faced with the political necessity of recompensing their most worthy collaborators, conferring upon them honors and gifts which could be inherited by their descendents. This would account for the origin of private land ownership and individual control of production enjoyed by the ruling class.

The Empire was continually adding new lands, through conquest, swamp drainage, expansion of irrigation works, or the terracing of hillsides. The emperor always felt it necessary to anticipate the Empire's demographic development and assure sufficient land and food reserves for its inhabitants. On the coast, production was increased by fertilizing the soil with guano and fish heads; in the highlands, farmers used llama dung and human excrement. Irrigation works were built in the arid zones. The goal was always the same—better utilization of all resources so as to maintain an equilibrium between production and consumption, and augment food reserves. Collier remarks that in this respect we can consider the Inca civilization triumphant, since it conquered the eternal problem of maximum use and conservation of the soil (Collier, 1960). The communities, however, depended on themselves for their subsistence and only during periods of poor harvest received support from the government.

The amount of land worked by each community depended on the number of its inhabitants. Upon their marriage, each couple received a unit of land called a *tupu*. Its production served to feed them, and its size varied according to the quality of the soil. When they became parents, the couple received another *tupu* for each son and half a *tupu* for a daughter. Every family in the community had the right to the produce from their annually reallotted parcel of land. Once the community lands were assigned, the remaining area was divided between the Sun and the Emperor—religion and the state. But the communal lands could be expropiated by the Emperor without compensation to increase the estates of the ruler and the nobles (Métraux, 1970).

Farming was a collective activity in which men and women worked together, performing clearly specified tasks. The man plowed, or more accurately, he made holes in the earth with the *taklla*, a pointed digging-stick, while the woman broke up the clods and planted the seed. All agricultural work was organized according to an immutable yearly rhythm. The farmer plowed in August and in September he planted maize to be harvested the following May. In December, he planted potatoes for a June harvest. During the month of July, he helped fill the storehouses with produce. In January, irrigation canals were cleaned and llama wool was spun. October was for making house repairs and seeing to the pasturing of the animals. During the remaining months, the Indian watched over his fields, shooed away marauding birds, went hunting, if he had permission, or took part in the annual hunt organized by the emperor for his own entertainment and to provide meat for the public storehouses. If he lived near a river or a lake, the Indian fished or, if harvest time was over, he journeyed to market with products for exchange.

Military service and compulsory service for the Emperor could unexpectedly change the tempo of a man's life. It has been estimated that one-tenth of all adult males served time in the army (Bennett and Bird, 1949), the ranks of which were continually swelled by new recruits from incorporated peoples. Except for its leaders, it was not a professional army, since actual warfare was a circumstantial event in the life of the Indian. He took part in war as he did in other activities, collaborating in a program for a purpose he could not understand.

SOCIAL ASPECTS OF THE INCA EMPIRE

While individual ownership increased among the aristocracy, the commoner retained the same collective economic structure. Private property was forbidden him. His most valued possession was the pair of llamas he received at his marriage, which supplied him with wool. His clothing and that of his family, of course, as well as some farming tools were his, and he may even have owned some domestic animals such as guinea pigs and dogs, which provided meat to vary his diet. The family's dwelling was a miserable hut with stone walls and perishable roof.

Year after year, generation after generation, the Indian fulfilled his cycle. Physically tough from the first days of life, his arrival was greeted as a happy occasion. A boy, and to a lesser degree a girl, was an economic asset that the Empire, even more than the *ayllu*, needed for its development. Because of this, children born out of wedlock during the trial period of marriage, or *servinacuy*, a common practice among Inca youth, were not unwelcome (Baudin, 1955).

Every Indian commoner, man or woman, inevitably accepted the marriage arranged by his parents. Up to a certain age, the youth was allowed to choose his partner, but if he failed to do so, he was asked to form a family or was simply assigned a mate.

Celibacy existed only among the Virgins of the Sun, or *mamacunas*, who were dedicated from infancy to religious service and kept a vow of chastity. Priests, too, made a vow to remain celibate. Concubinage was enjoyed only by the emperor and a few high-ranking persons, but like adultery and rape, was punishable by death when it occurred among the commoners.

In addition to the ruling class who administered the Empire, other important groups of Inca society were the priesthood and the military. The High Priest, or *Villac Umu*, was a close relative of the emperor and lived in Cuzco, which made that city the religious as well as the administrative capital of the Empire. He was assisted by a Council, the members of which belonged to one of the royal *ayllus*.

In Cuzco, and in other principal cities of the Empire, there were temples to the Sun attended by large groups of priests and servants. Minor sanctuaries serving smaller population centers had only one representative of the official religion, who was occasionally supported by the *ayllu* rather than the state, which sponsored the more important temples. The Empire had one state religion which served as a unifying force for its territory. The Sun, called Inti, was the god of the people. The Moon, Thunder, and the Earth, or Pachamama, were also deities for popular veneration and special offerings.

The supreme god was Viracocha, lord of creation. The cult of Viracocha was apparently restricted to the ruling class. Religion in Inca Peru never had the obsessive and bloodthirsty character it took on in the central Valley of Mexico, nor did the priesthood seem to enjoy such an exalted position as their Mexican colleagues.

During the Empire's last century, the importance of the military class grew and the successes of some of the generals began to disquiet the emperor. Capac Yupanqui, brother of The Inca Pachacuti, and the general of the army who expanded the Empire's northern frontier, was executed by order of The Inca who seemed to fear the repercussions of his brother's military glory (Mason, 1957). I assume that the emergence of private property was, in part, a way of controlling those persons nearest The Inca, including the principal generals. In some cases, it could be that the *mitimaes* fulfilled a political as well as military purpose by decentralizing certain groups of soldiers and keeping them far from the capital.

The Inca emperors fought their wars with a large, well-organized army, headed by a group of career officers elected from among the members of the royal family. Only by chance would a commoner have been able to join their ranks. By the end of the Empire, this military élite may have acquired the character of a permanent body.

Commerce was totally under state control. This discouraged the development of a merchant class with the drive and organization of that which existed among the Maya and, even more so, among the Aztecs. On the other hand, competent craftsmen were in demand. When a people had been conquered, their best artisans were taken to Cuzco to manufacture the goods prized by the ruling class.

From the coastal peoples, the highland women learned their skillful and diversified techniques of weaving cotton and llama or alpaca wool. The Virgins of the Sun made the art of weaving their specialty.

Metallurgy was dominated by the manufacture of objects in gold, silver, copper and, to a lesser degree, platinum. This was an ancient, established industry, as the Andean region was the principal, if not the oldest, metallurgic center in America (Mason, 1957). Copper and tin were alloyed to produce bronze, but like other peoples of America, the Inca did not have iron. Metal tools contributed little toward raising the people's standard of living, as metals were mainly used for decoration and later only to increase the efficiency of military weapons.

Inca pottery had great variety of form, yet it never acquired the decorative brilliance and originality characteristic of earlier coastal cultures, especially the Mochica and Nazca. Like the Chimú, the Inca seem to have used mass production techniques. Today we can still find similar ceramic pieces among the various products for sale in any Indian market in the highlands.

For his own use, the Indian made objects in wood, leather, bone, or stone. When not working in his fields or serving the state in public works programs or warfare, he turned artisan. The raw materials he used came from existing storehouse reserves, and the finished products were returned to the storehouses for eventual redistribution. In this way, simple, utilitarian articles without artistic merit were produced, to be used by the people in their daily lives and occasionally during festivals.

1. Rowe, who some twenty-five years ago wrote one of the best general summaries of Inca culture, says about its influence in Andean history: "the whole Andean culture was given a new orientation and turned into paths of development which it is still following after four centuries of alien domination" (Rowe, 1946).

2. Tawantisuyu means "the four parts of the world," or "the land of the four quarters."

3. Hatun Tupac Inca is also called Viracocha Inca. Sarmiento de Gamboa explains that while The Inca was in the "sumptuous *huaca* of Ticci Viracocha" in a town named Urcos near Cuzco, Viracocha, supreme god of the Inca, appeared to him. Upon learning this, one of the nobles around him gave him the name of Viracocha Inca, which has come down in history. He may also have dedicated his life to Ticci Viracocha (Sarmiento de Gamboa, 1943).

4. The first Samnite war took place between 343 and 341 B.C. Before that time, Rome only held political control over a league of cities located in the territory immediately north and south of the city. The league was dissolved in 338 B.C. and the cities came to form part of the Roman State (Hadas, 1956).

5. I am adopting thirteen as the most probable number, although several authors have questioned it, as well as the chronological order generally accepted. Thirteen Incas is the figure adopted by Mason (Mason, 1957), in agreement with the history of Garcilaso de la Vega. Imbelloni believes the lists to be fictitious (Imbelloni, 1946). Even the sixteenth century Spanish authors differ widely on the number of years each Inca reigned. Zuidema mentions eleven emperors before Huascar, the son of Huayna Capac who was defeated by his half-brother Atahuaellpa shortly before Pizarro arrived in Cajamarca. Huascar was the twelfth Inca and Atahuallpa the thirteenth (Zuidema, 1964).

6. Cuzco means "navel."

7. From the long list of authors writing in the first decades after the Conquest who passed down the history of the Inca Empire and its people, the reader will find the following of especial interest: Pedro de Cieza de León, the two parts of *La Crónica del Perú*; Garcilaso de le Vega, *Comentarios Reales*; Pedro Sarmiento de Gamboa, *Historia de los Incas*; Juan Polo de Ondegardo, *Relación del Linaje de los Incas*; the *Suma y*

Narración de los Incas, by Juan de Betanzos; the *Relación* by Cristobal de Castro; the *Noticia del Perú* by Miguel de Estete; the *Relación* by Pedro Sancho; and the *Historia del Nuevo Mundo* by Father Bernabé Cobo.

8. Paccarictampu means "camp of dawn."

9. To Pardo, the four Ayar brothers were actual persons (Pardo, 1946). He apparently based this opinion on the report of Sarmiento de Gamboa (Sarmiento de Gamboa, 1947), especially on parts nine to fourteen inclusive of *Historia de los Incas*. He even identified the stories with the place names of the region.

10. There is a certain parallel between the origin of the Inca and that of the Aztecs. In both cases the tribes were foreign to the environment in which they definitively settled. After a period of adaptation, they threw themselves into a series of conquests that allowed them to prosper, expand their borders, and develop the two most important political experiments and cities in America at the time of the Conquest.

11. The valley of Cuzco was occupied by a pre-Inca culture called Chanapata. Remains of this culture were found in a site located to the northwest of modern Cuzco (Bennett, 1946b).

12. "The first six or seven Incas were no more than *sinchis* (warrior chiefs) engaged in raiding their neighbors or defending themselves from outside attacks" (Métraux, 1970).

13. By order of Pachacuti, Inca history was revised and set down pictorially.

14. Virachocha Inca was an old man and his successor, Inca Urcon, had already been appointed when the Chanca launched the attack that took them to the suburbs of Cuzco. Urcon and Viracocha left the city thinking that defense was hopeless. Two of Viracocha's generals and two of his sons led the defense. After the defeat of the Chanca, Yupanqui replaced Urcon. He became the ninth Inca and took the name of Pachacuti.

15. John Collier comments that whereas in that epoch none suffered material want, today millions are in chronic need (Collier, 1960).

16. The true structure of the Inca Empire is being reviewed. Some years ago the socialist theory of the Empire was already in question, at least as applied to the territory as a whole (Moore, 1958). "Centralization of power," writes Métraux, "was combined, after a fashion, with the exer-

cise of indirect rule, if such an anachronistic phrase may be allowed"
(Métraux, 1970).

17. The first conquistadors had the opportunity to observe how trade was
conducted along the coast. One of the men who accompanied Pizarro
when he captured Atahuallpa describes the commercial activity as follows: "They trade by sea; these people are dedicated to trade. Their boats
are made by joining ten or twelve poles of a kind of corklike wood that
grows in this land, securing them with ropes and putting sails on them.
And so they sail, from coast to coast" (Ruiz de Arce, 1953).

18. The llama cannot serve as a mount since it can carry only fifty kilos for
moderate distances. For a brief synthesis of the value of the llama in the
economy of the Inca Empire, read the fourth chapter, pages 102 to 105,
of *El Imperio Socialista de los Incas*, by Louis Baudin (Baudin, 1953).

19. Maize will not ripen above an altitude of 2,000 meters. Only under exceptional ecological conditions was maize harvested above such an altitude
(Murra, 1968). The Inca Empire in the highlands was generally at altitudes higher than this, and it was only in the final decades of its history
that the Inca armies controlled the coast.

20. There is a good summary of the different population estimates for the
Inca Empire in *La Población Indígena y el Mestizaje en América* (Indian
population and racial mixture in America) by Angel Rosenblat, pages
309-315; (Rosenblat, Volume I, Editorial Nova, Buenos Aires, 1954).

21. Moore tells us there is clear evidence that the Inca bureaucracy, totally
government supported and so often admired, may not, in fact, have existed (Moore, 1958).

22. The Incas occupied some territories such a short time that they probably
used and improved the local roads they found. The Chimú, and other pre-
Inca cultures, had built roads connecting valleys or forming valley systems along the coast.

23. Stone bridges were used to cross narrow channels and suspension bridges
spanned wider rivers. A toll was charged to cross.

24. Manco Capac's first five descendents seem to have respected the tradition
introduced by the founders of the Inca dynasty, in which the first-born
son was designated as heir. During the dynasty's first 150 or 180 years,
all sons of The Inca, without exception, had the right to succeed him,
which occasioned many an intrigue and violent revolt. In those centuries,

it was The Inca himself who chose his successor, and in an emergency this decision could be made by the Council. First-born daughters do not seem to have figured in the uncodified law accepted by Inca royalty. See a recent documented work (Diez Canseco, 1960).

25. The real leader in the reign of Yahuar Huacac seems to have been his brother, Vicaquirao, who conquered several neighboring peoples near Cuzco.

26. Yahuar Huacac named his second son, Pahuac Gualpa Mato, as his successor. Due to the latter's death, Viracocha Inca ascended the throne.

27. In the last reigns, the right to rule was reinforced by limiting the succession to those valiant and able among the sons of the *coya*, the only queen among The Inca's many women (Diez Canseco, 1960).

28. It is generally agreed that Pachacuti mounted the throne in 1438 and ruled until 1471. Topa Inca Yupanqui reigned between 1471 and 1493 and Huayna Capac from 1493 to 1527.

29. According to Baudin, privately owned land was more common in the Yucay Valley, on the outskirts of Cuzco, where the highest percentage of the Inca ruling class undoubtedly lived. He adds that the masses, meaning the communities, lived and worked under a collective system but that the élite were on the road toward individual ownership as a result of the system of land awards (Baudin, 1953). There is evidence that some valleys on the north coast were the property of Inca lords, who demanded a percentage of the produce from the farmers who worked the land (Moore, 1958).

30. Metals were seldom used for the manufacture of weapons (Salas, 1950).

·12

THE INCA SOCIETY – CUZCO

"Then out spoke our Inca to his sister and wife: Our Father the Sun rules in this valley. Let us stop and make it our dwelling place in fulfillment of his will. Therefore, sister and wife, it is fitting that each of us call together these people, to instruct them and carry out the work entrusted to us by Our Father the Sun."

GARCILASO DE LA VEGA
(COMENTARIOS REALES)

□ **12**

ANY CITY WHICH BECOMES THE CAPITAL of an important political entity usually reflects its uncertain early stages of growth in the location and general order of its central district. The majority of the capitals of great preindustrial empires were not originally established for this purpose. Certainly the first inhabitants of Rome, London, Cuzco, and Madrid could not have envisioned the future development of these settlements which had clung to their modest character for several generations.[1] Only when they attracted those functions belonging to the capital city of an expanding empire, did the demographic and physical growth of these cities respond to their increasing political and commercial importance. This set them above the other cities of their respective states. In short, the evolutions of an empire and its capital tend to coincide. New districts added over a period of time often reflect the limitations of the original site and the spontaneous urban development that overtakes such a city, spurred on by its state's changing fortunes. The more or less rapid and successful territorial expansion of a state will determine the physical structure of its capital in the general elements of design introduced in each stage of its development. We need not remind ourselves that the capital of an empire does not always represent the best that that civilization can offer in the way of urban planning.

The capitals of the Roman and Inca Empires were centers of intense political and economic activity, and held the largest populations of their respective territories. Urbanistically, however, they do not mirror the technical level reached by these peoples. Perhaps none of the great cities of these empires provides a satisfactory urban example since, due to the rapid expansion of these two states and their need to concentrate the greater part of their resources in political and economic consolidation of

427

conquered territories, existing urban centers were pressed into service as provincial capitals. These were generally a far cry from the type of city either the Romans or the Inca would have built from the ground up.

During their imperial period, the Romans launched a vast program of urban construction, utilizing the well-known basic planning principles that they applied to Timgad, Volubilis, Aosta, Lincoln, Verulanium (St. Albans), Silchester, Autun, Turin, Trier, and other cities scattered around Asia, Europe, and North Africa.[2] Many of these were frontier cities built to defend the Empire against invasion, or they were colonies of veterans dedicated to a combination of agricultural and military tasks, or even important rest-stops along the highways that interconnected various regions of the Empire. These were not, by any means, the only cities built for a special purpose. Each time Rome needed to establish a group of settlers to serve as a particular cog in the governmental machinery, she sent engineers and surveyors to lay out the new city according to principles which might vary in different regions but were, on the whole, tested by time and experience.

We need not look at the Empire's outer borders to observe Roman theoretical urban principles translated into reality. We need only pass through the streets of Lucca and Sorrento, or visit the excavations at Ostia and Pompeii, to confirm the fact that even near the capital, cities were created in accordance with plans which, for many reasons, were inapplicable in Rome herself or in the major regional capitals of the Empire.

The Roman city plan was based on the crossing of two main perpendicular axes, which determined a simple lattice-work arrangement of secondary streets parallel to the major ones, thereby setting the shape and proportion of the city blocks. This model, influenced by the ideas of Hippodamus, was repeated throughout the western world.

Rome and the great existing capitals of Asia Minor continued to develop in tune with their empires. In large cities, Rome in particular, monumental constructions were introduced: forums, thermal baths, roadways, and amphitheaters emerged as an attempt at urban remodeling on a scale hitherto unknown. Throughout the duration of the Empire, however, Rome's basic urban pattern incurred no major modifications and remained an intricate, dark and filthy network of small streets.

If we consider the technical differences and the disparity of cultural levels reached by the Romans and the Inca, we will understand the chasm between one civilization, ruler of what was then the known world during its centuries of glory, and a people of the South American highlands who, while dominating the most developed cultures of the time in America, were hampered by their cultural and technical limitations. Even so, the factors that promoted conquest and the founding of new cities in both empires are markedly similar, as is the use they made of those cities already in existence in the territories they absorbed.

Ollantaytambo is the best known example of the technical level reached by Inca engineers and urban builders as applied, specifically, to a city of varied and complex functions, military and economic among others. Cities such as this were essential in the administrative machinery of the Inca Empire as well as fundamental to the success of a political and socio-economic program of a scope never seen before in America. Compared to other cities within the Empire, however, Ollantaytambo cannot be considered a great city.

The Inca Empire's great cities were Cuzco, the capital; Quito, in the far north of the Empire; Chan Chan, the ancient Chimú capital of the north coast; Túmbez, also on the north coast; Pachacamac, the shrine city of the central coast and Mecca of Peru's Indian peoples; Cajamarca, the north highland administrative center from which Atahuallpa directed military campaigns against his brother, Huascar; Tumebamba, near Cuenca, in Ecuador;[3] Huánuco Viejo, Bonbon, Jauja and Vilcashuaman, in the central highlands; and Pucará and Potosí, south of Cuzco. Many of these cities were founded, built and inhabited by civilizations that had profoundly influenced the Inca culture and were later absorbed into the Empire (Plate No. 65, page 253 and Plate No. 45, page 191).

The population of the Inca Empire was essentially rural and the percentage of urban population, though high for that epoch and cultural level, must have been low in actual fact. Nevertheless, the Empire's rural inhabitant was not exposed to the isolation that prevailed in other regions which, like the Peruvian highlands, depended exclusively on an agricultural economy. Without being urban, the highland farmer, yesterday as today, can not be considered socially isolated. We might best describe him as a villager.

The isolation that still exists in vast reaches of Ecuador, Peru and Bolivia is that of the village, but not of the individual. Throughout the centuries, the *ayllu* has continued to serve the highland population as a social and economic union acting as an integrating element. In addition, agrarian collectivism and the periodic reapportionment of land owned by the *ayllu* and its members were factors that tended to unite the rural population. Consider how the limited size of the *tupu*, the unit of economic production for each family, fostered high rural densification. Think of the organization of the work force needed to undertake the public works decreed by the emperor or the provincial governor, or the labor required to farm the land set aside for the Emperor or the Sun, of the annual seed distribution and yearly harvest of The Inca's land and the gathering of this produce into the state storehouses for use when the people suffered harvest losses. All these activities were made possible by the solidarity of the highland Indian's traditional social unit, the *ayllu*. As Métraux points out, the community took account of each family's needs (Métraux, 1970).

Highland agriculture was, and is today, based on intensive exploitation of an ungenerous soil which requires constant fertilization and extensive irrigation to insure a satisfactory yield. Agrarian collectivism, therefore, for historical, geographic and socio-economic reasons, has always been the Peruvian farmer's traditional way of life. It was not a system imposed by the Inca, but one which developed spontaneously centuries before. The Inca rulers found this social and economic structure ready-made, and managed to coordinate it, without much modification, over vast territories. This system of community ownership of property, in which each farmer had the use of what he grew on his own parcel, was so deeply engrained in the Indian that it still endures today.

So tight are the bonds uniting the *ayllu* that neither the claims of the Inca rulers, nor the injustices of Colonial times with its introduction of the *encomienda*, grants of large tracts complete with control over the Indians living there, nor the continuation under the Republic of a large-estate system, have been able to banish them. A lone man cannot survive in the highlands. To understand this, we need only read the bitter yet beautiful pages of Ciro Alegría and Jorge Icaza, or visit the highland towns and villages where the traditional Indian structure lingers into the twentieth century and local labor undertakes the public works which should be the responsibility of the central government.

During the Inca Empire, wherever there was a fertile valley or a strip of land capable of yielding a harvest, villages appeared, most of them small but some of medium size. It is quite possible that the distribution pattern of these highland villages has not changed for centuries and that many of them predate the development of the Inca Empire. Only with the real expansion of the Empire after 1438, and especially with the generalized system of *mitimaes* some decades later, did the ancient pattern suffer significant transformation. This transference of large population groups undoubtedly benefited certain regions which became settled almost completely in this way.

Under Inca rule, the great bulk of the population was offered one way of life only—a rural one—just as they had one state religion and accepted a body of unwritten laws. This in no way affected the physical characteristics of the ancient Indian villages where one or more *ayllus* lived within precisely defined territorial boundaries. During the fifteenth century, the typical highland village was probably no larger than that existing in pre-Inca times. Without an overall plan, spreading along the pathways that led the farmers to their nearby fields, the village must have looked like a jumble of houses, bound together by low stone or adobe walls that bordered the irregular alleys traveled by man and llama. The uneven shape and layout of the village was the spontaneous result of haphazard growth and topography.

In the location of a village, security reasons were apparently the first consideration, explaining the choice of rugged terrain.[4] Available sites were limited by the scarcity of arable land, which meant that any terrain relatively level and free of rocks had to be kept available for cultivation. This restricted the village population to a few hundred inhabitants, and made large-scale public works a necessity.

By order of the emperor, so many irrigation canals and terraces were built that some valleys, such as the Pisaj and Ollantaytambo among others, were considerably remodeled. Toward the same goal of making maximum use of cultivable land, coastal cities and villages were almost always built on the fringe of the irrigated areas. The appearance and layout of the coastal villages differed from those in the highlands, however, as the valleys' relatively level ground made for a more orderly plan. The different construction materials used in the coastal valleys also distinguished them from the highland centers. "The houses of the Indians are made of cane; those of the chiefs are of adobe with branches as roofs because it does not rain in this country" (Pizarro, 1953).

Plazas in highland villages, when they existed at all, were formed by the juncture of two or more intersections. The communal corral to hold the llamas was built on the village outskirts. Houses were of one story and rectangular. They had no windows and the low, narrow doors kept out the cold. Walls were of stone, the floor of earth and the roof was straw. In regions with frequent heavy rains, as in the Urubamba Valley, the slope of the roofs was pronounced. The interior of the house was dark and dirty, and there was no furniture other than some llama hides that served as bed and cover. The woman cooked on an open fire at one end, and the family ate sitting on the floor (Baudin, 1955).

When the crops began to ripen, around February or March, the Indian lived in a small shelter of branches built on his parcel of land, from which, alone or accompanied by some member of his family, he watched patiently, ready to protect his harvest from the ravages of birds and animals.

Throughout the first stages of urban evolution on the coast, and even during the Inca Empire, the deserts in between the valleys remained uninhabited. At the time of the brief Inca domination on the coast, the Empire gained control over a number of important existing urban centers such as the Chimú cities, which had previously been occupied by governmental representatives, the aristocracy and artisan groups.

On the whole, the population of the north coast not only seems to have diminished during Inca rule, but tended to live in more concentrated groupings. Less than twenty years after the conquest of Peru, Cieza de León traveled along the coast and found the valleys sparsely inhabited, either as a result of events precipitated by the Conquest or perhaps due to some migratory process originating in the Chimú Period.

In the Virú Valley, which I have used earlier in this book as an example of the possible urban evolution in the north coastal valleys, the Inca Period is called Estero, lasting from 1470 to 1532. All sites inhabited during Inca domination in the Virú had been occupied prior to that period (Willey, 1953). However, this was not proof that such was the case all over the north coast.

CUZCO

The origin of Cuzco and that of the Inca dynasty are tightly interwoven. The symbolic founding of Cuzco took place around 1200 when, according to legend, Manco Capac decided to make this site the center of the educational mission entrusted to him by his creator, the Sun. This would make Cuzco the oldest continuously inhabited city in South America and perhaps even in the Western Hemisphere (Rowe, 1944). For more than two centuries after its founding, Cuzco was probably no more than a modest village. Archeology has revealed little or nothing about it. According to Sarmiento de Gamboa, Manco Capac and the four Inca rulers who succeeded him lived and died in the House of the Sun, or "Hindicancha" (Sarmiento de Gamboa, 1947), which was almost certainly the principal building during those years.

In the middle of the fourteenth century, under the rule of Inca Roca, sixth in the dynasty, the city witnessed a number of important events. Inca Roca conquered Caitomarca, four leagues distant from Cuzco, and "channeled the waters above and below Cuzco, which to this day irrigate Cuzco's farmland" (Sarmiento de Gamboa, 1947). Inca Roca was also the first to break the custom of living in the House of the Sun and built his own palace in the upper part of the city or Hanan Cuzco.[5]

From that time on, each ruler built a palace where he lived with members of the royal *ayllu*, of which he became the head at the time of his coronation. "As the son did not wish to live in the houses where his father had lived, he left them as they were at his father's death, complete with servants, relatives and *ayllu* and lands, so that they could maintain themselves and keep the buildings in repair" (Sarmiento de Gamboa, 1947). The real reasons were quite different, as no ruler could inherit anything owned by his predecessors (Rowe, 1967).

The city seen by Pizarro's three ambassadors, around the middle of the year 1533, was that laid out by Pachacuti, the ninth Inca.[6] Work on the city began shortly after his coronation in 1439, undoubtedly with the emphasis on beautifying and expanding it rather than transforming its general organization. "He made the principal streets that were there when the Spaniards entered Cuzco, and set aside ground for community, public and private houses, ordering them built of highly polished masonry" (Sarmiento de Gamboa, 1947).

Pachacuti also resolved to enlarge and embellish the House of the Sun, retrieving it from the neglect it had suffered at the hands of the previous rulers. His works did not end there; he built a number of terraces on the sides of neighboring hills to augment the agricultural production of the valley; drained a swamp north of the former residential site of the first rulers, where a large ceremonial plaza called Huacapata began to develop, and constructed a kind of sun clock to measure time and determine the harvest seasons.

THE OUTER DISTRICTS

The Temple of the Sun, or Inti-Cancha, standing in lower Cuzco, was the central point of the ring which marked the circumference of the city (Valcárcel, 1925). Following this circular arrangement, outer and inner districts formed, differentiated by the semi-rural character of the former and the more urban nature of the latter, as seen in their respective architectures in adobe and stone.

The reigning *ayllu* was established in the central quarters. The outer districts were inhabited either by commoners, or by groups belonging to conquered peoples. Also in the outer districts lived the members of some of the *ayllus* of the first Incas and the provincial nobility, as Cuzco was their place of residence during some months every year (Rowe, 1967).

Analysis of the names, locations, and characteristics of Cuzco's outer districts affords us the best means of understanding its urban organization (Plate No. 66). We see the twelve districts or quarters laid out like a clock face and the order of their descriptions follows the movement of its hands. According to Garcilaso, the first quarter, also the principal one, was called Collcampata (Garcilaso, 1943). Taking the center of the city as the site where Manco Capac built the Temple or House of the Sun,[7] the quarter of Collcampata was located to the northwest, on the side of the same hill where Sacsahuamán was built. It served as granary and storehouse for the taxes and tribute.

East of Collcampata was the quarter of Cantutpata, sparsely populated, and a center for the cultivation of carnations, the Inca's favorite flower. Continuing eastward, we see the quarter of Pumarcucu, where the large felines presented to the emperor were tethered to stakes and tamed. Nearby was the quarter of Tococachi, now the San Blas neighborhood, which was densely populated during the Empire.

East of the Temple of the Sun were two quarters, one called Munaycenca, and farther south, the Rimacpampa, where large public gatherings were held.

The Pumapchupan quarter lay to the south, where the Huatanay River joins the Tuyumayo, leaving a spit of land in the shape of a puma's tail,

66 *Cuzco: Plan of center and suburbs, drawn in the last half of the past century. The location of the districts forming a circle around the Huacapata corresponds to the description given by the Inca Garcilaso. (Credit: Squier, E. George: Peru*. Incidents of Travel and Explorations in the Land of the Incas, *Harper and Brothers, New York, 1877.)*

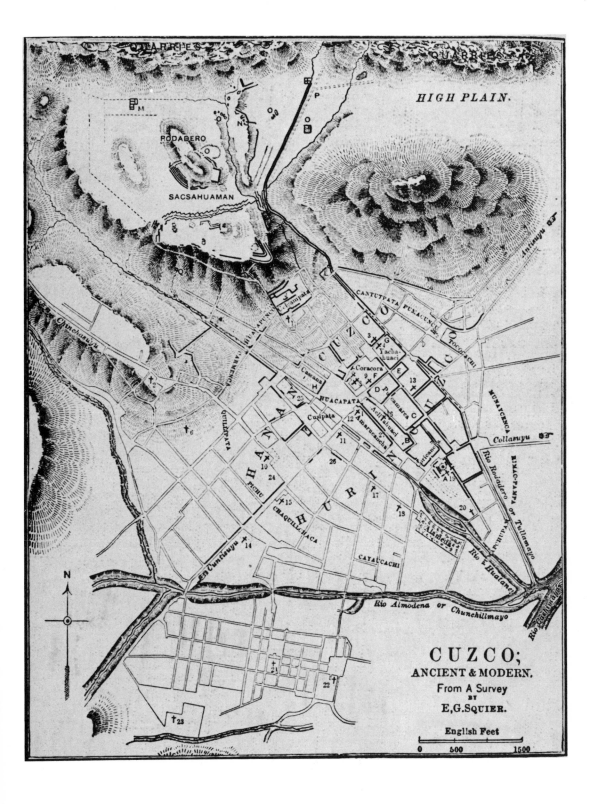

CUZCO;
ANCIENT & MODERN.
From A Survey
BY
E.G.SQUIER.

English Feet

0   500   1500

which earned this district its name. West of the Pumapchupan quarter and outside what was then Cuzco proper, was the town of Cayaucachi, which remained integrated as part of the city after the conquest and corresponds to the present neighborhood and plaza of Belén.

Also to the southwest was the quarter of Chaquillchaca, shown in Squier's plan above, as is Cayaucachi (Squier, 1877), a few hundred meters from the Temple of the Sun. Garcilaso, however, tells us that it lay some thousand paces outside the city. The Chaquillchaca district must have been absorbed into Cuzco's urban area several decades after the arrival of the Spaniards and today forms the neighborhood and plaza of Santiago.

The Inca quarter of Pichu, today a popular district, was formerly terraced and under intense cultivation. It was located to the west of the Temple of the Sun.

Between the present church and convent of San Francisco and the first foothills northwest of the city was an agricultural zone called Quillipata. The quarter of Carmenca lay more to the north, part of it on the same hills occupied by the Quillipata zone, today the Santa Ana district.

Between the Huatanay River and the site of Collcampata lay the last of the twelve quarters that made up Inca Cuzco. It was called Huacapuncu, a name which literally translated means "doorway to the shrine," perhaps indicating the locale of some symbolic entrance to the city. Today this district is known as the Saphi neighborhood. The Huacapuncu and Collcampata quarters were situated on the lower flanks of the hill where the Sacsahuamán fortress was built. As Garcilaso says, this made the full circle (Garcilaso, 1943).

THE CENTER

After Pachacuti remodeled the city, Cuzco's center was fixed by the location of public buildings and the palaces belonging to the succession of Inca emperors who, following the example of Inca Roca, established themselves around the new plaza, Huacapata. Several palaces of the last emperors directly surrounded Huacapata with their solid stone walls; those of the other royal *ayllus* were distributed in an arc across the northwest-southeast sector of the city, with the course of the Huatanay River as a base. The term palaces may be inaccurate but, in any event, they were large stone buildings with no openings other than doorways. The rooms were grouped around interior courtyards, and the cold and luminous climate of the highlands rendered windows unnecessary.

The richness of the palaces was seen in the fine stonework, admirably cut and fitted, and in the restrained interior decoration of tapestries and gold and silver objects. Walls were generally left unplastered, and the smooth stone surface[8] was broken only by trapezoidal niches. The palaces, and undoubtedly all public works, were planned by engineers who made clay or stone models of the project as a guide for the workmen who were to build it. Labor for these works was secured under the *mita* system. The examples of such models we see in museums are simple and generally no larger than any ordinary ceramic piece shown in the case. These provide us with a precise synthesis of the basic elements needed to direct construction, such as overall size, placement of apertures, fences and walls, the shape of the towers, etc. (Pardo, 1936).[9]

Some exterior and interior palace walls are still standing, most of them examples of the type of stone masonry that prevailed during the latter stages of the Inca Empire, probably from between 1440 and the fall of the Empire (Rowe, 1946). The walls were built of regular stone blocks, generally rectangular in shape. The quality and color of the stone used varied with the function of the building; a dark grayish to black stone was used in the Temple of the Sun and in the palaces, while in ordinary works and fortifications, easily obtainable common stone was used, such as diorite and limestone. Great blocks of hard mud or *adobon* were the basis of less important buildings, often topping a wall that had its lower courses in stone.

Adobon structures were more frequent in Pisac, Yucay, and other centers outside Cuzco and in buildings which, in view of their function, would have been built of stone had they been in the capital. What we find most astonishing in Inca stone masonry is the perfection of fit and the curious habit of emphasizing the edges of the blocks by beveling. These were the only decorative features of walls which would otherwise have been completely smooth. Today, we find the main beauty of this architecture in the nobility of its stone. In some blocks a series of protuberances seems the result of incomplete dressing of the stone, but it is difficult to determine whether these are intentional decorative elements or only technical requirements for easier transportation.

We can imagine the austere aspect of Inca Cuzco as we take stock of the simplicity of the architectural and urban features of the city's design.

An Inca plaza, such as Huacapata, was merely the space outlined by the sheer walls of the buildings, over which jutted their slanting straw roofs.[10] The majority of the streets were steep, straight, short, narrow alleys, irregularly laid out between stone walls that, even today, stand more than six meters high. These were the central quarters of the city, the area we consider urban Cuzco, which contained the best laid out and constructed of the palaces belonging to the royal *ayllus*. The outer districts were much more modest, and in these, stone construction seems to have been almost nonexistent.

Despite its simplicity, Cuzco was an extraordinary, even luxurious, city to the Spaniards. Pedro Sancho, who arrived in Cuzco November 15, 1533, described the city in these terms: "It is so beautiful and large that it would be something to see in Spain . . ." (Sancho, 1938). Another conquistador speaks of "many good houses" (Ruiz de Arce, 1953). Cieza de León, who traveled through Peru around 1547 when the effects of the Conquest and Spanish occupation could not yet have obliterated Cuzco's Inca architecture, describes the city as follows: "And in no part of this kingdom of Peru can any city be found with such noble design as Cuzco, the capital of the Inca Empire and its royal seat." He later adds, "Cuzco had a great manner and quality; it must have been founded by people of great worth" (Cieza de León, 1945). Garcilaso compares Cuzco to Rome, although he acknowledges that Rome was superior (Garcilaso, 1943). Estete, a witness to the capture of Atahuallpa, praises the buildings of hewn stone "in this city which are better than those of Spain" (Estete, 1938), and Betanzos, who lived in Cuzco during the 1540's describes it as "the great city of Cuzco" (Betanzos, 1880).[11]

At the beginning of the sixteenth century, Cuzco was unique among the cities of the Inca Empire for its activity, population, quality of construction, and its concentration of accumulated wealth. Nevertheless, as we will see later in this chapter, we can not compare Cuzco's architecture, city plan or activity with the great cities of the Mesoamerican civilizations. Cuzco was the political and religious capital of a society that had become what Toynbee describes as a universal state. The multiple states which preceded the Inca Empire in the control of the coast and highlands

67 *Cuzco: Plan of the plaza. The solid fine lines indicate the outline of the modern city as laid out in the first years of Colonial rule. (Credit: Reconstruction of the architect, Emilio Harth Terré.)*

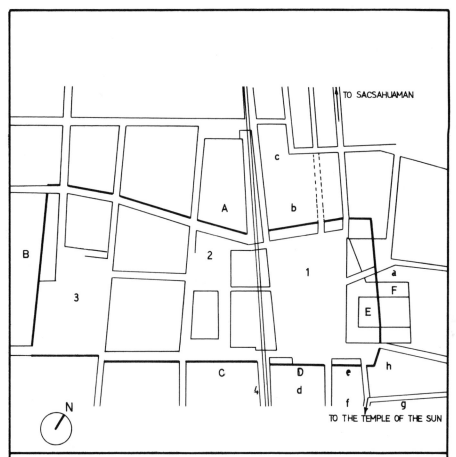

TO SACSAHUAMAN

N

TO THE TEMPLE OF THE SUN

THE SQUARE OF CUZCO BEFORE AND AFTER THE CONQUEST

——————— LIMITS OF THE INCA SQUARE

0   100   200m

INCA BUILDINGS

COLONIAL BUILDINGS

a- PALACE OF VIRACOCHA INCA
b- PALACE OF PACHACUTI
c- SCHOOL OF NOBLES
d- PALACE OF AMARUCANCHA
e- PALACE OF HUASCAR
f- PALACE OF THE VIRGINS OF THE SUN
g- PALACE OF TUPAC YUPANQUI
h- HATUM CANCHA
1- AUCAIPATA (PLAZA DE ARMAS)
2-3 SQUARE OF JOY (PLAZA DE REGOCIOSOS)
AND SQUARE OF SAINT FRANCIS
4- THE CANAL OF THE RIVER HUATANAY

A- TOWN HALL
B- SAINT FRANCIS
C- LA MERCED
D- THE UNIVERSITY AND THE
COMPANY OF JESUS
E- THE CATHEDRAL
F- THE HOLY FAMILY

had become fused into a single political entity, ruled by a supreme monarch. In that sense, the Inca Empire was an isolated phenomenon in America, although the Aztecs also might have ultimately become centralized enough to form a universal state if unforeseen events had not cut short this process. The urban structure of the two capitals reflects the difference between both societies: the Inca, static, materialistic and rural in its attachment to the land, while the Aztec was dynamic, still decentralized but becoming increasingly urban.

The palaces in the center of Cuzco were inhabited exclusively by members of the royal *ayllus* and their servants and, perhaps, by important guests of the emperor or his allies. This was Upper Cuzco or Hanan Cuzco. One type of palace has been described as a quarter by some authors because of its vast size and complex ground plan. It consisted of a number of small structural groups, cut through and outlined by narrow alleys that connected various courtyards surrounded by chambers. Besides the chambers, interior patios and passageways, each palace or quarter had its gardens, baths, and storehouses. The whole compound was enclosed by a high wall, described by Velarde as a true sign of exclusion, authority, and defense (Velarde, 1946). Some authors mention only eight palaces, or central quarters (Pardo, 1937; Valcárcel, 1925).

Earlier in this chapter, I mentioned that the Inca Pachacuti had ordered the draining of a swamp about five hundred meters north of the Temple of the Sun and crossed by the Huatanay River. This site gradually took the form of a large trapezoidal plaza. Called Huacapata, the plaza's main axis ran northeast-southwest, and served as the focal point around which the Inca rulers built palaces and temples.

Pachacuti built the only palace, called the Cassana, on the northwest side of the plaza. The ground where it stood is now the site of the National Museum of Archeology (Plate No. 67). Across the plaza from the Cassana were three groups of buildings. The *ayllu* of Huayna Capac, the eleventh Inca, lived in the quarter called Amarucancha, occupied today by the University of Cuzco and the Church of La Compañia. Next to the Amarucancha stood the buildings that included houses for the Virgins of the Sun, or *Acclahuasi*.[12] Beyond these, forming one of the corners of the present Plaza de Armas, was the palace of Pumarca belonging to the lineage of Topa Inca Yupanqui, the tenth Inca.

There was no building on the southwest side of the plaza. The northeast side, however, where the Cathedral and the Chapel of Santiago were later built, was occupied by a building called Cuyusmanco, belonging to the *ayllu* of Viracocha Inca, eighth in the dynasty. Next to it stood the Caroca palace where the lineage of Sinchi Roca was established.

Other royal palaces were built on the land between the inner palaces around the Huacapata Plaza proper and the outlying districts, forming a second, outer half-circle. The Satunrumiyoc palace, built by the sixth emperor, Inca Roca, stood to the east; to the southeast was Jatuncancha, occupied by Inca Yupanqui's *ayllu*. Since this lineage seems to already have had its quarter northwest of the plaza in the Cassana, I can find no reason for this duplication. Perhaps the Jatuncancha palace belonged to the *ayllu* of the seventh Inca, Yahuar Huacac, the only one of Inca Roca's successors whose palace I have found no location for in descriptions of Inca Cuzco. All these palaces belonged to the *ayllus* of Inca Roca and his successors.

The Collcamptata quarter on the hillside of Sacsahuamán has already been discussed as one of the outer districts. It was here that Manco Capac's lineage resided.

We see here an urban division which clearly defines the two great groups that made up Inca society. In the central sector were the palaces, inhabited by the families of those Incas who had already succeeded to the throne, as well as the reigning *ayllu,* or Kapac Ayllu. This concentration of royalty around the Huacapata Plaza dated from Pachacuti's reign.

Several of the outer districts, or suburbs, were occupied by upper class members of Inca society, such as the *curacas*, or governors, and by the foreign nobility who lived in the capital, enjoying privileges in exchange for their total subordination. The king of Chan Chan, for example, resided in the capital while his son governed his people, the Chimú, as the representative of The Inca of Cuzco. There were even foreign princes who had married princesses of the reigning *ayllu* in the interest of political consolidation.

Though lacking the prestige of the palaces, we can be sure that the *curacas'* houses reflected the rank due prominent members of the Empire who were required to spend long periods of time in Cuzco. One of the conquistadors tells us, "The reason the houses are so good is because the king of the land ordered all his lords to build houses in the city, and for four months of the year they were obliged to live in Cuzco where the king resided. There was one lord whose lands were six hundred leagues away, yet he had to live in the city as decreed. Lords whose lands were distant were given the order to bring people from their lands to settle in a town near Cuzco, that they might serve their lords when these were living at court" (Ruiz de Arce, 1953).[13]

I suspect Ruiz de Arce's reports were somewhat exaggerated, as I doubt that the annual visit was obligatory for the *curacas* and foreign nobles from the more remote corners of the Empire. Even assuming that a subjugated ruler was allowed the rare privilege of traveling in a litter with bearers, such a trip would still have been quite an undertaking at the prevailing travel rate of twenty kilometers per day. A journey to Cuzco from some distant principality might well have required over a hundred days in each direction. The Inca himself, with all the means at his disposal, chose to travel in stages of twelve to fifteen kilometers a day. Barring compelling military reasons, the ruler's journeys were almost always inspection tours. We can logically assume that the annual visit was only demanded of those princes or provincial governors relatively near the capital, as it would have been contrary to the administrative efficiency sought by The Inca to encourage some of his most important subjects to lose time in prolonged journeys. Cieza de León also refers to this politically motivated custom imposed by the rulers, "From all the provinces came the sons of lords to reside in this court with their servants and possessions" (Cieza de León, 1945).

Although the privileged members of Inca society and their servants occupied a good part of the outer districts, it was the humble working-class population that inhabited the suburban areas. Such apparent unity was, in reality, designed to concentrate the manpower necessary to produce the goods required by the ruling class and to build the public works that were under continuous construction in Cuzco during its last hundred years as the Inca capital.

For many years, Cuzco lacked an urban physiognomy, and was undoubtedly little more than a simple, not-too-populated settlement around the Temple of the Sun. Shortly after his coronation, Pachacuti had plans drawn up and "depopulated all the towns within two leagues of the city. He then allotted the lands of these towns to Cuzco and its inhabitants, sending the despoiled peoples to other parts. The citizens of Cuzco were much pleased by this, as it gave them that which cost them little, and thus he (Pachacuti) made friends using other people's land" (Sarmiento de Gamboa, 1947).

Other territories were gradually incorporated as the Empire expanded and these were occupied by the overflow of those groups which had formerly clustered around the city's original site, as well as by members of conquered tribes, headed by their own chiefs. In this sense, Inca Cuzco was the result of the *mitimaes* system, and the foremost example of the political and economic fruits of such a program.

Cuzco's outer quarters were gradually built up in this manner until they surrounded the Huacapata Plaza in a wide circle. The significance and purpose of this division into quarters is clearly explained by Montesinos: ". . . because if an uprising broke out in the city, it would not involve all the people. With the city divided into different quarters and governments, better account could be kept of the populace in the event they were needed by the king either for war or some public works or any other thing including paying tribute. It made it possible to keep informed about everyone without confusion" (Montesinos, 1882).

THE PLAZAS AND STREETS

"After the (coronation) festivities were ended, he (Pachacuti) laid out the town in the order it used to have, and made the principal streets that existed when the Spaniards entered Cuzco. He allotted land for community and private houses, ordering them built in highly polished masonry" (Sarmiento de Gamboa, 1947).

The Huacapata Plaza emerged from this new plan of the city. The Inca plaza was considerably larger than the present Plaza de Armas dating from Colonial times. Running northeast-southwest, it measured 550 meters by 250 meters, with an open area that included over ten hectares. The Huatanay River cut across the plaza, forming trapezoidal halves which correspond to the division into an upper and lower city. Each of these two sectors had its own distinct functions. North of the Huatanay lay the smaller trapezoid with the shape and approximate area of today's Plaza de Armas. It was called Aukaipata, and was used for those ceremonies witnessed by The Inca from a special stage. These were generally important community events such as saluting the rising sun, collective marriages, military or religious parades, and the symbolic distribution of bread and *chicha*, the fermented maize drink. This area also served as a market place. On the southwest side of the river was the larger of the two trapezoids, called Cusipata or Platform of Joy, where popular dances and festivities took place. This section of the plaza also had cultivated beds of maize. The Cusipata sector was broken up after the first land distribution among the Spanish conquistadors in October, 1534. In time, several residential blocks dating from Colonial times as well as the plazas of San Francisco and Regocijo filled in the ancient Cusipata (Harth Terré, 1958).

The city's principal building and most sumptuous construction was the Temple of the Sun, or *Curicancha* "which was one of the richest in gold and silver in the world" (Cieza de León, 1945). The Temple of the Sun and the neighboring buildings inhabited by priests and the Virgins of the Sun constituted the religious center of the Empire and served as a model for other religious constructions. Here the first seven Inca rulers were interred until the day when Pachacuti had them exhumed and, after celebrating their memory in feasts and sacrifices for four months, ordered them bedecked in gold ornaments and placed in highly decorated niches. "By which he endowed them with such authority that they were adored and held as gods by all strangers who came to see them" (Sarmiento de Gamboa, 1947), After the Conquest, the Spaniards built the church of Santo Domingo, here making use of the stone blocks from the Inca temple. The foundations and apse of this Christian church rise atop a beautiful curved wall which once served as the temple base.[14]

Palaces and temples formed the city's center, but along the main thoroughfares "were great arsenals for the Indian soldiers, containing lances, clubs and their arrows, regular as well as special long ones. There were sheds filled with ropes ranging in thickness from that of a finger to a thigh, with which they dragged building stones. There were sheds full of copper bars, tied in tens, from the mines. There were great storehouses of clothing of all sorts and storehouses of coca and chili and even of the skins of flayed Indians" (Trujillo, 1953).

The city's two main axes crossed at the Huacapata Plaza. These axes are indicated today by the direction of the secondary streets. Smaller streets were long and narrow, with steep grades due to the uneven terrain of the expanding city. Prescott's description of the street arrangement as being perfectly regular and crossing each other at right angles is most misleading.

One interesting map that attempts to portray Cuzco at the arrival of the Spaniards is found in the British Museum in London. It shows an overall city plan of absolute regularity; even the sectors near the Huacapata Plaza appear as a precise checkerboard. This plan, too, is far from representing the Inca city as it actually was.[15] Not only would any such attempt at a regular layout have been thwarted by topography, but we would find traces of it today, since the Spaniards adopted various Inca stone walls to determine their Colonial streets. The plan of modern Cuzco retains much of the character of the Colonial city, and the remains of those Inca walls still standing disprove the existence of any original gridiron pattern of streets.[16] Pachacuti tried to impose some sense of order in the city plan by introducing certain organizing features. The Huatanay River, crossing Cuzco in conduits today, was made the city's main axis, and its northwest-southeast direction determined the arrangement of the three principal streets that ran from the Huacapata Plaza to the Temple of the Sun.[17]

The Huatanay River also marked the division between Hanan-Cuzco, or Upper Cuzco, and Hurin-Cuzco, or Lower Cuzco. However, on this point we find disagreement. Some authors support this division (Horkheimer, 1943) while others, in agreement with Garcilaso, hold that the dividing line was the prolongation of the royal roads that ran from the Huacapata Plaza toward the northeast, or Antisuyu, and down to the southwest, or Contisuyu (Squier, 1877), which would give us an axis with a 90 degree shift from the previous one. We also find divergent opinions as to the significance of this division, but it is evident that the half located northeast of the Huatanay, which we consider the upper city, included the ceremonial part of the Huacapata Plaza and all palaces of the last royal *ayllus*. Rather than a territorial division based on a desire to separate a growing aristocracy from the people, it may well have been that this arbitrary segregation, mentioned by almost all the chroniclers, developed for reasons entirely political after the ascension of Inca Roca, the sixth Inca. Sarmiento de Gamboa says that Inca Roca "decreed that from then on, those persons coming from that sector form another band and faction to be called Hanancuzcos, which means the Cuzcos from the upper band" (Sarmiento de Gamboa, 1947).

CHARACTERISTICS OF THE INCA CAPITAL

Can we call Cuzco a city by the definitions adopted for this book? It is obviously harder to establish a criterion for Cuzco than for Teotihuacán, Tenochtitlán, the Maya centers or even Chan Chan. Comparing its size and population with South American urban centers prior to Inca domination, Cuzco was almost unique, with possible similarities only with Chan Chan, Pachacamac, and Cajamarquilla. If we include in the city's area some of the surrounding towns or suburbs such as Cayancanchi and the quarter of Chaquillchaca, two of the most distant sectors, we find that Cuzco occupied an area not less than one kilometer in radius, with the Huacapata Plaza as its center.[18]

The size of the population that lived in Cuzco is hard to estimate. One witness of the Conquest, Juan Ruiz de Arce, calculated that "Cuzco must have had four thousand residential houses" (Ruiz de Arce, 1953). Father Valverde, one of the three Dominican priests who came to Peru with Pizarro, confirmed in a letter written in 1539 that there were three or four thousand houses in the city at the time of its occupation by the Spaniards, and nineteen or twenty thousand houses in the suburbs.[19]

We have no way of knowing how far the suburbs extended, whether they were only the outer quarters or if they included other villages in the valley. Pedro Sancho mentions the existence of a hundred thousand houses in the valley, and other conquistadors calculated that the city had forty thousand residents (or about two hundred thousand persons, bearing in mind that to the Spaniards a "resident" meant the head of a family), and that another two hundred thousand were scattered within a radius of fifty to sixty kilometers. With this data, it is impossible to determine even an approximate density.

Early descriptions suggest that Cuzco had a certain similarity to a contemporary garden-city, formed by a concentrated center of urban character and density, ringed by a series of modest residential suburbs that were in turn surrounded by cultivated fields. The permanent occupation of this city, which continued uninterrupted for eight centuries, makes Cuzco a unique example in America of a center occupied first by an Indian culture, next by a preindustrial population and finally by a specialized and technologically advanced society.

The Spaniards thought of moving the city to the Yucay Valley, which offered a more temperate climate (Cieza de León, 1945; Herrera, 1945) but, in the end, they kept to their custom of governing from existing Indian cities, to avoid the expense and effort entailed in building a new city and to take advantage of the concentrated manpower needed by the Colonial economy.

The Inca ruler decreed that craftsmen and technicians from all over the

Empire come to live in Cuzco. With a large group of lower ranking administrators who already lived and worked in the city, they constituted an important percentage of specialists in the total number of city dwellers.

Above this distinctly middle-class urban group was the ruling class, which was almost impossible to break into for a man of modest origins. Beneath the middle class was the bulk of the population that worked as farmers and occasional soldiers or as laborers, constructing the public works that Inca expansionism required.

Cuzco's population, like that of any Indian city of America, was partially agricultural, but as the city grew, following the reign of Pachacuti, it began to depend on neighboring valleys for provisioning. The importance of the administrative and artisan groups also grew during this period. Craftsmen may have been organized in some way, since the administration emphasized mass production of utilitarian objects to the detriment of quality, which was inferior to that of the work of artists and artisans of more ancient Peruvian cultures and even of some contemporaneous peoples incorporated into the Empire during the fifteenth century.

The Huacapata Plaza was an urban space where the kind of varied and elaborate events took place which could only have occurred in one of the Empire's principal cities. Streets, too, were urban in their layout, which was to be adopted by the Spaniards, some of these in use today. In the center of the city, at least, streets outlined a pattern of trapezoidal and elongated blocks, occupied by the royal palaces and religious buildings. These were the typically urban characteristics of Inca cities found only in the Empire's principal centers or in especially planned settlements.

Prescott describes Cuzco as the metropolis of a great empire, the seat of the court and nobility, the military garrison and the meeting place for migrants coming from the most distant provinces. Cuzco was all these, and a market as well—the most important in both the region and the Empire.[20] It was also the political and administrative capital of a vast territory. But Cuzco was never a fortress. During its early years, its defenses depended on the natural advantages offered by its location in a valley protected by rugged mountain passes. The fortress of Sacsahuamán was built later, more as a refuge in case of attack than for defense.

In this ordered city, without luxury or ostentation, lived a society that maintained its various strata according to custom accepted by all. A man was born an Inca of the royal blood, a member of the provincial royalty or belonged to the great anonymous masses. In Cuzco lived people from all the provinces of the Empire in different social classes with no expectation of changing their respective positions. Under Inca rule, the Indian was born and died within his group.

From Cuzco evolved the most complete social and economic experiment ever attempted in pre-Columbian America and the best program of colonization and urbanization ever initiated during the Indian centuries on that Continent. The precise objectives of the Empire have been analyzed in a previous chapter. These goals and the means to achieve them were planned in Cuzco.

The Inca Pachacuti may have entrusted men from his own *ayllu* with the work of enlarging and remodeling Cuzco. Perhaps this represents South America's first Commission of Public Works. Without delegating authority, the emperor could never have fulfilled his innumerable responsibilities. During Pachacuti's reign, the capital was totally transformed by such ambitious projects as the canalization of the Huatanay River which, according to one chronicler, stretched several leagues beyond the city limits. These works would have required careful planning and constant supervision.

Certain urban institutions were needed to reach the Inca civilization's cultural level, and Cuzco was the logical place to locate the school for members of the royal *ayllu* and future administrators of the Empire. Cuzco was also the religious center of the state, and possibly of other typically urban institutions.

In summary, we know little about the outer districts with their houses of modest construction and perishable materials, or about the lives of the people who lived in them. To reach the center by any of the four main roads, these people had to cross over an extensive, disorderly suburb which stretched along the surrounding hillsides toward the valley. The center of the city, however, must have acquired an urban aspect that probably included the zone occupied by the rulers' palaces, the Temple of the Sun, the large rectangle 260 by 70 meters taken up by the *Acclahuasi,* or House of the Virgins of the Sun, and by the public buildings surrounding the central plaza. The center also differed in its great rectangular or trapezoidal city blocks, enclosed by high stone walls with almost no apertures (Plate No. 68). Outlined by these walls were the long, narrow and utilitarian paved streets that converged on the Huacapata Plaza.

68 *Inca stone work today. (Credit: Hardoy, Jorge E.)*

Cuzco's city plan lacked monumental constructions. In fact, I do not believe there was ever any attempt made to create vistas and variety by bringing into play the natural differences in elevation. The pedestrian walking from the upper sector down to the Huacapata Plaza would encounter a minimum of changing views and visual sequences as he passed through the long, confined street to the plaza, which might seem exaggeratedly large, yet of dimensions suitable for its various functions. Such a walk would not have been much different in feeling than a similar stroll through a highland Indian town today. Building materials have changed, the tempo is somewhat swifter, but the same sense of order and visual continuity is there.

Above the stone walls and straw roofs, the pedestrian would see the mountains, forming a majestic amphitheater above the city. Perhaps he gazed around him, filled his lungs with the sharp, clear air of the highlands, then returned home to his modest house on the outskirts where his family lived. He made his home in a city built with the sense of permanence characteristic of America's Indian centers, manifested in the architecture and in its very building materials. This same durability is the essence of the Indian race.

SACSAHUAMÁN

Cuzco was never walled. At some point in its history, the ruler ordered the construction of the Sacsahuamán fortress as well as the smaller forts and strongholds that have been found in the valleys leading into the Cuzco Valley.

The origin of the fortress, even the meaning of its name, lay obscured in mystery until Valcárcel excavated its ruins about thirty years ago. He reported that the entire construction of the fortress was Inca in period and style, with no pre-Inca work, its massive walls no different than the others that surround the site on its east, south, and western sides (Valcárcel, 1946).

Sacsahuamán is an excellent example of Inca architectural technique. Built as a refuge rather than for defense, the ruins of Sacsahuamán lie

69 *Sacsahuamán: Aerial view of the fortress. Note triple lines of saw-tooth defensive walls. (Credit: Servicio Aerofotográfico Nacional, Lima, Peru.)*

north of Cuzco on a hill rising over two hundred meters above the city's center.[21] The fortress includes chambers and storehouses capable of withstanding a protracted siege. These structures, as well as an unusual circular base which has been assigned such diverse roles as cistern or temple, were protected by a triple row of walls on the east, west and north sides. A steep ravine descending toward Cuzco rendered the south side impregnable (Plate No. 69).

The three ramparts formed mounting terraces and were built of gigantic stones to present an almost insurmountable obstacle to any attackers of that epoch. Three towers or lookouts completed this system of defenses. The ramparts, notched in outline like the teeth of a saw, could be entered only through the clefts, so that to reach the first platform, the enemy would have to elude the rain of projectiles hurled from the front and sides. If the attackers managed to survive this hazard, they were confronted with a second and third onslaught at the inner walls before they could enter the fortress. Even then, they would have to dominate the towers, one of which was several stories high.

Some authors state that the first urban settlement of Cuzco was in Sacsahuamán itself, since they find it more logical that the founder of the Inca Empire would have descended from Sacsahuamán to establish his palace at the foot of the Cuzco acropolis (Pardo, 1937). Valcárcel writes that Sacsahuamán was undoubtedly some other city, the Janan Kosko of Inca history transformed into a true acropolis, a *sanctum sanctorum* of the solar religion, stronghold of the imperial court and castle of The Inca (Valcárcel, 1934-1935). If we consider the uncertainties assailing the first Inca rulers confronted with the military and political weakness of their people in the early years of their beginnings in the Cuzco Valley, such a theory is not improbable, although we have no evidence to confirm it. All peoples who evolve into advanced cultures require natural or artificial defenses to protect them during their fledgling years. At the culmination of a culture, the capital, often the center of cultural radiation, usually remains unfortified, trusting in its prestige and in the military might of its armies to keep enemies at a distance.

My own unconfirmed hypothesis is that, urbanistically, the decline of a culture provokes its return to one of the initial stages of its evolution. At some point, the members of such a culture assure the security of their capital city by building defensive walls, or they even go back to a site they had originally occupied or some place similar, where natural defenses might provide a last refuge in case of invasion. Consider the evolution of urban cultures in Crete, where this cycle was completed after the destruction of what once had been proud and prosperous cities. Remember, too, that fortification of all the cities in the Roman Empire was ordered only during the rule of Dominiciano Aureliano, about 270-275 A.D., when Rome was in decline and the *Pax Romana* challenged. Faced with the collapse of the central government, Roman cities were thrown on their own resources. We find another example in the Maya cities of Yucatán, which were fortified during their declining centuries after the rupture of the League of Mayapán and the inevitable conflicts that ensued. In this case, various Maya groups returned to the Petén to reoccupy some of the old Classic centers, or to settle in new and easily defended sites.

Cuzco's urban development coincided with the politico-geographical expansion of the Inca Empire and brought a long period of peace to the inhabitants of the Cuzco Valley and the surrounding valleys. The wars of conquest, undertaken by the rulers following Pachacuti, were fought hundreds, even thousands of kilometers from Cuzco. The armies and their generals, and on occasion even The Inca himself, were away from the capital for years at a time. Eventually, the ranks of the Inca army, like those of the Roman army in its day, came to consist almost exclusively of recruits from the conquered peoples. Battles of conquest and consolidation must have seemed remote to the inhabitants of the capital.

At the beginning of the fifteenth century, during the reign of Viracocha Inca, the Inca capital was attacked for the last time. The Chanca, a tribe living west of Cuzco, advanced on the capital and even managed to penetrate some of its quarters. Again and again, the Chanca were driven back, until they were finally conquered and absorbed into the Empire. From that time on, the Inca were aware of their power and prestige. They also found that they had a new leader, the war hero Pachacuti, who soon thereafter succeeded his father, Viracocha Inca.

Perhaps it was the mounting awareness of Inca power that encouraged Pachacuti to remodel and enlarge the capital. Cuzco, as the Spaniards saw it, was the work of this ruler. It was no longer a stronghold, but a political and religious center. The Sacsahuamán fortress stood on a neighboring hilltop as a reminder of the uncertain times when the Inca fought for their survival. In the unlikely event of future attack, it remained as a refuge.

The conquest and occupation of Cuzco by the Spaniards involved neither war nor siege. The capture of the last emperor, Atahuallpa, points up the weaknesses in the governmental structure imposed by the rulers, as it took Pizarro only twelve months to take him prisoner in Cajamarca, execute him, consolidate Spanish power, and enter Cuzco in triumph.[22] A few weeks later, Pizarro organized the city's municipal government, and with the customary distribution of urban lots among the conquerors, Cuzco's physiognomy began to change as its Inca identity faded.

NOTES ON · 12

1. ONLY IN 1561, did Philip II decide to establish his court in Madrid, which had been a small insignificant city of Arab origin until then. Madrid was chosen as the official residence because of its location in the geographic center of the peninsula.

   "Rome was not built in a day." It was founded, according to legend, in 753 B.C. In 396 B.C., well into the Republican Period, the Romans captured Veii, a wealthy Etruscan city twenty kilometers north of Rome, thus taking the first step toward the unification of Italy.

   We do not know whether there had been an existing settlement on the site where the Romans established London. Throughout medieval times, London was an important commercial port in which the kings lived for periods of time, yet it was never made a royal seat. The crown and the city existed independently (Steen Eiler Rasmussen; *London, the Unique City*; A Pelican Book, A. 486; Harmondsworth, Middlesex, England, 1961).

2. On this subject we have a well-documented work with excellent cartographic reconstructions based on aerial photographs, by Ferdinando Castagnoli, *Ippodamo de Mileto e l'Urbanistica a Pianta Ortogonale*; De Luca Editores; Rome, 1956. To understand Rome's colonizing efforts and the extent of its trade, the reader will find the following books helpful: *Rome Beyond the Imperial Frontiers*; Sir Mortimer Wheeler; A Pelican Book; A. 335; Harmondsworth, Middlesex, 1955, and *The Cambridge Ancient History*; The Cambridge University Press.

3. Cieza de León tells us that Tumebamba "was like the head of a kingdom or bishopric." According to his chronicle, the "famous buildings of Tumebamba, that . . . were some of the richest and most splendid in all Peru," as well as the Temple of the Sun, had been built with stones brought from Cuzco by order of "King Guaynacapa (Huayna Capac) and the great Topainga (Topa Inca), his father." The author adds that Topa Inca lived for long periods in Tumebamba (Cieza de León, 1945).

4. Rowe suggests that it was probably "the policy of the Inca emperors to suppress the fortified villages, choosing a site on the plain as residence for the people" (Rowe, 1957).

5. Cuzco was divided into the Upper City, or Hanan Cuzco, and Lower City, or Hurin Cuzco. Six rulers built their palaces in the Upper City, the last of them being Huayna Capac.

6. Under pressure from Pizarro, Atahuallpa decided to show his good will by permitting a few Spaniards to travel to Cuzco to verify the state of tranquility that reigned in the country and to hasten the sending of the ransom which would restore his freedom. Three Spaniards journeyed to the capital on Pizarro's orders, and returned sometime around June of 1533, confirming the reports that had been circulating among the Spanish forces as to the wealth and population of the city. After Atahuallpa's execution on August 29 of that year, Pizarro and his army marched to Cuzco, arriving the morning of November 15, "at the hour of high mass" (Sancho, 1938).

7. Over the ruins of the House or Temple of the Sun, situated about five hundred meters southeast of Cuzco's modern cathedral, the Colonial monastery and church of Santo Domingo were built.

8. Prescott describes the walls as stained or painted in brilliant colors, and the doorways as being of reddish marble. The chroniclers in general give us few details of Inca architecture.

9. In his chronicle, the Conquistador Anónimo mentions that when de Soto was in Caxas, a large town to which he had gone as Pizarro's advance guard, a captain sent by Atahuallpa approached the Spaniards with gifts, among them "two very strong fortresses made of clay, saying that there were others ahead like them" (Conquistador Anónimo, 1938). Jerez confirms this event (Jerez, 1938).

10. The roofs of the houses in the outer districts, like those of the chambers forming palaces, were all of straw. The difference in rank was seen in the quality of workmanship. The Inca did not have roof tiles, as a number of chroniclers and historians have pointed out.

11. The reader will find a useful collection of descriptions of the city of Cuzco in *Antología del Cuzco*, edited by Paul Porras Barrenechea, Librería Internacional del Perú, Lima, 1961.

12. The ruins of this large monastery can be seen today. Here lived a group of servants of the Sun, or *mamacunas*, who had made vows of perpetual chastity. The *mamacunas* are not to be confused with the Chosen Women, or *acclacunas*, who could become concubines of the emperor, or of a noble if the ruler so willed. The *acclacunas* also served in the Temple of the Sun.

13. The northern frontier of the Empire was less than 2,500 kilometers from Cuzco. The undefined southern frontier was the most distant. By the

456

Inca's royal road it must have been about 3,000 kilometers from the capital. The distance from Quito to Talca, south of Santiago, Chile, traveling via Cuzco, was approximately 5,200 kilometers by the Andes route. The coastal road was more direct and perhaps quicker, but its northernmost point stopped at Túmbez, several hundred kilometers south of the Empire's northern frontier. Between Túmbez and Talca there was a distance of about 4,000 kilometers. The present Pan-American Highway, which crosses Peru from north to south along the coast, runs parallel in many places to the Inca road (Von Hagen, 1958). In a direct line, distances are considerably shorter.

14. Garcilaso describes the Temple of the Sun as follows: "The roofing was of wood and very high because there was much wind; the covering was of straw, because they did not know how to make tile. All four walls of the temple were covered from top to bottom with sheets and planks of gold. In the front, on what we would call the great altar, they had placed the figure of the Sun, made of a plank of gold twice as thick as those on the walls. The figure was formed with a rounded face and with its rays and flames of fire, all of one piece, neither more nor less than artists paint it. So large it was that it took up the whole front of the temple from wall to wall" (Garcilaso, 1943).

15. This refers to a plan 11 by 15 inches, presumably from the seventeenth or eighteenth century, a photostatic copy of which I found in the Library of Congress in Washington. A caption on it reads: "This shows the City of Cuzco and its great plaza when our Spanish forces came to it at the time of the Conquest." The original is found in the British Museum in London. I had the opportunity of examining it in 1968.

16. The Peruvian archeologist Chavez Ballón states that "the city maintains the Inca plans in its streets and plazas" (Manuel Chavez Ballón, *La ciudad calendario*, El Comercio, Lima, 19 de enero de 1965).

17. During the sixteenth and seventeenth centuries, views of Cuzco were included by most cartographers in their collections. There were drawings for instance, by Ramusio, who presented a view that became the prototype for most later collections, by Braun and Hogenberg, de Bry, du Pinet, Münster, and others. Damian Bayón, in a paper presented to the XXXVIII International Congress of Americanists, Stuttgart, 1968, and entitled "The ancient views of Cuzco in the Bibliotheque Nationale of Paris," includes the results of a preliminary research. All these "ideal" views of Cuzco bore no relation to reality.

18. "The ancient city of the Janan and Urin Cuzco had a perimeter of three

kilometers" (Manuel Chavez Ballónz *Tratan de reproducir plan arquitectónico del Inca Pachacutec*; El Comercio; Lima, 23 de enero de 1964).

19. According to William H. Prescott; *ibid;* note 30 of Chapter 8.

20. Valcárcel tells us that markets, one of the economic practices of Peru's native populations, existed from pre-Columbian times through the period of Spanish rule of the sixteenth to the nineteenth centuries, up to the present (Valcárcel, 1946). Transactions were made by bartering products, a system that still persists. Nevertheless, judging by the small importance the chroniclers attached to them, Inca markets seem to have been less prominent than those in Mesoamerica, and were limited to the barter of handcrafts or surplus products from the periodic distributions (Mason, 1957). In Inca Peru there was no merchant class such as that among the Maya and the Aztecs.

21. The Sacsahuamán fortress is 3,750 meters above sea level.

22. Prescott describes the arrival of Pizarro and his men in the Inca capital as follows: "The little army was formed into three divisions, of which the centre, or 'battle,' as it was called, was led by the general. The suburbs were thronged with a countless multitude of the natives, who had flocked from the city and the surrounding country to witness the showy, and, to them, startling pageant. All looked with eager curiosity on the strangers, the fame of whose terrible exploits had spread to the remotest parts of the empire."

·13

THE INCA CITY

"The ruins of what we now believe was the lost city of Vilcapampa the Old, perched on tip of a narrow ridge lying below the peak of Machu Pic-chu, are called the ruins of Machu Picchu because when we found them no one knew what else to call them."

HIRAM BINGHAM
(THE LOST CITY OF THE INCAS)

□ 13

THE TWO EXTREME EXAMPLES of urban concentrations emerging from the Inca civilization are represented by the capital and the simple rural villages where the bulk of the population lived. The capital reflected the Empire's power and wealth; the life of the people was seen in the innumerable small villages scattered wherever environmental conditions offered them a living. Neither represents a good example of the Inca's knowledge of urban planning.

The majority of the principal Inca urban centers developed without a plan. To this group belong all the cities following Cuzco in importance and which, at the zenith of the Empire, were regional capitals of major urban centers—Quito, Cajamarca, Tomebamba, Túmbez, Pachacamac, Chan Chan, Vilcashuaman, Cochabamba, Huánuco Viejo, Bonbon, and Jauja, to name a few (Plate No. 45, page 191). Several of these cities were pre-Inca settlements, taken over by the Empire for political, administrative, and economic reasons and later remodeled to fit their new functions. All of them were joined by the Inca road network, which shows that their importance did not vanish following their incorporation into the Empire. Some chroniclers mention them in passing, but rarely bother to describe them in detail as they do Cuzco. No doubt they found these cities less impressive than the Inca capital.

Cajamarca was one of the principal cities of the northern part of the Empire, and here the ruler, as was his custom, had built himself a spacious "pleasure house . . . of four rooms with a courtyard in the middle. In the courtyard was a pool fed by two pipes for water, one hot and the other cold. These pipes issued from springs which were close together. The Inca and his women bathed in that pool. Beyond the doorway of this house was a lawn" (Ruiz de Arce, 1953). This arrangement of a regular ground plan with a central patio was common in the principal buildings

461

of the Empire.

It was in this pleasure house that Atahuallpa received Pizarro's first emissaries, among whom was Ruiz de Arce, and it was from Cajamarca that he directed the final stages of the war against his brother, Huascar. This city was apparently Atahuallpa's official residence at the end of his life.[1]

Cajamarca was built on a mountainside (Jerez, 1938), with a fortress as defense. It seems to also have been a favorite place for Atahuallpa's predecessors, as "they thought so highly of it that they built their palaces here and erected an important temple to the Sun as well as a large number of storehouses" (Cieza de León, 1945). The House of the Virgins of the Sun completed the group of principal buildings.

The chroniclers tell us nothing about the location of Cajamarca's plaza, but were obviously impressed by its size, "larger than any in Spain" (Jerez, 1938). It was triangular in shape, outlined by three huge sheds or "lodgings" each two hundred paces long; the streets of the town began at the corners thus formed (Ruiz de Arce, 1953).[2] Another chronicler reports ten streets, all originating at the plaza (Trujillo, 1953). To the east stood a raised, truncated pyramid of regular base (Tello, no date).

All Inca cities seem to have had some characteristics in common. Although they may not have been fortified, there was often a place of refuge on a nearby elevation. In their choice of sites, relatively level locations appear to have predominated, close by a flow of water.

A wide space or plaza, appearing in archeological maps, was called a *Kancha*, mentioned in almost all the Spaniards' descriptions. The plazas in Cuzco, Huánuco, and Cajamarca were enormous; that of Jauja was "large and measures a quarter of a league" (Pizarro, 1953); at Túmbez the plaza was "of good size" (Ruiz de Arce, 1953); a rough estimate of the plaza at Vilcashuaman shows an area slightly less than three hectares;[3] the plazas of Tambo Colorado and Machu Picchu were also sizeable. As we shall see later in this chapter when we study the planned cities, these too had plazas. It is hard to ascertain, however, whether or not the plazas of some of the Empire's principal cities were of pre-Inca origin, since the cities themselves in their later histories were Inca. Considering the plazas' different shapes—trapezoidal in Cuzco and Tambo Colorado, almost rectangular in Huánuco Viejo, triangular in Cajamarca, pentagonal in Vilcashuaman, irregular in Machu Picchu and apparently irregular in Bonbon—I believe that in some cases Inca engineers took advantage of those existing areas with undefined forms and functions and converted them into the centers of the new settlements.[4] They then built the principal administrative buildings around these spaces, creating the layouts seen by the first Spaniards. The plazas of Cuzco, Huánuco, Vilcashuaman and others did not have pre-Inca origins, of course, as the cities themselves did not. The large *kanchas* were generally absent in the small villages.

All cities of a certain rank had well-constructed public buildings and many had palaces for the emperor and his retinue. These palaces, like that of Atahuallpa at Cajamarca, were on the outskirts of the city. "In what they call Guanuco (Huánuco Viejo) there was a royal house of admirable construction, with large and most skillfully fitted stones. This palace or lodging was the seat of the neighboring province of the Andes, and near it stood the Temple of the Sun, housing a number of virgins and ministers; it was such a large place in the time of the Incas that more than thirty thousand Indians were kept in its service" (Cieza de León, 1945).

Cuzco and other cities had several elements in common. The Temple of the Sun, probably a building formed by three groups of two rooms each, was found in Cuzco as well as in Huánuco Viejo and Tambo Colorado. All three cities were apparently divided in four *barrios* or districts. The two central *barrios* corresponded to the upper and lower halves of the city in Machu Picchu, with the upper half located to the west of the plaza and the lower half to the east. The *usñu* or platform from which the Inca administered justice, was also a common element in these cities (Zuidema, 1969), as were the houses of the priestesses of the Sun.

Determining the population of these regional centers and provincial capitals is difficult. Ruiz de Arce calculated that Túmbez, which he calls a town, "must have a thousand houses," or around five or six thousand inhabitants. When you consider that this same author wrote in his *Advertencias* that "the city (Cuzco) . . . must have four thousand lodging-houses," you begin to understand the different categories of cities. "House" and "lodging-house" clearly meant two distinct things to this chronicler; perhaps he understood a "house" to be some kind of dwelling, however modest, and a "lodging-house" to refer to a dwelling of a better class. Even so, we are left with this discrepancy between Ruiz de Arce's count and estimates of Cuzco's population by other chroniclers, as discussed in the preceding chapter. Cajamarca probably occupied an intermediate position between Túmbez and Cuzco.

When Francisco Pizarro sent his brother, Hernando, from Cajamarca to Pachacamac, which he described as "a town . . . very large and with great buildings," and which the Conquistador Anónimo qualified as "a town larger than Rome," he passed through the city of Jauja on his return trip. Upon sighting it from a neighboring hill, he was amazed to see in the plaza a "great black mass, which we thought was something burned. When we asked what it was, they told us that it was Indians." He later adds, "Some of the people who had been in the plaza came the next morning. They were simple Indians, and truly there were over a hundred thousand souls" (Pizarro, 1953). Another conquistador, Miguel de Estete, who accompanied Hernando Pizarro on his trip to Pachacamac, also estimated that "each day a hundred thousand persons came together in the Great Plaza (of Jauja)." Remembering Cieza de León's description of the thirty thousand Indians who served Huánuco's Temple of the Sun (Cieza de León, 1945), we wonder whether, aside from possible exaggeration, these figures might not represent masses of people gathered for some special event, rather than the regular inhabitants of these cities.

The majority of Inca settlements, despite their size and importance, evolved with no apparent fixed design, although, as I have mentioned, they had some common elements. Urban planning was used on several occasions toward the end of the Empire in a series of towns built by order of The Inca for administrative, economic, and political purposes. To this group belong Incahuasi, Tambo Colorado, Ollantaytambo and perhaps others as yet undiscovered. A number of *tambos,* or rest houses, were also planned and constructed in all corners of the Empire, following certain general principles of layout.[5] Those planned settlements we have found are admirable examples of definite urban organization and proof of the technical level reached by Inca engineers and masons.

The decision to build a city, the choice of site and when to start construction were almost certainly responsibilities of the emperor and his council. To facilitate matters, the principal administrators accumulated detailed information about the needs and potential of the territory to be conquered, incorporated and colonized.

The Inca lacked paper for sketching the preliminary plans of a project, but they substituted stone or clay models to show structural details. I have mentioned the importance of these mock-ups, which indicate the weight Inca technicians gave to planimetric and volumetric studies before undertaking a project. Repetition of rectilinear principles and the inclusion of such standard urban features as plazas and regular-shaped blocks of buildings are further proof that physical planning existed among the Inca.

The Inca had few measuring instruments and developed only crude construction methods. Stone, which they used in the important buildings, was quarried by the primitive expedient of cracking the rock, inserting wedges, and slowly and laboriously hauling out large chunks. These were then moved by log rollers, inclined planes and crowbars of bronze and wood. The stone was later cut into blocks by stone hammers and axes and bronze chisels. Finally it was polished with sand and water. Measuring instruments were simple and consisted of two superimposed rulers on which a scale had been marked.

The majority of civil engineering works all over the Empire from Pachacuti's reign up to the Conquest were possible only through the organized efforts of large groups of laborers, working to fulfill their *mita*. Thanks to the *mita*, most of the terraces, storehouses, roads, canals, and rest houses were built and, of course, the palaces and temples in Cuzco and the principal cities.

INCAHUASI

Unlike other Inca cities, we know why and when Incahuasi was built. It belongs to the period when the armies of Topa Inca Yupanqui began the conquest of the south coastal valleys and found themselves confronted by the Yunga, a warlike tribe led by their famous chieftain, Chuquimanco. The Yunga occupied the Cañete River Valley, and their strategically placed fortresses enabled them to resist the Inca armies for many years.

The building of Incahuasi was related to this campaign. When Topa Inca Yupanqui realized that the siege would be long, he ordered his armies to settle in and established himself with his retinue. Incahuasi was apparently formed by an observatory; a complex of barracks; storehouses for food, clothing and arms; a palace for The Inca; the Temple of the Sun and the house of the chosen priestesses, plus other minor structures. The city stood not far from the fortress of Chancari where Chuquimanco

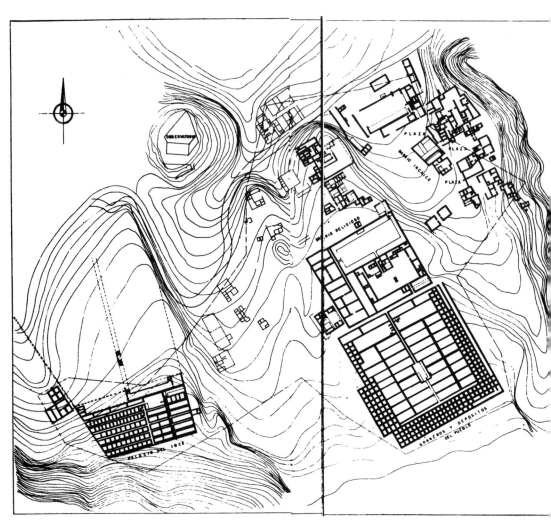

70 *Incahuasi: Incahuasi was built by order of Tope Inca Yupanqui to serve as a military camp and base of operations in his campaign against the Yunga. From west to east on the plan, we see the Palace of the Inca, the state granaries, and a complex of barracks and chambers. On a hill to the north stood an observatory. The town was completed by the Temple of the Sun and the house of the priestesses.* (Credit: Belaunde Terry, Fernando: La Conquista del Perú por los Peruanos, *Ediciones Tawantisuyu, Lima, 1959.)*

decided to make his last stand. It was planned in four main structural groups, separated from each other by several hundred meters of rugged terrain (Plate No. 70). The palace of The Inca, the state granary and the barracks were laid out in that order in parallel sections running from west to east, and the observatory stood on an elevation north of these structures. I do not know the location of a fifth group of religious structures in relation to the rest as we have no general plan of the whole settlement, only individual plans of each group and one diagram of several groups but without the religious sector (Harth Terré, 1933).

The Inca's palace consisted of a series of chambers forming a building of trapezoidal ground plan that continued on to a broad, raised platform of the same shape. The platform measured 15,000 square meters and was made of packed earth (Plate No. 71). It was divided into two similar sections by a raised walkway, in the middle of which stood a simple altar of stone and mud. According to Harth Terré, who has studied and measured Incahuasi's ruins, the platform was used for military inspections and ritual food distribution to married couples, a ceremony witnessed by the emperor or his *curacas* (Harth Terré, 1933). The living quarters of the palace were of simple construction, and a good part of the area was taken up by the emperor's private storerooms and the chambers of his servants. The Inca and his concubines lived in some of the rooms; others were occupied by the captains of his army. The palace had several guardrooms. At the front of the building overlooking the platform was a raised gallery of honor, roofed in an arrangement of poles and cloth. From here the emperor presided over ceremonies.

The second group of buildings was composed of the *colccahuasi*, or granary, where we observe a repetition of several of the geometric features found in other centers. The granary itself was an almost square building, 115 meters on each side, enclosed by a high wall of stone and mud. Within the wall were forty great chambers of regular shape in addition to 256 silos, four scant meters square, where maize, coca, potatoes, salt, chili peppers, and other foodstuffs essential to Inca diet were stored. Animal products and a storehouse for liquids were next to the granary. The guard lived in a separate building, elevated to facilitate vigilance. Administrative employees and porters made up the permanent personnel that undoubtedly lived in the neighboring chambers. One important feature of the *colccahuasi* was a courtyard, surrounded by columns, next to the storehouse for liquids. Here the solemn ceremony of *chicha* distribution took place, and llamas and other animals were sacrificed on a small altar.

Incahuasi's third group was that of the houses of the Chosen Women, or *acllahuasi*. A semi-circular arrangement of dwellings around a plaza with an altar bearing the sacred fire, this group constitutes an unusual example of known Inca architecture. The structures near it may have been those of the temple (Harth Terré, 1933).

The fourth group runs almost the length of the northwest side of the *colccahuasi* and consisted of a series of regular structures of different sizes, grouped around various irregular plazas, interconnected by short, narrow passageways. These may have been the houses of the chiefs and perhaps some of the soldiers.

Incahuasi was one of the most important coastal stations built by the Inca. Its ruins cover a large and arid area.[6] Since the palace ruins are on a steep hill, we can assume that its construction required extensive terracing of the site. The builders took advantage of the more level space between hills for the other structures. The overall plan indicates that the various groups were planned individually according to Inca architectural principles, but their disposition does not reveal previous planning of the complex as a whole.

TAMBO COLORADO

On a hill near the Pisco River, eight hundred meters above sea level, lie the ruins of Tambo Colorado. These remains are among the best preserved ruins of Peru. The Inca settlement is divided by a dirt road that runs along the cultivated banks of the river (Plate No. 72).

Tambo Colorado also dates from the late pre-Inca period, or the epoch when Inca armies invaded the south coast during the reign of Topa Inca Yupanqui. The basic purpose of Tambo Colorado is not clear. It may have been built to serve as a palace or a military camp, or an administra-

71 *Incahuasi: Plan of the Palace of the Inca. The almost square chambers to the right of the central corridor of the living area were the private store rooms of the Inca. The rooms to the left were occupied by the Emperor and his retinue. (Credit: Harth Terŕe, Emilio: "Incahuasi: ruinas inkaicas del valle de Lima-huana"; Revista del Museo Nacional; II-2; Lima, 1933.)*

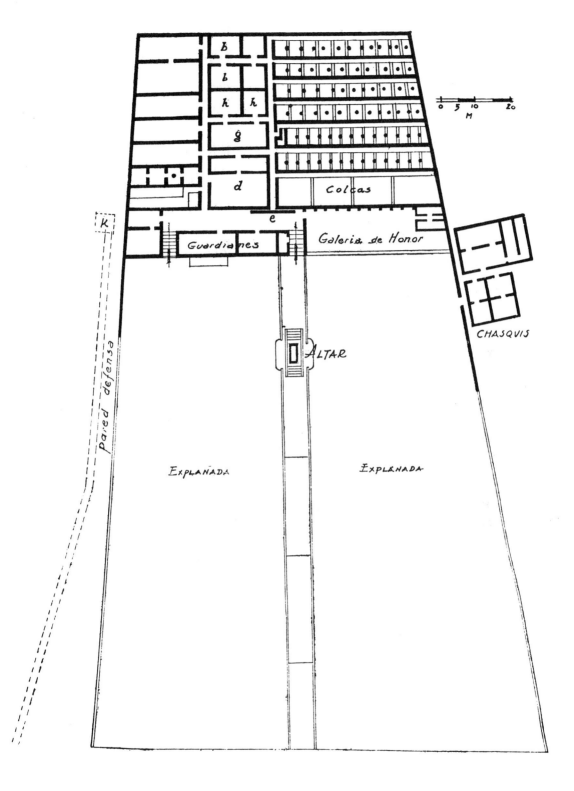

72 *Tambo Colorado: Model of Tambo Colorado. (Credit: Museum of Anthropology and Archeology, Lima.)*

73 *Tambo Colorado: Tambo Colorado may have been built as a military camp and administrative center. Its ruins lie in southern Peru next to the ravine of the Pisco River. Building C probably served as the residence of the principal chiefs. (Credit: Urteaga, Horacio H.; "Tambo Colorado"; Boletín de la Sociedad Geográfica; LVI-2; Lima, 1934. After a design by Emilio Harth Terŕe.)*

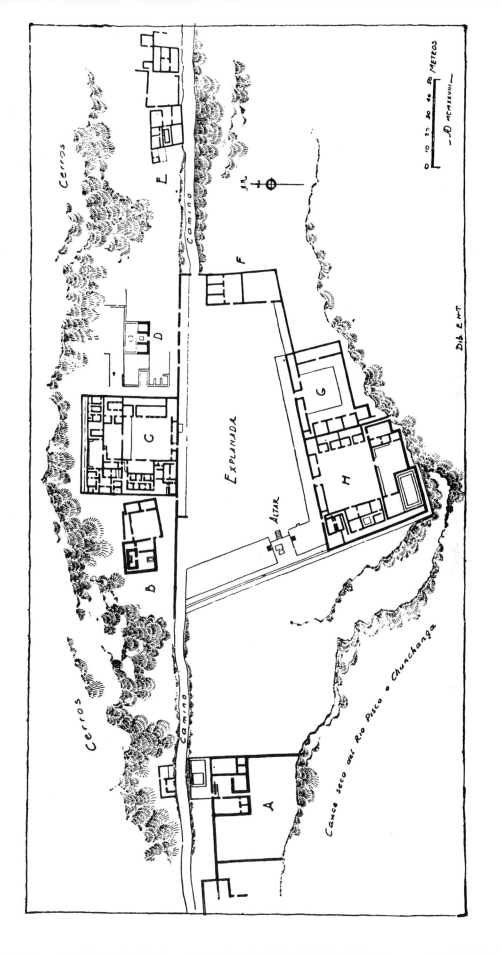

Cerros

Cerros

Camino

Camino

E

D

B

C

F

Explanada

Altar

G

H

A

Cauce seco del Rio Pisco o Chunchanga

Dib. E.H.T.

0 10 20 30 40 50 METROS

JD MCMXXXVIII

74 *Ollantaytambo: Aerial view. (Credit: Servicio Aerofotográfico Nacional, Lima.)*

tive center, a depot, or even as a combination of two or more of these functions.[7] The site was easily defended, since the spurs of the Cordillera rose to the north and on the south was the ravine of the Pisco River.

An adobe wall protected the central complex with its structures surrounding a large trapezoidal esplanade, probably used for drilling troops and for certain festivals. Tambo Colorado's trapezoidal shape may have been determined by the narrowness of the site and an understandable desire to expand the useable area to its maximum by taking advantage of a projection of the bluff overlooking the river.

The esplanade divided the buildings into two groups (Plate No. 73). The principal structure of the north group was an almost square edifice about fifty-five meters on each side, formed by several chambers around an interior court. This building, the most important of the group, had painted walls and was decorated with adobe friezes in geometric figures of great beauty and simplicity, some of which are still preserved. Perhaps this was the residence of the chiefs (Urteaga, 1939). Bordering the esplanade on the south, southwest, and western sides are ruins of several more structures of undetermined use.

The structural style predominating in Tambo Colorado is typically Inca with rooms arranged around regular courts. These quarters were probably used as housing for the general population or the troops.

OLLANTAYTAMBO

Ollantaytambo is a classic example of Inca urban planning (Plate No. 74). From the railroad that runs through the Urubamba River Valley between Cuzco and Machu Picchu, we can see cultivated terraces and the fortifications that once defended the city, as well as the Inca and modern constructions of Ollantaytambo on the plain below. The ruins of the Inca city and modern town are about seventy kilometers from Cuzco. Ollantaytambo is one of the few smaller urban centers of South America to be inhabited continuously since before the arrival of the Spaniards.

Ollantaytambo served several functions. First of all it was an important advance outpost in Cuzco's defense system. The Urubamba Valley was a natural entrance to the heart of the Empire and to Cuzco, and the Inca were ever fearful of advances by the jungle tribes that they never succeeded in dominating. This accounts for the many ruins of forts we see on the sides of the mountains forming the Urubamba Valley, which testify to the importance the Inca assigned to this threat. Another possible function of the zone of Ollantaytambo was that of producing food for the capital, aided by the valley's excellent climate and favorable environmental conditions. At some point in its brief history during the Inca period, Ollantaytambo must also have served as a royal residence, for the quality of construction, efficient water services, fountains and buildings such as small temples were not usual in Inca towns of small size. Judging by the style of stone construction found at the site, Ollantaytambo was established early in the second half of the fifteenth century, perhaps even begun during Pachacuti's reign.

The Patacancha River divides the city into two sectors, different in function and layout. East of the river lay the city proper, trapezoidal in shape, while west of the Patacancha was probably the reserved district. The outline of the ancient city shows a checkerboard pattern with an emphasis on perfect symmetry. Most of the interior streets cross each other at almost right angles, although an intentional deviation at the beginning of the third row of blocks, running north to south, allowed the street system, and therefore the city, to accommodate itself to the elongated terrain bounded by river and mountains (Plate No. 75).

Four longitudinal streets, the principal ones with central conduits, ran parallel to the river. Only the doors of the houses opened on to them. Eight transverse streets, each about two meters wide, lacked conduits. The slightly open pattern of the checkerboard gave the blocks different trapezoidal proportions. Each block was surrounded by a high blind wall belonging to two dwellings, and each dwelling was built around a central patio with its rooms opening onto it. I suppose that during the Inca Period, these houses were occupied by administrators in charge of harvests and some artisans, since their layout and type of construction makes it seem unlikely that farmers would have occupied them. The farmers probably lived in small huts on the cultivated terraces or in mod-

75 *Ollantaytambo: Ollantaytambo is the best example of Inca planning as applied to a small town which has survived to our times. It was built on both sides of a tributary of the Urubamba River, to serve as a defense for the Cuzco Valley, a residential center, and perhaps as a storage center for the Inca capital. The gridiron layout is clear in the residential sector which is still occupied today. The reserved district was on the other side of the river. On the sides of the mountains were many terraces, fortresses, and residential complexes for the chiefs. (Credit: Guía del Cuzco.)*

LEYENDA   LEGEND

1– INCAHUATANA
2– CAMINO AL INCAHUATANA
    ROAD TO INCAHUATANA
3– EDIFICIOS DEL NOROESTE
    BUILDINGS OF THE NORTH WEST
4– FUENTES
    FONTAINS
5– ESPLANADA DE LOS MONOLITOS
    MONOLITHS' ESPLANADE
6– ANDENERIAS AGRICOLAS
    AGRICULTURAL TERRACES
7– ANDENERIAS FORTIFICADAS,
    FORTIFIED TERRACES
8– ESCALINATAS
    STAIRWAYS
9– HABITACION: CENTRAL
    CENTRAL ROOM
10– GRUPO DE HABITACIONES DEL SUDOESTE
    SOUTHWEST GROUP OF ROOMS
11– EDIFICIO DE LA ESPLANADA
    ESPLANADE BUILDING
12– ESPLANADA
    ESPLANADE
13– ÑUSTATIANA
    PRINCESS THRONE
14– PLAZA MANYARAQUI
    MANYARAQUI'S PLAZA
15– PRIMER ADORATORIO
    FIRST ADORATORY
16– SEGUNDO ADORATORIO
    SECOND ADORATORY
17– TERCER ADORATORIO
    THIRD ADORATORY
18– CUARTO ADORATORIO
    FORTH ADORATORY
19– ACEQUIA DE REGADIO
    WATER CONDUITS
20– BAÑO DE LA ÑUSTA
    PRINCESS BATH
21– RIO PATACANCHA
    PATACANCHA RIVER
22– POBLACION ANTIGUA
    OLD CITY
23– AREA COLONIAL Y MODERNA
    COLONIAL AND MODERN AREA

est structures clustered in nearby agricultural villages.

This sector had its own plaza. Like many other Inca plazas, the space was outlined by the smooth walls of the buildings. Ollantaytambo's engineers did not try to emphasize this space with any structure of a different size. Its area equalled two rectangular blocks, bare of construction, so that the overall proportions made almost a square.

A second plaza, outside the planned sector, was connected to the other part of the city by a bridge. This may have been added during Colonial times, although in the Inca Period some similar connection between the old city and the reserved district must certainly have existed. The Plaza in the reserved district was a large space enclosed on three sides by rectangular buildings, perhaps storehouses, and by a wall on the fourth side. It was open at the corners. Located west of the river where other structures of a military, religious, and civil nature were built at different elevations above the plaza or on the terraced mountainsides, the Plaza probably served social and religious functions and was the scene of most of the town's activities.

HUÁNUCO VIEJO

Huánuco Viejo, in the present Department of Huánuco, was a highland administrative center built by order of The Inca. The ruins are located on a treeless plateau near the Huallaga River, 3,600 meters above sea level. The site was briefly occupied by the Spaniards in 1539 and described by Estete, Sancho and Cieza de León and subsequently by several historians and travelers. Between 1962 and 1965 the Institute of Andean Research, the University of Huánuco and the University of Wisconsin undertook a field investigation directed by John Murra which advanced our knowledge of provincial life in the Peruvian highlands at the time of the Inca expansion (Murra, 1962a).

Huánuco Viejo was one of several centers with administrative and storage functions in the Tawantisuyu. It was probably built during the early years of the second half of the fifteenth century in a territory previously occupied by the Yacha, the Chupacho, and the Wamali. After the conquest the area was resettled with *mitimaes* or colonists. It is interesting as a measure of Inca policy toward the people they conquered, that the three tribes mentioned above retained their settlements and ceramic styles while the Inca built their own centers and installations where they used the imperial type of architecture, masonry, and pottery (Thompson, 1968).

As in other Inca cities the main urban element of Huánuco Viejo was its huge central plaza, measuring 350 by 550 meters approximately (Harth Terré, 1964; Morris and Thompson, 1970; Shea, 1966) (Plate No. 76). The Inca highway crossed the city and the plaza in a southeast-northwest direction. In the center of the plaza was a low stone platform. It was identified as the *ushnu* or *usnu*, and its use was related to administrative and political functions (Morris and Thompson, 1970; Shea, 1966). The entire plaza was surrounded by a residential district. To the east was the best housing complex, frequently called the Incahuasi or Casa del Inca, not only the largest building of the city but the one with the best stone masonry in the Inca imperial style. The design is also typically Inca, with long narrow buildings forming internal courtyards.

To the north and south of the plaza were residential districts of inferior quality. Houses were built with *pirka* or undressed field stone, and the fine masonry of the eastern section is absent. Many streets provided access from these districts to the plaza but they do not form a regular pattern as in Ollantaytambo. The street layout in the residential districts is quite irregular although some straight stretches are found. Houses are smaller than in the eastern section but also built around a courtyard. To the north a fine housing sector was built following a more regular design. The design of the northwest and western districts is less clear but both seem to have had the same irregular layout.

Some six hundred meters to the south of the plaza were the storehouses. Morris and Thompson report that the storage zone at Huánuco Viejo, overlooking the site from a hill to the south, contained 497 storehouses and a series of thirty nonstorage buildings apparently connected with storage processing and administration (Morris and Thompson, 1970). Storehouses were built with *pirka* walls and all had a drain. Those in Huánuco Viejo had a volume capacity of 37,900 cubic meters and were probably used to store potatoes, oca, sweet potatoes, and other highland crops as well as maize and perhaps charcoal. (Morris and Thompson, 1970). Storehouses were frequently located in relation to provincial centers, such as Huánuco Viejo, Vilcashuaman, and Pumpu, a smaller

76 *Huánuco Viejo: General plan of Huánuco Viejo. (Credit: After a design by Emilio Harth Terré.)*

0　　　100　　　200　　　300　　　400　　　500　　MTS.

Inca center south of Huánuco Viejo.

Incahuasi, Tambo Colorado, Ollantaytambo, and Huánuco Viejo are all examples of the use of Inca urban concepts. In these cities, the repetition of certain principles of architectural composition probably guided the overall urban organization. Inca engineers leaned toward centralized groupings and massive architecture of stone, or stone and mud if built in the highlands. We see an obvious geometric arrangement of the structural groups and especially of individual edifices. Buildings generally surrounded a small patio or plaza and each of them was formed by a series of chambers or multiples of elements which determined the proportions of the structural group. Multiple elements in Inca construction were more regular and better proportioned than in Chan Chan and other coastal cities. As these elements only appear in Inca urban planning after the Empire's first contacts with the coastal peoples, their origin may be found in the Chimú influence rather than in the highlands.

I know of no study that has attempted to systematize those principles used by Inca architects in planning new settlements.[8] Such principles certainly existed, and knowledge of them would reveal new aspects of the Empire's administration, politics, and social and economic structure. I can not believe that the few examples of planned settlements that I have included are the only ones built by the Inca. The large-scale colonization programs, because of their intensity and the enormous territory involved, undoubtedly necessitated the planning of entire towns to accommodate groups of colonists in orderly and secure surroundings. A planned administration in the broadest sense, despite its well-known technical limitations, would not have left to chance the location of such important productive elements of the population. Although it is next to impossible to prove, my belief is that the stabilization of set frontiers must have been another reason for establishing military groups, since from a strategic point of view, Inca territory was vulnerable even in areas near the Empire's principal centers.

The urban examples discussed date from the last eighty years of the Inca Empire. These cities were of varied dimensions, and only Ollantaytambo, and perhaps Huánuco Viejo, were occupied permanently by civilian groups. Whatever their functions may have been, there is no doubt but that they were wholly or partially preconceived and that a systemization of layout was emphasized.

MACHU PICCHU AND ITS
NEIGHBORING TOWNS

Between 1940 and 1942, several sites near Machu Picchu in the Cordillera Vilcabamba were explored (Fejos, 1944). During their examination of an area about thirty square kilometers, members of the expedition discovered the ruins of six villages and such minor remains as forts and isolated houses. They also found evidence that they were dealing with one of the most populated regions of Inca Peru.

Some villages, Inty Pata and Wiñay Wayna for instance, covered large areas (Plate No. 77). Fejos considers the six largest sites to have been cities and expresses surprise that they could all have been occupied at the same time in such rugged, mountainous terrain (Fejos, 1944). The towns communicated with each other by roads that followed the contours of the mountain sides or by steps when drops in elevation were too severe. Between Inty Pata and Choquesuysuy, separated by only 1,200 meters in a direct line, was a seven hundred meter drop. Villages were built on stepped terraces on the sides of mountains, apparently seeking the proximity of some ravine with a flow of water, since in the majority of these sites, we find an efficient water supply system for domestic use and crop irrigation, and even drainage ditches to carry off waste water.

Dwellings were generally rectangular, grouped either in complexes around an open space or strung out in rows, the latter arrangement being better adapted to narrow terraces. It is hard to calculate the number of inhabitants of these groups of dwellings which, in no sense of the word, can be called cities. None of the sites has been excavated, not even superficially, and only a few of the housing groups have been partially uncovered. Judging by their ground plans and the number of chambers they show, we assume that these were villages inhabited by several dozen families who farmed the land on the nearby terraces.

The number and size of such terraces indicates that the greatest agricultural activity was concentrated around Inty Pata, Phuyu Pata Marka, Choquesuysuy, and Sayac Marka. Religious activity seems to have been centered at Chacha Bamba. Fejos suggests that this site was a shrine with its buildings clustered around a great carved granite rock near the river (Fejos, 1944). For reasons we have yet to learn, the various villages specialized in specific, mutually complementary functions.

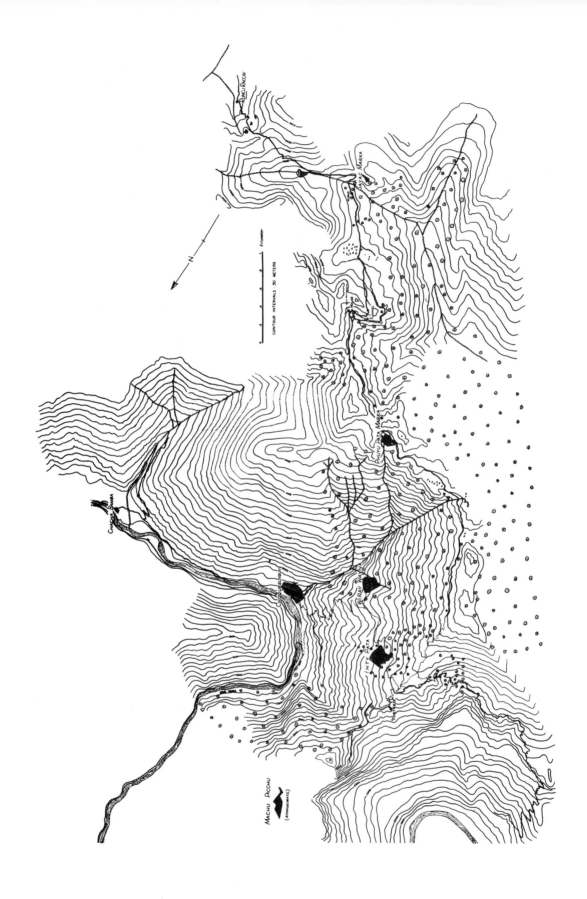

Less than two kilometers in a straight line north of Inty Pata stands Machu Picchu, unquestionably the most famous of all Inca ruins and those most visited by tourists. Nevertheless, Machu Picchu is not a good example of the Inca Empire's characteristic pattern of human concentration, that is, the planned city, the administrative center, or the agricultural village. Its size and limited number of dwellings, moreover, show it to be a city of much sparser population than the great cities of the Empire. It appears to be an intermediate specimen, the origin and function of which have been the subject of endless and fantastic speculation.

Machu Picchu's inhabitants, like those of the Empire in general, did not know writing, and the only way to establish the city's time of occupation and the characteristics of its people is through a comparative examination of its architecture, ceramics, textiles, and artifacts. Valcárcel states that not only are the ceramic and structural remains Inca, but that the architectural style itself, involving the use of huge rectangular stones, polished and perfectly joined, as well as the use of trapezoidal niches, is similar to that of Cuzco (Valcárcel, 1964). Other such Americanists as Rivet, Kubler (Kubler, 1960), Mason (Mason, 1957), Velarde (Velarde, 1946) and Pardo (Pardo, 1941) all agree with Valcárcel that Machu Picchu belongs to the Inca Period.

Bingham, who devoted several years of his life and a number of books to the study and interpretation of these ruins (Bingham, 1930, 1951), always believed that Machu Picchu's origin was pre-Inca and declared that the Inca had set forth from this site, which he connected with Tampu-Tocco, the legendary rock with the three openings, on their migration in quest of fertile lands (Bingham, 1930).

Machu Picchu was occupied during the Inca Period and abandoned in the years following the Empire's disintegration, probably after 1572 (Valcárcel, 1964). For centuries it lay forgotten except by a few local farmers. Around 1870, during a visit to Ollantaytambo, the French explorer, Weiner, was told of other important ruins in the region. Weiner's informants described a "Huaina Picchu" and a "Matcho Picchu," arousing his curiosity to the point where he decided to make a last excursion toward the east rather than continue his intended route to the south

77 *Machu Picchu: Plan of a sector of the valley of the Urubamba River near Machu Picchu. (Credit: Fejos, Paul: "Archaeological explorations in the Cordillera Vilcabamba, Southeastern Peru"; Publication in Anthropology No. 3: Viking Fund; New York, 1944.)*

78 *Machu Picchu: Aerial view of the promontory showing Urubamba River below. (Credit: Servicio Aerofotográfico Nacional, Lima.)*

79 *Machu Picchu: Lateral view of housing sector and terraces on prom-ontory between the two peaks. (Credit: Servicio Aerofotográfico Nacional, Lima.)*

(Weiner, 1880). After leaving Ollantaytambo, Weiner crossed the high sierras and descended into the valley of a tributary of the Urubamba River, penetrating this valley beyond the town of Santa Ana and unwittingly bypassing the famous city. Finally, forty years later, in 1911, the ruins of Machu Picchu were discovered by Dr. Hiram Bingham, who began his systematic study of the city the following year.[9]

MACHU PICCHU

Machu Picchu was not a large city, nor did it have a great number of inhabitants. Its uniqueness lies in the site its builders chose and in the marvelous, still visible harmony between the architecture of different structural groups and the topography (Plate No. 78).

The city stands on a promontory 2,700 meters above sea level, surrounded to the north, east and west by the deep canyon of the Urubamba River, which runs four hundred meters below at the present time. Built on the east side of the promontory where the slope was gentler, the city lies between two peaks, Huayna Picchu to the north and Machu Picchu to the southeast. The entire top of the promontory and large parts of the sides of the mountain were artificially modified by terraces, some used for farming and others as bases for buildings (Plate No. 79).

Today we can reach Machu Picchu by road or the railroad that runs along the Urubamba Valley. From the small station, a bus makes the trip to the ruins. In Inca times, paths led along the mountainsides or over the peaks to avoid crossing the torrential rivers. A high road, passing the ruins of several forts, connected Machu Picchu to neighboring towns and to Cuzco.

The only entrance to Machu Picchu was through a well-defended gateway at the far southwestern end of the city. Two walls, about one hundred fifty meters apart, protected the city to the south, the only side from which attack was to be feared. The east and western sides were guarded by precipices hundreds of meters deep, and on the north, the passage to the equally inaccessible peak of Huayna Picchu consisted of a narrow, easily defended footpath. Between the two walls on the south side

80 *Machu Picchu: Top of promontory with houses; streets separate structures; hillside heavily terraced. (Credit: Servicio Aerofotográfico Nacional, Lima.)*

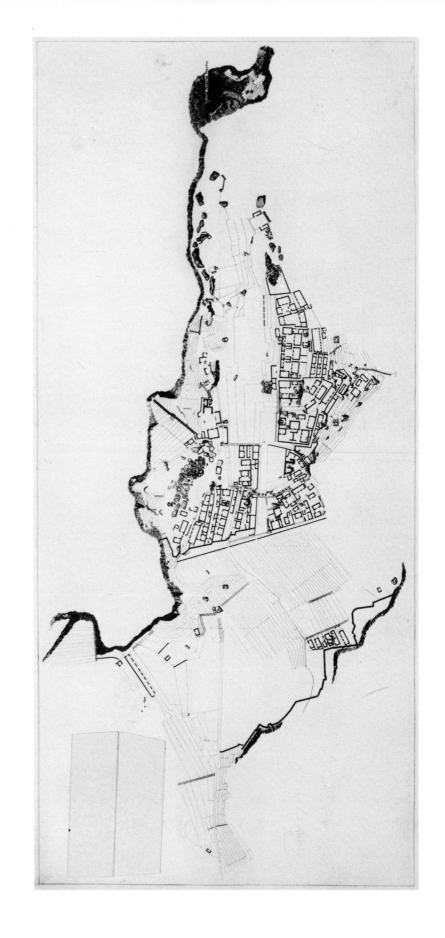

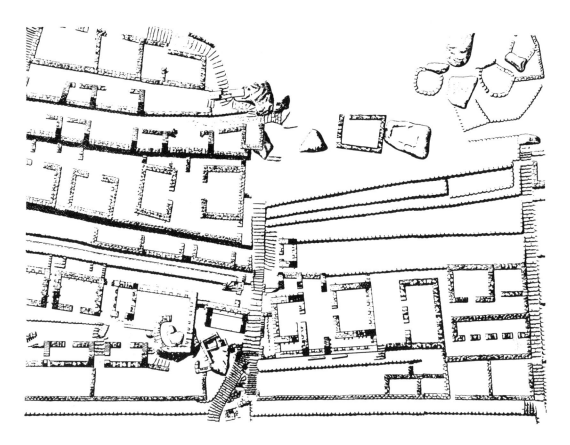

PLAN OF THE CENTRAL PART OF MACHU PICCHU

On the right is the King's Group. In the middle, the Stairway of the Fountains. The Royal
Mausoleum Group is in the lower left, with the Semicircular Temple and the Most
Beautiful Wall. The Upper City is partly shown in the upper
right corner. The Snake Rock region is also
in the upper right corner.

82 *Machu Picchu: Plan of the central district of Machu Picchu. (Credit:
Bingham, Hiram, Machu Picchu,* Citadel of the Incas, *Yale University
Press, New Haven, 1912.)*

81 *Machu Picchu: General plan of the ruins. (Credit: Fejos, Paul: "Archeological explorations in the Cordillera Vilcabamba, Southeastern
Peru"; Publication in Anthropology No. 3; Viking Fund; New York,
1944.)*

was an extensive zone of farming terraces where a few house ruins have also been found.

Machu Picchu lacked an overall plan. Its development was based on the repetition of certain similar elements which varied in accordance with the different sectors of housing that made up the city. Topography was the dominant factor in the distribution and relative hierarchy of the various sectors, and Machu Picchu's builders made skillful use of it. The site resembles an immense elongated receptacle with open ends, and its sides—in this case the eastern and western edges of the promontory—rise abruptly above the central depression which contains a broad, open space that obviously served as a plaza (See Plate No. 79).

The sectors are differentiated by the quality of their stone architecture and by the size of the houses. Archeologists usually hold that the south sector was where the nobility lived, as it occupies the highest position and its ruins show the best quality of building. It was bounded to the southeast by the inner defensive wall and by a parallel roadway with flights of stairs descending from the main gateway in a northeast direction to the lowest level of the city. This housing sector was formed by five or six parallel rows of dwellings having one, two, or three rooms. These rested on terraces and were separated by narrow streets running into stairways that led down to the central plaza (Plate No. 80). The larger houses formed the lowest row, where the most important social group in the city may have lived. This is the complex that Bingham calls the King's Group.

The eastern part of the city was occupied by three sectors built at different levels. The northernmost sector of the three lay along the plaza's eastern terraces, several hundred meters above its floor. It was composed of repeated complexes formed by a covered entrance and a courtyard around which were built four or five chambers which may have housed the same number of families. Surrounded by narrow streets, these units were interconnected from the inside, literally constituting a block of houses. From its simple architecture and estimated density, I believe this to have been a popular district[10] (Plate No. 81).

The layout of the city's central district was the most disorderly of the housing groups, but its quality of construction is inferior only to that of the King's Group. Bingham describes this district as characterized by in-

83 *Machu Picchu: Aerial view showing housing sectors, terraces, and flights of steps connecting the lower and upper sectors of the city on both sides. (Credit: Servicio Aerofotográfico Nacional, Lima.)*

tricate and ingenious stonework (Plate No. 82).

At the southeast corner of the city was a sector built against the inner defensive wall, extending down along the terraces to a level lower than that of the other sectors. The group was made up of thirty chambers, some forming courtyards, others in rows, and a few bearing no relation to the rest of the compound. This is generally known as the working class sector.

The northern sector of the city, where the promontory narrows to form a saddle leading to Huayna Picchu, had no housing, but we find a number of terraces and some large-sized constructions. Huayna Picchu is a formidable peak north of Machu Picchu that looms like an immense, isolated sculpture. On its summit, archeologists have found the remains of terraces and some structures.[11]

The total number of chambers in Machu Picchu is under two hundred. Considering that some of these may have been used for storage or public uses, a less than average population is indicated, even for a medium-sized Inca city. As all buildings are of stone, it is unlikely that we will discover more chambers in the future. There is no doubt, however, that a good proportion of the agricultural population serving or dependent upon Machu Picchu lived in the outlying areas rather than in the city itself. It is impossible to calculate the city's population with the data we have. Judging by the number of chambers, it could not have been greater than 1,000 or 1,200 persons. As Machu Picchu's function in the machinery of the Empire is still obscure, it is even difficult to conjecture about the degree of occupation in the areas outside the city walls, which must have been thickly settled.

As we see the city today, the lack of thatched roofs and the deteriorated condition of the masonry in most of the houses accentuate the importance of the terraces, small plazas and the central amphitheater. The visitor is also made aware of the prominence of stairways in the city. Bingham considers them Machu Picchu's outstanding feature and counts a hundred in all, both large and small, within the limits of the citadel (Bingham, 1930). There were stairways of one hundred and fifty steps and others of only three. Some were monolithic like the steps near the tower, but whatever their size, they were all of stone (Plate No. 83).

The whole western sector of the city, between the large central plaza and the terraces that run from the west of the promontory down to the river, is formed by a long, narrow, natural elevation which Machu Picchu's inhabitants transformed by building platforms at different levels to support various religious constructions. On the summit of this western hill, to the north of the series of small plazas, terraces and structures, stood a small temple around the sundial stone, or *intihuatana,* where, it was said, the priests symbolically tied the sun to a stone pillar with a mystical cord to prevent its disappearance—and with it the end of mankind.[12]

South of the religious sector was the Sacred Plaza, unquestionably Machu Picchu's most original and interesting urban feature. This was a semienclosed space of slightly trapezoidal form, surrounded by three stone structures. One of these had three windows, a rare feature which has given rise to yet another myth about the origin of the city as they suggest the Tampu-Tocco of legend with its three openings, through which Manco Capac and his brethren passed. The plaza is raised and closed off from the large surrounding central space, but if we look to the west, we are rewarded by a splendid view of the Urubamba Valley and the mountains beyond. Machu Picchu's central amphitheater was so irregular that we might describe it as natural. Closed to the north, east and west by hills completely altered by terracing, its only long vista was toward the southeast. The terraces may have had a religious significance as, perhaps, did the plaza itself, since it is doubtful that it served as a marketplace. Whether by chance or by design, this central space gives the impression of having been left unfinished.

A variety of functions have been attributed to Machu Picchu: a fortress built by order of one of the last emperors for the defense of Cuzco; a center of learning for the ruling class; an agricultural town; a religious center, an *acclahuasi,* or house of the chosen women, and the city of the pre-Inca kings. These are only some of the possibilities I have encountered in the course of this study, and there must be many more. Machu Picchu's role in the Inca Empire is still the subject of speculation, but the following points stand out. The number of terraces indicates that agriculture was of prime importance and that the population may have been self-sufficient. Machu Picchu's connections with Inty Pata, Phuyu Pata Marka and the other neighboring settlements constituted a simultaneously colonized and cultivated region. The city's population was small. Fortifications appear as outgrowths of the topography rather than dominant architectural features.

— *NOTES ON · 13* —

1. ATAHUALLPA WAS BORN in the province of Quito, one of the last regions to be added to the Inca Empire by his father, Huayna Capac. When his army engaged the forces of Huascar, his stepbrother, outside of Cuzco, in what was to be the decisive battle of the civil war, Atahuallpa was in Cajamarca. These events took place in 1532, a few months after the arrival of the Spaniards in Peru. Following the death of his father in 1527, Atahuallpa had administered the Empire's northern provinces, and he did not begin the war against Huascar until about 1530. Cajamarca was apparently a supply center for the Inca army (Jerez, 1938).

2. Harth Terré attempted a reconstruction of the central district of Cajamarca. As a result of his research he concluded that the main square of Cajamarca was trapezoidal in shape. The temple was in one corner and facing it were three sheds. The whole square was surrounded by a high wall cut by several doors. From one of the corners a narrow street led to a smaller, rectangular square, also surrounded by walls (Emilio Harth Terré, *La plaza incaica de Cajamarca,* El Comercio, Lima, September 30, 1962).

3. I made the calculation based on the plan of Vilcashuaman published by Victor Von Hagen in *Realm of the Incas*, New York, A Mentor Book, The New American Library, 1959.

4. The Inca centers on the south coast of Peru had rectangular or trapezoidal plazas (Menwel, 1959).

5. According to Poma de Ayala, there were royal *tambos* (tampu) along the emperor's roads as well as other, simpler rest-houses of one room used by ordinary travelers. Some *tambos* even had several individual rooms. *Tambos* serving as provision depots were large enough in some cases to house and feed an army on the march. The ground plan and method of construction were standardized, and the buildings' low height, symmetrical proportions, and solidity are representative of the utilitarian architecture developed by the Inca.

6. The occupied area must have been at least twenty hectares, although not all of it had buildings.

7. Lanning writes that Tambo Colorado "was remotely near being a city" (Lanning, 1967); Zuidema calls it a "colonial city" (Zuidema, 1969); Menzel defines it as a big Inca site (Menzel, 1959).

494

8. The best attempt that I know is by Zuidema (Zuidema, 1969) and in a series of articles written by Donald Thompson, individually or in collaboration (Thompson, 1969; Morris and Thompson, 1970).

9. "It fairly took my breath away. What could this place be? Why had no one given us any idea of it?" and later he adds, "Could this be 'the principal city' of Manco and his sons, that Vilcapampa where was the 'University of Idolatry' which Friar Marcos and Friar Diego had tried to reach? It behooved us to find out as much about it as we could" (Bingham, 1951).

10. None of the three housing groups I have mentioned should really be called a sector. The northern group barely covers 4,000 square meters and according to the number of chambers which might have been used as lodgings, I do not think that more than twenty families could have lived there.

11. Bingham believed that Huayna Picchu was used as a signal station (Bingham, 1951). This belief was confirmed by Valcárcel who adds that the peak of Huayna Picchu played "a principal religious, magic and military role" (Valcárcel, 1964).

12. Bingham refers to this elevation as the Intihuatana hill (Bingham, 1951). The stone pillar to which Machu Picchu's Priests of the Sun tied this heavenly body each year is a stupendous monolithic rock cut to form a pillar, a trapezoidal prism on an almost square base.

·14

NORTH AND SOUTH ANDEAN CITIES IN SOUTH AMERICA

□ **14**

DURING THE EIGHTY YEARS PRIOR to the conquest of their Empire by the Spaniards, the Inca incorporated a series of neighboring peoples who had attained the cultural level necessary for their rapid integration and consequent participation in the socio-political, economic experiment directed from Cuzco. Inca territorial ambitions were limited to the central section in the west of the South American continent. The elongated shape the Empire acquired after successive conquests by Pachacuti, Topa Inca, and Huayna Capac was directly dependent on the outermost boundaries of the conquered peoples' lands.

The central highlands of the South American Andes will always be associated with the Inca Empire. The Inca may have conquered the arid coast of the Pacific Ocean, but theirs was basically a highland culture. It was there that their society was born and took form, and there too the final fate of the Empire was determined. The conquest of Ecuador's southern coast, the coastal valleys of Peru, northwest Argentina, and the vast deserts of northern Chile that extended down to the fertile central valleys seems to have been prompted by political and strategic considerations, perhaps even cultural, rather than by economic motives.[1] The peoples living on the outer borders of the Inca Empire only occasionally constituted a regional economy, since their meager technological level and environmental limitations did not permit the development of any economy on a larger scale. The Inca Empire had nothing to gain, then, by incorporating under a single government cultures so far removed that their only possible contribution to the Empire's economy would be products not only difficult to transport, but similar to those already produced in more accessible, populated regions.

499

In other words, after the conquest of the highlands, the scene of the Inca's first imperialist experiments, it was a logical step, from many aspects, to the subsequent incorporation of the urban cultures on the north and central coast of Peru where technology and the level of living were higher than those of the inhabitants of the highlands. Nevertheless, we cannot discard the possibility that Cuzco's first expansionist efforts were motivated by certain undetermined deep needs which may well have been endowed with religious significance.

Given other geographical circumstances, the Inca Empire might have limited itself to the highlands, but militarily it became impossible to disregard the danger represented by two flanks thousands of kilometers long and difficult to defend. Although by the fifteenth century the coastal civilizations had lost the thrust of the previous centuries (Mason, 1957), the Inca, skillful strategists after Pachacuti's reign, could no longer ignore the existence of the Chimú, Chancay, and Chincha cultures occupying respectively the north, central, and southern coastal valleys of Peru.

The Inca also attempted to conquer the jungle that lay east of the highlands, and at the end of the fifteenth century or early in the sixteenth they may have promoted colonization along the jungle's edge (Bonavía and Ravines, 1969). It remains uncertain if this incursion was inspired by the same political, strategic, economic, and cultural reasons that had motivated the Empire in its first stages of expansion, whether the Inca merely wanted to suppress the primitive, warlike peoples who posed a continual threat, or if it was an attempt to establish a better line of outer defenses to protect the heart of the Empire against hostile advances. The Inca launched several expeditions into the jungle in which they achieved only partial successes or defeats. During its brief occupation, the Inca's jungle frontier suffered a series of advances and withdrawals. Cuzco soon became aware that further efforts in the jungle offered no compensations and that they could not hope to suppress an enemy who melted away into a hostile territory, vast and far different from the Inca's familiar highlands. For this reason, the Inca attitude toward the jungle peoples during the last years of the Empire seems to have been defensive rather than offensive.

The conquests of Huayna Capac, the last of the fifteenth century's great emperors, reflect the plan that his predecessors must have established. Huayna Capac's long reign spanned more years than those of his celebrated father and grandfather together. He received the Empire at its height of power, already composed of almost all those peoples who had reached the urbanist stage in western South America. This meant that all South America's urban cultures, except the Chibcha and other groups of Colombia, formed part of the Inca Empire when Huayna Capac inherited it in the year 1493. Huayna Capac's attitude was quite different from that of the preceding rulers. He conquered the Chachapoya who lived east of Peru's northern highlands, he controlled a pocket of the swampy coast of southwest Ecuador and the Island of Puná which had been left aside during his father's campaigns, and he conquered the Cayambi of northern Ecuador. When he reached the Ancasmayo River, which today separates Ecuador and Colombia, he fixed the Empire's northern frontier (Rowe, 1946; Mason, 1957) (See Plate No. 45, page 151).

All Huayna Capac's conquests tended to consolidate those regions already incorporated into the Empire. Territorially he added only a fifteenth or twentieth part of its total area. An attempt to conquer the Chibcha meant extending, by some thousand kilometers, a northern frontier that was already more than two thousand kilometers from the capital. To pursue conquests southward involved confronting the Araucanians, one of the most warlike and courageous peoples the Inca had encountered. To the east lay the jungle and toward the southeast roamed the belligerent nomadic tribes of the Bolivian and Paraguayan Chaco. There seemed no justification for new conquests, and for these compelling reasons, apparently, Huayna Capac did not undertake any.

In the outer reaches of the Empire, where the influence of Inca culture was felt late and possibly less intensely, existed cultures that had evolved within smaller geographic limits and with more restricted possibilities in reaching the urbanist stage. This chapter deals with cultures such as these, incorporated late into the Inca Empire or which remained on the fringe of its expansion.

AGRICULTURAL TOWNS ON THE EDGE OF THE PERUVIAN JUNGLE

The decade following 1960 saw a number of expeditions to the rim of the jungle of north and central Peru. These confirmed the existence of agricultural towns built and occupied during the Late Horizon. Two principal groups were reported: the ruins of Abiseo in the Department of San Martín, northeast of the city of Pataz in the northern Andes, and a group of settlements in the far north of the Department of Ayacucho, in the central Andean region (Bonavía, 1968a, 1968b).

The ruins of Abiseo lie in a rainy, mountainous area with severe climatic contrasts between day and night. This is the region known as Selva Alta, formed by abrupt ridges and deep valleys, with altitudes over 2800 meters above sea level. There are no maps of the area. Although access is difficult, we find pre-Columbian and Colonial ruins there, and some forty-five kilometers directly northeast are the remains of the Colonial town of Pajatén, founded by missionaries in the eighteenth century (Bonavía, 1968a). The declivity toward the east is steep so that the ruins of Pajatén are 400 meters above sea level, a difference of almost 2500 meters from Abiseo. The entire zone is encompassed in the basin of the Huallaga River, with its tributaries running through gorges between ridges covered by thick vegetation. The existence of Abiseo's ruins was revealed by inhabitants of Pataz in 1964. They were explored in 1965 and 1966, but only preliminary clearing and reconnaissance work was accomplished. In June of 1966, Bonavía dug a test excavation, subsequently publishing his findings (Bonavía, 1968a). He found the remains of an agricultural town or settlement consisting of sixteen structures of circular shape and some rectangular structures erected on the top of a partially leveled ridge, the entire complex of ruins covering an area somewhat larger than one hectare.[2] The circular structures were undoubtedly dwellings, built with slate slabs held in place by clayey mud. The larger structures had a diameter of about 14.8 meters and the smaller measured less than four meters across. Roofs were probably conical in form, made of straw resting on wood frames, perhaps with a wooden central support. Some houses were decorated with geometric motifs and larger-than-life carved wooden heads. On the plan, the structures show no overall order. The only criterion seems to have been to respect the natural slope of the site, which obliged the builders to dig into the hillside to level the floors of their houses.

The housing area was modified by terraces, which were also built for cultivation. The site lacks natural sources of water and no water storage systems were found. One unnamed river, a tributary of the Abiseo which, in turn, flows into the Huallaga, runs hundreds of meters below the site. Access to this river is difficult. On the other hand, the site is healthy and, possibly, much safer than others nearer water.

The ruins of five agricultural towns, discovered in 1963 on the fringe of the jungle in the Department of Ayacucho, also belong to the Late Horizon. Three of these towns, Caballoyuq, Matukalli, and Raqaraqáy, were built in the transition zone between the high grassy plain, or *puna*, and the jungle's edge. The other two, called Condorucchko and Uchuihuamanga, lie in the zone of Puna. The zone forms part of the basin of the Mantaro River, a tributary of the Apurimac. These five towns were explored by Guzmán and Bonavía in the middle of 1964 (Bonavía, 1968b, 1969). Their size and population are estimated to have been greater than those of Abiseo, as the number of structures recorded varies between about 300 in Caballoyuq and 50 in Matukalli and Raqaraqáy (Bonavía, 1969), indicating a maximum of around 1500 inhabitants and a minimum of 250. All five towns were inhabited at the same time, probably by a predominantly agricultural population, as suggested by the number of terraces found in the area, especially around Condorucchko and Uchuihuamanga. Pathways wound through these towns and some had canals to facilitate drainage from the abundant rainfall of the region.

In common with the ruins of Abiseo, the remains of these five settlements show a similar urban pattern and are located on the eastern slope of Peru's Cordillera Central at altitudes which range from 3400 to 3600 meters above sea level (Bonavía, 1969). The structures are circular, though smaller in diameter than those in Abiseo. The larger ones are no more than eight meters across and the smaller may measure around four meters. Walls were of slate, although granite was used occasionally. Due to the topographical variations existing in the sites chosen, the houses were half sunken to achieve a horizontal floor level. Roofs were probably conical and made of straw over a wooden framework. The overall arrangement of these structures was irregular, and in none of these towns do we find streets other than the pathways between buildings.

All these ruins belong to the period of Inca expansion and seem to be connected with a process of colonization along the jungle's edge, possibly initiated by settlers from other regions (Bonavía and Ravines, 1969). We can then assume that the advance and retreat of the frontier of civilization of the Inca Empire must be explained by factors other than a result of environmental changes related to soil depletion. Apparently the exhaustion and loss of cultivable land—and hence the conquest of the lower jungle—were subject, up to a point, to the existence of a central power having a tightly controlled administration during the last years of the Empire. Once this central power was broken, control of the outer regions crumbled rapidly and it is probable that in less than a hundred years weeds once again invaded the agricultural terraces (Bonavía and Ravines, 1969).

CITIES OF THE ATACAMA PUNA

The north coast of Chile is as arid as that of Peru, but without the latter's natural protections. The scarce rivers running into the ocean from the Cordillera constitute the sole surface source of fresh water. As they dry up frequently and carry a small volume of water, they permit irrigation of limited areas only. Fishing, too, must not have been easy for the Pre-agricultural inhabitants of the region, as the sea is heavy and gathering shellfish difficult (Bird, 1946a). Conditions grow gradually worse descending from the wide coastal valleys of northern Peru down toward the south. Chile's north coast is inhospitable and uninviting. Conditions then improve somewhat farther south where there is more water and certain vegetation.

The people originating here progressed toward agriculture and ceramics, but they could never have done without fishing and shellfish gathering to complete their diet. Corn, squash, potatoes, beans, and cotton were their main crops. Bird points out that the scarcity of arable soil impeded the growth of large settlements, while other factors even further limited their cultural development (Bird, 1946b).

The principal coastal sites were Arica, Taltal, and Punta Pichalo (Bird, 1946a; Mostny, 1954). In Arica a site was found dating from the Pre-agricultural Period that yielded a find of fishhooks made of shell, stone or bone, bone harpoons and fishing implements. Occupation of the site lasted until agriculture and such crafts as pottery, basket making, and textiles reached a development in keeping with the inhabitants' precarious possibilities.

Contemporaneous with this coastal culture, in the high *punas* of the modern Chilean provinces of Tacna, Arica, Tarapacá, Antofagasta, and Atacama, and of the Argentine provinces of Salta and Juyjuy developed a culture of shepherds and farmers known as the Atacameño (Bennett, 1946c). Its existence partially coincided with the Classic Period of Tiahuanaco, but little is known about its earlier stages. It lasted, under various influences, up to the Inca period (Bennett, 1946c). With the Diaguita who lived to the south, these people constituted the two most evolved groups of pre-Hispanic Chile.[3]

The Atacameño culture developed in the Atacama desert, an inhospitable, cold and arid *puna* at an altitude of over three thousand meters above sea level in the latitude of the Tropic of Capricorn. Today it is one of the largest and most desolate deserts of America, with vast open stretches and mountains with snow-capped peaks reaching over five and six thousand meters high. Plant and animal life is scarce. Before the sixteenth century, the principal animals were the llama, guanaco, alpaca, and possibly the vicuña (Gilmore, 1950). The Atacameño gathered llamas and alpacas into sizeable herds.

Although the level of humidity may have been greater during pre-Inca centuries, the Atacama desert or *puna* was and is today a region which requires irrigation for any kind of agriculture. It is not surprising, then, that in the face of such difficulties, the inhabitants of the *puna* congregated in small groups around the infrequent oases and other favorable places. Utilizing irrigation, they cultivated maize, quinoa, squash, potatoes, cotton, and other plants common to the Peru-Bolivian highlands.

The Atacameño were active merchants. Salt, which they supplied to part of the Bolivian territory (Serrano, 1947) and to the Diaguita, tobacco, and llama wool were the principal products that they exchanged for dried fish and shells from the coast and for the coca grown in the Bolivian valleys. Atacameño textiles found on the *puna* are superb, and they also carved gourds with geometric incisions and naturalistic motifs (Serrano, 1947), but they never developed stone architecture and sculpture, arts in which their neighbors to the north excelled.

Certain of the Pre-agricultural Atacameño settlements were still inhabited. The most important of these were in the Chilean Province of Antofagasta and in the Argentine Province of Juyjuy. The smaller settlements, of limited size and population, were built near those fields irrigated by a flow of water that encouraged the continuous establishment of a restricted number of farming families. Zapar and Peine were two such settlements. Other small settlements, such as Turi, San Pedro de Atacama, and Lasana, were situated in relation to a larger, well-fortified town built in a strategic place (Mostny, 1949). These settlements may have enjoyed local autonomy.

Smaller settlements, like Zapar, had no defensive walls. Others, like Peine, were no more than a cluster of dwellings and storehouses along both sides of a street. The small settlements were generally more spread

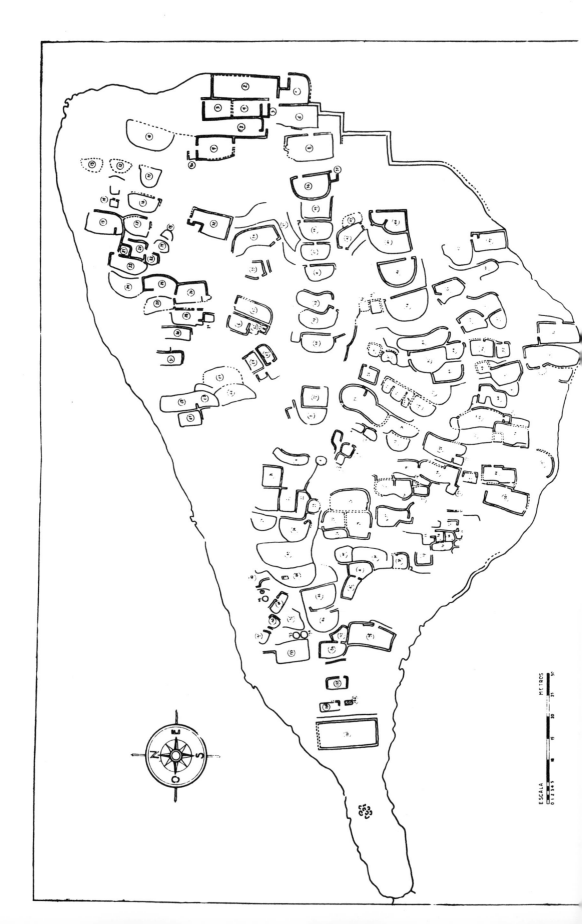

ESCALA   METROS
0 1 2 3 4 5   5   10   15   20   25   50

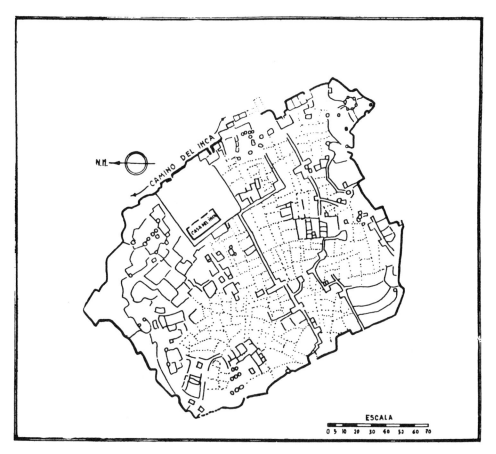

85 *Turi: Turi was a station along the Inca road which may have had pre-Inca origins. An almost square plaza and some streets were imposed on the tortuous layout characteristic of fortified Atacameño settlements. (Credit: Mostny, Grete; "Ciudades atacameñas"; Boletín del Museo Nacional de Historia Natural; XXIV: Santiago de Chile, 1948.)*

84 *San Pedro de Atacoma: The* pucará *of San Pedro de Atacoma is a good example of the fortified groupings built as residential centers and places of refuge in the northeast of Chile and northwest of Argentina during the centuries prior to the Spanish Conquest. (Credit: Mostny, Grete; "Ciudades atacameñas"; Boletín del Museo Nacional de Historia Natural: XXIV: Santiago de Chile, 1948.)*

out than the fortified towns and consequently had a lower population density.

The fortified town, or *pucará*, was a grouping characteristic of the north of Chile and of northwest Argentina. The *pucará* of San Pedro de Atacama offers a good example (Plate No. 84). It was built on a hilltop of difficult access and was enclosed by a wall. Dwellings were constructed on artificially leveled terraces according to two basic designs: the individual chamber and the chamber with an adjacent silo. The houses had almost no household appurtenances, and those objects found were simple utensils for domestic use. In none of the known settlements do we find evidence of an intentional urban layout. The structural shapes, rounded, rectangular or irregular, determined a series of alleys and broad spaces that could not qualify as actual plazas.

The ruins of Lasana lie in the Loa River valley. In this *pucará*, Mostny reports that the agglomeration was so large that access to houses situated on different levels was made through the roofs of those lower down. The final phase of urbanistic development, which apparently never fully evolved, was the construction of two-storied houses (Mostny, 1954). The reason for this concentration lay in the topography. A *pucará* would gradually fill in the entire top of a hill and then had limited possibilities to spread out without embarking on difficult and costly works of terracing and defense. Like other settlements concentrated in walled cities, an upward development inside the intramural area seems to have been the Atacameño's solution to their natural demographic growth.

A different case, perhaps unique among Atacameño settlements, is presented by Turi, where we find suggestions of an earlier concept (Plate No. 85). Built on a hill rising some thirty meters above the valley floor, Turi was a settlement of rectangular shape, covering an area of scarcely four hectares and surrounded by a stone wall almost three meters high. Turi may have ranked higher than the other Atacameño settlements. Two elements of its layout are important for the area. The first of these, possibly introduced during the pre-Inca period, is found in the two parallel streets running in a northeast-southwest direction, following the natural slope of the terrain and connecting what appears to have been the only gateways to the city. The second element was a walled plaza, called by Grete Mostny the Plaza of the Inca, almost square in shape and enclosed by an interior wall that bounded it on three sides, its fourth side being the defensive wall of the city. I do not know if a free space had previously existed in that same location, but the fact is that the Inca road, which in these latitudes measured about four and a half meters wide, passed tangent to Turi on its northeast side. To judge by its appearance, Turi's plaza may well have been created in answer to the commercial needs growing out of Inca occupation of the territory since it does not seem to have been employed as an urban element by either the Atacameño culture or by the peoples of northwest Argentina. The plaza's space was ample, an area of some two thousand square meters, and was completely closed except for two gateways, one of which connected with the road and the other with the principal street. Inside the plaza stood an unusually large rectangular structure which may have served as a *tambo*, or inn.

The rest of the city was crossed by short, narrow alleys, running in the habitual disorder of Atacameño settlements. Houses, on the other hand, had a more regular shape than those in the other settlements and *pucarás* mentioned. At the crossways of the alleys formed by the blind building walls, many small irregular plazas were formed. In all Atacameño cities the houses were built with roughly cut stone held together by mud mortar. Roofs were flat and later gabled, made of branches and mud over *algarrobo* and *chañar* beams, the only trees of a flora characterized by its scarcity and lack of variety.

CITIES OF NORTHWEST ARGENTINA

The northwest of Argentina is composed of the mountainous zones of the provinces of Juyjuy, Salta, Tucumán, La Rioja, Catamarca and the north of San Juan. It comprises several subareas (González, 1963). The Argentine *puna* to the north and west, a prolongation of the deserts and cold plateaus of Chile and Bolivia, is known as the Atacameño region. To the south appear a series of mountain-ringed, elongated valleys with flat floors that remain dry throughout the better part of the year. This is the Valliserrana region, of scarce rainfall, and it is here the Diaguita culture developed. To the south and east is the Selvas Occidentales region that extends to the vast plains and semi-tropical forests, and here the Candelaria culture evolved (Heredia, 1970). Embedded in the spurs of the Cordillera like a giant natural roadway runs the Quebrada de Humahuaca, the continuation of other deep ravines of southern Bolivia's mountain system. The climate of the northwest is dry. Altitudes are generally over 2500 meters above sea level. In this region, partially marginal to the development in the principal nuclear area of South America, there evolved a series of agricultural-herding cultures that had reached their urban stage only a few centuries before their lands were incorporated into the Inca Empire. This region had never been densely populated. Places favorable for human habitation were relatively few and small in size.

Despite the environmental limitations imposed on these cultures of northwest Argentina, they produced some ceramic works and stone and bronze pieces of artistic interest. Their architecture, like their sculpture, was simple and evinced a little-evolved technology. Their cities never achieved great importance, most of them remaining farming villages, some sizeable, and *pucarás* or fortresses.

Archeological information is as yet incomplete. We find few vestiges of the hunters and gathers who once lived in the region during the Pre-Ceramic Period. During the first millennium B.C., the techniques of pottery making and agriculture were known here, but among the principal cultures that employed them, such as the Condorhuasi in the Calchaquí valleys, the El Alamito culture (Núñez Reguiero, 1970) in the modern Department of Andalgalá in Catamarca Province, and the Tafí culture in the Province of Tucumán, no traces of the influence of Chavín artistic style are found. Tiahuanacoid influence is reflected in the agricultural culture of La Aguada (González, 1964) which developed between 650 and 850 A.D. in the eastern part of Catamarca Province and in the north of La Rioja. Artistically, this was the most advanced culture of the Middle Period. It was replaced by local cultures with a certain stylistic unity, outstanding among which are the Santa María culture, the Belén, and Tilcara and Pozuelos in the Puna. Belonging to this Late Period, lasting from approximately 900 A.D. up to the Conquest, are some of the Atacameño centers we have already discussed. Around the year 1480, during the reign of Topa Inca Yupanqui, Inca armies invaded and conquered the region. One of the Inca roads ran across the *puna* from Tupiza and Talina in a north-south direction, passing west of the Quebrada de Humahuaca, where another road may have existed. The road turned toward the southwest, running by Cachi, Angastaco, Punta Balasto, Quinmivil, and Calingasta to reach Uspallata, from where it crossed the Cordillera to arrive at the central valley of Chile. Another road, along the Pacific coast, touched at the Pica oasis and turned southeast to reach Turi and San Pedro de Atacama, turning again to the southwest past Copiapó and El Molle to join the first road in the Aconcagua Valley (Strube, 1963).

Although Inca culture had existed in northwest Argentina for barely half a century, we see its presence in the construction of *tambos* and fortresses, the exploitation of certain ore deposits, the gradual diffusion of the Quechua language and in the forms and decorative styles of pottery and bronze objects. While Inca influence is observed throughout the northwest, it was more dominant in certain zones of San Juan Province, such as Barrealito, Paso de Lámar and Angualasto, as well as Chilecito in La Rioja Province and such forts as the Pucarás of Andalgalá in Catamarca and Tilcara in Juyjuy Province.[4]

Between the Middle and Late Periods, in the subarea of the Argentine *puna* and immediate subareas, a population growth occurred which was reflected in the predominance of conglomerated nuclei of settlements rather than the dispersed nuclei characteristic of the Early and Middle Periods.[5] These conglomerated towns were more compact, removed from the agricultural fields and many of them were naturally or artificially walled.[6] Of this order were such towns as Tastil in the Quebrada del Toro in Salta Province and Los Amarillos in the Province of Juyjuy among others. Tastil, or Santa Rosa de Tastil, a hundred kilometers from the city of Salta, is one of the most important settlement nuclei of northwest Argentina. Eric Boman, who studied the region in 1901 as a member of a Swedish scientific mission directed by Erland Nordenskiol, and again in 1903 as a member of the Créqui Montfort and Sénéchal mission, described the site and published a map of it.[7] In 1967, an interdisciplinary team from the University of La Plata began a systematic study and restoration of the ruins.[8]

According to its researchers, Santa Rosa de Tastil was a permanently occupied urban center between the years 1349 and 1418 approximately, or before the Inca invasion. Extending over an area of twelve hectares, the ruins cover the top and sides of a hill rising two hundred meters above the level of the ravines of the Las Cuevas and Tastil Rivers, in all, some 3200 meters above sea level. Boman estimated the town's population at a minimum of three thousand inhabitants, assuming that each of the eight hundred enclosures was a dwelling occupied by four persons. The University of La Plata team calculated the population at somewhat more than 2200 inhabitants. This center corresponds to the Late Period which, from the ceramic remains and funerary practices found, probably belonged to the Santa María culture originating in the valley of the same name in the center and north of Catamarca Province. Nevertheless, the site's cultural

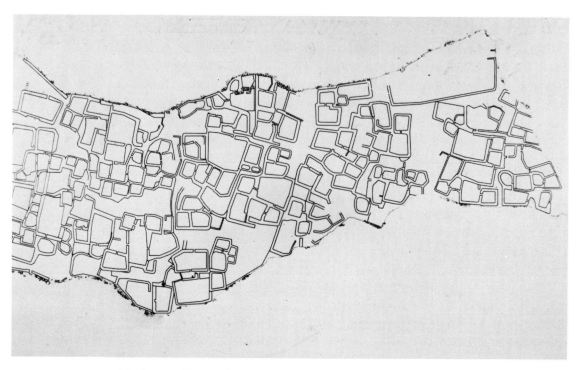

86 *Loma Rica: Plan. (Credit: Collection Muñiz Barreto, Museum of La Plata, Buenos Aires.)*

characteristics indicate that the inhabitants of Santa Rosa de Tastil had contact with the cultures of Quebrada de Humahuaca, the Puna and the Calchaquí valleys. This led Cigliano and Palma to believe that Santa Rosa de Tastil had been a reception and distribution center for products, which made it into an important commercial center.[9]

The houses were built with stone walls. Although the layout of the settlement was imposed by topography, we can distinguish principal streets opening onto large unbuilt spaces or plazas, as well as secondary streets.

The Santa María culture occupied the valleys of Catamarca Province during the Late Period, extending to the provinces of Tucumán and Salta. Linguistically it belonged to the Diaguita group. For the region, it represented a culturally advanced people who valiantly resisted the foreign invaders. They utilized irrigation, built roads and agricultural ter-

87 *Cerro Mendocino: Plan. (Credit: Collection Muñiz Barreto, Museum of La Plata, Buenos Aires.)*

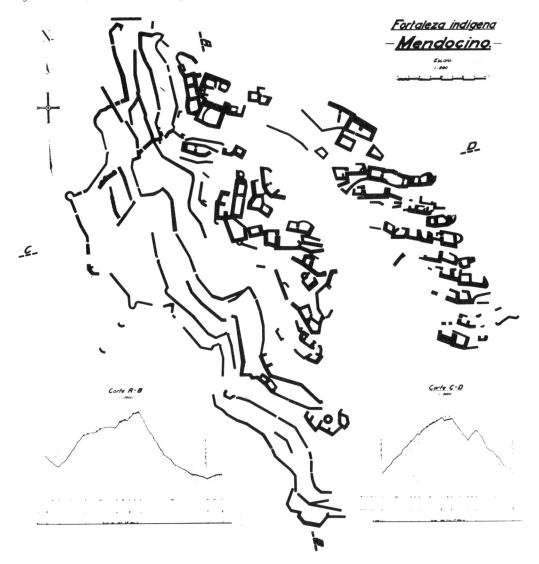

races, and lived near their fields in large settlements such as Loma Rica, Quilmes, and Cerro Mendocino. Probably none of these settlements was as large as Santa Rosa de Tastil. The ruins of Loma Rica, for example, are composed of some 250 enclosed spaces, and assuming an occupancy of four persons per enclosure, or house ruin, we would have a probable population of one thousand inhabitants (Plate No. 86). Cerro Mendocino was a fortified town located northwest of Punta de Balasto. Its ruins lie on a hilltop about 420 meters above the Santa María River and some 2600 meters above sea level (Plate No. 87). The site had natural defenses and its inhabitants reinforced it with no less than seven lines of walls made of mortarless stone slabs, embrasures, posts, and other defensive systems, but unlike other *pucarás,* Cerro Mendocino seems to have been permanently occupied (Anthropological Institute of the University of the Littoral, 1960). The ruins are in good condition. The distribution of the houses, built with double walls of stone slabs filled with rubble, follows the slope of the hill. Their size and shape vary. Almost rectangular enclosures predominate, consisting of two or more intercommunicating units and a single exterior door, although we also find circular house ruins. The size of those almost rectangular enclosures excavated and reconstructed is about 16 to 18 square meters. Roofs were straw and branches resting on a wooden framework supported by several central posts.

Inhabitants of the Santa Maria culture were farmers. Maize, beans, peanuts, potatoes, and varieties of squash were their main crops. They resorted to extensive irrigation with surface waters and constructed dikes and drainage ditches. To augment the cultivable area, they built terraces, preferably near the settlements where they lived. They also raised llamas and alpacas, building up large herds. The Santa María urns, used for the burial of children, are of considerable size and are characterized by their conical base and cylindrical body with decoration based on the stylized human face. Works in stone, on the other hand, were small, mainly plaques and circular disks. Metallurgy was advanced and varied in form, comprising utilitarian objects and those intended for religious rites, arms, and decorative articles.

The Belén culture was contemporaneous with the Santa María with which it shared similar cultural traits, both in its economy and ceramic forms, while remaining inferior in metallurgic development. This culture was centralized in the Hualfín Valley, south of the Santa María Valley, extending up to the boundaries of the modern provinces of Catamarca and La Rioja.

In the Quebrada de Humahuaca we find the ruins of several fortified nuclei. The best known and studied of these are the Pucará de Tilcara (Debenedetti, 1930), the Huichaires *pucará* (Casanova, 1934) and the Hornillos *pucará* (Casanova, 1942).

The remains of the Pucará de Tilcara cover an area of 170,000 square meters. We have abundant evidence to indicate that it was densely occupied. The ruins lie on a hilltop named after the ravine, and the only accessible side was protected by walls which, in some places, formed stepped lines of defense.

The Pucará de Tilcara had an irregular outline imposed by the terrain and by the necessity of constructing terraces to support the houses. The builders fully utilized the entire site, but the greatest crowding of structures was to be found at the summit. Streets and alleys were formed by the spaces left between houses, with some straight stretches of ground determined by the alignment of several buildings on a terrace. A study of the layout shows the existence of principal streets up to four meters wide that joined the various districts. Narrow, irregular secondary streets branched off from these main thoroughfares.[10]

Small plazas with no determined use abound, formed by widenings in the streets or at crossroads. Houses were generally rectangular, seldom exceeding sixteen square meters in size. A few houses had round or irregular ground plans, and some were even semi-subterranean. Undressed fieldstone masonry, held in place by its own weight, was the predominant building technique. Doorways were small and roofs were made of cane and mud laid over beams.

In all known *pucarás*, a basic scheme has been observed, probably the result of the growth imposed by having to absorb an increasingly large number of settlers. We do not know, however, if all houses of a *pucará* were continuously occupied. Possibly, the only permanent population was one composed of a stable garrison, the leaders, and those of the inhabitants engaged in various activities in the immediate vicinity.

THE CHIBCHA

The basins of the Bogotá and Sogamoso Rivers, tributaries of the Magdalena, constitute one of the most favorable regions for human life in South America. The climate encourages agriculture with no need of irrigation, the soil is fertile and encircling mountain chains provide natural defenses for this high savanna in the middle of Colombia—a propitious place for the evolution of an advanced culture.

The Chibcha, or Muisca, occupied this region up to the arrival of the Spaniards, establishing forty-two settlements in which were concentrated some of the urban functions characteristic of most pre-Columbian cities.

Chibcha territory stretched over some 40,000 square kilometers and was inhabited by over fifty tribes grouped in five principal confederations. The *caciques*, or chiefs, of each tribe elected the chief of the confederation and could also depose him. The Zipa, the principal confederation, dominated the southern territory, the central region was controlled by the Zaque, and the northeast zone by the Iraca confederation. These three confederations, the largest, grew to number 300,000, 240,000 and 175,000 persons respectively. Smaller confederations together totalled another 260,000 people (Kroeber, 1946).[11] The Chibcha were essentially farmers, as well as skillful goldsmiths, if bad builders. They left almost no monuments. Their cities were defended with palisades and their houses had walls of cane and mud with straw roofs. Size alone distinguished palaces and temples from the dwellings of the general population.

Chibcha cities served as centers of commercial exchange and seats of government for the confederation chiefs. Among the most important cities were Teusaquillo, belonging to the Zipa confederation, which may have been the Chibcha capital on which site the Spaniards built Bogotá; Muequetá, also Zipa, now modern Funza; Sugamuxi, an Iraca city where Sogamoso stands today; Hunsa, a city of the Zaque confederation, is the modern Tunja; and Boyacá and Zipaquirá, among many others (Kroeber, 1946).

1. IN SEVERAL PASSAGES, Garcilaso refers to the Inca rulers' plans to send their relatives to educate these idolatrous peoples and instruct them in the laws and ways of the Empire. Also, according to Garcilaso, local *caciques* petitioned the Inca Emperor to teach them the religion of the Sun and to incorporate them into the Empire.

2. Bonavía included a topographical survey of the ruins of Abiseo in the report of his expedition (Bonavía, 1968a).

3. Apparently the Atacameño were influenced stylistically by the more advanced art of the Diaguita and the Inca (Steward and Faron, 1959).

4. In reference to Inca influence, see the work of Alberto Rex González, *Arqueología de San Juan*, Etnia, No. 6, pp. 16-28, Olavarría, July to December, 1967. The most up-to-date information on northwest Argentina and northern Chile can be found in the works presented at the Symposium "Area Andina Meridional," coordinated by Alberto Rex González and Víctor Núñez Regueiro, Actas del XXXVII Congreso Internacional de Americanistas, Vol. II, pp. 1-369; Buenos Aires, 1968.

5. Marta Ottonello de García Reinoso and Guillermo Madrazo offer a good synthesis in *Instalación y economía prehispánica tardía en la puna argentina y su borde*, in Hardoy and Schaedel, 1969.

6. Ottonello de García Reinoso and Madrazo, *op. cit.,* p. 86.

7. Eric Boman, *Antiquités de la région andine de la République Argentine et du désert d'atacama*, Imprimerie Nationale, Paris, 1908. A description of Tastil is included on pp. 367-378.

8. The team directed by Dr. Eduardo Cigliano is preparing to publish the results of their work. A general report has been published in article form; Eduardo M. Cigliano and Nestor H. Palma, "Santa Rosa de Tastil. Una ciudad prehispánica en la provincia de Salta," Autoclub, Año XI, No. 58, pp. 79-84; Buenos Aires, May-June, 1971.

9. Cigliano and Palma, *op. cit.,* p. 84.

10. All *pucarás* had a disproportionate number of streets and alleys as a result of the topographical limitations to a more rational arrangement. The Pucará de Tilcara had 1600 linear meters of streets (Casanova, 1946).

517

11. Calculations of other authors vary. Sierra has calculated a total population varying between one and two million persons (Sierra, 1959). Steward and Faron estimate that there were only 300,000 inhabitants at the time of the Spanish Conquest (Steward and Faron, 1959).

15

GENERAL CONCLUSIONS ON PRE-COLUMBIAN CITY PLANNING AND DESIGN

□ 15

PRE-COLUMBIAN URBANISM had its own individual characteristics which distinguished it from that which evolved during the same centuries in other continents. As it was produced with human and technological resources indigenous to the American continent, we can isolate it from foreign influences and analyze it within the context of the regional cultures which advanced it and with its particular geography.

The evolution of these pre-Columbian urban cultures was interrupted at the beginning of the sixteenth century by Spanish conquest and colonization. Spanish culture was superimposed on Indian cultures. This produced a gradual fusion whereby native cultural traditions lost much of their essential character, resulting in hybrid cultures that rarely exhibited the vitality and authenticity of the originals. Nor was this fusion total. Two worlds coexisted throughout the Colonial Period. The Spanish world prevailed in the cities, represented by imported urban models where the new institutions were most securely entrenched. While in rural villages and in the country, the Indian world retained many of its values and its psychology, these were being partially adapted under pressure of Spanish institutions and a work regime imposed by force.

Indian urbanism was continued into Colonial urbanism (Hardoy, 1965). Its influence might pass unnoticed if we do not analyze in detail the reasons which led the early conquistadors and governors to select certain locations for America's first Spanish cities. The pre-Columbian cultures' basic criteria for urban planning and design were not respected by the Spaniards who brought quite different concepts of city life and urban architecture. In spite of this, for political and economic motives, the Spaniards made use of the principal Indian cities to establish the Col-

521

ony's first regional urban centers.

Two aspects of the pre-Columbian urbanization process are fundamental. First, the territory occupied by Indian urban cultures encompassed no more than eight percent of those twelve million square kilometers of Latin America where Spanish is the official language, or less than five percent of the total territory, if we include Brazil, Haiti and foreign colonies. Second, urbanization came about in almost simultaneous stages in Mesoamerica and South America. The fact should be emphasized, however, that although there was some exchange of products between Mesoamerica and South America during the Classic and Post-Classic centuries, perhaps earlier, and logically there must have been a parallel interchange of ideas, we have no proof that adoption of similar urbanistic criteria in both areas signifies a direct influence of one upon the other.

From the time sequence, we can deduce that urbanistic trends took root in the north and spread southward. Furthermore in the different important stages of the process—agricultural villages, ceremonial centers, early cities and the Great City—Mesoamerican urbanism, especially in central Mexico, appears as a more mature and better integrated process than that in South America.[1] At present, it is hard to draw valid conclusions on this subject. Although much progress has been made in recent years in establishing the periods of occupation of different sites, there has been no corresponding increase in the number of surveys of cities, sectors of cities and complexes of monuments, despite the excellent studies of the past decade in San Lorenzo, Tenochtitlán, Teotihuacán, Tikal, Dzibilchaltún, Chan Chan, Huánuco Province, Altar de Sacrificios, the Oaxaca region, and in Tiahuanaco, to name a few.

We cannot, then, speak of a single pre-Columbian urbanism that evolved following the stages mentioned. In site utilization, monumental perspective, linear progression, urban planning and organization in general: use of the street-passageway and certain urban forms, the grouping of architectural masses, and the concept of urban spaces, we find coexisting—regionally and in time—quite disparate urbanistic conceptions: Mayan and Teotihuacan, Aztec and Tarascan, Chimú and Inca. Different criteria also coexisted in the utilization of sculpture, bas-relief, murals, and color, even within a noticeable similarity in use of architectural forms.

PLANNED AND UNPLANNED CITIES

Almost all Classic and Post-Classic cities were unplanned and grew up spontaneously.[2]

A significant number of principal cities seem to have had their origins in an agricultural settlement, or the construction of a temple or more elaborate ceremonial complex around which houses and other architectural groups subsequently rose. Such seems to have been the case of Teotihuacán, Tula, Monte Albán, Xochicalco, El Tajín and, of course, Tenochtitlán in Mesoamerica. South American examples of this process can be found in Tiahuanaco, Pachacamac, and Cuzco. In other words, unlike contemporaneous European cities, in which a castle, a river crossing, the intersection of two roads or the presence of a spring might be factors that spurred the growth of an urban center, among America's Indian cultures in general the determining agent was a combination of ecological and religious motives.[3] In this sense, the prevailing reasons in America seem to have been similar to those existing in Sumeria in the third millennium B.C., when that country constituted a religious unit with one principal religious center.[4]

Water, of course, was the predominant factor in the choice of location for pre-Columbian cities in the different stages of their evolution. All large Indian cities were located near permanent sources of water and their inhabitants worked to improve water collection and storage facilities.

Examples of cities planned from their beginnings are few and belong almost exclusively to the Middle and Late Horizon in Peru. These cities conceived from the ground up were smaller in size and population than unplanned ones and were, in general, centers with a specialized function, rather than regional capitals where a series of complex and varied activities were concentrated. Nor did any preplanned cities attain political or commercial importance among pre-Columbian cultures. Viracochapampa and Pikillacta, for example, situated and planned during the Middle Horizon, were built to serve specific functions. Ollantaytambo, though small in scale, provides the best known example of Inca, or Late Horizon urban planning.[5]

In the three centers mentioned, builders adopted a plan of complete regularity, if not to the point of forming a perfect checkerboard. This gridiron plan, as we find it applied by the Greeks following the reconstruction of Miletto or the Romans in their colonies, as it was put to use in the French *bastides* or in small villages in northern Spain and in military encampments during the Reconquest, and as it was employed elsewhere in Europe during the Middle Ages or by the Spanish in America, was not used by South America's Indian cultures. Nevertheless, the interior arrangement of Chan Chan's citadels and that of other urban centers on the north and central coast of Peru during the intermediate Late Period, Ollantaytambo's plan, the division of lots in the *chinampa* districts around Tenochtitlán's island core, all indicate that Indian builders were aware of the organizing possibilities of a right-angled layout. There is no reason why the checkerboard as a city plan should not have been considered a natural solution for urban order adopted independently by cultures having no contact with one another.

Already during the Middle Horizon, in the irrigated valleys of the Peruvian coast and, perhaps, in the highlands, we find systems of grouping houses that might indicate an attempt at urban planning. During the period of Tiahuanacoid influence on the coast, walled enclosures of regular ground plan first appeared, becoming prevalent in the Chimú period. Chimú builders of that epoch on the coast based their cities on the use of multiples of these walled precincts, called citadels or wards. Although the city as a whole was not planned, we can see that the citadels themselves were, since they display a similar general orientation and a common pattern of inner organization. Chan Chan's scheme was repeated with variations derived from the particular sites utilized and with different scales and densities, in other south and central Peruvian coastal centers.

The Classic cities of central Mexico exhibit preconceived criteria which changed gradually to reach their maximum complexity in the Templo Mayor of Tenochtitlán. Among the Maya, though at first glance the temples comprising any of their Classic ceremonial centers seem to have been set out with no overall plan, we see that the builders worked with a subtle awareness of the characteristics of each site and a search for vistas and structural sequences of notable value in city planning.

It seems paradoxical, then, that in Maya cities, where buildings were grouped around the principal ceremonial center and secondary centers, no general organization was attempted. None appears among the Classic Maya, nor do we find any in Monte Albán, El Tajín, or Xochicalco where buildings seem to have been placed haphazardly according to the topographical exigencies of the site.

Teotihuacán undoubtedly offers the best example of urban planning during the Classic Period, not only for the monumental concept of its main axis, but for its application of a regular layout formed by similar blocks of housing complexes. In Teotihuacán, however, as in later urban centers of Central Mexico, these regularizing measures seem to have been incorporated in a city already partially built and inhabited.

During the Post-Classic centuries, and among the Aztecs in particular, these principles of order were imposed on existing cities, perhaps with the idea of using them as a basis for a gradual urban organization. The complexity of the functions concentrated in Tenochtitlán and the size of the population who either lived there or came into the city each day to visit its markets and attend ceremonies, would have been reason enough for an efficient urban layout. The Aztecs used a cruciform scheme of monumental scale that served as a point of reference for the rectilinear street network and, in the case of Tenochtitlán, the canal system as well. Where the two axes met, they built the ceremonial center of each city.

Aztec builders must have realized the importance of urban cartography, although no examples have come down to us. The Inca, on the other hand, perfected the use of models, a technique probably initiated by their predecessors on the coast. The Inca also relied on adequate technical personnel and specialized teams.

URBAN FORMS

The possibilities of a morphological classification of pre-Columbian cities before the arrival of the Spaniards are restricted by lack of specific archeological studies of the physical aspects of these cities, by the superposition of Colonial cities over the Indian ones in some fundamental examples, by the degree of durability of structural materials used by demographically larger pre-Columbian societies in their houses, and by urban cultures in general in any building other than temples, certain palaces and city walls, as well as by the predominantly rural way of life that prevailed. To further complicate matters, with some exceptions, economic and technical limitations make it feasible to explore only partial sectors of pre-Columbian cities, which yields an incomplete picture of their urban plan and the spatial relationship between their various components.

A preliminary classification that includes only sites of permanent or prolonged occupation, thereby excluding those built for defense purposes, might consist of:

Irregular Forms: This shape appears in the majority, distributed all over Latin America wherever an urban way of life emerged and throughout the successive stages of the pre-Columbian urbanization process.

The location of the principal Classic and Post-Classic cities was not, in general, determined by a site's defensible advantages. Security considerations rarely influenced the form of a city. Teotihuacán, El Tajín, the Maya centers in the Petén, Chan Chan and Cuzco, etc., were not directly defended.

The first agricultural villages probably belong to this group. Lacking a specific layout, streets were merely the spaces left between buildings, they had no predetermined orientation nor distinguishable pattern.

From the Classic and Post-Classic epochs, we find examples of walled cities and villages of secondary importance, whose builders made skillful use of topography for defense. In many cases, defensive enclosures were left incomplete, utilizing the natural inaccessibility of the site itself. La Quemada in Mesoamerica, Marca Huamachuco in northern Peru and Machu Picchu offer examples of naturally protected centers located in strategic places on certain advantageous elevations. Among instances of the irregular city form, whether imposed by the characteristics of a site or by general trends of growth, we would include the principal Classic and Post-Classic Mesoamerican cities and many belonging to the Middle and Late Horizon in the Peru-Bolivian highlands.

Tenochtitlán had a changing irregular form due to its unplanned peripheral expansion resulting from the addition of new *chinampas* to the city's central core (see Plates No. 24 and 25, pages 120 and 121). On the other hand, construction of the causeways connecting the center of the island with the mainland did not inspire a star-shaped growth. The *chinampa* land extensions were determined by variations in the lake's depth around the island and by a natural tendency to be as near as possible to the mainland on the closest side, the west, toward Tacuba.

Cuzco's growth also came about naturally and, although its districts seem to have sprung up spontaneously in a ring around the center, there is no overall radial-concentric scheme. In Tenochtitlán and Cuzco some elements were incorporated after both cities were already in existence as important political centers of considerable population. These elements introduced better order in the internal traffic, reinforced the locations of the respective centers, and may have influenced future planning.

Ovals: The circle is the simplest defensive shape to employ wherever the lack of topographical advantages makes some sort of protection necessary. As a form, it may have had symbolic implications as well. I do not know whether, in America's Formative Period, there were any circular villages in which the houses surrounded a central edifice, such as we find among the Slavs and certain African tribes.

The circular shape is common in the corrals built by shepherds or by nomadic groups in their encampments. The absence of herds in Mesoamerica, however, would exclude this as an origin for the circle-oval, nor did the corrals used to pen llamas and alpacas in the Peru-Bolivian highlands, and later on the coast, seem to have had this shape.

In Yucatán during the Post-Classic Period, coinciding with a time of great political unrest, the Maya built at least two centers which had an enclosing wall that formed an imperfect oval. It is not even certain that these city walls were actually constructed for defense purposes. Neither in Mayapán (See Plate No. 39 on page 175) nor in Chacchob do we find an interior city plan, and house ruins are distributed in the haphazard, low-density settlement pattern characteristic of the Maya.[6] The wall surrounded a housing zone which, in the case of Mayapán, covered an extensive area and had no particular order, the number of buildings increasing in density in the vicinity of the principal centers, the secondary centers, or the *cenotes*. The wall itself appears as an accessory element of dubious defensive value. Construction stops abruptly at the wall.

Regular Forms: Rectangular and octagonal shapes have been characteristic of planned cities for more than two thousand years in cultures at different stages of development and in various continents. In reality this has not been true of planned cities only, as in many cases centers with regular outlines emerged spontaneously, their organization a result of the systems of land tenure or existing irrigation canals, among other reasons. Urban planning is the premeditated act of cultures that have satisfied certain social and political prerequisites and which possess the necessary organization to carry it out (Hardoy, 1968). In pre-Columbian America, those cities we might classify as totally planned from the ground up are few and belong to the Middle and Late Horizon in Peru. As explorations progress, other examples may come to light, since analysis of the plans of

Viracochapampa and Pikillacta show two versions of basic ideas in urban planning. We find, for instance, the regular plaza surrounded by houses, the rectangular, slightly squared external shape, internal features such as *canchones* and other vacant spaces either square or rectangular, the rectilinear layout of city streets crossing at right angles and the outer city wall.

Flying in an airplane at low altitude along the lateral spurs of the Cordillera, you can see, half buried by sand, a number of regular-shaped centers of different sizes. I am not discarding the possibility that, coinciding with the expansion of their kingdoms or empires, the rulers of the Huari, Chimú and Inca may have embarked on a program of founding cities in different regions to serve as supply and colonization centers, acclimatization stations and administrative and military headquarters. These reasons are most logical, if we bear in mind the Inca's apparent objectives, their need to consolidate the economy and the Empire's expansionist policy.

In discussing planned cities in this chapter, I mentioned that among the pre-Inca cultures of Peru's north and central coast, possibly from the Middle Horizon, builders adopted an independent structural unit which they then repeated throughout a site, constituting the fundamental anatomy of a number of sizeable cities. Chan Chan is the best example of this (Plates No. 55 and 56, page 250), although Tocume on Cerro Purgatorio (Plate No. 64, page 242) and Pachacamac (Plate No. 54, page 225) among others, also belong to this group.

The unit or citadel was bounded on its four sides by a wall, usually rectangular in shape. We find the same use of terrain inside each unit, with individual variations in the percentages of ground used for the same purpose. We observe clear similarities in the rectilinear pattern of streets along which chamber dwellings were aligned, the zones designated as housing built around a plaza, the frequent location of *huacas* within the housing districts, and utilization of the remaining area in *canchones* with a considerable number of *pukios,* or large reservoirs. This use of regular-shaped units does not signify that the city itself had a defined form corresponding to that of its components, nor was there any overall city plan other than the adoption of a general orientation.

We have found no regular-shaped urban examples in Mesoamerica, with the single exception of a Post-Classic city of the Yucatecan Maya, all the more surprising for belonging to a people who did not utilize the street-passageway as it was known among other cultures. In Tulum, a rectangular wall seems to have been the determinant in a rectilinear pattern applied to an already existing center (Plate No. 40, page 117).

All examples in this group pertain to strongly centralized governments, and the Chimú and Inca use of stereotyped forms and layouts may well have been part of a far-reaching political policy.

Trapezoidal: A trapezoidal shape was generally determined by the limitations of the site where the town was built. Nevertheless, as palaces and urban sectors having this form were common among the Inca, the shape of Ollantaytambo, for instance, may have been due to other reasons. The housing district, or town to be exact, of Ollantaytambo was built in a trapezoidal form, yet with a rectilinear tendency in its street pattern, and although we find a trapezoidal plaza, this was situated in the characteristic centralized location of a checkerboard urban plan (Plate No. 75, page 290).

Other: Linear or star-shaped schemes were nonexistent. As in pre-Columbian America the technology of transport was undeveloped, linear groupings used to spring up along traveled routes or at crossroads. The star-shaped plan, on the other hand, is an advanced variant of the circle and its adoption was always due to defensive considerations among preindustrial societies.

A pure star-shaped form was unknown in American Indian cultures. Pre-Inca and Inca military engineers knew the value of bastions, as we see in the fortress of Paramonga in which a star-like shape is suggested (Plate No. 63, page 240). Paramonga was not a city according to the criteria used in this book, and may have been merely the residence of a garrison.

THE ELEMENTS
OF PRE-COLUMBIAN CITIES

In a contemporary city as in a baroque, medieval, Roman, or Greek city, the basic visual elements of the urban scenery are its structural volumes—isolated, forming complexes or grouped into blocks of various shapes—and its spaces, represented by streets, plazas, parks, and undefined areas. The combination of these two elements in a particular site and the relation that emerged, spontaneously or intentionally, between them and the topography, constitute the essential features of a city's physiognomy.

Various cultures, in different epochs, have utilized these three elements
—site, structural volumes, and space—to compose the individual urban
fabric of their cities.

The Street:

The importance, width, and layout of streets varied with cultures and
epochs. In Mesoamerica the first works serving the function of true
streets may have been the Maya causeways built as an approach to a ceremonial center or to some isolated structure of religious importance. This
criterion was undoubtedly that used by the Maya. In Tikal, this type of
paved way was built to unite the complex surrounding the Great Plaza
with Temple IV, with the Temple of the Inscriptions and with the North
Group (Plate No. 43, page 181). In addition, the causeway must have
been built to enhance the visual perspective of a particular temple, since
we find examples of pyramids with their corresponding causeways completely unconnected to the causeway system of a neighboring ceremonial
complex.[7] Spatially, these causeways seem to have been roads rather
than streets, despite their short stretch. Though bordered by a sort of low
wall, in no case do we find houses, religious buildings, or palaces set out
in a more or less continual line along their sides.

The concept of the street-passageway, of urban size and built to accommodate the movement of people and products, is clearly defined in
Teotihuacán. Like many other features that are found already in full
maturity in Teotihuacán this too probably had its antecedents. The
Avenue of the Dead, the two great axes and the streets that bounded the
blocks of houses on four sides fall into this category. They constitute the
oldest known example in America of a hierarchical street network. We
also find one case among the Maya in Tulum, where two or three parallel
streets suggest some kind of urban spatial arrangement.

Tiahuanaco's causeways may have served functions similar to those in
Teotihuacán. In South America, however, there was no contemporaneous
example equivalent to Teotihuacán's urban pattern. In Chan Chan and in
the cities of Peru's north and central coast, we find streets inside the citadels, but neither in Chan Chan, Tacume, Pachacamac, nor in any of the
principal Post-Classic centers was there a general plan of the complex as
a whole.

A hierarchical, ordered street network reappeared in Mesoamerica toward the middle or end of the fifteenth century, coinciding with the development of the Great City, as defined in the context of its time and place. Cuzco's street system was less clearly delineated than that of Tenochtitlán, where the population could move along the access causeways to the city center, or use the alternating secondary streets and canals. The visual impressions received by an Aztec traveling along such routes would have been much more spread out than those familiar to his contemporary in Europe or to today's pedestrian.

The explanation for the relative lack of importance given to streets in urban nuclei of such size and population as Tenochtitlán and Cuzco, may lie in the absence of a means of transport in pre-Columbian cultures which would have made them necessary. In Tenochtitlán, complementary systems of streets and canals were established for porters and canoes. The porters and llamas of Cuzco walked at the same pace. I am sure the volume of cargo which must have come into the markets of Tenochtitlán and Tlatelolco, as well as into those of Cuzco, could not conceivably have been as great, considering weight per capita, as that entering London or Paris during the same period. Even on the occasion of important ceremonies, the total absence of carts and mounts would have facilitated the efficiency of the existing street systems.

The Plaza:

The center of pre-Columbian life focused around plazas and ceremonial centers. Plazas offered a variety of activities, and in general there was a clear differentiation between those places used for religious festivals, commercial transactions and popular celebrations. This division of function was quite distinct, at least in the Indian cities the Spaniards saw.

The plaza of Inca Cuzco was divided into a ceremonial sector and a popular sector, separated by the canalized bed of the Huatanay River. In Tenochtitlán and Tlatelolco, the functions carried out in the religious precinct and those taking place in the plaza where the daily market was held differed markedly. Such a division may have prevailed in other principal Aztec and Inca cities, although in the smaller centers it seems more logical that both activities might have been merged in one place.

Since the remodeling of the centers of Cuzco and Tenochtitlán came about after the middle of the fifteenth century, coinciding with Emperor

Pachacuti's renovation project for the Inca capital and, in Mexico perhaps with ideas that Moctezuma I put into practice in the Aztec capital, we can speculate that the differentiation of urban functions came about at this time. On the other hand, little is known about the role of urban plazas during the Classic Period. All principal cities of this period had a number of plazas and in view of the different functions—administrative, religious, and commercial—concentrated in Classic urban centers, there may have been some degree of specialization among these plazas.

We find pre-Columbian plazas in a variety of shapes, sometimes totally independent of the form of the city and its plan. The regularity of the market-plaza of Tenochtitlán and the Templo Mayor's precinct bore close relation to the direction of the city's principal axes yet not to the pattern of the surrounding area. Cuzco's plaza took on, perhaps spontaneously, the shape of two trapezoids joined at their smaller ends. Apparently the plaza at Cajamarca was triangular and somewhat irregular. Bonbon's plaza was almost an open field.

In the planned ceremonial complexes following La Venta—Teotihuacán, for example—the right-angled pattern of urban composition was reflected in square and rectangular plazas.

Houses:

During the Pre-Classic or Formative centuries, there were probably no great differences among types of houses in the majority of rural villages. Class distinctions would have been represented in the greater proximity of those houses occupied by the ruling groups to the ceremonial centers.

In Classic Maya centers we find constructions called generically palaces, which may have served as the permanent or temporary residences of priests and other governing groups. The housing of the general population out in the country, in the territory of Maya expansion during the Classic and Post-Classic centuries, was not much different from that used today by people living in rural villages.[8] In the nunnery quadrangle at Uxmal, in the Temple of the Warriors and Temple of the Jaguars at Chichen Itzá, in Labná and other Maya sites, we find carved representations of the simple one-roomed house with straw roof as it is still built today.

In Teotihuacán, within what is considered its urban area along the Avenue of the Dead and in regular-shaped blocks, we find complex buildings such as the Viking Group, Atetelco, Zacuala and others that were evidently residences, called palaces by some authors. The district of Tlamimilolpa constituted an intermediate level of housing between the residences mentioned and the dwellings of the rural population.[9]

The incorporation of Indian states into two political experiments of such unprecedented scope as were the Aztec confederation and the Inca Empire gave rise to accentuated class distinctions, as has been pointed out in previous chapters. This differentiation is observed in the types of houses used by the ruling class as compared to those of the ordinary citizen.

The urban palaces of the Aztecs were described by the conquistadors, notably by Cortés and Díaz del Castillo, or represented in sixteenth century drawings. The basic floor plan seems to have been that of a series of chambers surrounding one or more plazas, depending on the importance of the palace. The residence of the last Aztec kings, like that of king Nezahualcóyotl in Texcoco, covered a considerable area and also served as a government seat, storehouse and for complementary functions. The general population lived in simple adobe houses, the more modest consisting of a single chamber, although there were others having several rooms designated as kitchen, bedroom and for other purposes.

From the time of Pachacuti's reign, Cuzco's central district was filled by the palaces of the emperors. These too were complexes of rooms intended for various functions. In the suburbs, not far from the center, the rest of the people lived in simple houses of perishable materials.

Architecture was not one of the outstanding arts in pre-Columbian cultures. Those buildings of greatest architectural value are found among the temples and other ceremonial edifices rather than the palaces. In its spatial aspects particularly, pre-Columbian architecture shows up the Indian builders' technical limitations. It was in the painting and sculpture integrated into the architecture where the great skill and inventiveness of anonymous regional artists reached one of the culminations in pre-Columbian art. We find prominent examples of this among certain Mesoamerican cultures in particular regions, such as central Mexico during Periods II and III of Teotihuacán, in the Usumacinta Valley around the seventh and eighth centuries A.D., and again in central Mexico coinciding with Tula's brief flowering.

In spite of its limited technical level, engineering was more advanced than architecture and some public works can be compared, in significance and scale, with those existing contemporaneously in Europe. Of course Indian engineers compensated for serious technical deficiencies by a massive use of manpower, which would have been impossible in Europe at that time. All in all, the road network of the Inca Empire reflects a thorough study of topography, and both Tenochtitlán's access causeways and the dike that protected the city bear witness to a knowledge of lake movements and the disadvantages of saline water. Both in Mexico and Peru, engineers built aqueducts, extensive irrigation works of swamp drainage and canalization, agricultural terracing and large granaries. Military engineers knew the use of bastions and double walls as exemplified by the saw-tooth defense system of Sacsahuamán, which may well have been one of the most advanced for its epoch.

The problems entailed in extracting stone, transporting it to a given place and erecting it in a temple, must have presented the greatest challenge to the energies and inventiveness of Indian engineers. Construction methods employed in these temples suggest that the technical level of pre-Columbian engineers was probably no greater than that of their Egyptian colleagues who built the great pyramids. This provides a strong contrast with the development achieved by pre-Columbian cultures in other arts and sciences.

—— *NOTES ON · 15* ——

1. SEE CHAPTER 1 of this book.

2. See Jorge E. Hardoy, *Centros ceremoniales y ciudades planeadas de la América precolombina*, Ciencia e Investigación, pp. 387-404; Buenos Aires, September, 1964.

3. The origin and spontaneous growth of European medieval cities is treated in detail by Pierre Levedan in his *Histoire de l'urbanisme*, Volumes I and II, Paris, 1926 and 1941.

4. See Jacques Pirenne, *La civilisation sumérienne*, Guilde du Livre, Paris, 1944.

5. See Chapter 13 of this book.

6. A schematic plan of Chacchob can be found in Pollock and Stronsvik, 1953.

7. See the example of the Morley Causeway and the corresponding structural group located in square B6 of the Plan of Tikal, in Carr and Hazard, 1961 (Plate No. 43, page 181).

8. See various works by Wauchope, 1934, 1938 and 1940.

9. See Armillas, 1950 and Séjourné, 1959.

Abbreviations used in the Bibliography

A	Archaeology
AA	American Anthropologist
AATQ	American Antiquity
AI	América Indígena
AMNH-AP	American Museum of Natural History. Anthropological Papers.
BAE	Bureau of American Ethnology
CA	Cuadernos Americanos; Mexico D.F.
CS	Ciencias Sociales; Unión Panamericana; Washington, D.C.
CIW	Carnegie Institution; Washington, D.C.
E	Expedition; Philadelphia.
ECM	Estudios de Cultura Maya; Mexico D.F.
EMA	El México Antiguo; Mexico D.F.
HMAI	Handbook of Middle American Indians
HSAI	Handbook of South American Indians
INAH	Instituto Nacional de Antropología e Historia; Mexico D.F.
IPGH	Instituto Panamericano de Geografía e Historia; Tacubaya, D.F.
ISA	Institute of Social Anthropology
MARI	Middle American Research Institute; Tulane University.
NGM	National Geographic Magazine
NP	Ñaupa Pacha; Berkeley.
PA	Publications in Anthropology; Yale University.
PM	Peabody Museum; Harvard University.
PSP	Prehistoric settlement patterns; Gordon Willey, editor.
RMEA	Revista Mexicana de Estudios Antropológicos; Mexico D.F.
RMIH	Revista del Museo e Instituto Histórico; Cuzco.
RMN	Revista Museo Nacional; Lima.
SI	Smithsonian Institution; Washington, D.C.
SWJA	Southwestern Journal of Anthropology
TPR	Town Planning Review; University of Liverpool.
VF	Viking Fund; Wenner Gren Foundation; New York.

BIBLIOGRAPHY

Acosta, Jorge R. "La ciudad de Quetzalcóatl; exploraciones en Tula, Hidalgo." *C.A.*, I-2 (Mexico, 1942): pp. 121-131.

---"Interpretación de los datos obtenidos en Tula relativos a la época tolteca." *R.M.E.A.*, XIV (Mexico, 1956-57): pp. 75-110.

---"La doceava temporada de exploraciones en Tula, Hidalgo." Anales del *I.N.A.H.*, XIII-42 (Mexico, 1961).

Adams, Robert M. "Some hypothesis on the development of early civilizations." *A.A.T.Q.*, XXI-3 (1953): pp. 227-232.

---"The origin of cities." *Scientific American*, CCIII-3 (1960): pp. 153-172.

Albright, William F. *The archaeology of Palestine*. Harmondsworth, Middlesex, England: Pelican Books, 1954.

Alcocer, Ignacio. *Apuntes sobre la Antigua México-Tenochtitlan*. Tacubaya, Mexico: *I.P.G.H.*, 1935.

Andrews, E. Wyllys. "Dzibilchaltún: lost city of the Mayas." *N.G.M.*, CXV-1 (Washington, D.C., 1959): p. 90.

---"Excavations at Dzibilchaltún, Northwestern Yucatán, Mexico." *Proceedings of the American Philosophical Society*, LIV-3 (Philadelphia, 1960): p. 254.

---*Dzibilchaltún program*. New Orleans: Tulane University, M.A.R.I., 1961.

Aparicio, Francisco de. "The comechingon and their neighbors of the sierras de Córdoba." *H.S.A.I.*, S.I., B.A.E. Publication 143, II-3 (Washington, D.C., 1946): pp. 673-685.

Arai, Alberto T. *La arquitectura de Bonampak*. Mexico: Ediciones del Instituto Nacional de Bellas Artes, 1944.

Armillas, Pedro. "Fortalezas mexicanas." *C.A.* VII-5 (Mexico, 1948): pp. 143-163.

---"Teotihuacán, Tula y los Toltecas; las culturas postarcaicas y preaz-
tecas del centro de México. Excavaciones y estudios, 1922-1950."
Runa III (Buenos Aires, 1950): pp. 37-70.

---"Tecnología, formaciones socioeconómicas y religión en Mesoamérica." In *Selected Papers of the 29th International Congress of Americanists*. Edited by Sol Tax. Chicago: University of Chicago Press,
1951.

---"Cronología de la cultura teotihuacana." *Tlatoani* I-2 (Mexico, 1952):
pp. 11-16.

Armillas, P. and West, R. "Las chinampas de México." *C.A.* IX-2
(Mexico, 1950): pp. 165-182.

Bartholomew, Harland. *Land uses in American cities*. Cambridge: Harvard University Press, 1955.

Batres, Leopoldo. *Teotihuacán o la ciudad sagrada de los toltecas*. Mexico: 1906.

Baudin, Louis. *El imperio socialista de los incas*. Santiago de Chile: Editorial Zig Zag, 1940.

---*La vida cotidiana en el tiempo de los últimos incas*. Buenos Aires:
Librería Hachette, 1958.

Beltran, Enrique. *El hombre y su ambiente. Ensayo sobre el valle de
México*. Mexico: Fondo de Cultura Económica, 1958.

Bennett, Wendell C. "Excavations at Tiahuanaco." *A.M.N.H.-A.P.*
XXXIV-3 (New York, 1934): pp. 359-494.

---"Excavations in Bolivia." *A.M.N.H.-A.P.* XXXV-4 (New York,
1936).

---"The Andean Highlands; an introduction." *H.S.A.I.*, S.I., B.A.E.
Publication 143, II-1 (Washington, D.C., 1946): pp. 1-60.

---"The archaeology of the Central Andes." *H.S.A.I.*, S.I., B.A.E. Publication 143, II-2 (Washington, D.C., 1946): pp. 61-147.

---"The atacameño." *H.S.A.I.*, S.I., B.A.E. Publication 143, II-3 (Washington, D.C., 1946): pp. 599-618.

---"The archaeology of Colombia." *H.S.A.I.*, S.I., B.A.E. Publication
143, II-4 (Washington, D.C., 1946): pp. 823-850.

---"The Gallinazo Group, Virú Valley, Peru." *P.A.*, Yale University No.
43 (New Haven, 1950).

---Introduction to *Edition of the selected papers of the XXIX International Congress of Americanists*. Chicago: University of Chicago
Press, 1951.

---"Excavations at Wari, Ayacucho, Peru." *P.A.*, Yale University No. 49 (New Haven, 1953).

Bennett, Wendell C., ed. *A reappraisal of Peruvian archaeology.* A.A.T.Q., Supplement to Vol. XIII-4: part 2 (1948).

Bennett, Wendell C. and Bird, Junius B. *Andean Culture History.* A.M.N.H., Handbook Series, No. 15. New York: 1949.

Bernal, Ignacio. *Mesoamerica.* I.P.G.H. Publication 152. Tacubaya, Mexico: 1953.

---"Ils vivaient a Tlatilco." *L'Oeil* VI (Paris, 1955).

---"Evolución y alcance de las culturas mesoamericanas." In *Esplendor del México Antiguo* I, pp. 97-124. Mexico: 1959.

---*Tenochtitlán en una isla.* Mexico: I.N.A.H., 1959.

---*Bibliografía de arqueología y etnografía.* Mexico: I.N.A.H., 1962.

Betanzos, Juan de. *Suma y narración de los incas.* Madrid: Biblioteca Hispano-Ultramarina, 1880.

Bingham, Hiram. *Vitcos, the last Inca capital.* Worcester, Mass.: American Antiquarian Society, 1912.

---"In the wonderlands of Perú." *N.G.M.* XXIV (Washington, D.C., 1918): p. 397.

---*Machu Pichu: a citadel of the Incas.* New Haven: Yale University Press. 1930.

---*Lost city of the Incas.* New York: 1951.

Bird, Junius. "Antiquity and migrations of the early inhabitants of Patagonia." *Geographical Review* XXVIII-2 (New York, 1938): pp. 250-275.

---"The cultural sequence of the north chilean coast." *H.S.A.I.*, S.I., B.A.E. Publication 143, II-3 (Washington, D.C., 1946): pp. 587-594.

---"The historic inhabitants of the north chilean coast." *H.S.A.I.*, S.I., B.A.E. Publication 143, II-3 (Washington, D.C., 1946): pp. 595-597.

---"Preceramic cultures in Chicama and Virú." In *A reappraisal of Peruvian Archaeology*. Edited by Wendell C. Bennett. *A.A.T.Q.*, Supplement to vol. XIII-4, part 2 (1948).

Black, G.A. and Johnston, R.B. "A test of magnetometry as an aid to archaeology." *A.A.T.Q.* XXVIII-2 (1962): p. 199.

Bonavía, Duccio. "A mochica painting at Pañamarca, Peru." *A.A.T.Q.*, XXVI-4 (1961): pp. 540-543.

---*Las ruinas del Abiseo.* Lima: Universidad Peruana de Ciencia y Tecnología, 1968.

---"Investigaciones arqueológicas en el Mantaro Medio." *R.M.N.*

XXXV (Lima, 1968): pp. 211-294.

---"Nucleos de población en la ceja de selva de Ayacucho, Perú." In *El proceso de urbanización en América desde sus orígenes hasta nuestros días*. Edited by Jorge E. Hardoy and Richard P. Schaedel. Buenos Aires: Editorial del Instituto Di Tella, 1969.

Bonavía, Duccio and Ravines, Roger. "Villas del horizonte tardío en la Ceja de Selva all Perú." In *El proceso de urbanización en América desde sus orígenes hasta nuestros días*. Edited by Jorge E. Hardoy and Richard P. Schaedel. Buenos Aires: Editorial del Instituto Di Tella, 1969.

Bordone, Benedetto. *Libro di Benedetto Bordone. Nel quale si ragiona de tutta l'isole del mondo con li lor nomi antichi y moderni*. Venice: 1528.

Borhegyi, Stephan F. de. "Settlement patterns in the Guatemalan highlands: past and present." In *Prehistoric settlement patterns in the new world*. Edited by Gordon R. Willey. Wenner-Gren Foundation for Anthropological Research Publication 23. New York: 1956.

---*Precolumbian cultural connections between Mesoamerica and Ecuador*. *M.A.R.I.*, Records II-6. New Orleans: Tulane University, 1959.

Brainerd, George W. "Changing living patterns of the Yucatan Maya." *A.A.T.Q.* XXII-2 (1956): pp. 162-164.

Bullard, W.R. *Residential property walls at Mayapán*. C.I.W., Department of Archaeology, Current Report No. 3 (1953).

---*Boundary walls and house lots at Mayapán*. C.I.W., Department of Archaeology, Current Report No. 14 (1954).

---"Maya settlement patterns in Northeastern Petén, Guatemala." *A.A.T.Q.* XXII-2 (1956): pp. 162-164.

Burr, C. Brundage. *Empire of the Inca*. University of Oklahoma Press, 1963.

Bushnell, G.H. *Peru*. New York: Frederick A. Praeger, 1957.

Calancha, Fray Antonio de la. *Crónica moralizadora del orden de San Agustín en el Perú*. Paris: Biblioteca de Cultura Peruana; Primera Serie, No. 4, 1938.

Callen, E.O. and Cameron, T.W. "A prehistoric diet revealed in coprolites." *The New Scientist* VIII-190 (1960): pp. 35-40.

Callnek, Edward. "Urbanization at Tenochtitlán." Research report read at the 68th Annual Meeting of the American Anthropological Association, New Orleans, 1968.

---"Subsistence agriculture and the urban development of Tenochtitlán." Paper presented at the 69th Annual Meeting of the American Anthropological Association, Boston. 1969.

Canals Frau, Salvador. *Prehistoria de América.* Buenos Aires: Ed. Sudamericana, 1950.

---*Poblaciones indígenas de la Argentina.* Buenos Aires: Ed. Sudamericana, 1953.

Cano, Washington. *El lago Titicaca.* Buenos Aires: Ed. Moreno, n.d.

Cardich, Augusto. "Los yacimientos de Lauricocha. Nuevas Interpretaciones de la prehistoria peruana." *Studia Praehistorica* I (Buenos Aires, 1958).

---"Investigaciones prehistóricas en los Andes Peruanos." In *Instituto de Etnología y Arqueología de la Universidad de San Marcos.* Lima: 1960.

Carr, R.F. and Hazard, J.E. *Tikal Report No. 11; Map of the ruins of Tikal, El Petén, Guatemala.* Philadelphia: Museum Monographs, The University Museum, University of Pennsylvania, 1961.

Carrasco, Pedro. "The civil-religious hierarchy in Mesoamerican communities: pre-spanish background and colonial development." *A.A.* LXIII-3 (1961): p. 483.

Carrera Stampa, Manuel. "Planos de la ciudad de México." *Boletin de la Sociedad Mexicana de Geografía y Estadística* LXVII-2 & 3 (Mexico, 1949): pp. 265-427.

Carrión Cachot, Rebeca. "La cultura Chavín—Dos nuevas colonias: Kuntur Wasi y Ancón." *R.M.N.* II-1 (Lima, 1948): pp. 99-172.

Casanovas, Eduardo. *Nota sobre el pucará de Huichairas.* Buenos Aires: Museo Argentino de Ciencias Naturales, 1934.

---*La arqueología de Coctaca.* Buenos Aires: Museo Argentino de Ciencias Naturales, 1934.

---"La Quebrada de Humahuaca." In *Historia de la Nación Argentina,* pp. 207-249. Edited by the Junta de Historia y Numismática Americana. Buenos Aires: 1936.

---"El pucará de Hornillos." *Anales del Instituto de Etnografía Americana.* Mendoza: 1942.

---"The cultures of the Puna and the Quebrada of Humahuaca." *H.S.A.I.*, S.I., B.A.E. Publication 143, II-3 (Washington, D.C., 1946): pp. 619-631.

Casavilca, Alberto. "La ciudad muerta de Cajamarquilla." *Boletín de la Sociedad Geográfica* LVI-2nd. trimester (Lima, 1939): pp. 100-109.

Caso, Alfonso. "Monte Albán, richest archaeological find in America." *N.G.M.* XXXVI (Washington, D.C., 1932).

---*Las exploraciones de Monte Albán. Temporada 1934-35.* I.P.G.H., Publication 18. Tacubaya: 1935.

---"¿Tenían los teotihuacanos conocimiento del tonalpahualli?" *E.M.A.* IV-344 (Mexico, 1937): pp. 131-143.

---*Exploraciones en Oaxaca, temporada 1936-1937.* Mexico: 1938.

---*Culturas mixteca y zapoteca.* Mexico: Ediciones El Nacional, 1942.

---"El paraíso terrenal en Teotihuacán." *C.A.* VI (Mexico, 1942): pp. 127-136.

---"Mapa de Popotla." *Anales del I.N.A.H.* II (Mexico, 1948): pp. 315-320.

---"El mapa de Teozacoalco." *C.A.* VIII (Mexico, 1949): pp. 145-181.

---*El pueblo del Sol.* Mexico: Fondo de Cultura Económica, 1953.

---"New World Culture history: Middle America." In *Anthropology Today.* Edited by A.L. Kroeber. Chicago: University of Chicago Press, 1953.

---"Los barrios antiguos de Tenochtitlán y Tlatelolco." *Memoria de la Academia Mexicana de la Historia* XVI (Mexico, 1953).

Castagnoli, Ferdinando. *Ippodamo di Mileto e l'urbanistica a pianta ortogonal.* Roma: De Luca Editor, 1956.

Castro Pozo, Hildebrando. "Social and economic-political evolution of the communities of Central Peru." *H.S.A.I.*, S.I., B.A.E. Publication 143, II-2 (Washington, D.C., 1946): pp. 483-499.

Centro de Investigaciones Antropológicas. *Esplendor del México Antiguo.* Mexico, 1959.

Chang, K.C. "Study of the neolithic social grouping: examples from the new world." *A.A.* CX-2: p. 298.

Chapman, Anne M. "Trade enclaves in Aztec and Maya civilizations." In *Trade and market in the early empires.* Edited by Karl Polanyi, G.M. Arensberg and H.W. Pearson. Glencoe, Illinois: The Free Press, 1957.

Chevalier, Francois. *La formation des grands domaines au Mexique.* Travaux et memoires de l'Institut d'Ethnologie, Université de Paris. Paris: 1952.

Childe, V. Gordon. "The urban revolution." *T.P.R.* XXI-1 (1950).

Cieza de León, Pedro. *Del señorío de los incas.* Buenos Aires: Ediciones Argentinas Solar, 1943.

---*La crónica del Perú.* Buenos Aires: Espasa-Calpe Argentina, Colección

Austral, No. 507, 1945.

Clark, J.D.G. *Archaeology and society*. Cambridge: Harvard University Press, 1957.

Cobo, Bernabé. *Historia del nuevo mundo*. Sevilla: Ed. Marco Jiménez de la Espada, 1890-95.

Codice Osuna. Facsimile reproduction of this work edited in Madrid in 1878. Mexico: Ediciones del Instituto Indigenista Interamericano, 1947.

Codice Ramirez. Manuscript of the 16th Century titled: *Relación del origen de los Indios que habitan esta Nueva España según sus historias*. Mexico: Ed. Levenda S.A., 1944.

Coe, Michael D. "Archaeological linkages with North and South America at La Victoria, Guatemala." *A.A.* LXII-3 (1960): pp. 363-393.

---*Mexico*. New York: Frederick A. Praeger, 1966.

---*The Maya*. New York: Frederick A. Praeger, 1966.

---"San Lorenzo and the Olmec civilization." *Dumbarton Oaks Conference on the Olmec* (Washington, D.C., 1968): pp. 41-78.

Coe, Michael D.; Diehl, R.C. and Stuiver, M. "Olmec civilization, Veracruz, Mexico: Dating of the San Lorenzo Phase." *Science* CLV-3768 (1967): pp. 1399-1401.

Coe, William R. *Piedras Negras Archaeology: artifacts, caches and burials*. Philadelphia: The University Museum, University of Pennsylvania, 1959.

---"Tikal 1959." *Expedition* I-4 (1959): p. 7.

---"A summary of excavation and research at Tikal, Guatemala: 1956-61." *A.A.T.Q.* XXVII-4 (1962): pp. 479-507.

---"Tikal: ten years of study of a maya ruin on the lowlands of Guatemala." *E.* VIII-1 (1965): pp. 5-56.

Collier, Donald. "The Archaeology of Ecuador." *H.S.A.I.*, S.I., B.A.E. Publication 143, II-4 (Washington, D.C., 1946): pp. 767-784.

---"Development of civilization on the coast of Peru." In *Irrigation civilizations: a comparative study*. Edited by Julian H. Steward. Pan American Union, Department of Cultural Affairs, Social Science Monograph, No. 1. Washington, D.C.: 1955.

Collier, John. *Los indios de las Américas*. Mexico: Fondo de Cultura Económica, 1960.

Conquistador Anónimo. *La conquista del Perú llamada la nueva Castilla*. Paris: Biblioteca de Cultura Peruana, Primera Serie, No. 2, 1938.

Cook de Leonard, Carmen. "Excavaciones en la plaza No. 21, Tres

Palos, Teotihuacán." *Boletín del Centro de Investigaciones Antropológicas de Mexico* IV (Mexico, 1957): pp. 3-5.

Cook, Sherburne F. "The interrelation of population, food supply and building in preconquest Central Mexico." *A.A.T.Q.* XIII-1 (1947): pp. 45-52.

Cook, Sherburne F. and Simpson, Lesley B. *The population of central Mexico in the XVI century.* Berkeley: University of California Press, 1948.

Cooper, John M. "The araucanians." *H.S.A.I.*, S.I., B.A.E. Publication 143, II-3 (Washington, D.C., 1946): pp. 697-750.

Cortés, Hernán. *Cartas de relación de la Conquista de Mexico.* Buenos Aires: Espasa-Calpe Argentina, Colección Austral, No. 547, 1961.

Covarrubias, Miguel. *Indian Art of Mexico and Central America.* New York: Alfred A. Knopf, Inc., 1957.

Cowgill, Ursula M. "Soil fertility, population and the ancient maya." Proceedings of the National Academy of Sciences XLVI-8: pp. 1009-1011.

Cressman, L.S. "Man in the New World." In *Man, culture and society.* Edited by Harry L. Shapiro. New York: Oxford University Press, 1960.

Dávalos Hurtado, Eusebio. "La alimentación entre los Mexicas." *R.M.E.A.* XIV (Mexico, 1954-55): pp. 103-118.

Day, Kent C. "Walk in wells and water management at Chan Chan, Peru." Paper presented at the XXXIX International Congress of Americanists, Lima, 1970.

Debenedetti, Salvador. *Las ruinas del Pucará.* Buenos Aires: Archivos del Museo Etnografico II-1st. part, 1930.

Dewey, Richard. "The rural-urban continuum: real but relatively without importance." *A.J.S.* LXVI-1 (1960): pp. 60-66.

Dickinson, Robert E. *City, region and regionalism.* New York: Oxford University Press, 1947.

Díaz del Castillo, Bernal. *Historia verdadera de la conquista de la Nueva España.* Buenos Aires: Espasa-Calpe Argentina, Colección Austral, No. 1274, 1955.

Diez Canseco, Maria R. "Succession, cooption to kingship, and royal incest among the Inca." *S.W.J.A.* XVI-4 (1960): pp. 417-427.

Di Peso, Charles C. "Cultural Development in Northern Mexico." In *Aboriginal cultural development in Latin America: an interpretative review*. Edited by Betty Meggers and C. Evans. Washington, D.C.: Smithsonian Institution, 1963.

Dobyns, Henry F. "Estimating aboriginal American population: an appraisal of techniques with a new hemispheric estimate." *Current Anthropology* VII-4 (1966): pp. 395-416.

Drucker, P.H.; Heizer, R.F. and Squier, R.J. *Excavations at La Venta, Tabasco*. S.I., B.A.E. Publication 170. Washington, D.C.: 1955.

Duncan, Otis Dudley. "Community size and the urban rural continuum." In *A Reader in Urban Sociology*. Edited by J. Hatt and A. Reiss. Glencoe, Illinois: The Free Press, 1957.

Durán, Fray Diego. *Historia de las indias de Nueva España e Islas de Tierra Firme*. Mexico: 1951.

Eaton, George F. "The collection of osteological material from Machu Pichu." *Memoirs of the Connecticut Academy of Arts and Science* V (New Haven, 1916).

Ekholm, Gordon F. "Regional sequences in Mesoamerica and their relationships." Paper commented by Shook and McNeish in *Middle American Anthropology*, Symposium of the American Anthropological Association, Pan American Union. Washington, D.C.: 1958.

Engel, Frederick. "Early sites on the peruvian coast." *S.W.J.A.* XII-1 (1957): pp. 54-68.

---*Paracas—Cien siglos de cultura peruana*. Lima: Juan Mejía Baca, editor, 1966.

---*Las lomas de Iguanil y el complejo de Haldas*. Lima: Universidad Nacional Agraria, La Molina, 1970.

Estete, Miguel de. *Noticia del Perú*. Paris: Biblioteca de Cultura Peruana, Primera Serie, No. 2, 1938.

Estrada, Emilio and Meggers, Betty J. "A complex of traits of probable transpacific origin on the coast of Perú." *A.A.* LXIII-5 (1958): p. 913.

Fejos, Paul. *Archaeological explorations in the Cordillera Vilcabamba, southeastern Peru*. V.F., Publications in Anthropology No. 3. New York: 1944.

Flannery, K.V.; Kirby, A.V.T.; Kirby, M.J. and Williams, A.W. "Farming systems and political growth in Ancient Oaxaca." *Science* CLVIII-3800 (1967): pp. 445-453.

Frankfort, Henri. "Town planning in ancient Mesopotamia." *T.P.R.,*

XXI-2 (1950).

---*The birth of civilization in the Near East.* New York: Doubleday, 1956.

Frenguelli, Joaquin. "The present status of the theories concerning primitive man in Argentina." *H.S.A.I.*, S.I., B.A.E. Publication 143, VI-1 (Washington, D.C., 1950) pp. 11-17.

Galindo y Villa, J. *Historia sumaria de la ciudad de Mexico.* Mexico: Editora Nacional, 1955.

Gamio, Manuel. *Guía para visitar la ciudad de Teotihuacán.* Mexico: Secretaría de Agricultura y Fomento, 1921.

---*La población del valle de Teotihuacán.* Mexico: Secretaría de Agricultura y Fomento, Dirección de Antropología, 1922.

García, José Uriel. "Sumas para la historia del Cuzco." *C.A.* XVIII-3, 4 & 5 (Mexico, 1959).

Gasparini, Graziano. "Visión arquitectónica de Tiwanaku." *Revista Shell*, No. 44 (Caracas, 1962): pp. 11-24.

Giesecke, Alberto. "Las ruinas de Paramonga." *Boletín de las Sociedades Geográficas de Lima* LVI-1st trimester (Lima, 1939).

Gillin, John. *Moche, a Peruvian Coastal Community.* S.I., I.S.A., Publication 3; Washington, D.C.: 1947.

Gilmore, Raymond M. "Fauna and ethnology of South America." *H.S.A.I.*, S.I., B.A.E. Publication 143, VI-4 (Washington, D.C., 1950): pp. 365-464.

Gomara, Francisco López de. *La conquista de México.* Mexico: Imprenta de H. Escalante y Cia., 1870.

González, Alberto Rex. *La estratigrafía de la gruta de Intihuasi (Prov. de San Luis, R.A.) y sus relaciones con otros sitios precerámicos de Sudamérica.* Córdoba: Revista del Instituto de Antropología de la Universidad Nacional de Córdoba, I, 1960.

---"Cultural Development in Northwestern Argentina." In *Aboriginal cultural development in Latin America: an interpretative review.* Edited by Betty Meggars and C. Evans. Washington, D.C.: Smithsonian Institution, 1963.

---*La cultura de La Aguada del N.O. Argentino.* Córdoba: Revista del Insitituto de Antropología, Universidad Nacional de Córdoba, II-III, 1964.

González Rul, F. and Mooser F. "La calzada de Iztapalapa." *Anales del I.N.A.H.*, XIV-43 (Mexico, 1962).

Graham, Ian. "A newly discovered classic maya site deep in the rain-forest of northern Guatemala: splendid stelae from the first exploration of Aguateca." *The Illustrated London News;* April 22, 1961.

Guillemin, George F. "The ancient cakchiquel capital of Iximche." *E.,* IX-2 (1967): pp. 22-35.

Gutkind, E.A. *Revolution of environment.* London: Kegan Paul, Trench, Trubner and Co., 1946.

Haag, William. "The Bering Strait land bridge." *Scientific American* CCVI-1 (1963): pp. 112-123.

Hackett, Brian. *Man, society and environment.* London: Percival Marshall, 1950.

Hadas, Moses. *A history of Rome.* Garden City, New York: Doubleday and Co., Inc., Anchor Books, 1956.

Hagen, Victor von. *Los caminos del Sol.* Buenos Aires: Editorial Hermes, 1958.

Hardoy, Jorge E. *Bibliografía anotada sobre la evolución de las ciudades de America Latina.* Berkeley: 1962.

---"Las ciudades precolombinas." *Revista de Arquitectura y Planeamiento* I-1, Rosario, 1963.

---"La influencia del urbanismo indígena en la localización y trazado de las ciudades coloniales." *Ciencia e Investigación,* XXI-9 (Buenos Aires, 1965): pp. 386-405.

---*Urban planning in precolumbian America.* New York: George Braziller, Inc., 1968.

Hardoy, Jorge E. and Schaedel, Richard P., eds. *El proceso de urbanización en América desde sus orígenes hasta nuestros días.* Buenos Aires: Editorial del Instituto Di Tella, 1969.

Harth Terré, Emilio. "Incahuasi: ruinas inkaicas del valle de Lima-huaná." *R.M.N.* II-2 (Lima, 1933).

---"Fundación de la ciudad incaica." *Revista Histórica* XVI, issues I-II (Lima, 1945).

---*Piki-llacta, ciudad de pósitos y bastimentos del Imperio incaico.* Cuzco: Revista del Museo e Instituto Arqueológico, Universidad del Cuzco, 1959.

---"Fundaciones urbanas en el Perú." Paper presented in 1959 at the Congreso de Historiadores Españoles, Madrid.

---"El asiento arqueológico de la ciudad de Lima, las 5 huacas de la Plaza de Armas." *El Comercio* (Lima. January 18, 1960).

---*Construcciones civiles del Incanato; los graneros de Pikillacta.* Author's edition.

---"El pueblo de Huánuco Viejo." *El Arquitecto Peruano* 320-321 (Lima, 1964): pp. 1-20.

Hatt, J. and Reiss, A., eds. *A reader in urban sociology.* Glencoe, Illinois: The Free Press, 1957.

Haverfield, F. *Ancient town-planning.* Oxford: The Clarendon Press, 1913.

Haviland, William A. "Prehistoric settlement at Tikal, Guatemala." *E.* VII-3 (1965): pp. 14-23.

---"Stature at Tikal, Guatemala: implications for ancient Maya demography and social organization." *A.A.T.Q.* XXXII-3 (1967): pp. 316-325.

---"A new population estimate for Tikal, Guatemala." *A.A.T.Q.* XXXIV-4 (1969): pp. 429-433.

Heizer, Robert F. and Cook, Sherburne F., eds. *The application of quantitative methods in archaeology.* *V.F.*, Publications in anthropology No. 28. New York: 1960.

Heredia, Osualdor. "La cultura Candelaria." *Rehue* 3 (Concepcion, 1970): pp. 55-82.

Herrera, Antonio de. *Historia de las Indias.* Buenos Aires: Editorial Guarania, 1945.

Hester, Joseph A. "Agriculture, economy, and population densities of the Maya." *C.I.W., Yearbook* No. 51 (1951-52), pp. 266-271; *Yearbook* No. 52 (1952-53), pp. 288-292.

Holstein, Otto. "Chan-Chan: capital of the great chimu." *The Geographical Review* XVII-1 (New York, 1927): pp. 136-161.

Horkheimer, Hans. *Historia del Perú; Perú prehispánico.* Trujillo, Peru, 1943.

---*Vistas arqueológicas del Noroeste del Perú.* Trujillo, Peru, 1944.

---*El Perú prehispánico*, Vol. I. Lima: Ed. Cultura Antártica, 1950.

Howells, William W. "Estimating population numbers through archaeological and skeletal remains." In *The application of quantative methods in archaeology.* Edited by Robert F. Heizer and Sherburne F. Cook. V.F. Publications in Anthropology No. 28. New York: 1960.

Huntington, Ellsworth. *Mainsprings of civilizations.* New York: The New Library, Mentor Book, 1945.

Hutchinson, R.W. "Prehistoric town planning in Crete." *T.P.R.* XXI-3 (1950).

Ibarra Grasso, Dick E. "Un nuevo panorama de la arqueología boliviana." In *Arqueología boliviana*. Edited by Carlos Ponce Sangines. La Paz: Biblioteca Paceña, 1957.

---"Antiguedad y cronologia de Tiwanaku." In *Arqueologia boliviana*. Edited by Carlos Ponce Sangines. La Paz: Biblioteca Paceña, 1957.

---*Lenguas indígenas americanas*. Buenos Aires: Editorial Nova, 1958.

---"Novedades sobre la verdadera historia de los incas." *Journal of Interamerican Studies* V-1 (Gainesville, 1963): pp. 19-30.

Ibarra Grasso, D.E.; Mesa, J. de and Gisbert, T. "Reconstrucción de Taypicala, Tiahuanaco." *C.A.* XIV (Mexico: 1955): pp. 149-176.

Imbelloni, J. *La segunda esfinge indiana*. Buenos Aires: Librería Hachette, 1956.

Instituto de Antropología de la Universidad del Litoral. *Investigaciones arqueológicas en el valle de Santa María*. Publication No. 4, Rosario, 1960.

Instituto de Estudios de Administracion Local. *Planos de ciudades Iberoamericanas y Filipinas existentes en el Archivo de Indias*. Madrid: 1951.

Instituto de Etnología y Arqueología de la Universidad de San Marcos, Peru. *Antiguo Perú; espacio y tiempo*. Lima: Librería-editorial Juan Mejía Baca, 1960.

Instituto Nacional de Antropología e Historia. *Guía oficial de Chichen Itzá*. Text by Alberto Ruz Lhuillier, Mexico, 1955.

---*Guía oficial del Museo Nacional de Antropología*. Edited by Eusebio Dávalos Hurtado and Jorge Gurría Lacroix. Mexico: 1956.

---*Guía oficial de Uxmal*. Text by Alberto Ruz Lhuillier. Mexico: 1956.

---*Guía oficial de El Tajín*. Text by José García Payón. Mexico: 1957.

---*Guía oficial de Tula*. Text by Pablo Martinez del Río and Jorge R. Acosta. Mexico: 1957.

---*Guía oficial de Monte Albán y Mitla*. Edited by Jorge Gurría Lacroix. Mexico: 1957.

---*Guía oficial de Copilco-Cuicuilco*. Text by Roman Piña Chan and Eduardo Noguera. Mexico: 1959.

---*Guía oficial de Palenque*. Edited by Alberto Ruz Lhuillier. Mexico: 1959.

---*Guía oficial de Teotihuacán*. Edited by Jorge Gurría Lacroix. Mexico: 1959.

---*Guía oficial de Tulúm*. Text by Alberto Ruz Lhuillier. Mexico: 1959.

---*Guía oficial de Calixtlahuaca*. Mexico: 1960.

---*Guía oficial de La Quemada y Chalchihuites*. Text by Eduardo Noguera. Mexico: 1960.

---*Zonas arqueológicas del Estado de Morelos (includes Tepoztlán, Teo-
panzolco and Xochicalco)*. Text by Eduardo Noguera. Mexico: 1960.

---*Guía oficial de Zempoala*. Edited by Jorge Gurría Lacroix. Mexico:
1960.

---*Official Guide—Tenayuca*. Mexico: n.d.

Instituto Panamericano de Geografía e Historia. *Atlas arqueológico de
la República Mexicana*. Publication 41. Mexico: n.d.

Iturribarria, Jorge F. *Las viejas culturas de Oaxaca*. Edited by Ferrocar-
riles Nacionales de Mexico. Mexico: 1952.

Jerez, Francisco de. *Verdadera relación de la conquista del Perú y provincia del Cuzco*. Biblioteca de Cultura Peruana, Primera serie, No. 2.
Paris: 1938.

Jijon y Caamaño, Jacinto. "Orígenes del Cuzco." *Revista del Museo e
Instituto Arqueológico* XVIII (Cuzco, 1959).

Jiménez Moreno, Wigberto. "El enigma de los olmecas." *C.A.*, I-5
(Mexico, 1942): pp. 113-145.

---*Introducción a la Guía Arqueológica de Tula*. Mexico: Ateneo Nacional de Ciencias y Artes de México, 1945.

---"Síntesis de la historia precolonial del valle de México." *R.M.E.A.*
XIV (Mexico, 1954-55): pp. 219-236.

---"Mesoamerica before the Toltecs." In *Ancient Oaxaca*. Edited by
John Paddock. Palo Alto, California: Stanford University Press, 1966.

Jones, Morris R. *Map of the Ruins of Mayapán, Yucatán, Mexico*.
C.I.W. I-1. Washington, D.C.: 1953.

Keleman, P. *Medieval American Art*. New York: The Macmillan Co.,
1943.

Kelley, David H. and Bonavia, Duccio. "New evidence for preceramic
maize on the coast of Peru." *N.P.* I (Berkeley, 1963): pp. 39-41.

Kelly, Isabel and Palerm, Angel. *The Tajin Totonac, part 1: History,
subsistence, shelter and technology*. S.I., I.S.A. Publication 13. Washington, D.C., 1952.

Kidder, Alfred V. "Settlement patterns; Peru." In *Prehistoric settlement
patterns in the new world*. Edited by Gordon R. Willey. Wenner-Gren
Foundation for Anthropological Research, Publication 23. New York:
1956.

Kidder, A.V.; Jennings, J.O. and Shook, Edwin. *Excavations at Kaminaljuyú.* C.I.W. Publication 561. Washington, D.C., 1946.

Kidder, Alfred V. and Samayoa Chinchilla, Carlos. *The art of ancient maya.* New York: Thomas Crowell, Co., 1959.

Kirchhoff, Paul. "Mesoamerica." *Acta Americana* I-1 (1943): pp. 92-107.

---"Land tenure in ancient Mexico." *R.M.E.A.* XIV, 1st part (Mexico, 1954-55): pp. 351-361.

Klove, Robert C. "The definition of standard metropolitan area." In *Readings in urban geography.* Edited by H. Mayer and C. Kohn. Chicago: University of Chicago Press, 1960.

Korn, Arthur. *History builds the Town.* London: Lund, Humphries and Co., 1953.

Kosok, Paul. "The role of irrigation in ancient Peru." *Proceedings of the VIII Congress of American Scientists* (1940): pp. 169-178.

---"Transport in Peru." In *The Royal Anthropological Institute,* editor, 1952.

---*Life, land and water in ancient Peru.* New York: Long Island University Press, 1965.

Krickeberg, Walter. *Las antiguas culturas mexicanas.* Mexico: Fondo de Cultura Económica, 1961.

Kroeber, A.L. "The chibcha." *H.S.A.I.,* S.I., B.A.E. Publication 143, II-4 (Washington, D.C., 1946): pp. 887-909.

Kroeber, A.L., ed. *Anthropology today.* Chicago: University of Chicago Press, 1953.

Kubler, George C. "The Quecha in the Colonial World." *H.S.A.I.,* S.I., B.A.E. Publication 143, II-2 (Washington, D.C., 1946): pp. 331-410.

---*Cuzco: reconstruction of the town and restoration of the monuments.* Paris: UNESCO, 1952.

---*The design of space in maya architecture.* Mexico: Miscellanea Paul Rivet, 1958.

---"Machu Pichu." *Perspecta: The Yale Architectural Journal* VI (New Haven, 1960): pp. 49-55.

---*The art and architecture of ancient America.* Harmondsworth, Middlesex, England: Penguin Books Ltd., Pelican History of Art, 1962.

Langlois, Luis. "Paramonga." *R.M.N.* VII-1 (Lima, 1938): pp. 21-52 and VII-2 (Lima, 1938): pp. 281-307.

Landa, Diego de. *Relación de las cosas del Yucatán.* Mexico: Librería

Robredo, 1938.

Larco Hoyle, Rafael. "La escritura peruana preincaica." *E.M.A.* VI-7 & 8 (Mexico, 1944): p. 219.

---"A culture sequence for the north coast of Peru." *H.S.A.I.*, S.I., B.A.E. Publication 143, II-2 (Washington, D.C., 1946): pp. 149-175.

Las Casas, Fray Bartolomé. *Historia de las Indias.* Mexico: Fondo de Cultura Económica, 1951.

Lanning, Edward P. "A pre-agricultural occupation on the central coast of Peru." *A.A.T.Q.* XXVIII-3 (1963): pp. 360-371.

---*Peru before the Incas.* Englewood Cliffs, New Jersey: Prentice Hall Inc., 1967.

Le Corbusier. *Urbanisme.* Paris: Editions Crès, 1924.

Lee, Rose Hum. *The city.* New York: J.B. Lippincott and Co., 1955.

Lehmann, Henri. *Las culturas precolombinas.* Buenos Aires: Editorial Universitaria de Buenos Aires, 1960.

Leipziger, Hugo. *The architectonic city in the Americas.* Austin: The University of Texas, 1944.

Lenz, Hans. "Las fibras y las plantas del papel indígena mexicano." *C.A.* IX-3 (Mexico, 1949): pp. 157-169.

Linné, Sigvald. *Archaeological Researches at Teotihuacán, Mexico.* Stockholm: Etnographical Museum of Sweden; Publication No. 1, 1934.

---*Mexican highland cultures; Archaeological Research at Teotihuacán, Chalpulalpan and Chalchicomila, in 1934-35;* Etnographical Museum of Sweden, Publication No. 7. Stockholm: 1942.

---"Radiocarbon dates in Teotihuacán." *Ethnos* XXI-3-4 (Stockholm, 1956): pp. 180-193.

Linton, Ralph. "Crops, soils and cultures in America." In *The Maya and Their Neighbors.* New York: 1940.

---*The tree of culture.* New York: Alfred Knopf, 1957.

Llanos, Luis A. "Ollantaitampu." *R.M.N.* V-2 (Lima, 1936): p. 123.

Longyear III, John M. "A historical interpretation of Copán archaeology." In *Selected Papers of the 29th International Congress of Americanists.* Edited by Sol Tax. Chicago: University of Chicago Press, 1951.

---*Copán ceramics.* C.I.W. Publication 597. Washington, D.C.: 1952.

López de Gomara, Francisco. *Historia de las Indias.* Buenos Aires: n.d.

Lothrop, S.K. *Tulúm, an archaeological study of the east coast of Yucatán.* C.I.W. Publication 335. Washington, D.C.: 1924.

---"The diaguita of Chile." *H.S.A.I.*, S.I., B.A.E. Publication 143 II-2 (Washington, D.C., 1946): pp. 633-636.

Lorenzo, Jose L. *La revolución neolítica en Mesoamérica.* Mexico: I.N.A.H., 1961.

Lowie, Robert H. "The tropical forest, an introduction." *H.S.A.I.*, S.I., B.A.E. Publication 143 III-1 (Washington, D.C., 1948): pp. 1-56.

Lumbreras, Luis G. "Esquema arqueológico de la sierra central del Perú." *R.M.N.* XXVIII (Lima, 1959): pp. 63-116.

---"Algunos problemas de arqueología peruana 1959." In *Insitituto de Etnología y Arqueología de la Universidad de San Marcos, Peru.·* 1960.

---"Espacio y cultura en los Andes." *R.M.N.*, XXIX (Lima, 1960): p. 222.

---*La cultura de Wari, Ayacucho. Etnología y Arqueología.* Universidad Nacional Mayor de San Marcos I, pp. 130-226. Lima: 1960.

---*De los pueblos, las culturas y las artes del Antiguo Perú.* Lima: Francisco Moncloa Editores, 1969.

---*Los templos de Chavín. Guía para el visitante.* Lima: Corporación Peruana del Santa, 1970.

Lundell, C.L. "The flora of Tikal." *E.* III-2 (Philadelphia, 1961): pp. 38-43.

Márquez Miranda, Fernando. "The diaguita of Argentina." *H.S.A.I.*, S.I., B.A.E. Publication 143, II-3 (Washington, D.C., 1946): pp. 637-654.

---"The Chaco-Santiagueño culture." *H.S.A.I.*, S.I., B.A.E. Publication 143, II-3 (Washington, D.C., 1946): pp. 655-660.

Marquina, Ignacio. "City planning by ancient Mayas." *El Palacio,* XXXIX (Santa Fe, New Mexico, 1930): pp. 314-316.

---"Las ciudades." In *México prehispánico.* Edited by Jorge A. Vivo. Mexico: 1946.

---"Arquitectura prehispánica." *I.N.A.H.* (Mexico, 1951).

---"El Templo Mayor de México." *I.N.A.H.* (Mexico, 1960).

Mason, J. Alden. *The ancient civilizations of Peru.* Harmondsworth, Middlesex, England: Pelican Books, 1957.

Maudslay, A.P. *Archaeology.* Biologia Centrali-Americana; ed. by F. Ducane Godman and Osbert Salvin, Vol. 1-4. London: 1889-1902.

---*Plano hecho en papel de Maguey que se conserva en el Museo Nacional de México.* (Mexico: Anales del Museo Nacional de Arqueología,

Historia y Etnología I, 1909): p. 49.

---"The valley of Mexico." *The Geographical Journal* XLVIII (London, 1916): p. 11.

Mayer, H. and Kohn, C., eds. *Readings in urban geography.* Chicago: University of Chicago Press, 1960.

Mayer Oakes, William J. "A Developmental Concept of Pre-Spanish Urbanization in the Valley of Mexico." *M.A.R.I.* II-8 (New Orleans: Tulane University, 1960): pp. 167-177.

MacGowan, Kenneth. "The orientation of middle american sites." *A.A.T.Q.* XI (1945): p. 118.

Mackie, Evan W. "New light on the end of classic maya culture at Benque Viejo, British Honduras." *A.A.T.Q.* XXVII-2 (1961): p. 216.

MacNeish, Richard S. "Ancient Mesoamerican civilization." In *Prehistoric agriculture.* Edited by Stuart Struever. New York: American Museum Sourcebook in Anthropology, 1971.

Mangelsdorf, Paul C.; MacNeish, Richard S. and Galinat, Walton C. "Domestication of corn." *Science*, CXLIII-3606 (1964): pp. 538-545.

Marti, Samuel. "Canto, danza y música precortesianos." Mexico: Fondo de Cultura Económica, 1961.

McBride, George and Merle, A. "Highland Guatemala and its maya communities." *The Geographical Review*, XXXII-2 (New York, 1942): p. 252.

McCown, Theodore. *Pre-incaic Huamachuco.* University of California Publications in American Archaeology XXXIX-4; Berkeley and Los Angeles: University of California Press, 1945.

---"The antiquity of man in South America." *H.S.A.I.*, S.I., B.A.E. Publication 143 VI-1 (Washington, D.C., 1950): pp. 1-9.

Means, Phillip. *Ancient civilizations of the Andes.* New York: Charles Scribner and Sons, 1931.

Meggers, Betty, ed. *Anthropological archaeology in the Americas.* Washington, D.C.: The Anthropological Society of Washington, 1968.

Meggers, B.J. and Evans, C. "The machalella culture: an early formative complex on the Ecuadorian coast." *A.A.T.Q.*, XXVIII-2 (1962): p. 186.

Meggers, Betty and Evans, C., eds. *Aboriginal cultural development in Latin America: an interpretative review.* Washington, D.C.: Smithsonian Institution, 1963.

Méndez, Amalia Cardos de. "El comercio de los mayas antiguos." *Acta Anthropológica, Epoca 2* II-1 (Mexico, 1959).

Mendieta y Núñez, Lucio. *Los zapotecos: monografía histórica, etnográfica y económica.* Mexico: Instituto de Investigaciones Sociales, Universidad Nacional Autónoma de México, 1949.

Menghin, Osvaldo F.A. *Origen y desarrollo racial de la especie humana.* Buenos Aires: Editoral Nova, 1958.

Menzel, Dorothy. "The Inca occupation of the south coast of Peru." *S.W.J.A.* XV-2 (1959): pp. 125-142.

---"Style and time in the Middle Horizon." *N.P.* II (Berkeley, 1964): pp. 1-105.

Mesa, José and Gisbert, Teresa. "Akapana, la pirámide de Tiwanacu." In *Arqueología boliviana.* Edited by Carlos Ponce Sanginés. La Paz: Biblioteca Paceña, 1957.

Métraux, Alfred. "The Guaraní." *H.S.A.I.*, S.I., B.A.E. Publication 143, III-1 (Washington, D.C., 1948): pp. 69-94.

---"The Tupinambá." *H.S.A.I.*, S.I., B.A.E. Publication 143, III-1 (Washington, D.C., 1948): pp. 103-133.

---*The history of the Incas.* New York: Schocken Books, 1970.

Michels, Joseph W. "Pattern of Settlement in and around Kaminaljuyú, Highland Guatemala." Paper presented at the 134th Annual Meeting of the American Association for the Advancement of Science, Boston, 1969.

Miles, S.W. "Maya settlement patterns: a problem for ethnology and archaeology." *S.W.J.A.* XIII-3 (1957): pp. 239-248.

---"An urban type: extended boundary towns." *S.W.J.A.* XIV-4 (1958): pp. 339-351.

Millé, Max and Ponce Sanginés, Carlos. *Las andesitas de Tiwanaku.* La Paz: Academia Nacional de Ciencias de Bolivia, 1968.

Millon, Rene F. "Irrigation at Teotihuacán." *A.A.T.Q.*, XXX-2 (1954): pp. 177-180.

---"Irrigation systems in the Valley of Teotihuacán." *A.A.T.Q.*, XXIII-1, part I (1957): pp. 160-166.

---"New data on Teotihuacán I, Teotihuacán." *Boletín del Centro de Investigaciones Antropológicas de México*, IV (Mexico, 1957): pp. 12-17.

---"The beginnings of Teotihuacán." *A.A.T.Q.* XXVI-1 (1960): pp. 1-10.

---"Extensión y población de la ciudad de Teotihuacán en sus diferentes períodos, un cálculo provisional." Paper presented at the Eleventh Mesa Redonda de la Sociedad Mexicana de Antropología, Mexico, 1966.

---"El problema de integración en la sociedad teotihuacana." Paper presented at the Eleventh Mesa Redonda de la Sociedad Mexicana de Antropología, Mexico, 1966.

---"Cronología y periodificación; datos estratigráficos sobre períodos cerámicos y sus relaciones con la pintura mural." Paper presented at the Eleventh Mesa Redonda de la Sociedad Mexicana de Antropología, Mexico, 1966.

---"Teotihuacán." *Scientific American*, CCXVI-6 (1967): pp. 38-48.

---"Urbanization of Teotihuacán; the Teotihuacán mapping project." In *El proceso de urbanización en America desde sus orígenes hasta nuestros días*. Edited by Jorge E. Hardoy and Richard P. Schaedel. Buenos Aires: Editorial del Instituto Di Tella, 1969.

Millon, Rene F. and Drewitt, Bruce. "Earlier structures within the pyramid of the Sun at Teotihuacán." *A.A.T.Q.*, XXVII-3 (1961): pp. 371-380.

Miró Quesada, Luis. "Chan Chan, estudio de habilitación urbanística." Report presented to the Organización Nacional de Planificación y urbanismo; Lima, 1957.

Molina, Cristobal de. *Ritos y fábulas de los incas*. Buenos Aires: Editorial Futuro, 1959.

Molins Fábrega, N. *El Codice Mendocino y la economía de Tenochtitlán*. Mexico: Ediciones Libre-Mex, 1956.

Montesinos, Fernando. *Memorias antiguas, historiales y políticas del Perú*. Madrid: Colección de Libros Españoles Raros o Curiosos, 1882.

Moore, Sally Falk. *Power and property in Inca Peru*. New York: Columbia University Press, 1958.

Moreno, Manuel M. *La organización política y social de los aztecas*. I.N.A.H. Mexico: 1960.

Moriarty, James R. "Floating gardens (chinampas) agriculture in the old lakes of Mexico." *A.I.*, XXXVIII-2 (Mexico, 1968): pp. 461-484.

Morley, Sylvanus. *The inscriptions at Copán*. C.I.W. Publication 219. Washington, D.C.: 1920.

---*Guide Book to the ruins of Quirigua*. C.I.W. Publication 16. Washington, D.C.: 1935.

---"Yucatán, home of the gifted Maya." *N.G.M.* LXX-5 (Washington, D.C., 1936): p. 590.

---*The inscriptions of Petén*. C.I.W. Publication 437. Washington, D.C., 1937-38.

---*La civilización maya*. Mexico: Fondo de Cultura Económica, 1956.

Morris, Craig. *El tampu real de Tunsucancha*. Huanuco: Cuadernos de

Investigación de la Universidad Nacional Hermilio Valdizán I, 1966.

Morris, Craig and Thompson, Donald E. "Huanuco Viejo: an Inca administrative center." *A.A.T.Q.* XXXV-3 (1970): pp. 344-362.

Morris, E.H.; Charlot, J. and Morris, A.A. *The temple of the warriors at Chichen Itza, Yucatán.* C.I.W. Publication 406. Washington, D.C.: 1931.

Mostny, Grete. "Ciudades atacameñas." *Boletín del Museo Nacional de Historia Natural* XXIV (Santigo de Chile, 1948): pp. 125-211.

---*Culturas precolombinas de Chile.* Santiago de Chile: Editorial del Pacífico, 1954.

Motolinia (Fray Toribio de Benavente). *Historia de los indios de la Nueva España.* Mexico: Editorial Salvador Chavez Hayhoe, 1941.

Mumford, Lewis. *The culture of cities.* New York: 1938.

Mundy, J.H. and Riesenberg, P. *The medieval town.* Princeton, New Jersey: D. Van Nostrand Co., Inc., 1958.

Murra, John. "An archaeological restudy of an andean etno-historical account." *A.A.T.Q.*, XXVIII-1 (1962): pp. 1-4.

---"Cloth and its functions in the Inca State." *A.A.* LXIV-4 (1962): p. 70.

---"La papa, el maiz y los ritos agrícolas del Tawantisuyu." *Amaru* VIII (Lima, 1968): pp. 58-62.

Noguera, Eduardo. "Antecedentes de la cultura Teotihuacana." *E.M.A.* III-5-8 (Mexico, 1935): pp. 1-181.

---"Exploraciones en Xochicalco." *C.A.*, XIX-1 (Mexico, 1945): pp. 119-157.

---*La cerámica arqueológica de Cholula.* Mexico: Editorial Guarania, 1954.

---"Extraordinario hallazgo en Teotihuacán." *E.M.A.* VIII (Mexico, 1955): p. 43.

---"Un edificio preclásico en Cholula." In *Estudios antropológicos*, published in honor of Doctor Manuel Gamio (Mexico, 1956): pp. 213-224.

Noguera, Eduardo and Leonard, Juan. "Descubrimiento de la Casa de las Aguilas en Teotihuacán." *Boletín del Centro de Investigaciones Antropológicas de México* IV (Mexico, 1957): pp. 6-9.

Núñez Regueiro, Victor. "The Alamito culture of Northwestern Argentina." *A.A.T.Q.* XXXV-2 (1970).

Nuttall, Zelia. "The gardens of ancient Mexico." *Smithsonian Report*, 1923 (Washington, D.C., 1925): pp. 453-464.

Olivé, Julio C. and Barba, Beatriz. "Sobre la desintegración de las culturas clásicas." *Anales del I.N.A.H.* IX-38 (Mexico, 1957): p. 57.

Oviedo, Gonzalo Fernández. *Historia general y natural de las Indias.* Madrid: Ed. José Amador de los Ríos, 1851-55.

Padden, R.C. *The Hummingbird and the Hawk. Conquest and sovereignty in the Valley of Mexico, 1503-1541.* New York: Harper and Row, 1970.

Paddock, John, ed. *Ancient Oaxaca.* Palo Alto, California: Stanford University Press, 1966.

Palerm, Angel. "La civilización urbana." *Historia Mexicana* II-2 (Mexico, 1952): pp. 184-209.

---"The agricultural basis of urban civilization in Mesoamerica." In *Irrigation civilizations: a comparative study.* Edited by Julian H. Steward. Pan American Union, Department of Cultural Affairs, Social Science Monograph No. 1. Washington, D.C.: 1955.

---"Notas sobre las construcciones militares y la guerra en Mesoamérica." *Anales del I.N.A.H.* VIII-37 (Mexico, 1958): p. 123.

Palerm, Angel and Wolf, Eric. "La agricultura y el desarrollo de la civilización en Mesoamérica." *Revista Interamericana de Ciencias Sociales, Segunda época,* I-2. Washington, D.C.: Union Panamericana, 1961.

Pardo, Luis A. "Maquetas arquitectónicas en el antiguo Perú." *Revista del Instituto Arqueológico del Cuzco* I-1 (Cuzco, 1936): pp. 6-17.

---*Ruinas precolombinas del Cuzco.* Cuzco: Editora Cuzco Imperial, 1937.

---"Machupijchu." *Revista del Instituto Arqueológico del Cuzco* V-8 & 9 (Cuzco, 1941).

---"La metrópoli de Paccarictampu." *Revista de la Sección Arqueológica de la Universidad Nacional del Cuzco* II (Cuzco, 1946): pp. 3-46.

---*Historia y Arqueología del Cuzco.* Cuzco: 1957.

Parsons, Jeffrey R. "The archaeological significance of mahamaes cultivation on the coast of Peru." *A.A.T.Q.* XXXIII-1 (1968): pp. 80-85.

---"An estimate of size and population for Middle Horizon Tiahuanaco, Bolivia." *A.A.T.Q.* XXXIII-2 (1968): pp. 243-245.

---"Teotihuacan, Mexico, and its impact on Regional Demography." *Science* CLXII (1968): pp. 872-877.

---*Sunken fields on the Peruvian coast. Preliminary Reconnaissance.* Ann Arbor: University of Michigan, Museum of Anthropology, 1969.

Paso y Troncoso, F. del. *Papeles de Nueva España,* vols. I-VII. Madrid: 1905.

Patterson, Thomas C. "The emergence of food production in Central Peru." In *Prehistoric agriculture.* Edited by Stuart Strueuer. American Museum Sourcebook in Anthropology. New York: 1971.

Perez, Jose R. "Exploraciones del túnel de la pirámide del Sol." *E.M.A.,* III (Mexico, 1935): pp. 5-8.

Peterson, Frederick. *Ancient Mexico.* London: George Allen and Unwin Ltd., 1959.

Pichardo Moya, Felipe. *Los aborígenes de las Antillas.* Mexico: Fondo de Cultura Económica, 1957.

Piggot, Stuart. *Prehistoric India.* Harmondsworth, Middlesex, England: Pelican Books, 1952.

Piña Chan, Román. *Las culturas preclásicas de la cuenca de Mexico.* Mexico: Fondo de Cultura Económica, 1955.

---*Mesoamérica.* Memorias, I.N.A.H., VI. Mexico: 1960.

---*Campeche antes de la conquista.* Campeche: Publicaciones del gobierno del Estado de Campeche, 1970.

Pizarro, Hernando. *Carta de los oidores de la audiencia de Santo Domingo.* Buenos Aires: Espasa-Calpe Argentina; Colección Austral; No. 1168, 1953.

Pizarro, Pedro. *Relación del descubrimiento y conquista del Perú.* Paris: Biblioteca de Cultura Peruana, Primera Serie, No. 2. 1938.

Polanyi, Karl; Arensberg, G.M. and Pearson, H.W., eds. *Trade and market in the early empires.* Glencoe, Illinois: The Free Press, 1957.

Polo, Marco. *The travels of Marco Polo.* Harmondsworth, Middlesex, England: Penguin Classics, 1958.

Pollock, H.E.D. and Stromsvik, Gustav. *Chacchob, Yucatán.* C.I.W.; Department of Archaeology, Current Report 6, I. 1953.

Poma de Ayala, Felipe Guaman. *Nueva crónica y buen gobierno.* Paris: Institut d'Ethnologie, 1936.

Ponce Sanginés, Carlos. *Informe de labores (octubre 1957-febrero 1961).* La Paz: Centro de Investigaciones Arqueológicas en Tiwanaku, 1961.

---"Restauración del templete semisubterráneo de Tiwanaku." *Ultima Hora,* June 2, 1961 (La Paz, 1961).

---"Fechas radiocarbónicas de Bolivia." *Ultima Hora,* June 24, 25, 26, 27 & 30, 1961 (La Paz, 1961).

---*El templete subterráneo de Tiwanaku.* La Paz: Academia Nacional de

Ciencias de Bolivia, 1969.

---"La ciudad de Tiwanaku." *Arte y Arqueología* I (La Paz, 1969): pp. 5-32.

---*Tunupa y Ekako: estudio arqueológico acerca de las efigies precolombinas de dorso adunco.* La Paz: Academia Nacional de Ciencias de Bolivia, 1969.

---*Wankarani y Chiripa y su relación con Tiwanaku.* La Paz: Academia Nacional de Ciencias de Bolivia, 1970.

Ponce Sanginés, Carlos, ed. *Arqueología boliviana.* La Paz: Biblioteca Paceña, 1957.

Poole, D.M. "The Spanish Conquest of Mexico: some geographical aspects." *Geographical Journal* CXVII: pp. 27-42.

Portilla, Miguel L. *Visión de los vencidos: relaciones indigenas de la conquista.* Mexico: Universidad Nacional Autónoma de Mexico, 1963.

---*Los antiguos mexicanos.* Mexico: Fondo de Cultura Económica, 1968.

Posnansky, Arthur. *Una metrópoli prehistórica en la America del Sur.* Berlin: Dietrich Reimer, 1914.

---*Tihuanacu—The cradle of American man.* vol. 1 & 2: New York: J.J. Augustin, Publisher; vol. 3 & 4: La Paz: Ministerio de Educación. Spanish and English edition.

Posner, Gerald S. "The Peru current." *Scientific American*, CXC-3 (1954): p. 66.

Prescott, William H. *History of the conquest of Peru.* New York: The Modern Library, n.d.

---*History of the conquest of Mexico.* New York: The Modern Library, n.d.

Proskouriakoff, Tatiana. *An album of maya architecture.* C.I.W. Publication 558. Washington, D.C.: 1946.

---"Mayapán: the last stronghold of a civilization." *Archaeology* VII-2 (1954): pp. 96-103.

Puleston, Dennis E. "The Chultuns of Tikal." *E.*, VII-3 (1965): pp. 24-29.

Puleston, Dennis E. and Callender, D.W. "Defensive earthworks at Tikal." *E.*, IX-3 (1967): pp. 40-48.

Queen, Stuart and Carpenter, David. *The american city.* New York: McGraw Hill Book Co., Inc., 1953.

Ramusio, Giovanni B. *Delle Navigationi et Viaggi.* Venice: 1556.

Rattray, Evelyn C. "An archaeological and stylistic study of Coyotlatelco pottery." *Mesoamerican Notes* VII-VIII (Mexico, 1966): pp. 87-211.

Recinos, Adrian, ed. *The annals of the Cakchiquels* and *Title of the Lords of Totonicapan.* Norman: University of Oklahoma Press.

Redfield, Robert. *The primitive world and its transformations.* Ithaca: Cornell University Press, 1953.

---*The folk culture of Yucatán.* Chicago: University of Chicago Press, 1959.

Redfield, Robert and Singer, Milton. "The cultural role of cities." *Economic development and cultural change* III (1954): pp. 53-73.

Reina, Ruben. "The abandonment of Primicias by Itzá of San José, Guatemala, and Socotz, British Honduras." *Tikal Report No. 10.* Philadelphia: University of Pennsylvania, The University Museum, 1961.

---"Milpas and milperos. Implications for Prehistoric Times." *A.A.* LXIX (1967): pp. 1-20.

Reyes, Alfonso. *Visión de Anahuac.* Mexico: El Colegio de México, 1953.

Ricketson Jr., Oliver G. "Astronomical observatories in the Maya Arc." *Geographical Review* XVIII-2 (1928): pp. 215-225.

Ricketson Jr., O.G. and E.B. *Uaxactún, Guatemala, group E, 1926-31.* C.I.W., Publication 477. Washington, D.C.: 1937.

Rivet, Paul. *Cités Maya.* Paris: Albert Guillot, 1954.

---*Los orígenes del hombre Americano.* Mexico: Fondo de Cultura Económica, 1960.

Robertson, Donald. *Precolumbian architecture.* New York: 1963.

Roosevelt, Cornelius Van S. "Ancient civilizations of the Santa Valley and Chavin." *Geographical Review* XXV-1 (1945): pp. 21-42.

Rosenblat, Angel. *La población indígena y el mestizaje en América.* Buenos Aires: Editorial Nova, 1954.

Rouse, Irving. "Settlement patterns in the Caribbean Area." In *Prehistoric settlement patterns in the New World.* Edited by Gordon R. Willey. Wenner-Gran Foundation for Anthropological Research, Publication 23. New York: 1956.

Rowe, John Howland. *An introduction to the archaeology of Cuzco.* Peabody Museum, XXVII-2. Cambridge: Harvard University Press, 1944.

---"Inca culture at the time of the Spanish conquest." *H.S.A.I.*, S.I., B.A.E. Publication 143, II-2 (Washington, D.C., 1946): pp. 183-331.

---"The kingdom of Chimor." *Acta Americana,* VI-1 & 2 (Mexico, 1948): pp. 26-59.

---"La arqueología del Cuzco como historia cultural." *R.M.I.H.* X-16 (1957): pp. 34-48.

---*Chavin Art. An inquiry into its form and meaning.* New York: The Museum of Primitive Art, 1962.

---"Urban settlements in Ancient **Peru**." *N.P.*, I (Berkeley, 1963): pp. 1-27.

---"What kind of settlement was Inca Cuzco?" *N.P.* V (Berkeley, 1967): pp. 59-77.

---"The sunken gardens of the peruvian coast." *A.A.T.Q.* XXXIV-3 (1969): pp. 320-325.

Rowe, John H. and Menzel, Dorothy, eds. *Peruvian archaeology. Selected Readings.* Palo Alto, California: Peek Publications, 1967.

Rowe, John; Collier, D. and Willey, Gordon. "Reconnaissance notes on the site of Huari, near Ayacucho, Peru." *A.A.T.Q.* XVI-2 (1950): pp. 120-137.

Ruiz de Arce, Juan. *Advertencia a sus sucesores.* Buenos Aires: Espasa-Calpe Argentina, Colección Austral, No. 1168, 1953.

Ruppert, Karl. *Chichen Itza—Architectural notes and plans.* C.I.W., Publication 595. Washington, D.C.: 1952.

Ruppert, K.; Thompson, J.E.S. and Proskouriakoff, T. *Bonampak, Chiapas, Mexico.* C.I.W. Publication 602. Washington, D.C., 1955.

Ruz Lhuillier, Alberto. *Guía arqueológica de Tula.* Mexico: Ateneo Nacional de Ciencias y Artes de Mexico, 1945.

---"La escritura indígena." In *Mexico prehispánico.* Edited by Jorge A. Vivo. Mexico: 1946.

---"Exploraciones arqueológicas en Palenque: 1957" and "Exploraciones arqueológicas en Palenque: 1958." *Anales del I.N.A.H.* XIV-43. Mexico: 1962.

Sahagún, Bernardino de. *Suma indiana.* Mexico: Imprenta Universitaria, 1943.

---*Historia general de las cosas de Nueva España.* Mexico: Editorial Nueva España, 1946.

Salas, Alberto. *Las armas de la conquista.* Buenos Aires: Emecé editores, 1950.

Sancho de la Hoz, Pedro. *Relación para S.M. de lo sucedido en la conquista y pacificación de estas provincias de la Nueva Castilla.* Biblioteca de Cultura Peruana, Primera Serie, No. 2. Lima: 1938.

Sanders, William T. "El mercado de Tlatelolco: un estudio en economía urbana." *Tlatoani* I-1 (Mexico, 1952): p. 14.

---"Estudios sobre el patrón de asentamiento del poblado de Xochicalco." *Tlatoani* I-2 (Mexico, 1952): p. 32.

---"The central mexican symbiotic region: a study in prehistoric settlement patterns." In *Prehistoric settlement patterns in the New World.* Edited by Gordon R. Willey. Wenner-Gren Foundation for Anthropological Research, Publication 23. New York: 1956.

---*The cultural ecology of the Teotihuacán Valley.* University Park, Pa.: Pennsylvania State University, 1965.

---"A profile of urban evolution in the Teotihuacán Valley." In *El processo de urbanización en America desde sus orígenes hasta nuestros días.* Edited by Jorge E. Hardoy and Richard P. Schaedel. Buenos Aires: Editorial del Instituto Di Tella, 1969.

Sanders, William T. and Price, Barbara. *Mesoamerica: the evolution of a civilization.* New York: Random House, 1968.

Sarmiento de Gamboa, Pedro. *Historia de los Incas.* Buenos Aires: Emecé Editores, 1947.

Sauer, Carl O. "Geography and plant and animal resources." *H.S.A.I.,* S.I., B.A.E. Publication 143, VI-4 (Washington, D.C., 1950): pp. 319-344.

---"Cultivated plants of South and Central America." *H.S.A.I.,* S.I., B.A.E. VI-4 (Washington, D. C., 1950): pp. 487-543.

Satterthwaite, Linton Jr. *Piedras Negras archaeology: architecture.* Philadelphia: University of Pennsylvania, University Museum, 1944.

Schaedel, Richard P. "Major ceremonial and population centers in northern Peru." In *Selected papers of the 29th International Congress of Americanists.* Edited by Sol Tax. Chicago: University of Chicago Press, 1951.

---"Mochica murals at Pañamarca." *A.,* IV-3 (1951): pp. 145-154.

---"The lost cities of Peru." *Scientific American* CLXXXV-2 (1951): pp. 18-25.

---"Urban growth and ekistics on the Peruvian Coast." *Acts of the XXXVI International Congress of Americanists.* Sevilla: 1966.

---"On the definition of civilization, urban, city and town in prehistoric America." In *El processo de urbanizacion en America desde sus orígenes hasta nuestros días.* Edited by Jorge E. Hardoy and Richard P. Schaedel. Buenos Aires: Editorial del Instituto Di Tella, 1969.

Séjourné, Laurette. *Palenque, una ciudad maya.* Mexico: Fondo de Cultura Económica, 1952.

---"Estudio del material arqueológico de Atetelco, Teotihuacán." *R.M.E.A.* XIV (Mexico, 1956-57): p. 15.

---*Pensamiento y religión en el México Antiguo.* Mexico: Breviario No. 128, Fondo de Cultura Económica, 1957.

---*Un palacio en la ciudad de los dioses.* Mexico: I.N.A.H., 1959.

Sellards, E.H. "Some early stone artifact development in North America." *S.W.J.A.* XVI-2 (1960): pp. 160-173.

Serrano, Antonio. *Los aborígenes argentinos.* Buenos Aires: Editorial Nova, 1947.

Shapiro, Harry. L., ed. *Man, culture and society.* New York: Oxford University Press, 1960.

Shea, Daniel. "El conjunto arquitectónico central en la plaza de Huanuco Viejo." *Cuadernos de Investigación de la Universidad Hermilio Valdizán* I (Huanuco, 1966): pp. 108-116.

Shipee, Robert. "A forgotten valley of Peru." *N.G.M.* LXV-1 (1924): pp. 110-132.

---"The great wall of Peru." *Geographical Review* XVII (1927).

Shook, E.M. *The great wall of Mayapán.* C.I.W.; Department of Archaeology; Current Report 2, I (1952-54).

---"The temple of the Red Stela." *E.* I-1 (Philadelphia, 1958).

---*Tikal report No. 1.* Philadelphia: The University of Pennsylvania, 1958.

---"Tikal stela 29." *E.*, II-2 (1960).

Shook, E.M. and Proskouriakoff, T. "Settlement patterns in Meso-America and the sequence in the Guatemala Highland." In *Prehistoric settlement patterns in the New World.* Edited by Gordon R. Willey. Wenner-Gren Foundation for Anthropological Research, Publication 23. New York: 1956.

Sierra, Jaime. "La civilización chibcha." *Revista de la Universidad de Antioquía,* No. 138 (1959).

Siren, Osvald. *The walls and gates of Peking.* London: Bodley Head Ltd., 1924.

Sjoberg, Gideon. *The pre-industrial city.* Glencoe, Illinois: The Free Press, 1960.

Smith, A. Ledyard. *Archaeological reconnaissance in Central Gua-*

temala. C.I.W., Publication 608. Washington, D.C.: 1955.

Solis, Antonio. *Historia de la conquista de México.* Buenos Aires: Espasa-Calpe Argentina, Colección Austral, No. 699, 1948.

Soustelle, Jacques. *La vida cotidiana de los Aztecas.* Mexico: Fondo de Cultura Económica, 1956.

Spence, Michael W. "The obsidian industry of Teotihuacán." *A.A.T.Q.* XXXII-1 (1967): pp. 507-514.

Spinden, H.J. "The population of ancient America." *Geographical Review* XVIII-4 (New York, 1928): pp. 641-660.

Squier, E. George. *Peru, incidents of travel and exploration in the land of the Incas.* New York: Harper and Brothers, 1877.

Stephens, John Lloyd. *Incidents of travel in Central America, Chiapas and Yucatán.* New York: 1841. ·

---*Incidents of travel in Yucatán.* New York: 1843.

Steward, Julian H., ed. *Handbook of South American Indians.* S.I., B.A.E. Publication 143, vol. I-VI. Washington, D.C.: 1946-50.

---*Irrigation civilizations: a comparative study.* Pan American Union, Department of Cultural Affairs, Social Science Monograph, No. 1. Washington, D.C.: 1955.

Steward, J.H. and Faron, I.C. *Native peoples of South America.* New York: McGraw Hill Co., Inc., 1959.

Stewart, T.D. "A physical anthropologist's view of the peopling of the new world." *S.W.J.A.*, XVI-3 (1960): pp. 259-273.

Stirling, M.W.; Ramey, F. and Stirling, M.W., Jr. "Electronics and archaeology." *E.* II-4 (Philadelphia, 1960): pp. 19-29.

Strong, W.D. *Cross sections of new world prehistory.* S.I., Publication 3739. Washington, D.C.: 1943.

Strong, W.D. and Evans, C. *Cultural stratigraphy in the Virú Valley, northern Peru.* Columbia studies in Archaeology and Ethnology, IV. New York: Columbia University Press, 1952.

Strube, Leon. *Vialidad imperial de los incas.* Córdoba: Instituto de Estudios Americanistas, Universidad Nacional de Córdoba, 1963.

Struever, Stuart, ed. *Prehistoric agriculture.* New York: American Museum Sourcebook in Anthropology, 1971.

Stumer, L. "The Chillon Valley of Peru." *A.* VII-3 (1954): pp. 172-178 and VII-4 (1954): p. 220.

---"Population centers of the Rimac Valley." *A.A.T.Q.* XX (1954): pp. 130-148.

---"Contactos foráneos en la costa central." *R.M.N.*, XXVII (Lima,

1958): p. 11.

Tamayo, Jorge L. *Geografía de América.* Mexico: Fondo de Cultura Económica, Breviario No. 66, 1952.

Tax, Sol, ed. *Selected papers.* XXIX° International Congress of Americanists. Chicago: University of Chicago Press, 1951.

---*Heritage of Conquest.* Glencoe, Illinois: The Free Press, 1952.

Tello, Julio C. "La ciudad inkaica de Cajamarca." *Chaski*, I-3 (Lima): p. 2.

---*Chavín: cultura matriz de la civilización andina.* Lima: Imprenta de la Universidad de San Marcos, 1960.

Termer, Franz. "The density of population in the southern and northern Maya empire as an archaeological and geographical problem." In *Selected papers of the 29th International Congress of Americanists.* Edited by Sol Tax. Chicago: University of Chicago Press, 1951.

Thompson, Donald E. "Formative Period Architecture in the Casma Valley." In *Actas y Memorias del XXXV Congreso Internacional de Americanistas,* I, pp. 205-212. Mexico: 1964.

---"Huanuco, Peru: a survey of a province of the Inca empire." *A.,* XXI-3 (1968): pp. 174-181.

---"An archaeological evaluation of ethnohistoric evidence of Inca culture." In *Anthropological archaeology in the Americas.* Edited by Betty Meggers. Washington, D.C.: Anthropological Society of Washington, 1968.

---"Incaic installations in Huanuco and Pumpu." In *El processo de urbanizacion en America desde sus orígenes hasta nuestros días.* Edited by Jorge E. Hardoy and Richard P. Schaedel. Buenos Aires: Editorial del Instituto Di Tella, 1969.

Thompson, Donald E. and Murra, John V. "The Inca bridges in the Huanuco Region." *A.A.T.Q.* XXXI-5 (1966): pp. 632-639.

Thompson, J. Eric. "Un vistazo a las ciudades mayas, su aspecto y función." *C.A.* XX-2 (Mexico, 1945): pp. 133-149.

---*Grandeza y decadencia de los Mayas.* Mexico: Fondo de Cultura Económica, 1959.

Thompson, J. Eric; Pollock, H.E.D. and Charlot, J. *A preliminary study of the ruins of Coba,Quintana Roo, Mexico.* C.I.W., Publication 424. Washington, D.C.: 1932.

Thurnwald, Richard. "The role of political organization in the development of man with suggested applications in the New World. " In

Selected papers of the 29th International Congress of Americanists. Edited by Sol Tax. Chicago: University of Chicago Press, 1951.

Torquemada, Juan de. *Monarquía indiana.* Mexico: Editorial Salvador Chavez Hayhoe, 1943.

Toussaint, M.; Gómez de Orozco, F. and Fernández, J. *Planos de la ciudad de México.* Mexico: Instituto de Investigaciones Estéticas de la Universidad Nacional Autónoma, 1938.

Trujillo, Diego de. *Relación del descubrimiento del reino de Perú.* Buenos Aires: Espasa-Calpe Argentina, Colección Austral, 1953.

United States Bureau of the Census. "Census areas of 1950." In *Readings in urban geography.* Edited by H. Mayer and C. Kohn. Chicago: University of Chicago Press, 1960.

Urteaga, Horacio H. "Tambo Colorado." *Boletín de la Sociedad Geográfica,* LVI (Lima, 1939): p. 85.

Vaillant, George C. "A correlation of archaeological and historical sequences in the Valley of Mexico." *A.A.* XL (1938): p. 544.

---*La civilización azteca.* Mexico: Fondo de Cultura Económica, 1955.

Valcárcel, Luis E. *El Cuzco Precolombino.* Cuzco: Revista Universitaria, 1924.

---*Del Ayllu al Imperio: la evolución político-social en el Antiguo Perú y otros estudios.* Lima: Editorial Garcilaso, 1925.

---"Final de Tawantisuyu." *R.M.N.* II-2 (Lima, 1933): p. 79.

---*Cuzco, archaeological capital of South America.* Lima: Banco Italiano, 1934.

---"Sajsawaman redescubierto." *R.M.N.* (Lima, 1934-35): II-1 & 2, pp. 3-36; III-3, pp. 211-233; IV-1, p. 24; IV-2, pp. 163-203.

---"Sobre el origen del Cuzco." *R.M.N.* VIII (Lima, 1939): pp. 190-233.

---"Cuzco Archaeology." *H.S.A.I.*, S.I., B.A.E. Publication 143, II-2 (Washington, D.C., 1946): pp. 177-182.

---"The Andean Calendar." *H.S.A.I.*, S.I., B.A.E. Publication 143, II-2 (Washington, D.C., 1946): pp. 471-476.

---"Indian markets and fairs in Peru." *H.A.S.I.*, S.I., B.A.E. Publication 143, II-2 (Washington, D.C., 1946): pp. 477-482.

---*Machu Picchu.* Buenos Aires: Eudeba, 1964.

Valle Arispe, Artemio de, ed. *La muy noble y leal ciudad de México, según relatos de antaño y hogaño.* Mexico: 1939.

Vallois, Henri V. *Vital statistics in prehistoric population as determined from archaeological data.* New York: V.F., 1960.

Van Zantwijk, Rudolf. "Principios organizadores de los mexicas, una introducción al estudio del sistema interno del regimen azteca." *Estudios de Cultura Nahuatl* IV (1963): pp. 187-222.

Vargas, Castelazo M. "La patología y la medicina entre los mixtecas." *R.M.E.A.* XIV (Mexico, 1954-55): pp. 119-143.

Varona, Esteban A. de. *Teotihuacán, Tula, Tenayuca.* Mexico: Unión Gráfica, 1959.

Vega, Garcilaso de la. *Los comentarios reales de los incas.* Buenos Aires: Emecé, 1943.

Velarde, Hector. *Arquitectura peruana.* Mexico: Fondo de Cultura Económica, 1946.

Verril, A. Hyatt. *Old civilizations of the new world.* New York: The New Home Library, n.d.

Villa, R. Alfonso. *The Yaxuna-Coba Causeway.* C.I.W., Contributions to American Archaeology, No. 9. Washington, D.C.: 1934.

Villagra, Agustin. "Las pinturas murales de Atetelco, Teotihuacán." *R.M.E.A.*, XIV (Mexico, 1956-57): p. 9.

Vinson, G.L. "Two important recent archaeological discoveries in Esso concessions, Guatemala." *Exploration Newsletter*, Standard Oil Company. New York: 1960.

Vivo, Jorge A., ed. *México prehispánico.* Mexico: 1946.

Vogt, Evon Z. "The genetic model and Maya cultural development." In *Desarrollo cultural de los Mayas.* Edited by Evon Z. Vogt and A. Ruz Lhuillier. Mexico: 1964.

Vogt, Evon Z. and Ruz Lhuillier, A., eds. *Desarrollo cultural de los Mayas.* Mexico: 1964.

Wauchope, Robert. *House mounds of Uaxactún, Guatemala.* C.I.W., Publication 436. Washington, D.C.: 1934.

---*Modern Maya Houses.* C.I.W., Publication 502. Washington, D.C.: 1938.

---"Domestic architecture of the maya." In *The maya and their neighbors.* New York: 1940.

---*A tentative sequence of pre-classic ceramics in Middle America.* M.A.R.I. Records I-14. New Orleans: Tulane University, 1950.

---*Implications of radio carbon dates from middle and South America.* M.A.R.I. Records II-2. New Orleans: Tulane University, 1954.

Wauchope, Robert, ed. *Handbook of Middle American Indians* I-IV.

Austin: University of Texas Press, 1964.

Weber, Max. *The city*. Glencoe, Illinois: The Free Press, 1958.

West, Michael. "Community settlement patterns at Chan Chan, Peru." *A.A.T.Q.* XXXV-1 (1970): pp. 74-86.

Westheim, Paul. *Arte antiguo de México*. Mexico: Fondo de Cultura Económica, 1950.

Wicke, Charles R. and Bullington, Maudie. "A possible andean influence in Central Mexico." *A.A.T.Q.* XXV-4 (1960): p. 603.

Wiener, Charles. *Perou et Bolivie: récit de voyage*. Paris: Librairie Hachette et Cie., 1880.

Willets, William. *Chinese Art*. Harmondsworth, Middlesex, England: Pelican Books, 1958.

Willey, Gordon R. "The culture of La Candelaria." *H.S.A.I.*, S.I., B.A.E. Publication 143, II-3 (Washington, D.C., 1946): pp. 661-672.

---"Peruvian settlement and socio-economic patterns." In *Selected papers of the 29th International Congress of Americanists*. Edited by Sol Tax. Chicago: University of Chicago Press, 1951.

---"The Chavin problem: a review and critique." *S.W.J.A.* VII-2 (1951): pp. 103-144.

---*Prehistoric settlements patterns in the Virú Valley*. S.I., B.A.E. Publication 155. Washington, D.C.: 1953.

---"The structure of ancient maya society: evidence from the Southern Lowlands." *A.A.* LVIII-5 (1956).

---"New World Prehistory." *Science*, CXXXI-3393 (1960): pp. 73-86.

---"Distribución cronológica de algunos tipos de artefactos en Altar de Sacrificios, Guatemala." *E.C.M.* V (Mexico, 1965): pp. 33-39.

---*An introduction to American archaeology*, vol. 1. Englewood Cliffs, New Jersey: Prentice Hall, Inc., 1966.

Willey, Gordon R., ed. *Prehistoric settlement patterns in the new world*. Wenner-Gren Foundation for Anthropological Research, Publication 23. New York: 1956.

Willey, Gordon R. and Bullard, William R. "Prehistoric settlement patterns in the Maya lowlands." *H.M.A.I.* II (Austin, 1965): pp. 360-377.

Willey, Gordon R. and Ford, James A. *Surface Survey of the Virú Valley, Peru. A.M.N.H.-A.P.* XI-III-1. New York: 1949.

Willey, Gordon and Phillips, Philip. *Method and Theory in American archaeology*. Chicago: University of Chicago Press, 1958.

Willey, Gordon; Bullard, W.R. and Glass, J.B. "The Maya community of prehistoric times." *A.* VIII-1 (1955): pp. 18-25.